WESTERN SAHARA

WESTERN SAHARA

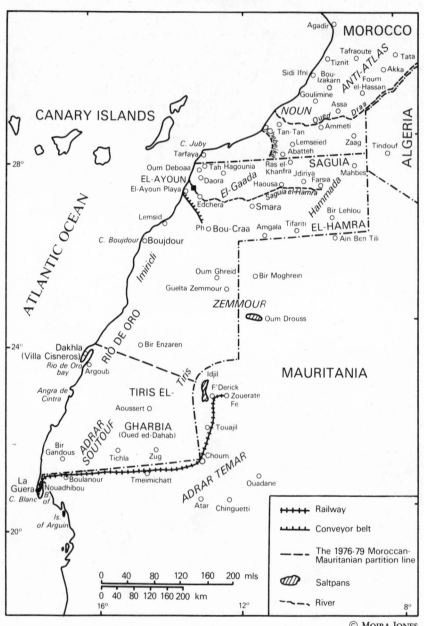

© Moira Jones

WESTERN SAHARA

The Roots of a Desert War

By Tony Hodges

LAWRENCE HILL & COMPANY
Westport, Connecticut 06880

To Sylvette

Published in the United States of America by
Lawrence Hill & Co., Publishers, Inc.,
520 Riverside Avenue, Westport, Connecticut 06880

Published in the United Kingdom by
Croom Helm Ltd
Provident House, Burrell Row
Beckenham, Kent BR 3 1AT

Library of Congress Cataloging in Publication Data

Hodges, Tony.
  Western Sahara.

  Bibliography: p.
  Includes index.
  1. Western Sahara—Politics and government.
I. Title.
DT346.S7H58   1983   964'.8   83-8565
ISBN 0-88208-151-9
ISBN 0-88208-152-7 (pkb.)

Croom Helm ISBN 0-7099-1295-1

1 2 3 4 5 6 7 8 9

Printed in the United States of America

CONTENTS

(Illustrations follow pages 54, 148, 228, and 336.)

INTRODUCTION

One of the most inhospitable places on Earth, the ex-Spanish territory of Western Sahara might seem the least likely tract of real estate to be coveted by anyone. Yet this bleak land on the western edge of the great Saharan desert has been the theatre of one of Africa's most bitter and intractable wars since 1975–76, when it was abruptly abandoned by Spain. Morocco, supported initially by Mauritania, has been battling for supremacy in the territory against a well-armed and highly motivated nationalist movement, the Frente Popular para la Liberación de Saguia el-Hamra y Río de Oro, known normally by its acronym "Polisario."

Inevitably, perhaps, given Western Sahara's isolation, the roots of this conflict are little understood, especially in the English-speaking world. This book's aim is to shed some light on the war's multiple, complex causes. Necessarily, it delves back into the past. It begins, thus, with a portrayal of the traditional nomadic way of life of the territory's indigenous inhabitants, the Saharawis, and an examination of their historical relations with their neighbors—the Moroccans to their immediate north and the tribes and emirates of what is now Mauritania, to their south. The historical background is completed with an account of the Saharawis' contacts with Europeans since the fifteenth century and of their ultimate colonization by Spain after a prolonged war of resistance that did not end until 1934.

A thesis of this book is that profound economic and social changes, spurred by the development of Western Sahara's important phosphate industry, laid the basis, along with changes in the political climate at home and abroad, for the rise of a modern nationalist movement, setting its sights on the creation of an independent nation-state. The first manifestation of this nationalism was Mohammed Bassiri's Harakat Tahrir Saguia el-Hamra wa Oued ed-Dahab (Liberation Organization of Saguia el-Hamra and Oued ed-Dahab), a short-lived urban movement which the Spanish authorities crushed in 1970. Three years later, Polisario was founded, principally by Saharawis living in the neighboring territories, to fight for independence arms in hand.

As Spain belatedly lost faith in its colonial "mission," in 1974–75, the Saharawi nationalists were destined, however, to face new enemies—though also to win the support of powerful new regional allies. The Moroccan occupation of Western Sahara was not spurred, as many observers have assumed, by a simple lust for its phosphates. Rather, an ideology of territorial expansion, founded on the ideal of recreating a supposed "Greater Morocco" of precolonial times, was deeply rooted in the Moroccan psyche. Fashioned by Moroccan nationalists in the fifties, this ideology had been appropriated by the monarchy, which consequently laid claim to Mauritania for the first nine years of its independence (1960–69) and briefly went to war with Algeria in 1963, in pursuit of a claim to much of the Algerian Sahara. The ground-swell of nationalist fervor in Morocco in 1974–75, which reached its highest pitch with the "Green March" in November 1975, was cleverly orchestrated by a king who saw no better way to outmaneuvre his domestic opponents and restabilize a regime that had been shaken by serious challenges, including two narrowly unsuccessful coups in 1971–72.

King Hassan II marched in Western Sahara in alliance with a foe of yesteryear, President Mokhtar Ould Daddah of Mauritania, who had previously counter-claimed Western Sahara to keep the Greater Moroccans at arm's length from his own country. Under the Madrid Accords of November 14, 1975, by which Spain agreed to cede Western Sahara, Moroccan and Mauritanian deputy governors joined the Spanish governor-general in a transitional tripartite administration, until the Spanish flag was finally hauled down for the last time in the colony's little capital, El-Ayoun, on February 26, 1976. The following April, Morocco and Mauritania formally partitioned their prize.

The Western Saharans had seen their country "decolonized" out of existence. They had not been consulted about their future—for King Hassan had dared not risk allowing a referendum, as the United Nations had been urging since 1966. Thousands of Saharawis fled to Algeria, whose president, Houari Boumedienne, had resolved, in his country's own national interest, to foil Morocco's territorial ambitions by opening Algeria's armories to the Saharawi nationalists and lobbying relentlessly on their behalf in the United Nations and the Organization of African Unity.

On February 27, 1976, one day after Spain's withdrawal from Western Sahara, Polisario proclaimed the birth of a new state, the Saharan Arab Democratic Republic (SADR). By 1983, it had been recognized by more than fifty African, Asian and Latin American governments. On the military front, meanwhile, Polisario proved one of the world's most resilient and effective guerrilla armies. By 1979 it had forced Mauritania, the weaker of its adversaries, to sue for peace. By 1982–83, the guerrillas roamed unchallenged over five sixths of Western Sahara, while eighty thousand Moroccan troops were boxed into two coastal enclaves, protected by a panoply of "electronic warfare" defenses. Apparently stalemated, the war was really one of attrition, a war that was gradually bleeding the Moroccan economy and undermining the very stability that the "recovery of the Moroccan Sahara" had recreated for Hassan's monarchy in 1975. For this, if no other reason, the war became cause for alarm in the capitals of the West, where Hassan is valued as an important third world ally, ruling a strategic country at the entrance of the Mediterranean.

This inter-African conflict has also become a challenge to Africa. In 1982, the OAU itself was thrown into one of the gravest crises in its history by a dispute over the admission of the SADR to its ranks. By agreeing to withdraw from the OAU's summit in Addis Ababa, Ethiopia, in June 1983, the SADR may have saved the OAU from self-destruction. However, the OAU's real challenge still lay ahead. This, as the Addis Ababa conference agreed by consensus, was to bring Morocco and Polisario to the negotiating table (an idea hitherto rejected on principle by Morocco), so that the two parties to this war could finally hammer out the terms of a ceasefire and make arrangements for a genuine, fair referendum.

It is ironical that a conflict with such broad regional and international implications should be fought out in such a remote, arid land as Western Sahara. To anyone visiting the Sahara for the first time, the landscape can seem as hostile as the ocean would to a shipwrecked sailor. It is eerily silent, apparently lifeless in its vastness. In most of Western Sahara, there appear to be nothing but rocks and stones, stretching interminably over monotonous plains, for mile upon mile. In all, the territory covers about 102,700 square miles, an area slightly larger than Great Britain. Its borders extend for 1,271 miles, of which 276 miles border Morocco in the north, 19 miles border Algeria in the northeast and 976 border Mauritania in the east and the south.

There are precipitous cliffs along a good part of the 660-mile seaboard, which has few natural harbors, hazardous sandbanks and shallow coastal waters, all factors which traditionally discouraged seafaring. Flanking the coast is a narrow belt of sand dunes, about ten to twenty miles wide. However, the rest of the territory belies the popular image of the desert as a succession of undulating dunes. Instead, most of Western Sahara consists of a series of rocky or gravel-strewn plains, which rise gradually from the coast to a maximum height of about 1,300 feet. These include El-Gaada in the northwest and, to its east, the great windswept Hammada, which extends far into Algeria, while in the south there is the plain of Tiris. There are two more mountainous zones—the Zemmour massif, which rises to 2,700 feet, in the center-east of the country, on the border with Mauritania, and Adrar Soutouf in the extreme southeast, where the highest peaks are about 1,700 feet. There is only one important river, the Saguia el-Hamra (the "Red River"), which flows east to west, from sources in the Zemmour massif to the Atlantic, across the northern part of the country, to which it gives its name. Like Western Sahara's other, smaller rivers, it is only seasonally in flow; for most of the year its bed is dry. After autumn rains, however, it floods the valley near El-Ayoun, and forces its way in channels through the coastal dune zone to reach the ocean.

The harshness of the Saharan climate is legendary. Even on the coast, where the aridity of the desert is tempered by the moisture brought by the Atlantic winds, annual rainfall rarely exceeds two inches. Very often it is even less. Temperatures soar to a blistering heat in the middle of the day (100°F on the coast or as high as 135°F inland in the summer) and then tumble in the course of the night, dropping to freezing point on winter nights inland. Besides these dramatic shifts in temperature and the extreme aridity, the Saharawi has to contend with the desert winds, which fill the air with fine particles of sand that, but for protective robes and turbans, clog hair, throat and eyes. The worst affliction is the *irifi*, a searing sandstorm, blown by powerful winds from the southeast. Becoming hotter and drier as it sweeps across the great plains, enveloping everything in a cloud of sand, it reduces visibility to a few yards.

There are no oases of any consequence in this blighted land. A study in 1952 showed that palm trees covered no more than 17 acres in the entire country. The only tree that really flourishes is the sturdy *acacia radiana*, of which the 1952 study estimated that there were about 6,350 acres. In valleys, like that of the Saguia el-Hamra and its tributaries, acacia trees provide considerable cover, of which the Polisario guerrillas have made good use, to avoid detection from the air. Apart from the acacias, however, vegetation is limited to a smattering of shrubs, thickets and small bushes. Scattered across this harsh landscape are jackals, hyenas, foxes and gazelles, besides an assortment of birds, small rodents, snakes and lizards. Ostriches, now extinct in Western Sahara, survived until fairly recent times in the south.

Despite the inauspicious climate and terrain, people have always lived in Western Sahara. Until about twenty years ago, before the development of phosphate mining and the political upheavals of the past decade, they were nomads, apart from the handful of Spaniards on the coast. These tough Saharans survived by migrating over vast distances in search of water and pastures for their camels and goats. In the hot summer months, when there was seldom any rain, the nomads would gather around wells or a *guelta*, a kind of natural rainwater cistern formed in a rocky hollow. In the winter months, when at least some rain usually fell, they would take advantage of the more abundant pastures. Ultimately, of course, the nomads were at the mercy of the weather. Rather appropriately, the camel drivers of the Western Sahara called themselves the ''sons of the clouds.''

ACKNOWLEDGMENTS

It would be impossible to name all those who, in one way or another, contributed to my research on Western Sahara between 1978 and 1983, while this book was under preparation. Several dozen people—among them many Western Saharans, Moroccans, Algerians and Mauritanians—gave invaluable advice and assistance, and I hope that they will forgive me if I extend my thanks to them *en bloc*. In particular, however, I would like to express my gratitude to both the Polisario Front and the Moroccan government for making it possible for me to travel widely in Western Sahara, despite the wartime conditions in the territory. I am also indebted to the Ford Foundation, whose generous grant made this project possible, and to my wife, Sylvette, without whose patience and encouragement it might never have been completed.

ABBREVIATIONS AND ACRONYMS

ALN	Armée de Libération Nationale (National Liberation Army), of Algeria
AMD	Alliance pour une Mauritanie Démocratique (Alliance for a Democratic Mauritania)
AOE	Africa Occidental Española (Spanish West Africa)
AOSARIO	Association des Originaires du Sahara anciennement sous Domination Espagnole (Association of Natives of the Sahara formerly under Spanish Domination)
BET	Borku-Ennedi-Tibesti region of Chad
BPL	Bone phosphate of lime
CAM	Confins Algéro-Marocains (Algerian-Moroccan Borderlands)
CCR	Council for the Command of the Revolution, of the SADR
CDT	Confédération Démocratique des Travailleurs (Democratic Confederation of Workers), of Morocco
CEAM	Confédération des Employeurs et des Artisans de Mauritanie (Confederation of Employers and Artisans of Mauritania)
CEPSA	Compañía Española de Petroleos (Spanish Petroleum Company)
CIA	Central Intelligence Agency, of the U.S.
CMRN	Comité Militaire de Redressement National (Military Committee of National Recovery), of Mauritania
CMSN	Comité Militaire de Salut National (Military Committee of National Salvation), of Mauritania
CNS	Conseil National de Sécurité (National Security Council), of Morocco
COA	Centre Opérationnel des Armées (Armed Forces Operations Center), of France
COMINOR	Comptoir Minier du Nord (Mining Agency of the North), of Mauritania
DGED	Direction Générale d'Etudes et de Documentation (General Directorate of Research and Documentation), of Morocco
DGS	Dirección General de Seguridad (General Directorate of Security), of Spain
DMA	Délégation Ministérielle à l'Armament (Ministerial Delegation for Armaments), of France
EEC	European Economic Community
ENMINSA	Empresa Nacional Minera del Sahara (National Mining Company of the Sahara)
FAR	Forces Armées Royales (Royal Armed Forces), of Morocco
FDIC	Front pour la Défense des Institutions Constitutionelles (Front for the Defense of Constitutional Institutions), of Morocco
FLN	Front de Libération Nationale (National Liberation Front), of Algeria
FLRSM	Front de Libération et du Rattachement du Sahara à la Mauritanie (Front for the Liberation and the Rattachment of the Sahara to Mauritania)
FLS	Frente de Liberación del Sahara bajo Dominación Española (Front for the Liberation of the Sahara under Spanish Domination)
FLU	Front de Libération et de l'Unité (Front for Liberation and Unity)
FMS	Foreign Military Sales
FNLC	Front National de Libération du Congo (National Liberation Front of the Congo)
Fosbucraa	Fosfatos de Bu-Craa, SA
Frolinat	Front de Libération Nationale du Tchad (National Liberation Front of Chad)
ICJ	International Court of Justice

IMF	International Monetary Fund
INI	Instituto Nacional de Industria (National Institute of Industry), of Spain
MICUMA	Mines de Cuivre de Mauritanie (Copper Mines of Mauritania)
MIFERMA	Mines de Fer de Mauritanie (Iron Mines of Mauritania)
MND	Mouvement National Démocratique (National Democratic Movement), of Mauritania
MOREHOB	Mouvement de Résistance 'les Hommes Bleus' (Resistance Movement 'the Blue Men')
MP	Mouvement Populaire (Popular Movement), of Morocco
MPAIAC	Movimiento para la Autodeterminación y la Independencia del Archipiélago Canario (Movement for the Self-Determination and Independence of the Canary Archipelago)
NATO	North Atlantic Treaty Organization
OAU	Organization of African Unity
OCP	Office Chérifien de Phosphates (Sharifian Phosphates Office), of Morocco
OCRS	Organisation Commune des Régions Sahariennes (Joint Organization of Saharan Regions)
OJE	Organización de Juventud Española (Spanish Youth Organization)
ONAREP	Office National de Recherches et d'Exploration Petrolières (National Office of Petroleum Research and Exploration), of Morocco
ONP	Office National de Pêche (National Fisheries Office), of Morocco
PCE	Partido Comunista de España (Communist Party of Spain)
PCM	Parti Communiste Marocain (Moroccan Communist Party)
PKM	Parti des Kadihines de Mauritanie (Workers Party of Mauritania)
PLO	Palestine Liberation Organization
PLS	Parti de Libération et du Socialisme (Party of Liberation and Socialism), of Morocco
Polisario Front	Frente Popular para la Liberación de Saguia el-Hamra y Río de Oro (Popular Front for the Liberation of Saguia el-Hamra and Rio de Oro)
PPM	Parti du Peuple Mauritanien (Mauritanian People's Party)
PPS	Parti du Progrès et du Socialisme (Party of Progress and Socialism), of Morocco
PRM	Parti du Regroupment Mauritanien (Party of Mauritanian Regroupment)
PRP	Partido Revolucionario Progresivo (Revolutionary Progressive Party)
PS	Parti Socialiste (Socialist Party), of France
PSOE	Partido Socialista Obrero Español (Spanish Socialist Workers Party)
PUNS	Partido de la Unión Nacional Saharaui (Saharawi National Union Party)
RNI	Rassemblement National des Indépendants (National Assembly of Independents), of Morocco
SADR	Saharan Arab Democratic Republic
SDR	Special Drawing Rights
SNIM	Société Nationale Industrielle et Minière (National Industrial and Mining Company), of Mauritania
SPLA	Saharawi People's Liberation Army
STM	Sindicato de Trabajadores del Mar (Seamen's Union), of the Canary Islands
UCD	Unión del Centro Democrático (Union of the Democratic Center), of Spain
UMT	Union Marocaine du Travail (Moroccan Union of Labor)
UN	United Nations
UNEM	Union Nationale des Etudiants Marocains (National Union of Moroccan Students)
UNESCO	United Nations Educational, Scientific and Cultural Organization
UNFP	Union Nationale des Forces Populaires
UNHCR	United Nations High Commissioner for Refugees
UPM	Union Progressiste Mauritanienne (Mauritanian Progressive Union)
USFP	Union Socialiste des Forces Populaires (Socialist Union of Popular Forces)
UTM	Union des Travailleurs Mauritaniens (Mauritanian Workers Union)

WESTERN SAHARA

1

The Sons
of the Clouds

THE SAHARA WAS NOT ALWAYS A DESERT. Through the ages, arid and humid periods have alternated in this now scorched and desolate land. Between about 5000 and 2500 B.C., for example, the western stretches of the Sahara were savanna country, roamed by such animals as the giraffes, elephants and rhinoceroses that archaeologists have found depicted in neolithic rock drawings in Western Sahara and Mauritania but which have long since vanished from this part of Africa.[1]

We know very little about the people who drew these animals. Local Saharan traditions recall that they were blacks, known as Bafour. But modern archaeological exploration suggests that, while most of southern and central Mauritania was inhabited by blacks in neolithic times, white peoples, of "Capsian" and "Iberomaurusian" stock, were predominant farther north.[2] In any case, the neolithic period ended in an ecological disaster when, from about the end of the third millenium B.C., the savanna began to give way gradually, over hundreds of years, to desert. Both cattle-raising and agriculture, which had been practiced by some of the western Sahara's neolithic inhabitants, became increasingly precarious; and according to local tradition, the Bafour began taking refuge in the oases or migrating to the south. But despite the increasingly inhospitable climate, new migrations into the western Sahara from the north began during the course of the first millennium B.C. The newcomers were Berber nomads. We do not know why they came. They may have been escaping enemies, or simply seeking new pastures; but whatever their motives, their use of iron and horses gave them the upper hand against the remnants of the neolithic population.[3] However, they might never have remained in the Sahara, as it finally evolved into true desert, had they not had the good fortune to acquire the one animal that could assure human survival there—the camel, which first arrived from the east in about the first century B.C.

Some of the Berbers of the western Sahara were converted to Islam, at least

3

superficially, during the eighth and ninth centuries, after the first Arab expeditions to the "far Maghreb," the Maghreb al-Aqsa. Atcording to medieval Arab
historians, Uqba Ibn Nafi, the governor of Ifriqia (Tunisia) for the Ummayad empire of Damascus, was the first Arab leader to reach Morocco—the regions of the
Draa River and the Souss, just to the north of the desert—in 681, but some
modern historians doubt that he really traveled farther west than central Algeria.[4]
Moussa Ibn Nusair, who was appointed governor of Ifriqia in 705, was the first
Arab to subdue parts of Morocco, and in 711 he dispatched a Berber army across
the Straits of Gibraltar which defeated the Visigoths and conquered Spain in the
name of Islam. By comparison, Arab interest in the forbidding and uninviting
Saharan desert was minor, though a later governor of Ifriqia, Abderrahman Ibn
Habib, is said to have ordered the construction of a line of wells from southern
Morocco to the trading city of Aoudaghost, on the other side of the desert, in
southern Mauritania, in 745. Indeed, the gradual spread of Islam into the desert
was probably made possible by the emergence for the first time, in the eighth and
ninth centuries, of regular, as opposed to sporadic, trading across the western
Sahara. The principal Arab states of the western Mediterranean, Ifriqia and
Spain, both needed the gold of black Africa to mint their coinage, and they competed, in alliance with local tribes, to control the principal trade routes.[5]

The tribes living at this time in the western belt of the Sahara were offshoots of
the two main Berber peoples of northwest Africa, the Zenata and the Sanhaja.
The former, despite their nomadic traditions, had become masters of the main
oases and trading centers on the northern fringes of the desert by the ninth century. Thus, in about 757, a branch of the Zenata, the Miknasa, who had embraced the revolutionary, egalitarian creed of Kharijite Islam, founded the city of
Sijilmassa among the palm groves of Tafilalet (southeastern Morocco).[6] By about
786, they had extended their influence westward to the palm oases of the Oued
Draa, the 550-mile-long river flowing from the Atlas Mountains to the Atlantic
which, along its southern course, forms part of the desert's natural northwestern
frontier. Sijilmassa itself remained a Kharijite state under the Miknasa for around
two hundred years and then, toward the end of the tenth century, came under the
sway of another Zenata tribe, the Maghrawa, who also extended their authority to
the oases of the Draa Valley. Sijilmassa was by then the key trading center on the
northern flank of the western Sahara.[7]

To the south, in the desert itself, the main tribes of camel-herding nomads
were of Sanhaja ancestry. Barred by the Zenata from migrating north toward the
Atlas ranges, the Saharan Sanhaja pushed southward in search of pastures and
competed with black African tribes for mastery of the steppes on the southern
edge of the Sahara. Early in the ninth century one of their greatest leaders,
Tilutan, succeeded in evicting the black Soninke from the city of Aoudaghost.
But these nomads' inherent disunity rendered Tilutan's victory ephemeral. The
Soninke kingdom of Ghana, which controlled the traffic in gold from the West
African forests, fought back against the Sanhaja and toward 990 recaptured
Aoudaghost, the main trading "port" on the southern borders of the desert.
So, by the end of the tenth century, the Sanhaja were on the retreat. They had
been barred by the Zenata and the Soninke from breaking out of their desert

wilderness to the more attractive pasturelands to the north and south, and they had likewise been excluded from the main market towns that controlled the lucrative trading across the Sahara from which they could benefit only marginally by offering their services as guides and transporters or by pillaging.[8]

Throughout history, the desert was a place of refuge or sanctuary for peoples fleeing tribal enemies or the exactions and repression of rulers. Conversely, the desert's limited pastoral resources, which could rapidly be exhausted in years of drought, encouraged periodic counter-migrations which, by virtue of the Saharans' warrior traditions, could profoundly mark the fertile regions they invaded. Such it was to be when, in the middle of the eleventh century, the Saharan Sanhaja rallied around a religious banner to drive their enemies, the Zenata and the Soninke, from the market towns on the fringes of the desert and then push remorselessly forward to crush the kingdom of Ghana and to conquer Morocco, Muslim Spain and much of western Algeria. The man who welded the Sanhaja into a powerful fighting force was a Soussi preacher from southern Morocco by the name of Abdallah Ibn Yacin, who had been invited to the Sahara to preach to one of the main Sanhaja tribes, the Gadala, who were then living along the Atlantic coast and in the region of the Saguia el-Hamra, by their chief, Yahya Ibn Ibrahim

NORTHWEST AFRICA

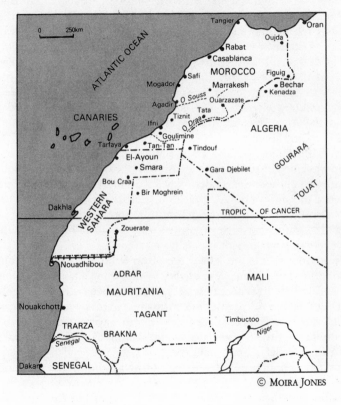

© MOIRA JONES

el-Gadali, who had become ashamed, after a pilgrimage to Mecca in about 1036, of his people's shallow knowledge of Islam. However, after being disowned by most of the Gadala, who took exception to his disciplinarian ways, Ibn Yacin turned to another tribe, the Lemtuna, then living farther south, in Tiris and Adrar (northern Mauritania), and gradually succeeded in recruiting a loyal band of followers, who came to be known as *al-murabitun*, the "Almoravids."⁹ By about 1040–42, he had assembled enough supporters to launch a *jihad*, or holy war, to eradicate the superstition, sorcery and animism still influential among the nomads; and after eventually forcing most of the Lemtuna, the Gadala and a third Sanhaja tribe, the Massufa, to submit to his leadership, he appointed a Lemtuna chief, Yahya Ibn Omar, to command the Almoravid army in further campaigns to impose the strict observation of Islamic principles on pagans and false Muslims alike. So, fired by religious zeal, the Sanhaja began raiding against their historic enemies, the Zenata and the Soninke, and in 1053–54 they scored a decisive double victory by seizing both Sijilmassa and Aoudaghost, thereby establishing their mastery over the main Saharan trading route. Then, the offensive logic of their war against the continuing Zenata resistance and their sense of religious mission impelled them onward into Morocco, in a campaign whose ultimate aim became the conquest of Morocco's fertile Atlantic plains. However, as the Almoravid army advanced northward, the original Saharan Sanhaja alliance began to break up, under the stress of old tribal frictions. Thus, when the Zenata of Sijilmassa rebelled against their new masters in 1054, shortly after the city's capture, the Gadala, who had been angered by the Lemtuna ascendancy in the Almoravid movement, refused to heed Ibn Yacin's pleas to ride anew against them and in 1056 killed Yahya Ibn Omar in battle. Yahya's brother, Abu Bakr Ibn Omar, who restored order in Sijilmassa the same year, succeeded to the Almoravid military command and, along with Ibn Yacin, advanced into the Souss and the Anti-Atlas mountains. By 1059 they had reached the Atlantic plains of northern Morocco.

However, the Almoravid advance into Morocco suffered a major setback when Ibn Yacin was killed in 1059 during a clash with the Berghwata tribe about twenty miles southwest of the site of modern-day Rabat. Moreover, intertribal strife once again sapped the unity of the Almoravids in their desert home-base; in 1061, Abu Bakr was obliged to return to the Sahara to restore order among the rebellious Gadala and Massufa, leaving his cousin, Yusuf Ibn Tashfin, in command of the Almoravid contingents in Morocco.¹⁰

After restoring order in the Sahara, Abu Bakr reforged a sense of common purpose among the quarrelsome desert tribes by proposing a holy war against pagan Ghana, which offered a chance to seize slaves and Ghana's legendary gold as well as to fulfill a religious duty. After fomenting rebellions by the Muslim aristocrats of Ghana's small vassal states, Abu Bakr began a concerted offensive in 1062 which culminated fifteen years later in the sacking of Ghana's capital, Kumbi Saleh, the flight of its last monarch, the *tunka*, the total collapse of his kingdom and, since they were allowed to retain their privileges only if they submitted to the new faith, the Islamization of the Soninke aristocracy.¹¹

Meanwhile, thousands of miles to the north, Yusuf Ibn Tashfin founded the city of Marrakesh in 1062 and then went on to complete the Almoravid conquest of Morocco, capturing the city of Fez in 1069. By 1082 his authority extended as far east as Algiers. From 1074 Ibn Tashfin received pleas from Muslim Spain, then divided into more than twenty weak independent principalities, to help beat back the Christian *reconquista* that had started in the 1050s. Finally, after the fall of Toledo to Alfonso VI of Castile in 1085, Ibn Tashfin crossed the Straits of Gibraltar with a powerful army and, on October 23, 1086, decimated the Castilian army at Zalaqa, near Badajoz. He then returned to Morocco, but when the Christians resumed their offensive, he landed once more in Spain, in 1090, and this time he began to act as master, rather than ally, of the cultivated but bickering rulers of Muslim Spain. By 1094 he had assumed control of all of Muslim Spain except Saragossa, which was absorbed into the Almoravid empire four years after his death in 1106.[12]

Nominally, the Almoravid empire now stretched from Saragossa to the River Senegal. But the reality was very different. There were in fact two "empires." The state founded by Yusuf Ibn Tashfin in Morocco had no direct control over the Saharan *al-murabitun*, and likewise Abu Bakr was powerless to influence events to the north of the desert, as he discovered to his cost in 1062 when, after restoring order among the Saharan Sanhaja, he returned to Morocco with the intention of resuming the command he had entrusted to Ibn Tashfin the year before. Yusuf "presented himself before Abu Bakr with rich presents and a strong escort. When the two chiefs met each other, Abu Bakr expressed surprise at the gifts: 'They are to make sure you lack nothing in the desert,' Yusuf Ibn Tashfin replied. Abu Bakr understood and returned to the land of the Lemtuna. He had remained a Saharan; Yusuf Ibn Tashfin had become a Moroccan."[13] While Abu Bakr proceeded to the conquest of Ghana, the Almoravid conquerors to the north of the desert gradually lost touch with their Saharan roots and fell under the cultural influence of Morocco and Spain. Then, less than four decades after Ibn Tashfin's death, the northern Almoravid state started to collapse, under multiple challenges in both Spain and Morocco. The Christian *reconquista* resumed its onward march, and in 1143–44 the Spanish Muslims rebelled against Almoravid rule. In Morocco, Masmuda Berbers from the Atlas Mountains rose in revolt in 1125, under the leadership of a new religious movement, the Almohads, who had conquered most of Morocco by 1143 and finally seized Marrakesh in 1147.

In the Sahara the fragile unity forged by the Almoravid leaders rapidly dissolved into intertribal conflict after Abu Bakr's death in a battle in Tagant, Mauritania, in 1087. Two centuries later, when the Saharan Sanhaja began facing a serious external challenge, the first incursions of tribes of Arab bedouins who had migrated all the way across North Africa, they were unable to put up effective resistance.

Though the early Arab invasions of the Maghreb, in the seventh and eighth centuries, had resulted in the conversion of the local populations to Islam, they had not altered its Berber character. Very few Arabs had settled in the Maghreb, and Arabic was rarely spoken outside the cities. In the desert regions to the south, the Arab influence was even less evident. The Berber nomads there met no Arabs apart from the occasional traveler or trader. But in the eleventh century there began a series of invasions by Arab bedouin tribes which were to transform the Maghreb. The invasions started because the Fatimid caliph of Egypt induced two large and troublesome nomadic peoples, the Beni Hilal and the Beni Sulaim, who had recently settled in the Nile Delta, to stop disturbing the tranquillity of Egypt and instead satisfy their urge to raid by attacking Ifriqia, whose local rulers, the Zirids, had just renounced Fatimid sovereignty. The Beni Sulaim settled first in Cyrenaica, Libya, and did not reach Ifriqia until the thirteenth century, but the Beni Hilal fell upon the fertile Tunisian plains in 1052 and sacked Qairuan, the Zirid capital, five years later. "Like an army of grasshoppers, they destroyed everything in their path," remarked the fourteenth-century Arab scholar, Ibn Khaldun.[14] By the 1150s some of the Beni Hilal had reached the Atlantic plains of Morocco. An important repercussion of the influx of these bedouins into the Maghreb was the displacement of the Berber languages by Arabic in most rural areas except the mountain ranges, which they bypassed.

Neither the Beni Hilal nor the Beni Sulaim reached the western Sahara. However, another bedouin Arab people, the Maqil, who apparently originated in Yemen, migrated across North Africa in their wake, skirting the edge of the desert, and by about 1218 some of them had reached as far west as the oases of the Draa Valley and the Atlantic coast.[15] The Maqil were a new threat to the states of the Maghreb. Though poorer and weaker than their forerunners, the Beni Hilal and the Beni Sulaim, they too hoped to push their way into the most fertile regions. Yaghmorasan Ibn Ziyan, the founder of the Ziyanid state of Tlemcen in northwestern Algeria in 1235–86, is said, doubtless with exaggeration, to have conducted no less than seventy-two expeditions against a Maqil tribe, the Dawi Ubaid Allah, to bar them from his lands. Farther west, the Beni Merin, Zenata Berbers from southeast Morocco, allied briefly with Maqil tribes during their war against the Almohads in the mid-thirteenth century; but when they finally defeated the Almohads, by capturing Fez in 1248 and Marrakesh in 1269, Morocco's new Merinid rulers had to confront attempts by the Maqil to break through the Atlas ranges into the Atlantic plains. So, while allowing some to settle in northern Morocco, the Merinid sultan, Abu Yusuf (1258–86), posted military units on the main passes across the Atlas Mountains and in 1271 sent a punitive expedition against the Maqil in the Draa Valley. Three years later, the Merinids besieged Sijilmassa, which was then under Maqil dominance.[16]

On account of these Merinid expeditions against them, or perhaps simply to find new pastures, some of the Maqil, from a group of tribes known collectively as the Beni Hassan, began migrating southward from the Draa Valley into the western Sahara, from about the end of the thirteenth century. This was not so much a full-blown invasion as a gradual infiltration, spread over as long as two or three centuries. Gradually, groups of Beni Hassan defeated or allied with, submerged or vassalized, or fused and intermarried with the Sanhaja, to give rise to a new Arabic-speaking people, known to us today as the "Moors," a people of mixed ethnic origins—Arab, Berber and, due to miscegenation with slaves and their descendants, black African too—who lived as pastoral nomads over a vast swath of the Sahara, from the Draa River in the north to the banks of the Senegal and the bend of the Niger, and from the Atlantic seaboard to a series of almost impenetrable dune zones, the Erg Iguidi, the Erg Chech and the Majabat al-Kubra, in what is now eastern Mauritania. To the Moors, this was the *trab el-beidan*, the land of the "whites," by contrast to that of the black Africans to their south, though it comprised numerous regions with their own distinct characteristics. One of them, known as the Sahel, or "littoral," since it bordered the Atlantic coast, roughly corresponded to the region that was later to be colonized by Spain, and its inhabitants came to be known as the Ahel es-Sahel, the "people of the Sahel."[17]

The genesis of the Moors was a long and complex process of interaction between the Sanhaja and the Beni Hassan, spread over hundreds of years and complicated by regional variations. In the fifteenth and sixteenth centuries, explorers and travelers noted that the Znaga language of the Sanhaja was still very widely spoken. The great chronicler of the early Portuguese discoveries of the fifteenth century, Gomes Eannes de Azurara, recorded that João Fernandes, an explorer who had traveled with groups of nomads into the Saharan hinterland from a point on the coast near Dakhla in 1445, found that "the writing of these people and their language are not like those of the other Moors; but they all belong to the sect of Mohamet and they are called Alarves and Azanegues and Berbers."[18] In the sixteenth century Leo Africanus and Luis de Mármol y Carvajal, who traveled into the western Sahara from Morocco in 1512 and 1556 respectively, reported the presence of both Sanhaja and an Arab tribe, the Oulad Delim ("Sons of Delim"). "The Delim live in the desert of Libya along with the Znaga, an African people," Leo Africanus wrote. "They possess neither dominion nor tribute, as a result of which they are reduced to an extreme poverty which obliges them to convert themselves into robbers. They frequently go to the region of the Draa to exchange their livestock for dates."[19] Claiming descent from Delim, one of the sons of Hassan, the supposed ancestor of all the Beni Hassan, the Oulad Delim emerged eventually as the dominant tribe in what was to become the southernmost part of Spanish Sahara, Adrar Soutouf, and they are probably among the purest Arabs of the Sahel.[20] By contrast, it appears that the Tekna tribes on the northwestern borders of the Sahara were the product of a process of fusion between Arab and Berber groups.[21]

In western Mauritania, between Tiris and the Senegal River, the Sanhaja united under the leadership of a Lemtuna man of religion, Nasser ed-Din, in 1644, to wage a long war, known as Shar Boubah, against the Beni Hassan, but were finally forced by internal divisions and successive defeats to sue for peace in 1674. Though conflicts between tribes of Arab and Berber origin continued over the following centuries, the war of Shar Boubah seems to have marked a turning point in Arab-Berber relations over much of the *trab el-beidan*. The agreement of Tin Yefdad, which ended the conflict, required the defeated Sanhaja to "abandon the sword for the book."[22] Thus it was that some Sanhaja tribes agreed to forsake war and dedicate themselves instead to religion and teaching as *ahel ktub*, or "people of the book." These tribes, which took on the character of religious fraternities, were known as *zwaya*, and the most respected among them, the aptly named "*zwaya* of the sun," prospered greatly from the offerings of their students and disciples (*telamid*). The lesser "*zwaya* of the shade" would pay a modest tribute, the *ghaffer*, to gain the protection of warrior tribes. These *ahel mdafa*, or "people of the gun," were of predominantly Arab descent, and acquired much of their wealth by raiding enemies and extracting tribute or labor from vassal tribes. The latter were known as the *znaga*—a clear enough indication of their ethnic origin—or, more derogatively, as *lahma*, "flesh without bones," and were forced, family by family, to pay a regular tribute, the *horma*, in the form of livestock or labor services, to designated families in the warrior tribe to whom they were subservient. They were often ruthlessly exploited.

Within each tribe, whether of warrior, *zwaya* or tributary status, there often lived, apart from the tribe's own members, families belonging to lower, hereditary castes. There were, first, the *maalemin*, craftsmen and artisans who worked for their host tribes as jewelers, blacksmiths, carpenters, saddlemakers, weavers, leatherworkers and the like; and secondly, though less frequently in the western Sahara than in Mauritania, there were the *iggawen*, or bards. At the very bottom of the social scale were the black slaves, or *abid*. The neolithic Bafour had possibly provided an original source of slaves to the Berbers when they first reached the Sahara; but over the centuries black slaves from the south were procured through trade and war. They were occasionally freed, to become *haratin*, but would remain dependent on their former masters, to whom they would frequently have to furnish labor or tribute, like the *znaga*.

Broadly speaking, this stratified social system existed throughout the *trab el-beidan*, though there were some regional variations, including in the coastal Sahel, or the western Sahara.[23] There, the main tribes of "warrior" status were to be the Oulad Delim and, despite a strong admixture of Berber blood, the Tekna. The Oulad Tidrarin, a tribe of predominantly Sanhaja origin which reached its apogee under the leadership of Sidi Ahmed Bou Ghambor at the end of the seventeenth century, were *zwaya* until, much weakened, about a hundred years later, they were forced to submit to the Oulad Delim and began paying the *horma*. They remained *znaga* throughout the nineteenth century until, in 1887, they rebelled and fought a long but ultimately unsuccessful war against their Oulad Delim oppressors.[24] However, most of the Western Saharan tribes of predominantly Sanhaja origin were neither *zwaya* nor *znaga*. They were "free," like the *zwaya* elsewhere, but they were often as warlike as the *ahel mdafa*, and ironically, in view of their mainly Berber origins, they claimed not only to be Arabs but even to descend directly from the Prophet Mohammed, and so to be *shorfa*.[25] Among them were the Reguibat, now the largest Western Saharan tribe, and the Arosien. Their "founders," Sidi Ahmed Reguibi and Sidi Ahmed el-Arosi, were celebrated sixteenth-century holy men; and this is the key to the puzzle of their claim to sharifian ancestry. In theory, the members of any tribe, or *qabila* (plural *qabael*), could trace their descent, patrilineally, from a common ancestor at the apex of the tribal genealogical tree. The *qabila* was subdivided into a series of fractions (*afkhad*, singular *fakhd*), with their own common ancestors, and in turn into smaller sub-fractions or "extended families."[26] There was a very strong sense of agnatic solidarity, or *asabiya*, because the tribe constituted the ultimate source of security for the individual in the anarchic world of the desert, where raiding between tribes was frequent. Nonetheless, the *qabael* were not as pure as their neat genealogical schemas might imply, and solidarity was not always based strictly on ties of blood. By means of a solidarity pact (*asaba*), individuals, groups or even whole tribes could be incorporated into a *qabila* by adoption and a sense of agnatic solidarity artificially created. Such a pact could even serve to bring a new *qabila* into existence, by bonding together "foreign" elements, perhaps around a prestigious family, holy man or warrior; and it is not at all surprising that in such cases the whole *qabila* could end up, after several generations, believing that it had an origin or genealogy which, at the outset, was that of only a dominant family or individual.[27] This, it seems, is what happened, for example, after Sidi Ahmed Reguibi, a holy man who claimed descent from a famous Moroccan saint of the twelfth and thirteenth centuries, Moulay Abdal-Salam Ibn Mashish, and ultimately from the Prophet Mohammed, arrived in the Draa Valley in 1503, gathered around himself a coterie of *telamid* and married a woman of the Sellam, a local nomadic tribe, by the name of Kaouria Mint Mohammed, whose sons Ali, Amar and Qacem were later said to have engendered the main branches of the Reguibat.[28] Often linked to Sufi lodges like the Qadiriya, such holy men, or "marabouts," seem to have provided important leadership to the Sanhaja groups in the western Saharan region in the fifteenth and sixteenth centuries as they came under challenge from both the Beni Hassan and Portuguese and Spanish raiders along the coast.[29]

By the nineteenth century, Hassaniya, the dialect of Arabic introduced by the Beni Hassan, had been adopted by all the *qabael* of the *trab el-beidan,* though a few isolated pockets of Znaga-speakers remained in Mauritania.[30] A product of the long history of wars, alliances, fusions and intermarriage between Beni Hassan and Sanhaja, this Arabization gave credence to the genealogies. To the Moors it confirmed their Arab identity and delineated the *trab el-beidan* from the neighboring regions to north and east, where Berber languages—Tashelhit, spoken by the Berbers of the Souss, the Anti-Atlas and the High Atlas, and Tamashagh, the language of the nomadic Tuareg of the central Sahara (Algeria, Niger and Mali)—remained dominant.

In the western Sahara, besides, most of the tribes of predominantly Sanhaja ancestry not only came to think of themselves as Arabs and *shorfa*, but, by and large, were no less "warriors" than the *ahel mdafa*, the "real" Arabs. The distinction between *shorfa* and warriors was, to say the least, blurred. Indeed, the nineteenth century saw the rise of the Reguibat as the largest and most powerful of all the *qabael* of this part of the desert. The Reguibat went to war with and defeated many of the tribes of the northern stretches of the *trab el-beidan*, one after another. The Tadjakant, a trading people, with whom hostilities began in 1820, were practically wiped out in 1895 when a force of a thousand Reguibat descended upon their capital, the trading town of Tindouf (which is now in southwestern Algeria) and massacred almost all its inhabitants.[31] Tindouf was then abandoned and remained almost continually deserted until the French army arrived there forty years later, in 1934. In 1866, meanwhile, the Reguibat helped another sharifian tribe, the Oulad Bou Sbaa, to defeat an invading force from Adrar and the Hodh (southeastern Mauritania) led by the marabout Sidi Ahmed el-Kounti. In 1888 the Reguibat joined the Oulad Tidrarin's war against the

Oulad Delim but they finally sold out these *znaga* by making a separate peace with the Oulad Delim in 1892. In 1897 they began another long struggle, against the Oulad Jerir of Adrar, whom they finally crushed in 1909. Simultaneously, they had been fighting against the Oulad Ghailan of Adrar in 1899–1904 and then, in 1905–10, against the Oulad Bou Sbaa, whom they severely defeated at the battles of Foucht (1907) and Lemden el-Hauat (1910).[32] Divided into two broad subgroups, the Reguibat es-Sahel, or "coastal Reguibat," and the Reguibat esh-Sharg, or "eastern Reguibat," their zone of nomadism extended over thousands of square miles of territory, from the Saguia el-Hamra and the Zemmour massif in Western Sahara, across the extreme north of Mauritania, into southwestern Algeria and as far as the northwestern tip of Mali.

Desert societies have always been prone to intertribal strife and raiding.[33] By virtue of their migrations, nomadic tribes would enter into frequent contact, and they were in competition for scarce pastoral resources, water sources and livestock. Moreover, since the creation of large-scale forms of human organization was discouraged by the inhospitality and vastness of the desert and by the sparseness and dispersion of its population, there was no effective supratribal state authority to maintain order in the western Sahara. The nomads had ample means of war (camels, firearms) and skills of evident military application (riding ability, knowledge of terrain), and success in battle appeared to the young to be the surest route to fortune and honor. The immediate objective of the raid (*ghazzi*), which might be staged against a tribe living hundreds or even more than a thousand miles away, was to seize livestock. It was organized as a commercial enterprise, with the wealthier members of the tribe investing in its success by loaning out equipment (*selb*)—camels, saddles, rifles and ammunition—to the young raiders in return for a fixed share in their booty. However, since the blood-debt (*diya*) incurred by a murder fell upon the killers' relatives, and not just on the killer himself, it could give rise to a blood-feud, or vendetta, and so generate a self-perpetuating spiral of raids and counter-raids that would only end when one side finally sued for peace, exhausted. Nonetheless, there were also constraints on raiding. Conflicts might be resolved by the patient diplomacy of a negotiating party (*sorba*). Payment of the blood-debt in camels or goats would prevent the spilling of more blood, and the practice of *meniha,* the lending of livestock by wealthy herd owners to the less fortunate of their kinsmen, not only provided security (the right to use the products of the loaned animals) to nomads with no animals of their own, but also, by dispersing the herds, reduced the risk of theft for the wealthy.[34]

The insecurity of the violent desert world would, besides, encourage or force tribes to enter into alliances and pacts for protection or mutual assistance. For example, the Tekna tribes were traditionally divided into two mutually antagonistic but unstable alliances—the Ait Jmel, who by the beginning of the twentieth century comprised the principal western Tekna tribes (the Ait Lahsen, Izarguien, Yagout and Ait Moussa Ou Ali), and the more easterly Ait Atman (the Azouafid, Id Ahmed, Id Brahim and Ait Oussa). Rarely were these Tekna "political parties" at peace with one another for more than five years at a time.[35] Sometimes these alliances could be broadened temporarily to include non-Tekna tribes, as in 1901, when, during a war triggered by an Azouafid *ghazzi* against a group of

Izarguien, both Ait Jmel and Ait Atman ended up recruiting allies among rival Berber tribes far to the north, in the region of Ifni.[36]

Protection pacts could range from mutually beneficial, evenhanded agreements between powerful tribes to the most exploitative and involuntary arrangements between strong and weak. Among the former, for example, were agreements, symbolized by the sacrifice (*debiha*) of a goat or camel, by which the right of passage and protection in "foreign" territory could be acquired. They were commonplace between groups of Reguibat and Tekna, since the Reguibat needed to cross Tekna country to reach the markets of the Draa Valley and the Oued Noun and some Tekna tribes needed to drive their herds south toward the Saguia el-Hamra. Sometimes, however, the *debiha* could imply submission, as, for example, when it was made by the small poor fishing tribes of the coast, such as the Fouikat, Lemiar and Mejat, to the powerful Tekna tribe, the Izarguien. However, no form of tribute was more systematic and demeaning than the *horma*.[37]

Despite the exploitation of tribute-paying *znaga* and of slaves, western Saharan society was relatively egalitarian. Indeed, it was much more so than parts of Mauritania to the south. Numerically speaking, the tribute-paying or enslaved component of the population was very small. The *znaga*, of whom the Oulad Tidrarin comprised the overwhelming majority, besides the few tiny fishing tribes, constituted no more than one eighth of the total population, and slaves probably accounted for less than 5 percent.[38] Only the very weakest of tribes could not successfully resist or escape the enforced payment of tribute through armed resistance, the exploitation of tribal rivalries to establish opportune alliances, or emigration; and whereas slaves were a valuable labor force, especially in the date-palm oases in parts of Mauritania, they were of little practical use and difficult to maintain in the exceptionally arid western Sahara, which has no oases of consequence and required long-distance migration in relatively small groups to take maximum advantage of the rare pastures. At the same time, very few families amassed a real fortune, despite the private ownership of livestock, in this desolate country where a serious drought could decimate the herds; and the practice of *meniha* alleviated cases of real hardship.

In such a pastoral desert society, the camel was, of course, the key to survival. With a stomach capacity of as much as sixty gallons, the camel can travel without drinking for five days in the hottest weeks of the summer or even several weeks in winter months if pastures are plentiful, and its ability to travel as far as forty miles a day allows maximum advantage to be taken of the sparse and scattered pastures. The camel was excellent as a pack animal for both normal nomadic migrations and long-distance trading, since it could carry loads up to three hundred pounds. Its hair was used to weave the nomads' tents (*khaimat*), its skins were fashioned into leather, and camel's milk—of which the females can furnish twelve pints a day or even twenty-four pints at maximum, six months after giving birth—was the foundation of the nomads' diet. The camel was also an instrument of war, a means and unit of exchange and, besides the salt mined in the Saharan *sebkhat* (salt pans), the nomads' principal "export."[39] Though of much less importance, the nomads also herded goats, which provided milk, meat, skins and hair.

They could suffer dreadfully from a prolonged drought, and in their constant stuggle against nature they knew that the slightest error of judgment could decimate their herds and perhaps result in starvation and death. It was thus a matter of survival to possess a quite remarkable sense of direction and knowledge of terrain—skills which, incidentally, have contributed to the Western Saharans' success as guerrillas in the twentieth century. The nomad was like a living compass. He could guide a caravan across an immense monotonous plain or lead his herds to a distant well or new pastures by using his knowledge of the stars and his memory of the most minute details of landscape.[40]

The cultivation of crops was marginal to the economy of the Ahel es-Sahel. There were almost no important oases between the Draa Valley and Adrar, though very small quantities of barley were grown in rain-collecting depressions.[41] It was mainly cultivated by slaves since agricultural labor was despised by the nomads. Furthermore, though Western Sahara has a coastline of some 720 miles, with rich fishing banks that have attracted the Canary Islanders for the past five centuries, only the small impoverished tribes of *znaga* along the coast engaged in fishing and their techniques were primitive in the extreme. They did not use boats but instead fished along the beach, wading in shallow waters with large nets. The lack of wood for boatbuilding, the steep coastal cliffs, the rarity of natural harbors and a dangerous stormy coastline seem to have combined to impede the development of fishing.[42]

The products of the camel and the goat could not satisfy all the nomads' needs. They would therefore frequent such trading centers as Tindouf or Goulimine, to the north of the Draa, to exchange their camels, or their wool and skins, for such "imports" as cereals, tea, sugar, weapons and other manufactured goods. They also participated, as guides, escorts or traders in their own right, in the long-distance caravan commerce which, depending on the epoch, would bring such prized commodities as gold, slaves, ostrich feathers and gum arabic from the savanna and forests to the south of the Sahara to the markets of the Maghreb and Europe and, in reverse direction, manufactured goods such as cloth.

Politically, each Western Saharan tribe and fraction regulated its affairs through an assembly (*djemaa*) of the heads of its most distinguished families—men who, by virtue of their valor, age, wisdom, piety or wealth, enjoyed the greatest respect. The *djemaa* selected the group's sheikh, established its own body of laws, the *orf,* to complement the basic Islamic judicial code, the *sharia,* and appointed a *qadi,* or judge, to administer justice.[43] At the tribal level this assembly was often known as the *ait arbain,* or "council of forty." Presided over by a *moqadem,* it would usually be called into session in time of war or grave crisis, to organize the tribe's defense or a raid and to appoint a military commander, the *dahman.*[44]

Except in times of insecurity it was rare for a whole tribe to gather together in one place. The limited and dispersed pastures required migrations in much smaller groups, so tribes were usually spread over huge distances in a large number of scattered encampments (*firqan,* singular *friq*). Outside times of war, political and judicial decisions were likely to be made at the level of the fraction or subfraction, rather than the tribe. Under such conditions of dispersal, in an exceptionally arid and hostile environment, no single group could draw on sufficient power or resources to establish even a semblance of supratribal government. By contrast, farther south in the plains of the south and center-west of Mauritania, which enjoy somewhat greater rainfall (3 to 5 inches a year, compared to less than 2 inches in Western Sahara) and whose oases and relatively better pastures could support a much higher concentration of population, embryonic supratribal emirates were created from about the seventeenth century by the stronger Beni Hassan tribes in Trarza, Brakna, Tagant and Adrar, but even they were exceedingly precarious.[45] They had no fixed capital, held but the most tenuous control of their subject tribes and were frequently torn apart by internal conflicts. Even such limited forms of supratribal organization were unknown in the ultra-arid and thinly populated swath of desert between Adrar and the Draa River. This was the domain of totally independent Saharawi tribes who never submitted to either the weak Mauritanian emirs or, as we shall see in Chapter Three, the state to the north of the desert, the sultanate of Morocco.

NOTES

1. Julio Caro Baroja, *Estudios Saharianos* (Instituto de Estudios Africanos, Madrid, 1955), p. 78.

2. R. Vernet, "La préhistoire de la Mauritanie," in *Introduction à la Mauritanie* (Editions du Centre National de la Recherche Scientifique, Paris, 1979), pp. 29–30.

3. Horses bearing riders or pulling carts or chariots are depicted, sometimes in association with inscriptions in the old Berber script, Tifinagh, in numerous western Saharan and Mauritanian rock drawings of the first millennium B.C. See *ibid.*, p. 41; Christine Vanacker, "La Mauritanie jusqu'au XXe siècle," in *Introduction à la Mauritanie*, p. 43; John Mercer, *Spanish Sahara* (George Allen and Unwin, London, 1976), pp. 64–65.

4. Charles-André Julien, *History of North Africa*, tr. John Petrie (Routledge and Kegan Paul, London, 1970), pp. 8–10.

5. Vanacker, *loc. cit.*, p. 51.

6. The Kharijite sect, which had originated in the Near East, proclaimed the right of Muslims to remove from office any *imam* who deserted the right path. Kharijism attracted many Berbers who saw in its doctrine religious sanction to oppose despotic Arab governments. See Julien, *op. cit.*, pp. 19–20, 33.

7. F. de La Chapelle, "Esquisse d'une histoire du Sahara occidental," *Hespéris*, Vol. XI, 1930, p. 58.

8. *Ibid.*, pp. 60–61.

9. Following accounts of Abdallah Ibn Yacin by Ibn Abi Zar (died 1326) and Ibn Khaldun (died 1406), it was for long believed that *al-murabitun*, the men of the *ribat*, were organized on an island retreat, probably off the Mauritanian coast. However, earlier Arab writers—Al-Bakri (*Kitab al-Masalik*, 1068) and the Qadi Iyad (died 1149, *Kitab al-Madarik*)—make no reference to such an island retreat, which seems likely to have been a myth of later creation. See H. T. Norris, "New Evidence on the Life of 'Abdullāh b. Yāsin and the Origins of the Almoravid Movement," *Journal of African History*, Vol. XII, No. 2, 1971, p. 257.

10. Jamil M. Abun-Nasr, *A History of the Maghrib* (Cambridge University Press, Cambridge, 1971), p. 96; Julien, *op. cit.*, p. 81; La Chapelle, *loc. cit.*, p. 648.

11. Alfred G. Gerteiny, *Mauritania* (Pall Mall, London, 1967), pp. 27–28.

12. Julien, *op. cit.*, pp. 86–87.

13. Henri Terrasse, *Histoire du Maroc* (Editions Atlantides, Casablanca, 2 vols., 1949–50), Vol. 1, p. 223.

14. Ibn Khaldun, *Kitab al-'Ibar*, in M. de Slane (tr.), *Histoire des Berbères* (Algiers, 4 Vols., 1852–56), Vol. 1, p. 34, cited in Julien, *op. cit.*, p. 72.

15. F. de La Chapelle, *Les Teknas du Sud marocain* (Comité de l'Afrique Française, Paris, 1934), p. 33.

16. La Chapelle, "Esquisse d'une histoire du Sahara occidental," *loc. cit.*, p. 68.

17. The term Sahel is relative. It could refer strictly to the coast, in which case the Ahel es-Sahel

would be the small fishing tribes. See Caro Baroja, *op. cit.*, pp. 65–66; Francis de Chassey, *La Mauritanie 1900–1975: de l'ordre colonial à l'ordre néo-colonial entre Maghreb et Afrique noire* (Editions Anthropos, Paris, 1978), pp. 25–29; Francis de Chassey, "Des ethnies et de l'impérialisme dans la genèse des nations, des classes et des Etats en Afrique," *L'Homme et la Société*, Nos. 45–46, July–September and October–December 1977, pp. 114–16.

18. Gomes Eannes de Azurara, "The Chronicle of the Discovery of Guinea," in Virginia de Castro e Almeida (ed.), *Conquests and Discoveries of Henry the Navigator* (George Allen and Unwin, London, 1936), p. 216. By "Moors," Eannes de Azurara meant North Africans in general.

19. Leo Africanus, *Descripción de Africa* (Madrid, 1952), p. 25, cited in Juan Bautista Vilar Ramírez, *El Sahara y el hamitismo norteafricano. Estudios antropo-históricos sahárico-magrebíes* (Instituto de Estudios Africanos, Madrid, 1969), p. 85. Libya was Leo Africanus' term for the Sahara.

20. Bertrand Fessard de Foucault, "La question du Sahara espagnol (I)," *Revue Française d'Etudes Politiques Africaines*, 10th Year, No. 119, November 1975, p. 103.

21. La Chapelle, *Les Teknas du Sud marocain*, pp. 33–34.

22. Gerteiny, *op. cit.*, p. 34. See also Vanacker, *loc. cit.*, pp. 58–59.

23. On the social stratification of Moor and Saharawi society, see Caro Baroja, *op. cit.*, pp. 25–48, Vilar Ramírez, *op. cit.*, pp. 106–9; A. Leriche, "Notes sur les classes sociales et quelques tribus de Mauritanie," *Bulletin de l'Institut Français d'Afrique Noire*, Series B, Vol. XVII, Nos. 1–2, January–April 1955, pp. 173–76; Ahmed Baba Miské, "Al-Wasit (1911): Tableau de la Mauritanie à la fin du XIXe siècle," *Bulletin de l'Institut Fondamental d'Afrique Noire*, Series B, Vol. XXX, No. 1, January 1968, pp. 131–40.

24. Caro Baroja, *op. cit.*, pp. 135–43.

25. Singular *sharif*, from which the English adjective "sharifian."

26. Caro Baroja, *op. cit.*, pp. 12–17.

27. *Ibid.*, pp. 18–22; Ahmed Baba Miské, *loc. cit.*, p. 144.

28. Caro Baroja, *op. cit.*, pp. 53–54; David M. Hart, "The Social Structure of the Rgibat Bedouins of the Western Sahara," *The Middle East Journal*, Vol. 16, No. 4, Autumn 1962, pp. 518–20.

29. Pious mystics who supposedly possessed divine grace (*baraka*) and usually claimed descent from the Prophet Mohammed, Sufi marabouts (a corruption of *murabitun*) became commonplace in Morocco and the western Sahara at this time. They were closely identified with the struggle against the European "unbelievers" who began attacking along the coast of Morocco from the end of the fourteenth century and along the western Saharan coast early in the fifteenth century. One of the main Sufi orders to reach the *trab el-beidan* was the Qadiriya, which had been established in Baghdad in the eleventh century by Abdal-Qadir al-Jilani. See Julien, *op. cit.*, pp. 210–11; A. Traoré, "L'Islam en Mauritanie," in *Introduction à la Mauritanie*, p. 158.

30. Caro Baroja, *op. cit.*, pp. 425–31; Ahmed Baba Miské, *loc. cit.*, p. 142.

31. For a detailed account of the war, see Caro Baroja, *op. cit.*, pp. 348–50.

32. *Ibid.*, pp. 350–59.

33. See Pierre Bonte, "La guerre dans les sociétés d'éleveurs nomades," *Cahiers du Centre d'Etudes et de Recherches Marxistes*, No. 133, 1977, pp. 42–67.

34. Caro Baroja, *op. cit.*, pp. 103–4, 339–47.

35. La Chapelle, *op. cit.*, pp. 67–69.

36. Caro Baroja, *op. cit.*, pp. 367–71.

37. *Ibid.*, pp. 22–23; La Chapelle, *op. cit.*, pp. 74–77.

38. Vilar Ramírez, *op. cit.*, p. 124; Caro Baroja, *op. cit.*, p. 175.

39. Caro Baroja, *op. cit.*, pp. 82–90; Mercer, *op. cit.*, pp. 166–67.

40. *Ibid.*, p. 517; Caro Baroja, *op. cit.*, p. 64; Angel Flores Morales, *El Sahara español: ensayo de geografía física, humana y económica* (Ediciones de la Alta Comisaría de España en Marruecos, Madrid, 1946), pp. 111–12.

41. Caro Baroja, *op. cit.*, pp. 113–14.

42. Mercer, *op. cit.*, pp. 175–76.

43. Caro Baroja, *op. cit.*, pp. 23–24, pp. 43–45; La Chapelle, *op. cit.*, p. 90.

44. *Ibid.*, p. 89; Hart, *loc. cit.*, pp. 523–25.

45. In Tagant a tribe of essentially Sanhaja origin, the Idou Aich, displaced the Beni Hassan from control of the emirate at the end of the eighteenth century.

2

Seamen from Renaissance Europe

U NTIL THE FIFTEENTH CENTURY most of the Saharan coast had been beyond the reach of European seamen. Since antiquity they had known of the Canaries, which lie about 150 miles out to sea from the northern edge of the desert, but there had been no direct contact with the islands during the European Middle Ages until the early fourteenth century, when seamen from Majorca and Genoa "rediscovered" them, to trade with their primitive inhabitants, the Guanches, or carry them off into slavery. In 1341 a Portuguese fleet reached the islands. Three years later, Luis de la Cerda, who had the support of King Pedro IV of Aragon, was crowned king of the Canaries by Pope Clement VI in Avignon, but he never succeeded in reaching his "kingdom." The other main contestant for the islands was the kingdom of Castile. A Castilian fleet landed there in 1393 to seize slaves, and in May 1402 a Norman knight, Jean de Bethencourt, sailed from La Rochelle to begin the islands' conquest in the name of Castile.[1] Bethencourt conquered Lanzarote in 1402 and Fuerteventura, the nearest island to the African coast, in 1405. He then set sail to return to Europe, but first he landed on the Saharan coast, somewhere near Cape Bojador (Boujdour) in 1405 and attacked a caravan of traders. It was the first of the raiding expeditions, known as the *entradas* or *cabalgadas*, that were to become one of the main activities of Spaniards from the Canaries on the Saharan coast for the following two centuries.[2]

Cape Bojador had been the southernmost landmark on the Saharan coast to be charted by medieval European seamen and cartographers. Legend had it that beyond the cape lay the dreaded Mare Tenebrosum, the "Sea of Darkness," from which no European or Arab seaman had been known to return. There had been occasional attempts to sail beyond the cape. In 1291, two Genoese brothers, Guido and Ugolini Vivaldi, had sailed into the Atlantic in the hope of reaching India by circumnavigating Africa and had disappeared; and the "Catalan Atlas" (1375) of the Majorcan Jewish geographer, Abraham Cresques, depicted a Catalan, Jaime Ferrer, vanishing into the unknown beyond the cape in 1346.[3]

It would be almost a century before European navigators finally succeeded in sailing beyond the cape and returning, despite the strong currents, to tell the tale. By then, the inquiring spirit of the Renaissance was inspiring ambitious attempts to push beyond the narrow geographical confines known to medieval Europe. The age of the great European voyages of discovery was beginning. The sponsors of the early fifteenth-century voyages hoped to find the sources of the gold and slaves brought by the trans-Saharan traders whom Cresques had depicted crossing a pass in the Atlas Mountains on the way from "the land of the Negroes of Guinea," and the explorers themselves sought loot, slaves and personal fame.⁴ But sailors and patrons alike often believed too that they were accomplishing a religious duty. There was a crusader spirit about the voyages. They would save the souls of infidels and pagans, outflank the Muslim world, and perhaps even find the fabled kingdom of Prester John, a descendant of the Three Wise Men who, it had widely been believed in Europe since the twelfth century, ruled a distant Christian land, somewhere in Africa or Asia.⁵

The sense of religious mission was particularly strong in the Iberian peninsula, where the Christian *reconquista* was then approaching its final stages and was to culminate in the capture of Granada in 1492. Some dreamed of carrying the *reconquista* across the sea into North Africa. As early as 1399 Enrique III of Castile had landed an army in northern Morocco, seized Tetuan and massacred half its inhabitants; and in 1415 João I of Portugal had captured and pillaged Ceuta, the prosperous Moroccan trading city overlooking the Straits of Gibraltar. It was one of King João's sons, Prince Henry, who, after participating in the sacking of Ceuta, began organizing the remarkable voyages of the seamen who were to set out from the Algarve to sail on beyond Cape Bojador, down the coast of Africa, toward Guinea. According to Gomes Eannes de Azurara, the Portuguese royal chronicler, Henry the Navigator was driven by curiosity as to what lay beyond the daunting cape. He hoped that his sailors would find harbors so that "ships could bring back to the realm many merchandises at little cost." He wished also to discover the extent of Muslim power in Africa, to know "whether in those regions there might be any Christian princes" who might aid him against the Muslims, and "to increase the holy faith in Our Lord Jesus, and to lead to this faith all souls desirous of being saved."⁶ So, in 1419, Henry founded a settlement at Sagres, a rocky promontory at the southwest tip of the Algarve, which he made the base for what was to become a systematic campaign of exploration. He built a fortress, an observatory, a chapel, houses and boatyards for the building of three-masted caravels, seventy-five feet long, which were said to be the best sailing ships of the day. Soon, he was sending out annual expeditions to the islands of the Atlantic (Madeira, the Azores and the Canaries) and to the African coast.

However, it was not until 1434 that one of Henry's captains, Gil Eannes, finally summoned up the courage to sail south of Cape Bojador. "Disdaining all peril," recorded Eannes de Azurara, "he passed beyond the cape, where he found matters very different from what he and others had imagined."⁷ A year later, Henry sent Gil Eannes out to sea again, this time with another of his navigators, Afonso Gonçalves Baldaya. They reached a bay 110 miles south of Cape Bojador, which they called the "Bay of the Mullet," Angra dos Ruivos. After hearing upon their return home that they had found footprints there, Henry dispatched Afonso Gonçalves Baldaya again, in 1436, with instructions "to go as far as is possible, and to do your best to contrive to speak with these people, or to take some of them, for it would be a great thing, and according to my desire, to have some person of these countries who could give me intelligence."[8] This time, he sailed sixty miles farther south than in 1435, reaching a bay he named Angra dos Cavalos since two members of his crew disembarked there with their horses and unsuccessfully chased after a group of nomads into the desert. It was fifty miles farther south, on the Dakhla peninsula, in 1441, that some of Henry's expeditionaries, under the command of Antão Gonçalves and Nuno Tristão, finally succeeded in capturing some nomads, twelve in all. Nuno Tristão continued down the coast, as far as Cape Blanc, while Gonçalves returned to Portugal with the captives, all but one of whom could not communicate in Arabic since "their language is not Moorish, but the azenague of Zaara."[9]

Thenceforth, the manhunts were on. In 1440, Henry secured papal indulgences for those fighting the Africans, and so he gave them a crusade banner that absolved those who died fighting beneath it.[10] The main targets of Henry's raiders were isolated groups of nomads along the Saharan coast, mainly small fishing communities that had no more than spears and stones with which to fend off the surprise attacks of the archers and crossbowmen landed by the caravels. In 1443, for example, a fleet of caravels sighted a nomad camp on Naar Island, forty miles south of Cape Blanc. "Our men, crying 'Santiago! San Jorge! Portugal!' fell upon them, killing and capturing as many as they could," Eannes de Azurara recalled. "Then you might see mothers abandoning their children and husbands abandoning their wives, each thinking only to flee as speedily as might be. And some drowned themselves in the sea, others sought refuge in their huts, others hid their children under the mud, thinking that thus they could come to seek them later. And at length Our Lord God, who rewardeth all that is well done, ordained that in return for the work of this day done by our men in His service they should have their victory over their enemies and the reward of their fatigues and disbursements, in the taking of one hundred and sixty-five captives, men, women and children, without reckoning those that died or that killed themselves."[11] They then continued raiding along the coast and on nearby islands and eventually returned to Portugal with 235 captives. On arrival in the city of Lagos, they were assembled in a field and divided into five lots, one for Henry. "They began to part them, one from another, in order to form companies, in such manner that each should be of equal value; and for this it was necessary to separate children from their parents, and women from their husbands, and brothers from brothers. There was no law in respect of kinship or affection; each had perforce to go whither fate drove him."[12]

Despite the slave raids, which had netted a total of 924 captives by 1448, the Portuguese did establish peaceful relations with some of the nomads. One brave explorer, João Fernandes, disembarked near Dakhla in 1445 and spent seven months traveling in the interior with groups of nomads.[13] Three years earlier had come the first recorded instance of peaceful trade between Portuguese and nomads. Landing on the Dakhla peninsula, Antão Gonçalves set free three high-ranking Saharawi captives in return for ten black slaves and some gold dust. He was told that traders brought gold there from "the country of the Negroes called Ouangara."[14] Thereafter, the twenty-five-mile-long inlet at Dakhla was to be known to the Portuguese as the Rio de Ouro, which in its Spanish form, Río de Oro, was to give its name to the colony founded four and a half centuries later.

The Portuguese soon grasped that slaves could be acquired by bartering as easily as by raiding. The Saharawis were willing to trade their own black slaves for such valued merchandise as cloth and grain. The main center for this traffic became Arguin, an island forty miles south of Cape Blanc which had been discovered by Nuno Tristão in 1443 and fortified by the Portuguese in 1448. "You should know," wrote Alvise da Ca da Mosto, a Venetian who embarked for Africa on one of Henry's caravels in 1455, "that the said Lord Infante of Portugal has leased this island of Arguin to Christians, so that no one can enter the bay to trade with the Arabs save those who hold the licence. These have dwellings on the island and factories where they buy and sell with the said Arabs who come to the coast to trade for merchandise of various kinds, such as woollen cloths, cotton, silver and 'alchezeli', that is cloaks, carpets and similar articles and above all corn, for they are always short of food. They give in exchange slaves whom the Arabs bring from the land of the Blacks, and gold *tiber*."[15] Ca da Mosto reported that "Portuguese caravels are coming and going all the year to this island" and that most of the trade was conducted with the city of Ouadane, "about six days inland by camel." Black slaves, brought to Ouadane by the caravans, were sent on to Arguin, and "as a result every year the Portuguese carry away from Arguin a thousand slaves."[16] The island remained one of the principal commercial-cum-naval strongpoints of Portugal's mercantile empire for almost two centuries.

Castile was Portugal's main European rival on the northwest African coast during the fifteenth century, as it was in the Canaries, where four of the seven islands (Lanzarote, Fuerteventura, Hierro and Gomera) had been brought under Castilian control by 1443. The Canaries provided the Castilians with a base from which to raid and trade along the nearby Saharan coast. In July 1449, Juan II of Castile awarded the coast, from Cape Aguer (Agadir) to Cape Bojador, to Juan de Guzmán, the Duke of Medina Sidonia, only six years after Pope Eugene IV had issued a bull recognizing Portugal's claim to the same coast—a bull confirmed in 1454 by Pope Nicholas V. The duke did not attempt to make use of his "rights," and in April 1468 Juan II's successor on the Castilian throne, Enrique IV, transferred them to Diego García de Herrera, the Castilian master of the Canaries, who did take an active interest in the African coast opposite the islands. In 1476 he sent an armed force there to build a fortress, Santa Cruz de Mar Pequeña.[17]

Herrera's intention was to use the fort as a base from which to raid for slaves for the plantations of Fuerteventura and Lanzarote, where labor was scarce due to the earlier massacres of their native populations.[18] Within two years of its construction, Santa Cruz was under siege from local tribes, but Herrera managed to relieve the garrison by sending seven hundred troops in a fleet of five ships. The manhunts followed one after the other, with the Castilian Crown receiving a fifth of the profits. One slave-raider, Juan Camacho, was said to have made forty-six raids by the time of his death in 1491.[19]

Three years after the founding of Santa Cruz, the Portuguese and Castilians finally came to an understanding on the division of their respective spheres of influence. By the Treaty of Alcáçovas, in September 1479, Portugal recognized the Castilian claim to the Canaries, whose conquest was then completed by the occupation of Grand Canary in 1483, Palma in 1493 and Tenerife in 1496. In return, Castile recognized Portuguese "rights" to the coasts of Guinea and the Kingdom of Fez, while the coast between them was left undelineated. The treaty was confirmed in May 1840 by the Treaty of Toledo and then endorsed by Pope Sixtus VI the following June. In 1485 Herrera died and shortly thereafter Santa Cruz was abandoned. However, another Portuguese-Spanish treaty, signed at Tordesillas in June 1494, recognized Spanish rights along four hundred miles of the African coastline, from Massa, in southern Morocco, to Cape Bojador, while confirming Portuguese rights farther north and south. Two years later, shortly after the occupation of Tenerife, the governor of the Canaries, Alonso Fajardo, sent a force back to the African coast to rebuild Santa Cruz, at the behest of Isabel I and Fernando II, the "Catholic Kings" who had unified Castile and Aragon in 1479. This infuriated Herrera's widow, Inés Peraza, who had intended to rebuild the fort on her own account, and in 1498 she persuaded her Portuguese son-in-law, Diego da Silva, to set sail with eight ships to sack the newly reconstructed fort.

Nonetheless, Spanish activity on the coast opposite the Canaries was now reaching its zenith, with the accent on peaceful trade rather than slave raids. The main goods sought by the Spanish were slaves, gold, skins, orchil, a valuable dye extracted from rock-plants along the coast, and cowrie shells, which were then used as money in West Africa. In 1497 the Crown banned slave-raiding in the vicinity of Santa Cruz, to encourage Muslim traders to direct their caravans to the fort, and the trade in cowrie shells and orchil was declared a royal monopoly. Santa Cruz was then linked to the Casa de Contratación of Seville, the pivot of the Spanish Crown's trading activities in both Africa and the Americas, after its founding in 1503.[20] Meanwhile, steps were taken to extend Spanish influence. In February 1499, the governor of Grand Canary, Lope Sánchez de Valenzuela, landed on the coast, traveled inland to the important trading center of Taghaost, in the region of the Oued Noun, and, so it is said, persuaded the chiefs of a Berber tribe, the Ait Bou Tata, to become subjects of Castile.[21] The following October an Andalusian knight, Alonso Fernández de Lugo, who had taken part in the conquest of the Canaries, received the grandiose title of Captain-General of Africa and was instructed by the Catholic Kings to establish three new forts, at Taghaost, at the mouth of the nearby Assaka River, to be baptized San Miguel de Saca, and, much farther south, at Cape Bojador. However, the earlier *entradas* had made many many of the local tribes wary of the Spaniards, and so when Lugo landed at the mouth of the Assaka in 1500 to erect the first of the new forts, his four hundred men were attacked by a large hostile force. About three hundred of the

Spaniards were killed. Lugo himself was rescued by some loyal Ait Bou Tata and brought to Taghaost, whence he made his way to Santa Cruz.[22]

Another of Lugo's ventures, an attempt to set up a fort farther north near Agadir in 1502, also had to be abandoned, this time because the Portuguese protested that this was in their zone. Three years later they set up their own fort there, Santa Cruz de Cabo Aguer. Despite the Treaty of Tordesillas, the rivalry between Spain and Portugal had not abated on either the Mediterranean or Atlantic coasts of North Africa. In 1508 a Spanish force seized the Peñón de Vélez, an islet off Morocco's Mediterranean coast, despite Portuguese protests that it was part of the Kingdom of Fez, and so a year later, in September 1509, Spain renounced its remaining rights along the Atlantic coast, with the sole exception of Santa Cruz de Mar Pequeña, by the Treaty of Cintra.

Four years earlier the worsening labor shortage in the Canaries had obliged the Spanish Crown to relax the ban on slave-raiding. The *entradas* resumed, with Lugo entitled to a half-share in the Crown's fifth of the profits, until in 1525 Carlos I gave added encouragement to the raiders by waiving his share.[23] The Spanish and Portuguese attacks aroused the fury of the coastal tribes of southern Morocco and the western Sahara who rallied behind marabout leaders to wage a *jihad* against the Christians. In August 1517 Santa Cruz was seized by local tribes, though it was quickly recaptured by the Spanish. Then in 1524 it was sacked again, and this time a plague in the Canaries prevented a relief force being sent out to drive the attackers away.[24]

The fort was abandoned and the Spaniards were not to establish another settlement on this coast until more than three and a half centuries later, in 1884. The Portuguese were evicted in turn from their fort at Agadir, in 1541, though they retained control of the island of Arguin, a little to the south of present-day Western Sahara, until 1638, when it was seized by the Dutch.[25] Spain's imperial focus switched to the Americas in the sixteenth century. However, the *entradas* from the Canaries continued, as ventures of the Crown, the *adelantado* (governor) or private individuals, who sometimes grouped together into slave-catching cooperatives. But in 1566 the Sanhaja of Santa Ana Island, near Arguin, routed a Canary expedition and captured its ships. Three years later Moroccan corsairs began raiding the Canaries, taking villagers off into slavery. In the hope of pacifying the Moroccan pirates, the Spanish Crown banned the *entradas* in 1572, but illegal raids continued until 1593.[26]

Meanwhile, the fishermen of the Canary Islands had begun to appreciate the rich fishing banks off the Western Saharan coast, where the Spanish Crown had first granted fishing rights to two of its subjects in 1490.[27] The islanders continued to fish there over the following centuries and they would occasionally land on the Saharan shore to mend their nets, dry their catch or barter with local tribes.

Though the activity of these fishermen was Spain's sole contact with the Saharan coast from the end of the sixteenth century until the "scramble for Africa" at the end of the nineteenth, the authorities in Madrid and the Canaries resented meddling there by other European powers, out of fear perhaps for the security of the Canaries. So when a Scotsman, George Glas, set up a trading post, which he called Hilsborough, on the coast opposite Fuerteventura in 1764, the Spanish government was incensed. Glas was jailed when he crossed from Hilsborough to Lanzarote to buy a boat and recruit new workers. He was detained for almost a year, during which time a group of nomads took Hilsborough by storm and put to death several of his men. His wife and daughter managed to escape with the help of their interpreter and reached the Canaries where, following diplomatic exchanges between London and Madrid, Glas was set free. This was not, however, to be the end of his tribulations. While sailing back to Britain with his gold dust, he was murdered and flung overboard.[28]

NOTES

1. Tomás García Figueras, *Santa Cruz de Mar Pequeña, Ifni, Sahara. La acción de España en la costa occidental de África* (Ediciones Fe, Madrid, 1941), pp. 25–26; Boies Penrose, *Travel and Discovery in the Renaissance, 1420-1620* (Harvard University Press, Cambridge, 1952), pp. 17–18.

2. F. de La Chapelle, "Esquisse d'une histoire du Sahara occidental," *Hespéris*, Vol. XI, 1930, p. 69.

3. Penrose, *op. cit.*, p. 17.

4. Alvise da Cadamosto, in G. R. Crone (ed.), *The Voyages of Cadamosto* (The Hakluyt Society, London, 1937), p. xii.

5. Penrose, *op. cit.*, pp. 12–13.

6. Gomes Eannes de Azurara, "The Chronicle of the Discovery of Guinea," in Virginia de Castro e Almeida (ed.), *Conquests and Discoveries of Henry the Navigator* (George Allen and Unwin, London, 1936), pp. 130–32.

7. *Ibid.*, p. 136.

8. *Ibid.*, p. 138.

9. *Ibid.*, p. 148.

10. John Mercer, *Spanish Sahara* (George Allen and Unwin, London, 1976), p. 80.

11. Eannes de Azurara, *loc. cit.*, pp. 160–61.

12. *Ibid.*, p. 170.

13. For an account of João Fernandes' travels into the Sahara, see *ibid.*, pp. 215–23.

14. *Ibid.*, p. 152.

15. Cadamosto, *loc. cit.*, p. 17. Gold *tiber* was gold dust.

16. *Ibid.*, p. 18.

17. Its exact location is no longer known. There are several ruins along the coast and historians have debated as to which might be those of Santa Cruz. Most have opted for the ruins at Puerto Cansado, which is midway between Tarfaya and the mouth of the River Chebeika.

18. F. de La Chapelle, *Les Teknas du Sud marocain* (Comité de l'Afrique Française, Paris, 1934), p. 34.

19. García Figueras, *op. cit.*, p. 33; Mercer, *op. cit.*, p. 84.

20. Antonio Rumeu de Armas, "La provincia española del Sahara," *Africa*, Vol. XVII, No. 228, December 1960, p. 4.

21. *Ibid.*, p. 5.

22. García Figueras, *op. cit.*, p. 34; Mercer, *op. cit.*, p. 86.

23. *Ibid.*, p. 88.

24. García Figueras, *op. cit.*, p. 34.

25. The Dutch, who were particularly interested in procuring the gum arabic extracted from the Mauritanian *Acacia verek*, which was widely used in the textile industry at this time, established a second trading base farther south at Portendick at the beginning of the eighteenth century. However, the gum traffic aroused strong competition from other European powers. In 1666 Arguin was seized by the English. In 1667 the French took the island. Between 1685 and 1721 it was in the hands of the Dutch and the Elector of Brandenburg. Portendick was captured by the French in 1723, recaptured by the Dutch and then regained by the French in 1724. By the Treaty of The Hague in 1727, Holland finally ceded both Arguin and Portendick to France. Thereafter, the main contenders were France and

England. In 1762, the English took Portendick. However, the Treaty of Versailles in September 1783 gave France sovereignty along the West African coast from Cape Blanc to Senegal, and after further belligerency during the Napoleonic Wars, this was confirmed by the Treaty of Paris in 1814.

26. Mercer, *op. cit.*, pp. 88–89; Francisco Hernández-Pacheco and José María Cordero Torres, *El Sahara español* (Instituto de Estudios Africanos, Madrid, 1962), p. 120.

27. Rumeu de Armas, *loc. cit.*, p. 4.

28. García Figueras, *op. cit.*, pp. 46–47.

3

Morocco
and the Sahara

U NTIL THE TWENTIETH CENTURY Morocco was not a unified nation-state. Rather, it was a mosaic of tribes, many of whom were often no more than nominally ruled by the sultan's government, the *makhzen*. The regions which were under the sultan's direct administration, normally the plains and the towns, were known as the *bilad el-makhzen*, the "government lands," while the regions beyond the sultan's control, usually regions of difficult access such as the mountains of the Rif and the three Atlas ranges, were known as the *bilad es-siba*, the "lands of dissidence."[1] Very few of Morocco's precolonial sultans had sufficient power or resources to bring the Berber mountain tribes under their direct control or to levy taxes on them. Most were preoccupied with fending off threats from palace rivals, rebellious tribes or foreign enemies, such as the Portuguese or Spanish in the fifteenth and sixteenth centuries, the Turks, who ruled the Algerian coast from the sixteenth to the nineteenth centuries, or France, which began its conquest of Algeria in 1830, and other European powers in the nineteenth century.

Consequently, intervention by Moroccan sultans in the distant Sahara was limited and ephemeral. When a sultan did pursue an active Saharan policy, in a rare period of security at home, his aim was usually to secure control of the trade across the desert and in particular to ensure that the caravans headed toward Morocco rather than such rival destinations as the Turkish-controlled Mediterranean ports to the east or European trading posts on the Sahara's Atlantic coast. The key to this was to control the strategic oases, market towns, salt mines and wells, upon which the Saharan trade hinged; and so, during the reigns of the most powerful of the Moroccan sultans, the *makhzen* did temporarily administer a few far-flung oases, such as those of the Gourara, Touat and Tidikelt regions which extend in an almost continuous line from the Tafilalet oases of southeastern Morocco for about five hundred miles into the Algerian Sahara, from where the trading caravans would head south toward the Niger Valley.[2] Likewise, the *makhzen* sometimes briefly controlled the southwestern "gates" to the Sahara—the oases and market towns of the Noun and the Bani valleys—in the pre-Saharan zone of transition and exchange between the worlds of the Tashelhit-speaking farmers of the Anti-Atlas and the Arabophone nomads of the western Sahara desert.[3] At times, governors and *caids* were appointed by the sultans to administer such strategic areas as the Noun and Touat, and garrisons would be posted there; but there were other periods, often lasting several decades or even a century, when the sultans were too weak to exercise direct control over these remote oasis regions, which accordingly became parts of the *bilad es-siba* like the Atlas and Rif mountains.

Their temporary administration was only possible at all because they had towns and villages with sedentary populations. But to the south of the Draa, in the swath of desert encompassing modern-day Western Sahara which reaches to the Adrar Temar in northern Mauritania, there were neither significant oases nor settlements of any kind except at Tindouf, where the Tadjakant built their trading city in 1852.[4] This was, above all, the domain of the long-range camel-herding nomads, the "sons of the clouds," whom the *makhzen* neither attempted nor would have been able to subdue effectively. These nomads may have held the Moroccan sultans in awe, as the most powerful rulers in the Maghreb, or respected their claim to the guardianship of western Islam as *amir al-muminin* (commander of the faithful), a title first taken by the Almohad sultans in the twelfth century. Some nomadic tribes briefly struck up alliances with a Moroccan ruler, by agreeing perhaps to help him achieve his strategic or commercial objectives in the Sahara in return for booty or assistance against tribal enemies. On a few occasions a tribe might even find it wise or opportune to declare its allegiance (*bayaa*) to the sultan, who, in return, might issue a royal decree (*dahir*) naming the tribe's leader as an official *caid*. However, such *dahirs* would never do more than give royal endorsement to independently established leaders; and pledges of allegiance to the sultan were both exceedingly rare and of very little and short-lived practical significance. The largest of the tribes now living in Western Sahara, the Reguibat, seem never to have recognized the sultan's suzerainty and they have a legend, symbolic in its own right of their sense of independece, that their founder, Sidi Ahmed Reguibi, bought their rights to the desert zones south of the Draa from a Moroccan sultan in the sixteenth century.[5] Some other tribes' legends, such as those of the Arosien, the Ait Lahsen and the Oulad Bou Sbaa, tell of their ancestors or founders fleeing into the desert, as a place of refuge, from the repression of Moroccan sultans.[6] There they were beyond the *makhzen*'s reach. In the western Sahara the tribes chose their own leaders and took their own decisions, whether of a political, judicial or military nature, through such sovereign assemblies as a *djemaa* or an *ait arbain*. No attempt was ever made by even the strongest of Moroccan rulers to administer or tax these tribes, or to halt their incessant intertribal raiding; and to have attempted to do so would have been utterly utopian, if only because the nomads were constantly on the move, scattered in small groups over enormous, distant tracts of exceedingly inhospitable territory.[7] It was European colonialism, with far greater resources and military means, that finally "pacified" the nomads in the twentieth century, and even then only with great difficulty.

Among the few Moroccan rulers to play active roles in the Sahara were two of the earliest sultans of the Saadian dynasty, Mohammed esh-Sheikh (1548–57) and Ahmed el-Mansour (1578–1603). *Shorfa* who succeeded in fighting their way to power in Morocco during the first half of the sixteenth century, in large part by virtue of their prominence in the resistance to the Christians along the Altantic coast, the Beni Saad were natives of the Draa and so were well aware of the economic importance of the caravan trade across the Sahara, which at that time was mainly conducted with the wealthy empire of the black Songhay, who had established their supremacy along the Niger Valley at the end of the fifteenth century. Their aim was to bring this trade under their direct control; and this, in part, is why they attacked the Portuguese trading forts along the Atlantic coast, among them Santa Cruz de Cabo Aguer (Agadir), which they seized in 1541 and then converted into their own maritime commercial outlet in the Souss.[8] One of the problems they faced was that most of the trade from the Niger at this time was bypassing Morocco completely. Instead it was flowing from the Niger to the Turkish-controlled cities of Tlemcen and Oran in Algeria, via the Touat oases.[9] Additionally, the Songhay rulers, the *askia*, whose capital was at Gao, near Timbuctoo, had taken control of the principal Saharan salt mines, at Teghazza (now in northwestern Mali), a resource of great value since salt was one of the main commodities for which the blacks of the sub-Saharan forests would part with their gold.[10]

So, as early as 1526, the Saadians sent troops to Touat, and from about 1544 they began claiming rights over the Teghazza mines, to which Askia Ishaq I responded by dispatching a force of Tuareg to raid the oases of the Upper Draa. In 1557 the black governor of Teghazza was murdered by Saadian agents; and sometime during his reign Mohammed esh-Sheikh himself is said to have led a force into the Sahara which reached as far as the trading city of Ouadane, in Adrar, but then had to withdraw to Morocco after learning that a large black army had gathered to bar its way to the Niger.[11] However, it was Ahmed, the third of Mohammed esh-Sheikh's sons to succeed him on the throne, who was to pursue the most vigorous Saharan policy. He was unusually well-placed to do so. After the crushing of an invading Christian army at the historic "Battle of the Three Kings" near Tangier in 1578, in which King Sebastião of Portugal was killed, Morocco was freed from external dangers and regarded as a power to be reckoned with by both the Christians and the Turks. Ahmed received the honorific title of *el-mansour*, "the victorious." He amassed a fortune from ransoming the prisoners captured in 1578, built up a strong, disciplined army, and, unlike the other eleven sultans of the Saadian dynasty, eight of whom were murdered, faced no serious revolts at home.

His first initiative in the Sahara, in 1581, was to restore the Saadians' lapsed authority in the Touat and Gourara oases. Then, in 1584 he sent a force toward the Niger, via Ouadane, which failed to reach its destination after most of its soldiers died of hunger or thirst in the middle of the desert. A year later, however, a small detachment of two hundred Moroccan troops succeeded in seizing the Teghazza mines. After this success, Ahmed el-Mansour resolved to take direct control of the commercial centers of the Niger by conquering the Songhay empire itself. Disregarding the advice of his religious officials, the *ulama*, who warned that "between the Sudan and our country lies an immense desert with neither water nor plants," whose crossing would be perilous in the extreme, the sultan assembled an expeditionary force of about three thousand men, mainly European Muslims, who set off on an epic trek to the Niger in October 1590 under the command of a Spaniard, Pasha Judar. After crossing about thirteen hundred miles of desert and losing at least half of his men on the way, Judar finally reached the Niger on February 28, 1591. There on March 12 his remaining troops had little difficulty in routing with musket fire a huge army of twenty thousand Songhay warriors armed with spears. After entering Gao, they turned west to Timbuctoo, which the Spanish pasha made his capital.[12] Loads of looted gold and slaves were hauled back to Morocco immediately after the conquest, and over the following years more gold was procured by trading the salt mined at the sultan's Saharan mines, but the invaders were never able to exploit directly the gold mines, which were located far from Gao.[13]

To Ahmed el-Mansour, the desert itself must have been rather like an ocean. It had to be crossed to reach the Eldorado on the banks of the Niger. Within the desert the only places of interest to the sultan were its "islands," the oases, and the salt mines, upon which the trade with the black gold producers so heavily depended. He had neither the means nor the ambition to rule the desert's nomadic tribes, though alliances were useful to protect the caravans; and even his control of the Anti-Atlas and the Souss, in southern Morocco, was relatively precarious.[14] Moroccan rule in Timbuctoo itself did not last long. Judar was recalled to Morocco in 1599, to be succeeded by governors of lesser caliber; and, after Ahmed el-Mansour's death in 1603, Morocco entered a half century of virtual anarchy, marked by fratricidal palace conflicts, the breakup of the Saadian kingdom into two states based in Marrakesh and Fez, the secession of several independent statelets elsewhere and renewed threats from Spain along the coast. Drained of its former wealth by the pillaging, Timbuctoo was abandoned to its conquerors and their descendants, who intermarried with local black women, forming a ruling caste known as the *arma*. From 1612 the city's pashas were no longer appointed by the sultan. Instead, they were placed in office, and as frequently deposed, by the troops. Twenty-one pashas succeeded one another between 1612 and 1660 and 128 followed between 1660 and 1750, some of them ruling for only a few hours before being assassinated by rivals.[15] The last contingent of military reinforcements from Morocco arrived in 1618, by which time the traffic in gold and slaves from the Niger to Morocco had been reduced to a trickle. Much of the trans-Saharan trade had been diverted elsewhere, to the Turkish cities of Algeria and Tunisia, via the Touat oases, which had slipped from Saadian control shortly after Ahmed el-Mansour's death, or to the Europeans on the Atlantic coast, notably at Arguin.[16]

Moreover, the statelets that came into being in southern Morocco at this time undermined Saadian involvement in the Saharan trade still further. Abu Mahalli, a marabout who became the effective ruler of Tafilalet and the Draa after Ahmed el-Mansour's death and briefly seized Marrakesh, controlled much of the trade between southern Morocco and black Africa until his death in 1614. To defeat him, the Saadians called on the assistance of another marabout, Yahya Ibn Abdallah el-Hahi, who in turn became a quasi-independent ruler in the Souss. He was eliminated in 1626 by Abu Hassun el-Samlali, who established an autonomous principality at Tazeroualt, in the Anti-Atlas, with a port at Massa at which ships from Europe traded with caravans arriving from the Sahara.[17] Tazeroualt only lost its independence after Abu Hassun's death in 1659 and the more or less contemporaneous rise to power of the Alawites, the dynasty which has ruled Morocco to the present day.

Presumed *shorfa* who had lived in Tafilalet since the thirteenth century, the Alawites were as familiar with the caravan trade across the Sahara as the early Saadians had been. They had gained control of the strategic Touat oases in 1645, long before the first Alawite sultan, Moulay Rashid (1664–72), was able to enter Fez (1666) or Marrakesh (1669); and in about 1670 Rashid is said to have sent an expedition into the Sahara as far as Ouadane to pursue a rebellious marabout from the Souss.[18] However, Rashid's successor, Moulay Ismail (1672–1727), whose mother was a black Saharan slave, was the only Alawite ruler to play a really major role in the Sahara, a role made briefly possible, as in Ahmed el-Mansour's time, by the unusual security of his realm at home. After five years of war, he had succeeded in establishing an iron grip over most of Morocco by 1677, though it took him another twelve years to subdue the Souss. Thereafter he succeeded in terrorizing would-be opponents or rebels into passivity and forcing even the traditional *bilad es-siba* to recognize his authority. The Turks were kept at bay and Morocco's Atlantic coastline was almost entirely freed of Christian enclaves. Such successes required a powerful and loyal army. Moulay Ismail therefore built up a regular army of some 150,000 men, all of whom were black *abid* who had no roots in Morocco's divided tribal society; and it was above all to obtain additional recruits for these *abid* regiments, as well as to reorient the trans-Saharan trade caravans toward Morocco, that he organized a series of expeditions into the desert during his long reign.[19] One of the first was sent in 1572 to gather slaves in Timbuctoo, where the pashas appear to have recognized the sultan's nominal sovereignty once again while remaining *de facto* independent.[20] Governors were regularly appointed to administer the Touat oases from 1676 until Moulay Ismail's death in 1727; and a *caid* was sent to Teghazza in 1694.[21]

Farther west, in what is now Mauritania, the sultan acquired thousands of slaves by exploiting tribal conflicts to forge beneficial alliances with some of the stronger Beni Hassan tribes. For example, a Moroccan force was sent to Trarza in 1672, two years before the end of the war of Shar Boubah between the Beni Hassan and the Sanhaja, to aid its emir, Terrouz, resist the Sanhaja rebels. Its return to Morocco with a large supply of slaves seems to have encouraged Moulay Ismail himself to lead another expedition in person in 1679. After a pacification campaign in the Souss, he took his army south to Adrar, married the daughter of the Emir of Brakna and, after sending envoys throughout Mauritania, "brought back from these regions 2,000 mulattoes and their children."[22] The following year a Moroccan force is said to have reached Tagant to arbitrate between the Idou Aich Berbers and the Beni Hassan.[23] In about 1724 the Emir of Trarza, Ali Shandora (1703–27), traveled to Meknes to seek Moulay Ismail's support against his enemies, among whom was the neighboring Emir of Brakna, and so made the *bayaa*. The sultan agreed to help and asked a Tekna chief from the Noun, Hammou Said el-Azergui, to travel to Trarza with an armed force, which helped Ali Shandora assure his ascendancy in southwestern Mauritania.[24] However, Moulay Ismail could not be said to have ruled the tribes and emirates of the *trab el-beidan*. Tribal leaders such as Emir Ali Shandora nominally recognized his suzerainty to buttress their own independent power; and the sultan's military expeditions into the *trab el-beidan* were brief and infrequent. Moreover, they reached only some parts of the "land of the Moors." They appear to have had almost no impact at all on the region now constituting Western Sahara, though the sultan's troops would have normally crossed the Hammada, the gravel plain to the south of the Draa and to the east of the Saguia el-Hamra, en route to the more populous regions farther south, in Adrar, Brakna, Trarza and Tagant. As for Timbuctoo, the sultan had no real control over the pashas, eighty-five of whom ruled the city during his reign, none of them with royal investiture.[25] By 1740 Timbuctoo was being forced to pay tribute to the Tuareg, who eventually occupied the city in the 1790s.[26] In fact, Moroccan influence in the Sahara and the Niger Valley rapidly dissolved after Moulay Ismail's death in 1727, though Thomas Pellow, an Englishman who became a commander in the Moroccan army, led an expedition as far south as the River Senegal in about 1730 to obtain slaves, gold and ivory on behalf of one of Moulay Ismail's sons, Moulay Abdallah.[27] Morocco plunged once more into anarchy as the *abid* army crowned and deposed sultans almost at will. Moulay Abdallah ruled on no less than four separate occasions, being deposed three times by pretenders, between 1729 and 1757.[28] Once again, the Berber tribes of the Rif and the Atlas mountains took advantage of the weakening of royal power to enter a state of *siba;* and they were not to be subdued effectively again until after the imposition of the Franco-Spanish "protectorate" in 1912. The Touat oases slipped from the Alawites' grasp toward the end of the eighteenth century, and the trade routes shifted once more to the east, to the benefit of the Turks, or to the southwest, to the French in Senegal.[29]

The sultans' chances of maintaining direct contact with the *trab el-beidan* vanished as the regions to its immediate north, the Noun, the Anti-Atlas and the southern Souss, reverted to their old status as part of the *bilad es-siba*. These regions were seething with discontent as a result of the diversion of the Saharan trading caravans from the southern ports of Agadir and Massa to the new port of Mogador, built due west of Marrakesh by Sultan Mohammed Ben Abdallah (1757–90) in 1765; and so the principality of Tazeroualt was reborn and another independent statelet was founded in Goulimine, the main market town of the Noun, by Ali el-Hadj.[30] Sultan Mohammed was quite candid about his lack of power in these regions when the King of Spain, Carlos III, sought his approval for the establishment of a fishing station on the coast opposite the Canary Islands, where Santa Cruz de Mar Pequeña had been abandoned two and a half centuries earlier. The idea was a reaction to the Hilsborough affair and had been suggested to Carlos III by the governor of the Canaries, Domingo Bernardi, who had jailed Glas in 1764–65. In 1765 the king sent a Franciscan priest, Bartolomé Girón, to Morocco to request the sultan's permission for the founding of a Spanish fishing port at the mouth of the Assaka River, in the Noun. Girón was unable to put the proposal directly to the sultan; and Carlos III's secretary of state, the Marquis of Grimaldi, made no further headway when a Moroccan ambassador visited Madrid in 1766 to negotiate the terms of a treaty of peace and commerce. The following year, Carlos III sent Admiral Jorge Juan as Spanish ambassador to Marrakesh, with instructions to negotiate the incorporation of a clause on the fishing base into the treaty. However, he too was unsuccessful. Indeed, when he signed the treaty on May 28, 1767, its eighteenth article explained why. Its Arabic text stated: "His Imperial Majesty warns the inhabitants of the Canaries against any fishing expedition to the coasts of Oued Noun and beyond. He disclaims any responsibility for the way they may be treated by the Arabs of the country, to whom it is difficult to apply decisions, since they have no fixed residence, travel as they wish and pitch their tents where they choose. The inhabitants of the Canaries are certain to be maltreated by those Arabs. . . ."[31] The sultan then wrote an apologetic letter to Carlos III. Referring to the inhabitants of "the coast of the River Noun," he informed the Spanish king that "they are neither subordinate to nor fearful of anyone, because they are greatly separated from my dominions and I do not have power over them" and that "these Arabs have no fixed abode and move around as it pleases them without submitting to government or any authority."[32] If this was the situation in the pre-Saharan Noun region, some hundred miles north of the present Western Saharan border, it could not have been less so in the desert itself, farther south.

Moulay Suleiman, who ruled Morocco from 1792 to 1822, was as frank as Mohammed Ben Abdallah about his lack of power over the peoples of the Noun. On March 1, 1799, his government signed a new peace and trade treaty with Spain which, in its twenty-second article, stipulated that "if any Spanish ship is shipwrecked on the Noun River and its coast, where His Moroccan Majesty does not exercise his domination [*sus dominios*], he nonetheless offers, to prove how much he appreciates the friendship of His Catholic Majesty, to employ the most appropriate and effective measures to save and set free the crews and other individuals who have the misfortune to fall into the hands of those natives."[33] Such shipwreck clauses were included in several other treaties between the sultanate and such maritime powers as Spain, Britain, and the United States between the late eighteenth century and the 1860s on account of the frequency of shipwrecks along the dangerous coastline of the Noun and the regions to its south which almost invariably ended in the enslavement of the survivors by local tribes.[34] Article 38 of a Moroccan-Spanish treaty of commerce signed on November 20, 1861, required, for example, that "if a Spanish vessel be wrecked at Oued Noun or on any other part of its coast, the Sultan of Morocco shall make use of his authority to save and protect the master and crew until they return to their country."[35] The maritime powers knew that the sultans had no means of enforcing their writ directly over the tribes of the Noun, let alone those of the Sahara, but they did hope that, since shipwrecked seamen were often sold by their captors to traders who would take them north in the hope of ransoming them for a sizable profit, the sultans would help to arrange for their eventual ransom or even ransom them personally.[36] This they would often do to enhance their prestige or improve relations with the maritime powers; but the fact that they would have to buy or help arrange for the purchase of enslaved sailors reveals that until the end of the nineteenth century they could not simply order their release, to comply with the shipwreck clauses of the treaties. They did not have the power to enforce such orders to the south of Agadir and so had to resort to commercial transactions.[37] Moreover, European governments sometimes decided to bypass the sultan altogether by dealing directly with the real masters of the Noun and the southern Souss, the rulers of Goulimine and Tazeroualt.

Both Sidi Hashem, the ruler of Tazeroualt, who had eighteen European mariners in his hands in 1816, and Sheikh Beyrouk of the Ait Moussa Ou Ali, the predominantly sedentary Tekna tribe that controlled Goulimine at this time, carried on a lucrative business in the ransoming of shipwrecked sailors. They also had a considerable stake in the Saharan caravan traffic, and Beyrouk was represented by commercial agents in all the main market towns of Mauritania and the "Sudan." To avoid the heavy customs duties levied by the *makhzen* in its port at Mogador, both these local rulers and European traders had an interest in trying to establish direct commercial relations. So, in 1835-36, Beyrouk tried to interest the British government in a plan to open a port at the mouth of the Draa, but a British warship, the *Scorpion*, which tried to bring gifts to the sheikh, failed to negotiate a landing on the coast. Then, in 1840, after negotiations between Beyrouk and the French consul in Mogador, a French ship, *La Malouine*, anchored in the mouth of the Draa. Its commander disembarked to hold further talks with Beyrouk and his chief adviser, Bou Azza. The negotiations continued when two other French warships, *L'Alouette*, and *La Vigie*, visited the Noun coast in 1841 and 1843 respectively. In 1845, Bou Azza traveled to France. However, the dangers of the coast between Cape Noun and the mouth of the Draa discouraged the French and, by about 1845, Beyrouk himself was backing away from his plans for a port, under the enticement of Sultan Moulay Abderrahman (1822-59), who had taken alarm at the sheikh's dealings with France for both commercial and political reasons. This was a time of serious French military pressure on the sultanate. A Moroccan army had been crushed by French forces in the plain of Isly, near Oujda, in August 1844, and Tangier and Mogador had been bombarded by the French navy in retaliation for Moroccan support for the Algerian resistance leader, the Emir Abdal-Qadir. In return for a promise to break off relations with the Europeans, Beyrouk was allowed to set up his own trading house in Mogador and receive two thirds of the customs duties paid on goods transiting through the port to or from the Noun. Shortly afterwards, however, Beyrouk died, to be succeeded by an oligarchy of his eleven sons, of whom the most influential were Habib, Dahman and Mohammed. They continued their father's inconsistent policy, oscillating between agreements with the *makhzen* and attempts to renew direct relations with European traders and governments. In 1853 the Beyrouk family's contacts with France finally ended when the sultan prevented a ship of the Marseilles company Altaras et Cohen from reaching the Noun.[38] But new relations were established with Spanish and British traders. In 1860 a Spanish businessman, Francisco Puyana, arrived in the Noun to negotiate a trade agreement and in 1862 returned to Lanzarote, in the Canaries, with Habib Ben Beyrouk, who gave him an official authorization to trade in the Noun. In 1864 a

Spanish doctor, Joaquín Gatell, was asked by the Spanish government to re-
connoiter the coast. He made three journeys in 1865, disguised as the "Caid
Ismail," and reached as far as Tarfaya (Cape Juby), where he narrowly escaped
death at the hands of a group of nomads who discovered that he was really a
Christian. The following year Habib Ben Beyrouk sent an envoy to Cadiz to sign a
trading agreement with Puyana and the Cadiz merchants Butler Hermanos. However, in a new swing of the pendulum, Jacobo Butler, Puyana and their
interpreter suddenly found themselves thrown into jail when they visited
Goulimine in 1867 to implement the deal. Habib had turned on his would-be
commercial partners to ingratiate himself with the sultan, Sidi Mohammed
(1859–73), who had just rescinded the Beyrouks' trading concession at Mogador.
Finally, Habib settled for a ransom of twenty-seven thousand duros and released
his prisoners in September 1874. Madrid then barred Spanish citizens from
visiting the Souss or the Noun.[39]

Despite the Beyrouks' inconstancy a Scotsman by the name of Donald Mackenzie, who had seen the importance of the caravan trade during a trip to southern
Morocco in 1872, surveyed the coast opposite the Canaries in 1876 and 1878 and
then signed a trading agreement with Mohammed Ben Beyrouk in July 1879
under which his North-West Africa Company established a trading post at Tarfaya. The following November, Mackenzie accompanied one of Habib's sons to
England.[40] Mackenzie's relations with the Beyrouks and the Tekna were founded
on mutual self-interest and escaped the complications that confounded the
trading initiatives of Butler and Puyana. "The commercial operations have
gathered momentum and the caravans sent by the tribes of the interior have
brought large quantities of wool, skins, ostrich feathers and gum to the North-
West Africa Company," noted a Belgian cavalry officer, Baron Lahure, who
visited Tarfaya in September 1888 on behalf of King Leopold II, who briefly considered buying out Mackenzie's interests there in order to found a transit station
between Belgium and the Congo.[41] In return, Mackenzie was selling tea, sugar
and cloth from Manchester. His relations with the Tekna were sound enough to
permit extensive traveling into the interior: in August 1883 he set off from Tarfaya with two British colleagues and a Tekna escort to visit the ruins at Puerto Cansado, which may be the remains of Santa Cruz de Mar Pequeña, and a month later
he accompanied a group of Izarguien on a much longer journey overland to their
tribe's fortified grainstores at Daora, thirty miles south of Tarfaya, and to the
Saguia el-Hamra.[42]

However, Mackenzie soon aroused the ire of the Moroccan sultan, Moulay
Hassan (1873–94), who began protesting about his activities in 1880 to the British
consul in Tangiers, Sir John Drummond Hay, and offering Mackenzie large
financial inducements to go away. "The sultan," Mackenzie later wrote, "saw
that the establishment of an independent British settlement at Cape Juby completely free from Moorish custom-house authorities would be a very serious blow
to the southern trade of Morocco. He foresaw also a political danger. Arms and
ammunition, he feared, might be poured in at Cape Juby for the use of the
natives hostile to Moorish rule."[43] Moulay Hassan therefore sent envoys to Tarfaya, and when they arrived in July 1880, they burnt down Mackenzie's trading

house, warned the local Tekna not to trade with him and, in Mackenzie's words, "declared to us and the people that the whole country belonged to the sultan."[44] For greater security Mackenzie then built a stone fort, which he baptized Cape Juby Castle but which the Spanish were later to call the *Casa Mar*, because, being built on a small islet off the beach, it seemed to rise out of the sea.

It was above all to resist the growing threats to Moroccan independence from the European powers that Moulay Hassan was determined to restore the *makhzen*'s administration to the regions of the *bilad es-siba* on the fringes of his empire and stop their inhabitants from dealing autonomously with men like Mackenzie. After the defeat of Isly in 1844, Morocco had fallen victim to a Spanish invasion in 1859–60 which had culminated in the Spanish occupation of Tetuan in February 1860 and the imposition of humiliating peace terms in a treaty signed the following April 26. Besides the payment of a large war indemnity, after which Spanish troops eventually evacuated Tetuan in 1862, and the enlargement of Spain's presidios on Morocco's Mediterranean coast (Ceuta, which had been occupied by Portugal in 1415 and by Spain since 1578, and Melilla, which had been conquered in the name of the Duke of Medina Sidonia in 1496 and incorporated into Spain sixty years later), the treaty required the sultan, under Article 8, "to concede in perpetuity to His Catholic Majesty, on the coast of the ocean, near Santa Cruz de Mar Pequeña, enough territory for the founding of a fisheries establishment like that which Spain used to possess there of old."[45] In fact, the Moroccan government was able to stall the implementation of this commitment. An immediate stumbling block was that nobody, in Spain or Morocco, had the slightest idea where Santa Cruz de Mar Pequeña had been located. The *makhzen*, meanwhile, warned Spain that it did not exercise effective control of the tribes along the coast opposite the Canaries and so could not guarantee the security of foreigners who went there. Many influential Spaniards were far from convinced of the profitability of a post there in any case, while others, like Puyana and Butler, initially saw greater advantage in dealing directly with the Beyrouks. However, after the jailing of Puyana and Butler had lowered the Beyrouks' stock and Mackenzie's activities had aroused fears that Britain might establish a presence on the coast opposite the Canaries, the Spanish government began urging the sultan to appoint the Moroccan members of the joint commission required under the 1860 treaty to determine the location and borders of the new Santa Cruz. In April 1877, during a visit to Fez, the Spanish counsul in Tangier, Eduardo Romea, persuaded Moulay Hassan to do so; and so a party of Spanish and Moroccan commissioners sailed down the coast in the *Blasco de Garay* in January 1878 and reached agreement on a site at Ifni. However, since the local inhabitants appeared menacing, it was deemed too dangerous to go ashore, and when the Spanish commissioners presented proposals for the cession of seventy square kilometers at Ifni, Moulay Hassan refused to give his assent, on the grounds that Santa Cruz had been farther south.[46] In April 1881, the sultan offered Spain financial compensation if it would agree to the annulment of Article 8 of the 1860 treaty.[47]

However, it was difficult for Hassan to thwart the ambitions of either Mackenzie or the Spanish in the Noun and its adjacent coasts, if only because, as the contemporary Moroccan historian, Ahmed el-Nasiri, put it, "their inhabitants had not been subject to the imperial authorities in a regular form for a long time."[48] So in the summer of 1882 the sultan headed south at the head of a large army, which reached Tiznit in the southern Souss in August. There he received the chiefs of the tribes of the Souss and the Noun, among them Dahman Ben Beyrouk from Goulimine, whom the sultan appointed as a *caid*. He promised to promote regional economic interests by opening a port at the mouth of the Assaka River and appointed a regional governor, who took up residence in Tiznit.[49] A special mission was dispatched to Tarfaya, but when it arrived on September 12, it failed to dissuade Mackenzie and the local Tekna from continuing their mutually beneficial trading.

The following year Hassan was finally obliged to accept Ifni as the site of Spain's proposed fishing base, after a new Spanish-Moroccan commission had surveyed the coast again, aboard the *Ligera*.[50] But the sultan was fortunate that the Spanish government once again dragged its feet; the next Spanish expedition to Ifni was not organized until twenty-five years later, in 1911. As for Mackenzie, the future looked darker after Dahman's appointment as *caid* and the death a year later of his chief ally among the Beyrouks, Mohammed, who had resided at Tarfaya. In 1884 a squad of Moroccan soldiers arrived at Tarfaya and "trade was brought to a standstill."[51] Two years later Hassan headed a second expedition to the southwestern fringes of his empire, this time reaching Goulimine, where the Beyrouks' autonomy was now definitively ended and a permanent garrison established. The sultan invested many of the chiefs of the sedentary or seminomadic Tekna tribes of the Noun and the Bani as official *caids,* and a similar stamp of royal approval was bestowed on some more distant chiefs, such as Mohammed Laamech, the leader of the Tadjakant of Tindouf, with whom the Tekna of the Noun had close trading relations.[52] A little later, in 1889-90, Hassan sent envoys to the Gourara, Touat and Tidikelt oases, where the *makhzen*'s administration had ceased some ninety years earlier, to forestall attempts by the French army in Algeria to push southward into the Sahara. By 1892 a complete system of Moroccan administration had been reestablished by the *makhzen* throughout these oasis regions; but the sultan was unable to prevent the French occupying them in 1899-1900.[53]

To the south of the Noun, Hassan was unable to bring the nomads of the desert even nominally under his authority. The sultan himself traveled no farther south than Goulimine in 1886. He sent agents to Mauritania in an attempt to induce the emirs of Trarza, Adrar, Tagant and Brakna to recognize his authority, but none were willing to do so. Nor were the Reguibat; and even the main nomadic Tekna tribes to the south of the Noun, the Izarguien, Ait Lahsen and Yagout, did not really submit. Baron Lahure, whose visit to Tarfaya came two years after Hassan's expedition to Goulimine, observed that the Tekna were divided into two wings, the "Moroccan Tekna," who lived mainly in the Noun and were predominantly sedentary or seminomadic, and the "free Tekna," nomads who migrated in the desert regions to the south, between the Draa and Cape Bojador and were beyond the sultan's reach.[54] The free Tekna continued to trade with the North-West Africa Company and so Moroccan troops raided Tarfaya in 1888, murdering the manager of Mackenzie's settlement.[55] In 1899 a force of Moroccan and Ait Moussa Ou Ali soldiers, sent out from Goulimine by Dahman Ould Beyrouk to chastize the Izarguien, was routed at Daora.[56] Dahman's authority over most of the Tekna tribes that had acknowledged the sultan's suzerainty in 1886 soon proved to be very precarious, and when the Ait Oussa, a partly nomadic Tekna tribe centered on the oasis of Assa in the Djebel Bani, joined the Reguibat in sacking Tindouf in 1895, nothing was done, by either the sultan or Dahman, to aid the Tadjakant or prevent the Ait Oussa from aiding the Reguibat.[57]

The sultan did finally get his way over Tarfaya, however. By the early 1890s trading there was in decline. Much of the Saharan traffic had been diverted to Saint-Louis, in Senegal, as shipping freight by sea had become very much cheaper, outbidding overland transport, and the French had gained control of the main departure points for the caravans along the Niger, including Timbuctoo, in 1894. Moreover, some of the commodities traditionally traded across the desert were no longer available or in demand. Gold was very scarce, and the trade in ostrich feathers was ruined by competition from southern Africa. Slaves were no longer wanted by the Europeans, of course, and Mackenzie himself was a commissioner of the Anti-Slavery Society, on whose behalf he left Britain for East Africa in February 1895. So the British government began negotiations on the transfer of the North-West Africa Company's interests at Tarfaya to the sultan. On March 13, 1895, Britain and Morocco finally signed an agreement by which the sultan purchased the trading station at Tarfaya for £50,000 and Britain recognized Moroccan sovereignty over "the lands that are between Wad Draa and Cape Bojador." Though none of the nomadic tribes to the south of the Draa were subject in any real way to the *makhzen,* such recognition suited British purposes. It was intended to keep rival European powers away from this coast and accordingly the agreement added that the Moroccan government "shall give its word to the English Government that they will not give any part of the above-mentioned lands to anyone whatsoever without the concurrence of the English Government."[58] However, it was Spain, one of the weakest of the European powers, that would eventually acquire Tarfaya. It had already established a presence on the coast, 370 miles farther south, on the Río de Oro bay.

NOTES

1. Charles-André Julien, *History of North Africa* (Routledge and Kegan Paul, London, 1970), pp. 229–30.

2. B. Marie Perinbam, "Trade and Society in the Western Sahara and the Western Sudan: an Overview," *Bulletin de l'IFAN,* Series B, Vol. 34, 1972, No. 4, p. 782.

3. On this pre-Saharan zone of transition, see Robert Montagne, "La limite du Maroc et du Sahara atlantique," *Hespéris,* Vol. XI, 1930, pp. 111–18, and Frank E. Trout, *Morocco's Saharan Frontiers* (Droz, Geneva, 1969), pp. 144–50.

4. On the city of Tindouf, see Julio Caro Baroja, *Estudios Saharianos* (Instituto de Estudios Africanos, Madrid, 1955), pp. 348–49.

5. Trout, *op. cit.,* p. 153. On the legend of Sidi Ahmed Reguibi's purchase of the territory to the south of the Draa, see Caro Baroja, *op. cit.,* p. 399.

6. According to a legend of the Arosien, Sidi Ahmed el-Arosi was thrown into the sultan's dungeons after being accused of sorcery in Marrakesh, where the marabout had been preaching and giving ablutions. A long-deceased saint is said to have spirited him away from his cell, carrying him

across the skies by the belt of his trousers until they reached a place about twenty miles west of Smara where the belt snapped and Sidi Ahmed fell to earth, to dedicate himself to a saintly life in the desert and marry three local women, whose sons begat the main fractions of the Arosien. See Caro Baroja, *op. cit.*, pp. 401–2. According to a legend of the Ait Lahsen, one of the main Tekna tribes, their founder was another sixteenth-century fugitive from a Moroccan sultan. To punish his mischievous behavior as a child, it is said, he had been sentenced by the sultan in Tafilalet to have one of his hands amputated; but, to avoid the punishment, he was taken by his mother to the region of the Oued Chebeika, between the Draa and Tarfaya, where they met and requested protection from Sidi Ahmed Reguibi, the founder of the Reguibat. However, the sultan himself is said to have arrived in person in Farsia and demanded payment in gold coins in return for the boy's pardon. Sidi Ahmed, it is said, threw to the ground the only three coins he had with him. Instantly, they were transformed into a heap of gold coins and the boy was set free. See Caro Baroja, *op. cit.*, p. 401. The Oulad Bou Sbaa appear to have migrated into the Sahara during the reign of Moulay Ismail (1672–1727), after an unsuccessful rebellion against the sultan. Fearing a massacre at the hands of the sultan's troops, they left their traditional lands near Marrakesh. One group, the Oulad el-Hadj, marched to the northeast, to the Oran region, but later returned to the Marrakesh region after being pardoned. But another wing of the tribe, the Oulad Brahim, drove their herds south into the desert, halting first in the region of the Saguia el-Hamra and then pushing on to Tiris. See Juan Bautista Vilar Ramírez, *El Sahara y el hamitismo norteafricano. Estudios antropo-históricos sahárico-magrebíes* (Instituto de Estudios Africanos, Madrid, 1969), p. 116, and Galo Bullón Díaz, "Los Ulad Bu Sba del Sahara," *Africa*, Vol. IV, Nos. 37–38, January–February 1945, pp. 40–41.

7. Trout, *op. cit.*, pp. 137–38; Francisco-Lorenzo Díaz del Ribero, *El Sahara occidental, pasado y presente* (Gisa Ediciones, Madrid, 1975), pp. 61–62; International Court of Justice, *Western Sahara, Advisory Opinion of 16 October 1975* (The Hague, 1975), pp. 45–48.

8. Jamil M. Abun-Nasr, *A History of the Maghrib* (Cambridge University Press, Cambridge, 1971), p. 207. Mohammed esh-Sheikh may have aided the forces that sacked Santa Cruz de Mar Pequeña in 1524 and the alliances forged during this period may explain why later in the century, after the Saadian conquest of Morocco, the Tekna became *guish* tribes, furnishing military contingents for the defense of the new dynasty in return for land in the fertile Haouz of Marrakesh. See F. de La Chapelle, *Les Teknas du Sud marocain* (Comité de l'Afrique Française, Paris, 1934), pp. 43–44, 63–64.

9. Díaz del Ribero, *op. cit.*, p. 46.

10. Writing in the mid-fifteenth century, Alvise da Ca da Mosto gave a graphic account of the trade between the Teghazza mines and the empire of Mali, a black state that reached its zenith in the fourteenth and fifteenth centuries, when it controlled the upper Niger and the city of Timbuctoo, which had been founded by the Sanhaja in the twelfth century. "Beyond the said mart of Edon (Ouadane), six days journey further inland, there is a place called Tagaza, that is to say in our tongue, 'cargador', where a very great quantity of rock-salt is mined. Every year large caravans of camels belonging to the above mentioned Arabs and Azanaghi, leaving in many parties, carry it to Tanbutu (Timbuctoo); thence they go to Melli, the empire of the blacks, where, so rapidly it is sold, within eight days of its arrival all is disposed of at a price of two to three hundred mitigalli [one mithqal equals about one-eighth ounce of gold—T.H.] a load, according to the quantity; then with the gold they return to their homes." Alvise da Cadamosto, in G. R. Crone (ed.), *The Voyages of Cadamosto* (The Hakluyt Society, London, 1937), p. 21.

11. F. de La Chapelle, "Esquisse d'une histoire du Sahara occidental," *Hespéris*, Vol. XI, 1930, p. 78; Odette du Puigaudeau, *Le passé maghrébin de la Mauritanie* (Ministère d'Etat chargé des affaires islamiques, Rabat, 1962), p. 26; Abun-Nasr, *op. cit.*, p. 213.

12. For accounts of the expeditions sent by Ahmed el-Mansour into the Sahara, see Julien, *op. cit.*, pp. 232–33; La Chapelle, *loc. cit.*, pp. 78–79; Puigaudeau, pp. 26–27; Abun-Nasr, p. 213; Lloyd Cabot Briggs, *Tribes of the Sahara* (Harvard University Press, Cambridge, 1960), pp. 46–47.

13. Julien, *op. cit.*, p. 234.

14. Díaz del Ribero, *op. cit.*, pp. 46–47.

15. Julien, *op. cit.*, pp. 233–34.

16. Abun-Nasr, *op. cit.*, p. 217; Díaz del Ribero, *op. cit.*, p. 48.

17. *Ibid.*, pp. 51–53; La Chapelle, *Les Teknas du Sud Maracain*, p. 45.

18. La Chapelle, "Esquisse d'une histoire du Sahara occidental," pp. 80–81; Trout, *op. cit.*, pp. 141–42.

19. *Ibid.*, p. 139; Julien, *op. cit.*, pp. 249–51; Díaz del Ribero, *op. cit.*, pp. 54–57.

20. Trout, *op. cit.*, p. 141.

21. Díaz del Ribero, *op. cit.*, pp. 57–58.

22. Aboulqâsem Ben Ahmed Ezziâni, *Ettordjemân elmo'arib 'an douel elmachriq ou 'lmaghrib*, extracts translated by O. Houdas as *Le Maroc de 1631 à 1812* (Ernest Leroux, Paris, 1886), p. 32. See also Trout, *op. cit.*, p. 140.

23. Puigaudeau, *op. cit.*, p. 29.

24. This incident reveals that the Tekna had again become *guish* tribes during Moulay Ismail's reign, probably after his pacification of the Souss and the Noun. The emirs of Trarza continued to express their gratitude to Hammou Said's descendants, the Izarguien, until the twentieth century by sending as annual *ghaffer* a gift of camels. See La Chapelle, *Les Teknas du Sud marocain*, p. 45; Puigaudeau, *op. cit.*, pp. 29–30.

25. Trout, *op. cit.*, p. 141.

26. *Ibid.*, p. 144; G. M. Désiré-Vuillemin, *Les rapports de la Mauritanie et du Maroc* (Service des Archives de Mauritanie, Saint-Louis, 1960), p. 26.

27. Trout, *op. cit.*, p. 143; Puigaudeau, *op. cit.*, p. 31.

28. See Julien, *op. cit.*, pp. 262–63.

29. Trout, *op. cit.*, pp. 24–25.

30. La Chapelle, *op. cit.*, pp. 45–46.

31. Cited in International Court of Justice, *op. cit.*, p. 50. The Spanish text of Article 18, whose wording was markedly different, reads: "His Imperial Majesty refrains from expressing an opinion with regard to the trading post which His Catholic Majesty wishes to establish to the south of the Noun River, since he cannot take responsibility for accidents and misfortunes, because his domination (*sus dominios*) does not extend so far. . . ." (*Ibid.*, p. 50.) Both Arabic and Spanish versions of the article went on to grant Spain fishing rights from Agadir (Santa Cruz de Cabo Aguer) northward. On the Treaty of Marrakesh and the negotiations preceding it, see also Díaz del Ribero, *op. cit.*, pp. 77–86, and Rachid Lazrak, *Le contentieux territorial entre le Maroc et l'Espagne* (Dar el-Kitab, Casablanca, 1974), pp. 44–45, 133–134.

32. Letter of Moulay Mohammed Ben Abdallah, Sultan of Morocco, to Carlos III, King of Spain, 1 moharrem 1181, in legajo 4310, Archivo Histórico Nacional de Madrid, cited by Díaz del Ribero, *op. cit.*, p. 83.

33. *Colección completa de tratados y convenios entre España y Marruecos, 1799–1895* (El Telegrama del Rif, Melilla, 1904), p. 28, cited in Díaz del Ribero, *op. cit.*, p. 86. See also Lazrak, *op. cit.*, pp. 45–46, 134–35.

34. Treaties with such clauses were signed with Morocco by the United States in 1786 and 1836, Great Britain in 1856 and Spain in 1861. Among the many sailors to be enslaved after a shipwreck were Alexander Scott, a British seaman who was shipwrecked between Cape Noun and Tarfaya in 1810 and spent over five years as a slave of the Taoubalt before escaping to the Anti-Atlas, where he was rescued by a British official from Mogador in 1816. See Major Rennell, "Account of the Captivity of Alexander Scott among the Wandering Arabs of the Great African Desert, for a Period of Nearly Six Years, with Geographical Observations on His Routes, and Remarks on the Currents of the Ocean on the North-Western Coast of Africa," *The Edinburgh Philosophical Journal*, Vol. IV, No. 7, January 1821, pp. 38–54, and No. 8, April 1821, pp. 225–43.

35. Cited in International Court of Justice, *op. cit.*, p. 51.

36. The tale of one such ransomed seaman is recounted by James Riley in *Loss of the American Brig Commerce Wrecked on the Western Coast of Africa in the Month of August 1815 with an Account of Timbuctoo and the Hitherto Undiscovered Great City of Wassanah* (Murray, London, 1817). The *Commerce* had been shipwrecked near Cape Blanc in 1815 and James Riley, who was its captain, was enslaved with several of his crew by local nomads. He was eventually sold to a cloth merchant, who took him north to Mogador and freed him there for a ransom of $920.

37. Díaz del Ribero, *op. cit.*, pp. 88–91.

38. La Chapelle, *op. cit.*, pp. 47–51; Tomás García Figueras, *Santa Cruz de Mar Pequeña, Ifni, Sahara. La acción de España en la costa occidental de África* (Ediciones Fe, Madrid, 1941), pp. 54–57.

39. *Ibid.*, pp. 80–87; La Chapelle, *op. cit.*, pp. 51–52; John Mercer, *Spanish Sahara* (George Allen and Unwin, London, 1976), p. 103.

40. Donald Mackenzie, *Khalifate of the West* (Simpkin, Marshall, Hamilton, Kent and Co. Ltd., London, 1911), pp. 163–67.

41. Joaquín Portillo, "El sultán confirmó a Londres que su soberanía acababa en el río Draa," *El País*, November 12, 1978.

42. Mackenzie, *op. cit.*, pp. 178–88.

43. *Ibid.*, p. 168.

44. *Ibid.*, p. 169.

45. Cited in Lazrak, *op. cit.*, p. 401.

46. *Ibid.*, p. 97; García Figueras, *op. cit.*, p. 96.

47. Robert Rézette, *The Western Sahara and the Frontiers of Morocco* (Nouvelles Editions Latines, Paris, 1975), p. 58.

48. Ahmed el-Nasiri, *Kitab elistiqsâ li-akhbâri doual elmagrib elaqsâ*, extracts translated by E. Fumey as "Chronique de la dynastie alouie au Maroc," *Archives Marocaines* (Vols. IX, 1906, pp. 1–399, and X, 1907, pp. 1–424), p. 327.

49. Díaz del Ribero, *op. cit.*, pp. 99–101.

50. García Figueras, *op. cit.*, pp. 110–11.

51. Mackenzie, *op. cit.*, p. 189.

52. Trout, *op. cit.*, p. 152.

53. *Ibid.*, pp. 27–32.

54. La Chapelle, *op. cit.*, p. 57.

55. Mackenzie, *op. cit.*, p. 189. The sultan eventually paid £5,000 compensation.

56. Caro Baroja, *op. cit.*, p. 366.

57. Trout, p. 155.

58. Cited in Trout, pp. 154–55. In its advisory opinion in 1975 on Morocco's claim to precolonial sovereignty in Western Sahara, the International Court of Justice commented on the 1895 Anglo-Moroccan agreement: "Numerous documents show that the position repeatedly taken by Great Britain was that Cape Juby was outside Moroccan territory, which in its view did not extend beyond the Dra'a. In the light of this material the provisions of the 1895 treaty invoked by Morocco appear to the Court to represent an agreement by Great Britain not to question in future any pretensions of the Sultan to the lands between the Dra'a and Cape Bojador, and not a recognition by Great Britain of previously existing Moroccan sovereignty over those lands."

4

The Origins
of Spanish Sahara

A s THE EUROPEAN POWERS "SCRAMBLED FOR AFRICA" at the end of the nineteenth century, Spain, which was by then one of Europe's weakest states, renewed its interest in the coast opposite the Canaries, three and a half centuries after the loss of Santa Cruz de Mar Pequeña. With the French on the island of Arguin, near Cape Blanc, and Mackenzie at Tarfaya, there were fears in Madrid that France, England or some other European power might secure control of this coast so close to the Canaries. It would be prudent, some argued, to raise the Spanish flag to forestall such rivals. At the same time, the Spanish government was encouraged to stake a claim by fishing interests in the Canaries, which valued the fishing resources off the Saharan coast, and by trading enterprises who, in the manner of the North-West Africa Company, hoped to tap the Saharan caravan traffic. Moreover, the traumatic loss of the colonies in America earlier in the century had left a sense of wounded pride that some Spanish nationalists now hoped to dispel by pursuing new imperial glories in Africa. The victory in Morocco in 1859–60 brought wind to their sails.

The Spanish colony on the Río de Oro was founded during the premiership of Antonio Cánovas del Castillo, a conservative royalist who had assumed the reins of government after the restoration of the Spanish monarchy in 1874 and remained in office until 1885 except for a brief period in 1881–83. Personally skeptical about the practical benefits of a colony on the Saharan coast, he authorized its founding under strong pressure from a well-connected and influential "Africanist" lobby backed by powerful business groups.

In the 1870s the proponents of Spanish colonial ventures in Africa began to organize societies to summon public support, prod the government into action and sponsor expeditions to Africa by Spanish explorers. Among them was the Asociación Española para la Exploración de Africa, which had sufficient political clout to be able to hold its first meeting, on September 16, 1877, under the presidency of King Alfonso XII. The meeting resolved to start surveying the coast opposite the Canaries.[1] Another group was the Sociedad de Geografía de Madrid, which was founded in 1876 and had among its leading lights one of the foremost ideologues of Spanish imperialism, Joaquín Costa. At a session of the society in May 1883 he proposed that a "congress of mercantile and colonial geography" be held to discuss such matters as the sending of explorers to Africa, the establishment of trading posts on the African coast and a campaign to rally public opinion and government support behind the colonial cause. The idea was approved and the congress duly met in Madrid on November 6–10, 1883, concluding its deliberations with the approval of a series of measures, ranging from the implementation of Article 8 of the 1860 Spanish-Moroccan treaty to the establishment of fishing stations on the coast opposite the Canaries and the creation of "a society of Spanish Africanists, whose purpose shall be to enlighten and arouse public opinion with regard to the problems of Spanish African policy and to influence the public authorities by the modern methods of mass meetings, discussions with the government, propaganda publications, etc."[2] The following month, the Sociedad Española de Africanistas y Colonistas was founded, and on March 30, 1884, it held its first public meeting in the Theater of the Alhambra. In January 1884 the society urged Cánovas del Castillo's government to occupy the Río de Oro and, the following June, it sent a petition to the Cortes advocating a vigorous colonial policy. The society had supporters in high places, not least among them Alfonso XII, who contributed three thousand pesetas to the society's first fund, launched by the Alhambra meeting, for the exploration of the Sahara and West Africa. In all thirty-seven thousand pesetas were collected, enough to send Manuel Iradier, Amado Ossorio and Bernabé Jiménez to Río Muni (Equatorial Guinea) and, in November 1884, Emilio Bonelli Hernando to the Río de Oro.[3]

Among the society's supporters were a number of businessmen who hoped to reap commercial rewards from the expansion of Spanish influence in Africa. Some imagined that, by establishing trading posts on the Saharan coast, conveniently close to the Canaries, they would be able to attract the Saharan caravans. Others wanted to establish bases from which to exploit the fishing resources off the Río de Oro, which were known to be far superior to those farther north off Ifni. In 1876, for example, a Sociedad de Pesquerías Canario-Africanas was set up and granted a royal concession to fish off the Saharan coast, and in September 1881 it established a pontoon in the Río de Oro bay after taking three local tribal leaders to Arrecife, the capital of Lanzarote, where they "ceded" to the company the Dakhla peninsula, the tongue of land sheltering the bay from the ocean. Two years later, in 1883, the Compañía Comercial Hispano-Africana was founded, under the chairmanship of General Manuel Cassola, "to develop Spain's commercial relations with Africa by establishing trading posts and creating a regular steamship service," and by February 1884 it was sending schooners from the Canaries to trade with the nomads at the Río de Oro and Cape Blanc.[4] The prime mover behind the new company, in which several Barcelona firms had interests, was one of Spain's most powerful business empires, López y López, which controlled about a quarter of the total tonnage of Spanish shipping at this time and owned such diverse companies as the General Tobacco Company of the Philippines, the Sociedad Española de Crédito Comercial, the Banco Hispano-Colonial and the Compañía Transatlántica. Not surprisingly for a business conglomerate of this size, López y López had good connections in the world of politics. Among its principal shareholders, for example, were Romero Roblero, a deputy in the Cortes who was to become minister of overseas affairs in the 1890s, and General Cassola, who also held a seat in the Cortes and was minister of war from 1887. Furthermore, financial backing for the Compañía Comercial Hispano-Africana came from the Banca General de Madrid, whose founder, Segismundo Moret, was appointed foreign minister in November 1885.[5]

So, by 1884 there was a formidable, interlocking nexus of business interests and Africanist propagandists who, with the ear of the royal family and several prominent politicians and the backing of influential sections of the press, could bring considerable pressure to bear on the Spanish government. Meanwhile, the Congress of Berlin was laying down the ground rules for the division of Africa. Unless Spain laid claim to the Saharan coast soon, another European power was certain to do so. The colonial lobby warned that, if Spain was upstaged, the security of the Canaries might be at risk, as well as Spain's prospects in Morocco. France had already aroused Spanish jealousy by occupying Algeria and Tunisia, and in April 1883 the Spanish government contested French rights to Arguin. There was also alarm at French attempts to establish trading relations with the Noun and at Mackenzie's activities at Tarfaya; and there was speculation that Mackenzie might try to establish a second trading post, perhaps on the Río de Oro, which he had visited in December 1880.[6]

It was to thwart such rivals that the Sociedad de Africanistas y Colonistas decided to send Emilio Bonelli to the Saharan coast in November 1884. The Cánovas del Castillo government agreed to support his mission by arranging for a Spanish warship, the *Ceres*, to land him along the coast. Having lived for six years in Morocco, in 1868–74, Bonelli was fluent in Arabic and so found it easy to make contact with local tribes. He suggested to them that Spanish trading posts could be established at the Río de Oro, Cape Blanc and Angra de Cintra, a bay about fifty miles south of the tip of the Dakhla Peninsula. The nomads stood to gain from such trade, as they did at Mackenzie's trading post, and it was doubtless with such commercial considerations in mind that a *sorba* of the Oulad Bou Sbaa signed a fateful treaty with Bonelli on November 28: "Don Emilio Bonelli, representing the Society of Africanists who reside in Madrid, the city of His Majesty the King of Spain, has arrived in the territory of the Oulad Bou Sbaa, on the coast of the sea with the goal of trading, selling and buying. He has constructed on our land a house where flies the Spanish flag, and we have given over to him the territory called Madibu or Cape Blanc of the coast, so that this territory finds itself uniquely under the protection and government of His Majesty the King of Spain, Don Alfonso XII."[7] Little could the three representatives of the Oulad Bou Sbaa who signed this declaration have realized that they were providing Bonelli with a pretext by which the Sociedad de Africanistas y Colonistas and the Compañía Comercial Hispano-Africana could persuade the Spanish government to "place under the protection of Spain the territories of Río de Oro, Angra de Cintra and the Bay of the West" in December 1884.[8]

Nonetheless, this colonial enterprise had a far from auspicious start. The idea of establishing trading posts at Angra de Cintra and the Bay of the West (Cape Blanc) was rapidly forgotten, and though the Compañía Comercial Hispano-Africana began erecting a fortified building at Dakhla in January 1885, it had to be abandoned when, on March 9, 1885, a hostile force of Oulad Delim arrived, murdered several of the company's employees and looted its stores. The survivors fled by ship to the Canaries.[9] However, Cánovas del Castillo pledged on March 27, under pressure in the Cortes, to maintain his government's support for the Río de Oro venture. In May the Compañía Comercial Hispano-Africana was able to issue twenty thousand new government-guaranteed shares of five hundred pesetas each.[10] A month later, a military detachment commanded by Captain José Chacón reoccupied Dakhla, which was baptized Villa Cisneros in memory of an archbishop who, four centuries earlier, had advocated the continuation of the *reconquista* into Africa. Then, on July 10, a royal decree placed the entire coast between Capes Blanc and Bojador under the administrative responsibility of the overseas ministry in Madrid. Bojador was chosen as the protectorate's northern limit, it would appear, because of the North-West Africa Company's presence at Tarfaya, while the southern limit was set at Cape Blanc because France held Arguin and had a claim to the coast between Senegal and Cape Blanc under the Anglo-French Treaty of Versailles, of September 1783. The decree, which was doubtless motivated by the need to comply with Article 35 of the General Act of the Congress of Berlin (February 26, 1885), requiring the colonial powers to establish an effective administration in their colonies, specified that a resident royal commissioner, responsible to the overseas ministry, would administer the protectorate, "pass treaties with the natives and . . . take possession of lands which have no known owner" and command "the land and sea forces which are stationed there for the maintenance of order and the defense of the protected territories."[11] Bonelli was given the job.

Official backing for the colonial enterprise at Villa Cisneros became further pronounced when Moret, one of the Compañía Comercial Hispano-Africana's most prominent supporters, was appointed foreign minister in November 1885 after the fall of Cánovas del Castillo's government. In January 1886 a naval division was based in the Canaries to "consolidate Spanish sovereignty on the west coast of Africa."[12] Then, on April 6, 1887, a decree extended Spanish jurisdiction 150 miles into the interior and transferred the administration of the colony, which was no longer described as a protectorate, to a "politico-military sub-governor," resident in Villa Cisneros and responsible to the captain-general of the Canaries.[13] One of his principal preoccupations in these early days was to fend off attacks by hostile Saharawis. From 1885 a tiny garrison of about twenty-five soldiers was posted in Villa Cisneros, to be relieved every three months when the supplies of drinking water arrived by ship from the Canaries. But the little settlement was raided on March 24, 1887, and again in March 1892, when two ships, the *Tres de Mayo* and *Las Marías*, were attacked, and on November 2, 1894.[14] The raiding finally halted after an agreement had been reached on March 2, 1895, with Sheikh Ould Laroussi, a leader of the Oulad Delim, the most powerful local tribe, who promised "to protect the transactions and not forbid relations of any kind between the natives and the Spaniards and to compensate the damages which might be caused by whomsoever among our subjects."[15] Ould Laroussi doubtless anticipated that the Oulad Delim stood to gain more by trading with Villa Cisneros than by attacking it. However, from the vantage point of the Compañía Comercial Hispano-Africana, Villa Cisneros turned out to be ignominious commercial failure. Hopes that the settlement would attract caravans laden with wealth from the African interior were quickly dashed. Villa Cisneros was far from the traditional caravan routes; and, as Mackenzie discovered to his cost, the trade northward across the Sahara was diminishing significantly by the early 1890s. The Saharawis sold the Spaniards little more than animals, wool and skins and, from time to time, a few ostrich feathers, but the price they fetched on the world market was tumbling by then because of the competition from South Africa. To acquire additional capital, the Compañía Comercial Hispano-Africana attempted, on Moret's advice, to interest German financial circles in its Rí de Oro venture in 1885–86, but to no avail.[16] It was the Spanish government that came to the rescue. Unable to make a profit from the colony, the companies with interests there began exploiting their political connections to milk subsidies and cheap credit from the government, which also had to bear the costs of administering and defending the settlement. The Compañía Transatlántica, for example, was granted a subsidy in 1887 to run a regular steamship service from the Canaries; in 1892 it was awarded an interest-free loan of five million pesetas by the overseas minister, Romero Roblero.[17] The Compañía Transatlántica, which took over the installations of the Compañía Comercial Hispano-Africana when the latter went into liquidation in 1893, could argue, of course, that its services were vital to the settlement's survival; and, to avoid the embarrassment of having to haul down the Spanish flag, the government felt obliged to foot the company's bill.

In a fruitless attempt to attract more trade to Villa Cisneros, three Spaniards set off from the settlement into the desert hinterland in May 1886, under the auspices of the Sociedad Geográfica Comercial, to which the Sociedad de Africanistas y Colonistas had changed its name in 1885. Julio Cervera Baviera, a thirty-two-year-old army captain, Francisco Quiroga, a professor at Madrid's natural history museum, and Felipe Rizzo, a diplomat experienced in African affairs who acted as interpreter, made their way across the sands of the Tiris plateau and, after some 220 miles, reached the salt pans of Idjil. There, on July 12, 1886, they signed two treaties, one with local Saharawi chiefs and the other with the Emir of Adrar, Ahmed Ould Mohammed Ould Aida, which supposedly ceded to Spain a vast area of desert, including Adrar Temar; but the treaties did not prevent the three travelers being set upon as they made their way back again to the coast, and they were lucky to escape with their lives. Meanwhile, another envoy of the Sociedad Geográfica Comercial, José Alvárez Pérez, a former Spanish consul in Mogador who had participated in the voyage of the *Blasco de Garay* to Ifni in 1878, had explored the regions between the Draa and Cape Bojador in March–April 1886, persuading chiefs of two Tekna tribes, M'barek Ould Mohammed of the Ait Moussa Ou Ali and Mohammed Ould Belal of the Izarguien, to place themselves under the society's "protection" and allow it to establish whatever installations it desired on the coast. Both tribes had had beneficial relations with Mackenzie and probably expected the Spanish to engage in similar commercial pursuits. However, despite the Sociedad Geográfica Comercial's petitioning, none of the new agreements was endorsed by the Madrid government, which recognized that it had neither the material means to give them practical meaning nor the diplomatic leverage to get them accepted by the major colonial powers. Spain could not lay claim to the Tekna regions while Mackenzie was installed at Tarfaya, and Adrar Temar was due east of Arguin and so within France's sphere of influence according to the decisions of the Congress of Berlin, which had given European powers the right to the territory inland from the points under their control on the African coast.

Even before the departure of the Sociedad Geográfrica Comercial's explorers, a Franco-Spanish commission had been set up in Paris to discuss border questions in the Sahara. On October 26, 1886, the talks ended with the signing of a protocol which divided Cape Blanc between Spain and France, from its southern tip to parallel 21°20', but then vaguely stipulated that the frontier between their possessions would "continue into the interior along the above-mentioned parallel."[18] This implicitly gave Adrar Temar to France.

French troops had gradually been penetrating into parts of the Algerian Sahara since 1854, while to the south of the desert there had been occasional clashes between French troops and Moor tribes near the Senegal River. However, it was at the very end of the nineteenth century that certain French military officers and politicians began to dream of conquering the Sahara. There were even proposals to build a railway from Algeria to Senegal. In 1899 forces from French Algeria marched south to occupy the Touat, Gourara and Tidikelt oases; and in December that year, the French colonial ministry voiced support for a plan, drafted by Xavier Coppolani, to establish a French protectorate over the whole of the *trab el-beidan* from the Senegal to the Draa. Spain's Saharan pretensions were an irritant to Paris, and reports during the 1890s that Spain was trying to interest German financiers and politicians in its colony, possibly with a view to selling it, were added grounds for displeasure. However, the French foreign minister, Thomas Delcassé, preferred to woo rather than challenge Spain and reminded the colonial ministry of Spain's Saharan interests and the 1895 Anglo-Moroccan agreement.[19] In 1899 he began talks with the Spanish ambassador in Paris, Fernando León y Castillo, which culminated on June 27, 1900, in the signing of a convention defining the borders of Spain's Saharan territory and French-to-be Mauritania. This confirmed the partition of Cape Blanc and extended the 1886 demarcation by defining the southeastern frontiers of the Spanish colony as far as the intersection of the Tropic of Cancer with the meridian 14°20' west of Paris (12° west of Greenwich), whence the border would "continue on that latter meridian in a northerly direction."[20] The northern borders were left deliberately vague on account of the 1895 Anglo-Moroccan agreement. Interestingly, Delcassé was careful to ensure that France received two zones of economic interest from the division, first the salt pans of Idjil, which were assigned to Mauritania by giving Spain's colony the curious kink in its southeastern border, and secondly the rich fishing waters of the Bay of Levrier, which was enclosed entirely within the French zone as a result of the partition of the Cape Blanc peninsula.[21]

THE DEMARCATION OF THE BORDERS
OF WESTERN SAHARA

© Moira Jones

The demarcation of the northern border of Spain's Saharan territory was inevitably bound up with the much larger question of the fate of Morocco, which was coveted by all the main European powers at the opening of the twentieth century. France, which had already conquered most of Algeria and Tunisia and was about to advance into Mauritania, had the most ambitious designs on Morocco but faced competition from the other powers, notably Britain and Germany. Spain too had ambitions, in view of its presidios at Ceuta and Melilla, its victory over Morocco in 1859–60 and the concessions it had wrung from Morocco in the ensuing peace treaty of April 1860. Spain, however, had little bargaining power of its own and so tried to oblige France to take its interests into account by exploiting the rivalries of the main contestants; but, as France's principal rivals successively decided to accept French predominance in Morocco, in return for concessions from France elsewhere in Africa, Spain's leverage and French generosity diminished.

After Italy had renounced colonial objectives in Morocco, in return for a free hand from France in Tripolitania (Libya), in an agreement signed in December 1900, France tried to strike a deal with Spain. The negotiations culminated on November 8, 1902, in agreement on a draft convention stating that, if the Moroccan government proved unable to maintain the *status quo*, "the Government of the French Republic and the Government of His Majesty the King of Spain will determine as follows the limits in the interior of which each of them will have the exclusive right to reestablish the tranquility, to protect the life and possessions of people and to guarantee the freedom of commercial transactions."[22] Article 3 then defined the Spanish zone of Morocco as including much of northern Morocco, including the Rif, Fez and Taza, and, in the south, a large swath of territory from the southern Souss and the Anti-Atlas to parallel 26°, just south of Cape Bojador. Both the Draa and the Saguia el-Hamra were thus to become part of Spanish Morocco. However, Spain withheld ratification of the convention, for fear of adverse British reaction to a unilateral Spanish agreement with France.[23]

Unfortunately for Madrid, the French government was to prove less generous when a new round of Franco-Spanish negotiations began in 1904. These had been preceded by a pact, signed on April 8, 1904, by which France and Britain had finally resolved their colonial disputes, the former accepting British hegemony in Egypt and the latter French predominance in Morocco. However, Article 8 of this Anglo-French agreement stipulated that Spain's interests in Morocco would be respected, and to keep France at a strategically safe distance from Gibraltar, Britain obliged the French government to accept a secret clause assigning the northern Moroccan coast to Spain. Negotiations followed between Lord Lansdowne, the British foreign secretary, and Paul Cambon, the French ambassador in London, on the matter of the 1895 Anglo-Moroccan agreement. Cambon informed Lansdowne that a Spanish sphere of influence was projected in southern Morocco and the Sahara; and on April 27 the British government gave Cambon a memorandum assuring France that Britain had no intention of claiming "any special position or influence" in the territory "in the neighbourhood of Cape Juby" and "will not oppose any arrangements in regard to it," especially since it understood that France was "negotiating with the Spanish Government on the basis that this territory shall fall within the sphere of influence of Spain should the Sultan ever cease to exercise authority over it."[24] However, with Britain no longer an obstacle to the achievement of their Moroccan ambitions, the French could afford to strike a much tougher bargain with the Spanish than in 1902. They simply prescribed the terms of a new Franco-Spanish convention. Signed on October 3, 1904, this included a bland and deceitful public declaration that France and Spain "remain firmly attached to the integrity of the Moroccan empire under the sovereignty of the sultan" and, of much greater importance, a set of secret accords, not published until 1911, which, like the unratified 1902 convention, permitted France and Spain to intervene in Morocco in the event of a breakdown of the *status quo* and accordingly divided Morocco into French and Spanish spheres of influence. As in 1902, Spain was to receive zones in both northern and southern Morocco, but they were less extensive than those proposed in 1902. In northern Morocco, Spain lost Fez and Taza to the French, while Tangier was to become an "international zone." In the south Spain was no longer to receive any of the Souss Valley but it was still to get most of the Anti-Atlas and the territories to its south.[25] Article Four recognized Spain's "special rights" over Santa Cruz de Mar Pequeña, which was arbitrarily located at Ifni and given fixed frontiers. Article Six concerned the western Sahara. Whereas the 1902 draft convention had defined the territory directly to the north of the 26th parallel as part of the Spanish sphere of influence in Morocco, Article Six of the new convention stated that "Spain has henceforward full liberty of action in regard to the territory comprised between 26° and 27°40' north latitude and the eleventh meridian west of Paris, which are outside Moroccan territory."[26] So Morocco's southern frontier was set farther north by France and Spain than in 1902. France, it seems, wanted to compensate Spain for its loss of important territories in northern Morocco and the Souss by recognizing its full sovereignty between parallels 26° and 27°40', the territory that later came to be known as Saguia el-Hamra, after the name of its principal river. And, as Cambon had been informed in London in April 1904, Britain, having renounced colonial intentions in North-West Africa, no longer wished to uphold the clause in its 1895 agreement with the *makhzen* which recognized Moroccan sovereignty as far south as Cape Bojador. Moreover, both France and Spain knew that no Moroccan officials or troops were posted farther south than the trading post that Mackenzie had abandoned in 1895 at Tarfaya, thirteen miles north of parallel 27°40'.[27]

Spain's "full liberty of action" in Saguia el-Hamra was confirmed eight years later, on November 12, 1912, by the final convention demarcating the French and Spanish zones in Morocco and the Sahara. This followed the Franco-German agreement of November 4, 1911, by which Germany, France's one outstanding rival, had finally accepted French predominance in Morocco, and five months later, the Treaty of Fez, of March 30, 1912, by which Sultan Moulay Hafid handed over his country to French "protection." The Treaty of Fez empowered France to delegate the guardianship of parts of the sultan's realm to Spain, but by 1912 the French were feeling even less generous to Spain than in 1904. Spain had almost no bargaining power now that both Germany and England had come to terms with France over Morocco's future, and, since France had been obliged to give up one hundred thousand square miles of the French Congo to Germany to get its way in Morocco, it was willing to give Spain only the crumbs of Moulay Hafid's empire. So the Spanish protectorate zone in northern Morocco was reduced to a small strip of coastline and a portion of the Rif Mountains, while in the south Spain had to give up its previous hopes of acquiring some of the Anti-Atlas range and accept a small protectorate zone sandwiched between the Draa and parallel 27°40'. Known later as Spanish Southern Morocco, this was divided by French-ruled territory from Spanish Ifni, a tiny enclave of about 580 square miles. To the south of parallel 27°40', the 1912 convention ratified Article Six of the 1904 convention, thus confirming that Saguia el-Hamra was "outside Moroccan territory" and could become an outright Spanish colony rather than part of Spain's protectorate zone in Morocco.[28]

Spain had been too weak to play more than a marginal role in the world powers' scramble for colonies. By 1914 the six largest powers had seized twenty-five million square miles of colonial territory; Britain alone had acquired thirteen million square miles.[29] Spain, by contrast, had managed to annex only about 135,000 square miles, of which almost six-sevenths were desert and the rest was divided between Río Muni and Fernando Po in West Africa, Ifni and the generally barren protectorate zone in northern Morocco, while in the 1890s Spain had been forced out of its two remaining American colonies, Cuba and Puerto Rico, as well as the Philippines. In the Sahara, Spain acquired 112,000 square miles under its agreements with France—a little under 9,900 square miles in Spanish Southern Morocco, about 31,650 square miles in Saguia el-Hamra and just over 71,000 square miles in Río de Oro. All of this, however, was simply on paper. In practice the Spanish presence remained entirely restricted at this time to the Lilliputian settlement at Villa Cisneros; and though two more settlements were established along the Saharan coast in 1916 and 1920, no attempt was made to control points in the interior until 1934, almost fifty years after the founding of Villa Cisneros.

While the desperate effort to hang on to Cuba and Puerto Rico exercised the minds of Spanish politicians and generals in the 1890s, the bitter resistance of the Rifians in northern Morocco drained Spanish colonial energies for most of the first quarter of the twentieth century. Even before the imposition of the Franco-Spanish protectorate on Morocco, Spanish forces had been engaged in fierce fighting with the tribes of northern Morocco. By 1909 there were forty thousand Spanish troops in Melilla.[30] In the first seven years of the protectorate, Spain made no significant progress in extending its sway beyond three little enclaves around Ceuta, Melilla and Larache. Many Spaniards began to express doubts about the wisdom of establishing a Spanish protectorate in Morocco at all. The left-wing Spanish parties were unequivocally opposed and even Miguel Primo de Rivera, the general who was to become dictator of Spain in 1923, suggested in March 1917 that Spain should try to regain Gibraltar rather than colonize Morocco.[31] However, pressures from the army officers in northern Morocco and international commitments to France and Britain obliged the Spanish government to redouble its efforts to "pacify" its protectorate zone after the First World War. In 1920 the Spanish Foreign Legion was founded to assist the conquest. The Rifians resisted bitterly, under the leadership of Mohammed Abdelkrim, who founded a republic in the Rif in 1921. Eventually it took half a million Spanish troops, backed up by French forces from 1925, to subdue them. Abdelkrim surrendered in May 1926 but the last Rifian resistance fighters held out until July 1927.

It is little wonder that successive Spanish governments felt it unwise to open a second front to the south, in Ifni or the Sahara; and so until 1934 the Spanish governors in the Sahara never tried to do more than consolidate the Spanish presence along the coast while cultivating the best possible relations with the nomads of the interior to keep them at bay. One man, Francisco Bens Argandoña, practically personified this policy for twenty-two years. A veteran of the Cuban war, Bens was appointed politico-military governor of Río de Oro in

1903, upon the recommendation of the military high command in the Canaries, and arrived in Villa Cisneros to take up his duties on January 17, 1904. From the beginning his aim was to win the Saharawis' confidence. One of his first decisions was to organize a sumptuous feast at Villa Cisneros for the local nomads. Two hundred sheep were slaughtered to feed hundreds of Oulad Delim, Oulad Bou Sbaa and Arosien. It was symbolic of Bens's "sugar-lump" policy toward the nomads. He assured them that Spain harbored no aggressive intentions and would not attempt, like the French in Mauritania, to extend its presence into the interior and subjugate the tribes. In April 1906 he even persuaded several sheikhs of the Reguibat, the Oulad Delim and other tribes to travel by steamer with their camels to take part in a day of pageantry in Las Palmas de Gran Canaria during a visit to the city by King Alfonso XIII.[32]

Bens nurtured such confidence among the nomads that he was able to travel widely in the desert without Spanish military escort at a time of fierce resistance by some of the tribes of the western Sahara and northern Mauritania to the northward thrusts of the French army. In 1907, for example, he visited Argoub, on the opposite side of the Río de Oro Bay from Villa Cisneros, with a group of Oulad Delim; and in November–December 1910 he spent forty-two days on an overland mission that took him as far south as Adrar.[33] A little later, in 1913, a Spanish explorer, Enrique d'Almonte, also traveled widely in the desert hinterland on behalf of the Real Sociedad Geográfica of Madrid.[34]

By assuring the Saharawis of his peaceful intentions, Bens hoped to facilitate his plans to found the new coastal settlements that he believed were needed in order to dissuade other European nations from establishing a presence on the coast. But Bens's plans were repeatedly frustrated by cautious, vacillating politicians in Madrid who either feared acting independently of France, prior to 1912, or worried about getting embroiled in new conflicts with hostile tribes while the troubles continued in northern Morocco. So when, after his trip to Adrar, Bens reconnoitered the coast in 1911 and then suggested that bases be established at both Tarfaya and Cape Bojador, the Madrid authorities rejected his proposal as premature, since the negotiations that were to lead to the 1912 Franco-Spanish border demarcation convention were about to begin. Similar hesitations led to the abandonment of an attempt by Bens to occupy Ifni in 1911. In July 1914 Bens finally secured the approval of the Spanish prime minister, the Count of Romanones, for the founding of a post at Tarfaya. The onset of World War I, which provided the Spanish garrison at Villa Cisneros and a few local nomads with the spectacle of a naval battle offshore between two German cruisers and a warship of the Royal Navy at the end of August, delayed execution of his plans, but on October 15, Bens set sail in the *Río de Oro* with a small contingent of Spanish soldiers, seventeen Saharawis and enough supplies to last three months. Meanwhile, however, the commander of the Spanish naval forces in the Canaries, Admiral Pidal, advised the Madrid government that conditions were not right for landing at Tarfaya and that resistance could be expected from local tribes. So, as Bens sailed northward up the coast from Villa Cisneros, a steamship returning to Spain from Fernando Po, the *Antoñica*, passed on orders from the admiralty to halt the expedition. Infuriated, Bens landed in a bay to the south of Cape Bojador and, ignoring the orders, set off overland, reaching Tarfaya seventeen days later, on November 6. But on November 16, Admiral Pidal arrived in person at Tarfaya aboard the cruiser *Cataluña* and ordered the unfortunate Bens to embark. He was dispatched back to Villa Cisneros.[35] It was not until June 29, 1916, that the intrepid governor was finally able to run up the Spanish flag at Tarfaya with Madrid's assent. Since Tarfaya was in Spanish Southern Morocco, Bens received the title there of "delegate" of the Spanish high commissioner in Morocco, whose capital was in Tetuan, while remaining politico-military governor of Río de Oro at Villa Cisneros.[36]

In April 1919 Bens was back again on the Ifni coast, after sailing north once more in the *Río de Oro*, but after negotiating with local tribes, he was ordered by the government to depart since France had protested his appeasement of the great anti-French resistance leader in the Anti-Atlas, Ahmed el-Hiba.[37] On October 30, 1920, however, Bens received instructions from the ministry of state to occupy La Guera, on Cape Blanc, so that a Spanish firm, Marcotegui, Guedes y Compañía, could set up a fishing industry there. Preparations were made in the Canaries, from where Bens set sail aboard the gunboat *Infanta Isabel* on November 27 with three fellow officers, fifty soldiers of the 66th Infantry and some construction workers. After picking up a machine gun and an interpreter from Villa Cisneros the next day, the *Infanta Isabel* arrived off La Guera on the morning of the thirtieth. Bens disembarked and ran up the flag.[38]

So, by 1920, Bens was administering three tiny settlements along the coast—Villa Cisneros, Tarfaya and La Guera. The Rif war, which drained Spain's military resources from 1921 to 1927, prevented him from launching new initiatives, and when he left the governorship in 1925, even Villa Cisneros was still only a tiny settlement of less than a thousand inhabitants, most of them Saharawis who camped in their *khaimat* around the Spanish fort and the buildings of the Compañía Transatlántica. "The future of Spanish Sahara does not promise much success," commented a British Foreign Office report in 1919. "Lack of fresh water and the consequent infertility of the soil, lack of harbours on the coast, the instability of the native population and of trade, and the laxity of Government control combine to make capitalists shy of investing money in this tract of country. In fact the only outstanding advantage which has hitherto accrued to Spain from its possession is the convenience afforded to the Canary and Balearic Islands' fishing fleets by Río de Oro, as a curing station and fishing depot. As a colony or dependency, and in part a Protectorate of Spain, the country is, to all intents and purposes, still in its infancy and does not show sign of growing into maturity."[39] Even the important fisheries opportunities were largely wasted. About seventy-five boats from the Canaries were operating off the Western Saharan coast in 1919, but the fishermen adhered to "sixteenth-century methods," complained a deputy in the Cortes, Castro Cazaleiz, who described the fish dried at the factory of the Compania Transatlántica at Villa Cisneros as "fit only for feeding Negroes."[40] Most of it was exported to Río Muni. In all, only 260 tons of fish were exported in 1913. Since there were virtually no other exports, total export revenue that year was only £4,020; but imports, which consisted mainly of clothes, food, cartridges and fresh water from the Canaries, cost only £4,250.[41] Writing a few years later, in 1926, a doctor of the colonial health service described Villa Cisneros as a village of twenty houses and twenty-eight tents. "The native population does not reach 150 persons. To that must be added a military detachment (thirty-five soldiers), a captain-governor, a lieutenant, a doctor, a policeman, a chaplain and the manager of the Transatlántica and that is the complete breakdown of the population of Villa Cisneros."[42] La Guera was much the same size, overshadowed by nearby Port Etienne, the French fishing port founded on the Cape Blanc peninsula in 1906.

Most of the Spaniards in Western Sahara at the time of Bens's departure were soldiers, but there were still only 703 of them—159 in La Guera, 121 at Villa Cisneros and 423 at Tarfaya, where a larger garrison was needed to guard the airfield built there in 1923.[43] Additionally, six Spanish air-force planes were based at Tarfaya and Villa Cisneros from 1928. During the twenties the Spanish authorities also began recruiting Saharawis into special paramilitary police units modeled on the French *groupes nomades*. The first Saharawi police unit was formed in 1926 and a mounted Saharawi camel corps was added two years later, when the Tropas de Policía del Sahara were officially constituted. But this force was modest in size. By 1930 it had thirty Europeans, including six officers, and 198 Saharawis, with sixty-two horses and 183 camels.[44]

Indeed, so little importance was attached to Western Sahara in Madrid that upon Bens's departure, in November 1925, a decree was published stipulating that his job should not in the future be held by an officer with a rank higher than lieutenant colonel or major.[45] The new man was Lieutenant Colonel Guillermo de la Peña Cusi, who, from his headquarters in Tarfaya, combined the titles of governor-general of Spanish Sahara, delegate of the high commissioner in the southern zone of the Protectorate of Morocco and inspector-general of the military forces in the Sahara. He received his orders and his budget from the Dirección General de Marruecos y Colonias, a subbody, set up in December 1925, of the presidency of the Council of Ministers in Madrid. He, in turn, delegated authority to run the three little Spanish settlements on the Saharan coast to a subgovernor in Tarfaya, a politico-military governor in Villa Cisneros and a delegate, responsible to the latter, in La Guera.[46] One of the territory's few benefits to the authorities in Madrid was its use as a dumping ground for political prisoners. A penal colony was founded at Villa Cisneros in 1932, presumably on the premise that it would be virtually impossible for its inmates to escape from their remote desert exile. Nonetheless, on December 31, 1932, twenty-nine prisoners made a dramatic breakout and fled in a fishing boat to Portugal.[47]

Until 1934 Bens's successors realistically continued his policy of a pacific *modus vivendi* with the nomads of the interior. They had neither the means nor the will to police them, so long as they left the little Spanish settlements on the coast at peace. The nomads were thus left to their own devices; but, though they did little to bother the relatively peacable Spaniards, they used the hinterland of Spain's nominal colony as a sanctuary from which to resist France's much more aggressive and determined attempt to subdue its nearby zones of desert.

NOTES

1. Tomás García Figueras, *Santa Cruz de Mar Pequeña, Ifni, Sahara. La acción de España en la costa occidental de Africa* (Ediciones Fe, Madrid, 1941), p. 123.
2. *Ibid.*, p. 125.
3. *Ibid.*, p. 127.
4. *Ibid.*, p. 126; J. L. Miège, "Les origines de la colonie espagnole du Río de Oro," in *Le Sahara: rapports et contacts humains, 7ème colloque d'histoire organisé par la faculté des lettres d'Aix-en-Provence* (Faculté des Lettres, Aix-en-Provence, 1967), p. 203.
5. *Ibid.*, pp. 202-3.
6. *Ibid.*, pp. 200-201; Donald Mackenzie, *Khalifate of the West* (Simpkin, Marshall, Hamilton, Kent and Co. Ltd., London, 1911), p. 178.
7. Cited in Miège, *loc. cit.*, pp. 208-9.
8. *Ibid.*, p. 210. The establishment of this protectorate was communicated to the French government on December 26, 1884, and to the British government on January 9, 1885. The Bay of the West, or, as the French called it, the Baie du Lévrier, is sheltered by the Cape Blanc peninsula.
9. García Figueras, *op. cit.*, p. 128.
10. Miège, *loc. cit.*, p. 211.
11. *Ibid.*, pp. 216-17.
12. French foreign ministry archives, Espagne 908, Madrid, January 21, 1886, cited in Miège, *loc. cit.*, p. 218.
13. García Figueras, *op. cit.*, p. 128.
14. *Ibid.*, p. 129.
15. Cited in Ramón Criado, *Pasión y muerte de un sueño colonial* (Ruedo Ibérico, Paris, 1977), p. 84.
16. Miège, *loc. cit.*, pp. 212-15.
17. *Ibid.*, pp. 218-19.
18. Cited in *Le Sahara occidental devant la Cour Internationale de Justice: mémoire présenté par le Royaume du Maroc* (Moroccan Government, Rabat, 1975), p. 15.
19. Frank E. Trout, *Morocco's Saharan Frontiers* (Droz, Geneva, 1969), pp. 165-66.
20. Article One of the Franco-Spanish convention of 1900 stated: "On the coast of the Sahara, the limit between the French and Spanish possessions will follow a line which, departing . . . on the western side of the Cape Blanc peninsula, between the extremity of that cape and the Bay of the West, will reach the middle of the aforesaid peninsula, then, in dividing the latter in half as much as the terrain will permit, will go to the north as far as the point of encounter with the parallel 21°20' north latitude. The frontier will continue to the east along 21°20' until the intersection of this parallel with the meridian 15°20' west of Paris (13° of Greenwich). From that point, the line of demarcation will run in the direction of the northeast by making a curve, between the meridians 15°20' and 16°20' west of Paris (13° and 14° west of Greenwich), which will be traced in a way to leave to France, with their dependencies, the salt pans of the region of Idjil, from whose external bank the frontier will be kept at a distance of at least 20 kilometers. From the intersection of the aforesaid curve with the meridian 15°20' west of Paris (13° west of Greenwich), the frontier will reach as directly as possible the intersection of the Tropic of Cancer with the meridian 14°20' west of Paris (12° west of Greenwich), and will continue on that latter meridian in a northerly direction." Cited in *Spanish Sahara (Río de Oro)* (Foreign Office, London, 1919), p. 33.
21. However, Article Two of the convention did grant Spanish fishermen the right to fish in the Bay of Lévrier and land on its shores, and Article Three provided that salt exported from Idjil into the Spanish zone would not be subject to French export duties.
22. Cited in Trout, *op. cit.*, p. 169.
23. *Ibid.*, p. 168.
24. *Ibid.*, p. 174-75.
25. Article Five stated: "In order to complete the delimitation set out in Article One of the convention of June 27, 1900, it is understood that the line of demarcation between the French and Spanish spheres of influence will start from the intersection of the meridian 14°20' west of Paris with 26° latitude north, which it will follow eastward as far as its intersection with the meridian 11° west of Paris. It will follow this meridian as far as the Oued Draa, then the thalweg of the Oued Draa until its meeting with the meridian 10° west of Paris, and finally the meridian 10° west of Paris until the crest line between the basins of the Oued Draa and the Oued Souss, and then follow in a westerly direction

the crest line between the basins of the Oued Draa and the Oued Souss, and then between the basins of the Oued Mesa and the Oued Noun as far as the nearest point to the source of the Oued Tazeroualt.'' Cited in Rachid Lazrak, *Le contentieux territorial entre le Maroc et l'Espagne* (Dar el Kitab, Casablanca, 1974), p. 413.

26. *Ibid.*, p. 414.

27. Trout, *op. cit.*, p. 177.

28. With regard to southern Morocco and the Sahara, Article Two of the 1912 convention stated: "The frontier of the French and Spanish zones will be defined by the thalweg of the Oued Draa, which it will follow from the sea as far as its intersection with the meridian 11° west of Paris; it will follow this meridian southward until its intersection with the parallel 27°40' latitude north. To the south of this parallel, Articles Five and Six of the convention of October 3, 1904, will remain applicable." Cited in Lazrak, *op. cit.*, p. 423.

29. V. I. Lenin, *Imperialism, the Highest Stage of Capitalism* (Foreign Languages Publishing House, Moscow), p. 134.

30. Miguel Martín, *El colonialismo español en Marruecos* (Ruedo Ibérico, Paris, 1973), p. 238. In July 1909, over a thousand Spanish soldiers were killed in a battle with the Rifians on Mount Gurugú.

31. *Op. cit.*, pp. 57, 90–97.

32. García Figueras, *op. cit.*, pp. 185–86.

33. *Ibid.*, p. 188.

34. See Enrique d'Almonte, "Ensayo de una breve descripción del Sahara español," *Boletín de la Real Sociedad Geográfica*, No. 56, 1914, pp. 129–347.

35. García Figueras, *op. cit.*, pp. 217–20.

36. *Ibid.*, p. 227. The governorship lost its politico-military qualification in 1923.

37. *Ibid.*, p. 231.

38. *Ibid.*, p. 232–33.

39. *Spanish Sahara (Río de Oro)*, p. 19.

40. *Ibid.*, p. 29.

41. *Ibid.*, p. 31.

42. Guillermo Rocafort, "La colonía española del Sahara occidental," *Revista Hispano-Africana*, Vol. V, November–December 1926.

43. The airfield was built by a French company to provide a landing strip for the first French flights between Casablanca and Dakar. Saharawi hatred of the French, who were then trying to subjugate the tribes of southern Morocco and northern Mauritania, required the stationing of a relatively large Spanish force there. See García Figueras, *op. cit.*, pp. 241–43.

44. *Ibid.*, p. 287.

45. *Ibid.*, pp. 251–52.

46. *Ibid.*, pp. 269–70.

47. *Ibid.*, p. 275.

Pro-Polisario demonstrators during a visit to Western Sahara by a United Nations mission of inquiry, El-Ayoun, May 1975

Polisario demonstrators, Aoussert, May 1975 Y. NAGATA, UNITED NATIONS

Ibrahim Ghali, minister of defense of the Saharan Arab Democratic Republic

Moroccan soldiers captured by Polisario guerrillas

Polisario guerrillas with seized Moroccan ammunition crates

Moroccan troops in Western Sahara on American-made personnel carriers SHARON I. SOPHER

King Hassan II address-
ing the United Nations
General Assembly, Oc-
tober 1982 SAW LWIN,
UNITED NATIONS

President Chadli Bendjedid of
Algeria, at the OAU summit in
Monrovia, Liberia, July 1979
JOE MARGOLIS

5

Resistance and Pacification

THE SAHARAWIS WERE AMONG THE LAST African peoples to submit to colonial domination. However, it was not the Spanish who finally brought them to heel but the French. From the turn of the century, as the French gradually conquered Mauritania, northward from Senegal, the center of anti-French resistance shifted across the border to the unpoliced Spanish Sahara, from which long-range raiding parties could set forth to harass the French to the south and loot the tribes that had allied with them. The Spanish, who remained closeted in their tiny coastal settlements, did nothing to stop those *ghazzian* and made no attempt to occupy the the interior of their colony until after the French had broken the back of the Saharawi resistance, in 1934.

This long war between the French and the northern tribes of the *trab el-beidan* really began in 1904 when one of the Mauritanian emirs, Bakar of Tagant, appealed for aid to fend off a threatening French invasion. Over the preceding two years, Xavier Coppolani, a Corsican who had been brought up in Algeria and spoke fluent Arabic, had subjugated the two southernmost Mauritanian emirates, Trarza and Brakna.[1] He had then been named French commissioner-general of Mauritania and had started assembling troops for a march into the two more northerly emirates, Tagant and Adrar. Desperate for help against Coppolani, the octogenerian Emir Bakar, who had ruled Tagant since 1836, sent envoys to the foremost religious leader of the Saguia el-Hamra, Sheikh Ma el-Ainin, who immediately pledged support and, over the next six years until his death in 1910, was to become one of France's most resolute foes, not only in Mauritania but, at the very end of his life, in Morocco too.

Mohammed Mustafa Ould Sheikh Mohammed Fadel, who received the nickname Ma el-Ainin, "water of the eyes," as a child, was by all accounts a man of quite remarkable stature, and his ability to unite many of the disparate and normally quarrelsome nomadic tribes in a crusade against the French might fairly be compared with that displayed eight and a half centuries earlier by Abdallah Ibn

Yacin in the early days of the Almoravid movement, when the Saharan Sanhaja united in a *jihad* against the Zenata and Ghana. Ma el-Ainin was not himself a native of the Saguia el-Hamra. Indeed, he had been born about a thousand miles away near the banks of the Niger, in the Hodh, in about 1830–31.[2] His kinsmen, the Ahel Taleb el-Mokhtar, claimed to be *shorfa* whose ancestors had migrated from Tafilalet, in southeastern Morocco, to the Hodh in the seventeenth century; and his father, Mohammed Fadel Ould Mamin, was one of the Hodh's most respected marabouts and the founder of the Fadeliya wing of the great Sufi order, the Qadiriya.[3] It was in 1859, at the age of about twenty-eight, that Ma el-Ainin first made his home in the northwestern Sahara, settling initially in Tindouf, which had been founded seven years earlier by the Tadjakant, and then migrating as a nomad and trader in the region between the Draa and Adrar. He was to return only twice to the Hodh, for very brief visits, in 1864, when his father probably invested him formally as a sheikh of his order, and in 1879, on the eve of his mother's death.[4]

From the beginning he seems to have held an almost magnetic appeal to the nomads of the northwestern Sahara. He arrived not only with the prestige of being the son of the revered Mohammed Fadel and thus the inheritor of his *baraka*, but had just returned from the *hadj* to Mecca, a pilgrimage which very few Saharan nomads could undertake in those days.[5] A man of evident erudition as well as religious zeal, who, it was said, had learned to recite the Koran by heart at the age of seven and had been sent as a youth to Morocco by his father to pursue his education in Marrakesh, he quickly attracted *telamid* seeking instruction. By his death, claimed one of his sons, Taleb Khiyar, he had authored "313 or 314 books" treating "all the matters known by men."[6] He was also, it seems, an accomplished sorcerer, a healer of the sick, an exorciser of evil spirits and a rainmaker, who was constantly surrounded in the later part of his life by nomads seeking his blessing or favors. He was, besides, a man of almost boundless stamina, a camel rider of the first order, who, it was recorded, could ride the 520 miles from Tindouf to Ouadane in just twelve days.[7]

Ma el-Ainin's reputation extended even beyond the desert, to Morocco, where, since at least 1858, he had established relations with the ruling Alawites that were to stand him in good stead later in his life. In fact, he may have accompanied some of Sultan Moulay Abderrahman's sons on his *hadj* to Mecca in 1858.[8] In 1874 he met Abderrahman's successor, Mohammed, in Marrakesh. However, it was during the reign of Moulay Hassan that common interest cemented his relations with the *makhzen*. To Moulay Hassan, a virulently anti-Christian marabout of Ma el-Ainin's standing was a valuable ally in his attempt to curb European activities on the Saharan fringes of his empire. So, when Ma el-Ainin visited Marrakesh in 1887, a year after Hassan's expedition to Goulimine, the sultan named him as his caliph (*khalifa*) in the western Sahara and provided him with weapons.[9] When Moulay Abdelaziz succeeded Hassan in 1894, at the age of fourteen, Ma el-Ainin's influence at the Alawite court reached its peak. Then sixty-four, the sheikh acted almost as the young sultan's uncle. He visited him seven times during his reign, and the trading post at Tarfaya was entrusted to his care after its sale to the sultan under the 1895 Anglo-Moroccan agreement.[10] More important, Moulay Abdelaziz sent craftsmen and materials to help Ma el-Ainin achieve one of his greatest ambitions, the founding of a city that would serve as a commercial and religious center in the heart of the northwestern Sahara where, apart from Tindouf, there had hitherto been no permanent settlements between Adrar and the oases of the Noun and the Djebel Bani. Ma el-Ainin chose a site for his city five miles south of the Saguia el-Hamra, on one of its tributaries, midway along the caravan routes from Adrar to the Noun, in a region of relatively good pastures. An abundance of rushes suggested the city's name, Smara, as well as plentiful local water sources. The city's construction, during which thousands of nomads lent a hand, began in 1898.[11] Palm groves were planted and about 50 wells sunk, while building materials were shipped from Morocco and the Canaries to Tarfaya and then transported overland by camel. The main buildings had been completed by 1902, when Ma el-Ainin took up residence in the city and made it his principal base of operations.

Meanwhile, Ma el-Ainin had become increasingly alarmed by the growing penetration of the western Muslim world by the European "infidels." In the 1880s he had encouraged the Ahel es-Sahel to harass the Spanish settlement at Villa Cisneros and in 1886 he tried, albeit without success, to prevent the Emir of Adrar and several Saharawi sheikhs from treating with the Spanish explorers, Julio Cervera Baviera, Francisco Quiroga and Felipe Rizzo, at Idjil. "Envoys from Negchir, sent by Me-Lainin, a religious leader of great influence," wrote Cervera later, "spread around false information regarding our intentions, information prejudicial to us, and incited the Arabs to impede our expedition in the Sahara, a territory which, in their view, we were staining with our ungodly feet, drawing the wrath of the Prophet and the curse of Allah on the faithful."[12]

However, it was the colonial ambitions of the French that really roused Ma el-Ainin's fury. Cloistered in Villa Cisneros, the Spanish were not very troublesome; but France had already conquered Algeria and Tunisia and by 1903 both Trarza and Brakna had fallen to Coppolani. Ma el-Ainin had been scandalized by the support offered to the French against the *ahel mdafa*, the warrior tribes, in southern Mauritania by the local *zwaya* tribes and the great spiritual leader, Sheikh Sidiya Baba of Trarza, his greatest rival among the marabouts of the *trab el-beidan*, and he feared that the French planned to push on northward to subjugate Tagant, Adrar and perhaps even the Saguia el-Hamra. Moreover, he was well aware that France had designs on Morocco too. So he did not hesitate to respond positively to Emir Bakar's plea for help by turning to the sultan of Morocco for military aid. He sent is oldest son, Sheikh Hasseina, to Tagant to assure Bakar that arms would arrive from Morocco; but, before such aid materialized, French forces, including units of Senegalese and Moor troops, routed the Idou Aich, the dominant tribe of Tagant, and killed the aged emir, on April 1, 1904.[13]

Coppolani was now set to embark on the conquest of the next emirate, Adrar, but on the night of May 12, he was struck down in the French camp at Tidjikja, Tagant, by a squad of assassins led by Sidi Seghir Ould Moulay Zein, the *moqadem* of a militant religious sect, the Ghoudfiya, who were apparently acting at Ma el-Ainin's behest.[14] This was a tremendous psychological boon to the anti-French forces, who believed that the tide would now turn in their favor. Ma el-

Ainin proclaimed a general *jihad* and tried to arrange for shipments of arms to reach the centers of the resistance, at Smara and in Adrar, where Hasseina was then acting as tutor and regent to the boy emir, Ahmed Ould Ahmed Ould Aida. A shrewd tactician who was familiar with the rivalries of the European powers, Ma el-Ainin successfully negotiated with such arms suppliers as the Woermann Company of Hamburg and Torres of Barcelona, which began shipping arms to Tarfaya with the connivance of their governments.[15] Moreover, Moulay Abdelaziz decided in 1905 to send his uncle, Moulay Idris Ben Abderrahman Ben Suleiman, with a consignment of arms to join the sheikh's forces. Traveling down the coast in a rented Spanish vessel, the *Ríos*, in the autumn of 1905, Moulay Idris landed at Tarfaya and then joined Ma el-Ainin at Smara.[16] Meanwhile, to counter the French pretensions to Mauritania, flatter Moulay Abdelaziz and impress the tribes that they had the sultan's support in their struggle against the French, Ma el-Ainin blandly declared that the entire *trab el-beidan* was part of Morocco. Thus, in November 1905, Hasseina wrote to Sheikh Sidiya Baba "to let you know that Muslims such as Ould Aida, Emir of Adrar, the Mechdouf, the Idou Aich of Tagant, have addressed complaints to Sheikh Ma el-Ainin against the Christians and have asked him to intervene with the Sultan. Informed by the sheikh, the Sultan let it be known to the Christians that the *trab el-beidan* was his and that they must not appropriate it. Today the sultan has sent a mission commanded by his cousin, accompanied by his *qadi* and his secretary, to receive the submission of the Muslims and to aid with troops and munitions those who desire them. If the Christians do not leave this country it will be *jihad*. Those who defend the cause of Islam will be supported; those who ally with the Christians will be considered enemies."[17]

Seen out of context, this recognition of the sultan's suzerainty may seem strange in view of the almost total absence of direct Alawite influence in this part of the Sahara since Moulay Ismail's death almost two hundred years earlier. However, it was only logical, as well-armed Christian forces pushed northward into the "land of the Moors," that the resistance movement should declare its allegiance to the caliph of western Islam. It was a way of challenging the legitimacy of the French presence in Mauritania and, more important, of encouraging the only powerful Muslim government in the region to provide military assistance. In no practical way did the tribes lose their political independence and, though Moulay Idris transmitted *dahirs* from the sultan formally investing tribal leaders as his *caids*, these did no more than endorse the position of existing leaders. Moreover, as we shall see, Ma el-Ainin later did not hesitate to turn against Moroccan sultans who failed in their duty to defend Islam against the Europeans. Meanwhile, in 1905–8, his personal authority among the anti-French Saharan tribes was enhanced by his privileged position as chief interlocutor with Moulay Abdelaziz, as well as with the arms dealers of Germany and Spain. Nonetheless, neither he nor Moulay Idris, whose stay in the Sahara was very brief, established anything even remotely resembling a centralized supratribal administration. Rather, they were leaders of a disparate and inherently unstable tribal coalition that came together to confront a grave external threat.[18]

As summons to resistance were brought by envoys to all parts of the *trab el-*

beidan during 1905, the French authorities got wind of Ma el-Ainin's feverish activity. On November 14, the French commissioner in Mauritania reported to the governor-general of French West Africa: "These past few days, the great sheikh of the Saguia el-Hamra addressed a call to rebellion to certain tribes which have already freely accepted our influence. . . . Furthermore, thanks to the support of the Moroccan government, he is procuring rapid-firing weapons and munitions for the people of Adrar and he is even offering some of them to those administered by us who are prepared to abandon our cause."[19] In June–July 1906, Moulay Idris proceeded south to Adrar, to prepare a campaign with Sheikh Hasseina and Emir Ould Aida against the French units in Tagant. The first clash, at Niemilane, in October 1906, was a victory for Moulay Idris's forces who then began a long siege of the French post at Tidjikja from November 5. Eighty French and Senegalese soldiers held out heroically until December 1, when a large relief column broke through to Tidjikja, forcing Moulay Idris to lift the siege and retreat to Adrar.[20]

After this setback, Ma el-Ainin returned to Morocco to request additional support, but he was appalled to find Moulay Abdelaziz weakening in his resolve to face up to the growing European pressure on his empire. He had accepted the Act of Algeciras, an agreement reached by thirteen powers in April 1906 which placed Morocco's ports, police and finances under Franco-Spanish control. At France's insistence, Abdelaziz agreed to recall Moulay Idris from the Sahara in May 1907, thereby closing the brief chapter of direct Moroccan participation in the anti-French struggle in Mauritania, and, the following July, he ordered his *caid* at Goulimine, Dahman Ould Beyrouk, to intercept a caravan carrying arms for Ma el-Ainin's forces from Tarfaya.[21] Moreover, when French forces occupied Oujda in March 1907 and three thousand French and Spanish troops landed at Casablanca in August, Abdelaziz was unable to offer any resistance. Dismayed by the sultan's compromises with the French, Ma el-Ainin declared his support for Abdelaziz's brother, Moulay Hafid, when he rose in rebellion in August 1907. Defeated in August 1908, Abdelaziz abdicated; but, to Ma el-Ainin's horror, Moulay Hafid, once victorious over his brother, signed the Act of Algeciras on January 5, 1909, to obtain the European powers' recognition.

A week earlier Ma el-Ainin had begun to face a new challenge in the south. Forces commanded by Colonel Gouraud swept into Adrar at the end of December 1908 and, after defeating anti-French forces at Amati, entered Atar, one of the main oasis settlements of Adrar, on January 9. The following April, forces commanded by Ould Aida and two of Ma el-Ainin's sons, Hasseina and El-Oueli, inflicted their revenge by decimating a French column at Ras er-Remt; but Chinguetti and the remaining date-palm oases were then occupied by the French and the remnants of the resistance forces were pursued as far north as the *sebkha* of Idjil in August. Though the emir managed to escape, Adrar was now in French hands.[22]

Ma el-Ainin abandoned Smara and settled in Tiznit, in the southern Souss. Then, on March 4, 1910, Moulay Hafid was obliged by the French to sign a convention which, by its tenth article, "on the subject of Sheikh Ma el-Ainin and the enemies of France in the Sahara," pledged the sultan to "prevent these agitators receiving encouragement and aid in money, arms and ammunition.''[23] However, anarchy was now spreading through Morocco itself, as French and Spanish encroachments undermined the *makhzen*'s authority and tribes rebelled. To save the Caliphate of the West from the Christians, Ma el-Ainin decided to try to take Morocco's destiny into his own hands. He made a personal bid for power, which some historians have likened to Abdallah Ibn Yacin's advance into Morocco from the desert in the eleventh century, but he had to contend with the French, a more formidable foe than the Almoravids had faced.[24] Ma el-Ainin was proclaimed sultan by his supporters in Tiznit and rode out of the city in June 1910 at the head of a six-thousand-strong army to challenge Moulay Hafid at Fez. But en route in the Plain of Tadla his army was routed by French forces under General Moinier on June 23. Vanquished, the would-be sultan fled back to Tiznit, where he died a few weeks later on October 28.[25]

After Ma el-Ainin's death, one of his most illustrious sons, Ahmed el-Hiba, was nominated head of his family, the Ahel Sheikh Ma el-Ainin, who, on account of the sheikh's numerous progeny, came to constitute a *qabila* of their own.[26] Like his father, el-Hiba was to make a bid for power in Morocco, which slid further into chaos when tribes rebelled in many parts of the country after Moulay Hafid's signing of the Treaty of Fez in March 1912. El-Hiba was proclaimed sultan in Tiznit and set forth, on July 15, to march on Marrakesh with an army of Saharawis and Soussis. The Blue Sultan, as he came to be known, because of the Saharawis' traditional blue-dyed robe, the *draa*, entered Marrakesh on August 15. Three days earlier, the discredited Moulay Hafid had abdicated in Fez, to be succeeded by his French-supported brother, Moulay Ben Yusuf, the grandfather of Morocco's present ruler, Hassan II. In Marrakesh, meanwhile, the French consul was jailed and the city's dignitaries made the *bayaa* to el-Hiba. But a five-thousand-strong army under the command of Colonel Mangin marched against him, defeated his troops at Sidi Bou Othman on September 6 and entered Marrakesh four days later.[27]

Fleeing south, el-Hiba held out against the French in the Souss for a year, until May 1913, when the forces of General Louis Lyautey, the French resident-general in Morocco, seized Agadir and Taroudant.[28] He then fell back to the Anti-Atlas, where a guerrilla struggle continued intermittently against the French until 1934. With the outbreak of the First World War in 1914, Germany took advantage of its alliance with the Ottoman empire to encourage rebellions by the Muslim colonial subjects of its enemies, and el-Hiba was a natural candidate for support, like Ahmed el-Raisuni, the main anticolonial leader in northern Morocco at this time. On October 15, 1916, a German UC20 submarine slipped out of Heligoland to make a thirty-day voyage to the coast of the Noun with a consignment of six thousand guns for el-Hiba. On board were Edgar Probster, a former German consul in Fez, and a Turkish captain who bore a message for el-Hiba from the Ottoman sultan. But after landing Probster and some of the armaments at the mouth of the Draa, the submarine was forced to abandon its mission when a French gunboat made its appearance. Probster trekked overland to the Spanish post at Tarfaya, where he was detained and taken to the Canaries, and thereafter no German arms reached el-Hiba, who died shortly after the end of the First World War at Qerdus in the Anti-Atlas on May 23, 1919.[29] However, the standard of revolt was kept aloft in the Anti-Atlas by another of Ma el-Ainin's sons, Merebbi Rebbu, who had accompanied el-Hiba on his march to Marrakesh in 1912.

Farther south, in the Sahara, the French conquest of Adrar in 1909 had not ended hostilities. The centers of resistance had simply been pushed farther north. From sanctuaries in nominally Spanish territory, Saharawi tribes were to continue harassing the French in Mauritania until the 1930s. Drawing on their warrior traditions, they applied the time-tested tactic of the *ghazzi*, sometimes crossing hundreds of miles of desert to fall upon unsuspecting French camps or loot the livestock of tribes allied to the French as far away as Trarza or the Hodh. For more than two decades, this guerrilla war inspired the youth of the Sahel, who fought for the triumph of Islam and the defense of their freedom, as well as booty and personal glory. The principal commander of this holy resistance war after Ma el-Ainin's death was another of the sheikh's sons, Mohammed Laghdaf.

On January 2, 1913, some four hundred warriors of the Oulad Delim and the Reguibat gathered at Bir Moghrein. They planned at first to make a long-distance raid on the Hodh, but instead they fell upon a French camp at El-Boirat, forty miles west of Atar, on January 10, almost annihilating the French, Senegalese and Moor soldiers there, and then slipped across the border into "Spanish Sahara." When news of the massacre reached the French commissioner-general in Mauritania, Lieutenant Colonel Mouret, there were immediate fears that the attack might herald a general offensive against the French posts in northern Mauritania. So, on February 9, Mouret himself, with just under four hundred troops, headed off in pursuit of the raiders and, without bothering to obtain Spanish approval, crossed into Spanish territory. It was the first French "hot pursuit" raid into Western Sahara. Meanwhile, two hundred Oulad Ghailan, traditional enemies of the Reguibat from Adrar, left Chinguetti to join Mouret's counter-*ghazzi*. After crossing the Zemmour, Mouret's men entered Smara, which they found deserted, on February 12. After two days camped there, they blew up the dome of Ma el-Ainin's old council hall and destroyed much of his library. This wanton vandalism infuriated the nomads, who regarded it as an act of sacrilege; and in vengeance Mohammed Laghdaf rallied more than a thousand men, mainly Reguibat and Tekna, to drive Mouret back to Adrar. After a bitter engagement at the Oued Tagliatt on March 10, Mouret regained Adrar on March 28. During a month and a half of operations, his men had crossed about a thousand miles of desert.[30]

From about 1919 the French army in Mauritania occasionally received assistance, mainly against the Reguibat, from French Algerian forces, which were then still continuing their advance into the Sahara from the north. In April 1919, French troops of the Compagnie Saharienne of Touat attacked a Reguibat encampment, and in the winter of 1920–21 French troops from Algeria and Mauritania succeeded in making their first junction, in the Hank, in northeastern Mauritania. In 1925 French forces entered the abandoned city of Tindouf for the first time, though they did not establish a permanent garrison there until nine years later. Another liaison between French troops from Algeria and Mauritania, the Compagnie Saharienne of Touat and the Groupe Nomade of Atar, was achieved in 1929. Nonetheless, the anti-French raids continued during the 1920s. In 1923 a guerilla campaign was launched by one of Ma el-Ainin's nephews, Mohammed Taqi Allah Ould Ely, alias Ouadjaha, and a religious leader, Mokhri Ould Boukhari. On November 23, 1923, the Groupe Nomade of Chinguetti was decimated by a party of raiders; and on March 26, 1924, Port Etienne (Nouadhibou) was attacked. In April 1925, there was another battle, between the Groupe Nomade of Chinguetti and Saharawi guerrillas, at Treyfia, in which Ouadjaha was finally killed.[31]

Of all the *ghazzi* leaders, one of the most remarkable was a nephew of Ma el-Ainin, Mohammed el-Mamoun, one of six sons of Sheikh Mohammed Fadel Ould Abeidi, who had been a marabout of great standing in Adrar at the turn of the century. El-Mamoun was an intellectual and deeply religious man who had traveled widely, lecturing in the famous *medersa* (Islamic university) of Kairouane in Fez in 1907 and spending the following three years in the Middle East, visiting Mecca, Medina, Jerusalem, Beirut, Damascus and Alexandria. With the support of German agents he had organized guerrilla attacks against the French in northern Morocco during the First World War; and in August 1921 he had been with Abdelkrim in the Rif during his great victory over the Spanish army at Mount Arruit. He had later abandoned the resistance in the Rif and, after making amends with the French, settled in Taza as head of studies at the city's *medersa*. However, feeling insecure in French Morocco, he fled south to the desert in 1929 and, by 1931, he had become one of the chief Saharawi resistance leaders. On September 7, 1931, his raiders, mainly Reguibat and Oulad Delim, defeated the Groupe Nomade of Atar in a battle at Chaiman, fifty miles north of Atar, though they later suffered serious casualties at the hands of a pursuing force at Aghouenit. The following year, in March, Ould Aida, the Emir of Adrar, who had declared his support for the French and been allowed to regain his freedom and his emirate after his capture in 1912, fled Atar in a bid to join the anti-French forces in Spanish territory. He was intercepted and killed before he could reach the border. However, Mohammed el-Mamoun's raids continued. In August 1932, he gathered together a force of Oulad Delim and Reguibat to stage a long-distance raid into Trarza. Though illness prevented his own participation, his raiders descended on a French post at Oum Tounsi, near Nouakchott, on August 18. A French lieutenant, five French noncommissioned officers and several Senegalese and Trarza soldiers were killed. Another long-range *ghazzi* was dispatched to Trarza the following November.[32] Two even more ambitious raids were organized early in 1934 by a Reguibi, El-Aissawi et-Tibari. The first involved a trek right across Mauritania to the Hodh, where some four hundred camels were seized from the Oulad Hammonat; the other, which was El-Aissawi's thirty-seventh and last *ghazzi*, left the Saguia el-Hamra in March 1934 and culminated in an assault on the Groupe Nomade of Arawan near Timbuctoo. Another four hundred camels were driven back to the Western Sahara. In all, El-Aissawi and his men had covered more than three thousand miles in the space of three months during these two epic expeditions.[33]

But by the spring of 1934, the Saharawi resistance was petering out, demoralized. Only isolated bands, like El-Aissawi's twenty-five raiders, were still active.

Despite their brilliant guerrilla tactics, their exhaustive knowledge of the desert terrain and their use of sanctuaries in Spanish territory, they were ultimately no match for the French, who were not only better armed but able to coordinate their final offensive in 1934 from Morocco, Algeria and Mauritania, thereby closing in on the Saharawis from north and south. The will to resist was sapped meanwhile by a drought which afflicted the region in 1933, and as the French net drew tighter, the raids became more dangerous and less profitable, while compromise became an economic necessity in order to retain access to vital pastures. The resistance had been weakened, moreover, by the lack of sustained, unified leadership. Ma el-Ainin's prestige temporarily persuaded many of the tribes to sink their differences and unite against the French, and the sense of outrage occasioned by Mouret's destruction of Smara in 1913 brought about a similar unity under the leadership of Mohammed Laghdaf. But for most of the war, the raids were sporadic and uncoordinated, the work of independent groups of raiders who did not follow any overall plan or strategy. Worse still, the French were able to set tribe against tribe by exploiting traditional rivalries, fears and suspicions. They gradually "bedouinized" the war, by recruiting nomads into their forces and encouraging traditional enemies of the anti-French tribes, such as the Oulad Ghailan of Adrar and the Ait Oussa of the Djebel Bani, to mount their own *ghazzian* against them. These officially sanctioned raids were often seen by their practitioners as defensive or revenge attacks against those staged by the anti-French tribes, and they allowed the "pacified" *ahel mdafa* to continue, despite their submission to the French, to act out their traditional role as warriors.[34]

It was the completion of the French conquest of southern Morocco, early in 1934, that was to pave the way for the final pacification of the Ahel es-Sahel. In February 1930 the French government had established a unified Algerian-Moroccan military command, under the ultimate authority of the French resident-general in Morocco, to stamp out the remaining centers of dissidence in the border regions of southern Morocco and Algeria, the Confins Algéro-Marocains (CAM). In February–March 1934 a lightning French campaign flushed out the last pockets of resistance in the Anti-Atlas and then swept through the valley of the Draa. Qerdus, which had been Merebbi Rebbu's headquarters, was occupied on March 14, though the last Blue Sultan avoided arrest by slipping away to Tarfaya, where he submitted to the much less feared Spanish on March 15.[35] Two weeks later a motorized column of French, Algerian, Senegalese and Foreign Legion troops who had taken part in the Draa campaign left the oasis of Akka in the Djebel Bani and, under Colonel Trinquet, the commander of the CAM, drove onto the Hammada, the plateau leading south of the Draa toward Tindouf, which was reached on March 31. This time, unlike in 1925, French forces were to remain in the city. With its easy access to the Hammada, it was the ideal advance post from which to police several of the Reguibat fractions, and by the summer of 1934 much of the Compagnie Saharienne of Touat had been transferred there.[36] On April 7, 1934, troops from Tindouf joined up with forces from Mauritania at Hassi Bel Guerdane, halfway between Ain Ben Tili and Bir Moghrein, just as El-Aissawi et-Tibari was crossing the western Saharan border at the end of his last marathon *ghazzi*.[37] A coordinated pacification of the Saharan border regions was now possible and so on May 1 the French government widened the CAM to include the extreme north of Mauritania, above the 25th parallel, and added an officer from Mauritania to its unified command structure.[38]

It is ironical, perhaps, that it was after the fall of the Spanish monarchy in 1931 that Spain finally extended its colonial presence in Western Sahara. The new Republican regime was not anticolonial and, while it introduced democratic reforms in Spain, it took no steps to liberalize Spain's repressive rule in northern Morocco. By 1933, moreover, the Madrid government was coming under strong pressure from Paris to take effective control of both Ifni and the hinterland of its Saharan colony. Briefly, in 1931–32, it toyed with the idea of handing Western Sahara to the League of Nations. This may have been one of the options debated and rejected when the French prime minister, Edouard Herriot, consulted Spanish ministers, during a visit to Madrid in October 1932, about the strategy for the final pacification of southern Morocco and the Saharan border regions.[39] At any rate, the Spanish authorities began applying a more activist policy from 1933. In August 1933, for example, a unit of troops was landed on the Ifni coast by the *Almirante Lobo*, though they reembarked and sailed away when local Ait Ba Amaran gathered threateningly to resist them.[40] However, after the completion of the French conquest of the Anti-Atlas and the Draa, the French occupation of Tindouf and the junction of Hassi Bel Guerdane, the Spanish government finally decided, at French insistence, to complete the pacification by occupying Ifni and the interior of Western Sahara. The Spanish forces met no resistance, for both the Ait Ba Amaran Berbers of Ifni and the Saharawis had by then resigned themselves to the European presence and, given a choice, they preferred, like Merebbi Rebbu, to submit to the relatively peaceable Spaniards than to the French whom they had been bitterly fighting for so many years.

The French army had subdued most of the territory surrounding Ifni by the end of 1933, but a final truce between the Ait Ba Amaran and the French forces was not arranged until March 4, 1934.[41] On March 27, General Osvaldo Capaz, who had previously been delegate for native affairs in Tetuan, arrived at the Spanish post at Tarfaya to plan a new landing in Ifni. After sailing up the coast in the gunboat *Canalejas*, he disembarked with a small force on April 6 and established a beachhead without a shot being fired. Three days later he was named governor of Ifni and by the end of the month he had established a network of military posts across the enclave. Ifni had at last been occupied, a full seventy-four years after the Moroccan government had agreed in principle to cede to Spain some territory on its southwestern coast, near the old site of Santa Cruz de Mar Pequeña. News of the expedition to Ifni revived memories in Spain of the bitter struggle in the Rif and aroused fears of a new colonial war. There were immediate protests. On April 20 a communist deputy in the Cortes denounced the invasion of Ifni and appealed to Spanish soldiers to refuse orders to go there, and a few days later the Spanish Communist Party proposed to the socialists that a joint demonstration be held "against the war in Ifni and the assault by Spanish imperialism on the popular masses of Catalonia."[42] However, when it transpired that there had been no resistance from the Ait Ba Amaran, the criticism died away.

The occupation of the interior of western Sahara began immediately after the successful completion of the Ifni expedition and proceeded without a whisper of protest from the Spanish left. On May 1, 1934, a camel corps unit of the Tropas de Policía del Sahara rode out of Tarfaya under the command of Captain Galo Bullón and Lieutenant Carlos de la Gándara, to occupy Daora. They reached Smara on May 15 and for the first time installed a permanent Spanish garrison in Ma el-Ainin's old capital.[43] Toward the end of the year, December 17–21, Spanish officials joined Colonel Trinquet, the commander of the CAM, and other French officers from the CAM and French West Africa at a conference in Bir Moghrein on the policing of the Saharan border regions. At the end of the talks the French representatives adopted a convention defining the respective administrative responsibilities of the CAM and the Mauritanian authorities. Outside the Spanish zone the Reguibat esh-Sharg would be subject to the CAM, while the Reguibat es-Sahel would be attached to Mauritania, but the nomads would be allowed to continue migrating across the colonial frontiers. The Spanish officials, for their part, confirmed that they would keep a garrison permanently at Smara and send regular patrols through the Saguia el-Hamra and the Zemmour to keep watch on the Reguibat in their territory, while farther south posts would be established at Zug and Tichla and mobile patrols would operate in Tiris and Adrar Soutouf to monitor the Oulad Delim.[44] During the summer months of 1934, a few Reguibat fractions had already made contact with the French authorities in Tindouf or Goulimine, but most of the anti-French leaders, including Mohammed Laghdaf and Mohammed el-Mamoun, preferred to establish relations with the less menacing Spanish.

NOTES

1. For accounts of Coppolani's conquest of Trarza and Brakna, see, for example, Alfred G. Gerteiny, *Mauritania* (Pall Mall, London, 1967), pp. 103–6, or Geneviève Désiré-Vuillemin, "Aperçu historique de la Mauritanie du XIXe siecle à l'indépendance," in *Introduction à la Mauritanie* (Centre National de la Recherche Scientifique, Paris, 1979), pp. 84–86.

2. According to Julio Caro Baroja, *Estudios Saharianos* (Instituto de Estudios Africanos, Madrid, 1955), p. 292. Paul Marty, in "Les Fadelia," *Revue du Monde Musulman*, Vol. XXXI, 1915–16, pp. 137ff., claims that he was born near Oualata in the Hodh in 1838.

3. Mohammed Fadel, who was born around 1780, is said to have been a disciple of Sidi el-Mokhtar el-Kounti (1729–1811), chief of the Kounta of Timbuctoo and a leading marabout of the Qadiriya. After Sidi el-Mokhtar's death, he apparently introduced sensationalist modifications into the Qadiriya rites, to create artificial states of emotional excitement. He attracted numerous followers in the prosperous Niger Valley and amassed a considerable fortune. His *telamid*, among them many of his forty-eight sons, spread the Fadeliya's influence far and wide in the Sahara in the second half of the nineteenth century. See Caro Baroja, *op. cit.*, pp. 289–91.

4. *Ibid.*, pp. 299–300; F. de La Chapelle, "Esquisse d'une histoire du Sahara occidental," Vol. XI, 1930, p. 91.

5. Caro Baroja, *op. cit.*, p. 294, gives the date of his *hadj* as 1858, La Chapelle, *loc. cit.*, p. 91, as 1857.

6. Cited by La Chapelle, *loc. cit.*, p. 92.

7. *Ibid.*, p. 92.

8. Caro Baroja, *op. cit.*, p. 294.

9. *Ibid.*, p. 303.

10. *Ibid.*, pp. 304–5.

11. *Ibid.*, p. 306. La Chapelle, *loc. cit.*, p. 92, gives the date of the city's founding as 1888.

12. Cited in Caro Baroja, *op. cit.*, p. 300.

13. Gerteiny, *op. cit.*, p. 107.

14. Odette du Puigaudeau, *Le passé maghrébin de la Mauritanie* (Ministère d'Etat chargé des Affaires Islamiques, Rabat, 1962), pp. 44–45; Caro Baroja, *op. cit.*, p. 319.

15. Gerteiny, *op. cit.*, p. 111; Frank E. Trout, *Morocco's Saharan Frontiers* (Droz, Geneva, 1969), p. 159. Kaiser Wilhelm II, it should be noted, arrived in person in Tangier in March 1905 to demonstrate Germany's opposition to French hegemony in Morocco.

16. Puigaudeau, *op. cit.*, p. 97.

17. *Ibid.*, p. 95.

18. Trout, *op. cit.*, p. 159; Gerteiny, *op. cit.*, p. 109; Désiré-Vuillemin, *loc. cit.*, p. 88.

19. *Affaires du Maroc*, French diplomatic documents, Vol. III, 1906–1907, p. 5.

20. Puigaudeau, *op. cit.*, pp. 100–101; Caro Baroja, *op. cit.*, p. 319.

21. Robert Rézette, *The Western Sahara and the Frontiers of Morocco* (Nouvelles Editions Latines, Paris, 1975), pp. 82–83; Trout, *op. cit.*, p. 158.

22. Désiré-Vuillemin, *loc. cit.*, p. 89; Gerteiny, *op. cit.*, pp. 111–12. Ould Aida was eventually captured by the French in January 1912 after the French seizure of Tichit in eastern Mauritania.

23. Cited in *Le Sahara occidental devant la Cour Internationale de Justice. Mémoire présenté par le Royaume du Maroc* (Moroccan Government, Rabat, 1975), p. 59.

24. See Désiré-Vuillemin, *loc. cit.*, p. 89; La Chapelle, *loc. cit.*, p. 92; Caro Baroja, *op. cit.*, p. 334.

25. *Ibid.*, pp. 321–22; Trout, *op. cit.*, p. 313.

26. According to Caro Baroja, *op. cit.*, Ma el-Ainin had twenty-seven sons, as well as numerous daughters. Attilio Gaudio in *Le Dossier du Sahara occidental* (Nouvelles Editions Latines, Paris, 1978), p. 81, claims that he had thirty-three sons and thirty-nine daughters, while John Mercer in *Spanish Sahara* (George Allen and Unwin, London, 1976), p. 111, says he had sixty-eight children by twenty-six women.

27. Caro Baroja, *op. cit.*, pp. 326–27; Tomás García Figueras, *Santa Cruz de Mar Pequeña, Ifni, Sahara. La acción de España en la Costa occidental de Africa* (Ediciones Fe, Madrid, 1941), pp. 209–10.

28. *Ibid.*, p. 210.

29. For accounts of the UC20 mission, see *ibid.*, pp. 223–24, and Caro Baroja, *op. cit.*, pp. 329–30.

30. *Ibid.*, pp. 330–31; Trout, *op. cit.*, p. 211.

31. *Ibid.*, p. 232; Caro Baroja, *op. cit.*, pp. 331, 379–80; Désiré-Vuillemin, *loc. cit.*, p. 95; A. Traore, "Islam en Mauritanie," in *Introduction à la Mauritanie*, p. 164.

32. Caro Baroja, *op. cit.*, pp. 383–84.

33. Puigaudeau, *op. cit.*, p. 105; Gerteiny, *op. cit.*, p. 114.

34. Ahmed-Baba Miské, *Front Polisario, l'âme d'un peuple* (Editions Rupture, Paris, 1978), pp. 106–7.

35. García Figueras, *op. cit.*, pp. 291–2.

36. Trout, *op. cit.*, pp. 318–19.

37. *Ibid.*, p. 350; Gaudio, *op. cit.*, p. 138.

38. Trout, *op. cit.*, pp. 327–28.

39. Francisco Hernández-Pacheco and José María Cordero Torres, *El Sahara español* (Instituto de Estudios Políticos, Madrid, 1962), p. 125; García Figueras, *op. cit.*, p. 273.

40. *Ibid.*, pp. 278–79.

41. Rachid Lazrak, *Le contentieux territorial entre le Maroc et l'Espagne* (Dar el Kitab, Casablanca, 1974), p. 93.

42. Miguel Martín, *El colonialismo español en Marruecos* (Ruedo Ibérico, Paris, 1973), p. 128.

43. Hernández-Pacheco and Cordero Torres, *op. cit.*, p. 125; García Figueras, *op. cit.*, p. 305.

44. Gaudio, *op. cit.*, pp. 115, 140.

6

A Forgotten Colony

AFTER THE BELATED OCCUPATION of Ifni and strategic points in the interior of Western Sahara in the spring and early summer of 1934, both territories were integrated for reasons of convenience into the administrative structure of Spanish Morocco. Under a decree enacted by the Spanish Republican government on August 29, 1934, the high commissioner of the Spanish protectorate zone of Morocco, who was based in Tetuan, acquired the additional title of governor-general of the territories of Ifni, Spanish Sahara and Río de Oro. The chain of command passed from Tetuan to Sidi Ifni and Tarfaya, where two *delegados gubernativos* were responsible to the governor-general for the administration of Ifni and the Saharan territories respectively, and from Tarfaya to Villa Cisneros and La Guera, where local administration was supervised by two *comandantes*. In Tarfaya, the Saharan *delegado gubernativo* doubled as the high commissioner's delegate in Spanish Southern Morocco; and, likewise, the Tetuan caliphate, the Spanish Moroccan branch of the sultan's now powerless *makhzen*, had a delegate in Tarfaya, a post held for about two decades by Mohammed Laghdaf. The minuscule expenditure allocations for Ifni and the Sahara were simply annexed to the budget for the Spanish protectorate zone.[1]

The victory of the Popular Front in the Spanish general elections in February 1936 had no repercussions in the Sahara. Constituted by the socialists, the communists, Republican liberals and Catalan nationalists, the Popular Front said nothing in its program about Spain's colonies, and the following March, the new government appointed a tough, repressive high commissioner in Morocco, Juan Moles, who had no sympathy whatever for Moroccan nationalism. When the Spanish army in Morocco rose against the Republic under General Francisco Franco's leadership on July 17, 1936, the Republic's colonial policy was not among its complaints.[2] In Tarfaya, the *delegado gubernativo*, Antonio Del Oro, immediately sided with the Francoists when he received telegraphed instructions from Tetuan on July 17, unlike the *delegado gubernativo* at Ifni who refused to follow the orders from Tetuan and, after a confrontation with pro-fascist officers in his garrison, fled across the border into French Morocco.[3]

The long bloody civil war in Spain in 1936–39 left almost no mark on Western Sahara. The Saharawis were not recruited into the Francoist forces in significant numbers, like the Muslims of Spain's protectorate zone in northern Morocco, 14 percent of whom had been enlisted by 1937.[4] About the only ripple to reach the Sahara from the Spanish war was the incarceration of Republican political prisoners from the Canary Islands in the prison camp at Villa Cisneros, from which a group of detainees made a heroic breakout in March 1937, escaping down the coast to Senegal in a fishing boat.[5]

In the early years of the Second World War, as the Axis armies swept across Europe, the ideologues of the Spanish *Nuevo Estado* began to dream of imperial expansion in northwest Africa, at the expense of France. In 1942, for example, the Spanish government published a book, *Aspectos de la misión universal de España*, written by an eminent member of the Sociedad de Estudios Internacionales y Coloniales, José María Cordero Torres, which asserted that "Spain's vital space" included not only its existing small African possessions but also French-ruled Morocco, much of Mauritania and the Oran region of western Algeria and parts of the French-ruled territory adjacent to Río Muni. Regarding Western Sahara, Cordero Torres urged "a more complete and permanent occupation by means of the installation of a string of posts linked by roads along the coast and frontiers, and the expansion of the occupation forces on the basis of mixed units and special services," and he proposed that the 1886 treaty with the emir of Adrar justified the extension of Spain's desert colony into Mauritania, as far as Tichit, over three hundred miles from its existing frontiers.[6] However, Spain's sole attempt at colonial expansion during the war was its occupation of Tangier in March 1941, and even that was short-lived. Tangier was evacuated when the allies landed in Morocco in 1942, and as the Axis powers were thrown onto the defensive, the Falangist dream of imperial glory in Africa receded.

In fact, the destruction wreaked during the civil war had left Spain in poor shape for colonial expansion. The level of Gross National Product achieved in 1935 was not regained until as late as 1954.[7] Until the late 1940s, moreover, nothing was known about the mineral wealth of Western Sahara. It remained a prestige colony, of no economic or strategic value of any kind to Spain, which correspondingly invested almost nothing in it. Most Spaniards scarcely knew that the colony existed. Almost none settled in it, and under an ordinance published on February 8, 1947, Spaniards and other non-Saharawis had to file numerous forms to obtain a special permit to visit, live or work there.[8]

The *de facto* administrative unification of Western Sahara and Ifni with the Spanish protectorate zone in Morocco "brought a danger, however faint, from the more or less imminent awakening of nationalism in Morocco," observed a Spanish writer on colonial affairs, Angel Doménech-Lafuente, in 1945.[9] Indeed, Moroccan nationalism became a potent political force after the founding of the Istiqlal (Independence) Party in 1944. So the Madrid government thought it wise, two years later, to separate formally the administration of the colonies of Ifni and Spanish Sahara from that of its protectorate in Morocco. Thus, on July 20, 1946, a decree established Africa Occidental Española (AOE—Spanish West Africa), a new entity comprising Ifni, Saguia el-Hamra and Río de Oro. AOE was headed by a governor-general, who was resident in Sidi Ifni and directly responsible to the presidency in Madrid through its colonial office, the Dirección General de Marruecos y Colonias. He had overall responsibility for the military forces in AOE as well as the civil administration, in which he was assisted by a secretary-general. A ministerial ordinance of February 8, 1947, defined the Saharan part of AOE as comprising the "zone" of Saguia el-Hamra and the "colony" of Río de Oro. However, it did not include Spanish Southern Morocco, the strip of desert between the Draa and parallel 27°40'. The governor-general of AOE was responsible for its administration, but since it was considered part of Spain's protectorate zone in Morocco, he acted there as delegate of the high commissioner in Tetuan rather than as governor-general of AOE.[10]

By this time the Spanish still administered only a handful of settlements, none of which was larger than a medium-sized village. In 1940 a settlement had been founded twelve miles from the Atlantic in the valley of the Saguia el-Hamra at a place where Lieutenant Colonel Del Oro had found good fresh water sources (*ayoun*) two years earlier. After the creation of AOE, El-Ayoun became the administrative capital, under a resident subgovernor, of both Saguia el-Hamra and Río de Oro. In Villa Cisneros there was a subordinate *delegado gubernativo* with responsibility for Río de Oro. Otherwise, there were small settlements only in Smara and La Guera and military outposts at Bir Gandous, Guelta Zemmour, Tichla and Zug by 1946. Farther north in Spanish Southern Morocco, the main administrative center by 1946 was Tan-Tan, thirteen miles south of the Draa, though supplies arrived by sea or plane at Tarfaya, which was named Villa Bens after Francisco Bens's death that year. There were small garrisons at five other points in Spanish Southern Morocco at this time.[11]

Until the early 1960s the pace of change remained exceedingly slow. By 1952, for example, there were still only 216 civilian employees, 155 of them Saharawis, while the telephone service had just twenty-four subscribers in the whole territory.[12] As late as 1959 there were only six primary-school "sections," with just seven teachers, six Spanish and one Saharawi, and a total enrollment of 366 pupils, of whom 139 were Saharawi children, 105 Spanish children and 122 adults.[13] Another graphic indicator was that the territory's total budget in 1952 was a mere 19.7 million pesetas, of which more than half (10.2 million pesetas) was spent on the police force. It had grown only to 53.5 million pesetas by 1960.[14] Since water is such a basic resource for economic development, it is also revealing of the territory's extreme backwardness at this time that until 1960 there were only 130 wells in the whole country, an area larger than Britain, with a total water supply capacity of about forty thousand cubic feet, less than the amount of water consumed daily by many rural villages in Spain.[15]

The only real industry was fishing. A state-owned fishing company, IPASA, was set up in 1948 by the Spanish government's Instituto Nacional de Industria (INI), and it made some modest investment in a refrigeration and processing plant. During the 1950s between two thousand and six thousand tons of fish were landed annually, mainly at Villa Cisneros and La Guera.[16] The only other resource exploited by the Spanish was seaweed, which was collected from 1953 for use as fodder and fertilizer. The coast was divided into four zones which were assigned as concessions to Spanish companies, who paid the Saharawi seaweed collectors by weight. The territory's exports consisted almost entirely of fish, plus some seaweed and a few live animals. In 1958 they totaled some 523 tons and had a value of only 958,015 pesetas. Imports were more than twenty times as high, totalling 21.4 million pesetas.[17]

In many respects the Saharawis' way of life continued as it had for hundreds of years. Very few Saharawis came to live in the small Spanish settlements before the sixties. The vast majority remained nomads and, as such, they were more or less left to their own devices by the Spanish, who, despite establishing garrisons in the interior in 1934, could not hope to bring the dispersed nomadic communities under their direct administrative control and made no attempt to tax them. The Saharawi fractions continued to administer their own affairs through their traditional *djemaas* and to apply their own codes of justice, the customary *orf* law and the koranic *sharia*.

In order to maintain their pragmatic *modus vivendi* with the nomads, the Spanish officials naturally sought to maintain cooperative relations, above all, with the leading families and sheikhs of the principal "warrior" and sharifian tribes. Consequently, they had no interest in fostering modernizing or egalitarian reforms in Saharawi society, and they generally turned a blind eye to such practices as the *horma* and slavery, though both were formally banned. Spanish officials sometimes stopped the sale of slaves in their own settlements or offered sanctuary to slaves who fled their masters, but they made no attempt to stamp out slavery in general.[18] As late as 1975 a UN mission reported that it "encountered several persons who said they were slaves" and "also obtained copies of documents relating to the purchase, sale and freeing of slaves." Slaves were still being bought and sold, often to serve as domestic servants, and it was quite common for a master to rent out the services of a slave under a commercial agreement.[19]

Nonetheless, the Spanish presence did bring many subtle changes to Saharawi society. First, it halted the previously endemic intertribal raiding. This, in turn, allowed the nomads to migrate in smaller groups than in the past to take better advantage of the scattered pastures.[20] Their herds were therefore dispersed more widely and total livestock holdings probably grew. At the same time, the Spanish settlements, despite their small size, became centers of exchange, where the nomads could sell their animals, skins and wool and buy cloth, sugar, tea and flour. Previously almost all exchange had been in barter form; now money began to circulate significantly among the nomads for the first time.[21] Moreover, though still a very limited phenomenon before the sixties, there was some settlement by Saharawis on the edges of the Spanish towns and outposts. Some would find jobs on construction sites or in the police camel corps. Meanwhile, though not suppressed outright by the Spanish authorities, such practices as slavery and the *horma* were gradually eroded. The existence of the Spanish settlements and some job opportunities there allowed a few runaway slaves to seek Spanish protection or find work; and the ending of the *ghazzian* allowed the *znaga* to escape the humiliation of the *horma,* which had always rested on fear and insecurity. Once freed from the obligatory payment of "protection" tribute to the Oulad Delim, the Oulad Tidrarin prospered. By the 1950s they seem to have owned more livestock than their erstwhile oppressors, the Oulad Delim, many of whom, however, managed to maintain their rank as "people of the gun" by joining the paramilitary police.[22]

However, to the Saharawis, the *pax hispanica* had, in an important sense, made them all tributaries. Though they were not obliged to pay taxes, they no longer enjoyed the total freedom of the past. "All are *znaga* now," some Saharawis told the Spanish anthropologist, Julio Caro Baroja, when he was conducting the research for his monumental study of Saharawi society, *Estudios Saharianos,* in the early fifties. "That is to say, we all now have to adjust ourselves to laws which are not ours, put up with the control of arms, property and so on, imposed by more powerful people. The only 'man of the gun' now is the soldier of the government."[23] But, Caro Baroja also noted, the *ghazzian* had ended too recently to erode the warrior consciousness molded over generations.[24] At the end of the fifties the Saharawis were to return to their military traditions and fight once again to restore their lost freedom.

NOTES

1. Tomás García Figueras, *Santa Cruz de Mar Pequeña, Ifni, Sahara. La acción de España en la costa occidental de Africa* (Ediciones Fe, Madrid, 1941), p. 310.

2. Miguel Martín, *El colonialismo español* (Ruedo Ibérico, Paris, 1973), p. 142.

3. *Ibid.*, p. 173; García Figueras, *op. cit.*, pp. 315–16.

4. Martin, *op. cit.*, p. 175.

5. García Figueras, *op. cit.*, p. 316.

6. José María Cordero Torres, *Aspectos de la misión universal de España* (Ediciones de la Vicesecretaría de Educación Popular, 1942), pp. 33–46, cited by Juan Maestre Alfonso, *El Sahara en la crisis de Marruecos y España* (Akal, Madrid, 1975), pp. 124–35. Similar proposals were made by José María de Areilza (the Count of Motrico) and Fernando María Castiella in *Reivindicaciones de España* (Madrid, 1941). See Martín, *op. cit.*, pp. 207–8.

7. Ramón Criado, *Sahara, pasión y muerte de un sueño colonial* (Ruedo Ibérico, Paris, 1977), p. 92.

8. Francisco Hernández-Pacheco and José María Cordero Torres, *El Sahara español* (Instituto de Estudios Políticos, Madrid, 1962), p. 148.

9. Angel Doménech-Lafuente, *Africa*, June-July 1945, p. 20.

10. Hernández-Pacheco and Cordero Torres, *op. cit.*, p. 127.

11. Angel Flores Morales, *El Sahara español, ensayo de geografía física, humana y económica* (Ediciones de la Alta Comisaría de España en Marruecos, 1946), pp. 104–5.

12. *Resumen estadístico de Africa española* (Dirección General de Marruecos y Colonias e Instituto de Estudios Africanos, Madrid, 1954), pp. 345, 353.

13. John Mercer, *Spanish Sahara* (George Allen and Unwin, London, 1976), p. 203.

14. *Resumen estadístico de Africa Española* (1954), p. 346; Manuel Melis Clavería, "La provincia de Sahara ante el plan de desarollo económico y social," *Africa*, No. 295, July 1966, p. 4.

15. Maestre Alfonso, *op. cit.*, pp. 60–61.

16. Mercer, *op. cit.*, p. 181.

17. Hernández-Pacheco and Cordero Torres, *op. cit.*, p. 162.

18. Julio Caro Baroja, *Estudios Saharianos* (Instituto de Estudios Africanos, Madrid, 1955), pp. 97, 188.

19. Report of the United Nations Visiting Mission to Spanish Sahara, 1975, in *General Assembly Official Records*, 30th Session, Supplement No. 23, UN Document A/10023/Rev. 1, pp. 56–57.

20. Caro Baroja, *op. cit.*, p. 4.

21. *Ibid.*, p. 97.

22. *Ibid.*, p. 100. Despite their slightly fewer numbers, the Oulad Tidrarin were estimated by the colonial authorities in 1950 to have 5,173 camels, compared with 3,200 for the Oulad Delim.

23. *Ibid.*, p. 33.

24. *Ibid.*, p. 5.

7

The Army
of Liberation

I T WAS MOROCCO'S REGAINING OF INDEPENDENCE IN March–April 1956 and the insurrectionary appeals of commanders of the Jaich at-Tahrir (Army of Liberation) in southern Morocco which inspired the Saharawis to rise in revolt for the first time since the pacification of 1934. The Army of Liberation was a rural partisan movement that had begun recruiting support in the mountains of the Rif and the Middle Atlas in the summer of 1955, two years after Sultan Mohammed V had been arbitrarily deposed by the French and exiled to Madagascar in reprisal for his collaboration with the Istiqlal Party. In October 1955 it had launched an insurrection in the Rif and parts of the Middle Atlas, tying down large numbers of French troops. The Algerian Front de Libération Nationale (FLN) had also begun its armed rebellion, in 1954, and to avoid having to fight on two fronts, the French government had decided to seek a compromise with Mohammed V, who was flown back from Madagascar on October 31 and, after talks in France, allowed to return home in triumph on November 16. But instead of laying down its arms after this initial victory, the Army of Liberation had stepped up its pressure on France, while negotiations continued between the French government and the sultan. *Caids* lacking in patriotism had been killed and, in Oujda, several French soldiers captured. In the last weeks of the protectorate the guerrilla movement had grown rapidly in strength and influence, notably after recruiting thousands of former Moroccan auxiliaries of the French armed forces, the *goumiers* and *moghzanis,* when they were relieved of their French command in February 1956. France finally ended its protectorate and recognized Moroccan independence on March 3, but by then the Army of Liberation effectively controlled much of the Rif, the Atlas ranges and the extreme south of Morocco.

The ending of the French protectorate left the Spanish government, which had taken a softer line on Moroccan nationalism in the early fifties than the French authorities, with little alternative but to follow suit. The sultan held talks with

Franco in Madrid and then, on April 7, 1956, the Spanish government recognized
Morocco's full sovereignty and pledged to "respect the territorial unity of the empire, which the international treaties guarantee."[1] However, Franco was determined to hang on to Spain's remaining African possessions, including AOE
(Spanish West Africa). Responsibility for their administration was transferred to a
new Dirección General de Plazas y Provincias Africanas when the Dirección
General de Marruecos y Colonias was dissolved on August 21.[2] From a political or
ideological standpoint, Franco was not prepared at this time to countenance the
idea of Spain abandoning its "colonial mission" in Africa, and he also needed a
new stamping ground for the Foreign Legion after its withdrawal from northern
Morocco. The Spanish forces there had numbered no less than 175,000 men,
65,000 of them Spanish, and the officer corps had regarded the ending of the protectorate with disfavor. Many of the units were gradually to be relocated to Ifni,
the Sahara or the Canaries. Furthermore, though Ifni was of no economic value to
Spain, Franco had been aware of Western Sahara's potential mineral wealth for
several years. In 1950, during a visit to El-Ayoun, he had met the geologist
Manuel Alía Medina, who had discovered phosphates in the territory in the late
forties; and in 1952 the Dirección General de Marruecos y Colonias had set up a
mineral division, the Servicio Minero, which in turn had entrusted further
research work on the phosphates to Adaro de Investigaciones Mineras, a sub-
sidiary of the parastatal INI (National Institute of Industry).[3] Finally the fishing
resources off the Saharan coast were of enormous value to the Canary Islands. The
Franco regime claimed that it had solid legal rights to remain in both Ifni and
Western Sahara. Ifni, it said, had been ceded "in perpetuity" under the Spanish-
Moroccan treaty of 1860 and Spain had full sovereignty over Saguia el-Hamra and
Río de Oro under the Franco-Spanish conventions of 1904 and 1912. Only in
Spanish Southern Morocco, which had been part of Spain's protectorate zone in
Morocco under the 1912 convention, did Franco eventually acknowledge Moroc-
can rights and withdraw in April 1958.

However, news of the successful independence struggle in Morocco quickly
reached the desert. Nomads from the western Sahara and nearby regions often
visited Goulimine and other market towns of the Noun and the Bani and there
they heard of the guerrilla movement that had taken control of large tracts of the
Moroccan countryside. A guerrilla nucleus had first been formed in southern
Morocco as early as 1954, in Tiznit, by Ibrahim Namri (Ibrahim Tizniti), but it
was in 1956 that it really became a mass movement. In January 1956, at a conference of Army of Liberation leaders in Madrid, three operational zones were
created, in the Rif, the Middle and High Atlas ranges, and the south, where
overall command was entrusted to Benhamou Mesfioui, a guerrilla leader from
the Rif. As the former *moghzanis* and *goumiers* joined his forces, often after
raiding their local armories, the Army of Liberation took control of much of the
southern Souss, the Anti-Atlas and the regions to its south in the spring of 1956,
establishing its main headquarters in Tiznit, Bou-Izakarn and Goulimine. The remaining isolated French officials in these regions were in grave danger, and two
were kidnapped, never to reappear, in June and October 1956.[4]

Mohammed V's government in Rabat had very little control over events in these regions until almost two years after the ending of the protectorate. Yet, the king refused to allow the French army, which still had thousands of troops in Morocco, to undertake police action in the south, for fear of arousing nationalist anger; and, in a sense, he was not displeased to see the Army of Liberation's focus of activity shift during 1956 to the extreme south of his kingdom, far from Morocco's main population centers. Nonetheless, the leaders of the guerrilla movement were regarded with disquiet by both the top guard of the Istiqlal Party, which had great difficulty in bringing them under party control, and the Palace, which viewed the "irregulars" as a potential danger to the monarchy and wanted to integrate them into the new regular army, the Forces Armées Royales (FAR), which was constituted by former Moroccan troops of the French and Spanish armies, plus some two thousand French officers and noncommissioned officers, when it was founded in May 1956 with Crown Prince Hassan as chief-of-staff. Partisan leaders who brought more than one hundred guerrillas to lay down their arms were promised officer's rank in the regular army and by the end of 1956 about ten thousand former Army of Liberation men had joined the FAR, swelling its total strength to about thirty thousand troops.[5] But thousands of other irregulars, especially in the south, refused to lay down their arms and join the FAR. Furthermore, many of the partisan leaders became disillusioned by Mohammed V's compromises with the French after independence. "Some people are beginning to ask themselves whether our revolution did not run aground after the declaration of independence," noted the supreme body of the Army of Liberation and the urban resistance movement, the Conseil National de la Résistance, in August 1956. "The victories which we have obtained so far are only victories to the extent that they have had the effect of liberating Moroccan sovereignty in the diplomatic and juridical spheres. As to the internal situation, the expected transformations have not been achieved and no change worthy of note has appeared."[6] In particular, there was dismay at Mohammed V's willingness to allow several thousand French troops to remain in Morocco at a time when France was at war with the FLN in neighboring Algeria. Indeed, many of the guerrilla leaders had regarded the struggle for Morocco's independence as merely part of a broader pan-Maghrebian or pan-Arab liberation struggle. In July 1955 a coordinating committee of liberation armies of the Maghreb had been set up, and after Morocco's independence some Moroccan Army of Liberation groups began helping to smuggle arms to the FLN.

Likewise, Benhamou Mesfioui's men in the south of Morocco encouraged the Ait Ba Amaran of Ifni and the Saharawis to fight for their freedom and offered them assistance to do so. A small group of about twenty-five Saharawis, among them a young Reguibi by the name of Abba el-Sheikh, joined the Army of Liberation in southern Morocco in 1956 and were then sent south to the desert to inspire the nomads to revolt.[7] If France and Spain had been forced to grant Morocco independence, they suggested, they could surely be driven from the Sahara, which they had only subjugated two decades earlier. Many Saharawis were convinced that they would be able to regain their ancient freedoms by returning to their warrior traditions, and so many of the *djemaas*, particularly of the Tekna tribes and the Reguibat, resolved to follow the lead of the Army of Liberation. They began to form guerrilla units that were almost exclusively Saharawi in composition and, despite their use of some modern weapons provided by the Army of Liberation, modeled their tactics on the raiding techniques of old.

At first their main targets were French posts on the Hammada near Tindouf. From bases in the Draa valley, a guerrilla group attacked the French frontier post of Oum el-Achar, ninety miles due north of Tindouf, in June 1956, and shortly afterward the French evacuated an oil-exploration team from Hassi Sidi el-Mounir, some seventy-five miles farther to the northeast. In July a French convoy en route from Bechar to Tindouf was ambushed on the Hammada near Tinfouchy, about 180 miles northeast of Tindouf. Clashes continued in this region during 1957, with the Army of Liberation staging frequent attacks on the French posts at Oum el-Achar and Hassi Sidi el-Mounir.[8] However, the scope of the guerrilla war broadened when, on February 15, 1957, about two hundred guerrillas attacked a French patrol in northern Mauritania, at Agmar, a water source fifty miles northeast of the French post at Fort Trinquet (Bir Moghrein). Three French officers and twenty soldiers were killed, and the attackers then slipped across the border into Spanish Sahara.[9] The French authorities were horrified. A guerrilla war in northern Mauritania threatened to jeopardize plans made by the multinational consortium Mines de Fer de Mauritanie (MIFERMA), which had been founded in 1952 by French, British, Italian and West German steel companies and the French government's Bureau Minier de la France d'Outre-Mer, to set up a mining industry near Fort Gouraud (Zouerate), where iron ore had been discovered in 1935, and build such associated infrastructure as a railway line more than four hundred miles long to the coast and new port facilities at Port Etienne (Nouadhibou). French interests held about 55 percent of MIFERMA's equity and, to help finance the Zouerate project, the French government was seeking a major loan from the World Bank which was unlikely to be forthcoming in the event of a serious guerrilla war.[10] Politically, moreover, it did not relish the prospect of having to cope with an insurgency in the Sahara while it was trying to fight the FLN in Algeria. Guerrilla attacks in northen Mauritania also endangered French plans to introduce internal self-government in Mauritania in accordance with the *loi-cadre* on French Africa which had been enacted in June 1956 in the hope of sealing off France's black African colonies from the revolutionary winds blowing to the north of the Sahara and under which Mauritania's first university graduate, Mokhtar Ould Daddah, a member of a prestigious *zwaya* tribe from Trarza, the Oulad Birri, was to take office in May 1957 as vice-president of a new Conseil de Gouvernement presided over by the governor.[11]

So, within a few days of the Agmar attack, a military strategy conference was held in Tindouf. General Ely, the chief-of-staff of the French armed forces, was there, along with General Gabriel Bourgund, the commander of the French forces in French West Africa, General René Cogny, the commander of the French troops still in Morocco, and other high-ranking officers from French West Africa and Algeria. "The military conference that has just met in Tindouf," announced the French secretary of state for the armed forces on February 26, "has enabled security measures to be taken regarding the bands of the so-called Moroccan Army of Liberation, which, crossing Spanish Sahara and the Río de Oro, take refuge there after their incursions into French territory."[12] To the French, it looked as if the clock had been turned back to the days of the old *ghazzian* before 1934, when the anti-French raiders had also used Spanish territory as a sanctuary. Accordingly, Gaston Defferre, the minister for overseas territories in Guy Mollet's cabinet, gave the high commissioner of French West Africa, Gaston Cusin, the green light on February 20 to stage hot pursuit raids into Spanish territory. "The recent events in Mauritania have shown on the one hand that the rebels have taken advantage of facilities in Spanish territory to circulate, group themselves and establish supply and operational bases, and on the other hand that we have been unable to achieve the wiping out of these bands by virtue of being unable to pursue our action across the border. So I am deciding to authorize you, in the event of new aggression by the rebels, to pursue them and destroy them with all your means, without taking this frontier into account."[13] A tacit nod of approval for such hot pursuit actions had already been given by the commander of the Spanish forces in Western Sahara, General Rojo; and this was confirmed by the Spanish authorities at a meeting with French officials in Port Etienne on February 25. Two days later, Cusin announced in Dakar that "the Spanish authorities in Río de Oro have granted us their full cooperation in the recent events in Mauritania but they have only been able to do so to the extent of their military means which are very limited."[14]

The Moroccan government, for its part, disclaimed all responsibility for the Army of Liberation's attacks. Ahmed Balafrej, the foreign minister, remarked in Dakar, the capital of French West Africa, on March 8, after a meeting with Cusin, that the "incidents" had been the work of "elements that we have described as uncontrolled and difficult to control."[15]

In June, Madrid appointed a new governor-general to administer AOE. General Mariano Gómez Zamalloa arrived in Ifni to take up his new duties just as violence erupted in the previously peaceable enclave. On June 16, two Moroccan soldiers in the Spanish forces there were murdered by nationalists. The colonial authorities responded by closing down the local headquarters of the Istiqlal Party, arresting several of its leading militants and deporting them to the Canaries. Strikes and a boycott of the Spanish administration then started, and several anti-Spanish demonstrators were reportedly shot dead.[16] Gómez Zamalloa had reason to be worried. The disturbances in Ifni might be the prelude to attack by the Army of Liberation, which had previously left the Spanish alone, despite traversing Spanish territory in the Sahara to attack the French in Algeria and Mauritania; and, if the guerrillas did attack, he knew that he had insufficient troops and equipment to hold the smaller posts in Ifni or Western Sahara. Under such circumstances, Gómez Zamalloa was well disposed to military cooperation with the French. On July 12, soon after his appointment, he met General Bourgund at Villa Cisneros and agreed to allow French troops to advance up to fifty miles into Spanish territory in pursuit of guerrillas and to permit French aircraft to fly reconnaissance missions up to sixty-two miles inside Spanish borders. But to General Bourgund's dismay, Gómez Zamalloa failed to get reinforcements and had to abandon almost all the Spanish posts in the interior of Western Sahara, including even Smara, in order to provide adequate defenses for the coastal settlements, Villa Cisneros, El-Ayoun and Tarfaya.[17]

Meanwhile, Bourgund began to draft a plan for a joint Franco-Spanish counterinsurgency campaign, to be baptized Ouragan (Hurricane). At his next meeting with Gómez Zamalloa, in Dakar on September 20, he won the Spanish governor-general's support for the idea. The next step was to secure the approval of the governments in Paris and Madrid. Two months later Franco was to appreciate the real extent of the danger posed by the Army of Liberation when, on November 23, several hundred guerrillas launched a full-scale invasion of Ifni, attacking seven of its frontier posts simultaneously. Some fell at once into rebel hands, and Spanish reinforcements had to be rushed from the Canaries. Spanish air-force Messerschmitts of World War II vintage flew bombing sorties from the islands and, according to Crown Prince Hassan, attacked targets in the province of Agadir as well as in Ifni, while a flotilla of four Spanish cruisers arrived in the Canaries and then made a threatening appearance in Moroccan territorial waters, a mile off the beach at Agadir, on December 7. The same week, Spanish troops regained control of the main posts overrun by the guerrillas in November.[18] But all of a sudden, the Spanish government ordered a retrenchment. "All the isolated posts held by small garrisons in the territory of Ifni," it announced on December 11, "have been evacuated to permit coordinated action by Spanish troops against the bands of aggressors which are still to be found in the enclave and against those which could arrive there as reinforcements. Over the last forty-eight hours the Spanish troops have finished setting up new positions that should enable them to exercise control over the territory." The government added that sixty-two Spanish soldiers had already been killed there.[19] The seven thousand to eight thousand Spanish troops in Ifni had pulled back to a tiny strip of territory extending no farther than twelve miles from its capital, Sidi Ifni. For almost twelve years, until Ifni was finally ceded to Morocco in 1969, the Spanish forces remained ensconced in this essentially valueless little enclave that had a population of only twenty-four thousand and remained totally dependent on supplies from the Canaries. No attempt was ever made again to reoccupy any of the territory abandoned in December 1957.

Meanwhile, the Army of Liberation had also begun attacking targets in Western Sahara. On November 29, a group of guerrillas turned up at the virtually undefended lighthouse at Cape Bojador, kidnapped the seven Spaniards they found there and sabotaged the lighthouse, putting it out of action for several days. On December 3, the army ministry in Madrid announced that guerrillas had attacked a Spanish convoy at Arbaa el-Mesti, near El-Ayoun.[20] There was another clash, just twelve miles north of El-Ayoun, on December 22, and on January 3, 1958, the Army of Liberation attacked Spanish positions at Argoub, across the Río de Oro bay from Villa Cisneros.[21]

For the Spanish government, the idea of a joint military campaign with the French armed forces had by now become an attractive one, despite the humiliating implication that Spain's own military means were hopelessly inadequate. A supplementary advantage of such a joint operation, besides, was that it offered an exceptional opportunity to break free from the international opprobrium and isolation Madrid had endured since the Second World War. However, in Paris, Cusin and Bourgund still found a certain reticence on the part of the French socialists, who were strongly represented in the Félix Gaillard government that took office in November, to swallow the idea of a joint military operation with the Francoist army. Reportedly, Cusin and Bourgund therefore decided to arrange some "cinema" to force matters in Paris. Mokhtar Ould Daddah, it seems, was encouraged to fire off an ultimatum on December 16 demanding French military action against the Army of Liberation units in Río de Oro within forty-eight hours.[22] The next day at Atar, and on December 19 at Port Etienne, Cusin and Bourgund held briefing sessions with the French officers stationed in northern Mauritania. The troops and equipment had already been gathered for a major counterinsurgency sweep into Spanish Sahara; but additionally Cusin and Bourgund were told of an unexpectedly favorable development. A guerrilla leader had just turned up at Fort Trinquet, reported a split in the Army of Liberation and asked for arms to fight against it. He was Khatri Ould Said Ould el-Joumani, a sheikh of the Lebouihat, one of the largest subtribes of the Reguibat esh-Sharg, who, along with several other Reguibat, had apparently been arrested by the Moroccan commanders of the guerrilla forces.[23] He had managed to escape dressed as a woman. He wrote to Cusin a few weeks later, on January 15, 1958, "on behalf of all the chiefs of the Reguibat of Zemmour" to request "peace and your aid against the Army of Liberation which is attacking us on our territory, causing damage to the country, property and the people." He went on: "This aid would involve, in particular, the defense of our territory, which extends from the Kharawi to the Atlantic Ocean, and from the coast to Adrar Soutouf, and to the Kediat of Idjil, to Bir Moghrein, to Tindouf and to the Oued Draa. This is the country for whose defense we are soliciting your aid."[24] On January 19, another leader of the Reguibat esh-Sharg, Habouha Ould Lahbib, gave himself up to the French at Ain Ben Tili.

Very little is known about the causes of these defections. The western ways of the young radical Moroccans in the Army of Liberation's leadership may have alienated the austere and traditionalist nomads.[25] Perhaps too there was resentment among the Saharawi guerrilla fighters that they were being excluded from the overall command by these Moroccans, who were, besides, almost all Berbers. Moreover, an order to withdraw northward from the desert, given sometime in the winter of 1957–58, aroused suspicions that Benhamou Mesfioui and his fellow commanders were manipulating the Saharawis for ulterior purposes. Why, when the Spanish had been forced to pull back to the coast, were the guerrilla forces being told to reassemble to the north of the Draa?[26] Was it, perhaps, that the Moroccan commanders intended to use the Saharawis to halt the FAR's advance into southern Morocco?

Upon hearing of the infighting and demoralization in the Army of Liberation, Cusin was convinced that no time should be lost in launching Operation Ouragan. On December 30 he put his case in Paris to an interministerial committee meeting that had been summoned to discuss events in Mauritania. Mokhtar Ould Daddah's appeals, the Khatri affair and a hunch that Mohammed V would turn a blind eye to a campaign against the irregulars whom he so distrusted persuaded the ministers to give Ouragan the go-ahead. The French ambassador in Madrid, Baron Guy de La Tournelle, was instructed by Gaillard to seek an immediate meeting with the Spanish foreign minister, Fernando María Castiella.

Castiella endorsed Ouragan without hesitation and within days French and Spanish officers were meeting to begin joint planning. Meanwhile, to underline that it had no intention of bowing to the guerrillas, the Spanish government issued a decree on January 10, 1958, which abolished AOE and converted both Spanish Sahara and Ifni into fully-fledged Spanish provinces.[27] They were no longer colonies, but were now "part of Spain." While General Gómez Zamalloa, the former governor-general of AOE, became governor-general of Ifni, another senior army officer, General José Héctor Vázquez, was appointed governor-general of the new province of the Sahara.[28]

However, Spanish Southern Morocco was excluded from the two new provinces, giving rise to speculation that Spain would finally end its "protectorate" there. In fact, in talks with Mohammed V and Ahmed Balafrej in Tangier on September 15–17, 1957, Castiella had promised to withdraw from the territory between the Draa and parallel 27°40' as soon as the FAR had restored order in southern Morocco and halted the guerrilla attacks of the Army of Liberation.[29] Until then, however, Spain would stay put. On December 7 the Spanish government had proceeded to publish a communiqué recalling that it had "drawn the attention of the Moroccan authorities amicably but with insistence, for six months, to the anomalous situation, for a sovereign state, that it has failed to exercise effective control over a vast region to the south of the Atlas range, a situation which, besides, is not new in the history of Morocco." Spain, the communique added, "would fail in its sense of international responsibility if it abandoned the aforementioned southern zone to those who do not obey His Majesty the King of Morocco and who refuse to accept the law and the discipline of their legitimate sovereign."[30]

During January–February, as preparations for Operation Ouragan were finalized, Saharawi guerrillas kept up the pace of attacks. During the night of January 12, outlying Spanish posts near El-Ayoun were raided. The next morning Foreign Legionnaires moved out of the capital on a search-and-destroy mission and, after finding a large concentration of guerrillas at Edchera, twelve miles away, battled with them for most of the day. Fifty-one Spanish soldiers were killed or wounded, the authorities in Madrid announced a few days later.[31] Meanwhile, at meetings in Las Palmas and Dakar, French and Spanish officers were putting the finishing touches to the plans for Ouragan. It was to be a lightning, two-stage sweep, first through Saguia el-Hamra, where Smara was to be reoccupied, and then through Río de Oro. The Spanish maneuvers, involving nine thousand troops and sixty aircraft, were to be named after Mount Teide, the highest peak in the Canaries, while the French side of the campaign, in which five thousand troops and seventy aircraft were to be deployed, was code-named Ecouvillon (sponge). To avoid the risk of clashing with the regular Moroccan army, which was just beginning to move units into the regions of southern Morocco controlled by the Army of Liberation, orders were given not to cross parallel 27°40'. The whole operation was to be over within a fortnight. It was to deliver a short, sharp shock to the Saharawi guerrillas.[32] Overall command was assumed from the French side by General Bourgund and from the Spanish side by the captain-general of the Canaries, Lieutenant General López Valencia, and the new governor-general of

Spanish Sahara, General Héctor Vázquez. To offset potentially hostile foreign reaction, a pretext was required to launch the operation. At the end of January there was an incident, a relatively minor shootout between a group of guerrillas and some Mauritanian soldiers thirty-five miles from Fort Trinquet, which served Gaillard's purposes. D-Day was fixed for February 6, then postponed for four days because of poor weather.[33]

On February 10, while motorized units under the command of General Héctor Vázquez headed out of El-Ayoun and Tarfaya, French troops from Tindouf and northern Mauritania crossed the border into Saguia el-Hamra. Spanish paratroopers were dropped into Smara. By February 20, the first stage of the operation had been successfully completed. Though sandstorms had allowed many of the guerrillas to slip northward without detection toward the Army of Liberation bases in the Draa Valley, several points in the interior had been reoccupied by Spanish forces and a devastating blow had been struck to guerrilla morale. Between February 20 and 24, French and Spanish troops swept through Río de Oro, reoccupying Bir Enzaren, Aoussert, Agracha and other previously abandoned outposts. During the whole operation, only eight Spanish and seven French soldiers had been killed.[34]

Khatri Ould Said Ould el-Joumani wrote to Cusin to "thank him in the name of all the populations of the Sahara for what he has done and will do for them," while among the guerrillas demoralization sapped the will to fight on after Ouragan.[35] The divisions within the Army of Liberation became more serious and culminated in a revolt against the Moroccan guerrilla commanders at Tan-Tan, a settlement in Spanish Southern Morocco which Spanish forces had evacuated during 1957.[36] The movement was further weakened by desertions. Many guerrillas did not know what had become of their families during Ouragan and had lost much of their livestock. To ensure continued access to their traditional pastures, many disillusioned guerrillas began drifting back from the Draa to Saguia el-Hamra, Río de Oro or northern Mauritania. In Mauritania a special team of officials was set up, under Colonel Guibaud, to exploit the demoralization. Gifts totaling 4.15 million CFA francs were distributed to guerrilla deserters who gave themselves up at the French posts in northern Mauritania, and, including sums spent on handing out flour, sugar, tea, rice, cloth and other relief, about 20 million CFA francs were spent in all.[37] Three thousand Reguibat declared their loyalty at special ceremonies in Fort Gouraud and Fort Trinquet on April 10–11 attended by Mokhtar Ould Daddah, who eloquently argued that they had been right to give themselves in because, as *beidan,* they were Mauritanians, not Moroccans. "You Reguibat," he proclaimed at Fort Gouraud, "you are the people of this region of northern Mauritania, but you are members of Greater Mauritania because we want to create the Mauritanian nation, which implies that Mauritania will become a large tribe in which the present tribes are simply families. With unity, we can achieve everything by ourselves; disunited, we will be vulnerable and our disunity will merely encourage the lust of our enemies."[38] Shortly afterward, on May 2–5, Khatri Ould Said attended the constitutive congress of Mokhtar Ould Daddah's Parti du Regroupement Mauritanien (PRM) at Aleg.[39] Meanwhile, the World Bank sent its first team of experts to the iron-bearing region near Fort Gouraud in April and, after hearing of the restoration of security there, approved a $66 million loan to MIFERMA.

At much the same time, regular Moroccan forces were beginning to establish control in the extreme south of Morocco. On March 3, a week after Ouragan, the Moroccan Haut Comité de la Défense Nationale announced that it was sending "reinforcements" to Bou-Izakarn and Goulimine, which had been among Benhamou Mesfioui's key bases. Satisfied that the FAR would now discipline the remnants of the Army of Liberation, the Spanish government began talks with the Rabat regime about the handover of Spanish Southern Morocco. After preliminary conversations between the Spanish ambassador in Rabat, Alcover Sureda, and Balafrej on March 18, Castiella and Balafrej met in Cintra, Portugal, on April 1 and reached agreement that Tarfaya, the sole point in the zone which was still occupied by Spanish troops, would be transferred to Moroccan administration on April 10. The fifteen hundred Spanish troops in Tarfaya would remain there temporarily "under the same regulations as those in the rest of Morocco until the signing of an agreement concerning all these troops."[40] In fact, the April 10 handover ceremony at Tarfaya had to be postponed, because the column of Moroccan troops that set out from Goulimine under the command of Mohammed Oufkir could not get there. A large force of hostile Saharawis blocked Oufkir's men at the River Chebeika, ninety-five miles from Tarfaya.[41] The ceremony was finally held on July 22, when Crown Prince Hassan flew into Tarfaya by helicopter and held a reconciliation meeting with Saharawi sheikhs at Boukhcheibia, near the River Chebeika, at which he promised to release imprisoned Saharawi guerrillas.[42]

Practically all the Saharawis who had fought for the Army of Liberation and now found themselves under Moroccan administration were utterly destitute. Except for some of the Tekna, they were effectively refugees from the Spanish or French controlled zones farther south. Many had lost all or most of their herds, and a serious drought that began in 1959 added further hardship. Most were dependent for survival on relief from the Moroccan authorities.[43] Not surprisingly, many were only too glad to be offered the opportunity to enlist in the regular Moroccan army, and by the end of 1959 several thousand had signed up.[44] Farther north, the remnants of the Moroccan guerrilla groups were also gradually being disarmed and disbanded. They were encouraged to cooperate with the government by a combination of carrot and stick tactics, ranging from offers of jobs in the police force, the army or the administration and promises of *colon*-owned land to imprisonment and torture for the more recalcitrant or radical.[45]

The Spanish authorities in Western Sahara had little to fear from the Army of Liberation after Operation Ouragan and the entry of the FAR into Morocco's far south. The guerrilla attacks ceased, and on May 7, 1959, forty Spaniards who had been captured by the Army of Liberation in Ifni and Western Sahara in 1957–58 were released at a ceremony in the royal palace in Rabat.[46] There was one isolated incident two years later, on March 11, 1961, when an armed group kidnapped eleven American, French, Canadian and Spanish members of an oil-exploration team working for Union Oil and the Compañía Ibérica de Petroleos near the Moroccan border. However, they quickly ended up in the hands of the FAR and were released ten days after their capture.[47] The next guerrilla attacks were not to come until twelve years later, in 1973, after the founding of the Polisario Front.

NOTES

1. Cited in Rachid Lazrak, *Le contentieux territorial entre le Maroc et l'Espagne* (Dar el Kitab, Casablanca, 1974), p. 427.
2. Attilio Gaudio, *Le dossier du Sahara occidental* (Nouvelles Editions Latines, Paris, 1978), p. 112.
3. Alejandro Murillo Goñi, "Desarollo de la provincia del Sahara," *Africa*, Vol. XVII, No. 227, November 1960, p. 9.
4. Georges Chaffard, *Les carnets secrets de la décolonisation* (Calmann-Lévy, Paris, 2 Vols., 1965 and 1967), Vol. II, pp. 87–130.
5. John Waterbury, *Le commandeur des croyants* (Presses Universitaires de France, Paris, 1975), p. 236.
6. Cited in *ibid.*, p. 236.
7. *El pueblo saharaui en lucha: documentos del Frente Popular para la Liberación de Saguia el Hamra y Río de Oro* (Polisario Front, 1975), p. 10.
8. Frank E. Trout, *Morocco's Saharan Frontiers* (Droz, Geneva, 1969), pp. 420–23.
9. *Chroniques Etrangères: Espagne*, (La Documentation Française, Paris), No. 181, March 31, 1957, p. 19.
10. Pierre Bonte, "Multinational Companies and National Development: MIFERMA and Mauretania," *Review of African Political Economy*, No. 2, January–April 1975, p. 94; Chaffard, *op. cit.*, Vol. I, pp. 257–58.
11. *Ibid.*, pp. 256–57.
12. Cited in *Chroniques Etrangères: Espagne*, No. 181, March 31, 1957, pp. 19–20. See also Chaffard, *op. cit.*, Vol. I, p. 261.
13. Cited in *ibid.*, p. 260.
14. Cited in *Chroniques Etrangères: Espagne*, No. 181, March 31, 1957, p. 20.
15. Cited in Chaffard, *op. cit.*, Vol. I, p. 264.
16. *Chroniques Etrangères: Espagne*, No. 186, August 31, 1957, pp. 16–17.
17. Chaffard, *op. cit.*, Vol. I, pp. 267–68.
18. *Chroniques Etrangères: Espagne*, No. 190, pp. 4–13, December 31, 1957.
19. *Ibid.*, p. 8.
20. *Ibid.*, pp. 7–8.
21. *Chroniques Etrangères: Espagne*, No. 191, January 31, 1958, pp. 11, 17.
22. Chaffard, *op. cit.*, Vol. I, pp. 270–71.
23. *Ibid.*, p. 273.
24. The full text of Khatri Ould Said Ould el-Joumani's letter to Cusin is published in Chaffard, *op. cit.*, Vol. I, pp. 289–90. According to legend, it was the land from the Kharawi, in the Draa Valley, to "the seventh wave of the ocean" which Sidi Ahmed Reguibi bought from a Moroccan sultan in the sixteenth century. See Chapter 3, Note 5.
25. Virginia Thompson and Richard Adloff, *The Western Saharans* (Croom Helm, London, 1980), p. 314.
26. *El pueblo saharaui en lucha*, pp. 11–12.
27. Decreto por el que se reorganiza el Gobierno General del Africa Occidental Española, *Boletín Oficial del Estado*, (Madrid), January 14, 1958.
28. *Chroniques Etrangères: Espagne*, No. 192, February 28, 1958, p. 19.
29. *Chroniques Etrangères: Espagne*, No. 188, October 10, 1957, pp. 17–18.
30. *Chroniques Etrangères: Espagne*, No. 190, December 31, 1957, p. 12.
31. *Chroniques Etrangères: Espagne*, No. 192, February 28, 1958, p. 18.
32. Chaffard, *op. cit.*, Vol. I, p. 276.
33. *Ibid.*, p. 279.
34. *Ibid.*, p. 280; *Chroniques Etrangères: Espagne*, No. 193, March 3, 1958, pp. 5–6.
35. *La Semaine en AOF* (Dakar), April 19, 1958.
36. *El pueblo saharaui en lucha*, p. 12. In an interview with the author (Tindouf, November 1979), Mohammed Ali Ould el-Ouali (Omar Hadrami), a member of the Polisario Front's executive committee, said that an Algerian-born leader of the Army of Liberation, Si Saleh el-Jazairi, was detained by

the guerrillas in this incident, which came to be known by Saharawis as the "raiding of the armory."

37. Chaffard, *op. cit.*, Vol. I, p. 286.

38. *La Semaine en AOF*, April 19, 1958.

39. Bertrand Fessard de Foucault, "La question du Sahara espagnol (I)," *Revue Française d'Etudes Politiques Africaines*, 10th Year, No. 119, November 1975, p. 83.

40. *Efe*, dispatch from Lisbon, April 3, 1958, cited in *Chroniques Etrangères: Espagne*, April 30, 1958, p. 19. There were still thirty-five thousand Spanish troops in northern Morocco at this time and the last of them were not withdrawn until August 1961.

41. *El pueblo saharaui en lucha*, p. 12. According to Mohammed Ali Ould el-Ouali (interview with author, Tindouf, November 1979), Crown Prince Hassan, who was then chief-of-staff of the FAR, flew in by helicopter to negotiate with the Saharawi force at the Chebeika but failed to break the impasse. There was then a shoot-out between the guerrillas and Moroccan troops shortly after Hassan's departure, he claims. It was probably the confrontation at the River Chebeika to which Hassan was referring when fourteen years later, in a speech on August 20, 1972, shortly after an unsuccessful coup attempt by Moroccan air-force officers, he included the Saharawis among a list of previous rebels against the monarchy. See "Discours prononcé par le Roi Hassan II à l'occasion de l'anniversaire de la Révolution du Roi et du Peuple," *Le Matin* (Rabat), August 21, 1972, republished in *Annuaire de l'Afrique du Nord, 1972* (Centre National de la Recherche Scientifique, Paris, 1973), p. 791. To avoid the guerrilla forces at the Chebeika, Oufkir seems to have tried to follow an alternative route to Tarfaya through territory to the south of parallel 27°40' but to have been halted by Spanish forces. See *Chroniques Etrangères: Espagne*, No. 195, May 31, 1958, p. 5.

42. *El pueblo saharaui en lucha*, p. 12; *Chroniques Etrangères: Espagne*, No. 198, August 31, 1958, p. 12.

43. Even before the cession of Spanish Morocco, the Moroccan government had informed the UN secretary-general on March 18, 1958, that thirteen thousand refugees had arrived in its territory "following the Franco-Spanish police operations in the Sahara." Cited in *Chroniques Etrangères: Espagne*, No. 194, April 30, 1958.

44. Eight thousand Saharawis joined the FAR in 1959 according to *El pueblo saharaui en lucha*, p. 12. In particular, many Ait Oussa, Tekna who had played a prominent role in the Army of Liberation, joined the FAR at this time. So did some Reguibat, including Abba el-Sheikh.

45. Waterbury, *op. cit.*, pp. 238–41; *Amnesty International Briefing: Morocco* (Amnesty International, London, 1977), p. 2.

46. *Chroniques Etrangères: Espagne*, No. 207, May 31, 1959, p. 12.

47. For a detailed account of this strange incident, see "L'affaire de l'enlèvement des onze prospecteurs de pétrole," *Chroniques Etrangères: Espagne*, No. 230, March 1961, pp. 14–18.

8

Greater Morocco

*If Morocco is independent, it is not completely
unified. The Moroccans will continue the
struggle until Tangier, the Sahara from Tindouf
to Colomb-Bechar, Touat, Kenadza,
Mauritania are liberated and unified. Our independence will only be complete with the
Sahara! The frontiers of Morocco end in the
south at Saint-Louis-du-Sénégal!*

—Allal el-Fassi, June 19, 1956[1]

ON THE MORROW OF MOROCCO'S INDEPENDENCE, Allal el-Fassi, the principal leader of the Istiqlal Party, who had just returned
home from exile in Cairo, began to argue that only parts of the historic Alawite
empire had been freed and so the ending of the protectorate had only been a partial victory. "So long as Tangier is not liberated from its international statute, so
long as the Spanish deserts of the south, the Sahara from Tindouf and Atar and
the Algerian-Moroccan borderlands are not liberated from their trusteeship, our
independence will remain incomplete and our first duty will be to carry on action
to liberate the country and to unify it," he proclaimed on March 27, 1956.[2] By
June, he was insisting that Morocco's true southern border was the Senegal River.
His cousin Abdelkebir el-Fassi then drew a map of Greater Morocco, which was
published in the Istiqlal Party's daily newspaper, *Al-Alam*, on July 7 and
depicted Morocco incorporating a vast portion of the Algerian Sahara, including
the oases of Touat, Gourara and Tidikelt, the whole of Spanish Sahara and

Mauritania, and even a corner of northwestern Mali, in addition to such more plausibly Moroccan territories as the Spanish enclaves of Ifni, Ceuta and Melilla. The potential mineral wealth of the Sahara, which had recently been highlighted by the discovery of oil in the Algerian desert and MIFERMA's plans to exploit the huge iron deposits in Mauritania, was evidently an important influence on the ideologues of Greater Morocco; and a "commentary on the economic importance of the Sahara," which gave an inventory of its minerals, was published by Al-Alam alongside Abdelkebir el-Fassi's map.

In a series of articles, collectively entitled the Livre Rouge and published in the nationalist review Perspectives Sahariennes in 1959–60, Allal el-Fassi sought to prove that France and Spain had deprived Morocco of its historic Saharan provinces by imposing their arbitrary colonial frontiers at the beginning of the century and that they now intended to retain control of these desert regions to preserve their economic and strategic interests—among them, in France's case, plans to test nuclear weapons in the Algerian Sahara, as well as to exploit the desert's minerals. To Allal el-Fassi it was almost immaterial to ask whether the local inhabitants considered themselves Moroccan. To ask the population of Tindouf or Fort Gouraud (Zouerate) whether they were Moroccan, he wrote in Al-Istiqlal on September 17, 1956, had as little logic as "to ask the population of Fez or Marrakesh to say whether they are Moroccan or something else." If, however, the Saharans were duped by the colonialists into rejecting Morocco, he would later insist, the Moroccan government should act to stop them. "Mauritania has no right to separate itself from the rest of Morocco," he advised Crown Prince Hassan in September 1958. "In such an event, which God forbid, the King and the people would be duty bound to preserve the unity of the homeland."[3]

The extravagance of el-Fassi's proposals at first surprised most Moroccans. "Originally," he said in October 1957, "I was the only person to call for the liberation of the Sahara and I was greeted with laughter."[4] However, in the heady aftermath of Morocco's independence struggle, his stirring calls for renewed combat against colonialism and his idealized vision of the glories and conquests of precolonial Morocco quickly captured the hearts of Moroccan nationalists. The Istiqlal Party formally endorsed his territorial demands at its first post-independence congress in August 1956. King Mohammed V, for his part, could not afford to allow the principal nationalist party and its prestigious leader to outpace the monarchy in nationalist fervor during the delicate post-independence period when the Palace was attempting to consolidate its hold over the country to the disadvantage of the Istiqlal Party and such other components of the nationalist movement as the Army of Liberation and the trade unions. Moreover, since el-Fassi's theses glorified the conquests of the more powerful of Morocco's precolonial sultans, Mohammed V calculated that his doctrine could easily be turned to royal advantage, to boost the monarchy's prestige.

The Greater Morocco cause was officially embraced by the Moroccan government toward the end of 1957. At the United Nations, Morocco laid claim to Mauritania, Ifni and Spanish Sahara on October 14.[5] Then, on November 12, a dahir named Abdelkebir el-Fassi director of Saharan and frontier affairs in the ministry of the interior. A few days later Moroccan broadcasting transmitters

GREATER MOROCCO

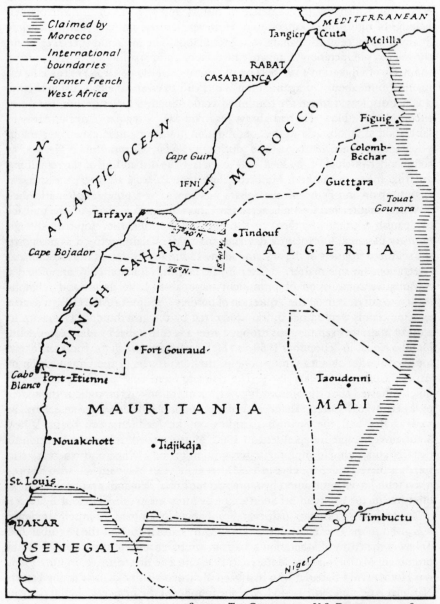

SOURCE: THE GEOGRAPHER, U.S. DEPARTMENT OF STATE

began beaming the "Voice of the Moroccan Sahara" to the desert.[6] Mohammed V himself first publicly endorsed the Saharan claims on February 25, 1958 when, in a speech in the market place at M'hamid, an oasis village in the valley of the Draa, he promised to "strive with all our power to recover our Sahara and everything which, by the evidence of history and the will of the inhabitants, belongs of right to our kingdom."[7] However, the real military struggle against Spain and France in the Sahara was petering out. The M'hamid speech came on the last day of Operation Ouragan, just as French and Spanish forces were routing the Army of Liberation's last pockets of resistance in Río de Oro. Yet the king remained mute about Ouragan, and it is difficult to escape the conclusion that he was not displeased to see the combined Franco-Spanish forces dealing the guerrillas a decisive blow. He had always regarded the "irregulars" of the Army of Liberation as an obstacle to the consolidation of a strong monarchical regime in post-independence Morocco, and during 1958–60, Crown Prince Hassan, as commander-in-chief of the FAR, was to oversee the disbanding of the remaining guerrilla forces in southern Morocco. Under the Palace's auspices, the struggle against Spain and France in the Sahara was now to be a purely diplomatic one.

When Balafrej and Castiella agreed at Cintra on April 1, 1958, on the transfer of Spanish Southern Morocco to the Rabat authorities, the Moroccan foreign ministry hastened to explain a day later that "Mr. Balafrej refused to recognize the southern frontiers of the aforementioned zone and expressed the most formal reservations on this matter."[8] Later in the month, Mohammed V appointed a consultative commission of prominent nationalist, trade union and religious leaders to advise him on the "question of borders."[9] Some of Allal el-Fassi's most extreme claims were rather quickly forgotten by the government. The claim to parts of Mali, for example, was dropped after a visit to Rabat by Mali's president, Modibo Keita, in September 1960 and Mali's participation in the conference that founded the Casablanca Group, one of the forerunners of the Organization of African Unity, in January 1961. The claim to Saint-Louis in Senegal was also quietly shelved. But the Moroccan government continued throughout the sixties to lay claim to Western Sahara, Mauritania and much of the Algerian Sahara, as well as Ifni and the Spanish presidios on the Mediterranean coast. When Mauritania became independent in 1960, Morocco tried to bar its admission to the UN and withheld diplomatic recognition for nine years; and when Algeria finally achieved independence in 1962 after eight years of bloody war with France, it too found itself confronted by Moroccan territorial demands and had to fight a brief war in 1963 to fend off an attempt by Morocco to seize Tindouf by force.

To many Moroccan nationalists and probably Mohammed V himself, credence was given to the Greater Morocco cause by the participation of the Reguibat and Tekna in the Army of Liberation's Saharan campaign and the defection of several prominent Mauritanians to Morocco in 1956–58. The first to arrive, in June 1956, was Horma Ould Babana, who had been Mauritania's first deputy in the French National Assembly, in 1946–51, and the founder of the first anticolonial party in Mauritania, the Entente Mauritanienne, in 1948. Then, on March 27, 1958, the Emir of Trarza, Mohammed Fadel Ould Oumer, and two Mauritanian cabinet ministers, Dey Ould Sidi Baba and Mohammed el-Mokhtar Ould Bah, arrived in

Morocco, to make the *bayaa* to Mohammed V and talk of "the whole Mauritanian people's desire to see Mauritania return within the fold of the mother country."[10] Horma Ould Babana appears to have believed that with Moroccan aid he could make a political comeback in Mauritania, where he had been politically out-gunned by the French colonial authorities and the traditional Moor oligarchy, who had taken exception to his reformist campaigning in the late forties and founded a conservative rival party, the Union Progressiste Mauritanienne (UPM), in 1948. Horma had easily been defeated in both the 1951 and 1956 elections for Mauritania's seat in the French National Assembly by the UPM's candidate, Sidi el-Mokhtar N'Diaye, and had then gone into voluntary exile in Cairo before arriv-ing in Morocco. In the late fifties, as Mauritania headed toward internal self-government and then independence, in accordance with French plans to balkanize French West Africa and at the same time keep iron-rich Mauritania out of the orbit of the turbulent Maghreb, latent rivalries between the *beidan* and black Africans threatened to undermine the tireless campaign waged by the UPM's leader, Mokhtar Ould Daddah, to forge a new unifying spirit of Maurita-nian nationhood. A number of small black-based parties emerged in 1956-59, some of them advocating association or integration with neighboring black states.[11] Likewise, some Moors oriented themselves politically to the Arab world, and in particular to Morocco, either from a radical pan-Arab perspective or out of fear of black domination. However, the UPM won an overwhelming victory in elections to Mauritania's Territorial Assembly in March 1957, capturing thirty-three of the thirty-four seats. The Entente was in disarray. Dey Ould Sidi Baba and Mohammed el-Mokhtar Ould Bah, who were both leaders of the Entente, agreed to join Mokhtar Ould Daddah's cabinet in January 1958 but fled to Morocco with the Emir of Trarza two months later when rumors spread of plans for a federation with Mali or Senegal.

"Compatriots," the Voice of the Moroccan Sahara appealed to the *beidan* of Mauritania in September 1958, "rise up and smash the chains which have broken you, cut the ropes which fetter you and march to victory."[12] But the Army of Liberation's guerrilla campaign in northern Mauritania had collapsed during Operation Ouragan in February. In May, moreover, the Entente's rump had fused with the UPM to form the Parti du Regroupement Mauritanien (PRM), and Moor fears of black hegemony receded as the predominantly Moor-led PRM, which won all forty seats in elections to a new National Assembly in May 1959 after banning the small opposition parties, ruled out federation with neighboring black states and led Mauritania to independence under Mokhtar Ould Daddah's presidency, on November 28, 1960.[13]

The Moroccan government's diplomatic efforts met with equal failure. An at-tempt to persuade the World Bank to withhold support for the plans to exploit the Zouerate iron deposits, upon which the new state's economic viability was largely to rest, ended in failure when a $66-million loan for MIFERMA was ap-proved in March 1960.[14] As France made the final preparations for Mauritanian independence, vigorous protests were lodged in Paris. "Morocco," the foreign ministry reminded France on August 20, 1960, "has never abandoned, implicitly or explicitly, its rights over regions which, at all times, have formed an integral part of the kingdom and which only the regime of the protectorate artificially separated from the national territory.''¹⁵ But Mohammed V had no effective leverage over President Charles de Gaulle. His government was still heavily reliant on French civil servants, economic ties with France had barely diminished at all since independence and the FAR were equipped with French weapons and still partially commanded by French officers.

With Mauritania's independence only days away, the Rabat government published a ''white book'' spelling out in detail the historical grounds for its claim to Mauritania.¹⁶ The Mauritanian government replied a few days later with a rival ''green book,'' which rebutted the Moroccan arguments point by point.¹⁷ On the eve of independence Mohammed V's government organized a ''day of protest and reflection'' throughout Morocco. ''France,'' it protested, ''is preparing to execute the plot hatched against our country by granting independence to a vast part of our territory on November 28. After installing a puppet government and putting true Mauritanian representatives in prison, she is seeking thereby to perpetuate her domination over Mauritania.''¹⁸

To increase the pressure on France, the Moroccan government tried to summon support from third world countries and the Soviet bloc. During a tour of the Middle East by Mohammed V in January-February 1960, most Arab governments publicly expressed support for the Moroccan claim to Mauritania, and on August 28, 1960, the political committee of the Arab League voted to ''support Morocco in its demand for the recovery of Mauritania as an integral part of its national territory.''¹⁹ With this backing from the Arab states, Morocco was then able, on October 19, to persuade the UN General Assembly to examine the dispute over Mauritania. M'hammed Boucetta, an Istiqlalian who represented Morocco in the ensuing debates, argued that France was trying to create an artificial state in Mauritania, run by handpicked yes-men, so that it could exploit its minerals. On November 15, he compared Mauritania to secessionist Katanga in the newly independent Congo (Zaire) and predicted that ''the territory of southern Morocco to which France wishes to give independence will be dominated by powerful companies, such as MIFERMA and MICUMA, whose financial power is matched only by political power.''²⁰ If France was so committed to Mauritanian independence, he asked the next day, ''why not grant it to Algeria where a war is raging and human life is being lost every day?''²¹ Arguments like these convinced a few of the more radical Afro-Asian states, but there was unease among many black African governments at Morocco's apparent disdain for Mauritania's right to determine its own future. Boucetta himself captured their mood of apprehension rather well when he remarked on November 25 that Morocco was being accused of wanting to ''crunch up Mauritania like chocolate.''²² Moreover, one Arab country, Tunisia, had already stepped out of line, probably under French pressure, and announced that it would sponsor Mauritania's application for UN membership.²³ A large majority in favor of Mauritania's entry to the UN seemed assured in the General Assembly, but Morocco's cause was saved by a Soviet veto in the Security Council on December 3.²⁴ Morocco chalked up another minor success when the founding conference of the Casablanca Group, held on January 4–7, 1961, adopted a resolution stating that ''France has amputated Morocco from its southern part in Mauritania, in order to extend its domination in the Sahara, exploit its wealth and secure outlets to the Atlantic for itself.'' It approved ''any action undertaken by Morocco in Mauritania to recover its legitimate rights there.''[25]

However, Mauritania was by now a reality. In December 1960, immediately after the Security Council veto, the Brazzaville Group, a bloc of formerly French-ruled African countries, protested that it was ''the duty of the UN'' to admit Mauritania.[26] When Mauritania's bid for UN membership came before the UN again a year later, most Arab states and members of the Casablanca Group continued to side with Morocco, but in the Security Council the western powers and the Soviet Union thrashed out a compromise by which Mauritania was recommended for UN membership in return for Mongolia's admission. Finally, the General Assembly voted by 68 to 13, with 20 abstentions, to admit Mauritania on October 27, 1961.[27]

Morocco was similarly rebuffed by the Organization of African Unity at its founding a year and a half later in May 1963. King Hassan II, who had succeeded to the throne in 1961, boycotted the founding conference in Addis Ababa because President Mokhtar Ould Daddah had been invited, and the Moroccan government delayed another four months before signing the OAU Charter. When it finally did so, on September 19, it felt it incumbent to inform the organization's first chairman, Emperor Haile Selassie, that ''in thus subscribing to all the objectives and principles of the Charter of the Organization, principles which it has always faithfully and resolutely upheld, the Government of His Majesty the King has in no way intended to renounce its legitimate rights with regard to the peaceful achievement and preservation of the territorial integrity of the Kingdom within its rightful frontiers.''[28]

A month later Morocco was embroiled in something far more serious than the diplomatic jostling over the Mauritanian question. War broke out on the border with Algeria. In its ''white book'' the Rabat government had recognized the Moroccan-Algerian frontier only along its northernmost stretch, from the Mediterranean to the city of Figuig. To the south, Morocco claimed vast tracts of Algerian territory, including Bechar, Tindouf and the oases of Touat, Gourara and Tidikelt, which it claimed had at times been administered by *caids* and governors appointed by the *makhzen* and at other times been part of the Moroccan *bilad es-siba*.[29] Moreover, on July 6, 1961, a year before the end of Algeria's independence war, Ferhat Abbas, the president of the Provisional Government of the Algerian Republic, had signed an agreement with Hassan II accepting that ''the territorial problem posed by the border imposed arbitrarily between the two countries by France will be resolved in negotiations between the government of the Kingdom of Morocco and the government of independent Algeria'' and that an Algerian-Moroccan commission should be set up and ''meet as soon as possible to proceed to the study and solution of this problem in a spirit of fraternity and Maghrebian unity.''[30] Ferhat Abbas' intention in signing this was to dissuade the Moroccan government from trying to negotiate a border agreement with France prior to Algeria's independence. The Evian negotiations between the FLN and the French government had opened on May 20 but rapidly run aground on the

Saharan question. While accepting the principle of Algerian independence, De Gaulle was hoping to retain control over the oil and minerals of the Algerian Sahara, either by maintaining French sovereignty there or, on the grounds that the desert was an "internal ocean," by involving other neighboring and less radical African states in determining its future. France had created an Organisation Commune des Régions Sahariennes (OCRS), "open to all the countries bordering the Sahara," on January 10, 1957, and had included in it the southern Algerian departments (Oasis and Saoura) and the French colonies of Soudan (Mali), Niger, Chad and Mauritania. It had also tried unsuccessfully to entice Morocco into the OCRS, while agreeing earlier, at the time of Morocco's independence, to set up a joint Franco-Moroccan commission to fix definitively Morocco's southeastern frontiers. Thus, while accepting the principle of bilateral Algerian-Moroccan frontier negotiations to discourage Morocco from negotiating separately with France, Ferhat Abbas secured the Moroccan government's commitment to "support the Provisional Government of the Algerian Republic without reservation in its negotiations with France on the basis of respect for the integrity of Algerian territory."[31]

However, the July 1961 agreement was never implemented. Ferhat Abbas himself was pushed aside in the complex power struggle which beset the FLN when Algeria finally achieved independence in July 1962. The victorious faction, headed by Ahmed Ben Bella, did not reject the idea of negotiating a border agreement with Morocco. However, it was preoccupied with tackling the huge problems inherited from the bloody independence war, during which several hundred thousand Algerians had lost their lives (out of a total population of about ten million) and almost two million peasants had been uprooted, and from the ensuing exodus of about eight hundred thousand Europeans, among them practically all of colonial Algeria's administrators, managers, technicians and skilled workers.[32] It is hardly surprising that Ben Bella was dismayed by Hassan II's rapid resort to force along the border and his attempt to exploit the conflict to undermine the revolutionary Algerian government in its hour of need.

Immediately after Algeria's independence, units of the FAR occupied several former French posts on the Algerian side of the *de facto* border, or "operational limit," established by French forces between Bechar and Tindouf during the Algerian independence war, and the Rabat authorities claimed that the population of Tindouf had declared its allegiance to Hassan II. Three days after independence, meanwhile, the Moroccan government sent a delegation to Algiers to demand the implementation of the July 1961 agreement. However, Algerian troops forced the FAR to withdraw from the posts they had occupied along the operational limit and on October 9 finally entered Tindouf, reportedly clashing with pro-Moroccan elements there.[33] Five months later, on March 13–15, 1963, King Hassan visited Algiers, to be told by Ben Bella that he could not discuss the border problem until after Algeria's first presidential elections, which were finally held the following September. "I ask Your Majesty to leave me the time to establish Algeria's new institutions," Hassan later recalled Ben Bella as telling him. "When this has been done, in September or October, then we will open this dossier on the frontiers together. It goes without saying that independent Algeria cannot be France's inheritor as far as the Algerian frontiers are concerned."[34]

However, Hassan was not to give Ben Bella the breathing space he needed. After a series of border incidents between July and September 1963, Moroccan troops crossed the operational limit on October 1 and occupied the former French posts of Hassi Beida and Tinjoub, about twenty to thirty miles south of M'hamid, thereby threatening to cut the main road link between Bechar and Tindouf in the vicinity of Tinfouchy. Five days later the Moroccan and Algerian foreign ministers, Ahmed Reda Guedira and Abdelaziz Bouteflika, met at Oujda amid mounting tension but failed to reach agreement, and on October 8–9 Algerian troops recaptured both Tinjoub and Hassi Beida after fierce fighting. However, Moroccan troops fought their way back into the two posts on October 14, prompting Ben Bella the next day to proclaim a general mobilization of veterans of Algeria's independence war and to launch a diversionary counteroffensive to the north in which Algerian forces seized the Moroccan post of Ich and the heights around the Moroccan city of Figuig. But Moroccan troops continued their advance farther south and by October 26 the Moroccan government was claiming that its forces had pushed forward to within ten miles of Tindouf.

The border demarcation dispute itself would appear, in view of Ben Bella's stated willingness to negotiate a border agreement, to have been merely a pretext for Hassan's decision to invade. His real purpose, without question, was to undermine the Algerian Revolution and stem its influence among his own subjects. Mohammed Harbi, who was a member of the FLN's central committee and one of Ben Bella's advisors at this time and had visited Morocco in the summer of 1963 to meet leaders of the antigovernment Union Nationale des Forces Populaires (UNFP), has observed that "there was a specific political desire in Rabat, to dismantle the foreseeable alliance between Ben Bella's Algeria, Nasser and the Moroccan opposition, more precisely the veterans of the Resistance," and that "it was necessary to act fast, before an Algerian army, properly speaking, had been set up."[35] Hassan had undoubtedly been alarmed by the contacts between the UNFP and the FLN and by comments made by Ben Bella to the Egyptian newspaper *Al-Ahram* in March 1963 that the Algerian Revolution would not halt at Algeria's frontiers. Furthermore, the FLN enjoyed enormous prestige among Moroccans after the success of its long, bitter war against France; and the revolutionary measures enacted during the first year of the Ben Bella government, among them the famous "March decrees" establishing workers' self-management of the estates and businesses abandoned by the departed *pieds noirs*, were applauded by many Moroccans who had been disillusioned by the slow pace of change since independence in their own country. Indeed, it is significant that the king's first and very modest land-reform measure, the nationalization of about 250,000 hectares, or approximately one quarter of the total of *colon*-owned land in Morocco, which was not adopted until more than seven years after Morocco's independence, was itself very much a reaction to what had been happening in Algeria and was announced only days before the outbreak of the border war, on September 26, 1963.[36] Hassan did not enjoy the personal popularity that his father had won during Morocco's independence struggle and his political fortunes had reached a decidedly low ebb. In May 1963 the royalist coalition, the Front pour la Défense des Institutions Constitutionelles (FDIC), had won only 34 percent of the votes in a general election; and two months later the king had resorted to sweeping repression against the opposition, arresting about 130 members of the UNFP, including twenty-one of its twenty-eight parliamentary deputies and the entire staff of its newspaper, *At-Tahrir*, on charges of plotting to overthrow the monarchy, and in a subsequent trial ten UNFP members, including the party's secretary-general, Mehdi Ben Barka, who had left the country and was tried in absentia, were sentenced to death. So it was in this context of political tension and repression at home that Hassan launched his border war. He hoped that a ground swell of war-time patriotism would diminish the political influence of the Algerian revolution among his own people and that by attacking now he could deal a hard blow against the Ben Bella government before it had the means to put up effective resistance. Not only was Ben Bella facing the awesome challenge of rebuilding Algeria's shattered economy, but his armed forces were still weak and faction-ridden and he was confronting a host of political challenges, of which the most important was an armed insurrection by the Berbers of Kabylia which broke out on September 29 under the leadership of Colonel Mohand Ou el-Hadj and Hocine Ait Ahmed.

The Kabyle rebellion almost certainly influenced Hassan's timing. However, instead of allowing the revolt to spread, the Moroccan advance toward Tindouf encouraged some of the rebels, including Mohand Ou el-Hadj, to join forces with Ben Bella to beat back the Moroccan threat. Moreover, as the Algerian population mobilized to resist the invasion and the Algerian army pursued its counteroffen-sive in the Figuig region, Hassan began to come under diplomatic pressure from his main allies, France and the United States, which wanted to woo Ben Bella and feared that continuation of the war might lead to intervention by Egypt and Cuba, both of which already had some troops in Algeria, or even the Soviet Union. The OAU, meanwhile, began a mediation attempt. Between October 16 and 25 Emperor Haile Selassie visited Morocco and Algeria in a bid to arrange a summit meeting between Hassan and Ben Bella. The two men finally met in Bamako, Mali, on October 29–30, and agreed that a cease-fire would take effect from midnight on November 1. They also accepted that a commission of Algerian, Moroccan, Ethiopian and Malian officers should be set up to establish a demilitarized zone, that Ethiopian and Malian officers should be posted there to guarantee its demilitarization and that the OAU should be requested to convene a conference of African foreign ministers as soon as possible so that an arbitration commission could be set up to study the frontier problem and propose a definitive solution. Fighting continued in the Figuig area after the November 2 deadline but the cease-fire finally took effect two days later. A fortnight later, on November 15–18, the OAU Council of Ministers met in extraordinary session and set up the proposed arbitration commission, appointing to it representatives of the governments of Ivory Coast, Ethiopia, Mali, Nigeria, Senegal and Tanzania; and the commission held its first sessions on December 3–5, 1963, in Abidjan and on January 23–27, 1964, in Bamako.

On February 20, 1964, Algeria and Morocco reached agreement on the extent of the demilitarized zone. Its terms were kept secret, but to the north of Tindouf both Moroccan and Algerian troops appear to have withdrawn about four and a half miles from the positions they had held before the outbreak of hostilities on

October 1, 1963. Hassi Beida, Tinjoub, Oum el-Achar and other points along the old French operational limit ended up in the demilitarized no man's land, while farther north, in the Figuig area, where the Algerians had made their main advance during the war, Algerian troops vacated Ich and the heights above Figuig on March 3, 1964.[37]

But the underlying border problem remained unresolved, despite repeated meetings of the arbitration commission between 1963 and 1967. Both the Moroccan and Algerian governments presented their views to the commission, but it was unable to produce an acceptable compromise. The Moroccan government produced old French maps to show that places like Hassi Beida and Tinjoub had once been considered part of Morocco; but these Moroccan claims, which could have been satisfied by minor border adjustments that might have proven acceptable to Algeria on their own terms, were confused with the much more extravagant claims still being made by Rabat radio to such places as Bechar and the Touat oases. The Ben Bella government was therefore not willing to open what looked like a pandora's box of territorial disputes and, having forced Morocco to abandon the territory it had seized in the autumn of 1963, it now confidently refused to make any concessions at all. It renounced the agreement signed by Ferhat Abbas and proclaimed its adherence to the principle of respect for the borders inherited by African states from the colonial powers which the OAU formally swore to uphold at a summit meeting in Cairo in July 1964 in order to prevent territorial claims undermining the continent's stability.

There was continuing tension between Morocco and Algeria after Ben Bella's downfall in the military coup led by Houari Boumedienne in June 1965. When the Algerian government decided in May 1966 to nationalize all mineral resources without making an exception for those in the disputed border regions, such as the iron ore at Gara Djebilet, near Tindouf, the Moroccan government was quick to protest; and during the same month the Moroccan press reported Algerian "provocations" at Oum el-Achar and Merkala, twenty miles to its south. As tension mounted, the OAU arbitration commission met once again, for its ninth session, on July 25 in Addis Ababa; but a fresh border incident occurred in the vicinity of Ain Chair, near Bechar, on January 22, 1967.[38] A month later, on February 28, Hassan wrote to the secretary-general of the UN, U Thant, to complain that Algeria was unwilling to respond positively to Morocco's territorial claims and was engaging in an arms buildup. Boumedienne responded by cementing ties with Mauritania; and on March 5, 1967, Mokhtar Ould Daddah arrived in Algiers on a state visit, decrying "Moroccan expansionism."[39]

Among the Moroccan political parties, the greatest enthusiasm for the claims to Mauritania and the Algerian Sahara continued to come from the Istiqlalians, who, after serving in Hassan's government until 1963, were in opposition for the following fourteen years. The small Parti Communiste Marocain (PCM), which was banned in February 1960 but succeeded in maintaining a semiclandestine organization and a legal press, embraced the Greater Morocco cause too throughout the sixties, apparently in the hope of proving its patriotic credentials to Moroccan nationalists, though it was uneasy about the October 1963 war.[40] However, the UNFP, which had been formed by the left wing of the Istiqlal Party in November 1959, rapidly took its distance from the Greater Morocco ideology. Its principal leader, Mehdi Ben Barka, described the government's territorial demands in May 1960 as an "operation of diversion and camouflage"; and on May 25, 1962, at its second congress, in Casablanca, the party declared that it supported the principles of independence and self-determination, would "not commit the blunder of making an exception for Mauritania" and would "take issue with Allal el-Fassi's annexationist propaganda."[41] The Union Marocaine du Travail (UMT), the main trade union federation, which had close links with the UNFP at this time, took a similar stance and refused, for example, to vote against Mauritania's admission to the International Labor Organization at an ILO conference in May 1961 while the Moroccan government delegation walked out of the proceedings in protest.[42]

During the border war with Algeria, moreover, Mehdi Ben Barka, who was then in exile, made an impassioned antiwar appeal. "This armed conflict which began several days ago in the Algerian-Moroccan borderlands," he declared on October 16, 1963, "constitutes a veritable betrayal not only of the dynamic Algerian Revolution but, in a general sense, of the whole Arab Revolution for liberty, socialism and union, and of the entire world movement of national liberation. It is my duty as spokesman of the UNFP and voice of the Moroccan people's aspirations to proclaim here that the Moroccan people will never approve entry into an armed conflict with their brothers, the Algerian people, whatever the pretexts prefabricated by governments for their particular and unavowable schemes."[43] Such pan-Arabist internationalism stood in the tradition established by the Moroccan nationalists who had worked to unify the liberation struggles against France in the Maghreb or who had attempted after Morocco's independence to assist the FLN or spread the anticolonial struggle into the Sahara. It was utterly at odds with the narrow chauvinism of the Greater Moroccans, whose ideology had been astutely appropriated by the monarchy to glorify the Alawite dynasty and divide the peoples of the Maghreb.

NOTES

1. Cited in Bertrand Fessard de Foucault, "La question du Sahara espagnol (I)," *Revue Française d'Etudes Politiques Africaines*, 10th Year, No. 119, November 1975, p. 78. Tangier, which had been placed under the combined administration of the main European powers following the Treaty of Fez and the Tangier Statute of 1923, was transferred to Moroccan administration in October 1956.

2. Cited in *ibid.*, p. 78.

3. Criticism of the Proposals Made by the Crown Prince, September 17, 1958, cited in Separate Opinion of Judge de Castro, *Western Sahara: Advisory Opinion of 16 October 1975* (International Court of Justice, The Hague, 1975), pp. 127–28.

4. Speech to the Beni Mestara, October 16, 1957, cited in *ibid.*, p. 119.

5. United Nations Document A/C.4/SR.670.

6. Françoise de La Serre, "Les revendications marocaines sur la Mauritanie," *Revue Française de Science Politique*, Vol. 16, No. 2, April 1966, pp. 320–21.

7. Cited in *Le Sahara occidental devant la Cour Internationale de Justice, Mémoire présenté par le Royaume du Maroc* (Moroccan Government, Rabat, 1975), p. 36.

8. *Chroniques Etrangères: Espagne* (La Documentation Française, Paris), No. 194, April 30, 1958, p. 16.

9. Rachid Lazrak, *Le contentieux territorial entre le Maroc et l'Espagne* (Dar el Kitab, Casablanca, 1974), p. 283. The commission included Allal el-Fassi, Abdelkebit el-Fassi, Mehdi Ben Barka (deputy secretary-general of the Istiqlal Party and president of the Consultative Assembly), Mahjoub Ben Sed-

dik (Union Marocaine du Travail), Hadj Mohammed Tetouani (representing the *ulema*), Mehdi Ouazzani (Union Marocaine du Travail), Fadil el-Mouquit (Parti Démocratique pour l'Indépendance), Ali Bou Aida (governor of the province of Tarfaya), Sheikh Mohammed Laghdaf Ould Sheikh Ma el-Ainin and Mohammed Basri (Conseil National de la Résistance).

10. Cited in La Serre, *loc. cit.*, p. 323.

11. They included the Bloc Démocratique du Gorgol, founded by Sarr Diawar, a former leader of the Entente, in 1956, the Union des Originaires de la Vallée du Fleuve, founded in 1957, and the Union Nationale Mauritanienne, which was created in 1959 and advocated integration with Mali.

12. Voice of the Moroccan Sahara, September 25, 1958, cited in La Serre, *loc. cit.*, p. 325.

13. After the dissolution of the Entente, one small party of predominantly Moor composition did continue to oppose the PRM. This was An-Nahda al-Wataniya al-Mauritaniya (Mauritanian National Awakening), which was founded in September 1958 by radical anti-imperialist youth led by Bouyagui Ould Abidine and Ahmed-Baba Miske. It was banned and its leaders jailed in 1959, but after independence the Nahda and other opposition groups fused with the PRM to form the Parti du Peuple Mauritanien (PPM) in 1961.

14. La Serre, *loc. cit.*, p. 326. Morocco had first informed the World Bank on March 17, 1958, that it opposed the provision of a loan to MIFERMA because of its claim to sovereignty in Mauritania. See also Fessard de Foucault, *loc. cit.*, p. 79.

15. *Ibid.*, pp. 79–80.

16. *Livre blanc sur la Mauritanie* (Ministère des Affaires Etrangères, Rabat, 1960).

17. *The Islamic Republic of Mauritania and the Kingdom of Morocco* (Mauritanian Government, Nouakchott, 1960).

18. Cited in La Serre, *loc. cit.*, p. 326.

19. Cited in Fessard de Foucault, *loc. cit.*, p. 80.

20. "Intervention de M. M'hamed Boucetta, chef de la délégation marocaine, devant le 1ère Commission, le 15 novembre 1960," *La Libération de la province mauritanienne et l'opinion internationale* (Ministère de l'Information et du Tourisme, Rabat, undated), p. 22. MICUMA planned to exploit the copper at Akjoujt, though mining did not begin there until 1971.

21. "Intervention de M. Boucetta, chef de le délégation marocaine, devant la 1ère Commission, le mission, le 16 novembre, 1960," *ibid.*, p. 32.

22. "Intervention de M Boucetta, chef de le délégation marocaine, devant la 1ère Commission, le 25 novembre 1960," *ibid.*, p. 33.

23. Morocco retaliated by recalling its ambassador from Tunis on November 24. Ambassadors were not exchanged again until 1964. For the Tunisian government's view of the Mauritanian question, see *Livre blanc sur le différend entre le gouvernement de la République tunisienne et le gouvernement chérifien du Maroc* (Secretaire d'Etat aux affaires etrangères, Tunis, 1961).

24. In fact, Soviet-bloc support for Morocco was qualified. The USSR backed Morocco's accusations that France had neocolonial designs on Mauritania but supported the idea of holding a referendum in Mauritania under UN auspices. This was opposed by Morocco. Cuba too supported the principle of self-determination, while accusing France of planning a phony independence for Mauritania. See "Intervention de M. Bisbe (Cuba)," *La Libération de la province mauritanienne et l'opinion internationale*, pp. 125–26.

25. "Conférence africaine de Casablanca, janvier 1961, Résolution sur la Mauritanie," *ibid.*, p. 133.

26. La Serre, *loc. cit.* p. 328.

27. *Ibid.*, p. 328.

28. *Note of September 19, 1963* (Ministry of Foreign Affairs, Rabat), Moroccan Government document 1222/CAB/MAE.

29. After the founding of its colony in northern Algeria in 1830, France had defined its borders with Morocco piecemeal as French authority was gradually extended southward. The first Franco-Moroccan border agreement, the convention of Lalla Marnia, was signed in 1845, one year after the French victory at Isly, and defined the frontier explicitly for only about 102 miles along the western limit of previous Ottoman influence from the Mediterranean to Teniet Sassi, the southern limit of the Tell and of the zone of unirrigated agriculture. Farther south no precise border demarcation was considered necessary since "the land cannot be tilled and can only be used as grazing grounds for the Arabs." Cited in Frank E. Trout, *Morocco's Saharan Frontiers* (Droz, Geneva, 1969), p. 19. However, a number of tribes and *ksours* (fortified desert villages) were defined as belonging to Morocco or Algeria, thus creating a kind of border zone.

In 1899 French troops moved south into the Sahara and began occupying the oases of the Touat,

Gourara and Tidikelt regions. Sultan Moulay Hassan, who had reestablished direct control of the oases in 1891–92 after a lapse in Moroccan administration since the end of the eighteenth century, was unable to halt the conquest. As the French extended their presence in the Sahara, a more precise definition of the Algerian-Moroccan frontier south of Teniet Sassi became necessary, in particular so that effective police action could be taken against the nomadic or seminomadic tribes that were resisting or raiding the French. So on July 20, 1901, France signed a protocol with the Moroccan government which defined a border zone, albeit still in tribal rather than strictly geographical terms, reaching as far south as the junction of the Oued Zousfana and the Oued Guir, the two tributaries of the Oued Saoura. However, French troops began advancing far to the west of the border defined in 1845 and 1901, to take action against tribes there who were raiding the French positions in Algeria or to prepare the way for the eventual imposition of French rule in Morocco itself. In December 1911, Maurice Varnier, who had been secretary-general of the French administration in Algeria, was appointed high commissioner in eastern Morocco, with a headquarters in Oujda, which French troops had occupied in 1907. In January 1912 he drafted a border line to demarcate his own "protectorate" in eastern Morocco from Algeria. The "Varnier Line," which was accepted by the French government and enacted by decree, coincided with the 1901 protocol's boundary between Teniet Sassi and Figuig, but farther south it enlarged French territory by several hundred square miles, notably by incorporating Bechar and Kenadza, which had already been occupied by French troops. It was for this reason that the Moroccan government only recognized the established Moroccan-Algerian border as far south as Figuig in its 1960 White Book. The Varnier Line tailed off into the Hammada of the Guir to the west of the Oued Guir. Beyond, no border demarcation was attempted, but as French troops from Algeria and Morocco gradually extended their presence southward, respective zones of police action were agreed at a series of "North African conferences" which began in 1923. Eventually, in 1930, the French government established the Confins Algéro-Marocains (CAM) for which there was a unified military structure involving troops from both Morocco and Algeria, under the ultimate authority of the resident-general in Morocco. Besides allowing coordinated military action against the dissident tribes in the southern Moroccan-Algerian borderlands, the CAM's creation obviated the need to define an exact frontier there. With the completion of the pacification of the Anti-Atlas and the Draa Valley and the occupation of Tindouf in 1934, the CAM were reorganised on May 1, 1934, The Draa came under the administration of the French protectorate in Morocco, while Tindouf was to be administered from Algeria. However, for military as opposed to strictly administrative matters, the CAM remained in being until February 18, 1956, less than a month before Morocco's independence. No formal border was established in the region of the CAM after the 1934 pacification. Administrative maps published by the Moroccan protectorate authorities between 1934 and 1953 showed a "presumed southern limit of Morocco" extending from the Hammada of the Guir (where the Varnier Line had ended) to the northeastern tip of Saguia el-Hamra.

In the late 1940s extensive mineral prospecting began in the CAM. In 1952–53 manganese was found in large quantities on the southern edge of the Hammada of the Guir and in 1953 huge iron deposits were discovered at Gara Djebilet, near Tindouf. In January 1954 plans were made for oil exploration near Tindouf. Meanwhile, however, the upsurge of nationalist agitation in Morocco after the exiling of the sultan in 1953 had aroused fears in Paris that the protectorate might have to be abandoned; and so, in order to assure French access to the minerals in the Saharan border regions, the protectorate authorities decided to shift Morocco's "presumed" southern border northward in 1953 to what came to be known as the "Trinquet Line," Trinquet having been the CAM's commander in the thirties. This more or less took the frontier to the escarpment of the Hammada of the Draa. However, when Morocco became independent, the French authorities in Algeria decided to move troops still farther north, beyond the Trinquet Line, to a string of advance posts which constituted a continuous police line, or "operational limit," stretching from Teniet Ariatne on the Varnier Line, along the western edge of the Hammada of the Guir, then along the northern edge of the Kem-Kem plateau and finally along the course of the lower Draa from near M'hamid to the 11th meridian west of Paris, the eastern limit of Spanish Southern Morocco. The French government agreed in March 1956 to establish a joint commission with the Moroccan government to fix the Algerian-Moroccan border definitively, but this never met, apparently because of France's negative reaction to the Moroccan government's insistence that the commission should also examine its claim to Mauritania. The 1956 police line therefore became Morocco's *de facto* but unrecognized southeastern border.

　　30. Cited in E. Méric, "Le conflit algéro-marocain," *Revue Française de Science Politique*, Vol. 15, 1965, No. 4, p. 744.

　　31. Ferhat Abbas' intention in signing the July 6, 1961, agreement with Morocco is clearly in-

dicated in an article entitled "Notre Sahara," which was published alongside the text of the agreement in the FLN's organ *El Moudjahid* on July 19, 1961. See Méric, *loc. cit.*, pp. 744–46.

32. Gérard Chaliand and Juliette Minces, *L'Algéerie indépendante* (François Maspero, Paris, 1972), p. 23.

33. Méric, *loc. cit.*, pp. 747–48.

34. Hassan II, *Le défi* (Albin Michel, Paris, 1976), p. 91.

35. Interview with Mohammed Harbi, *Jeune Afrique*, No. 881, November 25, 1977.

36. See Negib Bouderbala, "Aspects du problème agraire au Maroc," *Bulletin Economique et Social du Maroc*, August 1974, p. 204. The remaining *colon* farmland was not nationalized until nine years later, in 1972, by which time, however, most foreign-owned farms had already been sold to large private Moroccan landholders.

37. Trout, *op. cit.*, p. 427.

38. *Ibid.*, p. 430; Abdallah Laroui, *L'Algérie et le Sahara marocain* (Serar, Casablanca, 1976), p. 42.

39. *Ibid.*, p. 43.

40. The PCM's endorsement of the Istiqlal Party's territorial demands may ironically be contrasted with its initial opposition, in 1943–45, to the Istiqlal Party's campaign for Moroccan independence, which the PCM, aping the French Communist Party, considered to be a diversion from the fight against fascism.

41. La Serre, *loc. cit.*, p. 329.

42. *Ibid.*, p. 329.

43. The full text of Ben Barka's appeal of October 16, 1963, is published in Mehdi Ben Barka, *Option révolutionnaire au Maroc, suivi de Ecrits Politiques 1960-1965* (François Maspero, Paris, 1966), pp. 157–59.

9

Greater Mauritania

*I cannot help evoking the innumerable ties
which unite us: we bear the same names, we
speak the same language, we conserve the same
noble traditions, we honor the same religious
leaders, graze our herds on the same pastures,
give water to them at the same wells. In a word
we are referring to that same desert civilization
of which we are so justly proud. So I invite our
brothers of Spanish Sahara to dream of this
great economic and spiritual Mauritania.*

—Mokhtar Ould Daddah, Atar, July 1 1957[1]

I T WAS IN THESE CHALLENGING WORDS that a Mauritanian claim to Western
Sahara was first staked in 1957. Mokhtar Ould Daddah was
speaking six weeks after being sworn into office as vice-president—under the
presidency of the French governor—of Mauritania's first Council of Government,
on May 21. He was appealing to the tribes of the remote desert expanses of
Western Sahara and northern Mauritania to withdraw their support from the
Moroccan-led Army of Liberation, whose attacks in northern Mauritania endangered both France's experiment in internal self-government and MIFERMA's
plans for massive investment near Zouerate. "To these Reguibat es-Sahel and
esh-Sharg, nomads of the Saguia el-Hamra and the Río, Tekna, Arosien, Oulad
Tidrarin, Oulad Delim and Ahel Sheikh Ma el-Ainin, we say: Let us be united

and no longer allow ourselves to be divided by foreigners." Rather than follow these "foreigners," the Moroccan leaders of the Army of Liberation who regarded him as a puppet of French colonialism, Mokhtar Ould Daddah suggested that these tribes should join their fellow *beidan* to the south, Hassaniya-speaking nomads like themselves, in creating a "new Mauritania" which, with French aid, would soon join the "ranks of modern nations." This would unite "all the Moors, from the Atlantic to the Azaouad, and from the Draa to the banks of the Senegal." The border between Spanish-ruled Sahara and Mauritania was artificial, a "frontier which we want to see disappear from our hearts and then erased from the maps." Indeed, by placing the natural northern frontier of Greater Mauritania at the Oued Draa, Mokhtar Ould Daddah was laying claim not just to Saguia el-Hamra and Río de Oro, but also to Spanish Southern Morocco, which Spain was to hand over to the Rabat authorities nine months later but which, as the pastures of the Tekna nomads, was, in his view, very much part of the *trab el-beidan*. Mauritanians were not only becoming "conscious of belonging to the same community from the Atlantic to the Soudan," but "this solidarity extends beyond our frontiers, it encompasses the Moor populations of the Spanish Sahara and the Moroccan borders."[2]

A few months later, after the grim experience of Operation Ouragan, many of the Reguibat heeded Mokhtar Ould Daddah's advice and gave themselves up at the French posts in northern Mauritania. However, he faced a new challenge, of a political or diplomatic rather than military nature, after Mohammed V's endorsement of the Greater Moroccans' Saharan claims in his speech at M'hamid in February 1958. As Mauritania advanced toward independence, its architects had to justify its very right to existence, in the UN, to the Arab states, even to the World Bank. They argued that the *beidan* were a distinct people with their own language, Hassaniya, and a unique culture born of their pastoral nomadic society. By such criteria, the *qabael* of Spanish Sahara belonged also to this desert civilization; their zones of migration were merely part of the *trab el-beidan*. Conversely, if Morocco had a valid claim to Spanish Sahara, Mokhtar Ould Daddah knew, the identical premises of its claim to Mauritania could not be refuted. The idea that the Ahel es-Sahel might develop a national identity of their own and proceed eventually to independence occurred to neither Moroccans, Mauritanians, Spaniards nor even the Western Saharans themselves in the late fifties or early sixties.

Mokhtar Ould Daddah had another very practical reason to rebuff the Moroccan claim to Western Sahara. If the Rabat government succeeded in taking control there, Mauritania would have 980 miles of common border with its archenemy. The border would not, of course, be recognized by the Moroccan government, and it would be in remote desert terrain and impossible to patrol effectively. Moreover, the iron mines near Zouerate, which began production in 1963 and were accounting for about 85 percent of Mauritania's total export earnings by the mid-sixties, were sited less than thirty miles from this border, while the 419-mile railway line which was built to evacuate the ore from the mines to the coast ran alongside it, for most of the way at a distance of only about five miles, and ended at the port of Nouadhibou, which was right on the Western Saharan border, on the Cape Blanc peninsula. If Morocco annexed Western Sahara, it could practically hold the Mauritanian government to ransom.

A perfectly satisfactory arrangement, from Nouakchott's standpoint, was to uphold the *status quo*. As a Spanish colony, Western Sahara was a convenient buffer zone that kept the Moroccans at arm's length. Of course, this was never espoused as official policy. Western Sahara, it was said, was an integral part of Mauritania and Spain should begin negotiations on its transfer to Mauritanian administration. Addressing the United Nations General Assembly on October 14, 1963, Mokhtar Ould Daddah spoke of his hope of establishing, after talks with Spain, "our sovereignty over a vast part of our national territory which is still not liberated."[3] But privately the Spanish presence was accepted as a convenient military shield. Nouakchott's principal concern was to ensure that Madrid did not bow to Moroccan lobbying and come to terms with Rabat behind its back.[4] However, Mokhtar Ould Daddah was repeatedly reassured by the Spanish government that this would not happen, notably during a tête-à-tête with Fernando María Castiella when the veteran Spanish foreign minister visited Nouakchott on March 7–9, 1966.[5] Spanish-Mauritanian relations were reinforced, moreover, by Spanish aid for Mauritania's desperately backward economy, and in particular by Spanish investment from 1964 in the fishing industry at Nouadhibou, which one Spanish writer frankly described as a gift "to keep the Mauritanians' mouths shut."[6]

Paradoxical though it may seem, there were actually three distinct Mauritanian "policies" on Western Sahara during the sixties. There was the official claim to the territory; there was the quiet acceptance of the *status quo* to keep Morocco at bay; and from 1966, side by side with these, there was a third policy of support for self-determination, a policy destined for the attention of diplomats at the United Nations, where the General Assembly adopted its first resolution on Western Sahara in 1965.[7] In fact, all these apparently contradictory policies had the same *raison d'être*, the need to keep Morocco out of Western Sahara and so away from Mauritania's existing borders.

From 1963, when the UN's special committee on decolonization, the Committee of 24, began to examine the Western Saharan problem, the overriding concern of the Mauritanian delegation at the UN was to rebuff the attempts of Dey Ould Sidi Baba, the Moroccan permanent representative, to obtain UN recognition of its claim to the territory. An obvious way to prevent such a setback was to embrace the doctrine of self-determination, which had become the hallmark of the UN's approach to decolonization. At a special session of the Committee of 24 in Addis Ababa in August 1966, the Mauritanian representative mocked Morocco's claim to Western Sahara as being "as ridiculous as those which England might now make against France on the pretext that, at the time of Joan of Arc, Paris and a large part of France had been occupied by the English," and averred that, while historically part of Mauritania, Western Sahara "should be completely independent," of Morocco as well as Spain.[8] At a later session of the Committee of 24, held in New York on November 18, the Mauritanian delegate argued that "although the Sahara is an integral part of Mauritania, the right of its inhabitants to choose their future, without their being converted into tools of the internal problems of other countries, must be defended.''[9] Mauritania then voted on December 20, 1966, in favor of the first General Assembly resolution calling on Spain to allow a referendum to be held in Western Sahara under UN auspices. It voted for all six of the almost identical General Assembly resolutions which followed between 1967 and 1973. Mokhtar Ould Daddah may well have believed that the Western Saharans would have opted to join Mauritania in a free plebiscite. "If a referendum of self-determination had been faithfully organized," he was to claim some years later, in 1976, ''the Saharawis, for all sorts of reasons, could only have come out in favor of reunification.''[10] This might have been true in the early sixties; but a strong sense of Saharawi nationalism took root a decade later. In any event, the referendum was never held.

NOTES

1. "Discours prononcé par Maître Moktar Ould Daddah, vice-président du Conseil du Gouvernement de la Mauritanie, à Atar, le 1er juillet, 1957," in Moktar Ould Daddah, *Discours et interventions* (Nouakchott, 1966), p. 10.

2. *Ibid.*, pp. 9–11.

3. Bertrand Fessard de Foucault, "La question du Sahara espagnol (II)," *Revue Française d'Etudes Politiques Africaines*, 10th Year, No. 120, December 1975, p. 75.

4. William Eagleton, "The Islamic Republic of Mauritania," *The Middle East Journal*, Vol. 19, No. 1, Winter 1965, p. 52.

5. Fessard de Foucault, *loc. cit.*, p. 76.

6. Emilio Menéndez del Valle, *Sahara español: una descolonización tardía* (Editorial Cuadernos para el Diálogo, Madrid, 1975), p.43. The Spanish government's Instituto Nacional de Industria (INI) invested two hundred million ouguiyas in the industries Mauritaniennes de Pêche (IMAPEC), whose complex at Nouadhibou opened in 1970 with a capacity to process 105,000 tons of fish a year. However, actual output has been far lower because of marketing difficulties and inadequate landings of fish. See "Les industries existantes et les projects," *Europe-Outremer*, 55th Year, No. 574, November 1977, p. 35.

7. See Chapter 10.

8. Thomas M. Franck, "The Stealing of the Sahara," *American Journal of International Law*, Vol. 70, No. 4, October 1976, p. 702.

9. *ABC* (Madrid), November 19, 1966.

10. "Synthèse de la communication du Secrétaire Général du Parti devant le Conseil National du Parti du Peuple Mauritanien (29–30–31 janvier 1976)," in *1975-76, La réunification de la patrie: un objectif sacré pour le peuple mauritanien* (Ministère d'Etat à l'Orientation Nationale, Nouakchott, 1976), p. 7.

10

At the United Nations

HE UNITED NATIONS first began to turn its attention to Western Sahara in
the early 1960s. Most of the British and French colonies in Africa had already achieved independence or were on the verge of doing so; but Spain, like Portugal, had no intention of preparing its colonies for self-rule.

The UN Charter, to which Spain had adhered in 1955, obliged member states with colonies "to develop self-government, to take account of the political aspirations of the peoples, and to assist them in the progressive development of their free political institutions."[1] In 1960 the UN General Assembly had gone a step further to proclaim that "all peoples have the right to self-determination" in a Declaration on the Granting of Independence to Colonial Countries and Peoples, often better known as Resolution 1514. "Immediate steps," it required, "shall be taken, in Trust and Non-Self-Governing Territories or all other territories which have not yet attained independence, to transfer all powers to the peoples of those territories, without any conditions or reservations, in accordance with their freely expressed will and desire, without any distinctions as to race, creed or colour, in order to enable them to enjoy complete independence and freedom."[2] A year later, the General Assembly set up a special watchdog committee, known as the Committee of 24, to monitor progress toward decolonization.[3] In 1963 Western Sahara was included on the UN's list of territories to which Resolution 1514 applied, and in October 1964 the Committee of 24 adopted its first resolution on Western Sahara and Ifni, lamenting Spain's delay in implementing the provisions of Resolution 1514 and urging it to take immediate measures to do so.[4]

The General Assembly followed suit a year later, on December 16, 1965. By an overwhelming majority of 100 to 2 (Spain and its Iberian colonial ally, Portugal), with four abstentions (the U.S., Britain, France and South Africa), the General Assembly adopted its first resolution on Western Sahara and Ifni, endorsing the Committee of 24's resolution and requesting "the Government of Spain, as the administering power, to take all necessary measures for the liberation of the Territories of Ifni and Spanish Sahara from colonial domination and, to this end, to enter into negotiations on problems relating to sovereignty presented by these two territories."[5]

The resolution was ambiguous in that it failed to indicate either the nature of the "problems relating to sovereignty" or the parties with whom Spain was supposed to "enter into negotiations" about them; but the implication was that Spain should hold talks with Morocco about Ifni and with both Morocco and Mauritania about Western Sahara in view of their rival claims to the territory. Moreover, there was a more fundamental ambiguity in Resolution 1514, which, besides proclaiming the right of self-determination, also stated that "any attempt aimed at the partial or total disruption of the national unity and the territorial integrity of a country is incompatible with the purposes and principles of the Charter of the United Nations."[6] Thus, Morocco argued that Spanish occupation of Ifni and Western Sahara violated its territorial integrity and national unity. Resolution 1514 had been complemented in 1960 by another resolution, number 1541, which stated that a colonial territory's decolonization need not involve its emergence as a sovereign independent state but could, instead, be achieved by its "free association" or "integration" with an independent state, and it was this latter option which Morocco proposed for both Ifni and Western Sahara. However, Resolution 1541 added that a colony's boundaries could only be altered if that was what its inhabitants wanted.[7] Indeed, it had become a standard practice by the early sixties for the UN to organize or monitor elections or plebiscites in colonies where, on the eve of the colonial power's withdrawal, there was an element of doubt about their inhabitants' real desires. Examples were the UN-supervised plebiscites that led to the merger of British Togoland with Ghana in 1956, the merger of British-ruled Northern Cameroons with Nigeria in 1959 and of Southern Cameroons with formerly French Cameroun in 1961, the division of Belgian Ruanda-Urundi into two independent states in 1961, and the association between Western Samoa and New Zealand in 1962.[8]

There clearly was doubt about the wishes of the inhabitants of Western Sahara, if only because both Morocco and Mauritania had conflicting claims to the territory. By contrast, there was no evidence that the population of Ifni considered themselves anything other than Moroccan or would not wish to join Morocco. At the special session of the Committee of 24 held in Addis Ababa in June 1966, both the Moroccan and Mauritanian delegations upheld their countries' claims to Western Sahara but accepted that its inhabitants should be entitled to choose their destiny.[9] Accordingly, on December 20, 1966, the General Assembly adopted a resolution, by 105 votes to 2 (Spain and Portugal), with 9 abstentions, which explicitly distinguished the procedures to be followed in the decolonization of Western Sahara from those applicable to Ifni. While requesting Spain to "determine with the Government of Morocco, bearing in mind the aspirations of the indigenous population, procedures for the transfer of powers" in Ifni, the resolution recommended a very different approach to the Western Saharan problem. Spain was asked "to determine at the earliest possible date, in conformity with the aspirations of the indigenous people of Spanish Sahara and in consultation with the Governments of Mauritania and Morocco and any other interested party, the procedures for the holding of a referendum under United Nations auspices with a view to enabling the indigenous population of the Territory to exercise freely its right to self-determination.'' In order to create a favorable climate for such a referendum, Spain was asked to permit the return of all refugees, ensure that only indigenous Western Saharans could vote, and "provide all the necessary facilities to a United Nations mission so that it may be able to participate actively in the organization and holding of the referendum.'' Finally, the secretary-general of the UN was asked to appoint a special mission "for the purpose of recommending practical steps for the full implementation of the relevant resolutions of the General Assembly, and in particular for determining the extent of United Nations participation in the preparation and supervision of the referendum.''[10] Between 1967 and 1973 the General Assembly adopted six more resolutions, all of which repeated the proposal of a referendum.[11] From 1969, when Ifni was returned to Morocco, the resolutions concerned Western Sahara alone.

Spain refused to allow a UN special mission to visit Western Sahara until 1975 and never permitted the UN to hold a referendum. As Spain stalled, so the resolutions adopted in the General Assembly became tougher in tone. For example, Resolution 2711, adopted in December 1970, regretted the bloody events in El-Ayoun the previous June when the Foreign Legion fired on unarmed Saharawi demonstrators, and for the first time it invited "all States to refrain from making investments in the Territory.''[12] Resolution 2983, adopted by the General Assembly in December 1972, deplored Spain's failure to provide sufficiently clear information on the conditions and timetable for decolonization and for the first time explicitly recognized the Western Saharans' right to independence, though this had been implicit in the previous affirmations of their right to self-determination. The resolution expressed "its solidarity with, and support for, the people of the Sahara in the struggle they are waging in order to exercise their right to self-determination and independence" and requested "all States to give them all necessary moral and material assistance in that struggle" and to "refrain from helping to perpetuate the colonial situation in the Territory by means by investments.''[13]

In the late sixties the Organization of African Unity too began to express concern about Spain's uncompromising brand of colonialism in the Sahara, and like the UN it ended up supporting the idea of a referendum to allow the Western Saharans to determine their future freely. Besides declaring their "absolute dedication to the total emancipation of the African territories which are still dependent,'' the African states which signed the OAU's founding charter in Addis Ababa on May 25, 1963, feared that territorial claims would engender conflict and destabilize African states and so they included in the charter a commitment to "respect for the sovereignty and territorial integrity of each state and for its inalienable right to independent existence.''[14] The Moroccan government, which knew that this could be interpreted as a ban on the kind of claims it had made to Mauritania and parts of Algeria, delayed four months before signing the charter and, when it finally did so, on September 19, 1963, felt it advisable to inform the OAU's chairman, Emperor Haile Selassie, that its signature did not imply recognition of "*faits accomplis*" or renunciation of its struggle to achieve its "rights." To the contrary, Morocco argued, its own territorial integrity would remain compromised so long as its demands had not been satisfied. However, the charter's implicit ban on frontier disputes was made explicit in a resolution adopted by the OAU's first ordinary summit, which was held in Cairo on July 17–21, 1964. This described inter-African border disputes as a potentially dangerous source of conflict which could easily be exploited by outside powers. It noted that the frontiers inherited from colonialism at the moment of their independence were a "tangible reality" and concluded by pledging all OAU member states to "respect the frontiers existing at the moment when they acceded to independence."[15] This principle was then incorporated into a declaration known as the Proclamation of Cairo, though it was accompanied by a rider that portions of territory which had been amputated by colonial powers to serve their interests "must return to the country which accedes to independence."[16] There was no reason to question the application of this rider to the Ifni case; but with respect to Western Sahara, where there were conflicting territorial claims, the OAU endorsed the approach adopted by the UN. In 1969 and 1970 the OAU Council of Ministers adopted resolutions which simply urged Spain to implement the UN resolutions on Western Sahara.[17] By 1972, however, it was spelling out its policy on the territory in greater detail, explicitly endorsing the UN's calls for a referendum. At its nineteenth ordinary session, held in Rabat on June 5–19, 1972, the Council of Ministers called on Spain "to create a free and democratic atmosphere in which the people of that territory can exercise their right to self-determination and independence" and requested African states "to intensify their efforts vis-a-vis the Spanish Government to induce it to implement Resolution 2711 of the UN General Assembly and, in particular, its provisions relating to the holding, as soon as possible, of a referendum designed to enable the population of the Sahara under Spanish domination to freely exercise their right to self-determination, in accordance with the principles of the United Nations Charter, under the auspices and with the full guarantees of that international organization."[18] A similar resolution was adopted a year later by a session of the Council of Ministers in Addis Ababa; and the UN resolutions were additionally endorsed by both the nonaligned movement, at the nonaligned states' fourth summit, held in Algiers on September 5–9, 1973, and the world's Muslim states, at the fifth Islamic summit, held in Kuala Lumpur, Malaysia, on June 21–25, 1974.[19] However, all of these resolutions were to be ignored by Spain when, in November 1975, it finally decided to hand over Western Sahara to Morocco and Mauritania without first allowing a referendum.

NOTES

1. UN Charter, Article 73(b).
2. UN General Assembly (UNGA) Resolution 1514, *General Assembly Official Records (GAOR)*, 15th Session, Supplement 16, UN Document A/4864 (1960), pp. 66–67.
3. The committee's official title is the Special Committee on the Situation with Regard to the Implementation of the Declaration on the Granting of Independence to Colonial Countries and Peoples.
4. *GAOR*, 19th Session, Annex No. 8 (Part I), UN Document A/5800/Rev. 1 (1964), pp. 290–91.
5. UNGA Resolution 2072, December 16, 1965, *GAOR*, 20th Session, Supplement 14, UN Document A/6014, pp. 59–60.

6. UNGA Resolution 1514, *loc. cit.*, pp. 66–67.

7. UNGA Resolution 1541, *GAOR*, Supplement 16, UN Document A/4684 (1960), pp. 29–30.

8. Thomas M. Franck and Paul Hoffman, "The Right of Self-Determination in Very Small Places," *New York University Journal of International Law and Politics*, Vol. 8, No. 4, Winter 1976, p. 336.

9. "The Question of Western Sahara at the United Nations," *Decolonization* (UN Department of Political Affairs, Trusteeship and Decolonization, New York), No. 17, October 1980, p. 5.

10. UNGA Resolution 2229, December 20, 1966, *GAOR*, 21st Session, Supplement 16, UN Document A/6316 (1966), pp. 72–73.

11. See UNGA Resolution 2354, December 19, 1967, *GAOR*, 22nd Session, Supplement 16, UN Document A/6716 (1967), pp. 53–54; UNGA Resolution 2428, December 16, 1968, *GAOR*, 23rd Session, Supplement 18, UN Document A/7218 (1968), pp. 63–64; UNGA Resolution 2591, December 16, 1969, *GAOR*, 24th Session, Supplement 30, UN Document A/7630 (1969), pp. 73–74; UNGA Resolution 2711, December 14, 1970, *GAOR*, 25th Session, Supplement 28th UN Document A/8028 (1970), pp. 100–101; UNGA Resolution 2983, December 14, 1972, *GAOR*, 27th Session, Supplement 30, UN Document A/8730, pp. 84–85; and UNGA Resolution 3162, December 14, 1973, *GAOR*, 28th Session, Supplement 30, UN Document A/9030 (1973), pp. 110–11.

12. See supra Note 11.

13. See supra Note 11. Resolution 3162, adopted by the General Assembly on December 14, 1973, likewise explicitly recognized the Western Saharan people's right to independence by inviting Spain "to determine, in consultation with the Governments of Mauritania and Morocco and any other interested party, the procedures for the holding of a referendum under United Nations auspices to enable the indigenous population of the Sahara to exercise freely its right to self-determination and independence."

14. Charter of the Organization of African Unity, Article 3, paragraph 3.

15. Resolution 16, OAU Assembly of Heads of State and Government, Cairo, July 17–21, 1964.

16. Proclamation of Cairo, OAU Assembly of Heads of State and Government, Cairo, October 10, 1964, Article 5, paragraph 2. The rules of territorial integrity and the sanctity of colonial borders could be mutually contradictory under certain circumstances. Moreover, they could conflict with the right of self-determination, since the exercise of this democratic right, which was first enunciated in the eighteenth century, implies the right to secession from a state, thereby altering its territory and borders. However, the idea of secession, for example by ethnic minorities, was anathema to the rulers of the multi-ethnic and often unstable states which achieved independence in Africa.

17. See Resolution 206, on Decolonization and Apartheid, OAU Council of Ministers, 13th Ordinary Session, Addis Ababa, August 27–September 6, 1969; Resolution 209, on Decolonization and Apartheid, OAU Council of Ministers, 14th Ordinary Session, Addis Ababa, February 27–March 6, 1970; and Resolution 234, on Decolonization, OAU Council of Ministers, 15th Ordinary Session, Addis Ababa, August 25–31, 1970.

18. Resolution 272, on the So-Called Spanish Sahara, OAU Council of Ministers, 19th Ordinary Session, Rabat, June 5–19, 1972.

19. Resolution 301, on the Sahara under Spanish Domination, OAU Council of Ministers, 21st Ordinary Session, Addis Ababa, May 17–24, 1973. The fourth nonaligned summit conference, held in Algiers on September 5–9, 1973, reaffirmed "its unshakable attachment to the principle of self-determination and its concern to see it applied under conditions that would ensure to the inhabitants of the Sahara under Spanish domination the free and authentic expression of their will, in accordance with the relevant United Nations resolutions regarding this territory." Resolution on the Sahara under Spanish Domination, Fourth Conference of Heads of State and Government of Non-Aligned Countries, Algiers, September 5–9, 1973, published in *Western Sahara and the Struggle of the Saharaoui People for Self-Determination* (International League for the Rights and Liberation of Peoples, Rome), p. 110. The fifth Islamic summit, held in Kualur Lumpur on June 21–25, 1974, asked Western Sahara's neighboring countries "to pursue their consultations, to unite and to intensify their efforts to obtain the application of Resolution Number 3162 of the 28th General Assembly of the United Nations, notably regarding the arrangements for the organization as soon as possible of a referendum so as to allow the indigenous populations to express themselves in full freedom, in accordance with the Charter of the United Nations, under the auspices and guarantee of the international organization." *Reuters*, dispatch from Kuala Lumpur, June 27, 1974.

11

Hassan's Détente

*Spain and Morocco are the two pillars of
Hercules which guard the entrance to the
Mediterranean. It is upon our two countries
that, in large part, the destiny of the free world
depends.*

—King Hassan II, July 6, 1963

MOROCCO'S RELATIONS WITH SPAIN remained fraught until 1962. Besides the territorial disputes over Western Sahara, Ifni and the presidios of Ceuto and Melilla, there was tension about fishing rights, especially after Morocco decided to extend its fishing limit from six to twelve miles in June 1962. Spain responded by sending warships to Ceuta and Melilla to protect the Spanish fishing fleet off northern Morocco while farther south several Spanish boats were interned in Agadir for fishing illegally in Moroccan waters.[1]

However, Spain had not faced any serious military threat in Western Sahara since Operation Ouragan and the disbanding of the Army of Liberation by the FAR at the end of the fifties. Moreover, since his ascent to the throne in 1961, King Hassan II had wanted to set relations with Spain on a new, cooperative footing. Ideologically he had much in common with the Spanish dictator, General Franco; and, having personally supervised the disbanding of the remnants of the Army of Liberation when he was crown prince and chief-of-staff of the FAR, he had no intention of allowing an anti-Spanish guerrilla movement to be re-created on Moroccan territory. Moreover, as tension with revolutionary Algeria grew in 1962–63 and political friction sharpened at home, culminating in the mass arrests of UNFP leaders and activists in July 1963, he had no interest whatever in the presence of armed irregulars in his country or conflict on another front with Spain.[2] For its part, the Franco regime had nothing to gain from seeing its southern neighbor succumb to the radical nationalism promoted by Nasser, Ben Bella and the UNFP and so did not hesitate to proffer political solidarity with Morocco's conservative monarchy. At the same time it dangled an attractive economic carrot that Hassan readily welcomed.

So, though the claim to Western Sahara remained official Moroccan policy, nothing was done to give Madrid real cause for alarm until quite different circumstances in 1974. Economic and political collaboration, rather than the pursuit of the traditional territorial claims, became the hallmark of the king's relations with Madrid, much to the chagrin of Moroccan nationalists.

Ironically, however, the pragmatic détente with Spain began when the Istiqlal Party was still represented in the Moroccan government and an Istiqlalian leader, Ahmed Balafrej, was foreign minister. On September 14, 1962, Balafrej declared that the Moroccan government hoped that "His Majesty King Hassan II and General Franco would rapidly be able to meet each other in order to clear up the atmosphere and allow the two countries' diplomats to resolve the generally minor pendings problems."[3] The fishing boats detained at Agadir were immediately released; and Balafrej then visited Madrid on October 24-28, meeting Franco, his foreign minister, Fernando María Castiella, and the vice-president of the Spanish government, Captain-General Muñoz Grandes. Three weeks later, on November 16-22, Muñoz Grandes paid a return visit to Morocco to continue the talks, with Balafrej and the king, who decorated the general with the Alawite Military Order of the Throne, pressed him to arrange a summit meeting with Franco "here or in Spain" and recalled the help given the fascists by Moroccan soldiers during the Spanish civil war.[4] At the end of November, the Moroccan minister of the interior, Ahmed Reda Guedira, explained that Morocco would henceforth try to resolve its territorial disputes with Spain through diplomatic channels. "We are not renouncing any of our prerogatives in this matter, that goes without saying; but we do not think that the sound of gunfire is indispensable to back up well-founded demands."[5]

The departure of the Istiqlalian ministers from Hassan's government in January 1963 allowed Hassan to accelerate the new course.[6] The king's plans for a summit meeting with Franco were finalized by his information minister, Abdelhadi Boutaleb, during a visit to Madrid on May 24-29; and six weeks later, on July 6, Hassan finally flew into Madrid's Barajas Airport, to be greeted by a twenty-one-gun salute and an embrace from the *caudillo*. The two rulers talked privately for four hours in the airport terminal building, breaking only briefly for a formal luncheon. This was the first Spanish-Moroccan summit since Mohammed V's visit to Madrid in April 1956 to negotiate the termination of Spain's protectorate in northern Morocco. No details of what was said were released to the press, but a joint communiqué revealed that Franco and Hassan had resolved to "study all the problems of mutual interest with a view to finding solutions which can serve as a basis for subsequent agreements"; and the "spirit of Barajas," as Castiella described the new deétente a year later on July 3, 1964, was to set the tone of Hassan's relations with Franco for more than a decade.[7]

During the summer of 1963 the Francoists made common cause with the king as he confronted the UNFP. "We Spaniards," remarked the Spanish information minister, Manuel Fraga Iribarne, in Rabat on July 11, "will never be able to forget that numerous Moroccan friends helped us in our struggle against communism and I am sure that on their side numerous Moroccans remember the attitude of Spain and its *caudillo* at certain difficult moments of recent history. In the years to come these relations should be based on the same spirit, in the face of certain aggressors who are preparing for the subversion of all spiritual and traditional values."[8] The Francoist press chimed in. "The worst that could befall Europe," warned the Madrid daily *ABC* on July 13, "would be the installation of an African Castroism on the other shore of the Mediterranean."

Seven years later, on February 5, 1970, the Franco regime was to render political services to Hassan in a more tangible way by extraditing to Morocco two UNFP militants, Mohammed Ajar and Ahmed Benjelloun, who had fled to Spain as refugees. Ajar was sentenced to death on September 17, 1971, at the end of a show trial of 193 socialist oppositionists accused of plotting to overthrow the monarchy, though he was subsequently amnestied by the king the following May.[9]

Spain began offering substantial economic aid to the Hassan regime shortly after the Barajas summit. "I am sure that there are vast domains in which Morocco and Spain can work together," suggested the Spanish industry minister, Gregorio López Bravo, in Casablanca on March 2, 1964.[10] In particular, López Bravo proposed Spanish aid for the Moroccan chemical and pharmaceutical, textile, iron and steel industries. Hassan and his minister for economic affairs, Driss Slaoui, were impressed; and a few days later, on March 9–12, during a visit to Spain, the Moroccan information minister, Ahmed Alaoui, proposed that a tunnel or bridge be built across the Straits of Gibraltar.[11] The following summer, on June 2, a trade agreement was signed.[12]

Meanwhile, Guedira, who had succeeded Balafrej as foreign minister, had visited Spain in June 1964; Castiella reciprocated by arriving in Morocco in July. The following year, on February 12, Hassan was to converse directly with Franco again during a hunting expedition in the Sierra Morena in Andalucía; and in February 1966 he was to appoint a former general in the Spanish army who was a personal friend of Franco, Lieutenant-General Mohammed Ben Ameziane, as his ambassador to Spain.[13]

The Moroccan writer Rachid Lazrak has observed that the Spanish-Moroccan negotiations on territorial issues during the decade after Barajas were conducted almost entirely by Franco and Hassan themselves, in private conversations or by way of messages delivered by special envoys.[14] No direct pressure was brought to bear on Spain by Morocco. For example, the claim to Ceuta and Melilla was not brought before the UN, even though from 1963 Spain continually raised the analogous problem of Gibraltar at the UN; and both cities continued to receive their water supplies from Morocco.[15] The claims to Ifni and Western Sahara were voiced sporadically in diplomatic forums like the UN, but no attempt was made to organize an anti-Spanish struggle by their inhabitants, let alone to apply military pressure.

During the sixties and early seventies Hassan was much criticized by Moroccan nationalists for putting the struggle against Spain on ice. His cordiality with Franco seemed indefensible to the Istiqlal Party, the UNFP and the semi-clandestine PCM alike. The UNFP, which won the support of many veterans of the Army of Liberation after its split from the Istiqlal Party, was particularly scathing of royal policy. It regarded the dissolution of the Army of Liberation by the FAR as a betrayal of the anticolonial struggle, and though it had defended Mauritania's right to self-determination and opposed the war with Algeria in 1963, it assumed, like the Istiqlal Party and the PCM, that Western Sahara was as Moroccan as the presidios or Ifni, if only because the Saharawis had fought in the Moroccan-led Army of Liberation.

The king's secret diplomacy did finally succeed, though not until as late as thirteen years after Morocco's independence, in persuading Spain to sign a treaty in Fez on January 4, 1969, by which Ifni was ceded, or retroceded, to Morocco the following June 30, but unlike Western Sahara, Ifni had zero economic interest for Spain, and in any case the Spanish authorities had only controlled a tiny enclave around the capital, Sidi Ifni, since the withdrawal of Spanish troops from most of the territory in 1957 during the war with the Army of Liberation. In return, moreover, Franco secured a fishing agreement, signed the same day as the Treaty of Fez, which gave Spanish fishermen the right to fish in Moroccan waters, though it was to be revoked unilaterally by Morocco three years later.

On a purely verbal plane the Moroccan government had briefly revived its drumbeating about Western Sahara prior to the Treaty of Fez, in 1965–68, in response to the adoption of the first resolution on Western Sahara and Ifni by the UN's Committee of 24 in 1964. A ministry of Mauritanian and Saharan affairs was created in 1965 under Moulay Hassan Ben Driss, a cousin to the king. In 1966 he encouraged the formation of a Frente de Liberación del Sahara bajo Dominación Española (FLS), which sent a delegation led by a grandson of Sheikh Ma el-Ainin, El-Abadila Ould Sheikh Mohammed Laghdaf, to New York to lobby the UN in November–December 1966, on the eve of the adoption of the first General Assembly resolution on Western Sahara to advocate a referendum.[16] With the assistance of the ministry of Mauritanian and Saharan affairs, the FLS began publishing a journal, *Nuestro Sahara*, in March 1967 under the editorship of Brika Zaruali, an Istiqlalian who had been one of the group's lobbyists in New York.[17] A few weeks later, on May 7, General Mohammed Oufkir, the Moroccan interior minister, piqued Madrid by declaring at the annual Tan-Tan *moussem* that the tribes of the Western Sahara were ready to liberate their territory from foreign rule. Castiella lodged a protest with Ben Ameziane, the Moroccan ambassador in Madrid, and the Spanish army minister, Lieutenant-General Camillo Menéndez Tolosa, flew to El-Ayoun to give a suitably saber-rattling warning that Spain would not bow to the Moroccan "jackals" who coveted Western Sahara's minerals. In turn, the Spanish ambassador in Rabat, Eduardo Ibañez, was duly reprimanded by the Moroccan foreign ministry.[18] Yet there was a comic-opera air to all these verbose pronouncements and protests. The FLS itself was barely active. It was never more than a circle of Saharawi exiles in Morocco whose limited diplomatic and literary ventures depended entirely on the *largesse* of the Moroccan government. It never attempted to begin underground political work within Western Sahara, and in mid-1968 even *Nuestro Sahara* ceased publication. The front finally faded away in 1969 when King Hassan reached agreement with Spain on Ifni, dropped his claim to Mauritania and wound up the ministry of Mauritanian and Saharan affairs.[19]

Another Moroccan-based group, the Mouvement de Résistance "les Hommes Bleus" (MOREHOB—"The Blue Men" Resistance Movement), which took its colorful name from the *draa*, the Saharawis' flowing indigo-dyed robe, had even less political significance. Founded in Rabat by a former Moroccan policeman, Bashir Figuigui, who took the bizarre Christian pseudonym of Edouard Moha, it announced its birth in July 1972 by circulating a memorandum to foreign embassies promising a struggle against Spanish colonialism in both Western Sahara and the enclaves of Ceuta and Melilla until "their return to the mother country." Avowedly royalist, it took as its slogan the official Moroccan motto "God, Country, King" and claimed that its action would complement "the wise policy carried out by the government of the mother country."[20] Its charter spoke of recruiting anti-Spanish commandos and said that MOREHOB would link up with resistance groups within Western Sahara "on the sole condition that the latter are not against the fundamental principles of national unity."[21] However, MOREHOB never carried out political work in Western Sahara. A UN mission that visited Western Sahara in 1975, examining political conditions there in depth, reported that it did not meet a single MOREHOB supporter in the territory and that "the Spanish authorities and the political movements encountered within the territory consider that MOREHOB does not have many members and point to the fact that there is no evidence of it having engaged in armed activities within the territory."[22]

Moha himself was something of a maverick. In March 1973 he suddenly turned up in Algiers, claiming that he had "refused categorically" to play the role of a "fifth column" on behalf of the Moroccan government.[23] To fill the vacuum, another pro-Moroccan grouplet, styling itself the August 21 Movement, was set up in Rabat in July 1973 to "take action parallel to the policy conducted by the authorities of the motherland" and liberate "occupied Moroccan territories in conjunction with the people of the Sahara, Ceuta and Melilla."[24] Nonetheless, this group, which was led by Mohammed Abdou Ould Hassan, a Saharawi from Tarfaya who had worked in the Moroccan civil service, was totally inactive and disintegrated within a year.

King Hassan's downplaying of the Western Sahara question meshed from the late sixties with a muting of his enthusiasm for the whole Greater Morocco cause. He began to accept that the territorial claims to Mauritania and parts of Algeria were utopian and had become an unnecessary obstacle to potentially beneficial cooperation with the new military government in Algeria, headed by Houari Boumedienne, which had seized power from Ben Bella in 1965. A more pragmatic attitude toward Algeria was evident by September 1968, when the king traveled to Algiers to participate in a summit conference of the OAU. "We are certain," he told Boumedienne as he left for Morocco after the summit, "that the talks we have had with Your Excellency on the subject of the Moroccan-Algerian questions have opened wide perspectives before our two peoples and new ways to resolve what has not been settled and confirm what is in the process of being carried out."[25]

The king must have broached the idea of another summit, for four months later, on January 11, 1969, Boumedienne flew into Rabat with six Moroccan F-5 jets escorting his Ilyushin-18. From Rabat the Algerian president proceeded to Hassan's winter palace at Ifrane in the Middle Atlas, where, on January 15, a twenty-year treaty was signed, committing Morocco and Algeria to "submit all the questions in abeyance between them to bilateral commissions."[26] Accordingly, at another summit meeting, held in Tlemcen, Algeria, on May 27, 1970, Hassan and Boumedienne decided to set up a joint commission to "proceed to the fixing of the border line between the two countries." Hassan joined Boumedienne, moreover, in a joint commitment to "the intangibility of their frontiers," so there seemed little doubt that the commission would end up confirming the *de facto* border. In return, Morocco was rewarded with an opportunity to participate in "an Algerian-Moroccan company for the exploitation of the Gara Djebilet mine," eighty miles southeast of Tindouf, where iron ore had first been discovered in 1952.[27] One of the largest deposits of iron ore in the world, Gara Djebilet has over two billion tons of ore, of which about eight hundred million tons have a relatively high grade of 57–58 percent iron and could easily be mined by open-cast methods. Another large iron-ore deposit, of 750 million tons, 55 percent pure, has since been found at Abdelaziz Mecheri, 250 miles east of Tindouf.[28] The deposits near Tindouf are actually much larger than the total iron-ore deposits of Mauritania, which is by far the biggest iron producer in the Arab world.[29] Boumedienne agreed at Tlemcen to take Morocco into partnership regarding Gara Djebilet for sound economic as well as diplomatic reasons—the opportunity to cut costs by evacuating the ore via southern Morocco to the Atlantic, a distance of about 380 miles, rather than to the Mediterranean, 975 miles to the north.

The Istiqlal Party was not impressed. Gara Djebilet, it protested, was Moroccan by right and Algeria had no authority to expect Morocco to renounce its territorial claims in order to benefit from the exploitation of its iron. "Nothing has changed with regard to Morocco's sovereignty over its despoiled territories in the north, south and east," the party's executive committee declared on June 3, a week after the Tlemcen summit.[30] A similar view was taken by the much smaller Parti de Libération et du Socialisme (PLS), to which the PCM had changed its name in 1968, and whose secretary-general, Ali Yata, deplored at a press conference in Paris on March 10, 1971, that Tindouf and Bechar had "been purely and simply abandoned, and our southeast finds itself deprived of its mineral wealth, in particular the iron ore at Gara Djebilet."[31]

But Hassan was not deflected from his policy of détente by the protests of the Greater Moroccans. There were immediate economic advantages to be gained, and not only with regard to Gara Djebilet. In June–July 1970 Moroccan and Algerian officials met to discuss a plan to build a natural-gas pipeline from Algeria, which has the world's third-largest natural-gas reserves, to Europe via Morocco and Spain. Had the plan been implemented, the pipeline could have supplied energy to new industries that were then on the drawing board for northeastern Morocco, notably a huge steel mill at Nador.[32] Meanwhile, despite the generally noncomplementary character of their economies, Moroccan-Algerian trade tripled in value between 1968 and 1972, reaching £17.4 million, and on March 17, 1973, Morocco and Algeria signed a long-term trade agreement.[33]

The first session of the border demarcation commission met within a month of the Tlemcen summit, on June 24–26, in Rabat, with General Oufkir, the Moroccan interior minister, and Colonel Abdelkader Chabou, the secretary-general of the Algerian defense ministry, heading the two delegations.[34] Topographical studies were then carried out in June–July with the help of the Institut National Géographique de Paris.[35] Meanwhile, another commission began studies on the Gara Djebilet project, and after talks with the Algerian foreign minister, Abdelaziz Bouteflika, King Hassan announced on May 28, 1972, that an agreement had been reached to build a railway from Gara Djebilet to Tarfaya.[36]

Finally, a fortnight later, on June 15, 1972, during the closing session of an OAU summit conference in Rabat, the Algerian and Moroccan foreign ministers, Bouteflika and Ahmed Taibi Benhima, signed two conventions, one formally demarcating the Moroccan-Algerian border, the other setting out the basis for Moroccan-Algerian cooperation in the Gara Djebilet project, while Hassan and Boumedienne signed a joint declaration affirming their intention to "establish a permanent peace for centuries to come."[37] The Istiqlal Party was irate and its daily newspaper, *L'Opinion*, was barred from publication on the eve of the signing ceremony at the summit because it dared to reiterate the old claims to Touat, Saoura, Kenadza and Tindouf.

The border convention was the first to define *de jure* the entire frontier from longitude 8°40', Algeria's southwestern border with Western Sahara, to Teniet Sassi, the southernmost border point defined by the Franco-Moroccan Treaty of Lalla Marnia in 1845. In essentials it gave recognition to the *de facto* border and so amounted to an unconditional renunciation by Morocco of its claims to parts of Algerian territory. The signatories declared that "the provisions of the present convention definitively settle the frontier questions between Algeria and Morocco" and agreed that a joint commission should be set up by October 15 to mark the frontier, completing its work within three years.[38] The convention on Gara Djebilet created a joint company, in which the Algerian and Moroccan governments each held half the shares, for the transportation and marketing of iron ore. It was not actually to mine the ore at Gara Djebilet, which was to be an exclusively Algerian responsibility, but Algeria guaranteed to deliver seven hundred million tons of ore to the company over a period of sixty years.[39]

The détente with Algeria was accompanied by a belated recognition of Mauritania. Hassan broke the ice by inviting President Mokhtar Ould Daddah to a summit of Islamic nations in Rabat in September 1969. There, Boumedienne brought Hassan and the Mauritanian president face to face for the first time by inviting them to a private dinner. "It was not just to drink a glass of tea," quipped the king the next day, confiding to journalists that he had known ever since 1960 that the Moroccan claim to Mauritania was unattainable.[40] A day later Ould Daddah let it be known that there was now "no obstacle" to the development of normal bilateral relations.[41] The UNFP, which had always rejected the claim to Mauritania, welcomed the king's new policy; but the Istiqlal Party and the PLS were shocked. The editors of the two Istiqlalian newspapers, *L'Opinion* and *Al-Alam*, were jailed for eight days in October for committing the crimes of "offense to the dignity of His Majesty and threat to public order" when they published an editorial opposing the recognition of Mauritania under the banner headline "The People's Sovereignty Is Inalienable."[42]

A month after the Islamic summit, on October 30, the Mauritanian president dispatched a "goodwill" delegation, headed by Ahmed Ould Mohammed Salah, the PPM's political secretary, to meet Hassan in Rabat. General Oufkir, Ahmed Snoussi and Mohammed Jaidi, the Moroccan ministers of the interior, information and commerce and industry, then visited Nouakchott on January 13–16, 1970, and they were followed a few days later by a team of Moroccan trade and transport officials who drafted a commercial agreement and discussed plans for a direct maritime connection.[43] On February 2, 1970, Hassan appointed Morocco's first ambassador to Mauritania, Kacem Khiri; and a Mauritanian ambassador arrived in Morocco to present his credentials to the king the following April.[44] The fence-mending culminated with the signing of a "treaty of friendship, neighborliness and cooperation" in Casablanca on June 8, 1970, during a second visit to Morocco by Ould Daddah, and then, a month later, with the conclusion of four agreements for cooperation in trade, industry, fishing and maritime and air transport.[45] To cap it all off, Hassan made a personal gift of one million dirhams for the construction of a mosque in Nouakchott.

In return for his concessions to Mauritania and Algeria, Hassan may have anticipated that their governments would let Morocco have its way in Western Sahara. In fact, a secret understanding on the territory's future seems to have been reached at the OAU summit in Rabat in June 1972 when the Algerian-Moroccan frontier dispute was finally settled. "A new element entered the situation in 1972, during the meeting of the OAU summit in Rabat," Ould Daddah was to claim in 1976. "Taking into account the real situation in the Sahara, Mauritania and Morocco reached a bilateral solution of the problem, involving the idea of two zones of influence, one in the south for Mauritania and the other in the north for Morocco. Present in the Moroccan capital at the time, President Boumedienne alone was associated with this agreement, which received his approval and backing."[46] Such approval was implied, perhaps, when Boumedienne asked rhetorically on June 15, 1972, upon signing his joint declaration of peace and friendship with Hassan, whether "it is necessary to reaffirm our total solidarity with brotherly Morocco in the struggle it is waging to reestablish its sovereignty over those territories which still remain under colonial domination."[47] No mention was made of a partition between Morocco and Mauritania, but two years later, in a speech to an Arab League summit in Rabat in October 1974, Boumedienne revealed that he had been "present at a meeting with His Majesty the King of Morocco and the President of Mauritania, a meeting at which they found a means to resolve the problem of the Sahara which envisages a Moroccan and a Mauritanian zone." He added: "I was present; I gave my full endorsement without ulterior motives."[48]

However, if a tacit agreement to partition Western Sahara was reached in June

1972, it was no more than a verbal understanding, and until Boumedienne's speech to the Arab League summit in 1974 a secret one at that. Publicly, Morocco joined Mauritania and Algeria in endorsing the UN resolutions, which hinged on the proposal of a referendum of self-determination. Indeed, like Mauritania, Morocco had tailored its policy since 1966 to accommodate the UN's standard decolonization principles, while continuing to uphold its historic claim to Western Sahara. Recognizing that the UN would not give outright endorsement to Morocco's demand for "reunification," especially in view of Mauritania's counterclaim, Morocco's representative at the UN, Dey Ould Sidi Baba, had gone so far, despite his own background as a Mauritanian "renegade," to propose on June 7, 1966, at a special session of the UN's Committee of 24 in Addis Ababa, that Western Sahara and other Spanish colonies "should as soon as possible be granted their independence," thereby "enabling the people of those territories to exercise all the responsibilities of power themselves, without any colonialist presence," though he hastened to add that Morocco had not renounced its claim to Spanish-ruled territory in northwest Africa.[49] The nationalists of the Istiqlal Party were aghast. "We are absolutely opposed to any attitude, even one explicable for tactical reasons, which could engender confusion and put in question the integrity of Moroccan territory to the slightest extent," *L'Opinion* protested on July 22 in an editorial that reaffirmed the party's view that Morocco extended from Oujda to Senegal and from Tangier to Touat; and the PCM leader, Ali Yata, cabled the king to demand that "Dey Ould Sidi Baba be relieved of his functions."[50] But the ultras of the Istiqlal Party were quietly ignored. Speaking in the UN General Assembly on October 13, the foreign minister, Mohammed Cherkaoui, reaffirmed Morocco's support for Western Sahara's independence and said that this must be "a true independence that will put the future of these territories in the hands of their own nationals who, with their discretion and in fully recovered freedom, will know how to decide their destiny." Accepting the idea of a referendum in Western Sahara, Cherkaoui proposed that "prior to any consultation with a view to the application of self-determination, the following measures be taken: 1. Withdrawal of all the Spanish military forces from these territories. 2. Maintenance in these territories of the police forces deemed indispensable by UNO to assure public order there. 3. Withdrawal of the Spanish administration from these territories. 4. Free return of refugees native to these territories. These prior conditions met, the referendum can be organized either directly under the authority of UNO, or in collaboration with and under the joint supervision of the Moroccan and Spanish authorities."[51] Morocco accordingly voted in favor of General Assembly Resolution 2229 on December 20, 1966. Once again the Istiqlal Party showed its displeasure. "We were hoping," lamented *Al-Alam* on December 18, "that the United Nations would promulgate its resolution on the basis of the incontestable historical evidence, a resolution that would decide upon the restitution of these provinces to Morocco without having recourse at all to a referendum, the transfer of powers or consultation with the concerned parties." However, the Moroccan government went on to vote for all of the following six pro-referendum resolutions adopted by the General Assembly between 1967 and 1973 except, rather mysteriously, that adopted in 1972, on which Morocco abstained.[52]

Indeed, Hassan himself explained at a press conference on July 30, 1970, that, during his negotiations with Spain, "instead of going purely and simply to claim the territory of the Sahara, I went to request specifically that a popular consultation take place there, assured as I was that the first result would be the departure of the non-Africans and that then one would leave it up to the people of the Sahara to choose whether to live under the Moroccan aegis or their own aegis or any other aegis."[53] A few weeks later, on September 14, the king joined the presidents of Mauritania and Algeria for a trilateral summit meeting in Nouadhibou, on the Cape Blanc peninsula. Meeting in a Catholic mission school about three hundred yards from the Spanish border post at La Guera, the three leaders resolved to "intensify their close cooperation in order to hasten the decolonization of this region in compliance with the relevant United Nations resolutions" and, for this purpose, to set up a tripartite coordinating committee to "follow the process of decolonization in the territory in both the political and diplomatic fields."[54] But nothing really came of the Nouadhibou summit. No concrete plan of anti-Spanish action was adopted, and for the Greater Moroccans there was once again disappointment that no mention was made of Morocco's claim to the territory.[55] The tripartite coordinating committee, which was composed of the three countries' foreign ministers, failed to meet for more than a year. When at last it did, in Algiers on January 4–5, 1972, it approved a "program of action" to be put before Hassan, Boumedienne and Ould Daddah at a new summit, to be held in Rabat the following March.[56] However, the summit was canceled, apparently because Mauritania began to reassert its claims to Western Sahara particularly vigorously with the encouragement of one of Hassan's archenemies, Colonel Muammur Qadhafi of Libya, who offered military support to help liberate Western Sahara from Spain during a visit to Mauritania in February 1972. As a militant pan-Arabist, Qadhafi could have been expected to take a tough stand against Spain, but he had special reasons to side with Mauritania at this time. He had as much disdain for Hassan as for King Idris, whom he had overthrown in 1969; and Hassan had broken diplomatic relations with Libya in July 1971 when Tripoli Radio prematurely applauded the authors of an unsuccessful military coup against the king. By contrast, the Qadhafi government had provided considerable economic assistance to Mauritania, after establishing diplomatic relations in January 1970, and was to applaud Mokhtar Ould Daddah's nationalist economic reforms in the early seventies.[57]

In June 1972, Hassan, Ould Daddah and Boumedienne finally reached their informal understanding at the OAU summit in Rabat, but nothing was said in public about a deal to divide Western Sahara after Spain's departure, and though the Moroccan government continued to uphold the UN resolutions on self-determination, at times it could not disguise its disappointment that Algeria and Mauritania would not openly endorse Morocco's "rights" in Western Sahara. "Until now, Morocco, in the name of the Maghreb, in the name of Arab and Islamic solidarity, in the name of African unity, has made heavy sacrifices in order to normalize its relations, as much with Algiers as with Nouakchott," remarked a brother-in-law to the king, the newspaper proprietor Ahmed Alaoui, in an editorial in *Maroc-Soir* on May 10, 1973, a day after the tripartite coordinating committee had met again, in Nouakchott. "But we must state that it has been alone in making concessions," he complained. "It is up to our neighbors to give evidence in turn of the same solidarity, by offering for example to guarantee the total freedom of the referendum, without fostering hidden schemes, and by sincerely helping Morocco to recover the territories of which it has been plundered." Yet, the presidents of Mauritania and Algeria remained unwilling, when they met again for a tripartite summit with Hassan on July 24, 1973, in Agadir, to do more than join the king in reaffirming "their unwavering attachment to the principle of self-determination and their concern to ensure that this principle was implemented in a framework which guaranteed that the will of the inhabitants of Sahara was given free and genuine expression, in conformity with the United Nations decisions on this question."[58]

Hassan doubtless accepted the UN policy of self-determination as a second best to outright recognition of Morocco's claim to Western Sahara, which diplomatic realities had made unattainable, because until as late as 1974 he assumed that a referendum would in any case lead to Morocco's absorption of the territory. He was unaware that a Saharawi nationalist consciousness had germinated in the greatly changed economic, social and political conditions in Spain's desert colony in the late sixties and early seventies. He would almost certainly have concurred with Ahmed Alaoui's observation in *Maroc-Soir* on July 23, 1973, that "although the Moroccan character of this part of the Sahara is historically and geographically obvious," Morocco had accepted the idea of a referendum "certain that the population will vote in favor of returning to the motherland." Two months earlier a small group of young Saharawi militants had founded the Polisario Front and staged their first guerrilla raid against an isolated Spanish army post.

NOTES

1. Richard Comyns Carr, "Spain and Morocco: a New Phase," *Contemporary Review*, Vol. 205, No. 1183, August 1964, p. 409.

2. *Ibid.*, pp. 411–12.

3. *Chroniques Etrangères: Espagne*, No. 249, November 30, 1962, p. 9.

4. *Chroniques Etrangères: Espagne*, No. 250, December 31, 1962, p. 20.

5. *Le Monde* (Paris), November 30, 1962.

6. Rachid Lazrak, *Le contentieux territorial territorial entre le Maroc et l'Espagne* (Dar el Kitab, Casablanca, 1974), p. 289.

7. "Les relations hispano-marocaines," *Maghreb* (La Documentation Française, Paris), No. 3, May–June 1964, p. 11; *Le Monde*, July 9, 1964.

8. *Chroniques Etrangères: Espagne*, Nos. 7–8 (1963), July–August 1963, p. 35. "The attitude of Spain and its *caudillo* at certain difficult moments of recent history" was a reference to Franco's opposition to the French decision to exile Mohammed V in 1953–55.

9. *Reuters*, dispatches from Rabat, February 16, 1970 and May 15, 1972, and from Marrakesh, September 17, 1971.

10. "Les relations hispano-marocaines," *loc. cit.*, p. 11.

11. *Ibid.*, p. 12.

12. *Le Monde*, July 9, 1964.

13. *Chroniques Etrangères: Espagne*, No. 3 (1965), March 1965, p. 16; "La retrocession d'Ifni et les relations hispano-marocaines," *Maghreb*, No. 33, May–June 1969, p. 36.

14. Lazrak, *op. cit.*, p. 285.

15. *Ibid.*, pp. 310, 352.

16. *Reuters*, dispatch from Rabat, January 13, 1967.

17. For a bibliography of articles in *Nuestro Sahara*, see Attilio Gaudio, *Le dossier du Sahara oc-cidental* (Nouvelles Editions Latines, Paris, 1978), pp. 442–43.

18. *Reuters*, dispatches from Rabat, May 12, 1967, and May 16, 1967; *Africa Confidential* (London), April 20, 1968.

19. Author's interview with Mohammed Ma el-Ainin, Rabat, October 16, 1978.

20. Letter of Edouard Moha to ambassadors accredited to Morocco, July 1972. See also *Reuters*, dispatches from Rabat, July 15, 1972, and July 29, 1972. In an interview with the author in Rabat on August 8, 1978, Moha claimed that MOREHOB had been founded in 1969 and that, though born in Morocco and raised in Goulimine and Ouarzazate, he was a Reguibi of the Oulad Taleb fraction and his real name was Mohammed Ould Taleb. However, there is no independent evidence of MOREHOB's existence prior to the OAU summit in Rabat in June 1972. Not only the Polisario Front, but left-wing Moroccans have disputed his claim to Saharawi origins and claimed that he was born in the Middle Atlas—at Azilal, according to Abdallah Baroudi ("Le complot 'saharien' contre le peuple marocain et son armée," *Les Temps Modernes*, 34th Year, No. 394, May 1979, p. 1835). According to representatives of the Moroccan opposition group, Alikhtiar Athaouri (Revolutionary Option), interviewed by the author in Paris on October 10, 1979, Moha served in the Moroccan police at Benguerir for a while and was suspected by the Moroccan left of having links with the ministry of the interior and the secret police in 1972 during his brief period of MOREHOB activity in Rabat.

21. MOREHOB, *Charte du mouvement*, Articles 9 and 11.

22. Report of the United Nations Visiting Mission to Spanish Sahara, 1975, paragraph 228, in *General Assembly Official Records*, 30th Session, Supplement 23, p. 65.

23. *Reuters*, dispatch from Rabat, March 3, 1973.

24. *Reuters*, dispatch from Rabat, July 11, 1973.

25. Message de S. M. le Roi au Président Boumedienne, *Maroc-Documents*, March 1969, p. 41.

26. Traité de fraternité, de bon voisinage et de coopération conclu entre la République algérienne démocratique et populaire et le Royaume du Maroc, in *Journal Officiel de la République Algérienne Démocratique et Populaire*, 8th Year, No. 11, February 5, 1969, pp. 82–84.

27. *Communiqué commun algéro-marocain* (Ministère des Affaires Etrangères, Royaume du Maroc, Division Presse et Information, DAP/5, June 1, 1970).

28. Author's interview with M. Krachni, directeur des mines et de la géologie, ministry of heavy industry, Algiers, September 23, 1979.

29. According to *Metal Bulletin Monthly* (February 1969), Mauritania's iron-ore deposits total 1,915 million tons.

30. *Reuters*, dispatch from Rabat, June 3, 1970.

31. Ali Yata, *Le Sahara occidental marocain* (Casablanca, 1973), p. 286.

32. In December 1971 the Moroccan under-secretary of state for commerce, industry and mines, Abdelaziz Benjelloun, informed the Moroccan parliament that negotiations were proceeding on plans to pipe Algerian gas to the proposed Nador steel plant. (*Reuters*, dispatch from Rabat, December 3, 1971.)

33. *Reuters*, dispatch from Casablanca, March 16, 1973; *El Moudjahid* (Algiers), March 18–19, 1973. On the obstacles to greater inter-Maghreb economic cooperation and trade, see Abderrahman Robana, "The Maghreb Economic Cooperation in Retrospect," *The Maghreb Review*, Vol. 3, Nos. 7–8, May-August 1978, pp. 12–15; Abderrahman Robana, *The Prospects for an Economic Community in North Africa* (Praeger, New York, 1973); and Bruno Etienne, "L'unité maghrébine à l'épreuve des politiques étrangères nationales," *Annuaire de l'Afrique du Nord 1970 (CNRS, Paris, 1971)*, pp. 85–100.

34. *Reuters*, dispatches from Rabat, June 23, 1970, June 24, 1970, and June 26, 1970.

35. Marie-Françoise Labouz, "Le règlement du contentieux frontalier de l'Ouest maghrébin: aspects politiques et juridiques," *Maghreb*, September-October 1972, p. 52.

36. *Reuters*, dispatch from Agadir, May 28, 1972.

37. "La déclaration commune maroco-algérienne du 15 juin 1972," *Le Matin du Sahara* (Casablanca), October 14, 1978.

38. Convention relative au tracé de la frontière d'Etat établie entre le Royaume du Maroc et la République algérienne démocratique et populaire, *Journal Officiel de la République Algérienne Démocratique et Populaire*, 12th Year, No. 48, June 15, 1973, pp. 546–48.

39. Convention de coopération entre l'Algérie et le Maroc pour la mise en valeur de la mine de Gara Djebilet, *Journal Officiel de la République Algérienne Démocratique et Populaire*, 12th Year, No. 48, June 15, 1973, pp. 548–51.

40. *Reuters*, dispatch from Rabat, September 26, 1969.

41. *Reuters*, dispatch from Rabat, September 27, 1969.

42. *Reuters*, dispatch from Rabat, October 24, 1969.

43. "Relations avec la Mauritanie," *Maroc-Documents*, November 1970, p. 197.

44. Labouz, *loc. cit.*, p. 53.

45. Traité de fraternité, de bon voisinage et de coopération entre la République Islamique de Mauritanie et le Royaume du Maroc, *Journal Officiel de la République Islamique de Mauritanie*, 1970, pp. 233–34; *Reuters*, dispatch from Rabat, July 9, 1970.

46. "*Synthèse de la communication du secrétaire-général du parti devant le Conseil National du Parti du Peuple Mauritanien (29–30–31 janvier 1976)*," in Moktar Ould Daddah, *1975-1976, La réunification de la patrie: un objectif sacré pour le peuple mauritanien* (Ministère d'Etat à l'Orientation Nationale, Nouakchott, 1976), p. 8.

47. *Maroc-Documents*, June 1972, p. 78.

48. Cited by Hamdi Ould Mouknass, foreign minister of Mauritania, in a speech to the UN General Assembly on October 13, 1977. The citation was not challenged by the Algerian foreign minister, Bouteflika, when he took the floor later the same day to reply to the Mauritanian minister. "He has also spoken of an agreement between Morocco and Mauritania. But who more than Algeria," Bouteflika asked, "would rejoice at an understanding between Morocco and Mauritania, between Tunisia and Libya, between Libya and Egypt, or between Niger and Mali, if problems should arise?"

49. Cited in Thomas M. Franck, "The Stealing of the Sahara," *American Journal of International Law*, Vol. 70, No. 4, October 1976, p. 702.

50. "Telegramme addressé à Sa Majesté Hassan II, Roi du Maroc, 8 juin 1966," in Ali Yata, *op. cit.*, p. 195.

51. *Discours prononcé par S.E. Monsieur Mohamed Cherkaoui, ministre des affaires etrangères du Maroc, à la XXIème session de l'Assemblée Générale, 13 octobre 1966* (Moroccan Government).

52. This may have been because the resolution referred explicitly for the first time to the right of the Western Sahara people to independence rather than, as before, simply self-determination; but Morocco voted for the almost identical resolution adopted by the General Assembly a year later, in December 1973.

53. "Conférence de presse du Roi Hassan II, le 30 juillet 1970," *Annuaire de l'Afrique du Nord 1970* (CNRS, Paris, 1971), p. 807.

54. *Joint Communiqué Issued by the Governments of Algeria, Mauritania and Morocco on 14 September 1970 at Nouadhibou*, in UN Document A/10023/Rev. 1, p. 123.

55. See for example *L'Opinion* (Rabat), September 16, 1970.

56. *Joint Communiqué Issued by the Governments of Algeria, Mauritania and Morocco on 5 January 1972, at Alger*, in UN Document A/10023/Rev. 1, p. 124.

57. During a visit to Tripoli in September 1971, Ould Daddah was given Libyan aid totaling CFA 5.5 million; and during Colonel Qadhafi's return visit to Nouakchott in February 1972 the two heads of state set up a joint Libyan-Mauritanian commission, which, at its first meeting, in May 1972, reached an agreement on trade. A month later, on June 20, the Mauritanian and Libyan governments set up a jointly owned Banque Arabe Libyenne Mauritanienne pour le Commerce Extérieur et le Développement (BALM), which opened its doors the following November. See "La Mauritanie à un moment décisif de son histoire," *Europe-Outremer* (Paris), 50th Year, No. 519, April 1973, p. 26.

58. *Joint Communiqué Issued by the Governments of Algeria, Mauritania and Morocco, 24 July 1973, at Agadir*, in UN Document A/10023/Rev. 1, pp. 126–27.

12

Minerals
and Social Change

W E WILL NEVER extract the slightest material benefit here; and, on the other hand, we have given you as much as we have been able," swore Admiral Carrero Blanco, the vice-president of the Spanish government, on May 16, 1966, during a visit to El-Ayoun.[1] It was a characteristic Spanish pledge of colonial selflessness. In fact, Western Sahara was on the brink of a phosphate bonanza, had already been scoured by teams of oil explorers and was known to have substantial deposits of iron ore, as well as numerous other minerals, some of them, like vanadium, of strategic value.[2] By 1970 the Spanish government and state-owned companies were investing heavily in the territory, to explore for or exploit minerals and provide the necessary infrastructural backup. In turn, its social physiognomy was transformed. The small towns rapidly expanded as thousands of Spanish workers arrived from the Canary Islands and most of the Saharawis abandoned their precarious nomadic way of life to look for jobs, relief or education.

One of Western Sahara's resources had been appreciated by Spaniards from the Canary Islands for more than four and a half centuries. That was the fish off its coast, an extension of the Senegalese-Mauritanian continental shelf, which, along with the Gabon-Congo-Angola coast, is reputed to be the most valued fishing region in Africa. According to a recent Moroccan study, 2 million tons of fish could be caught annually in Western Saharan waters.[3] A Spanish estimate of the total catch in Western Saharan waters in 1969 by fishing boats from throughout the world was 1.28 million tons, of which the fishing fleet from the Canaries accounted for 250,000 tons, boats from the Spanish peninsula 200,000 tons, Japanese vessels 300,000 tons and Soviet boats 200,000 tons.[4] In 1974 the deep-sea fishing fleet from the Canary province of Las Palmas, which fishes almost exclusively off the Western Saharan coast, caught 197,227 tons, worth 4.8 billion pesetas.[5] This fleet, which comprised 273 vessels with a combined tonnage of 48,724 tons, accounted for 93 percent of the value of the fish landed in the province of Las Palmas and was a mainstay of the provincial economy. Including processing, the fishing industry's output was valued at 9.4 billion pesetas, second only to tourism in its contribution to Las Palmas' economy.[6]

The most important species caught in Western Saharan waters by the Canary Islands' fishing boats were sardines, of which about 90,000 tons were caught annually, and octopus and squid, of which the annual catch averaged around 70,000 tons, though many others, including tuna, lobster, anchovy, hake and red mullet, were also caught.[7] However, the Western Saharans themselves scarcely benefited at all from this huge industry off their coast. Fish-processing factories had been set up at Villa Cisneros and La Guera in the earliest days of the Spanish colony, but the industry remained primitive until after the Second World War, and as late as 1949 only 657 tons of fish were landed in the territory. In 1948, however, Spanish public and private capital was invested in a new Western Saharan fishing enterprise, IPASA, which built processing facilities in La Guera, and by the sixties the annual total fish catch by boats based in Western Sahara was oscillating between a low of 2,013 tons (1963) and a high of 6,661 tons (1968). From 80 to 90 percent of the catch was ground into fish flour. By 1974 the total catch by Western Saharan boats had reached a record 11,800 tons, worth $1.5 million, but this was still less than 1 percent of the total tonnage of fish caught off Western Sahara by boats from the rest of the world.[8]

TABLE 12.1

TONNAGE OF FISH LANDED IN WESTERN SAHARA, 1969–74

1969	1970	1971	1972	1973	1974
4,271	3,651	3,250	5,012	5,400	11,800

In the early sixties, meanwhile, the international oil companies had descended on Western Sahara in search of a bigger prize than fish. In 1956 the most important of the Algerian Saharan oil fields, Hassi Messaoud, had been discovered, and in Spanish Sahara the geological structures looked promising too. Interest centered on two large sedimentary basins, one running north to south along the coast, both on and offshore, the other straddling the border with southern Morocco, west to east, from the Atlantic to the Hammada. However, exploration had been precluded until Spain relaxed its protectionist investment laws at the end of the fifties. The green light to foreign oil companies was given by an oil investment law enacted on December 26, 1958, which allowed foreign companies to acquire concessions on Spanish territory, and by a subsequent decree, published on June 25, 1959, which spelt out the terms on which oil companies could search for and pump oil in Spanish-ruled Africa.[9] Western Sahara was to be divided into 108 rectangular blocks, each seventy by thirty-five kilometers, which would then be awarded to interested oil companies under six-year permits, which could be extended for an additional three years.

Meanwhile, the Servicio Minero y Geológico of the government's colonial office, the Dirección General de Plazas y Provincias Africanas, carried out an aeromagnetic survey that delimited 160,000 square kilometers where there appeared to be favorable oil prospects. Copies of the survey were put up for sale and within ten days more than twenty companies had paid out a total of sixty million pesetas to obtain them.[10] Eventually, in 1960–61, forty-three onshore blocks covering just over 100,000 square kilometers, 37 percent of the territory's total land area, were awarded to twenty companies grouped into eleven consortia. Most were Spanish subsidiaries of U.S. oil companies, but the Spanish state's Instituto Nacional de Industria (INI) had an interest in ten of the permits.[11] Drilling began almost immediately and by 1964 it was reported that 27 discoveries had been made, notably at Foum el-Oued, near El-Ayoun.[12] But by then most of the companies had decided to pull out, two years before the expiration of their exploration permits. No commercially viable deposits had been found. World oil prices were too low to warrant development perhaps, and the territory's meager infrastructure, in particular the shortage of water, might also have influenced the companies.

However, the oil search did not halt entirely. One consortium, grouping the Compañía Española de Petroleos (CEPSA) and Spanish Gulf Oil, retained its onshore blocks, and in 1966 exploration started offshore for the first time. In 1971 Gulf and CEPSA discovered oil offshore in the south, but it was reported to be of poor quality and difficult to extract.[13] When Spain withdrew from Western Sahara in 1976, nine concessions were still held by two groups, three offshore by the Spanish state companies ENPASA and ENPENSA, and six (three onshore and three offshore) by CEPSA, Gulf and CONOCO.[14]

Significantly, the oil search in Spanish Sahara was mirrored by exploration work farther north in the same sedimentary basins, across the border in the Moroccan province of Tarfaya, former Spanish Southern Morocco, which had been handed to the Rabat government after the Cintra accord of April 1958. There, Italy's ENI acquired exploration rights over thirty thousand square kilometers offshore and onshore on July 26, 1958, two days after the publication of Morocco's first petroleum code.[15] ENI carried out geological and geophysical surveys and in 1960 sunk its first well onshore, at Oum Doul. ENI then switched its attention offshore and began drilling in the mouth of the River Chebeika, about forty-five miles due north of the Western Saharan border in 1961.

ENI suddenly pulled out in 1963, but two years later Esso was awarded offshore exploration rights in the Tarfaya region and in 1968 began drilling there. Abraham Serfaty, a former official of the Moroccan Direction des Mines et de la Géologie, has claimed that, during a visit to Esso's drilling rig there in 1969, he found that the earlier ENI drillings, whose findings had been shrouded in secrecy, had proved positive and that the second of Esso's test wells, which had been drilled in 1968, had indicated the presence of a large oil-bearing zone, stretching down the coast from Tarfaya.[16] In March 1972 Esso was reported to have found oil again, this time on its eighth well off Tarfaya, two miles southwest of the second well. However, Esso too abandoned its leases. The oil was said to be very heavy and sulfurous, and in 1968–72 such oil could not have seemed a very attractive commercial bet.[17]

The upward spiral in oil prices which began in 1973 changed the picture. In March 1978, a little over two years after Spain's withdrawal from Western Sahara, the Moroccan government awarded seven offshore exploration blocks between El-Ayoun and Boujdour to British Petroleum and Phillips Oil Company.[18] But, although seismic work was carried out, no drilling took place and in 1980 the concession was abandoned, apparently because of the war between Morocco and Polisario, which was then attacking fishing boats along the coast and had condemned the companies' agreement with Morocco as an infringement of Western Sahara's sovereignty.[19] Since then, the oil search has shifted back across the border into the Tarfaya region. In February 1982 Morocco's petroleum office, ONAREP, awarded Mobil two exploration blocks covering 9,710 square kilometers offshore from Puerto Cansado, just north of Tarfaya, to the pre-1975 Western Saharan border, which, in view of the contested sovereignty farther south, Mobil was apparently unwilling to cross. Mobil, which planned to invest $117 million in seismic studies and exploratory wells, brought in one of the world's most advanced seismic vessels in May 1983. Meanwhile, interest turned also to the huge onshore shale-oil deposits in the Tarfaya region, which were first discovered in 1974. Morocco claims the fourth-largest shale reserves in the world and toward the end of the 1970s was encouraged by the rise in world oil prices to consider investigating the possibility of exploiting them. The main shale-oil deposits are at Timhadit, one hundred kilometers south of Fez in the Middle Atlas, where there are estimated to be ten to twenty million tons, with an 8 to 10 percent oil yield, and in the Tarfaya region, where the deposits have been estimated to be ten times larger. In an agreement with ONAREP in September 1981, Shell undertook to make a feasibility study of the Tarfaya deposits.[20] Like Mobil, Shell decided to restrict its activity to the north of the pre-1975 border, though the shale reserves are thought to stretch south across the border.

Though none of the earlier discoveries has yet been developed, it is striking that international oil companies remain interested in the Western Saharan-Tarfaya region more than two decades after the first exploration attempts there. By the early 1980s they had been obliged to focus their exploration work to the north of the pre-1975 border, for obvious political and security reasons, but there is considerable evidence that the regions to the immediate south of Tarfaya in the same sedimentary basins could have as promising petroleum prospects.

Since the 1950s there has also been interest in Western Sahara's iron-ore deposits. Iron ore was found in the fifties at Agracha, on the northwestern edge of the Tiris plateau, a few miles from the huge Mauritanian iron deposits near Zouerate. The deposit was said to total seventy-two million tons of ore with a grade of 57.3 percent iron and 13.6 percent titanium oxide, a component in the manufacture of paint. It also contains 0.6–0.8 percent vanadium, making Western Sahara one of the world's largest potential sources of this metal, which is used in the aerospace industry to make light, heat-resistant metal alloys. A Norwegian firm investigated methods of separating the titanium oxide and the valuable vanadium, and in the early sixties a hundred-mile railway route from Agracha to the Río de Oro bay was surveyed. Nevertheless, in 1964 INI announced that the world iron market was too depressed to warrant investment in the Agracha project. In the northeast, meanwhile, Manuel Alía Medina, the Spanish geologist who first discovered phosphates in Western Sahara, found iron too, in the east of Saguia el-Hamra in 1947, and suggested that the whole Tindouf Depression, which includes the massive iron deposits at Gara Djebilet across the Algerian border, could be iron-bearing. An aeromagnetic study was carried out in the early sixties, but Spain was secretive about the results of its prospecting in this region. Iron has also been found in a third zone, in the center of the country, where an aeromagnetic study in 1965 revealed forty-six possible sites, but few details of the prospecting there were released either.[21]

It is phosphate that has really put Western Sahara on the world mineral map. During the early 1940s, while most of Europe was plunged in war, Manuel Alía Medina, who was an adventurous young geology professor from the University of Madrid, crisscrossed the Western Saharan desert on the back of a camel to study the country's geological structure. His findings suggested propitious conditions for phosphates, and so, during an expedition to the north of the territory in 1945, he gathered samples of sediments from the Hammada which he brought back to Madrid for analysis. With the help of his brother, José, who was a chemist, he found that he had samples with a 24 percent phosphate content. On April 5, 1947, he sent a report of his discovery to General Franco. The Dirección General de Marruecos y Colonias immediately asked Alía to return to Western Sahara to make further investigations in the summer of 1947. It was the hottest and most trying part of the year in which to undertake such an expedition, but, Alía recalled later, "my natural impatience made up my mind not to postpone the expedition further."[22] With the help of a chemist from Ifni, he set up a small laboratory in El-Ayoun and then headed out into the desert to collect new samples. Soon they were finding that they had samples yielding 60 percent phosphate, rich enough to mine. This warranted a personal interview with Franco, to whom Alía presented one of his phosphate-rich specimens on October 1.

Franco met Alía again in 1950 during a visit to El-Ayoun, and two years later the Spanish government commissioned the state mineral prospecting company, Adaro de Investigaciones Mineras, a subsidiary of INI, to embark on more advanced studies. A pilot plant was built and several deposits south of El-Ayoun near Boujdour were identified and investigated. Finally, in July 1962, INI founded a special company, the Empresa Nacional Minera del Sahara (ENMIN-SA), to evaluate the prospects for exploiting the territory's phosphates. After completing a systematic survey, ENMINSA claimed that the country had about ten billion tons of phosphate, second in the world phosphate league to Morocco, which has about forty billion tons, out of a world total of about seventy billion tons.[23] At the same time, ENMINSA announced a proven deposit of 1.7 billion tons of ore at Bou-Craa, about sixty-seven miles southeast of El-Ayoun. It was one of the biggest deposits in the world. Moreover, most of the ore was of remarkably high grade, ranging between 75 and 80 percent bone phosphate of lime (BPL), or between 34.31 and 36.6 percent phosphorus pentoxide (P_2O_5), a higher grade than that mined in both Morocco and the United States.[24] It also promised to be particularly easy to mine by open-cast methods, since the deposit lay just below the surface, about 2.5 to 7 meters in depth, spread over about ninety square miles.[25]

ENMINSA set about trying to attract foreign capital for a project to open up the deposit. Several U.S. companies, among them Gulf Oil, W. B. Grace, Texaco and Standard Oil of California, showed interest in establishing a mining consortium, but in May 1967 the negotiations broke down. Another attempt, involving the International Mining and Chemical Corporation of Chicago and French and German companies, likewise ended in failure in January 1968. Apparently these firms were discouraged by the low price of phosphates on the world market, Western Sahara's uncertain political future and the Spanish government's insistence on maintaining full management control and sending the ore to Spain for processing into fertilizer.[26]

After the suspension of the talks with the International Mining and Chemical Corporation, the Spanish government decided to go it alone. A new INI subsidiary, Fosfatos de Bu-Craa, or Fosbrucraa for short, was founded in August 1969 with a brief to exploit the deposits. Loans were raised from the First Wisconsin National Bank and the U.S. Export-Import Bank, and by 1975, 24,476 million pesetas had been invested in the first phase of the Bou-Craa project, which provided an annual production capacity of 3.7 million tons of ore.[27] Since stripmining methods were possible, two giants draglines, each weighing three thousand tons, were shipped in from the U.S. to remove the topsoil. Bucketwheel excavators were brought to extract the underlying layer of ore and load it on to hundred-ton bottom-dump trucks. A storage area with a capacity to stockpile three hundred thousand tons of ore was built nearby, and most remarkable of all, a sixty-two-mile conveyor belt, the longest in the world, was constructed by Krupps of West Germany and the Continental Clouth rubber company at a cost of $72 million to transport the ore, at a rate of up to two thousand tons an hour, to the coast. Raised on stilts for protection against sand drifting, the conveyor belt clears the dune zone near the coast by means of a 5.5-mile bridge. Its 113,000 rollers are operated by eleven control stations, which are in turn monitored by a computerized control room at the coast.[28] There, at El-Ayouan Playa, twenty miles from the capital, the conveyor belt terminus adjoins another 300,000-ton storage area, where the ore can be stockpiled before being fed into a treatment plant. Nearby is a power station that generates the electricity needed to operate the whole system, from the draglines at Bou-Craa to the loading of ships at El-Ayoun Playa. The shallow coastal waters precluded the construction of a conventional harbor and so a two-mile-long pier, jutting out to sea at right angles from the coast, was built by the German firm Strabach. Three loading berths were built at its end, to receive ships of up to one hundred thousand tons, sixty thousand tons and twenty thousand tons respectively. The two larger berths can load ships at a rate of no less than four thousand tons an hour, the smallest at a rate of two thousand tons per hour.[29]

The first phosphate exports were shipped to Japan in May 1972. By 1975, annual production had reached over 2.6 million tons, making Western Sahara the world's sixth largest producer.[30] However, Fosbucraa's export capacity, which had already reached 3.7 million tons, was due to be increased by 1980 to 10 million tons, which would have been roughly equivalent to the quantity shipped annually by the U.S., the world's second largest phosphate exporter, and not far behind the first, Morocco, which exported 16.4 million tons in 1980.[31] For Spain, which had previously imported most of its phosphate rock from Morocco, the Bou-Craa mines ensured vital supplies of ore for its newly built phosphoric acid plants at Huelva, near Cadiz; and during the 1974–75 world phosphate boom, when Morocco quadrupled its export prices, the Huelva plants received their supplies from Bou-Craa at pre-boom prices.[32] Fosbucraa, meanwhile, was confident that it would be able to recover its investment in the first phase of the Bou-Craa project, which had established the initial production capacity of 3.7 million tons a year, within ten years; indeed, the company's proceeds from sales of phosphate reached 4,771 million pesetas in 1974 alone.[33]

In the early sixties the search for oil and minerals had been hampered by the primitive state of the territory's economic and administrative infrastructure. There were insufficient supplies of water and electricity, inadequate ports, roads and telecommunications, and not enough labor. Belatedly the government in Madrid took stock of the shortcomings and began pumping in the funds needed to take advantage of the colony's mineral potential. In 1960 Western Sahara's provincial budget had been a mere 53.5 million pesetas, of which subsidies from Madrid had accounted for four-fifths (42.3 million pesetas). A year later the budget had quadrupled to 207.3 million pesetas.[34] The Spanish government appointed a special commission in November 1964 to draft what was to become the territory's first development plan. The priority was to plug the most serious infrastructural gaps. The following February, Madrid approved an extraordinary budget of 225.7 million pesetas for public works projects, raising the province's total annual budget to 552 million pesetas, and in November 1965 a director of economic and social development was appointed to oversee investment in the territory. A 250-million-peseta development plan was finally launched in 1966.[35] By 1972 the provincial budget had risen to 1,276 million pesetas (Table 12.2). Two years later it had doubled again to 2,472 million pesetas, of which 1,310 million pesetas were allocated to capital projects. Subsidies from Madrid accounted for 1,701 million pesetas, 69 percent of the total budget, but as tax revenue from the phosphate industry was now coming on stream, the dependence on budgetary subsidies was expected to diminish rapidly.[36]

A prerequisite for development was the rapid expansion of the supply of water. Between 1960 and 1970 prospectors found 175 new water sources and 170 million pesetas were invested in increasing the supply, which rose fiftyfold during the decade, from a capacity of only 1,130 cubic meters a day to 54,300 cubic meters. El-Ayoun's water supply rose from a mere 200 cubic meters a day in 1960 to 3,000 cubic metres a day in 1970, though the water was salty and barely drinkable.[37] In 1972 a water desalination plant with a capacity of 3,500 cubic meters a day was completed at El-Ayoun Playa to service the phosphate industry.[38] In the south, near Villa Cisneros, which had previously had to import its drinking water from the Canaries, an oil-exploration team chanced upon a huge subterranean freshwater lake. It may be the largest to have been found anywhere in the world, for it reportedly extends over twenty-three hundred square miles, with a depth of between thirty and two hundred feet, about fourteen hundred feet below the surface. A well drilled there in the sixties produced five thousand cubic meters a day, and the Spanish authorities set up three experimental farms nearby. One day,

TABLE 12.2
WESTERN SAHARA'S BUDGET, 1972–74
(in million pesetas)

	1972	1973	1974
Revenue			
Territorial revenue	280	315	771
Subvention by Spain	703	957	1,701
Funds for reserve	293	325	—
Total	1,276	1,597	2,472
Expenditure			
Recurrent expenditure	575	909	1,150
Capital expenditure	702	690	1,310
Total	1,277	1,599	2,460

SOURCE: Report of the United Nations Visiting Mission to Spanish Sahara, 1975, in *General Assembly Official Records*, 30th Session, Supplement 23, UN Document A/10023/Rev. 1, page 52.

perhaps, the funds will be available, perhaps from phosphate revenue, to make at least this part of the desert bloom.[39]

Another indicator of Spain's infrastructural investment in the territory in the sixties is that installed electrical generating capacity rose from 1,150 kilowatts in 1963 to 3,430 kilowatts in 1969, by which date there were four power stations. Another power station had been built by 1972 to provide electricity for Fosbucraa.[40] Meanwhile, new port facilities were provided to handle the increasing volume of trade. A 450-meter quay was completed at Villa Cisneros in 1961, though access remained restricted to vessels under six thousand tons because of the sandbanks at the entrance to the Río de Oro bay. The first jetty to be built near El-Ayoun, at El-Ayoun Playa, was completed in 1961 too; until then cargo used to be brought to the beach by launches from ships waiting out to sea. The same year a twenty-three-million-peseta road was built from the Playa to the capital. A decade later the Fosbucraa port was built, and besides its three phosphate-loading berths, this also had an unloading berth for general goods which could accommodate ships of up to ten thousand tons.[41]

As investment in the phosphate industry and basic infrastructure proceeded, imports of machinery and fuel rapidly increased. So did imports of consumer goods, as thousands of Spaniards and Saharawis settled in the territory's small towns to take up jobs. Overall, imports rose almost tenfold between 1959 and 1971, from 170 million pesetas to 1.6 billion pesetas.[42] By contrast there was almost nothing to export, except some fish, until the first phosphate shipments in 1972. So, until then, there was an enormous trade deficit. By 1974, however, phosphate receipts had reached 4.7 billion pesetas, far outstripping imports.

As the modern sector of the economy expanded, thousands of Spanish workers began to arrive in the territory, mainly from the Canary Islands, where unemployment was rife. At first they came alone, without their families; but then, as schools and social amenities were provided, they started to bring their families over. Between 1958 and 1967 the number of Europeans, excluding temporarily posted military personnel, grew from 1,710 to 9,726; by 1974 the number had more than doubled, to 20,126.[43] El-Ayoun, where there had been little more than a military post and a few *khaimat* and shacks in the fifties, was gradually converted into a real town, with a population of over 40,000, one-third Spanish, by 1974; and by 1970 television repeaters in both El-Ayoun and Villa Cisneros were relaying Spanish TV from the Canary Islands.[44]

The phosphate industry was capital-intensive and so did not provide many jobs, but, of its work force of 2,620 in 1975, 65 percent were Europeans. They not only held 81 percent of supervisory and technical posts but many of the unskilled jobs too.[45]

Despite the influx of Spanish labor, many Saharawis too began arriving in the towns looking for work. By 1974 there were around 8,000 Saharawi wage-earners in all—5,465 of them unskilled laborers, 345 industrial workers, 707 drivers, 190 office employees, 141 teachers and 1,341 soldiers and policemen, among others.[46] Albeit still minuscule by international standards, a Saharawi working class was being born. Meanwhile, other Saharawis put their age-old commercial skills to use by setting up shop in the growing towns as traders, taking advantage of the expanding urban market and also of the opportunities, due to Western Sahara's status as an extension of the Canary Islands' special customs zone, to smuggle such goods as household electrical appliances, cigarettes and building materials at virtually duty-free prices across the long unpoliceable frontiers into Morocco, Mauritania or Algeria. By 1974 the Spanish census authorities could count 981 Saharawi traders in the territory.[47]

The territory's growing labor requirements and the settlement of European families prompted the colonial authorities to begin providing modern educational and training facilities, which had been almost nonexistent before the sixties. As late as 1959 there had been only seven primary-school teachers and 366 primary-school pupils in the whole country.[48] There was no secondary education at all until October 1963, when the General Alonso secondary school opened its doors in El-Ayoun. It had a branch in Villa Cisneros.[49] By 1974 there were 9,252 children in school, 6,170 of them Saharawis, though still only 111 of the 653 secondary-school pupils were Saharawi.[50] Meanwhile, the Spanish ministry of labor's Promoción Profesional Obrera (PPO) set up two training schools in El-Ayoun and Villa Cisneros in 1967; and, by 1972, they had trained 1,500 Saharawis in such fields as masonry, carpentry, catering, secretarial skills and electrical and mechanical trades.[51] By 1975, seventy-five Saharawis were studying in Spain on government grants, fifty-two of them at universities or other institutions of higher education.[52]

The availability of jobs, trading opportunities and educational and medical facilities in the towns all played a part in encouraging Saharawis to abandon their traditional nomadic way of life. The towns held out the promise of greater security and well-being than was possible in the desert, where fortune depended on the fortuities of the weather and where a serious drought could decimate the herds, leaving their owners destitute. A particularly harsh drought in 1959–63 is estimated to have killed off 46 percent of the country's camels, reducing their numbers from 44,848 to 24,300, and though there was a gradual recovery during the sixties, another great drought, in 1968–74, is thought to have wiped out 60 percent of the livestock.[53]

Sedentarization occurred on a mass scale throughout the Sahara during this period. In Mauritania, for example, the nomadic proportion of the population fell from 65 percent in 1965 to 36 percent in 1977, while the population of the capital, Nouakchott, grew tenfold, from a mere 12,300 to 134,986.[54] Though no totally reliable statistics are available, it would appear that a majority of Western Saharans had abandoned nomadism by 1974, when the last census was conducted. The number of Saharawis living in the three main towns, El-Ayoun, Smara and Villa Cisneros, had tripled since 1967, reaching 40,660 (Table 12.3), or 55 percent of the total number of Saharawis recorded in the 1974 census, which put the total population at 95,019, of whom 73,497 were Saharawis, 20,126 Europeans and 1,396 from other African countries. However, the nomadic element of the population may have been underestimated, as the census authorities themselves noted the reluctance of some Saharawis to cooperate with their efforts.[55]

TABLE 12.3

THE GROWTH OF THE URBAN SAHARAWI

POPULATION

	1967	1974
El-Ayoun	9,701	29,010
Smara	1,916	7,280
Villa Cisneros	2,364	5,370
Total, three main towns	13,981	40,660

SOURCES: *Resumen estadístico del Sahara español (Año 1969)* (Instituto de Estudios Africanos, Madrid, 1970), page 10; *Censo-74* (Servicio de Registro de Población, Censo y Estadística, El-Ayoun, 1974), page 44.

The census also took no account, of course, of the Saharawis living beyond Western Sahara's frontiers. However, sedentarization among the Ahel es-Sahel, the *qabael* with historic migratory, pastoral traditions in the belt of territory roughly encompassed by Western Sahara, had proceeded on as large a scale in southern Morocco, northern Mauritania and southwestern Algeria as within the Spanish colony. Political as well as economic factors had encouraged many thousands of Saharawis to settle in southern Morocco in 1958 after the collapse of the Army of Liberation and the Spanish withdrawal from the Tarfaya region. They had lost much of their livestock during the war with the Spanish and French, and many of their remaining animals perished in the ensuing 1959–63 drought. Impoverished, they squatted in such southern Moroccan settlements as Tarfaya, Tan-Tan, Zaag and Goulimine, where they could find relief, jobs and education. To avoid destitution, in fact, many joined the FAR after the disbanding of the Army of Liberation. By 1966 there were 27,976 members of Western Saharan tribes living in the province of Tarfaya, according to census results published by the Moroccan ministry of the interior.[56] There were certainly a few thousand more farther north, and it seems unlikely that there could have been less than forty thousand to fifty thousand Saharawis in Morocco by 1974. Likewise, several thousand Reguibat and other Saharawis settled in northern Mauritania in the sixties and early seventies, partly as a result of the growth of employment in Zouerate and Nouadhibou brought about by the opening of the iron-mining industry and the expansion of economic and administrative infrastructure there. Reguibat sedentarization also occurred in southwestern Algeria, mainly around Tindouf, with the assistance of the Algerian government, which launched a settlement program for drought-stricken Reguibat in 1966. In the early 1970s, Reguibat were helped to set up agricultural villages at Abadla, southwest of Bechar, and at Oum el-Assel, Ain Naga and Hassi Abdallah near Tindouf. By 1975 there were some 18,000 Reguibat in Algeria, of whom at least 10,000 were sedentary.[57] In all, perhaps, there could have been 200,000 Ahel es-Sahel, or Saharawis, by this date, about half of them living within Western Sahara, the rest beyond its borders.

Despite this dispersal across several countries, a marked sense of kindred continued to be felt by the members of families, fractions and tribes divided by the political frontiers. Except for those who had been born in the towns, almost all had previously migrated into or through Western Sahara as nomads, at least in their childhood, and very few Saharawis did not have close family relatives who had settled in one or more of the other countries with Saharawi communities. It is not surprising, in view of these strong bonds between Saharawis across state frontiers, that Saharawis who had settled in Morocco, Algeria and Mauritania were to come to play as important a part in the Saharawi nationalist movement as their relatives who had settled within the Spanish colony.

NOTES

1. Emilio Menéndez del Valle, *Sahara español: una descolonización tardía* (Editorial Cuadernos para el Diálogo, Madrid, 1975), p. 10.

2. Besides oil, iron, phosphates and vanadium, Western Sahara is reputed to have titanium oxide, tungsten, platinum, gold, chrome, tin, beryl and manganese, among others. See Pamela Smith, "Imbroglio in the Sahara," *Arabia and the Gulf* (London), November 21, 1977, pp. 8–9.

3. "La pêche maritime au Maroc," *Revue bimensuelle d'Information* (Banque Marocaine du Commerce Extérieur, Casablanca), No. 141, March 1979, p. 2. This referred, moreover, only to the coast of the zone of Western Sahara annexed by Morocco in 1975–76. It excluded the coast of the zone briefly held by Mauritania, which Morocco did not annex until August 1979.

4. Attilio Gaudio, *Le dossier du Sahara occidental* (Nouvelles Editions Latines, Paris, 1978), pp. 339–40.

5. *La importancia del sector pesquero en la economía de la Provincia de Las Palmas* (Organización Sindical de Las Palmas, Secretariado de Asuntos Económicos, Las Palmas, June 1975), p. 3.

6. *Ibid.*, p. 9.

7. *Informe sobre el Acuerdo Pesquero Hispano-Marroquí por lo que afecta a Canarias* (Las Palmas, undated), p. 2; Francisco Hernández-Pacheco and José María Cordero Torres, *El Sahara español* (Instituto de Estudios Políticos, 1962), p. 163.

8. Mowton L. Waring Jr., *Spanish Sahara, Focus of Contention* (Air War College, Air University, Maxwell Air Force Base, Alabama, 1976), p. 23.

9. *Decreto por el que se aprueba las normas reglamentarias especiales sobre la aplicación de la ley de hidrocarburos en las provincias españolas en África* (Presidencia del Gobierno, Madrid, June 25, 1959).

10. J. A. Comba, "Investigación minera en el Sahara español," *África*, 17th Year, No. 227, November 1960, pp. 18–20.

11. For details, see Hernández-Pacheco and Cordero Torres, *op. cit.*, p. 165, and *Rencontres Méditerranéennes*, August-October 1962, pp. 378–79. The companies acquiring concessions were Spain Cities Service Petroleum Co., Richfield Sahara Petroleum Co., Banco Español de Crédito, Phillips Oil Co., Compañía Española de Petroleos, Spanish Gulf Oil Co., Texaco Spain Inc., California Oil Co. of Spain, Instituto Nacional de Industria, Atlantic Exploration Co., Union Oil Co. of California, Hispanic Sun Oil Co., Champlin Oil Refining Co., Pan-American Hispano Oil Co., Gao of Spain Inc., Sohio Iberian Oil Co., Tidewater Oil Co., Magellan Petroleum Co., Oil Investments Inc. and Safrep.

12. John Mercer, *Spanish Sahara* (George Allen and Unwin, London, 1976), p. 191; Jamil Moulahid, "Les sahraouis et le phosphate," *Esprit*, No. 4, April 1976, p. 782.

13. *ABC* (Madrid), September 15, 1974.

14. *ABC*, January 28, 1976.

15. *Chroniques Etrangères: Espagne* (Paris), No. 198, August 31, 1958, p. 12.

16. Abraham Serfaty, "Le pétrole au Sahara occidental derrière les appétits impérialistes," *Souffles* (Paris), new series, No. 2, October 1973, pp. 3–5.

17. *Reuters*, dispatches from Rabat, March 23, 1972, and May 20, 1974.

18. *Middle East Economic Digest* (London), March 31, 1978.

19. See Tony Hodges and James Ball, "Oil and the Western Saharan Conflict," *Quarterly Energy Review: Africa* (Economist Intelligence Unit, London), 2nd Quarter 1982, p. 3.

20. For details, see *ibid.*, p. 4.

21. Mercer, *op. cit.*, pp. 88–89; Comba, *loc. cit.*, pp. 16–17.

22. "El descubrimiento de los fosfatos del Sahara fue una verdadera aventura," *Ya* (Madrid), November 9, 1975.

23. However, the U.S. Bureau of Mines puts Western Sahara's total identified phosphate resources at only 1.6 billion tons (presumably taking account only of the Bou-Craa deposits), sixth in rank behind Morocco (40 billion tons), the U.S. (8 billion tons), South Africa (7 billion tons) and Australia (2 billion tons). See *Phosphate* (Bureau of Mines, U.S. Department of the Interior, Washington, January 1979), p. 3.

24. *Fosfatos de Bu-Craa, SA* (Instituto Nacional de Industria, Madrid, 1972), p. 10. The average grade of phosphate produced in Morocco and the U.S. is 32.7 percent and 31.1 percent P_2O_5 respectively (1976 figures). See "Les phosphates et les engrais au Maroc," *Maghreb-Développement* No. 3, 1977, p. 2.

25. *Fosfatos de Bu-Craa, SA*, p. 8.

26. Elsa Assidon, *Sahara occidental, un enjeu pour le Nord-Ouest africain* (François Maspero, Paris, 1976), p. 34.

27. Report of the United Nations Visiting Mission to Spanish Sahara, 1975, in *General Assembly Official Records*, 30th Session, Supplement 23, UN Document A/10023/Rev.1, p. 54.

28. *Fosfatos de Bu-Craa, SA*, pp. 26–27.

29. *Ibid.*, pp. 36–40.

30. After the U.S. (44.3 million tons in 1975), the U.S.S.R. (24.1 million tons), Morocco 13.5 million tons), Tunisia (3.5 million tons) and China (3.4 million tons). See "Les phosphates et les engrais au Maroc," *loc. cit.*, p. 2.

31. Report of the United Nations Visiting Mission to Spanish Sahara, 1975, *loc. cit.*, p. 53. Note that, despite being the world's two largest phosphate producers, the U.S. and the U.S.S.R. export only a small proportion of their output, and so Morocco, which is the world's third largest producer, is the leader exporter.

32. *Ibid.*, p. 53.

33. *Ibid.*, pp. 53–54.

34. "Les territoires espagnols d'Afrique," *Notes et Etudes Documentaires* (La Documentation Française, Paris), No. 2951, January 3, 1963, p. 19. All budget figures in this chapter exclude expen-

diture on the Spanish armed forces stationed in Western Sahara except local police and paramilitary forces.

35. Manuel Melis Clavería, "La Provincia de Sahara ante el plan de desarollo económico y social," *Africa*, 23rd Year, No. 295, July 1966, p. 4.

36. Report of the United Nations Visiting Mission to Spanish Sahara, 1975, *loc. cit.*, p. 52.

37. Mercer, *op. cit.*, p. 191; Juan Maestre Alfonso, *El Sahara en la crisis de Marruecos y España* (Akal, Madrid, 1975), p. 191.

38. *Fosfatos de Bu-Craa, SA*, p. 12.

39. See *General Assembly Official Records* (UN, New York), 28th Session, Supplement 23, Chapter 12; *Middle East Economic Digest*, April 16, 1976.

40. *Resumen estadístico del Sahara español (Año 1969)* (Instituto de Estudios Africanos, Madrid, 1970), p. 15; *Fosfatos de Bu-Craa, SA*, p. 45.

41. *Ibid.*, p. 37; Santiago García Peñalver, "Realidades del Sahara," *Africa*, 18th Year, Nos. 236–37, August-September 1961.

42. "Les territoires espagnols d'Afrique," *loc. cit.*, p. 18; Virginia Thompson and Richard Adloff, *The Western Saharans* (Croom Helm, London, 1980), p. 123.

43. Hernández-Pacheco and Cordero Torres, *op. cit.*, p. 143; *Resumen estadístico del Sahara español (Año 1969)*, p. 10; Report of the United Nations Visiting Mission to Spanish Sahara, 1975, *loc. cit.*, p. 38.

44. Ramiro Santamaría, "La obra de España en el Sahara," Part II, *Africa*, 27th Year, No. 338, February 1970, p. 6.

45. Report of the United Nations Visiting Mission to Spanish Sahara, 1975, *loc. cit.*, p. 54.

46. *Censo-74* (Servicio de Registro de Población, Censo y Estadística, El-Ayoun, 1974), p. 74.

47. *Ibid.*, p. 74.

48. *Mercer, op. cit.*, p. 203.

49. "El enseñanza media en el Sahara," *Africa*, 24th Year, No. 310, October 1967, p. 11.

50. Report of the United Nations Visiting Mission to Spanish Sahara, 1975, *loc. cit.*, p. 57.

51. Ramiro Santamaría, "La cultura, arma de paz en el Sahara español," *Africa*, 24th Year, No. 363, March 1972, p. 8.

52. Report of the United Nations Visiting Mission to Spanish Sahara, 1975, *loc. cit.*, p. 58.

53. Maestre Alfonso, *op. cit.*, p. 190; *Report of the Special Committee*, UN Document A/9623/Add.4 (Part II), November 13, 1974, pp. 24–25.

54. *Seconds résultats provisoires du recensement général de la population (population au 1er janvier 1977)* (Bureau Central de la Population, Ministère du Plan et des Mines, Nouakchott), pp. 13, 17.

55. *Censo-74*, pp. 5, 44; Report of the United Nations Visiting Mission to Spanish Sahara, *loc. cit.*, p. 38. The census gave a tribal breakdown of the Saharawi population: 52 percent (32,792) were Reguibat, divided almost evenly between the Reguibat es-Sahel (18,347) and the Reguibat esh-Sharg (19,625). Two Tekna tribes, the Izarguien (7,984) and the Ait Lahsen (3,540), were the second and fifth largest groups. The other main groups were the Oulad Delim (5,382), the Oulad Tidrarin (4,842) and the Arosien (2,858). See *Censo-74*, pp. 52–57.

56. Gaudio, *op. cit.*, p. 45.

57. Eugénie Muret, *Le processus de sédentarisation des nomades reguiebat de la région de Tindouf (Algérie)* (unpublished dissertation), pp. 21, 74–79.

13

Spain's
Desert "Province"

FRANCOIST SPAIN was not admitted to the United Nations until as late as 1955. Then, as a new member, it was requested by the UN secretary-general on February 24, 1956, to provide information on its colonies. The Madrid government bided its time and, before replying, changed the legal status of its colonies in Western Sahara, Ifni, Río Muni and Fernando Po to Spanish "provinces." Western Sahara, as we have seen, was converted into a province upon the dissolution of Africa Occidental Española in January 1958, during the war with the Army of Liberation.[1] After this constitutional conjuring trick, Madrid blandly informed the UN on November 10, 1958, that "Spain possesses no non-self-governing territories, since the territories subject to its sovereignty in Africa are, in accordance with the legislation now in force, considered to be and classified as provinces of Spain."[2]

However, the Spanish government had difficulty in denying the colonial character of its African provinces, and on November 11, 1960, it finally announced that it would start reporting, as requested, to the UN about conditions in these territories. Madrid was shocked, however, when the General Assembly adopted its first resolution on Western Sahara and Ifni in December 1965. Only Portugal joined Spain in voting against it. The Franco government had strong incentives to conciliate the UN and reappraise its colonial policy. Though it had already succeeded, by and large, in breaking out of its postwar international isolation, it wanted to rally international support for its claim to Gibraltar, which Spain had been forced to cede to England under the Treaty of Utrecht in 1713. To summon third-world support at the UN, where it had been arguing its case since 1963, it was presenting the Gibraltar dispute as a colonial question. The Spanish government was embarrassed to be accused of practicing colonialism itself, and Jaime de Piniés, a member of the Spanish delegation to the UN, tried to soothe his country's critics during a debate on Western Sahara and Ifni in December 1966 by arguing that it was wrong to "suspect Spain's intentions in this field while we have a colonial problem on our own soil."[3] The Franco government was particularly anxious not to alienate Arab states, and especially those of the Maghreb. Its foreign policy had set great store on cultivating friendly relations with the Arab world, both to promote Spanish economic interests and muster Arab support at the UN, and Franco, who had always refused to recognize Israel, sent letters to all the Arab governments in 1966 to reaffirm Spain's support for their stand on the Palestinian question.[4]

In May 1966, therefore, four members of Franco's cabinet visited Western Sahara to examine conditions in the territory at first hand.[5] Four months later the Spanish government signaled a significant policy shift in a letter to the UN's Committee of 24 which proposed resolving the Ifni dispute through bilateral talks with Morocco and accepted the principle of self-determination in Western Sahara.[6] "We are prepared to apply the principle of self-determination in the Sahara," confirmed Spain's UN ambassador, Manuel Aznar, on October 12; and Jaime de Piniés went further on December 7, announcing that "my delegation is prepared to initiate discussions with the secretary-general with a view to studying the nomination of a commission to go to Spanish Sahara" in order to "observe the territory's situation directly and objectively" and "form an opinion on the problem, confirming Spain's sincerity regarding decolonization."[7] Nonetheless, the Spanish government could not bring itself to vote in favor of the resolution adopted in the General Assembly a few days later, on December 20, and justified its negative vote on the grounds that the resolution required Spain to consult the Moroccan and Mauritanian governments on the holding of the proposed referendum.[8] The Spanish delegation to the UN abstained on the four broadly similar resolutions adopted by the General Assembly in 1967–70 but voted against the much tougher resolution adopted in 1972 which called for a ban on foreign investment in Western Sahara.

On September 6, 1967, Jaime de Piniés informed the Committee of 24 that negotiations had started "at the highest level" with Morocco about Ifni.[9] Franco had exchanged messages with King Hassan, it seems, and a few days later, on September 23–24, the Spanish foreign minister, Fernando María Castiella, met his counterpart, Ahmed Laraki.[10] In a speech to the UN General Assembly three weeks later, on October 12, Laraki revealed that "an agreement in principle has just been concluded between the two governments for the practical implementation of the resolution regarding the territory of Ifni."[11] The following year, Spain withdrew from Fernando Po and Río Muni, which achieved independence as the state of Equatorial Guinea on October 12, 1968. Less than three months later, on January 4, 1969, Spain signed the Treaty of Fez, by which Ifni was handed over to Moroccan administration the following summer, on June 30. There was opposition to the cession of Ifni from the more blinkered Falangists, to whom it seemed a betrayal of Spain's African mission. In the normally pliant Cortes, sixty-five *procuradores* voted against ratification of the treaty and twenty-five abstained. It was an unprecedented display of dissent, but the government still had a majority of 230.[12] In Franco's view, Ifni had no strategic or economic value whatever. It was a precedent, perhaps, to give it up, but its cession scored Spain diplomatic points at the UN and, it would seem, a reprieve from Hassan with regard to Western Sahara, Ceuta and Melilla. Moreover, only the small enclave around Sidi Ifni had actually remained under Spanish control since 1957, and the

Treaty of Fez was coupled with a fishing agreement that gave Spanish fishermen the right to fish freely in Moroccan waters and so appeared to resolve Spain's long-running fishing dispute with Morocco.

As a result of the cession of Ifni and the independence of Equatorial Guinea, Western Sahara became Spain's sole remaining African colony, besides the presidios on Morocco's Mediterranean coast. Accordingly, the Dirección General de Plazas y Provincias Africanas changed its name to the Dirección General de Promoción del Sahara, which had a less colonial ring about it. However, despite repeatedly assuring the UN that it would allow self-determination in Western Sahara, the Spanish government had no intention of doing so in practice, since the discovery of the territory's huge phosphate deposits had by now made it hot property. While it made plans for massive investment to exploit the Bou-Craa deposits, Spain tried to convince the UN that, while it supported the principle of self-determination, the referendum could not be rushed because of the nomadic character of the population and the low level of economic development. A referendum, Spain said, would be organized when the territory was "ready" for it and the indigenous population wanted one. Indeed, it was not until August 1974, almost eight years after the UN General Assembly's first resolution calling for a referendum in Western Sahara, that Spain finally announced that a referendum would be held, and it was not until May 1975 that it allowed a UN mission of inquiry to visit the territory.

Madrid's post-1966 Western Saharan policy was thoroughly hypocritical, yet it appeared to carry no serious political risks for Spain within the territory, at least until the early seventies, since there was no powerful, organized nationalist movement there pressing for implementation of the self-determination pledges. Indeed, the Spanish authorities in El-Ayoun succeeded in persuading eight hundred sheikhs to address a petition to the UN on March 21, 1966, supporting continued union with Spain. "The Saharan people, through their authentic representatives, declare with total integrity that their wish is to remain indissolubly united with the Spanish state," it read. The sheikhs rejected the territorial claims of neighboring countries and added that "if one day we have the ability to build an independent country, we will come to an arrangement with the Spanish state alone."[13] The following October, the colonial administration organized a referendum on a similar document. The choice was to sign or abstain. At *djemaa* meetings held across the territory between October 3 and 20, 14,637 Saharawis, approximately 89 percent of the 16,433 men over eighteen who were entitled to vote, signed their support.[14] There was a dissenting minority, for only half the Reguibat esh-Sharg signed.[15] In November, however, the petition was taken to the UN by an eight-member Comisión Elegida por el Pueblo del Sahara, which was chaperoned by the Director General de Plazas y Provincias Africanas, General Díaz de Villegas.[16] "An improvized independence would lead us to chaos and disorder," the commission testified to the UN. "The consequences and damage of such haste would fall on us, and we cannot allow a small minority of adventurers backed by any other nation to disturb our peace and tranquillity."[17]

So, while endorsing the principle of self-determination, the Spanish government could see little risk of actually having to concede independence. At the same time, the notion of self-determination allowed Madrid to rebuff the Moroccan and Mauritanian claims to Western Sahara. The territory's future, it could argue, was a matter to be determined exclusively by the Saharawis, without external interference. In fact, given Mauritania's weakness and the absence of a strong indigenous Saharawi anticolonial movement, Spain's principal concern was to avoid having to hand its valuable desert territory to Morocco, which, it was assumed in Madrid, would quickly challenge Spanish economic interests if it succeeded in annexing it. First, Morocco's Office Chérifien de Phosphates (OCP), which is the largest exporter of phosphate rock in the world, could be expected to elbow Spanish interests out of Bou-Craa, and secondly, in view of the long history of disputes over Spanish fishing rights off Morocco, the Moroccan government might try to restrict Spanish fishing off the Saharan coast, where the fishing resources are much more important than those farther north.[18]

The rival claims advanced by Morocco and Mauritania allowed the Franco regime to engage in divide-and-rule diplomacy, exploiting their governments' mutual suspicions, and at the same time to parade hypocritically before the UN as defenders of the Saharawis against their predatory neighbors. Spain's diplomacy in the Maghreb was buttressed, moreover, by the promotion of economic relations with all the states of the Maghreb, in which the great architect of Spanish policy was Gregorio López Bravo, the minister of industry in 1962–69 and foreign minister from 1969 to 1973. López Bravo, it will be recalled, had proposed wide-ranging cooperation in industrial projects during his visit to Morocco in March 1964, a few months after the Barajas summit which had set Spanish-Moroccan relations on a new footing. On June 2, 1964, a Spanish-Moroccan trade agreement had been signed, and during a subsequent visit to Morocco, on July 3–7, Castiella, who was Spain's foreign minister from 1957 to 1969, had proposed Spanish investment in such major industrial projects as the scheme to build a steel plant at Nador, in northeastern Morocco.[19] Two years later, on June 1, 1966, three agreements were signed in Rabat setting up joint Spanish-Moroccan companies in the fields of textiles, paper manufacture and tourism.[20] During a visit to Madrid by King Hassan in July 1969, Franco even suggested that Morocco should join Spain in exploiting Bou-Craa.[21] The idea, which would have implied tacit Moroccan recognition of the Spanish position in Western Sahara, was pursued by López Bravo in Rabat in May 1970, but Hassan refused the bait. "There can be no bargaining on the sacred principles of our national sovereignty and territorial integrity," said the king's foreign minister, Abdelhadi Boutaleb.[22] López Bravo returned to Morocco, however, in March 1971, to sign an agreement setting up a joint Spanish-Moroccan commission for economic, cultural, scientific and technical cooperation, which held its first meeting the following May.[23]

Mauritania was repeatedly reassured, meanwhile, that Spain would not settle the Western Saharan dispute bilaterally with Morocco behind Mauritania's back, and it too was offered aid, notably for its fishing industry. Under an agreement signed in February 1964, Spanish fishing boats were granted access to Mauritania's territorial waters in return for Spanish investment in a joint fishing company, IMAPEC, whose installations in Nouadhibou were finally inaugurated in 1972. The most extensive economic relations, however, were with Algeria, which became a major market for Spanish industry, especially in view of European

Economic Community trade barriers. Algeria became Spain's largest export market in Africa and by 1971 the value of Spanish-Algerian trade had reached $60 million a year.[24] In February 1972, moreover, López Bravo signed an agreement in Algiers for the purchase of twenty-three billion cubic meters of Algerian natural gas over eighteen years, beginning in 1974, and this seemed destined to make Spain Algeria's third main export market, after the U.S. and France. At the same time Spain provided more than 2.5 billion pesetas of credit to Algeria.[25] Spain held out the option of importing another five billion cubic meters of gas a year if a direct pipeline could be laid from Algeria to Spain under the Mediterranean, and so, the following November, the Sociedad de Estudios del Gasoducto Mediterraneo Occidental (Segamo) was founded by the Algerian hydrocarbons company, Sonatrach, the Spanish gas company, Enagas, and Gaz de France.[26] For its part, the Spanish oil company, Hispanoil, signed an agreement with Sonatrach the following year, in June 1973, under which it planned to invest $33.6 million in oil exploration in Algeria.[27]

Though motivated by economic interests, the growth of this nexus of economic relations between Spain and the countries of the Maghreb had the added advantage, as far as López Bravo and other Spanish ministers were concerned, of dampening the militancy of northwest African states regarding Western Sahara. There can be little doubt that it did so.

Within Western Sahara, the January 1958 decree had made El-Ayoun the province's capital and placed overall responsibility for its administration in the hands of a governor-general, who had to be a military officer with the rank of brigadier-general or major-general. As a commander of the armed forces in Western Sahara he tok orders in military matters from the captain-general of the Canary Islands, but otherwise he was directly responsible to the presidency in Madrid, through its colonial office, the Dirección General de Plazas y Provincias Africanas, or, as it was known after 1969, the Dirección General de Promoción del Sahara. Despite its provincial status, the Spanish government was under no illusion that it could administer Western Sahara in the same way as the provinces of the peninsula. "The peculiarity of the various physical and human factors displayed by the Spanish province of the Sahara is unquestionable," acknowledged the preamble of a law on the province's organization, enacted on April 19, 1961. It cited the Saharawis' nomadism their adherence to Islam and the desert climate among special factors that had to be taken into account in adapting the normal Spanish administrative system to Saharan conditions.[28]

So long as the great majority of Saharawis were still nomads, migrating in search of pastures for their animals across a territory more than half the size of metropolitan Spain, the colonial authorities could not administer them directly. They had to work in harness with the tribes' own leaders and institutions. Thus, the April 1961 law gave official status to the tribal fractions in the province's system of local government and stated that they would be administered in accordance with "norms of customary character." A decree on the territory's local government, enacted on November 29, 1962, went into detail, specifying that the fractions would be administered by councils responsible to the traditional *djemaas* and headed by fraction leaders elected according to custom by heads of families and confirmed in office by the governor-general.[29]

Though they were still very small, the November 1962 decree gave the two main coastal towns, El-Ayoun and Villa Cisneros, the status of municipalities (*terminos municipales*), with the right to their own city councils (*ayuntamientos*), comprising elected *concejales*, twelve in El-Ayoun and eight in Villa Cisneros, and state-appointed mayors (*alcaldes*). Smara and La Guera were given the lesser status of "minor local entities" (*entidades locales menores*) and the right to elect four-man local *juntas*. For the territory as a whole, there was to be a fourteen-member Cabildo Provincial (provincial council); and the province was to be represented in the Cortes in Madrid.

The elections to these bodies were no more democratic, of course, than those held in metropolitan Spain in the Francoist period. The official Falange was the only legal party, and no Saharawis could stand for office on an openly anticolonial platform. The electorate was confined to male heads of families resident in the municipalities and the "minor local entities," and since so few Saharawis lived in the urban areas in the early sixties, a large proportion of the voters were Spaniards. In any case, only half of the *concejales* of the *ayuntamientos* were elected by these male family heads. In tune with classic Francoist principles, the rest were chosen by corporate groups, representing trade, industry, culture and the professions, in which, of course, Spaniards were predominant. Moreover, the corporate groups could not elect anyone they wanted. They had to submit names to the governor-general, who would then compile official lists of candidates, three times as many as the number of seats to be filled.

The Cabildo Provincial was indirectly elected. It had two representatives from the *ayuntamientos* and *juntas locales*, six representatives from the nomad fractions and six delegates representing trade, industry, culture and the professions, elected as at the local level from lists prepared by the governor-general with three times as many candidates as the number of seats.

None of these councils could choose their own leaders. The presidency in Madrid appointed both the president of the Cabildo Provincial and the *alcalde* of El-Ayoun, upon the advice of the governor-general, while the *alcalde* of Villa Cisneros and the presidents of the two *juntas locales* of Smara and La Guera were nominated directly by the governor-general.

When the first provincial elections were held in May 1963, seven Spaniards and five Saharawis were elected councillors in El-Ayoun and a Spaniard was appointed as the capital's mayor. In Villa Cisneros, four Saharawis and four Spaniards were elected, but a fifth Saharawi, a sheikh of the Oulad Delim by the name of Souilem Ould Abdellahi, was appointed *alcalde* by the governor-general. In La Guera and Smara two Saharawis and two Spaniards were elected to each *junta local*. In the subsequent elections to the first Cabildo Provincial, seven Spaniards and seven Saharawis won seats, and the government in Madrid chose to appoint another Saharawi loyalist as its president. He was Khatri Ould Said Ould el-Joumani, who, despite his decision to rally to the French in Mauritania in December 1957 during the Army of Liberation's insurgency, had since settled in Western Sahara and become a "Spaniard." Under the indirect, corporatist electoral system, Khatri, Souilem and the Spanish mayor of El-Ayoun, Pozo Crespo, then took their seats in the Spanish Cortes in Madrid on July 15, 1963.[30]

Under the November 1961 decree the elected members of the Cabildo Provincial, the *ayuntamientos* and the *junta locales* were to have a four-year mandate, but since half the seats were to come up for election every two years, the second elections were held in 1965. Khatri was replaced as president by another staunch supporter of the Spanish connection, Saila Ould Abeida Ould Ahmed, like Khatri a sheikh of the Reguibat. In 1967 the province's number of *procuradores* in the Cortes was raised from three to six.[31]

Neither the Cabildo Provincial nor the *ayuntamientos* had any real power. They were required to provide basic provincial or municipal services, but their decisions could be overruled by the governor-general and they were almost entirely dependent on subsidies from Madrid, where the cabinet retained the right to determine the territory's budget, took major decisions on its future development and decided which Spanish laws were compatible with the territory's special status. The governor-general was responsible in civilian administrative matters to the presidency in Madrid, rather than to the Cabildo Provincial, whose decisions he could veto whenever he deemed fit. The province's civil servants were responsible to him, rather than the council, and he had the power to issue special decrees for the territory.[32] Second in command was the secretary-general, who took day-to-day charge of the civil administration and deputized for the governor-general in his military duties whenever he was absent. Like the governor-general, he was therefore a senior military officer, as normally were the *delegados gubernativos*, the officials who headed the two *delegaciones regionales* for the northern and southern regions of the province, based at El-Ayoun and Villa Cisneros respectively.

There was no alternative to indirect rule through the traditional *djemaas* so long as most Saharawis remained nomadic. However, administrative reforms were required when large numbers of Saharawis began settling in the towns and political expectations began to grow among urbanized Saharawis. The colonial authorities soon recognized that neither the Cabildo Provincial, which had only six members in 1967, nor the *ayuntamientos* provided adequate channels of communication with the Saharawi population. However, rather than set up a democratically elected legislative council, in which younger, more politically conscious leaders might have come to the fore, the colonial authorities decided to create a purely consultative assembly stacked with conservative, elderly sheikhs, men who owed their status largely to their loyalty to Spain. This was the Asamblea General del Sahara, or the Djemaa, as it came to be known, though it had little in common with the tribal *djemaas* of old.

At the UN, Spain pointed to the creation of the Djemaa in 1967 as proof of its desire to give a greater voice to the Saharawis. However, the assembly had no real power. Its functions, according to the May 1967 decree that established it, were to examine and give an opinion on matters of general interest to the territory, such as budgets, public works projects, education, agriculture and livestock, water supplies or other aspects of economic and social policy, to make observations or suggestions on laws and decrees so that they were well suited to the territory's special conditions, and, on its own intitiative, to propose *normas*, or legislative measures, to the government.[33] However, the governor-general was under no obligation to endorse such *normas* or to submit legislation to the assembly for its approval, and the latter did not control the territory's budget, which continued to be drawn up and approved by the government in Madrid.

Initially the Djemaa had eighty-two members, all of them Saharawis, though the secretary-general of the provincial administration acted, without vote, as the assembly's official "adviser" and another nonvoting Spanish official served as its secretary. A narrow majority of its members were *ex officio*—the president of the Cabildo Provincial, the *alcaldes* of El-Ayoun and Villa Cisneros and the officially recognized *sheikhs* of tribal fractions. Only forty members were directly elected, and even these were not elected by universal adult suffrage in geographically defined constituencies but were chosen by the *djemaas* of the tribal fractions.[34] Moreover, all these representatives had to receive the governor-general's endorsement before taking up their seats.[35]

The first elections were held between July 14 and August 20, 1967, giving time for the *djemaas* to assemble and select their representatives. The tribes were represented in the Djemaa in rough proportion to their size. Of the eighty-two seats, the Reguibat alone held forty-five, divided almost equally between the Reguibat es-Sahel (twenty-three) and the Reguibat esh-Sharg (twenty-two). The Oulad Delim had twelve seats, the Izarguien nine, the Arosien five and the Oulad Tidrarin seven, while the smaller tribes shared the remaining seven.[36] The inauguration of the assembly in El-Ayoun on September 11 was an occasion for unusual ceremony and pomp. The Tercio Don Juan de Austria of the Foreign Legion was on hand, to parade with full colors and a band, as seventy-eight of the eighty-two representatives, bedecked in the traditional *draa*, arrived to take their seats in the Salón Oriental. After a speech from the governor-general, they proceeded to the election of the assembly's president and vice-president, who, according to the May decree, had to be chosen from among the nonelected members. A Reguibi, Saila Ould Abeida, who was then still president of the Cabildo Provincial, was elected president and a prominent sheikh of the Oulad Delim, Baba Ould Hasseina Ould Ahmed, as his deputy. "We are men who have a duty to join together and work for greater unity with Spain and the welfare of our land," appealed Saila Ould Abeida after the voting results had been read out by the territorial *qadi*, Sheikh Galaoui.[37]

Half the seats were supposed to be reelected every two years, but it was not until January 1971 that the next elections, for forty seats, were held. Saila Ould Abeida was then succeeded as president by Khatri Ould Said Ould el-Joumani, while Baba Ould Hasseina Ould Ahmed remained vice-president.[38] Two years later the Spanish government decided to bring the system of tribal representation under closer scrutiny. Under a statute on a "newly structured organization of sheikhs and *djemaas*," published in the *Boletín Oficial del Sahara* on April 30, 1973, the tribes were divided into 114 sections, known as "family units," formed by fractions or subfractions, and ruled that henceforth their sheikhs would be elected by men aged twenty-one or over who held Spanish identity cards. The elected sheikh had to promise to be loyal to Spain and carry out his duties in cooperation with the Spanish authorities and police.[39] Elections were duly held on June 10. Meanwhile, the membership of the Djemaa was raised to 102, comprising the president of the Cabildo Provincial, the *alcaldes* of El-Ayoun and Villa Cisneros, forty official sheikhs, forty representatives elected by male Saharawis over twenty-one within the "family units" and sixteen representatives of such corporate groups as workers, craftsmen and the professions.[40]

The UN mission of inquiry which finally visited Western Sahara in May 1975 reported that the Djemaa appeared to "depend considerably for guidance on the Spanish authorities" and to be "representative largely of the older and more conservative element of Sahara society," owing to the method whereby its members were elected.[41] Men like Khatri Ould Said Ould el-Joumani and Saila Ould Abeida formed a privileged elite who owed their positions primarily to Spanish patronage and their loyalty to the colonial authorities. Nonetheless, the members of the Djemaa were not just "yes men." They were repeatedly assured by the Madrid government and its local officials in El-Ayoun that, when the territory was ready for self-determination, a referendum would be held on its future. Meanwhile, they were told, Spain was defending their true interests by investing in the territory's economic development and modernization and by warding off the aggressive designs of neighboring countries who coveted its mineral wealth. "Spain is here to protect you like a jealous mother," promised the province's secretary-general, Manuel Melis Clavería, with characteristic paternalism, at the ceremony inaugurating the Djemaa in September 1967.[42]

The Spanish authorities did their best to appear benevolent. Relief was distributed to drought-stricken nomads, subsidies were provided to keep down food prices in government run *economarts*, and schools and clinics were built. Bank loans were made available, meanwhile, to Saharawi traders, who also benefited, like the import-export houses in the Canaries, from the territory's "free zone" customs status; and the provision of bank credit could be subtly employed as a form of patronage to buy the loyalty of the trading class, who were well represented in the Djemaa.

At the same time, the Spanish authorities were careful to show respect for the Saharawis' customs and, above all, for their religion. In 1957–58 the Catholic Spanish had paraded as devoted defenders of Islam against the allegedly Godless and communist Moroccans commanding the Army of Liberation, and the April 1961 decree on the province's organization had made a point of guaranteeing the Saharawis' "right to practice the Muslim religion, as well as their traditional customs and ways." State funds were invested in the construction of mosques and every year the colonial government would charter an aircraft from the Spanish airline Iberia to lay on free trips to Mecca for selected pilgrims. Once again, it was the loyalist sheikhs and the richer traders who profited from such patronage.[43]

The colonial government trod with particular care with regard to judicial matters. The April 1961 decree pledged that, while the judicial system would be adapted to the Spanish model, traditional Koranic justice would be retained "in its present field of application." Outside the towns, disputes were resolved and crimes punished much as they always had been, by the *djemaas* and *qadis*. Within the towns a dual system of justice had been created during the fifties. A decree enacted in 1953 had stipulated that where "both or one of the two parties are not natives," cases would be heard by Spanish-style courts, either *juzgados locales* in El-Ayoun or Villa Cisneros, or the higher *juzgado territorial*.[44] A quite separate system had been set up for the settled Saharawi population under two decrees designed to streamline the traditional systems of customary *orf* law and Koranic *sharia* law and bring them under state supervision. The first decree, enacted in December 1955, had set up *orf* courts comprising a local Spanish official and three Muslims in El-Ayoun, Smara, Villa Cisneros, La Guera and

Aoussert, to try cases where the maximum sentence was a fine of five thousand pesetas or a month in jail. Appeals or more serious cases went to a *tribunal territorial* where cases were heard by the regional *delegado gubernativo*, an official adviser on Islamic justice and two Muslims, or the *tribunal superior* in El-Ayoun, where the provincial secretary-general sat in judgment with his secretary and two Muslims. A parallel system of Islamic civil courts, or *qodat* based on the *sharia* law, was set up under another decree, published in March 1956, and a provincial *qadi* was appointed to hear the most serious cases and appeals.[45]

Yet, in other ways the Spanish authorities offended the Saharawis' dignity. Their paternalistic manner was insulting. Believing that they were on a civilizing mission, they tended to denigrate Saharawi society and culture and often spoke of their Saharawi subjects as if they were children who required parental protection and guidance. Moreover, there seemed no place for the Arabic language, whether in official documents, in the classroom or even on road signs. The Spanish presence seemed overwhelming, dominant and a threat to the Saharawi way of life and culture. Indeed, as Spanish soldiers, administrators, mining technicians, shopkeepers and workers arrived in ever-increasing numbers, often bringing their families with them, the Saharawis felt that they were being swamped by outsiders. By 1974 there were over twenty thousand Spanish civilian residents and at least twenty thousand Spanish troops in the country, and in view of the small size of their own community, there seemed to be a very real danger, in Saharawi minds, that a continuation of the influx might eventually lead to their being outnumbered. In El-Ayoun, where more than half the Europeans lived, there was at least one Spaniard for every two Saharawis in the early seventies, and the town center, where the Spanish civilians lived, was beginning to look like a desert outpost of the Canary Islands, with a luxurious Parador Nacional de Turismo, scores of bars and even a nightclub, whose manager used to fly in striptease girls from Las Palmas. Though many of the civilian immigrants had come to escape unemployment in the Canary Islands, they seemed relatively prosperous and privileged to the Saharawis, who lived, almost without exception, in ghetto-like suburbs on the edge of the capital. Though there was no formal *apartheid*, such *de facto* segregation was real enough, and it was mirrored by informal social barriers that prevented almost all Saharawis from entering such centers of European entertainment as the municipal swimming pool, the Parador and the Casino.[46]

Most of the Saharawis who arrived in the towns in the late sixties and early seventies were impoverished. They had lost much of their livestock in droughts and had to sell some or all of their remaining animals to acquire the money needed to survive in an urban environment. Large encampments grew spontaneously on the edges of towns and degenerated into shanties, and though the Spanish launched a modest housing program in 1971, the UN mission that visited Western Sahara four years later was still struck by "the acute need to increase the availability of permanent housing in most of the population centers."[46]

Discontent grew, meanwhile, among most sectors of the urban Saharawi population. Though Saharawi workers technically received the same wages as Spanish workers with equivalent jobs, they were by and large employed in the lowest and most poorly paid grades, while Spanish employees practically monopolized skilled, managerial and technical posts, received bonuses for working abroad and also enjoyed family allowances not available to Saharawis. At Fosbucraa, for example, 81 percent of the technical and supervisory posts were held by Spaniards, and it was not surprising, perhaps, that the UN mission in 1975 should have found that the phosphate workers were "among the more politically active groups in the territory."[48] As in metropolitan Spain, of course, trade unions were illegal.

The Saharawi soldiers in the Tropas Nómadas had their grievances too. They were not integrated into regular army units and were often posted for long periods to remote desert outposts. They had almost no prospects of promotion, since all their officers were Spanish; and even in the Policía Territorial there were still only two Saharawis with commissioned rank as late as 1975.[49] Moreover, as the anticolonial movement gathered in strength in the early seventies, the Saharawi troops and police suffered the indignity of being employed to repress or fight against their own people. As we shall see, there were to be cases of mutiny and numerous desertions during the last year of Spanish rule.

It was among the youth, above all, that hostility toward the colonial *status quo* became most marked. The young, better educated Saharawis were disgusted by the paternalism of the local Spanish officialdom, keenly felt the anomaly that Western Sahara alone remained under European rule, years after all the neighboring countries had achieved independence, and lost patience with the timid, collaborative sheikhs in the Djemaa. In the schools, moreover, Saharawi students resented that all the teachers, except for a handful employed to teach Koranic and Arabic studies, were Spanish, that almost all the instruction was in Spanish, that they were pressured to join Francoist youth movements like the Organización de Juventud Española (OJE), and, perhaps most insulting of all, that their textbooks glorified Spain and its colonial history. Furthermore, despite the expansion of educational facilities, there were still formidable educational hurdles. As late as 1974, only 37 percent of the school-age population was enrolled in school. The dropout rate was so high that, whereas there were over six thousand Saharawi children in primary school by 1974, only one hundred and eleven were in secondary school. There were five times as many Spanish secondary-school students. Educational opportunities were particularly limited for Saharawi girls. Overall, only about one-eighth of Saharawi girls were attending school in 1974, and of them just three were in secondary school.[50]

Like Spain itself in the Francoist era, Western Sahara was administered by a dictatorial regime that was intolerant of dissent and hounded anyone who dared to step out of line. None of the basic democratic rights, of free speech, assembly, political organization, press and the like, were respected, any more than they were in metropolitan Spain. In many respects Western Sahara was a military colony. The senior administrative officials were military men, and, after the 1957–58 emergency, there were large permanent garrisons in all the main settlements. In some, the soldiers seemed to outnumber the local civilian population. Much of the Foreign Legion had been transferred from northern Morocco to Western Sahara and Ifni during the 1957–58 war. Two *tercios*, or regiments, of the Legion were stationed permanently in the Sahara, the Tercio Don Juan de Austria in the northern region of the territory, and the Tercio Alejandro Farnesio in the southern region. Modeled after the French Foreign Legion, this was an elite volunteer force and by the 1960s about 5 percent of its troops were still non-Spanish "soldiers of fortune." The two *tercios* of the Legion were supplemented by other Spanish regiments that consisted mainly of conscripts, several thousand of whom were sent out to the Sahara every year to carry out their military service. In the event of an emergency, there were thousands of additional troops, as well as air-force units, in reserve in the Canary Islands. Finally, there were the predominantly Saharawi Tropas Nómadas, divided into two battalions, the "Saguia el-Hamra" in the north and the "Capitán de Gándara" in the south, and the paramilitary Policía Territorial.[51]

In addition to these military forces, the colonial regime had an intelligence service, the Servicio de Información y Seguridad, whose informers and spies kept tabs on the Saharawi population and reported suspicious behavior. The Madrid government tried to keep a veil of secrecy over events in the territory. Even though it was considered a Spanish province, Spaniards, like other foreigners, required visas to visit the territory, and, except for those with jobs there, these were often refused or only granted for very short periods after long bureaucratic delays. As for press reporting, an official note distributed to all Spanish news media in July 1972 warned that "since information or commentaries in the Spanish press could compromise the interests of the State, all stories about Spanish Sahara are considered classified information."[52]

NOTES

1. Decreto por el que se reorganiza el Gobierno General del Africa Occidental Española, 10 de Enero de 1958, *Boletín Oficial del Estado* (Madrid), January 14, 1958. See Chapter 7.
2. Cited in *Western Sahara, Advisory Opinion of 16 October 1975* (International Court of Justice, The Hague, 1975), p. 25.
3. Jaime de Piniés in the Fourth Committee of the General Assembly, December 10, 1966, cited in Bernard Jacquier, "L'autodétermination du Sahara espagnol," *Revue Générale de Droit International Public*, Vol. 78, No. 3, July-September 1974, p. 697.
4. "Our uninterrupted policy of friendship with the Arab countries has become a constant element of our diplomacy," remarked López Bravo, the Spanish foreign minister, on February 31, 1971. "It must not just be understood in sentimental, historic, cultural terms. It is a realistic policy, consistent with our past, and which in turn has an influence on problems derived from our geopolitical position relating to North Africa. The Arab countries have appreciated our conduct and their fourteen votes at the United Nations are one of our surest supports. . . ." Cited in Rachid Lazrak, *Le contentieux territorial entre le Maroc et l'Espagane* (Dar el Kitab, Casablanca, 1974), pp. 21-22.
5. *Chroniques Etrangères: Espagne* (La Documentation Française, Paris), No. 7-66, July 1966, p. 19.
6. Lazrak, *op. cit.*, pp. 301-2.
7. *Chroniques Etrangères: Espagne*, No. 11-66, November 1966; *ABC* (Madrid), December 9, 1966.
8. *ABC*, December 17, 1966.
9. "La retrocession d'Ifni et les relations hispano-marocaines," *Maghreb*, No. 33, May-June 1969, p. 36.
10. *Maghreb Arabe Presse* (Rabat), September 24, 1967.
11. *Chroniques Etrangères: Espagne*, No. 11-67, November 1967. Significantly, a decree enacted the same year on the election of the national councilors of the Francoist Movimiento omitted Ifni.
12. Lazrak, *op. cit.*, pp. 336-37.
13. *ABC*, November 19, 1966.
14. *Ibid.*
15. John Mercer, *Spanish Sahara* (George Allen and Unwin, London, 1976), p. 235.

16. *ABC*, November 18, 1966, and November 19, 1966.

17. *ABC*, December 8, 1966.

18. In 1957, after Morocco's independence, Spain and Morocco had drafted a fishing agreement that would have given Spanish fishermen the right to fish in Moroccan waters, but it was never ratified by Morocco. Then, on June 30, 1962, Morocco extended its territorial waters from six to twelve miles. There were immediately numerous incidents between Moroccan coast guards and Spanish fishing boats, which were often escorted by Spanish warships. The dispute was not really resolved until the signing of the convention of Fez, on January 4, 1969, at the same time as the signing of the treaty ceding Ifni to Morocco. This ten-year agreement allowed both countries' fishermen to fish freely in each others' waters, an arrangement that really benefited only Spain. However, in January 1972, Morocco announced that it would make use of its right to abrogate the convention, from the following December 31. Then, on January 31, 1973, Morocco announced that it would extend its territorial waters from twelve to seventy miles and that all fishing within twelve miles of the Moroccan coast would be outlawed. Since no Spanish-Moroccan fishing agreement was then in force, this meant that Spanish fishing boats could not even fish within seventy miles of the coast. Spain protested, but King Hassan signed the decree imposing the new restrictions on March 9. Spanish warships tried to protect Spanish fishing boats from arrest by Moroccan coast guards, while talks proceeded between Spanish and Moroccan officials, culminating in a new fishing agreement on January 2, 1974, which only temporarily resolved the problems.

19. *Chroniques Etrangères: Espagne*, Nos. 7-8-64, July-August 1964, pp. 21-23.

20. *Chroniques Etrangères: Espagne*, No. 6-65, June 1965.

21. *Reuters*, dispatch from Rabat, July 3, 1969.

22. *Reuters*, dispatch from Rabat, May 8, 1970.

23. *Reuters*, dispatches from Rabat, March 13, 1971, and May 10, 1971.

24. Virginia Thompson and Richard Adloff, *The Western Saharans* (Croom Helm, London, 1980), p. 14.

25. Zakya Daoud, "Sahara: le Maroc face aux visées etrangères," *Lamalif* (Rabat), No. 65, September 1974.

26. *To the Point International*, March 7, 1977.

27. *El Moudjahid* (Algiers), June 23, 1973.

28. Ley 8/61, de 19 de Abril, sobre organización y régimen jurídico de la Provincia de Sahara, *Boletín Oficial del Estado*, April 21, 1961, p. 6062.

29. *Decreto de la Presidencia del Gobierno de 29 de Noviembre de 1962 por el que se aprueba el Ordenamiento de la administración local para la Provincia de Sahara*, *Boletín Oficial del Estado*, December 12, 1962.

30. *Chroniques Etrangères: Espagne*, No. 63-9, September 1963, p. 13.

31. Mercer, *op. cit.*, p. 200.

32. Decree 2604/61, December 14, 1961, Articles 13, 18 and 19.

33. Decree 1024/67, May 11, 1967, Article 174.

34. "La Yemáa o Asamblea General del Sahara," *Africa* (Madrid), 24th Year, No. 309, September 1967, p. 18.

35. Decree 1024/67, Article 168.

36. Manuel Castilla Ortega, "Se constituye la Asamblea General de Sahara," *Africa*, 24th Year, No. 310, October 1967, p. 8. The Ahel Sheikh Ma el-Ainin and the Ait Lahsen had two seats each, while the Tendega, the Ait Moussa Ou Ali and the Filala each had one.

37. *Ibid.*, p. 9.

38. *Report of the Special Committee*, UN General Assembly, 27th Session, 1972, UN Document A/8723/Add.4/Part II, p. 29.

39. Robert Rézette, *The Western Sahara and the Frontiers of Morocco* (Nouvelles Editions Latines, Paris, 1975), pp. 106-7.

40. Report of the United Nations Visiting Mission to Spanish Sahara, 1975, *General Assembly Official Records*, 30th Session, Supplement 23, UN Document A/10023/Rev.1, p. 42.

41. *Ibid.*, p. 44.

42. Castilla Ortega, *loc. cit.*, p. 10.

43. Juan Maestre Alfonso, *El Sahara en la crisis de Marruecos y España* (Akal, Madrid, 1975), p. 205.

44. Decree of January 23, 1953. See Francisco Hernández-Pacheco and José María Cordero Torres, *El Sahara español* (Instituto de Estudios Políticos, Madrid, 1962), p. 152.

45. *Ibid.*, pp. 144-45.

46. Soledad Balaguer and Rafael Wirth, *Frente Polisario: la última guerrilla* (Editorial Laia, Barcelona, 1976), pp. 32–33.

47. Report of the United Nations Visiting Mission to Spanish Sahara, 1975, *loc. cit.*, p. 56.

48. *Ibid.*, p. 55.

49. *Ibid.*, p. 50.

50. *Ibid.*, pp. 57–58.

51. Ramón Criado, *Sahara, pasión y muerte de un seuño colonial* (Ruedo Ibérico, Paris, 1977), pp. 105–6; Mercer, *op. cit.*, p. 226.

52. *Report of the Special Committee*, UN General Assembly, 27th Session, 1972, UN Document A/8723/Add.4/Part II, p. 30.

Khatri Ould Said Ould el-Joumani, Saharawi member of the Spanish Cortes, 1963–75

Ahmed Ould Brahim Ould el-Bashir, Saharawi member of the Spanish Cortes, 1970–75

Camel troops of the Territorial Police, El-Ayoun Y. NAGATA, UNITED NATIONS

Mohammed Sidi Ibrahim Bassiri, leader of the Liberation Organization of Saguia el-Hamra and Oued Ed-Dahab. Disappeared and presumed murdered after his arrest by the Spanish authorities in El-Ayoun, June 1970

El-Ouali Mustapha Sayed, first secretary-general of the Polisario Front. Killed in combat, 1976

Mohammed Lamine Ould Ahmed, prime minister of the Saharan Arab Democratic Republic, 1976–82

Polisario guerrillas, 1973

Mahfoud Ali Beiba, a founder of the Polisario Front. He was a deputy secretary-general of the Front in 1973–76 and became prime minister of the Saharan Arab Democratic Republic in 1982

Khalihenna Ould Rashid, secretary-general of the Saharan National Union Party (PUNS), and Khatri Ould el-Joumani at the United Nations MIGUEL JIMÉNEZ, UNITED NATIONS

14

The Genesis of Saharawi Nationalism

LIKE MANY MODERN AFRICAN NATIONS, Western Sahara has no historical antecedent. The Saharawis never constituted a nation in precolonial times, and their present-day nationalism is a very recent phenomenon that took root only in the latter part of the Spanish colonial period.

Before the arrival of the Spanish, no supratribal authority had ever regulated Western Saharan society, except briefly in the early days of the Almoravid movement, nine centuries ago. The harsh world of the desert, in which small nomadic groups had to migrate over vast areas in search of pastures, was not conducive to the rise of large and complex state structures, and as we have seen, Saharawi society was traditionally prone to intertribal raiding. The Saharawis' prime loyalties were therefore to tribe, fraction and family, the social groups within which political, military and judicial leaders were appointed, assemblies like the *djemaa* or *ait arbain* would meet, collective defense or raids were organized, and civil disputes were resolved and crimes punished. Likewise, it was by virtue of his place on the genealogical tree of his *qabila* or *fakhd* that the Western Saharan acquired an array of rights and obligations relating to such matters as the finding of marriage partners and responsibility for blood debts. Moreover, tribal identity and conflict were reinforced by the caste inequalities between free and vassal tribes.

Not surprisingly, notions of blood loyalty (*asabiya*) were particularly strong, and though the final establishment of a *pax gallica/hispanica* in 1934 terminated intertribal raiding, eroded the protection system at the root of the caste inequalities between tribes, and also diminished the day-to-day significance of the *fakhd* by allowing migration in much smaller groups to make better use of scarce pastoral resources, notions of tribal or fraction identity and loyalty had changed little by the late 1950s. They remained much stronger than any incipient sense of supratribal national identity, whether Western Saharan, Moroccan or Mauritanian.

Nevertheless, as men of the desert, great camel-herding nomads and speakers

149

of the Hassaniya dialect of Arabic, the Saharawis did, in a broad cultural sense, regard themselves as a very different people from the predominantly Tashelhit-speaking sedentary or seminomadic Berbers to their immediate north, in the Noun, the Bani and the Anti-Atlas. The Saharawis were, of course, only a branch of the *beidan*, the Hassaniya-speaking nomads of mixed Arab, Berber and black African ancestry who lived in the vast desert expanses between the Noun and the valleys of the Senegal and the bend of the Niger; but they had a certain distinctiveness, as the Ahel es-Sahel, the people of the Atlantic littoral, an especially arid zone whose *qabael* had never been subservient to either the sultans of Morocco or the Mauritanian emirs to the south. Such a regional identity and history of complete tribal independence might not have had any great political significance for the latter part of the twentieth century. On the face of it, the Saharawis of Western Sahara might appear to have far more in common with the Moors across the border in Mauritania than do the latter with their fellow Mauritanians, of Pulaar, Soninke and Peul ancestry, and similarly there is no intrinsic historical reason why the cultural differences between the Saharawis and their Moroccan neighbors to the immediate north should have been any more of a barrier to political integration today than those, say, between Arabophone and Berberophone Moroccans. Indeed, thousands of Saharawis had become part of a broad, transfrontier anticolonial struggle when they responded to the insurrectionary appeals of the Army of Liberation in 1956–58. However, though the Saharawi combatants in the Army of Liberation had been inspired to rise against the Europeans by Morocco's independence and though their senior commanders were Moroccans, they may not have had, as it were, a "Moroccan national consciousness." It was through the traditional *djemaas* that Saharawi fractions gave their support to the movement, and though some Saharawi participants in the struggle may have embraced the ideal of becoming part of independent Morocco, it is probable that most saw the war as a resumption of the anticolonial *ghazzian* that had ended barely two decades earlier and as an attempt to restore the "total liberty" to which they had been accustomed before 1934. Yet, had the Army of Liberation succeeded in driving the Spanish from Western Sahara at the end of the fifties, the territory would have been integrated into Morocco and doubtless Saharawi nationalism would not have emerged as a political force, just as Tuareg nationalism has never become a significant political factor in southern Algeria.

In fact, the Saharawi wing of the Army of Liberation was crushed in 1958. The following decade saw no serious attempts by the Saharawis to oppose Spanish rule. However, it did see profound economic, social and political changes within the Spanish colony, and these, along with important changes in the regional and international political arenas, were to ensure that, when a new anticolonial movement did begin to take shape, at the end of the sixties, it had a decidedly different political complexion from that of the Saharawi units of the Army of Liberation.

Until the late fifties the colonial presence had not only been extremely recent, it had also left but a modest mark on traditional Saharawi society. Western Sahara had had minimal economic interest to Spain during this period, the pace of change had been exceedingly slow and none of the few Spanish settlements had really grown larger than village size. Indeed, since 1934, the Saharawis had continued to engage in their own pastoral economy, albeit with increased trading ties to the Spanish settlements, to apply their own justice, the customary *orf* and the Koranic *sharia* law, and to regulate their affairs through their *djemaas*, while coexisting pragmatically with the Spanish, except during the brief insurrection of 1957–58. However, since the late fifties, Western Sahara had experienced belated but rapid changes, due to the sudden awakening of interest in its mineral resources. The growth of employment and educational opportunities in the towns, as well as droughts, had encouraged a large part of the Saharawi population to abandon its precarious nomadic way of life and settle in the urban areas. Sedentarization brought the Saharawis into much more direct and permanent contact with the Spanish. Indeed, they really came within the purview of Spanish administrative bodies and the Spanish judicial system for the first time. They were no longer living in coexistence with Spanish settlements that were essentially external to their own nomadic world, but were now part of a Spanish-dominated urban society, even though the territory's towns were still very small by international standards. With its administrators and bureaucrats, soldiers and policemen, laws and regulations, schools and hospitals, Western Sahara started to look, to settled Saharawis, like a country—a country dominated, moreover, by the Spanish. In this new urban environment, Saharawis of different tribal and caste origins lived and worked, or went to school, side by side; and by contrast to the dominant Spanish, who were now the undisputed *ahel mdafa*, or "people of the gun," they all now shared the humiliating status of *znaga*.

Moreover, a series of political changes, introduced by the Spanish government from 1958, tended to reinforce the impression that the territory was becoming a consequential political entity. Following provincialization and the arrival of a resident governor-general in 1958, there were the elections to the Cabildo Provincial in 1963 and then the creation of the Djemaa in 1967 and though this latter assembly was not democratically elected and had no real legislative powers, its very existence and its debates on the territory's economic, social and other problems tended to reinforce the Saharawis' emerging sense of supratribal territorial identity.

The backdrop to these changes, besides, was Western Sahara's status as the sole remaining European colony in the region, following the successive achievement of independence by Morocco, Mauritania and Algeria. The Western Saharans were now living a distinct and unique colonial experience, and despite the Moroccan and Mauritanian territorial claims, neither the Rabat nor Nouakchott regimes played any significant role in assisting the birth of a new anticolonial struggle against Spanish rule in the territory. Furthermore, the Moroccan opposition parties, who vigorously expressed their displeasure at the Hassan regime's soft-pedaling of the claim to Western Sahara, limited their militancy in practice to the writing of editorials in party newspapers and the making of speeches. They made no attempt to begin political work underground within Western Sahara itself. It is, thus, one of the great ironies of the Western Saharan problem that it was partly as a result of the failure of the Moroccan and Mauritanian governments and of the Moroccan opposition parties to pursue their claims to Western Sahara with real vigor that, ten years after the demise of the Army of Liberation, anticolonial Saharawis began to organize on their own account and to turn as far afield as Algeria and Libya for external support. This self-reliance helped to mold the distinctively Saharawi nationalist character of the anticolonial movement that resurfaced toward the end of the sixties.

Meanwhile, many Saharawis knew, from the mid-sixties onward, that the United Nations and the OAU were now advocating self-determination for the Spanish Sahara through the mechanism of a referendum. Indeed, in response to the UN's growing pressure for decolonization and to rebuff the Moroccan and Mauritanian territorial claims, Spain had endorsed the UN doctrine of self-determination in 1966, albeit without the intention of putting it into practice. The future of the country, Spanish officials now said, was a matter to be determined exclusively by the Saharawis and Spain, without external interference. In Spanish progaganda much was made of Morocco's supposed desire to acquire Western Sahara's new-found mineral wealth. "It is certain that, with the scent of these riches, the jackals are beginning to prowl around your *khaimas*," Lieutenant-General Camillo Menéndez Tolosa, the Spanish army minister, warned the Saharawis during a visit to El-Ayoun on May 16, 1967. "But now more than ever," he promised, "you will have us by your side, to the end and to the last sacrifice, to guarantee your will, without foreign pressure or interference, to protect you against the maneuvers and false fraternity in whose name it is intended to bring you into a household to which you have never belonged and in which, if they achieved their goal (something they will never do), you would be considered a poor relative to be exploited like a domestic."[1] Hypocritical though they were, in view of Spain's own interest in the territory's minerals, the general's words struck a chord in the Saharawi soul. Why should the Moroccans, who had never had to cope with the rigors of the arid Sahara, now arrive from the north to reap the advantages of its newly discovered mineral wealth?[2] But why, for that matter, should the Spanish? Moreover, the development of the phosphate industry doubtless suggested to the Saharawis that an independent Western Sahara would be economically viable, indeed relatively prosperous.[3]

Ironically, then, the Spanish government's oft repeated yet hypocritically void commitments to self-determination and its paternalist defense of Saharawi rights against the predatory designs of neighboring governments played a significant part too in engendering a nationalist consciousness that was later to rebound against the Spanish. Even the declaration endorsed in the November 1966 referendum and taken to the UN by the Spanish-sponsored "Comisión Elegida por el Pueblo del Sahara" had ended by remarking that "the signing of this statement does not bar the possibility of the Saharan people reaching complete independence in the future, simply by requesting Spain for it when we have capable leaders and adequate economic means."[4] However, Saila Ould Abeida, Khatri Ould Said Ould el-Joumani, Souilem Ould Abdellahi and the other conservative sheikhs in the leadership of the Djemaa made little effort to pressure Spain to act upon its verbal commitment to self-determination and this timidity prompted young urban Saharawis to begin engaging in their own autonomous nationalist activity.

The legitimacy and practicality of the independence option were doubtless also confirmed in Saharawi minds by the decisions of both Morocco and Mauritania to endorse the UN proposal of a referendum of self-determination, though they knew that neither the Moroccan nor the Mauritanian government had abandoned its claim to Western Sahara. Furthermore, by dropping Morocco's claim to Mauritania and recognizing Mauritania's independence in 1969, King Hassan established a precedent that was not lost on the Western Saharans. If Mauritania could finally secure Moroccan recognition of its right to nationhood, why could not Western Sahara too?

The Western Saharans were becoming a rather well-informed people during this period. The role of Arabic as a common *lingua franca* and the spread of transistor radios enabled them to obtain access to a wide range of information and political ideas. In fact, the flood of cheap radios from the Canary Islands at minimal or no import duty under the territory's special customs "free zone" status meant that virtually no Saharawi family was without one. UNESCO statistics show that, for every thousand inhabitants, 340 Western Saharans possessed radios, compared to only 95 in Morocco and 47 in Algeria.[5] With the plethora of Arabic radio stations, it was therefore not difficult for Saharawis to hear of the UN resolutions, the neighboring governments' declarations on Western Sahara, or, of perhaps as great influence, the inspiring struggles for national independence being fought elsewhere in the third world, from Vietnam to Palestine, and Guinea-Bissau to Eritrea.[6] Furthermore, significant numbers of young Saharawis were able for the first time to receive a modern education during the late sixties when the Spanish authorities at last began to expand the colony's hitherto extremely restricted education system.

The leadership of the new anticolonial movement of the late sixties and early seventies was markedly different in background and experience from the nomads who led the Saharawi guerrilla forces in 1957–58. Though they had, by and large, spent much of their childhood in a nomadic environment, they had later settled in the small towns and gone to school. Some had proceeded on to university. It was a young Saharawi who had studied abroad, in the Middle East, who organized the first clandestine anticolonial movement to be founded in Western Sahara after the collapse of the Army of Liberation's insurgency. A Reguibi, Mohammed Sidi Ibrahim Bassiri had been born sometime in 1942–44 near Tan-Tan, which was then part of Spanish Southern Morocco. During the Army of Liberation's Saharan campaign he seems to have been living farther south, in Saguia el-Hamra, for he was one of several hundred Saharawi children evacuated by the guerrillas in September 1957 from Lemsid, near El-Ayoun, to Morocco, where he entered a school in Casablanca with the help of a government scholarship. After passing the baccalaureate exams, he traveled to the Middle East, to study at the universities of Cairo and Damascus, where he is said to have been influenced by the pan-Arabist ideas of the Baathists. He graduated with a diploma in journalism and returned to Morocco in 1966, to found a radical Saharawi journal, *Al-Chihab* (The Torch).[7]

Toward the end of 1967, however, Bassiri left Morocco for Western Sahara, where he managed to persuade the Spanish authorities to grant him a residence permit. He worked as a Koranic teacher in the mosque at Smara.[8] There he used his influence as a teacher to recruit the nucleus of an underground anticolonial movement that came to be known as the Harakat Tahrir Saguia el-Hamra wa Oued ed-Dahab (Organization for the Liberation of Saguia el-Hamra and Oued ed-Dahab), or more simply as al-Hizb al-Muslim (the Muslim Party). In an interview with the Algerian daily newspaper *La République*, published in January 1971, a few months after the movement had been severely repressed by the Spanish authorities, two of its exiled leaders said that it had three principal objectives—internal autonomy, an "agreement between the organization and the Spanish government fixing a time limit for the proclamation of the independence of the Sahara and the evacuation of the Spanish troops" and "no exploitation of mineral resources without the organization's consent." They approved the idea of a referendum, but only on condition that the Harakat Tahrir was recognized by the Spanish administration and there was "no military garrison between the population and the ballot boxes."[9]

As a small secret organization, the Harakat Tahrir produced little in the way of documents, relying primarily on word of mouth to spread its propaganda, and it appears to have had an informal system of leadership and decision-making. But it was, nonetheless, the country's first urban-based political party. It advocated wide-ranging social reforms as well as progress toward decolonization. According to a Spanish military intelligence report, written in June 1970, it advocated "the abolition of the sheikhs. not just the current ones, whose incapacity and incompetence are recognized, but the institution in and of itself." The movement's members were "seeking to destroy the tribal structure" and also wanted "the reorganization of the present institutions, including the Asamblea General."[10] By the spring of 1970, the colonial intelligence services had detected widespread support for the movement among younger Saharawis in the towns. Most alarming of all for the Spanish authorities, its supporters included "a considerable number of soldiers in the Tropas Nómadas, policemen, interpreters, drivers, administrative auxiliaries and teachers of the Koran, that is to say practically all the personnel in the confidence of the *jefes de puesto*," the *delegado gubernativo* of the colony's northern region, López Huertas, noted. He added that the movement's recruits paid dues and swore an oath on the Koran.[11]

Meanwhile, the movement had decided to request support from neighboring Arab governments. Taking advantage of the Tindouf *mouggar*, an annual trade fair that attracts visitors from throughout the Western Saharan region, the organization was able to submit a memorandum setting out its goals and appealing for aid to Algerian officials in Tindouf on May 8, 1970.[12] Similar appeals to the Moroccan and Mauritanian governments were also planned, but they had not been dispatched by the time the Spanish ax fell, in June 1970.

The movement's fate was sealed when a majority of its members decided to emerge from clandestinity and present their demands publicly to the colonial government. A minority, which included Bassiri, is said to have advised against such audacity, arguing that it would invite repression that the movement was still poorly equipped to survive, but then to have gone along with the majority's decision. The plan was to present a petition listing the movement's demands and hold a counterdemonstration to a pro-Spanish rally sponsored by the colonial authorities in El-Ayoun on June 17. "The authorities have refused to receive the memorandum or meet the members of the organization," Bassiri wrote on the eve of the two rival demonstrations. "The situation is dangerous, very dangerous."[14] Indeed it was. Early the next morning, while some five hundred people assembled in the Plaza de Africa in the center of El-Ayoun for the government-sponsored rally, a somewhat larger crowd, of about fifteen hundred gathered in the outlying suburb of Zemla, a neighborhood on the road leading out of town toward Smara, and demanded that the governor-general, General José María Pérez de Lema y Tejero, who was the star speaker at the official rally, come in person to receive the Harakat Tahrir's petition.

He eventually conceded to meet the demonstrators at Zemla, where the petition was read out in Arabic and translated into Spanish for the general's benefit. His reply was extraordinarily arrogant: "I am here in the Sahara, like Franco with the Spaniards, as the captain of a ship, to steer it to the best harbor," he told the crowd.[15] He then ordered the demonstrators to disperse and departed, bearing with him the petition. At five in the afternoon López Huertas returned to Zemla, accompanied by a sixty-strong squad from the Policía Territorial. Hoping that the *delegado gubernativo* was bringing a reply to the petition, three youths moved out from the crowd to meet him, but they were immediately arrested, whereupon the crowd began pelting the police with stones. One hit López Huertas, who rushed off to report a breakdown of law and order. In a later debriefing report, a captain in the Policía Territorial recalled what followed: "At 7:30 P.M., a company of the Tercio, commanded by Captain Arcocha, made its appearance. When asked about his presence in the aforementioned place, he replied to me that he had orders to dissolve the gathering. He ordered the deployment of his forces, going past our defense lines. . . . The company of the Tercio continued its slow advance. Already quite near [the demonstrators] and under attack from stones and sticks, like the police beforehand, they opened fire into the air, at which moment some natives fell to the ground, giving flight to all the demonstrators, who were pursued by the company of the Tercio."[16]

The Spanish government stated officially that two died.[17] However, the Mauritanian ministry of information claimed on June 20, after receiving eyewitness accounts from travelers arriving in Bir Moghrein, that twelve were killed, while the Moroccan government, which lodged a protest with the Spanish foreign ministry, claimed that ten were killed, and exiled leaders of the Harakat Tahrir later put the death toll at eleven.[18] The ensuing repression shattered the Harakat Tahrir. Hundreds were arrested, though most were released after a few days. A few were jailed for several months, among them ten militants who were held in the Alcandi Prison in Dakhla and six soldiers of the Tropas Nómadas who were detained in the Canary Islands until the beginning of 1971.[19] The night after the Zemla massacre, at three in the morning, security forces seized Bassiri, whom López Huertas described on June 23 as a "classic agitator" in a memorandum reporting his arrest.[20] He has never since been seen. Spanish officials later claimed that he was deported to Morocco a few days after his arrest. This has always been denied by the Moroccan government, and relatives of Bassiri living in Tan-Tan informed the UN in 1975 that they had had no news of him since 1970.[21] Many Saharawis assume that he was murdered by his Spanish captors.

NOTES

1. *Maghreb Arabe Presse* (Rabat), May 17, 1967.

2. Zygmunt Komorowski has argued that this attitude is shared by Saharans who constitute minorities in states dominated by "outsiders" from the black south or the Maghreb to the north. "The road transport and mining businesses situated in the desert sign on representatives of all the

tribes and natives of various regions. But, given the harsh climate, they are almost uniquely Saharans. This state of affairs creates an opposition between 'us' who have lived here for generations and 'them' who have come from the fertile and rich lands of the north or the south, where drought is not a threat, and only come here temporarily to administer and exploit." Zygmunt Komorowski, "Formation de la conscience sociale supratribale en partant des conditions ethniques du Sahara occidental," *Africana Bulletin* (University of Warsaw Center of African Studies), No. 23, 1975, p. 116.

3. Later, in May 1975, the Spanish government suggested to the UN that "on the basis of present population statistics, the phosphates when fully developed would furnish a per capita revenue equal to that of some developed countries in Europe." Report of the United Nations Visiting Mission to Spanish Sahara, 1975, in *General Assembly Official Records*, 30th Session, Supplement 23, UN Document A/10023/Rev.1, p. 72.

4. *ABC* (Madrid), November 19, 1966.

5. *Statistical Yearbook* (UNESCO, Paris, 1973), cited in Komorowski, *loc. cit.*, p. 115.

6. The influence of these nationalist struggles is particularly evident in the earliest issues of *20 de Mayo*, the bulletin published by the Polisario Front from 1973.

7. This account of Bassiri's early life is based on the author's interview with Mohammed Ma el-Ainin in Rabat on November 16, 1978, and on Federico Abascal, Sol Gallego and Enrique Bustamante, "Sahara: documentos secretos," *Cuadernos para el Diálogo* (Madrid), January 21, 1978, p. 17. See also Attilio Gaudio, *Le dossier du Sahara occidental* (Nouvelles Editions Latines, Paris, 1978), p. 237, and *El pueblo saharaui en lucha: documentos del Frente Popular para la Liberación de Saguia el Hamra y Río de Oro* (Polisario Front, 1975), p. 2.

8. Ahmed-Baba Miské, *Front Polisario, l'âme d'un peuple* (Editions Rupture, Paris, 1978), p. 119.

9. *Reuters*, dispatch from Algiers, January 21, 1971.

10. Informe del Estado Mayor del Sector del Sahara sobre 'el movimiento nacionalista denominado Organización del Pueblo Saharaui,' 13 de Junio de 1970, in Abascal, Gallego and Bustamante, *loc. cit.*, p. 16.

11. Informe del delegado gubernativo de la Región Norte, Señor López Huertas, sobre la 'Organización Avanzada para la Liberación del Sahara y los preparativos del día 17 de Junio de 1970', in *ibid.*, p. 15.

12. *El pueblo saharaui en lucha: documentos del Frente Popular para la Liberación de Saguia el Hamra y Río de Oro*, pp. 16–17.

13. *Ibid.*, pp. 15–17.

14. "La dernière lettre de Bassiri," *Sahara Libre* (Polisario Front, Algiers), No. 38, July 7, 1977, p. 2.

15. Cited in *El pueblo saharaui en lucha: documentos del Frente Popular para la Liberación de Saguia el Hamra y Río de Oro*, p. 18.

16. Cited in Abascal, Gallego and Bustamante, *loc. cit.*, p. 17. The above account is also based partly on an interview by the author in Las Palmas in October 1978 with Comandante Aguirre, who was an official of the Servicio de Información y Seguridad of the Gobierno General del Sahara in 1966–76.

17. *Reuters*, dispatch from Madrid, June 20, 1970.

18. *Reuters*, dispatches from Nouakchott, June 20, 1970, and Algiers, January 21, 1971; *Maghreb Arabe Presse*, June 18, 1970.

19. Interview with Mohammed Ali Ould el-Bachir (who was briefly placed under house arrest after the Zemla incidents), Tindouf, November 1979; *El pueblo saharaui en lucha: documentos del Frente Popular para la Liberación de Saguia el Hamra y Río de Oro*, p. 19.

20. Abascal, Gallego and Bustamante, *loc. cit.*, p. 17.

21. Report of the United Nations Visiting Mission to Spanish Sahara, 1975, *loc. cit.*, p. 72.

15

The Birth of the Polisario Front

T HE BLOODSHED AT ZEMLA shattered the illusions of those who had taken the
Spanish pledges of respect for self-determination at face value. The tragic
events of June 1970 caused much bitterness, and a new governor-general, General
Fernando de Santiago y Díaz de Mendívil, was dispatched to El-Ayoun on March
4, 1971, to replace the much maligned General Pérez de Lema. Some Saharawis
were now convinced of the wisdom of returning to the old tradition of the *ghazzi*
and the gun, but the immediate aftermath of Zemla was a period of demoralization. The Harakat Tahrir was shattered. Bassiri had disappeared, and many of the
movement's other leading activists had been jailed and then deported.
Reorganization would be slow and difficult, and it was initially from beyond the
country's borders that a new leadership would gradually be brought together, by
a charismatic young Reguibi studying law in Morocco.

El-Ouali Mustapha Sayed, or Lulei as he was known to his friends and comrades, was born in 1948, or thereabouts, somewhere on the Hammada.[1] A nomad
as a youngster, he had settled with his parents in Tan-Tan after the defeat of the
Army of Liberation in 1958, when he was about ten. Like many of the Saharawis
who camped or squatted around the little towns or villages of southern Morocco in
the aftermath of the 1957–58 rising, his family was more or less destitute. They
had few animals left, just one or two goats, and El-Ouali's father, Mustapha
Sayed, was handicapped and unable to work. His mother, Mbarka, brought in a
few dirhams as a seamstress, and the eldest of his four brothers, Labat, earned a
small wage as a road laborer. The going was so tough that the family often
depended for survival on the free flour and cooking oil that was distributed by the
Moroccan government in those days to the impoverished Saharawis in its
southernmost provinces.[2] Despite these hardships, El-Ouali began attending a
primary school in Tan-Tan in 1961–62, and though he was briefly expelled in
1963 for skipping class to shepherd his father's remaining goats, he eventually
managed to obtain his primary-school certificate and win a government scholar-

ship to attend the Lycée Ben Youssef in Marrakesh as a boarder. He read voraciously, immersing himself in the works of Arab poets and novelists, but apparently ran foul of the *lycée's* headmaster, who expelled him for indiscipline in 1965. After a brief stint as a laborer on a road-building gang in Tan-Tan, he succeeded in gaining admission, once again under a government scholarship, to another secondary school, in Taroudant, where he first began to take a keen interest in politics and, in particular, in the recently founded Frente de Liberación del Sahara (FLS). To keep abreast of political developments, he decided to leave Taroudant, a little town in the Souss about eighty miles east of Agadir, and move to Rabat, where he was admitted to one of Morocco's oldest and most prestigious of *lycées*, the Groupement Scolaire Mohammed V. By all accounts he was a brilliant student, and in 1970 he passed the baccalaureate with distinction. With yet another scholarship from the ministry of education, he entered the law school at Mohammed V University in Rabat.

This was Morocco's largest university and there were perhaps thirty to forty Saharawi students enrolled there by 1970. Their backgrounds were broadly similar—in most cases a nomadic childhood, followed by settlement in the extreme south of Morocco, often in great poverty after the traumatic events of 1957–58 and the ensuing drought, and then a successful schooling made possible by government grants. Of the thousand or so Saharawi children who had been admitted to Moroccan schools after the 1957–58 war, they were the academic elite, and by 1975 sixteen of them are said to have graduated from the university with a *licence*, the equivalent of a bachelor's degree.[3] Several of the Saharawi students in Morocco were to join El-Ouali in playing a major role in the birth of a new Saharawi liberation movement, among them Mohammed Lamine Ould Ahmed, who was later to be prime minister of Polisario's Saharan Arab Democratic Republic (SADR), Mohammed Ali Ould el-Ouali, who would later be an influential member of Polisario's ruling executive committee, and Mohammed Salem Ould Salek and Mohammed Ould Sidati, both later members of the SADR government, all of whom were enrolled at Mohammed V University in the early seventies, and El-Ouali's brother, Bashir Mustapha Sayed, then a *lyceéen* in Agadir, who was to become Polisario's deputy secretary-general in 1976.[4]

These students knew, indirectly at least, of Bassiri, the Harakat Tahrir and what had happened at Zemla, and they were also familiar with the UN's resolutions on Western Sahara. Moreover, they were greatly influenced by the Palestinian Resistance and other third-world national liberation movements, and by the political radicalization then sweeping their own campuses. Most Moroccan universities were repeatedly strikebound in 1969–73, and in 1972 the Union Nationale des Etudiants Marocains (UNEM) swung sharply to the left when the Marxist *frontistes* of the March 23 Movement and Ilal-Amam (Forward) displaced the union's hitherto predominantly UNFP leadership at its fifteenth congress.

In Rabat El-Ouali formed a loosely structured collective of Saharawi students. At first they did not specifically advocate the establishment of an independent Western Saharan state. Their focus, rather, was on ending Spanish rule.[5] Indeed, paradoxical though it may seem in hindsight, they worked hard in 1971–72 to lobby support from the Moroccan opposition parties that were the standard bearers of the Greater Morocco cause. This was only natural, for these parties had for long reproached the government for its cooperative relations with the Franco regime. El-Ouali and his associates met the leaders of the Istiqlal Party, including Allal el-Fassi, and of the UNFP, the PLS and the trade unions of the Union Maro-caine du Travail (UMT), and some of the Saharawi students joined or collaborated closely with one or other of these factions of the Moroccan opposition. Some, for example, participated in a conference on the Sahara sponsored by the Istiqlal Youth in March 1972, and El-Ouali himself maintained relations with the PLS, for whom he wrote a study of the Western Saharan problem which was published after editing by the party's secretary-general, Ali Yata, in its journal, *Al-Mabadi*, in May 1972.

However, the Saharawi student group in Rabat underwent a rapid political evolution between 1971 and 1973. It started to regard itself as the embryo of a new liberation movement that, arms in hand, would relight the flame extinguished at Zemla. As these students prepared for the launching of their armed liberation struggle, they lost patience with the Moroccan opposition par-ties, who, despite their verbal anti-Spanish militancy, were not prepared to pro-vide any practical support. Most of the Moroccan opposition leaders whom El-Ouali consulted, notably Allal el-Fassi and Ali Yata, seem to have told him not to expect Moroccan support until there had been a change of government in Rabat, a perspective tantamount to postponing the Saharawi liberation struggle in-definitely.

The focus of the Rabat student group's work gradually began to shift away from lobbying the Moroccan opposition parties to recruiting support among the Saharawis of southern Morocco and sending envoys out of the country to examine political conditions and muster support within Western Sahara itself, to make contact with like-minded Saharawis in other centers of the Saharawi diaspora, such as Tindouf and Zouerate, and also to request support from foreign Arab governments. Thus, El-Ouali, Mohammed Lamine and Mohammed Salem Ould Salek spent about a month in El-Ayoun on an exploratory mission in the summer of 1971, and the following October several of the Rabat students organized a clandestine meeting of about a hundred young Saharawis in Tan-Tan to discuss the formation of a new liberation movement.[6] Then, in March 1972, they first began soliciting aid from foreign governments. Letters were sent between March and June to Colonel Qadhafi, President Mokhtar Ould Daddah, President Houari Boumedienne and the government of Iraq.[7] The autonomous, self-reliant character of this work encouraged El-Ouali's student group to adopt an increas-ingly nationalist outlook, and, as they came into closer contact with the Saharawi community in Western Sahara itself, they established contact with former members or supporters of the Harakat Tahrir who had set their sights on in-dependence, rather than integration with Morocco.

Within Morocco, meanwhile, they had begun to suffer harassment from the Moroccan authorities by the spring of 1972. The early seventies were a period of considerable political tension in Morocco, marked by two military coup attempts in July 1971 and August 1972, political skirmishing between the Palace and the principal opposition parties, the UNFP and the Istiqlal Party, which had formed a national front (Kutlah al-Wataniya) in 1970, a rash of strikes by trade unions, and political turmoil on the campuses which culminated in the banning of UNEM in

January 1973.[8] Scores of Moroccan oppositionists and dissidents were detained in these tense years. The Rabat authorities were not prepared under such circumstances to run the risk of allowing an autonomous and militant Saharawi liberation organization—one intent, moreover, on beginning a guerrilla war against Spain—to take shape on its territory, though the El-Ouali group wrote formally to the Moroccan government in April 1972 to request its support.[9] A month earlier, on March 3, the Moroccan police had broken up an "unauthorized" anti-Spanish demonstration in Tan-Tan by a small group of Saharawis, including several students from Rabat, and briefly detained nine of the demonstrators, among them El-Ouali.[10] During a tour of southern Morocco in May, King Hassan felt obliged to defend his record on Western Sahara. Speaking in Agadir on May 23, after returning from Tarfaya province, he promised the Saharawis that they were "neither forgotten nor neglected" and that his policy toward Spain was "not in contradiction with our firm determination to link up again with our subjects who live in the Sahara."[11] However, when Saharawi students took to the streets of Tan-Tan again three days later, during the annual *moussem* (fair), forty-five were arrested. Several were kept in detention for a week.[12]

The Tan-Tan incidents confirmed the El-Ouali group's fears that the constitution of a Saharawi liberation movement on Moroccan territory would be impractical, if not dangerous. During May, meanwhile, El-Ouali had set off from Tarfaya province in a Land Rover to make his way across the Hammada to the annual *mouggar* in Tindouf, where he made contact with both local Saharawis and officials of Algeria's ruling Front de Libération Nationale.[13] Three other students from Rabat, Mohammed Lamine, Mohammed Ali Ould el-Ouali and Beyadillah Mohammed Sheikh, made a parallel investigative mission to El-Ayoun, while El-Ouali traveled on from Tindouf to Zouerate, where he came across a nucleus of Saharawi exiles, among them M'hammed Ould Ziou, a veteran of the Army of Liberation who had settled in Mauritania after the 1957–58 war, and Ahmed Ould Qaid, who had fought in the Army of Liberation, joined the Harakat Tahrir and then, after the Zemla massacre, been jailed in the Canaries and Dakhla until 1971, when he had been deported to Mauritania.[14] This group had rather good contacts with the Mauritanian government and so was able to arrange for residence permits to be issued to El-Ouali and some of his comrades. The Algerian government, by contrast, responded coolly to El-Ouali's approaches and in March 1973 allowed Edouard Moha to set up a MOREHOB office in Algiers.

It was in Zouerate therefore that El-Ouali assembled his small band of cadres, from southern Morocco and the original student group in Rabat, from the nucleus around M'hammed Ould Ziou in Zouerate itself, and from the towns of Western Sahara, whence came such recruits as Mahfoud Ali Beiba, who would later become a prominent member of Polisario's executive committee and its deputy secretary-general in 1974–76, and Ibrahim Ghali Ould Mustapha, a Reguibi who had served for six years in the Policía Territorial and was to become one of Polisario's principal guerrilla commanders and later the SADR's minister of defense.[15]

On May 10, at a secret congress, held somewhere near the Western Saharan-

Mauritanian border, the Frente Popular para la Liberación de Saguia el Hamra y Río de Oro was finally born. The congress elected El-Ouali secretary-general and appointed an executive committee, which issued a manifesto announcing that the front had been founded as the "unique expression of the masses, opting for revolutionary violence and the armed struggle as the means by which the Saharawi Arab African people can recover its total liberty and foil the maneuvers of Spanish colonialism."[16] The following November, the front began publishing a monthly journal, *20 de Mayo*, which was smuggled into the Spanish-controlled towns, but from the start the front's principal focus was on its guerrilla campaign. Indeed, the first attack was staged just ten days after its founding. The target was a small isolated post of the Tropas Nómadas at El-Khanga in the northeast of Saguia el-Hamra. According to Polisario accounts, the raid almost became a fiasco before it had started. In all, there were less than a dozen guerrillas, among them El-Ouali, and they were armed with a motley collection of ancient rifles and one small submachine gun. Success was to hinge totally on surprise, as they had enough ammunition between them to keep firing for about five minutes, but while camping near El-Khanga, two of the guerrillas, including El-Ouali, fell into the hands of an enemy patrol as they went to fetch water from a nearby well. They were taken back to El-Khanga, where the garrison, of exclusively Saharawi composition, reported the arrest of two suspicious-looking youths to the nearest Spanish base. After realizing what had happened, the guerrillas still at large decided to attack that evening, after sunset. Despite holding two prisoners, the Saharawi garrison had no idea that an attack was imminent; when it came, they surrendered without firing a shot. The two prisoners were rescued, a valuable new collection of firearms was stolen and the Saharawi soldiers were arrested, lectured on the front's political objectives and set free.[17]

Over the following two years, the front continued to stage small hit-and-run attacks. The Spanish captured their first five Polisario prisoners in an engagement at Guelb Lahmar, near the Mauritanian border, on January 26, 1974, and Polisario's first three martyrs fell in combat the following March, at the battles of Hassi Maitalla and Aoukeyra, in Saguia el-Hamra.[18] By mid-1975, Polisario had fought around twenty to thirty small battles, though the Spanish government did not break its silence about this remote desert war, far from the beaten paths of even the most itinerant of journalists, until after a rather serious Polisario ambush at Agjeijimat, near Tifariti, an important Spanish base near Saguia el-Hamra's border with Mauritania, on December 17, 1974, in which, according to official Spanish communiqués, five Spanish soldiers lost their lives.[19] In an attempt to stem the influx of Europeans into the colony, the front kidnapped a Spanish businessman, Antonio Martín, in El-Ayoun itself on March 11, 1975.[20] However, the most sensational and damaging of its operations was a sabotage attack on Fosbucraa's conveyor belt, which temporarily halted all phosphate deliveries to the coast. At half past ten on the night of October 20, 1974, two groups of saboteurs left El-Ayoun by car and headed for two of the belt's control stations, about twenty miles to the south. After breaking in, they sprayed gasoline over the station's sophisticated control equipment, lit fires and vanished into the night, leaving several million dollars' worth of damage.[21]

Nonetheless, the guerrilla campaign was hard-going. It was no longer possible to recruit large parties of raiders from nomad camps as before 1934 or in 1957–58. There were not many nomads left. In fact, most of the early militants were young, relatively well-educated Saharawis from the towns, whether from Western Sahara or the neighboring territories. Typical were the Saharawis arrested by the Spanish in October 1974 on charges related to the attack on the Fosbucraa conveyor belt. Most were young skilled workers in their early twenties, graduates of the General Alonso secondary school in El Ayoun or of the Promoción Profesional Obrera (PPO) who worked for Fosbucraa as electricians, computer staff and engineers.[22] But recruitment, for sabotage or guerrilla action at least, was slow at first, for the defeats of 1958 and 1970 had left a bitter taste and it was obvious that the Spanish armed forces in the territory were not only numerous, perhaps twenty thousand men by 1974, but incomparably better equipped than in the days of the Army of Liberation. The guerrillas, who still probably numbered no more than a couple of hundred by the beginning of 1975, had practically no modern weapons and enjoyed barely any external support.

Of all the Arab states, only Libya was really sympathetic. In June 1972, Colonel Qadhafi had publicly announced that he would back a "people's war" to liberate Western Sahara if Spain did not leave by the end of the year.[23] El-Ouali, who first visited Libya sometime in 1972 or early in 1973, shortly before the front's founding, later remarked that "we came to Libya barefoot, we left armed."[24] And Qadhafi himself remarked in 1976 that, when the Polisario guerrilla campaign began in 1973, "the Libyan Arab Republic fulfilled its Arab national duty by furnishing arms to the front and setting up an office for it in Tripoli."[25] In fact, Tripoli became the headquarters of Polisario's external-relations committee, and in 1974 Radio Tripoli began beaming Polisario broadcasts to Western Sahara.[26] But very little material support reached the front from Libya, mainly because no neighboring states were prepared to cooperate.

The Ould Daddah government had allowed the movement's main leaders to settle in Mauritania, and of course Polisario guerrillas could easily outwit pursuing Spanish forces by slipping across the border into the vast unpoliceable desert regions of northern Mauritania. Insofar as Polisario was not Moroccan-inspired, it could be construed in Nouakchott as another potential buffer to keep Morocco out of Western Sahara and away from Mauritania's borders, and this was sufficient grounds to justify harboring its militants and turning a blind eye to some of their activities. Ould Daddah was to acknowledge in 1976, referring to Polisario, that "the first operations by this movement against the Spanish presence were launched from Mauritanian territory."[27] However, his government never gave the movement military aid and it took care not to jeopardize its relations with Spain, which was not only a more consequential buffer between Morocco and Mauritania, but an important source of economic aid. On at least two occasions, in June and October 1973, Polisario guerrillas were arrested in Mauritania, on the latter occasion so that the captured members of a Spanish patrol could be rescued and handed back to the Spanish authorities.[28] For its part, the Algerian government remained suspicious of Polisario until at least the summer of 1974 and did not provide significant support until early in 1975. It refused to allow Libyan arms to transit across Algerian territory, and El-Ouali was even arrested and deported during a visit to Algiers in 1973.[29]

The front's founding manifesto had not explicitly mentioned independence as a goal. The formula of "total liberty" was perhaps deliberately ambiguous. As late as January 1973, in fact, El Ouali had written a memorandum, for the attention of UNFP exiles in Algiers, which seemed to approve the idea of Western Sahara's integration with Morocco.[30] And Polisario itself admitted two years later, in a balance-sheet of its progress, in July 1975, that "in effect the Revolution was not clear in its first year about certain of its goals."[31] Doubtless this reflected the different, contrasting backgrounds of the movement's earliest militants. It would appear that the group of ex-students from Morocco initially "lagged" in their Saharawi nationalism, but they had now cut loose from their links with the Moroccan opposition parties, with which they had become thoroughly disillusioned. They had forged the nucleus of a liberation movement with Saharawis of a quite different background and outlook from within the Spanish colony, as well as from Mauritania, and they were now being obliged to count only on their own strength and resources as they fought their difficult guerrilla war against the Spanish without the benefit of significant aid from any foreign government. It is not surprising that Polisario should have become embittered by what it described in March 1974 as "the silence of Arab countries and notably those of the Maghreb, and Morocco especially, with regard to colonialist Spain's action and its savage repression of the people."[32]

It was at its second congress, held on August 25–31, 1974, that the front came out unambiguously in favor of full independence. This congress, Polisario has observed, marked a "turning point," defining "clearly and scientifically the objectives of the Revolution in the short and the long term."[33] A manifesto adopted by the congress declared that "the Saharawi people have no alternative but to struggle until wresting independence, their wealth and their full sovereignty over their land."[34]

El-Ouali was reelected secretary-general, Mahfoud Ali Beiba was named deputy secretary-general, and a twenty-one member political bureau and seven-member executive committee were elected. The top leadership body, the executive committee, was subdivided into two specialized committees, one for political affairs and the other, headed by Ibrahim Ghali Ould Mustapha, to coordinate the guerrilla campaign.[35] Mohammed Lamine Ould Ahmed was put in charge of the external-relations committee.

The congress adopted a "program of national action" which set out the front's broad objectives. First and foremost, it was fighting for "national liberation from all forms of colonialism and the achievement of complete independence" and the "creation of a republican, national regime, with the effective participation of the masses."[36] The front saw itself as the voice of all Saharawis, wherever they lived, and did not disguise its regret that the borders of Western Sahara encompassed only part of their traditional zones of migration and only some of their contemporary centers of settlement, but despite the artificiality of the colonial borders, the front pledged to respect them in order to avoid transgressing the established OAU doctrine on African frontiers and to summon as wide diplomatic support as possible.[37] In the name of national unity, the front abhorred all forms of kinship loyalty, to the point that its members denied tribal affiliation together. Caste status, which had often been closely associated with tribal membership, was renounced with equal resolve, and there was a strong reforming, egalitarian streak in the front's philosophy. The program of national action called for the abolition of "every form of exploitation," and this meant in the first place the definitive eradication of such exploitative practices as slavery and the extraction of tribute from vassals. The front also wanted a "fair distribution of resources, to overcome the differences between the countryside and the towns," the provision of adequate housing and health facilities, the Arabization of education and the provision of free, compulsory schooling "at all levels and for all social layers." There was also, significantly, a strong commitment to the principle of women's emancipation. The front would struggle "to reestablish the political and social rights of the woman and open up all perspectives to her," the program of national action promised.[38] "It has become necessary for our struggle," 20 de Mayo had declared the previous April, "that the Saharawi woman bears all responsibilities and undertakes her duty in the national struggle by participating actively in the armed revolution like her sisters in the Palestinian, Algerian and Guinea-Bissau revolutions."[39] As for the collaborationist sheikhs in the Djemma, there was nothing but scorn in the front's propaganda.

Polisario saw itself as an integral "part of the Arab revolution and of the world movement of national and democratic revolution," and it identified closely with such nationalist guerrilla movements as those that had been fighting Portugal in Angola, Mozambique and Guinea-Bissau. It had particular empathy with the Palestinian Resistance. Indeed, it saw a parallel between Spain's desert colony in the Maghreb and the Israeli enclave in the Arab Mashrek, and it was surely no accident that the movement chose a flag, in red, white, black and green, which closely resembled that of Palestine.

NOTES

1. At Bir Lehlou, according to Leila Badia Itani, *Al-Polisario: qaid wa thawra* (Dar al-Masirah, Beirut, 1978), p. 128. Itani's account of the life of El-Ouali Mustapha Sayed and the origins of the Polisario Front is based on a lengthy interview with Mohammed Lamine Ould Ahmed, one of the founders and principal leaders of the movement and a close acquaintance of El-Ouali since childhood. El-Ouali's father was a member of the Thaalat fraction of the Reguibat es-Sahel.

2. *Ibid.*, p. 129, and author's interview in Rabat, October 16, 1978, with Mohammed Ma el-Ainin, a Saharawi who knew El-Ouali well as a fellow student in Rabat in the early seventies.

3. Itani, *op. cit.*, p. 130.

4. For their detailed biographies, see Tony Hodges, *Historical Dictionary of Western Sahara* (Scarecrow Press, Metuchen, New Jersey, 1982), pp. 54, 232–33, 236–37 and 239–41.

5. Author's interview with Malainine Ould Saddick, Polisario representative in Algiers, September 24, 1979.

6. Interview with Mohammed Ma el-Ainin, Rabat, October 16, 1978, and Itani, *op. cit.*, p. 20.

7. According to *El pueblo saharaui en lucha: documentos del Frente popular para la liberación de Saguia el Hamra y Río de Oro* (Polisario Front, 1975), pp. 23–24, the El-Ouali group sent letters to Colonel Qadhafi on March 20 and June 13, 1972, to President Mokhtar Ould Daddah on March 23 and April 14, 1972, and to both President Houari Boumedienne and the Iraqi government on March 24, 1972.

8. UNEM was not relegalized until 1978.

9. *El pueblo saharaui en lucha: documentos del Frente popular para la liberación de Saguia el Hamra y Río de Oro*, p. 23.

10. *Reuters*, dispatch from Rabat, March 5, 1972; Interview with Mohammed Ma el-Ainin, Rabat, October 16, 1978. The detainees were released after two or three days.

11. *Reuters*, dispatch from Rabat, May 24, 1972.

12. *Reuters*, dispatch from Rabat, May 30, 1972.

13. Author's interview with Mohammed Ali Ould el-Ouali, Tindouf, November 14, 1979. Itani dates El-Ouali's first contact with the FLN as being in the summer of 1972. Mohammed Ma el-Ainin (interview, Rabat, October 16, 1978) recalled El-Ouali's trip to Tindouf being "at the end of 1972." Possibly there were two trips.

14. Ahmed-Baba Maské, *Front Polisario, l'âme d'un peuple* (Editions Rupture, Paris, 1978), p. 136; *Dossier du Sahara occidental* (Association des Amis de la RASD, Paris, 1978). For biographies of Ahmed Ould Qaid and M'hammed Ould Ziou, see Hodges, *op. cit.*, pp. 26, 228.

15. For biographies of Ibrahim Ghali Ould Mustapha and Mahfoud Ali Beiba, see *ibid.*, pp. 178–79 and 218–20.

16. Political Manifesto of May 10, 1973, in *Sahara Libre* (Polisario Front, Algiers), No. 13, May 20, 1976, and in *Annuaire de l'Afrique du Nord 1975* (CNRS, Paris, 1976), p. 985. The front did not publicize its existence to the press until July 1973, when a communiqué was distributed in Nouakchott. This was reported on July 21, 1973, by four Moroccan newspapers, *Le Matin*, *L'Opinion*, *Al-Alam* and *Maghreb Informations*.

17. Miské, *op. cit.*, pp. 150–51.

18. *El pueblo saharaui en lucha: documentos del Frente Popular para la liberación de Saguia el Hamra y Río de Oro*, p. 126; *Sahara Libre*, No. 21, July 1975, and No. 37, June 5, 1977; *Maghreb Informations*, March 20, 1974, and April 20, 1974. Bashir Ould Lahlaoui was killed at Hassi Maitalla on March 8, 1974, and Abderrahman Ould Abdellahi and Laroussi Mahfoud on March 13, 1974, at Aoukeyra.

19. *Christian Science Monitor*, December 23, 1974; Stephen Hughes, report from Rabat to BBC Africa Service, Focus on Africa, December 20, 1974. King Hassan was later to claim, at a press conference on June 2, 1981, that if "Africans . . . had analyzed the genuine nature of the Polisario, they would have seen that it did not possess the criteria of liberation movements. If they had gone a few years back they would have found that it was a resistance movement that appeared after the Spanish departed and that it had never fired a bullet against a Spanish soldier." (Radio Rabat, June 2, 1981). However, the Moroccan press reported many of Polisario's early attacks in 1973–74. See, for example, *Maghreb Informations*, February 23, 1974, March 20, 1974, and April 20, 1974. Likewise, the trade-union affiliates of the UMT in Rabat and Salé held a public meeting on May 18, 1974, at the UMT club in Rabat to mark Polisario's first anniversary and issued a statement declaring: "The Saharawi masses have been waging heroic struggles against fascist colonialism for a year under the leadership of the Popular Front for the Liberation of Saguia el-Hamra and Oued ed-Dahab and their first operation was carried out on May 20, 1973. Since that date, it has been inflicting heavy losses on the enemy despite the latter's means of repression and the viciousness of its reprisals." (Cited in *20 Mai*, No. 9, July 1974.)

20. *20 Mai*, No. 18, April 1975.

21. *20 de Mayo*, No. 14, December 1974.

22. Biographical details of twelve of those arrested are given in *20 de Mayo*, No. 14, December 1974.

23. *Reuters*, dispatch from Rabat, June 18, 1972.

24. Press conference in Tripoli, October 29, 1975 (*El Moudjahid*, Algiers, October 30, 1975).

25. Letter from Colonel Qadhafi to King Hassan II, February 27, 1976, in *Jeune Afrique* (Paris), No. 796, April 9, 1976, pp. 36–37.

26. Miské, *op. cit.*. p. 160.

27. "Synthèse de la communication du secrétaire général du Parti devant le Conseil National du Parti du Peuple Mauritanien," in Moktar Ould Daddah, *1957–1976, La réunification de la patrie: un objectif sacré pour le peuple mauritanien* (Ministère d'Etat à l'Orientation Nationale, Nouakchott, 1976), p. 10. For Polisario's view of its relations with the Mauritanian government in 1973–76, see "Omar Hadrami, Polisario Representative, Interviewed by Tony Hodges," *Africa Report* (New York), March-April 1978, p. 42.

28. On June 30, 1973, Mauritanian security forces arrested two Polisario guerrillas near Ain Ben Tili and confiscated their weapons, then a significant part of the movement's entire stock of arms. (*20 Mai*, No. 21, July 1974.) On October 10, 1973, six guerrillas were arrested so that the members of a Spanish patrol whom they had captured in September could be set free. (*20 de Mayo*, No. 1, November 1, 1973.)

29. Author's interviews with Mohammed Ali Ould el-Ouali, member of the executive committee of the Polisario Front, Tindouf, November 14, 1979, and with members of the Moroccan opposition group, Alikhtiar Athaouri, who had been living in Algiers in 1973, in Paris on October 10, 1979.

30. In a memorandum he presented to the Algiers branch of the UNFP in January 1973, he wrote: "The succession of different [Moroccan] states, the struggle for power and tribal infighting led to an increase in emigration to this neutral and and safe area [the Sahara] and its use as a place of refuge by the oppressed. In addition, it was at many times a sanctuary for rebels fleeing their enemies. The consequence of these successive waves of emigration to the Sahara and countermigration to Morocco was that the area became integrally linked at most times with the existing authorities in Morocco. Often central powers were exercised by these governments over the inhabitants of these areas, especially in time of war, when many of them would recruit the inhabitants of this area to their ranks. And it is possible to say that the region was a Moroccan province just like all the other Moroccan provinces." ("Muthakkarat Mustapha el-Ouali haoul al-Sahra," *Alikhtiar Athaouri*, Paris, No. 19, October 1977, p. 7.) The memorandum was serialized in six parts by *Alikhtiar Athaouri*, the journal of the Moroccan left-wing "Basrists," in Nos. 19–23, October, November and December 1977 and January and February 1978, and No. 25, April 1978.

31. "Bilan de deux années de lutte de notre peuple," *20 Mai*, No. 21, July 1975, p. 15.

32. *Reuters*, dispatch from Rabat, March 20, 1974.

33. "Bilan de deux années de lutte de notre peuple," *loc. cit.*, p. 15.

34. "Manifeste politique, adopté par le deuxième congrès," in *Le peuple saharaoui en lutte* (Polisario Front, 1975), p. 50.

35. *ABC* (Madrid), June 3, 1975; Report of the United Nations Visiting Mission to Spanish Sahara, 1975, in *General Assembly Official Records*, 30th Session, Supplement 23, UN Document A/10023/Rev. 1, p. 97.

36. "Programme d'action nationale, adoptée par le deuxième congrès," in *Le peuple saharaoui en lutte*, p. 42.

37. "Our country should naturally include at least the present provinces of Nouadhibou and Zouerate," a Polisario spokesman told the African group at the UN in 1975. "The French and Spanish colonizers themselves had taken these boundaries to fix their respective zones of influence. But at the moment of negotiating the definitive treaties, Spain found itself in such a weak position that it had to abandon part of the country to France. On the Moroccan side, it was only in 1958 that Spain ceded the Saharawi province of Tarfaya." But once independent, Western Sahara "is not going to launch new territorial demands whatever distress their amputation may cause. The Sahara is most respectful of the rules of coexistence established by the international and African communities." ("El Sahara y la ONU," *Sahara Libre*, No. 2, November 25, 1975, pp. 16–17.)

38. "Programme d'action nationale, adopté par le deuxième congrès," *loc. cit.*, p. 43.

39. *20 de Mayo*, No. 6, April 1974.

16

A Statute of
Autonomy

ON FEBRUARY 20, 1973, the Djemaa sent a message to General Franco requesting "greater participation by the people of the Sahara in the functions and responsibilities relating to the internal administration of their territory."[1] It is doubtful that such a suggestion emanated spontaneously from such a pliant and subservient body as the Djemaa. It would seem, rather, that the territory's new secretary-general, Ricardo Duyos González, a lieutenant-colonel in the infantry, advised the assembly's officers that Madrid would look kindly on a request of this nature and suggested the idea of petitioning the *caudillo*. Franco replied promptly on March 6, assuring the Djemaa that he had instructed his government to study its request "with the utmost diligence" and "to propose appropriate measures."[2]

Six months later, on September 21, Franco wrote again to the Djemaa, to announce that his government would prepare Western Sahara for internal autonomy. His statement marked a turning point in Spanish policy. "The Spanish State reiterates and solemnly guarantees that the population of the Sahara will freely determine its future," he pledged. "This self-determination will take place when the population freely so requests." Meanwhile, to continue "the process of political advancement of the Saharan people and in preparation for its future, a system of gradually increasing participation by that people in the management of their own affairs will be instituted." Specifically, he proposed the devolution of legislative powers to the Djemaa, which, "as supreme representative organ of the Saharan people, shall be responsible for drawing up general provisions concerning the internal affairs of the territory, without prejudice to the power of sanction vested in the governor-general." If the Djemaa gave its assent, these proposals would be embodied in a statute of internal autonomy. "The acceptance of these basic provisions by the General Assembly of the Sahara neither replaces nor diminishes the right of the Saharan people to self-determination concerning its future, for which this stage is a necessary preparation."[3] Franco's proposals were duly endorsed by the Djemaa at a session held on November 13–15, 1973, and in accordance with the new policy, Spain abstained in the UN General Assembly's vote on Resolution 3162 on December 14, instead of casting a negative vote as in December 1972.[4]

Nothing was said about the speed at which the constitutional changes were to proceed, and no target date was given for the eventual exercise of self-determination. It is probable that a rather long drawn-out process, lasting several years, was initially envisaged but that later developments prompted Franco to telescope it into a much shorter period. By the spring of 1974 Polisario's guerrilla attacks could no longer be dismissed as a passing irritant. The war was still small in scope, but the attacks were becoming more frequent, the guerrillas could easily evade pursuit by slipping across the borders into Mauritania, and intelligence reports revealed growing sympathy for them among the Saharawi population, especially the young. Meanwhile, there were difficulties at home, the most dramatic being the assassination of the head of Franco's cabinet, Admiral Luis Carrero Blanco, by Basque nationalists on December 20, 1973.[5] Four months later came the revolution in Spain's Iberian neighbor, Portugal. To Franco, the downfall of the Salazarist regime of Marcello Caetano at the hands of the Movement of the Armed Forces not only threatened to encourage those fighting for democracy in Spain but also heralded the end of Portugal's ruinous colonial wars in Angola, Mozambique and Guinea-Bissau and, sooner rather than later, the granting of independence to all the Portuguese African colonies. Apart from the white-settler regimes in southern Africa, Spain might soon be alone in the African colonial field.

Franco's answer was to accelerate the plans for internal self-government and then proceed rapidly to a form of independence that would not appreciably endanger Spanish economic interests in Western Sahara. He did not doubt that the territory would be economically "viable" after independence, given its huge phosphate industry. There were plans at this time to increase phosphate exports to ten million tons a year, making Western Sahara the world's second largest exporter of phosphate rock, and as world phosphate prices were now soaring, quadrupling between 1973 and 1975, it was estimated that the territory could earn as much as $700 million a year from its phosphate exports. Yet Franco knew that an "independent" government in El-Ayoun would have been almost helplessly reliant on Spain for technical assistance. Among the handful of Saharawi graduates there was only one medical doctor and one lawyer. Very few of the territory's civil servants above intermediate level were Saharawis, and it was obvious that, even with accelerated promotion, Spanish civil servants would be needed to keep government departments functioning effectively. Most important of all, perhaps, a majority of Fosbucraa's employees were Spanish; indeed, they held 81 percent of supervisory and technical posts. Even if the company was nationalized after independence, the Spanish government had every reason to expect that INI would continue to run the phosphate industry in practice, perhaps under a management contract, and that Spain would thereby still effectively control one of the world's most important phosphate-mining centers. As for the country's lucrative fishing resorces, which were of such importance to the Canary Islands, there seemed little doubt that a Western Saharan government would allow Spanish boats to go on fishing off its coast, in return perhaps for Spanish aid for its own fledgling fishing industry.

What Franco was determined to avoid, however, was Western Sahara's integration with Morocco. Its state-owned Office Chérifien de Phosphates (OCP), the largest phosphate exporting company in the world, would have little difficulty from a technical standpoint in operating the Bou-Craa mines and so Moroccan annexation would almost certainly result, sooner or later, in Spain's losing control of the phosphate industry. Likewise, Spain's frequent fishing disputes with Morocco, one of its principal fishing rivals, had left Franco in no doubt that Moroccan control of Western Sahara would threaten Spanish fishing rights off its coast—a coast, moreover, which was much richer in fishing resources than Morocco's own waters farther north. Fortunately for Franco, there was very little popular support within Western Sahara by 1974 for the idea of integration with Morocco. The challenge was to fend off the inevitable Moroccan protests and simultaneously to keep the radical nationalists of Polisario at bay, while an administratively effective and politically trustworthy Saharawi government was installed in El-Ayoun and chaperoned through an intermediate stage of internal autonomy toward formal independence.

A new team was appointed to implement the plan. A security *apparatchik*, Colonel Eduardo Blanco Rodríguez, who had worked for fifteen years in the Dirección General de Seguridad (DGS) and since 1965 as its director-general, took overall responsibility as Director General de Promoción del Sahara from April 22, 1974. A career officer, General Federico Gómez de Salazar, was named governor-general on May 31, and in June a colonel in the Engineers, Luis Rodríguez de Viguri y Gil, became secretary-general of the provincial administration.[6]

"I had the immediate objective of securing the approval and implementation of a Statute of Autonomy," Colonel Rodríguez de Viguri later recalled.[7] This was the Estatuto Político, by which powers of internal self-government were to be transferred to a Saharan government as a first step toward independence. The statute, which was approved by the Djemaa at a session held on July 4–6, 1974, provided for the creation of a Governing Council, presided over by the governor-general and comprising seven other members, three appointed by the governor-general and four elected by the Djemaa from among its members, the Djemaa member with the highest number of votes becoming the council's vice-president. The statute also converted the Djemaa itself from a purely consultative body into a legislative assembly with powers to enact laws relating to internal affairs, including the territory's budget. Laws approved by the Djemaa were to be promulgated by the governor-general, and so long as they did not affect the powers reserved to Spain (external defense and, significantly, internal security), he could not refuse to do so, although he could, in consultation with the Governing Council, refer them back to the Djemaa for reconsideration, with suggested modifications. Moreover, the assembly was no longer to consist of tribal representatives. It was to comprise forty members elected from constituencies and up to twelve members designated by the governor-general. Accordingly, a commission of the Djemaa drafted an electoral law that provided for universal adult suffrage, thereby enfranchising women for the first time, and for the distribution of parliamentary seats between geographical districts rather than tribes and corporate groups as hitherto.[8]

At its July session the Djemaa also approved a development plan, drafted by the Spanish government for the years 1974–78. In all, about 20 billion pesetas were to be invested—some 8.3 billion pesetas by INI in the phosphate industry and almost all the rest in the development of social services (9 billion pesetas), economic infrastructure and industry, one of the main proposed projects being the construction of a new fish-processing factory at Villa Cisneros with sufficient capacity to produce twenty-seven thousand tons of fish and fish products a year.[9]

Meanwhile, on August 20, eight years after first being urged to do so by the UN General Assembly, the Spanish government informed the secretary-general of the UN, Kurt Waldheim, that it would hold a referendum under UN auspices during the first six months of 1975.[10]

Perhaps because there was now less to hide, the Spanish government decided to lift the veil of secrecy about developments within Western Sahara. The censorship of news in the Spanish press about the territory, which had been imposed in 1972, was ended on September 14, 1974.[11] Further measures to prepare for internal self-government and eventual independence were proposed by the Djemaa at a session held on November 19–22, after a month's postponement due to the Polisario attack on the Fosbucraa conveyor belt on October 20. Though still without real legislative powers, the assembly proposed laws on judicial reform, the creation of a Saharan civil service and, of special importance for the impending referendum, the criteria of Western Saharan nationality, all of which were subsequently endorsed by the governor-general and published as *normas*, or regulations, in the *Boletín Oficial del Sahara*.[12] The *normas* on judicial reform abolished the dual system of courts established by the Spanish authorities in the fifties and created a single, unified system of independent courts that were to have jurisdiction in civil, criminal, labor and litigious-administrative cases. An Organic Law of Justice was to be drafted by the Djemaa's judicial commission and submitted to the Djemaa for approval. The *normas* on the territory's civil service formally transferred overall control of government departments from the Dirección General de Promoción del Sahara to a commission responsible to the Governing Council. The *normas* also proposed the creation of a civil service training institute, since not one of the thirty government departments was headed by a Saharawi and (as late as May 1975) only five had Saharawi assistant heads. Even in the Policía Territorial only two Saharawis held commissioned rank, and nearly all the teachers were Spanish. The *normas* on nationality, which were promulgated by the governor-general on December 18, regulated the issuing of identity documents, a crucial matter for the coming referendum. They laid down that persons would be deemed Western Saharans if they were born of Western Saharan fathers or mothers or had been born in the territory though their parents were of foreign nationality (so long as the latter too had been born in the territory). Persons could opt for Western Saharan nationality if they were born in the territory or born outside it of Western Saharan parentage. Finally, the *normas* provided that non-Saharans could be granted nationality upon the recommendation of a commission of the Djemaa if they had resided in the territory for at least five consecutive years or, exceptionally, for three years if they had made a significant contribution to the territory—by introducing an important industry or directing a major enterprise, for example.[13]

At an extraordinary session in February 1975 the Djemaa selected its four members of the Governing Council and also appointed a permanent commission, including the assembly's president, Khatri Ould Said Ould el-Joumani, and fifteen other members, to act as the Djemaa's steering committee between full meetings and as a link with the Governing Council.[14]

While all these constitutional changes were being prepared, the colonial authorities contrived also to mold a Saharawi political leadership that could wrest the initiative from the Polisario Front and steer the country toward independence in close association with Spain. Though still important allies, the conservative and generally elderly sheikhs in the Djemaa were insufficient for this purpose. Younger, and better educated, blood was needed to run an effective government and marshal popular support. As early as 1970, during the confrontation with the Harakat Tahrir, Spanish officials had been toying wth the idea of creating a Saharawi party that could provide a safe, monitored avenue for political expression and involvement in the territory's affairs by the younger educated Saharawis whose ambitions could not easily be satisfied in the traditionalist framework of the Djemaa.[15] This became a much more urgent matter after the creation of the Polisario Front and the drafting of the Estatuto Político. So, during 1974, an officially sanctioned Saharawi party began to take shape, with the rare distinction of being the only political party besides the Falange to enjoy the privilege of legality in Francoist Spain. It first took the bombastic title of the Partido Revolucionario Progresivo (PRP), but then, in October, changed its name to the Partido de la Unión Nacional Saharaui (PUNS), as which it was formally registered in El-Ayoun on February 16, 1975.[16] The party adopted a fourteen-point program, which included commitments ''to attain Saharan independence through a process of accelerated self-determination'' and, with reference to Morocco and Mauritania, ''to reject any foreign claim''; but, unlike the guerrillas of the Polisario Front, the *Punsistas* championed the idea of a special relationship with Spain, their program pledging ''to preserve mutual friendship and cooperation with Spain in every field.'' A UN mission of inquiry which visited Western Sahara in May 1975 reported that the PUNS was ''opposed to radical social change''; and, in fact, the PUNS program included a committment ''to preserve and strengthen the religious and social traditions, adapting them to the institutions of a modern state.'' The UN mission noted also that most members of the permanent commission of the Djemaa identified themselves as party members and that the party derived ''much of its support from the traditional element of Saharan society, including the majority of sheikhs and notables, and from the older generation.''[17] Colonel Rodríguez de Viguri confided in July 1975 that ''more than 60 percent of the members of the Djemaa are *Punsistas*.''[18]

The party's secretary-general was a talented young engineer who was typical of the new breed of university-trained technocrats upon whom the Spanish officials in El-Ayoun were counting to head the new state-to-be. He was Khalihenna Ould Rashid, a twenty-seven-year-old Reguibi who had trained in Las Palmas and Madrid and married a Spanish woman. During 1974–75 it seemed as if he was being groomed by the Spanish authorities for the presidency of an independent

Saharan state, almost after the manner of France's elevation of the young lawyer Mokhtar Ould Daddah to the leadership of Mauritania in the late fifties; and Spanish officials gave considerable organizational and financial backing to his party.

The Polisario Front lambasted the PUNS as the vehicle by which "Spain and its allies intend to set up a seemingly national administration." It was a potpourri of "Arabs and officers of the Francoist police and administrators of the colony such as the secretary-general, Luis Rodríguez de Viguri, who brought it into being."[19] The Front's second congress, which met six weeks after the approval of the Estatuto Político by the Djemaa, denounced the internal autonomy plan as "a maneuver to save colonialism in a state of weakness, an attempt to dupe the people in order to continue its domination over our land and our national wealth." The referendum too was a "maneuver," but the front said that it would accept it if all Spanish troops had first been withdrawn and replaced by "the revolutionaries of the Polisario Front to ensure security," the Spanish administration had been replaced by a "national administration," political exiles had been allowed to return home, the Spanish "colons" had departed, the "plunder of national wealth" had halted, the referendum was controlled by the United Nations and the Arab League, and the referendum led immediately to independence.[20]

In fact, Franco's plans for a gradual devolution of powers to a Spanish-leaning Saharawi government came to nought. As we shall see, the Estatuto Político was never put into effect, the referendum was delayed and finally abandoned and, a few months after its founding, the PUNS began to disintegrate. Rapidly, the Spanish government was confronted with the choice of striking a deal with Polisario or handing its colony to Morocco and Mauritania.

NOTES

1. Cited in *Report of the Special Committee*, UN General Assembly, 28th Session, Vol. IV, p. 64.

2. *Ibid.*, p. 65.

3. *ABC* (Madrid), September 28, 1973.

4. *Report of the Special Committee*, UN General Assembly, 29th Session, UN Document A/9623/Add.4 (Part II), p. 23.

5. Minister of the presidency in 1965–67 and vice-president of the Council of Ministers in 1967–73, Carrero Blanco had been appointed president of the Council of Ministers only the previous June.

6. Ramón Criado, *Sahara, pasión y muerte de un sueño colonial* (Ruedo Ibérico, Paris, 1977), pp. 45–46, 259–60.

7. Speech in Madrid, November 14, 1979, published in *Sahara 14-nov, 1975, la traición* (Asociación Amigos del Sahara and IEPALA, Madrid, 1980), pp. 61–62.

8. Report of the United Nations Visiting Mission to Spanish Sahara, 1975, *General Assembly Official Records*, 30th Session, Supplement 23, UN Document A/10023/Rev. 1, pp. 44–46.

9. *Ibid.*, p. 55.

10. Letter dated 20 August 1974 from the Permanent Representative of Spain to the United Nations to the Secretary-General, UN Document A/9714.

11. *ABC*, September 15, 1974.

12. *ABC*, November 22, 1974, and November 23, 1974.

13. Report of the United Nations Visiting Mission to Spanish Sahara, 1975, *loc. cit.*, pp. 47–50.

14. *Ibid.*, pp. 43–45.

15. Federico Abascal, Sol Gallego and Enrique Bustamante, "Sahara: documentos secretos," *Cuadernos para el Diálogo* (Madrid), January 21, 1978, p. 16.

16. *Reuters*, dispatch from the UN, New York, March 10, 1975.
17. Report of the United Nations Visiting Mission to Spanish Sahara, 1975, *loc. cit.*, pp. 60–61.
18. *Arriba* (Madrid), July 19, 1975.
19. *Notre peuple face aux tout derniers crimes du fascisme impuni* (Polisario Front, December 1974), p. 10.
20. "Manifeste politique, adopté par le deuxième congrès," *Le peuple saharaoui en lutte* (Polisario Front, May 1975), p. 50.

17

Hassan's Riposte

WHEN HE HEARD of the Spanish government's internal autonomy plan, on July 4, 1974, King Hassan responded angrily the same day, by writing to Franco to warn him against taking "any unilateral action" in Western Sahara.[1] Four days later, in a speech in Fez, the king declared that he would not tolerate a "puppet state" in the "southern part of our country," and he appealed to his countrymen to make 1974 "a year of mobilization at home and abroad to recover our territories."[2]

After more than a decade of carefully nurtured Spanish-Moroccan cordiality, during which King Hassan had deliberately downplayed Morocco's territorial claim to Western Sahara to the displeasure of the Moroccan opposition parties, the king had now resolved to abandon the "spirit of Barajas." Western Sahara was no longer to be a matter for occasional private exchanges of views with Franco. The king was set upon thwarting the internal autonomy plan, which he rightly saw as a prelude to full independence. Over the following year, the "recovery" of the "Moroccan Sahara" became his overriding ambition.

It has often been said that Hassan's renewed interest in Western Sahara was motivated, in part at least, by a desire to control the territory's phosphate wealth. Morocco is, in its own right, the world's largest exporter of phosphate rock and the third largest producer, after the United States and the Soviet Union, which export only a small fraction of their output. In 1974, Morocco exported 18.7 million tons, 34 percent of world trade in phosphates. Control of Bou-Craa, where exports were scheduled at this time to rise from their 1974 level of 2.1 million tons to around 10 million tons by 1980, could have been anticipated, perhaps, to raise Morocco's share of world phosphate exports to more than 50 percent. That, the king may have hoped, would have given Morocco as much leverage over world phosphate prices as OPEC had over oil prices. Indeed, even without the Bou-Craa mines, Morocco's state phosphate company, the Office Chérifien de Phosphates (OCP), was exploiting the record world demand for fertilizers at this time to achieve dramatic increases in its export prices. The price of Moroccan phosphate rock quadrupled between November 1973 and January 1975, rising from $14 to $68 a ton, and Morocco's phosphate earnings soared from 788 million dirhams in 1973 to 4,075 million dirhams in 1974, encouraging optimistic prognoses of the country's economic future. However, Morocco could not sustain the high prices. As demand for fertilizers fell and Morocco's U.S. competitors undercut the OCP in its traditional European markets, the boom was punctured. World phosphate exports fell from 55 million tons in 1974 to 44 million tons in 1975 and Morocco's exports fell from 18.7 to 13.1 million tons. Export prices were halved and Morocco's phosphate earnings collapsed, from 4.1 billion dirhams in 1974 to only 2.1 billion dirhams by 1977.[3] Since then, recovery has been slow and erratic. So, despite the annexation of most of Western Sahara, including the Bou-Craa region, in 1975–76, Morocco proved unable to control the world phosphate market. Nonetheless, Bou-Craa did add to Morocco's overall export capacity, though only potentially since Polisario attacks kept the mines closed from 1976. Paradoxically, even their closure may have marginally protected the OCP's Moroccan mines by keeping a rival supply of ore off the glutted world market.

Like Spain, Morocco also had good reason to prize Western Sahara's extensive fishing resources. Fisheries are one of Morocco's most important industries, employing about fifty thousand workers, including twenty-five thousand in processing and canning plants, and fish is the country's fourth main export, after phosphates, citrus fruit and textiles. However, the fish catch, of which sardines account for well over three-quarters, has tended to stabilize around 200,000 to 250,000 tons a year after declining from a record of almost 400,000 tons in 1973, and Moroccan fisheries experts have regarded the much richer resources off the Saharan coast as offering the main potential for the industry's growth. "Any increase in sardine fishing must be achieved by exploiting the stocks situated between Oued Noun and El-Ayoun, whose potential is 400,000 tons a year," the Moroccan government's Office National de Pêche (ONP) was to suggest in 1977.[4]

However, despite the benefits of gaining control over Western Sahara's phosphate and fishing resources, there is little evidence that economic considerations played a significant part in kindling Hassan's Saharan ambitions in the summer of 1974. At most they were an added incentive; his principal considerations were entirely political in nature.

Since ascending the throne in 1961, the king had managed to conserve his grip on power more skillfully than many third-world monarchs. Nonetheless, he had been under serious political challenge on many fronts. He had never enjoyed the kind of prestige which his father, Mohammed V, had gained from his role in the independence struggle and his period of exile in Madagascar in 1953–55, and his patriotic credentials had been widely questioned by both the UNFP and the Greater Moroccans of the Istiqlal Party. As a supposed descendant of the Prophet Mohammed and the spiritual as well as temporal ruler of his people, as *amir al-muminin* (commander of the faithful), he retained a certain religious standing, but primarily in the rural areas, where political awareness remained low and the dense network of officials of the ministry of the interior had successfully prevented penetration by the urban-based opposition parties. The inexorable exodus of poor and landless peasants into the towns had gradually diminished the demographic weight of the country areas, however, and the progressive urbanization and modernization of Moroccan society had brought greater questioning of the king's claim to a divine right to rule. Moreover, his flamboyant, opulent lifestyle alienated many, and most educated Moroccans were appalled by the favoritism with which he habitually used his powers of patronage and appointment to create a clientele of supporters while refusing to yield real power and resorting to repression to silence critics and dissidents. Economic performance, particularly in agriculture, had been desultory, and there was criticism of the continued hold of foreign interests over much of the economy. Moreover, social inequalities had become stark and provocative in the cities, where up to two million people, around a quarter of the urban population, were living in extreme poverty in sprawling and unsanitary shantytowns by the mid-1970s.[5] In the huge Ben Msick shantytown on the edge of Casablanca, discontent had exploded, spontaneously and anarchically, into violent rioting in March 1965, which had only been suppressed by the army at the cost of several hundred lives.

An adept politician, Hassan had spent much of his reign fending off challenges to his regime by playing up the disputes and mutual suspicions of the country's rival political factions and subtly combining carrot and stick tactics to reward opponents prone to compromise and repress the more recalcitrant. Within certain carefully circumscribed bounds he had allowed opposition parties to organize, publish newspapers and, from time to time, contest elections and express their views in parliament, but when faced by determined opposition, he had employed his constitutional powers to dissolve the Chamber of Representatives and rule by decree, censored or banned opposition newspapers, outlawed opposition parties and thrown opposition politicians into jail. Three months after his army's bloody suppression of the March 1965 riots in Casablanca, he had declared a state of emergency, dissolved the Chamber of Representatives, which had been elected three years earlier, and ruled by decree for five years. In October 1965 his most forthright political opponent, the exiled leader of the UNFP, Mehdi Ben Barka, had been kidnapped and murdered in France, in a plot which a French court later traced back to Hassan's tough interior minister, General Mohammed Oufkir.[6] In 1970, Hassan had finally drafted a new constitution, but the main opposition parties had rejected it, since it conserved the royal grip on power and even reduced the proportion of directly elected parliamentary seats to only one-third (compared to two-thirds under the previous 1962 constitution). The Istiqlal Party and the UNFP formed a national front, the Kutlah al-Wataniya, and boycotted the ensuing elections. Meanwhile, a new wave of labor militancy had been heralded by two long strikes by phosphate miners in 1968 and 1971. The universities were almost continually strike-bound between 1969 and 1973, and, at its fifteenth congress, in 1972, the leadershp of UNEM passed to the Marxist groups, Ilal Amam and March 23.[7]

On March 3, 1971, Hassan described the monarchy as "the rock on which the waves of evil break and the unshakable edifice that resists the vicissitudes of the times." Less than four months later, on July 10, he narrowly escaped death when part of the army, which had hitherto been regarded as one of the bastions of royal power, tried to stage a coup. Acting on the orders of a group of generals who had apparently been angered by corruption, a force of cadets burst into the king's

palace at Skirhat, fifteen miles south of Rabat, and opened fire on guests attending a garden party held to celebrate his forty-second birthday. They surrendered
when one of the coup leaders, General Mohammed Medbouh, was killed, and the
king managed to survive unscathed. A year later, on August 16, 1972, he had
another close scrape when a group of air-force officers, flying American-built Northrop F-5 fighters, tried to kill him by strafing his private Boeing 727 as he flew
home from a vacation in France. Less menacing was a series of isolated guerrilla attacks in the Atlas Mountains and bomb blasts in Casablanca, Rabat, Oujda and
Nador carried out by an extreme left-wing faction of the UNFP in March 1973.[8]

After the shock of the Skirhat attack, Hassan tried to placate his critics with a
few cosmetic anticorruption measures. Six former cabinet ministers were arrested
in November 1971. At the same time, the king dispensed with the royalist-
dominated parliament, which had enjoyed very little credibility on account of the
opposition's boycott of the 1970 elections, and in March 1972 he promulgated a
new constitution that raised the proportion of directly elected parliamentary seats
to two thirds but nonetheless ensured that decisive power remained in royal
hands. It was condemned, like the 1970 constitution, by the opposition parties.
The king failed to call elections and so ruled for a further five years by decree.

Thousands were arrested on political grounds during these crisis years. In
September 1971, 193 members of the UNFP were tried in Marrakesh on charges
of endangering state security and five of the defendants received death sentences,
though these were later commuted. In January 1973 UNEM was outlawed and
scores of its leaders, including the union's president, Abdelaziz Menebhi, were
arrested. The following March, forty activists of a high school students' union, the
Syndicat National des Lycéens (SNL), were detained and held without trial for
two years, and in August eighty members of UNEM received jail terms ranging up
to fifteen years. Meanwhile, the guerrilla attacks in March 1973 provided a pretext
for a wide-scale clampdown on the UNFP, which had split in 1972 into a so-called
"Rabat faction" led by Abderrahim Bouabid and a "Casablanca faction" led by
Abdallah Ibrahim which retained close ties with the unions of the UMT. Some
two thousand people were rounded up in the immediate aftermath of the March
incidents.[9] The "Rabat" UNFP was formally banned on April 2, 1973, thereby
joining the pro-Moscow PLS, which had been declared illegal in 1969, in
semiclandestinity; and after two trials at Kenitra, in August 1973 and January
1974, several dozen UNFP members were given long jail sentences, some for life,
and twenty-two were condemned to death and executed. Sixty-four exiles, including the veteran left-wing UNFP leader, Mohammed Basri, were sentenced to
death *in absentia.*[10]

Meanwhile, the coup attempts and the purges that followed them decimated
the armed forces. No less than nine of the country's sixteen generals lost their lives
as a result of the 1971 coup attempt: five were killed during the fighting at Skirhat
and four more, along with six other officers, were summarily executed at the
king's orders three days later.[11] Hassan then named his trusted interior minister,
Oufkir, one of the few surviving generals, to take command of the armed forces as
defense minister and chief-of-staff, while a thousand soldiers were brought to
trial in January 1972 and given jail sentences ranging from one year to life.
However, a few hours after the August 1972 coup attempt, Oufkir too died. He

shot himself twice in the head, according to the minister of information, Moham-med Benhima, who described his death as "a suicide of treachery, not a suicide of loyalty"; but there were suspicions that he had been executed, either for master-minding the coup plot or for failing to detect it. Two hundred and twenty members of the air force were arrested, and after a trial in November, eleven of-ficers were sentenced to death and executed the following January.[12]

Three days after the Boeing incident, the king announced that he would take personal command of the armed forces. The post of defense minister was abol-ished.[13] With most of his generals now dead and only two of those surviving still on active service, Hassan henceforth kept a very close watch on the FAR. No cen-tralized intermediate command structure was permitted between the Palace and battalion and brigade commanders. Garrisons were kept constantly on the hop and shifted from one base to another. Indeed, the army was practically disarmed. It kept its weapons, but the ammunition was locked up in dumps scattered across the country and guarded by parallel security forces such as the Gendarmerie Royale, the Sûreté Nationale and the paramilitary Forces Auxiliaires. The king now took all major military decisions himself.[14]

From 1973, the king took a series of political measures to try to refurbish his regime's tarnished image. At the end of the year he made new overtures to the civilian opposition. The ban on the "Rabat" UNFP was lifted on December 17, and Bouabid was invited to a palace tête-à-tête on January 6, 1974. Two days later, orders were given for the release of 450 UNFP members who had been held without trial since the March 1973 incidents, and in March he hinted that he would call parliamentary elections.[15] At the same time, the king took advantage of the phosphate boom to embark on expansionist economic policies in the hope of stimulating faster growth and tackling some of the grave social problems that endangered his regime's stability. Since the phosphate boom raised export receipts by 84 percent and government revenue by 71 percent in 1974, the government radically revised its five-year plan for 1973–78, more than tripling its overall investment target, from 11.7 billion dirhams to 39.8 billion dirhams, though, as we shall see, this was precariously premised on the expectation that phosphate prices would remain at their record levels.

One of the most important of the king's new political initiatives was a decision to "Moroccanize" the farms and small businesses still owned by foreigners. In the countryside land hunger had become acute. Among rural families 56.5 percent owned less than five hectares of arable land each and a further 23.4 percent owned none at all, according to a rural census conducted in 1973–74. At the opposite end of the rural spectrum, 2.9 percent of rural families owned 33.9 percent of all the country's arable land.[16] For years the opposition parties had decried Hassan's failure to expropriate and redistribute most of the one million hectares of farmland acquired by European settlers during the Protectorate. Indeed, his first and exceedingly modest agrarian reform measure, enacted in 1963, had con-fiscated only about one-quarter of this land, and by 1971 only about 90,000 hec-tares had actually been redistributed to peasant farmers. Meanwhile, about 400,000 hectares of unconfiscated land were sold privately by their European owners to large Moroccan landlords. The Skirhat affair jolted the king into order-ing the distribution of another 90,000 hectares in 1972, and then in March 1973 he announced that the remaining foreign-owned land, then totaling only about 325,000 hectares, would be Moroccanized and redistributed.[17] In all, the Moroccanization and redistribution measures affected only a small fraction of the country's total of 7.2 million hectares of arable land and benefited less than 4 percent of the one million peasant families with no land at all or less than one hectare, "a drop in the ocean," as one agronomist remarked.[18] None of the large Moroccan-owned estates were confiscated or broken up, and no real dent was made in the rural exodus. But Hassan hoped that the Moroccanization measures would help disarm his critics and spawn a loyalist rural class of "middle peasants" who owed their prosperity to royal patronage.[19]

Another shrewd move on the king's part was the dispatch of several thousand Moroccan troops to Egypt and Syria in 1973, which, besides improving his hitherto somewhat suspect anti-Zionist credentials, had the advantage of distancing a significant part of his untrustworthy army and giving it a sense of mission. Part of the expeditionary force subsequently fought the Israelis on the Golan Heights during the 1973 Arab-Israeli war.

However, the crusade launched by the king in the summer of 1974 for the recovery of the "Moroccan Sahara" did more by far than any other of his initiatives to restore royal prestige. Since the fifties Moroccans had been conditioned by the government, the opposition parties and news media alike to consider the liberation and integration of the Spanish-ruled Sahara as a patriotic duty of the highest order, and so they responded to the king's calls for mobilization with enormous enthusiasm, as if they were preparing for a *jihad*, a holy war to free fellow countrymen from the oppression of colonial infidels. The king rode on the crest of a huge wave of patriotism. He played his cards brilliantly, using the media to capitalize on the patriotic fervor to restore his dynasty's image as the symbol of the nation's unity and the guarantor of its strength and defense. Like the Middle East expedition, the Saharan campaign provided another noble cause to occupy the minds of army officers and keep much of the FAR at a safe distance from the king's palaces, this time near the southern Moroccan border. Furthermore, the opposition parties were coopted and neutralized. Hassan invited the Istiqlal Party, the UNFP and even the leader of the previously banned PLS to join his great crusade, and they all eagerly agreed to do so. Having complained for years about the royal government's appeasement of Franco and its abandonment of the claims to Mauritania and parts of Algeria, it was not surprising that the Greater Moroccans of the Istiqlal Party and the former PLS should have applauded the king's about-turn in policy, but the UNFP's support was at odds with the tradition set by Ben Barka in its early years, when the party opposed the 1963 war with Algeria and upheld Mauritania's right to self-determination. However, the UNFP had always assumed, largely on account of the Saharawis' support for the Army of Liberation in 1956–58, that the Saharawis considered themselves to be Moroccan. Since its founding in 1959, when it recruited many Moroccan veterans of the Army of Liberation, it had had almost no contact with Saharawis, since it had made no attempt to organize clandestinely in the Spanish colony, and it was therefore ignorant of the new nationalist stirrings there since the late sixties. Moreover, after the years of repression it had endured since the early sixties, the party had little stomach for the kind of head-on confrontation with the Palace that opposition to the king's Saharan *jihad* might well have entailed. Only small clandestine Marxist factions, such as Ilal-Amam, which openly supported Polisario, dared to express their dissent as the main parties of the "opposition" climbed aboard the royal campaign.[20]

The king cemented his alliance with the main opposition parties by offering a liberalization of political conditions at home, confident as he was that they would not easily be able to challenge his new popularity. In August 1974, for example, he freed from detention two prominent leaders of the UNFP, Omar Benjelloun and Mohammed Lyazghi, who had been kept in jail despite their acquittal in the August 1973 Kenitra trial; and at about the same time he gave Ali Yata the nod to form a new legal communist party. On September 17, he let it be known that he might call parliamentary elections by October 1975.[21] In fact the elections were not held until 1977, and the liberalization was only partial. The more militant of the king's opponents were treated with as little clemency as ever: seven leftists who had been condemned to death in the Kenitra trials were executed in August 1974, just as the alliance between the Palace and the main opposition parties was being sealed, and the following autumn about one hundred Marxists, most of them members of the Ilal-Amam and March 23 groups, were detained, to be brought to trial only in 1977, when most received long jail sentences.[22] However, the concessions made by the king to the larger and more circumspect opposition parties in the summer of 1974, as the Saharan campaign got under way, were grasped like a breath of fresh air.

These parties may have anticipated, or at least hoped, that in the impending confrontation with Spain, the king's resolve would falter, giving them a chance to come to the fore as uncompromising nationalists and reap the political benefits of the crisis. Hassan was certainly playing for very high stakes. If he failed to force Spain's hand, his political fortunes would tumble even lower perhaps than they had been in 1971–73. His prestige and credibility would be seriously shaken, the opposition parties would subject his government to a barrage of criticism and, perhaps most dangerous of all, the army could be tempted to try to depose him again. By contrast, the prize for success seemed considerable to the king—the chance to be acclaimed as a national hero, as the "reunifier of the nation," to reassert the monarchy's prestige, placate the army and outmaneuver the opposition parties, and to increase his regime's regional and international stature to boot.

On July 16, 1974, the king summoned political leaders to a special conference, to plan a diplomatic blitzkrieg of the world's capitals. Besides the premier, Ahmed Osman, and numerous cabinet ministers, six party leaders attended— Abderrahim Bouabid, Ali Yata, M'hammed Boucetta, the secretary-general of the Istiqlal Party, Mahjoubi Aherdan of the predominantly Berber Mouvement Populaire (MP), and Abdelkrim Khatib of the small Mouvement Populaire Démocratique et Constitutionel (MPDC). The king requested them to undertake diplomatic missions as his personal envoys, to put Morocco's view of the Western Saharan problem to governments throughout the world. The opposition leaders readily agreed.[23] The foreign minister, Ahmed Laraki, left Morocco immediately to confer with President Boumedienne in Algiers, in the hope of securing Algerian support, or at least neutrality, in Morocco's impending confrontation with Spain, and then went on to Tunisia and Mauritania. The prime minister visited several European capitals, including Paris and Moscow, while Khatib, the MPDC leader, toured black Africa. The opposition leaders left Morocco on July 27. Boucetta went to Egypt, Somalia, Ethiopia and Sudan, while Bouabid traveled to Iran, China, India, Turkey and Indonesia. Hassan's Stalinist emissary, Ali Yata, was sent off, appropriately, on an eighteen-day mission to Eastern Europe.[24]

The military implications of the new Saharan policy were reviewed at a meeting of the king's National Defense Committee held the same day as the conference with political leaders. Hassan then appointed one of his closest confidants, Colonel Ahmed Dlimi, the director of his aides-de-camp and the boss of the Moroccan secret police, the Direction Générale d'Etudes et de Documentation (DGED), as commander of the third military region, bordering Western Sahara, and entrusted him with full civil, as well as military, powers there.[25] To prepare for the Spanish colony's eventual annexation, frantic efforts had to be made to compensate for the years of neglect to which Tarfaya province, one of Morocco's poorest regions, had been abandoned since its cession by Spain in 1958. A road had been built from Goulimine to Tan-Tan, where there was now a military base and an airfield, but to the south of Tan-Tan there was no tarmac road at all. The settlement at Tarfaya had lost even the little importance it had acquired when the Spanish were there. So, on September 3, during a tour of southern Morocco, Hassan announced an emergency development plan for the province, to make it "a solid link between the motherland and the despoiled Sahara once it has been recovered."[26] Work finally began on a road to Tarfaya, and at the beginning of 1975 the government announced that 420 million dirhams would be invested in the province.[27] By February 1975, Colonel Dlimi had an estimated twenty thousand troops under his command in southern Morocco.

Hassan may have calculated that Franco, who was now eighty-one years old, would not want to risk seeing his long era end in conflict and so would quickly bow to Moroccan pressure. Indeed, in July the aged dictator fell dangerously ill with phlebitis and was obliged to hand the reins of government to Juan Carlos de Borbón, the thirty-five-year-old prince whom he had named as heir apparent in 1969. Moreover, Hassan had offered concessions to Spain in return for its colony. "Once you have recognized Morocco's sovereignty over this part of its territory," he had promised in his July 8 speech, "we are prepared to put military bases at your disposal" and to allow Spain to retain an interest in the "extraction and marketing" of the territory's mineral and fisheries resources.[28] However, when he sent Osman and Ahmed Laraki, the foreign minister, to Madrid on August 12 for the first direct talks with Spanish leaders since his July 4 warning letter to Franco, it quickly transpired that, despite the *caudillo's* illness, the Spanish government was not inclined to compromise. After seven hours of talks with Prince Juan Carlos, the Spanish premier, Carlos Arias Navarro, and his foreign minister, Pedro Cortina y Mauri, on August 13, they flew home empty-handed, to report total failure to the king.[29] Worse still, they had been informed in Madrid of the imminent plans to announce the holding of a referendum. "Information has reached us," the king told Moroccans in a televised address a week later, on August 20, "that the Spanish state has decided to put an official request before the United Nations Organization to begin the process of self-determination" and "to fix a date not exceeding six or seven months at the most for the organization of the referendum."[30]

Hassan's rejoinder was frank and unambiguous. If the referendum included the option of independence, "it is evident that not only will Morocco reject it but it will be the first time that it disavows a decision emanating from the United Nations Organization." The king added a thinly veiled threat. "Morocco prefers to take a diplomatic, political and peaceful path, instead of resorting to no matter what other means; however, if Morocco ascertains that this path will not lead to the recovery of its territories, it will certainly not hesitate to find these other means."[31] The Spanish government, however, refused to back down. During August it placed its troops in Western Sahara on alert. Franco confounded Hassan, as well as many Spaniards, by recovering, resumed his functions as head of state and on August 30 presided at a cabinet meeting. Six days later, on September 5, the minister of the army, General Francisco Coloma Gallegos, flew to El-Ayoun to review his forces' state of readiness; and on September 7 the Dirección General de Promoción del Sahara issued a detailed policy statement, declaring that, while Spain wanted to "maintain close contact with the governments of the countries interested by the Saharan question," among them Morocco, it would not be deflected from its view that "only the indigenous population of the Sahara has the right to determine its own destiny."[32]

For its part, the Polisario Front, meeting at its second congress, on August 25–31, sent a message to Hassan warning him against embarking on an "expansionist war against a small people which has few resources but is deeply devoted to its country and its defense." If Hassan pursued his current policy, the front said, it would lead either to the crime of genocide or to a "war without perspectives" for the Moroccan people.[33] If the message ever reached the king, it made no impression. "We hope these subversive elements will put an end to their nefarious activities," he said in Agadir on September 3. "Let them know that the Sahara has been and will remain Moroccan. We shall not hesitate to punish them."[34] On September 17 he went further, revealing that he had "already asked the Spanish either to police their own territory, because it still is their own territory, or to leave me free to prevent the secessionists, because the FLS [sic] people, and particularly Ouali, who was one of the strike leaders in the law faculty, did all their studies here in Rabat."[35]

At home Hassan was now riding high on a groundswell of patriotism. For weeks, barely a day went by without some organization or other sending messages to the king, lauding his Saharan policy and renewing the *bayaa*, the traditional pledge of allegiance to the throne. If the opposition parties had expected to make capital from their new alliance with the Palace, it was Hassan who was really making the political running, as television, radio and progovernment newspapers poured out a torrent of propaganda, painting the king as the architect and commander of the country's campaign for reunification with its Saharan provinces. Once the king had aroused such popular enthusiasm, his campaign generated its own relentless force, like a "locomotive with a terrific head of steam ready to go rattling down the track," as one foreign journalist writing from Rabat at this time remarked.[36] Spain had refused to abandon its plans for internal autonomy and a referendum, yet retreat on Hassan's part seemed impossible. It would have betrayed his people's hopes and expectations, angered the army and emboldened the opposition parties. So, when palace officials suddenly summoned journalists to a royal press conference on September 17, there was such an air of crisis that some foreign correspondents expected to be told of the outbreak of hostilities on the Saharan border. Time was running out, for the referendum was to be held within a matter of months and it seemed certain to endorse the option of independence. Action had to be taken rapidly to get it halted or, at the very least, postponed. But, despite his calculated brinkmanship and rhetorical bellicosity, Hassan was enough of a realist to appreciate the costs of military conflict with Spain. In fact, he had invited journalists to his Rabat palace because he had hit on a brilliant time-buying stratagem. He would have the Western Saharan dispute submitted to the International Court of Justice at The Hague and thereby persuade the UN to postpone the referendum while the territory's legal status was under the court's laborious and time-consuming scrutiny.

So, while repeating his opposition to a referendum, which "would lead us into conflict with the United Nations Organization," and affirming that Moroccans "were ready to recover their soil by whatever means," he proposed that Spain should join Morocco in requesting the ICJ's arbitration. "You, the Spanish government, claim that the Sahara was *res nullius*; you claim that it was a territory or property left uninherited; you claim that no power and no administration had been established over the Sahara; Morocco claims the contrary. Let us then request the arbitration of the International Court of Justice."[37] If the ICJ found that Morocco had historically exercised sovereignty in Western Sahara, Hassan seems to have believed, the UN could be persuaded to make the principle of territorial integrity override that of self-determination. In any case, a period of delay would give Morocco time to argue its case abroad, build up its armed forces, which had been seriously weakened by the coup attempts, and, perhaps, await political changes in Spain.

It would also give the king time to do something about Mauritania's embarrassing counterclaim. "Becoming direct neighbors, it is entirely normal that we should open a dialogue with our Mauritanian friends to find out what our relations are going to be, what are frontiers will be," Hassan suggested at his press conference, hinting, as it were, that Mauritania might be offered at least some of the Spanish colony.[38] To Hassan's dismay, his vigorous assertions of the Moroccan claim over the previous two months had prompted President Mokhtar Ould Daddah to mount his own rival diplomatic campaign in defense of Mauritania's "rights" in Western Sahara. On August 3, his foreign minister, Hamdi Ould Mouknass, had reaffirmed the Mauritanian claim, sending the king's brother-in-law, Ahmed Alaoui, into spasms of rage in the pages of his evening paper, *Maroc Soir*. "Discordant voices can only provide support for Spain," he protested in an editorial on August 6, accusing the Nouakchott regime of ingratitude for Morocco's recognition of Mauritania. Three days later, Mokhtar Ould Daddah went personally to Fez, to meet Hassan, but they failed to reach an understanding, and on August 20, during a visit to Zaire, Hamdi Ould Mouknass once again spoke out in support of his country's claim, prompting Alaoui's morning newspaper, *Le Matin*, the next day to decry these "abhorrent declarations" as "collusion with colonialism."

The ICJ stratagem not only provided more time to come to terms with

Mauritania; it also made it all the more necessary, for Morocco had to ensure that Mauritania did not dispute its claims at The Hague. Some sort of compromise had to be negotiated, and the obvious solution was a partition. It was at the UN, in New York, a fortnight after the king's press conference, that the idea was first broached to the Mauritanian government. Hassan sent a special delegation, headed by Laraki but including also the two main opposition leaders, Bouabid and Boucetta, to New York on September 23 to offer the Mauritanians an olive branch. Boucetta was initially shocked by the idea of a deal with Mauritania, which his party still considered a Moroccan province, but Bouabid convinced Boucetta that it made tactical sense.[39] Laraki made his pitch to the Mauritanians in an address to the General Assembly on September 31. "Mauritania," he declared, "is interested in the future of the Sahara and, on account of its rights, it cannot but be associated with the settlement and the ending of the dispute which is opposing Morocco and Mauritania to Spain."[40] In his own speech to the General Assembly the next day, Hamdi Ould Mouknass said he "could not fail to respond favorably" to Laraki's remarks, now that "the Moroccan government has clearly recognized our rights in this region of the Sahara."[41] A month later, during a summit conference of the Arab League, held in Rabat on October 26–29, Hassan and Mokhtar Ould Daddah agreed, in Hassan's words, "not to leave any longer the possibility or the opportunity for anyone to say that we are not agreed" on Western Sahara.[42] The precise terms of the deal were never made public, but it is known that Ould Daddah agreed to back Morocco's approach to the ICJ and accept an eventual partition.

The Mauritanian president believed that he had compelling reasons to do so. At least Mauritania would get some of Western Sahara and perhaps even a share in its mineral wealth, whereas, if he rejected Hassan's offer, Morocco seemed so determined to prevent independence that it would probably take over the whole territory. It was better to get a slice of the pie than none at all; and, moreover, if Mauritania was fated to have Morocco as a neighbor in any case, it was advisable that they should be on friendly terms and that their common border should be well to the north of Mauritania's vital iron-ore region. To clinch his deal with Ould Daddah, besides, Hassan dangled an attractive economic carrot. At a meeting in Fez, on December 10, Hassan and Ould Daddah set up an Agence Mauritanienne et Marocaine de Coopération (AMAMCO), which was formally constituted on February 12, 1975, and launched a series of aid projects, ranging from the provision of a $15-million loan for the Mauritanian copper industry in March 1975 to the admission of four hundred Mauritanian students to Moroccan universities and colleges later in the year and, beginning in 1976, the construction of a magnificent mosque in Nouakchott.[43]

Predictably, the Spanish government rejected Hassan's proposal that Morocco and Spain jointly submit their dispute over Western Sahara to the adjudication of the ICJ. The king's recourse was to persuade the UN to request a nonbinding "advisory opinion" from the World Court. After extensive backstage lobbying in New York, Morocco and Mauritania finally persuaded thirty-three states to line up with them to cosponsor a draft resolution which, on the pretext that there was a "legal difficulty" over Western Sahara's precolonial legal status, requested the ICJ to give an advisory opinion on two questions:

" ' I. Was Western Sahara (Río de Oro and Sakiet El Hamra) at the time of colonization
    by Spain a territory belonging to no one (*terra nullius*)?'

"If the answer to the first question is in the negative,

" 'II. What were the legal ties between this territory and the Kingdom of Morocco and
    the Mauritanian entity?' "

The resolution went on to request the Committee of 24 to send a mission of inquiry to Western Sahara and urged Spain to postpone the referendum until the
ICJ had given its advisory opinion.[44]

Among third world and especially African governments, many of whom owed
their existence to the exercise of self-determination, there was considerable unease
about endorsing a resolution that not only took the curious stand of requesting
the colonial power to postpone the referendum urged by the UN for the previous
eight years, but also shifted the focus away from the UN's cardinal decolonization
principle, self-determination, to the historical question of whether Western
Sahara had belonged to Morocco or Mauritania a hundred years ago. "The people
of Spanish Sahara should be the court," declared a member of the Kenyan
delegation to the UN, Francis Njenga, expressing a fear that the UN was "being
asked to treat them as chattels and not as people."[45] Spain, which wanted to proceed without hindrance with its plan to devolve power to the PUNS, made much
of the paradox of a resolution which, as its ambassador to the UN, Jaime de
Piniés, put it, "requests both decolonization and postponement of the referendum to make decolonization possible."[46]

Most states, however, were more than pleased to have the Saharan dispute
shuttled off to the World Court. Most Arab states, besides, were now giving
strong support to Morocco. The secretary-general of the Islamic Conference,
Hassan Touhami, had openly endorsed the Moroccan claim on August 14, during
a visit to Casablanca, declaring that it was "imperative that the Sahara return to
the motherland, that is to Morocco."[47] Even the leader of the Palestine Liberation
Organization, Yasser Arafat, had lined up with King Hassan, announcing in
Rabat on July 22 that "the PLO is ready to lend its support to Morocco to help it
liberate the occupied Sahara."[48] Hassan's stock in the Arab world had been
enhanced considerably by the participation of Moroccan troops in the Arab-Israeli
war in 1973 and by his personal role in reconciling Jordan and the PLO at the October 1974 Arab League summit. Furthermore, hostility to "separatism," and
Arab unionist ideology, encouraged some of the Republican Arab regimes to support the king's bid for "reunification" with his "amputated" Saharan provinces,
while the imperative of regal solidarity sufficed for the Gulf monarchs.

To the leaders of the West, notably President Valéry Giscard d'Estaing of
France and Henry Kissinger, the U.S. secretary of state, who had visited Hassan in
Rabat in October 1974, there were strategic reasons to let the king have his way.
He was a fervent anticommunist, a traditional ally of the NATO powers, ruling a
country strategically located at the entrance to the Mediterranean. He had allowed the U.S. to maintain military facilities on his territory, permitted French
and other Western warships to call at his ports and tried over the years to moderate
Arab hostility to Israel. Moreover, the U.S. and French governments knew that
the stability of his regime hinged, after the internal dissension and crises of the
early seventies, on the success of his Saharan crusade.

On December 13, to Morocco's delight, the UN General Assembly approved the resolution requesting the ICJ's advisory opinion and urging postponement of the referendum. Eighty-seven states voted in favor of Resolution 3292 and none voted against, while forty-three states, including Spain, showed their disquiet by abstaining and two, Libya and China, did not take part in the vote.

The Saharawis themselves were not even to have the right to be heard by the court, which can only receive evidence from independent governments, and the Polisario Front therefore expressed astonishment at a decision to "convey the destiny of our peoples before the Court of The Hague in our total absence."[49] The questions addressed to the World Court concerned the ownership and legal status of Western Sahara in the nineteenth century, as if historical property rights, rather than the will of the territory's indigenous population, should determine its future. "In the mid-twentieth century," protested the deputy mayor of El-Ayoun, Ahmed Ould Brahim Ould el-Bashir, a leader of the PUNS, "the Saharawis will not accept the whole world speaking for them as if they were cattle."[50]

NOTES

1. *Message adressé par S.M. Hassan II au General Franco, chef de l'Etat espagnol, le 4 juillet 1974* (Ministère d'Etat chargé de l'information, Rabat).

2. Discours de SM le Roi à l'occasion de la Fête de la Jeunesse, 8 juillet, in *Discours de SM Hassan II, 3 mars 1974–3 mars 1975* (Ministère d'Etat chargè de l'information, Rabat), pp. 61, 63.

3. "Les phosphates et les engrais au Maroc," *Maghreb-Développement*, 1977, No. 3, p. 2; "Phosphate Market: Boom, Vacillation and Recovery," *Industrial Minerals*, November 1976, pp. 17–27; Banque du Maroc, *Rapport sur l'exercice 1977* (Rabat, 1978), Appendix 31.

4. *Situation du secteur de la pêche, 1977* (Office National de Pêche, Casablanca), p. 30. See also "La pêche maritime au Maroc," *Revue Bimensuelle d'Informations* (Banque Marocaine du Commerce Extérieur, Casablanca), No. 41, March 1979, pp. 2–19.

5. See Noël Cannat, *Analyse de la pauvreté urbaine au Maroc: Rabat, Salé, Kenitra, Casablanca. Etude qualitative*, report for World Bank, April–May 1978.

6. See Daniel Guérin, *Les assassins de Ben Barka, 10 ans d'enquête* (Guy Authier, Paris, 1975).

7. Led by Abraham Serfaty, an anti-Zionist Jew and veteran communist, Ilal-Amam had split from the PLS in August 1970, while the March 23 Group had been constituted the previous March, mainly by former members of the UNFP, such as Mohammed Ben Said, who had been a leader of the Army of Liberation. They had been influenced by the failure of the UNFP and the PCM (the forerunner of the PLS) to provide political leadership at the time of the March 1965 Casablanca events (after which the March 23 group took its name) and by the Arab defeat in the 1967 Middle East war. The two groups formed a front at the 14th UNEM congress in 1970 and so came to be known in student circles as the "frontistes." See *23 Mars*, Supplement to No. 10, June 1975, pp. 12–14; *Souffles*, New Series, No. 2, October 1973; and *Jeune Afrique*, December 14, 1974.

8. *The Times* (London), May 2, 1974.

9. *Amnesty International Briefing: Morocco* (Amnesty International, London, 1977), pp. 1–7.

10. *The Times*, May 2, 1974, and August 22, 1974.

11. *Reuters*, dispatches from Rabat, July 11, 1971, and July 13, 1971.

12. *Amnesty International Briefing: Morocco*, p. 3; *Reuters*, dispatches from Rabat, August 16, 1972, August 18, 1972 and August 21, 1972.

13. Dahir No. 1–72–258 du 9 rejeb 1392 (19 août 1972) relatif à la suppression du ministère de la défense nationale et des fonctions de major général et major général adjoint, *Bulletin Officiel du Royaume du Maroc*, No. 3121, August 23, 1972, p. 1149.

14. *Africa Confidential*, December 2, 1972; Harold D. Nelson, "National Security," in Harold D. Nelson (ed.), *Morocco, a Country Study* (U.S. Government Printng Office, Washington, D.C., 1978), pp. 260–62; *Washington Post*, January 25, 1976.

15. *Le Monde* (Paris), August 30, 1974; *Africa Contemporary Record*, Vol. 7, 1974-75, pp. B74-B75.

16. Paul Pascon, "le 'recensement agricole,' 1973-74," *Bulletin Economique et Social du Maroc*, Nos. 133-34, 1977, p. 218.

17. *Ibid.*, p. 221; Paul Pascon, "Le patrimoine de la colonisation privée en 1965," *Bulletin Economique et Social du Maroc*, Nos. 133-34, 1977, p. 201. The 1963 land reform applied only to the approximately quarter million hectares of so-called "official" settler farmland, which had been attributed to European *colons* by the French Protectorate government. The lands of *colonisation privée*, acquired by Europeans through land purchases without the direct intervention of the colonial government, covered 728,000 hectares by 1956 and were exempt from Moroccanization until 1973, by which time private sales to large Moroccan private landholders had disposed of around 400,000 hectares.

18. Negib Bouderbala, "Aspects du problème agraire au Maroc," *Bulletin Economique et Social du Maroc*, August 1975, p. 206.

19. *Libération* (USFP, Casablanca), May 26-June 1, 1978.

20. In the September 1974 issue of its clandestine journal, *Maroc Résistance* (No. 3, pp. 3-4), Ilal-Amam opposed the "arbitrary integration" of Western Sahara, accused Hassan of harboring neocolonial ambitions, supported "the Sahara's national independence, a genuine independence with regard to colonialism and neocolonialism and a reconstruction of unity with our people, free of exploitation and repression," and advocated "unconditional arming of the Saharan masses and political and military support to their national forces, notably the Popular Front for the Liberation of Saguia el-Hamra and Oued ed-Dahab."

21. Conférence de presse de S.M. le Roi sur le Sahara marocain, 17 septembre, *Discours de S.M. Hassan II, 3 mars 1974-3 mars 1975* (Ministère d'Etat chargé de l'information, Rabat), p. 81.

22. *Reuters*, dispatch from Rabat, August 26, 1974; *Amnesty International Briefing: Morocco*, p. 7. One member of Ilal-Amam, Abdellatif Zeroual, was tortured to death shortly after his arrest in November 1974.

23. *Reuters*, dispatch from Rabat, July 16, 1974.

24. *Al-Bayane* (Casablanca), August 21, 1974.

25. Dlimi had achieved notoriety in 1966 when, as DGED deputy director, he had been tried and then acquitted by a Paris court after the abduction and murder of Mehdi Ben Barka. He had been appointed director of the DGED in 1970 and director of Hassan's aides-de-camp in August 1972.

26. Discours de S.M. le Roi a Agadir, 3 septembre, *Discours de S.M. Hassan II, 3 mars 1974-3 Mars 1975* (Ministère d'Etat chargé de l'information, Rabat), p. 70.

27. Robert Rézette, *The Western Sahara and the Frontiers of Morocco* (Nouvelles Editions Latines, Paris, 1975), p. 141.

28. Discours de S.M. le Roi à l'occasion de la Fête de la Jeunesse, 8 juillet, *loc. cit.*, pp. 60-61. On September 17, Hassan reassured Spain that its investments in Western Sahara would be protected by Morocco's Investment Code.

29. *Reuters*, dispatches from Madrid, August 13, 1979, and August 14, 1979.

30. Discours de S.M. le Roi à l'occasion de la commémoration de la Révolution du Roi et du Peuple, *Discours de S.M. Hassan II, 3 mars 1974-3 mars 1975* (Ministère d'Etat chargé de l'information, Rabat), p. 66.

31. *Ibid.*, pp. 66-67.

32. *ABC* (Madrid), September 7, 1974.

33. Message du Deuxième Congrès tenu du 25-8-1974 au 31-8-1974 à Sa Majesté Hassan II, Roi du Maroc, in *Le peuple saharaoui en lutte* (Polisario Front, 1975), p. 52.

34. Discours de S.M. le Roi à Agadir, 3 septembre, *loc. cit.*, p. 71.

35. Conférence de presse de S.M. le Roi sur le Sahara marocain, 16 septembre, *loc. cit.*, p. 88.

36. *Africa Confidential*, October 18, 1974.

37. Conférence de presse de S.M. le Roi sur le Sahara marocain, 17 septembre, *loc. cit.*, pp. 93, 76.

38. *Ibid.*, p. 77.

39. Interview with Abderrahim Bouabid, *Jeune Afrique* (Paris), June 11, 1976, p. 21.

40. *Jeune Afrique*, November 16, 1974.

41. Cited in Emilio Menéndez del Valle, *Sahara español: una descolonización tardía* (Editorial Cuadernos para el Diálogo, Madrid, 1975), pp. 28-29.

42. Conférence de presse de S.M. le Roi sur les résultats de la 7ème conférence arabe au 'sommet', 30 octobre, *Discours de S.M. Hassan II, 3 mars 1974-3 mars 1975* (Ministère d'Etat chargé de l'information, Rabat), p. 114.

43. Taieb Bencheikh, "L'Agence Mauritanianienne et Marocaine de Coopération," *Remarques Africaines* (Brussels), 18th Year, Nos. 489–90, August 15, 1976, p. 12.

44. UN General Assembly Resolution 3292, December 13, 1974.

45. Cited in Thomas M. Franck, "The Stealing of the Sahara," *American Journal of International Law*, Vol. 70, No. 4, October 1976, pp. 706–7.

46. Cited in Rézette, *op. cit.*, p. 153.

47. *Reuters*, dispatch from Rabat, August 14, 1974.

48. *Esquisse d'une chronologie de l'action politique et diplomatique du Maroc pour le recouvrement du Sahara occidental, mois de mai-juin-juillet-août 1974* (Bureau de Documentation, Ministère d'Etat chargé de l'information, Rabat), p. 2.

49. *Notre peuple face aux tout derniers crimes du fascisme impuni* (Polisario Front, 1974), p. 11.

50. Cited in Virginia Thompson and Richard Adloff, *The Western Saharans* (Croom Helm, London, 1980), p. 130.

18

The Algerian Dimension

The route leading to the final decolonization of the Sahara is quite clear. The support that my government, together with Morocco and Mauritania, has always given to General Assembly resolutions on this question does not permit it to envisage any other way of putting an end to Spanish domination over the Sahara than through the holding of a referendum on self-determination, to be both supervised and guaranteed by the United Nations. Such a solution, incidentally, would not be in conflict with the Moroccan and Mauritanian claims, but if those claims are to be met it would appear that there is no better course to follow than that of the express choice of the population itself. Thus the opinion of the population directly concerned will always remain the primary and decisive element in any settlement.

—Abdelaziz Bouteflika, Algerian
minister of foreign affairs, speaking
in the UN General Assembly, October 9, 1975.[1]

ALGERIA, which shares a twenty-five-mile frontier with Western Sahara, some thirty-five miles west of Tindouf on the Hammada, had never laid claim, like Morocco and Mauritania, to the territory. Rather, it had consistently supported the Western Saharans' right to self-determination and it had voted in favor of all the UN resolutions advocating a referendum. However, President Houari Boumedienne's government at first refused to back Polisario, apparently because it doubted the movement's political maturity and popular support, and when King Hassan launched his Saharan crusade in the summer of 1974, it was initially reluctant to risk jeopardizing the détente that had been carefully constructed with Morocco since 1968–69. For a few weeks at the end of 1974 it seemed as if Boumedienne would support the Moroccan-Mauritanian plans for partition. But he swung Algerian support firmly behind Polisario early in 1975 when he became aware of the depth of the Saharawis' nationalist aspirations and greatly disturbed by Hassan's attempts to redraw Morocco's frontiers in defiance of their will. To Boumedienne, the Moroccan claim to Western Sahara was akin to those made earlier to Mauritania and parts of Algeria. It had the same parentage, in the Greater Morocco theses of Allal el-Fassi, and, as the king's Saharan drumbeats grew louder during 1975, they revived the memories of Morocco's attempt to seize Tindouf in 1963, when Boumedienne was head of the Algerian Armée de Libération Nationale (ALN). Now, as then, Hassan's vigorous pursuit of territorial claims seemed to the Algerian government to be a stratagem employed by the king to resolve his political difficulties at home. If he was allowed to seize Western Sahara, against its people's will, without challenge, the king might sometime be tempted to bid again for domestic political gain by reviving Morocco's old claim to parts of Algeria. An ominous sign was that Hassan had withheld ratification of the 1972 Algerian-Moroccan border convention. So, for the sake of Algeria's own national security, the Boumedienne regime decided to prevent a precedent being set in Western Sahara. His armed forces began to arm and train the Polisario guerrillas, while Madrid was lobbied to remain loyal to its promise of self-determination.

El-Ouali had first solicited aid from the Algerian government when he visited Tindouf in the summer of 1972. He had been cold-shouldered and so brought together his nucleus of militants in northern Mauritania instead. He had returned to Algeria in February 1973, meeting both Algerian officals and a group of UNFP exiles, followers of Mohammed Basri, who were then seeking Algerian assistance for plans to begin a guerrilla campaign in the Atlas Mountains.[2] But once again El-Ouali's pleas for aid fell on deaf ears. The Algerian authorities seem to have regarded him as an adventurer, a young student who had not lived in the Sahara for many years and could not have prepared the necessary political groundwork for a serious guerrilla campaign against Spain. Perhaps, they may have judged, he had the same putschist traits as the Basrists, who, like El-Ouali, had been promised arms by Libya. The Basrists, in fact, had done no preparatory political work among the Berber peasants in the Atlas Mountains, who immediately reported their arrival to the Moroccan authorities when they attempted to start operations there in March. They were quickly hunted down. The Algerian government, which believed that it had finally resolved its border dispute with Morocco, on

Algerian terms, was anxious not to disturb its détente with King Hassan and so refused to assist the Basrists and confiscated some of their arms. Likewise, it seems, the Algerian government did not wish to be associated with an ill-conceived guerrilla campaign against Spain, with which Algeria had substantial and growing economic relations, and sometime in the spring of 1973, on the eve of Polisario's founding, El-Ouali was briefly detained and deported by the Algerian authorities.[3]

Strangely, Edouard Moha, the leader of MOREHOB, had better luck than El-Ouali when he suddenly turned up in Algiers in March, dropping his erstwhile support for the Moroccan claim and accusing the Rabat regime of trying to "enslave" MOREHOB and convert it into a "fifth column."[4] Moha's real motives for shifting base to Algiers are shrouded in mystery. Possibly he had been disenchanted by the paucity of the patronage offered him by the Moroccan government or political parties.[5] However, El-Ouali believed that Moha had been deliberately sent by the Moroccan government itself to undermine his own attempts to secure Algerian support, and whatever the truth, the net result of Moha's success in obtaining permission to open an Algiers bureau for MOREHOB was that the Algerian government did continue to turn a blind eye to El-Ouali's requests for aid.[6]

The UNFP exiles in Algiers, however, knew of Moha's past as a Moroccan policeman and warned the government that he might have been sent by the Rabat regime as an agent. Then, during the summer, when El-Ouali returned to Algiers shortly after Polisario's founding, they apparently called Moha's bluff by bringing him face-to-face with the Polisario leader, in the company of Jelloul Malaika, the FLN official responsible for relations with liberation movements. In the course of their verbal confrontation, it became obvious that Moha had never set foot in the Sahara. He was deported almost at once and went to live in Belgium.[7] This did not clear the way for Polisario however. After their sorry experience with Moha, who also seems to have been suspected of financial dishonesty and had left the impression that the Saharawi liberation movement was weak and beset with factionalism, the Algerian authorities were doubly cautious about helping El-Ouali, with whose *curriculum vitae* and true intentions they were as unfamiliar as they had been with Moha's.[8]

A more sympathetic note was not sounded in Algiers until the summer of 1974. The Algerian government was perturbed by Hassan's sudden decision, early in July, after the unveiling of Spain's internal autonomy plan, to launch his emotive crusade for the recovery of Morocco's "amputated Saharan provinces." To the Algerian government, it not only looked as if the king had renounced his former commitment to the principle of self-determination and was deliberately conjuring back to life the old demons of Greater Morocco, but he had also turned his back on the tripartite coordination of policy which had been inaugurated at the Nouadhibou summit in 1970. Now, it seemed, the king was acting unilaterally. He was playing dangerously on the emotions of his subjects, for his personal political gain, and, since he had so far refused to ratify the 1972 frontier convention, which Algeria had ratified on May 17, 1973, President Boumedienne believed that he had cause for alarm.

On August 9, President Mokhtar Ould Daddah, who had been no less jolted by

Hassan's change of tune, arrived in Algiers to swap misgivings with the Algerian president.[9] And a little earlier, sometime in July, El-Ouali had been back in Algiers, with Mohammed Lamine Ould Ahmed, receiving a markedly more respectful reception than on his earlier visits in 1972–73. The disconcerting mood in Morocco and Polisario's proven, if modest, guerrilla track record over the previous year were sufficient grounds to express sympathy and hint that tangible support might be forthcoming. However, several more months were to pass before the Algerian government would throw its weight firmly behind Polisario. In the summer of 1974 support for the movement was still regarded as one of several reserve options, since there were still many imponderables. The Algerian government had insuffient information, for example, to gauge the real extent of Saharawi nationalist aspirations or to forecast the likely outcome of a referendum, if it was held.[10] It was still uncertain, moreover, about the course that Spanish and Mauritanian policies might take. So, despite its misgivings about Hassan's conduct, the Algerian government kept its options open. It refrained from endorsing or condemning what Hassan was doing, but its silent neutrality earned vigorous protests from the Moroccan press, which seemed to confirm Boumedienne's fears about the almost frenzied mood that had now gripped Morocco.[11]

His alarm at the hostile character of the Moroccan press campaign against Algeria, his desire to save the Algerian-Moroccan border convention and regional détente, and the news of the Moroccan-Mauritanian *rapprochement* in October combined to encourage Boumedienne to conciliate Hassan in the autumn of 1974. In the UN General Assembly on October 10, Abdellatif Rahal, Algeria's UN ambassador, declared his satisfaction that Mauritania had joined Morocco in proposing that the ICJ "throw light on the judicial and historical aspects" of the Western Saharan problem, in order to "facilitate the search for a final solution," though he hastened to add that "the opinion of the population directly concerned will always constitute the fundamental and determinant element in any settlement."[12] Later in the month, in a speech to the Arab League summit held in Rabat on October 26–29, Boumedienne was to go much further, committing himself openly to supporting the Moroccan-Mauritanian partition plan agreed by Hassan and Ould Daddah on the summit's eve. "If our brother presidents and kings endorse this formula for agreement between the two countries and for the achievement of the liberation and demarcation of what is to be the Moroccan zone and what is to be the Mauritanian zone, then I will be among those to subscribe to this formula," he promised.[13] Then, on December 13, in the UN General Assembly, Algeria voted in favor of the resolution requesting the ICJ to give an advisory opinion on Western Sahara, even though forty-three other states, mostly from the third world, abstained because the resolution urged Spain to postpone its referendum and asked the ICJ to examine historical legal matters of no evident relevance to Western Sahara's contemporary decolonization. Indeed, Algeria missed an opportunity to capitalize on the skepticism among many third world states, despite being in a strong position to do so. It enjoyed enormous prestige in the third world at this time, having hosted the fourth nonaligned summit in 1973 and spearheaded the South's efforts to secure a better deal from the industrialized North at the ensuing special session of the UN General Assembly on raw material prices. Algeria was respected for its record of support to national liberation movements, and the Algerian foreign minister, Abdelaziz Boutelflika, was presiding over the 1974–75 session of the UN General Assembly. Yet Boumedienne and Boutelflika scarcely questioned the legitimacy of Hassan's claim to Western Sahara.

It was not until early in 1975 that Algeria began aiding Polisario and voicing strong opposition to Moroccan policy. In February five hundred Polisario guerrillas began to receive training from the Algerian armed forces. The following April, Boutelflika was praised by Polisario and virulently rebuked by the Moroccan press for insisting at an Arab League council meeting in Cairo that the Saharawis be allowed to exercise their right to self-determination.[14] Meanwhile, Boumedienne asked his ambassador in Paris, Mohammed Bedjaoui, to represent Algeria during the ICJ's sessions on Western Sahara at The Hague. By May 29–30, when a UN mission of inquiry on Western Sahara visited the Tindouf region, Polisario was well installed there. The mission members met several of Polisario's top leaders, including El-Ouali, Ibrahim Ghali and Mahfoud Ali Beiba, the front's deputy secretary-general, who had now left Mauritania to make Tindouf their main external base, and they toured three Saharawi settlements, at Hassi Abdallah, Oum el-Assel and Tindouf itself, in each of which, the mission later reported, it "was met by large and vociferous demonstrations of several thousand people in which the flags of the Frente Polisario were prominently displayed."[15]

By now the Moroccan press was subjecting Algeria to unremitting attack. "If the populations of the Sahara agree that a part of the Sahara should go to Morocco and another to Mauritania," Boumedienne asked, by way of reply, on June 16, "why turn around then on the neighbor who claims neither the territory nor its division?" What Algeria would not tolerate, he warned, was the trampling of the Saharawis' right to determine their own future. Since the FLN's own struggle for Algeria's independence, he stressed, the principle of self-determination had become a "constant element of Algerian policy" and a "fundamental basis of our political philsophy." It would not be renounced.[16]

In an attempt to undercut Hassan's campaign, the FLN issued invitations on June 16 to the two main Moroccan opposition parties, the UNFP and the Istiqlal Party, as well as Ould Daddah's PPM, to an interparty conference on the Saharan crisis, but they refused to attend.[17] At the same time, the Algerian ambassador in Spain, who was summoned to Algiers for consultations with Boumedienne on June 18, began lobbying the Spanish government to remain true to its commitment to self-determination.

Nonetheless, there was still a certain ambiguity in Algerian policy. Possibly the foreign ministry did not see eye to eye with Boumedienne about the course to take. Boutelflika was particularly anxious not to allow the Western Saharan dispute to destroy the Moroccan-Algerian detente that had been so laboriously constructed since 1969, and he seems to have believed that a deal could be made with Hassan to preserve it. During a visit to Rabat on July 1–4, he apparently told Hassan that Algeria would accept a Moroccan-Mauritanian partition of Western Sahara on condition that Hassan ratified the 1972 Algerian-Moroccan border convention. Hassan, who seems to have held up ratification purposefully as a bargaining counter to secure Algerian acceptance of his Western Saharan ambitions, readily concurred. "The two parties agree to implement projects which have been adopted by mutual consent and have not yet been executed," a joint Moroccan-Algerian communiqué announced after the talks. As for Western Sahara, Algeria "warmly welcomed the agreement reached between the two fraternal countries, Morocco and Mauritania, concerning the region, an agreement which would consolidate security, tranquility, stability and cooperation."[18] Four days later, on July 8, King Hassan could claim, seemingly with good reason, that Algeria was now "on Morocco's side."[19] But, if Bouteflika really had struck a bargain with the king, it must have been repudiated by Boumedienne, for Algerian-Moroccan relations now steadily deteriorated, and in The Hague on July 29, Bedjaoui forcefully reaffirmed Algeria's support for self-determination before the ICJ. On the very day of Bouteflika's arrival in Rabat, moreover, the Tindouf region had been placed under the direct authority of the president's office, to prepare for a rapid buildup of military forces there.

Though he had abandoned his hopes of saving the Moroccan-Algerian détente with great reluctance, Boumedienne now believed that the only truly effective way to bury the Algerian-Moroccan border problem once and for all was to teach Hassan and the Greater Moroccans that attempts at territorial expansion would not pay. At stake, in fact, was a fundamental OAU principle, on the sanctity of the borders inherited from colonialism, to which Algeria had always subscribed in order to defend its own territorial integrity from Moroccan claims. If Hassan succeeded in flouting the principle in Western Sahara, against its people's will, to resolve his internal political problems, there was a real danger, whether he formally ratified the 1972 Algerian-Moroccan border convention or not, that he would be encouraged to revive the old claims to parts of Algerian territory if and when political circumstances at home once again required new diversionary patriotic causes abroad. Furthermore, if Hassan got his way in the Sahara, the FAR would be within striking distance of Tindouf from the west across the gravel plain of the Hammada, the king's international stature would increase and the Moroccan economy might be strengthened by control of the Bou-Craa mines. In a word, the regional "balance" between Algeria and Morocco would tilt dangerously to Hassan's advantage. Perhaps Boumedienne also feared that the U.S., which had good reason to disapprove Algeria's militancy on such matters as oil prices, North-South economic relations and Palestine, was condoning, or even encouraging, Hassan to engineer such a shift in regional power relations.[20]

Additionally, Boumedienne recognized that his government's credibility as a consistent supporter of national liberation movements would be knocked, to the detriment of its claims to third world leadership and revolutionary legitimacy, if it failed to defend the Saharawis' right to independence. However, Boumedienne's ideological differences with the Moroccan monarchy, wide-ranging though they may have been, played no part in motivating his challenge to Hassan's Saharan crusade, just as they had not constrained his policy of détente with Morocco in 1969–73, when the threat of Moroccan "expansionism" seemed to be receding. Nor did a supposed desire on Algeria's part to secure an outlet to the Atlantic for its iron ore at Gara Djebilet, as has sometimes been suggested, influence Boumedienne's Western Saharan policy, for he had reached a perfectly satisfactory arrangement with Hassan in 1972 for its shipment across southern Morocco and then, in November 1974, he had announced that Algeria no longer planned to export the ore but would build a railway from Gara Djebilet to northern Algeria to supply a new steel plant on the Mediterranean coast.[21]

The democratic validity of the Algerian government's stand on Western Sahara was indisputable, whether or not it was dictated by strategic interest or the government's democratic credentials could be faulted on such domestic matters as the language rights of the Kabyles and Algeria's other Berber minorities. Why, the Algerian government asked, had Morocco and Mauritania reneged on the commitments to self-determination made at the tripartite summits in Nouadhibou and Agadir?[22] If the Saharawis were really Moroccan or Mauritanian, why were the Rabat and Nouakchott governments so reluctant to let the Saharawis so declare themselves in a referendum? "The rejection of a referendum springs from a doubt about the results," charged the Algerian justice minister, Boualem Ben Hamouda, the following December. "If the Saharawi people really belonged to Morocco or Mauritania, how would they refuse to reintegrate the 'mother country'?"[23] The historical bases of Morocco's claim, besides, deserved only ridicule in Ben Hamouda's opinion. "Does Morocco demand the Sahara because some Moroccan traders transited through it to buy gold and slaves in what was then called the 'Soudan,' " he asked? "In this hypothesis, the Saharawis have the right to demand Morocco and Spain because their ancestors the Almoravids departed from this territory in the eleventh century to spread their authority over the whole region and Andalucía."[24]

NOTES

1. Provisional Verbatim Record of the 2382nd Meeting, UN General Assembly, UN Document A/PV.2382, October 9, 1975, p. 66.

2. El-Ouali presented a memorandum on Western Sahara to the UNFP branch in Algiers in February 1973. See Chapter 15, footnote 30.

3. Author's interview with members of Alikhtiar Athaouri, Paris, October 10, 1979.

4. *Reuters*, dispatch from Rabat, March 5, 1973; MOREHOB communiqué, Algiers, April 4, 1973.

5. Author's interview with Ali Yata, secretary-general of the PPS, Casablanca, November 14, 1978.

6. *El pueblo saharaui en lucha: documentos del Frente popular para la liberación de Saguia el Hamra y Río de Oro* (Polisario Front, 1975), p. 25; Ahmed-Baba Miské, *Front Polisario, l'âme d'un peuple* (Editions Rupture, Paris, 1978), pp. 157-59.

7. Interview with members of Alikhtiar Athaouri, Paris, October 10, 1979; *El pueblo saharaui en lucha: documentos del Frente popular para la liberación de Saguia el Hamra y Río de Oro*, p. 25; Paul Balta, "Le Sahara occidental suscite les convoitises de ses voisins," *Le Monde Diplomatique* (Paris), August 1975, p. 15; *Le Monde* (Paris), September 17, 1974.

8. Author's interview with Slimane Hoffman, president of the FLN commission on foreign affairs, Algiers, September 24, 1979.

9. *El Moudjahid* (Algiers), August 10, 1974.

10. Interview with Slimane Hoffman, Algiers, September 24, 1979.

11. *Reuters*, dispatch from Rabat, August 27, 1974.

12. *El Moudjahid*, October 12, 1974.

13. Cited in *The Legitimate Decolonization of Atlantic Western Sahara and the Plots of Algerian Rulers Aiming at Hegemony in North-Western Africa* (Ministry of State in Charge of Foreign Affairs, Rabat, 1977, published also in UN Document E/CN.4/Sub.2/391, June 15, 1977).

14. *Reuters*, dispatch from Rabat, April 29, 1975.

15. Report of the United Nations Visiting Mission to Spanish Sahara, 1975, in *General Assembly Official Records*, 30th Session, Supplement 23, UN Document A/10023/Rev.1, p. 95. See also *El Moudjahid*, May 30, 1975, and June 12, 1975.

16. *El Moudjahid*, June 22-23, 1975.

17. Paul Dessens, "Le litige du Sahara occidental," *Maghreb-Machrek* (Paris), No. 71, January-March 1976, p. 42.

18. Joint Communiqué Issued by the Governments of Algeria and Morocco on 4 July 1975, in Rabat, in UN Document A/10023/Rev.1, p. 128.

19. *Reuters*, dispatch from Rabat, July 8, 1975.

20. *Le Monde*, May 14, 1976.

21. The suggestion that Algeria aims to build a railway from Gara Djebilet to El-Ayoun is made, for example, in Robert Rézette, *The Western Sahara and the Frontiers of Morocco* (Nouvelles Editions Latines, Paris, 1975), p. 146. However, Algeria had signed a convention with Morocco in June 1972 setting up a joint company for the transportation of Gara Djebilet's ore by railway through southern Morocco. This convention had been ratified by President Boumedienne on May 17, 1973, and agreement in principle had been reached that the railway would lead to a new port, to be built at Tarfaya. Indeed, the Moroccan writer, Abdallah Laroui, has commented, with respect to Gara Djebilet, that "one cannot see how these interests would be endangered if Morocco replaces Spain in the Sahara, or if the iron of Gara Djebilet is evacuated through Tarfaya instead of by a port farther to the south, since the principle of Moroccan-Algerian collaboration has already been accepted for the transport via Morocco of both iron in the south and gas in the north." (*L'Algérie et le Sahara marocain*, Serar, Casablanca, 1976, p. 91.) The Tarfaya railway project was, in part, a casualty of the Western Sahara crisis, for King Hassan refused to ratify the 1972 convention on Gara Djebilet, just as he did not ratify the parallel convention settling the Algerian-Moroccan border problem, and the joint Moroccan-Algerian company for the transportation and marketing of Gara Djebilet's ore was therefore never set up. The Algerian government seems to have despaired of Moroccan unreliability and decided instead, despite the huge distances, to use Gara Djebilet's iron to meet its own growing steel needs. During a visit to Tindouf on November 27, 1974, Boumedienne announced that a railway would be built from Gara Djebilet to the Mediterranean coast and that 10 million to 12 million tons of ore would be mined annually, more than in Mauritania. (*El Moudjahid*, November 28, 1974.) "We do not need any access to the Atlantic for the iron ore of Tindouf because we want to process it ourselves," he said a year later. (*Nouvel Observateur*, Paris, November 8, 1975.) In fact, Algeria's Société Nationale de Sidérurgie (SNS) intends eventually to produce about 10 million tons of steel a year at a new steel plant at La Macta, in northwestern Algeria, to meet the country's projected increase in steel requirements. This third steel plant would supplement those at El-Hadjar, near Annaba, which was opened in 1969–72 and had a capacity of 2 million tons per year by 1980, and at Jijel, where production will commence in 1983, raising Algeria's national steel-producing capacity to between 3.5 and 4 million tons a year. Iron-ore output, from the existing mines at Boukhadra and Ouenza in northeastern Algeria, where there are 200 million tons of deposits, reached 3.5 million tons in 1980. Construction of the massive La Macta steel plant has not yet begun and the project does not feature in the 1980–84 development plan; however, since 1976, a series of contracts for feasibility and technical studies on the Gara Djebilet mines, the La Macta plant and a nine hundred-mile linking railway have been signed with such companies as Bechtel, Canadian Pacific Services, LKAB International of Sweden, Nippon Steel Corporation and the Soviet firm Tyazhpromexport. Gara Djebilet will probably be developed eventually, to feed a major new steel plant, since Algeria's steel consumption is expected to reach 8 million tons a year by 1990 and, according to the Algerian ministry of heavy industry, steel import requirements would reach 10 million tons a year by 2000 if a third steel plant is not built.

22. Boualem Ben Hamouda, *La question du Sahara occidental et le droit international* (Algiers, 1976), pp. 7–9.

23. *Ibid.*, p. 11.

24. *Ibid.*, p. 12.

19

Prelude to Crisis

THE UNITED NATIONS' DECISION to submit the Western Saharan problem to the International Court of Justice and urge Spain to postpone its referendum was a diplomatic coup for King Hassan. Reluctantly the Spanish government announced on January 16, 1975, that it would postpone the referendum and present evidence to the ICJ.[1] To placate King Hassan, Franco also delayed implementation of the Estatuto Político, even though it had already been endorsed by the Djemaa. The assembly therefore remained a purely consultative body and, though it nominated its four members of the projected Governing Council in February 1975, General Federico Gómez de Salazar froze the plans to bring the council into being.

These retreats by the Spanish government discredited the leaders of the Djemaa and the PUNS, who had encouraged Saharawis to take the Spanish promise of self-determination at face value, and greatly increased support for Polisario, which had hitherto been a rather small guerrilla group. "The local authorities were putting off the nomination of the autonomous government in accordance with received instructions," Colonel Luis Rodríguez de Viguri, who was then the provincial secretary-general, later recalled. "But the native population fell into a state of despair upon seeing the Spanish delaying tactics. Above all, the youth, who were very disillusioned, began to rally massively around the Polisario Front, and the desertions to its Algerian camps, especially by soldiers of the Tropas Nómadas and the Policía Territorial, escalated."[2]

Demonstrations by Polisario supporters had become increasingly frequent in the towns since the autumn of 1974. On October 13, a crowd of Saharawi workers and unemployed had demonstrated in El-Ayoun to demand wage rises and the extension of social security benefits to non-Europeans. A day later, secondary school students had gone on strike to demand the Arabization of education, better boarding conditions and increased grants. After unproductive negotiations between student leaders and Rodríguez de Viguri on January 2, several students were arrested, sparking off another round of strikes which lasted until mid-February. On November 18, 1974, meanwhile, Polisario supporters had marched on the governor-general's residence in El-Ayoun to protest against the arrests that had followed the sabotage attack on the Fosbucraa conveyor belt the previous October.[3]

There was growing unrest too in the Tropas Nómadas and the Policía Territorial, where Polisario agents were actively recruiting support at this time. The Spanish authorities were horrified when, on May 10–11, 1975, Saharawi troops in two separate patrols of the Tropas Nómadas in the remote northeast mutinied, killing one of their officers and imprisoning fourteen Spanish officers and soldiers, and then deserted to the Polisario Front with their prisoners and weapons. Two hundred Saharawi soldiers were immediately discharged from the Tropas Nómadas on suspicion that they were Polisario sympathizers. Just over a fortnight later, on May 27, Polisario guerrillas captured fourteen members of the Policía Territorial at Ain Ben Tili, near the Mauritanian border, and on June 14 almost the entire Policía Territorial unit at Guelta Zemmour joined Polisario after a guerrilla unit had overrun the police post there, capturing its commanding officer, a Saharawi.[4]

The May 10–11 mutinies came at a particularly embarrassing time for the Spanish authorities, as the UN mission of inquiry, which Madrid had finally agreed to allow into the territory after the debate in the General Assembly in December, was due to arrive in El-Ayoun on May 12, with a mandate to secure "firsthand information on the situation prevailing in the territory, including information on political, economic, social, cultural and educational conditions, as well as on the wishes of the people."[5] In fact, the reaction of the Saharawi population to the mission's tour of the territory, between May 12 and 19, came as an even greater shock to the Spanish government, and to the watchful governments of Morocco and Mauritania too, than the mutinies. General Gómez de Salazar probably had no idea what was in store when he welcomed the UN team, which was headed by the Ivory Coast's UN ambassador, Siméon Aké, at El-Ayoun's small airport. Along the road to the airport he had seen thousands of apparently loyal Saharawis waving PUNS banners. But the PUNS insignia had only been there to keep the Spanish in good humor. When the general drove back toward the city center, accompanying his UN guests, he was astonished to find that they had disappeared, to be replaced by a forest of Polisario flags and placards.

Over the following week, mass demonstrations were held wherever the UN mission members went. Aké and his two colleagues, diplomats from Cuba and Iran, traveled throughout the country, interviewing Saharawis from all walks of life—tribal sheikhs, leaders of the PUNS, the members of the permanent commission of the Djemaa, Polisario militants, students, soldiers of the Tropas Nómadas, traders, a delegation of women, phosphate miners and even Polisario prisoners in an El-Ayoun jail. The Spanish authorities were anxious to prove the sincerity of their commitment to decolonization and so made no attempt to restrict the mission's freedom of movement or to stop the Saharawis from demonstrating. "Owing to the large measure of cooperation which it received from the Spanish authorities," the mission noted in its subsequent report to the Committee of 24, "the mission was able, despite the shortness of its stay in the territory, to visit virtually all the main population centres and to ascertain the views of the overwhelming majority of their inhabitants. At every place visited, the Mission was met by mass political demonstrations and had numerous private meetings with representatives of every section of the Saharan community. From all of these, it became evident to the mission that there was an overwhelming consensus among Saharans within the territory in favour of independence and opposing integration with any neighbouring country."[6]

In many of the territory's towns, the mission reported, the demonstrations "appeared to represent the majority of the Saharan residents."[7] More than half the population of Smara came out on to the streets to greet the mission during its visit there on May 16; and at Bou-Craa, almost all of Fosbucraa's Saharawi work force had demonstrated two days earlier. "In all these manifestations in the northern part of the territory, the overwhelming majority of demonstrators carried the flags and emblems of the Frente Polisario or incorporated its colours in their apparel," the mission reported; and "on 13 May, in El Aaiún, the Mission attended the largest of the demonstrations, organized by the Frente Polisario, which was reported in the press to have amounted to 15,000 people."[8]

The outpouring of support for Polisario astonished Spanish officials. The movement had hitherto been entirely underground and it was still fighting a guerrilla war in the desert against Spanish troops. Yet it clearly enjoyed deep-rooted popular support and had an effective clandestine organization in the towns. "In the light of what it witnessed in the territory, especially the mass demonstrations, of support for one movement, the Frente Polisario," the mission believed that "its visit served as a catalyst to bring into the open political forces and pressures which had previously been largely submerged" and noted that "this came as a surprise to the Spanish authorities who, until then had only been partly aware of the profound political awakening of the population."[9] In El-Ayoun, some Spaniards were so enraged by the euphoria of the Polisario crowds that they began daubing such Falangist slogans as "*Arriba España*" and "*Viva la Legión*" on walls in the European quarters of the city. On May 15, two hundred Spanish women vented their anger outside the governor-general's office.[10]

The leaders of the PUNS were as shaken as some of the Spaniards. The party had been completely upstaged, except in the south. "Although the mission met privately with a number of groups in the northern region representing PUNS," the UN envoys noted, "it did not witness any separate public demonstrations in support of that party. This was in marked contrast to the Frente Polisario, whose supporters from the outset appeared en masse carrying the flags and emblems of their movement. It was not until the mission visited the southern region that PUNS, following the example of its opponents, organized mass demonstrations to greet the mission at each place visited."[11] At Villa Cisneros and other settlements in the south, Polisario and PUNS supporters staged separate, rival demonstrations, but "although both groups mustered a large number of supporters," the mission noted, "the preponderance was clearly in favour of the Frente Polisario." The placards of Polisario and PUNS were "similar," for "both demanded complete independence for the territory and opposed integration with neighbouring countries."[12]

The PUNS's disastrous performance in the capital and other towns and villages in the north shook the party's secretary-general, Khalihenna Ould Rashid. Fearing, it seems, that the Spanish government would jettison his party, which it had done so much to help set up, and would try to come to terms with Polisario, he decided upon an extraordinary exchange of loyalties and departed for Morocco before the UN mission had even completed its tour of the territory. On May 18 he turned up in Casablanca with two senior party aides and pledged allegiance to King Hassan. Two days later he claimed at a press conference in Rabat that Polisario was communist-backed and wanted to set up an "extremist state."[13]

The UN mission did not restrict its investigations to Western Sahara itself. It also visited Madrid on May 8–12 and May 20–22 to consult, among others, the prime minister, Carlos Arias Navarro, the foreign minister, Pedro Cortina y Mauri, and the minister of the presidency, Antonio Carro Martínez. Then the mission members toured Western Sahara's three neighbors. In Algeria, which they visited on May 28–June 1, they were received twice by President Houari Boumedienne, who assured them that Algeria had no interest in Western Sahara other than to see the Saharawis' right to self-determination respected.[14] They then traveled to the Tindouf border region where they were met by thousands of pro-Polisario demonstators in Saharawi settlements at Tindouf, Oum el-Assel and Hassi Abdallah. They interviewed El-Ouali Mustapha Sayed and other Polisario leaders and, on May 29, were driven into the desert by Polisario members to a rendezvous with the fourteen Spanish officers and soldiers captured by the mutionous Tropas Nómadas nearly three weeks earlier.[15] In their discussions with the UN team, the Polisario leaders argued that a referendum was unnecessary since it was now evident that the majority of Saharawis wanted independence, but they said that they would accept one, if the UN insisted, on condition that the Spanish administration had first been withdrawn and replaced by a "national" administration, that all Spanish troops had been withdrawn and replaced by Polisario soldiers under UN and Arab League guarantees, and that all refugees had been allowed to return to the territory.[16]

During their subsequent tour of Mauritania, on June 4–9, the mission members met President Mokhtar Ould Daddah, who argued his case for the integration of the southern part of Western Sahara into Mauritania, and then traveled north to the towns of Atar, Zouerate, Bir Moghrein and Nouadhibou, near the Western Saharan border, where they witnessed large rival demonstrations. Some, organized by the ruling Parti du Peuple Mauritanien, called for Western Sahara's unification with Mauritania, but others supported Polisario and its goal of independence.[17]

The mission members' other port of call was Morocco. There, between May 22 and 28, they were received twice by King Hassan in Fez, held meetings with several cabinet ministers and the leaders of the main political parties, interviewed Khalihenna Ould Rashid, who had absconded to Morocco four days before their own arrival, and witnessed large pro-annexation demonstrations in towns in the far south of the country, near the Western Saharan border. They left in no doubt about the depth of popular support in Morocco for Hassan's campaign for "reunification," as well as his government's determination to achieve its objectives. The mission was informed that Morocco would not accept the inclusion of independence among the options to be put to the Western Saharans in a referendum. The only acceptable question was: "Do you want to remain under the authority of Spain or to rejoin Morocco?"[18]

Yet, during its tour of Western Sahara, the mission had found almost no Saharawis who favored joining Morocco. "During its visit to the territory," it reported, "the mission did not encounter any groups supporting the territorial claims of neighbouring countries and consequently had no way of estimating the extent of their support, which appeared to be submerged by the massive demonstrations in favour of independence."[19] Besides Khalihenna Ould Rashid, the only Saharawi of note within the territorty to have opted publicly for unity with Morocco had been the *qadi* of El-Ayoun, Ibrahim el-Leili, who had slipped across the border into Morocco in November 1974 and made the *bayaa* to King Hassan in Fez on December 3.[20]

It was a matter of considerable embarrassment to the Moroccan government that the UN mission had not come across any political group within the territory that advocated integration with Morocco. Within Morocco, there had been the tiny August 21 Movement, but this had virtually vanished by 1974 and it had never attempted to begin political work or engage in military action within the Spanish colony. Edouard Moha, the leader of MOREHOB, who had been living in Brussels since his deportation from Algeria in 1973, made another of his curious political realignments in January 1975, sending a memorandum to the ICJ to declare that Morocco's claims were "well founded and irrefutable."[21] The UN mission met Moha during its visit to Morocco but "did not encounter any other members or supporters of MOREHOB either in the territory or elsewhere."[22]

In an attempt to make up for lost time, the Moroccan government had given its blessing to a new movement founded in February 1975, the Frente de Liberación y de la Unidad (FLU), which claimed that it would "smash the separatist movements and, in particular, the Polisario group," which, pushing credibility to the limit, it accused of simultaneously acting "in connivance with the Spanish occupier and its valets" and trying "desperately to open the door to international communism in our occupied Sahara."[23] This new group began infiltrating guerrillas and saboteurs into Western Sahara from bases in southern Morocco on the eve of the UN mission's visit, in the hope of pressuring Spain to abandon its referendum plans and impressing upon the UN mission that an anticolonial guerrilla campaign was being fought within the territory by an authentic Saharawi liberation movement that advocated unification with Morocco. But, though the FLU's attacks aroused the Spanish government's concern, the group made no attempt, or was unable, to mobilize popular support on the streets during the UN mission's tour of the territory. It was not until the mission arrived in Morocco that it met FLU members and supporters.[24]

At its first and only congress, held in Agadir on September 13–14, 1975, and hailed by the Moroccan prime minister, Ahmed Osman, as an expression of the "awakening of Saharawi youth" and their loyalty to the "glorious Alawite throne," the FLU voted to oppose self-determination, elected a seventy-nine-member central committee and a smaller permanent executive committee of seventeen members, and chose Rashid Douihi, a young Saharawi who had studied in Rabat with El-Ouali, as secretary general.[25] Both the Spanish government and Polisario regarded the FLU as a creation of the Moroccan government and claimed that its soldiers, who were estimated by the Spanish authorities to number about 1,500 by May 1975, were Saharawis serving in the regular Moroccan armed forces.[26] The Saharawi community of southern Morocco had indeed been an important source of recruitment for the FAR since the late fifties because of the intense poverty of Morocco's southernmost provinces and the Saharawis' military traditions; and several of the FLU's commanders, men like Captains Abba el-Sheikh and Mohammed Ould Khir, were veteran officers of the FAR who had fought the French and the Spanish during the Army of Liberation's Saharan insurgency.

The FLU began its guerrilla campaign, a week before the UN mission's arrival in El-Ayoun, by shelling a Spanish military post at Jdiriya, about thirty-five miles south of the Moroccan border, on May 4 and planting several bombs, one of which killed a thirteen-year-old Saharawi boy, in El-Ayoun on May 4–5.[28] On May 14, rockets were fired at two Spanish helicopters near the Moroccan border. The next day a Saharawi businessman returning home from the annual Tindouf *mouggar* died in a hail of bullets when his vehicle was ambushed by FLU guerrillas near Haousa, a small settlement on the Saguia el-Hamra; and on May 16 the FLU staged another attack near Hagounia, seventeen miles south of the Moroccan border. Thousands of troop reinforcements were flown in from the Canary Islands, to face up to the threats from both Polisario and the FLU, and on June 20 five Spanish soldiers were killed by a FLU landmine near Tah, two miles from the Moroccan frontier.[29]

But, despite the loss of life, FLU's guerrilla campaign was spectacularly incompetent. On June 8 an entire FLU unit of forty-four men, which had intended to occupy the Spanish post at Mahbes, in the extreme northeast of Saguia el-Hamra, near the Moroccan and Algerian frontiers, under the false impression that the Spanish army had evacuated its bases there, found itself surrounded by Spanish troops and surrendered. Documents found on the guerrillas proved that they were all regular soldiers of the FAR, and Captain Abba el-Sheikh was captured in the incident. A few weeks later, on July 22, sixteen more FLU guerrillas were taken prisoner by a Spanish patrol near Hagounia.[30]

The FLU campaign was just one of a series of levers used by the Moroccan government during 1975 to pressure Spain to abandon its plans for a referendum. At the same time it revived the previously dormant claims to the Spanish presidios on the Moroccan coast and began once again to harass Spanish fishing boats in its waters. Making much of Madrid's inconsistency in claiming Gibraltar while refusing to withdraw from Ceuta and Melilla, Hassan wrote to the Committee of 24 on January 27, 1975, to request that it examine the problem of "these enclaves within Moroccan territory" and place them on its list of non-self-governing territories.[31] The Spanish government immediately accused the Moroccan government of trying to "disturb Spain's traditional unity and territorial integrity."[32] On February 8, a Spanish fleet, including four destroyers, three helicopter squadrons and a force of marines, sailed into Ceuta and Melilla to show the flag.[3] The following April, the foreign ministers of the Arab League formally endorsed Morocco's claim to the presidios.[34] Then, in May, Moroccan saboteurs started planting bombs in the enclaves, complementing the FLU's exploits in the Sahara.

On May 31 three bombs exploded in a Melilla cafe, injuring twelve Spaniards; on June 19 a Spanish worker was killed in Ceuta when bombs exploded outside the city's military and naval headquarters; and two more died in Melilla the next day, apparently while trying to plant a bomb in an oil depot. Tension remained high in the presidios for the rest of the summer, and in a speech to the UN General Assembly on October 7, the Moroccan foreign minister, Ahmed Laraki, called on Spain to open negotiations about the enclaves' future.

In the spring the Moroccan navy had renewed attempts to intercept Spanish fishing boats off its coast. On April 2 a Moroccan patrol boat was reported to have fired on two Spanish fishing boats, and five days later coast guards intercepted two Spanish fishing boats within Morocco's seventy-mile territorial limit, near Larache. Two Spanish warships intervened, forcing the Moroccans to abandon one of the fishing boats, but the other was towed into Tangier.[35]

Throughout these tense months, thousands of Moroccan troops were massed, under Colonel Ahmed Dlimi's command, in the border regions of southern Morocco. General Gómez de Salazar estimated that Dlimi had twenty-five thousand men there.[36] King Hassan, moreover, was openly threatening to use force if necessary to get his way. On April 28, for example, he told a French radio station that he had massed troops in southern Morocco "to provide a framework, at all levels, for the inexorable march that the Moroccan people will not fail to undertake with their king at their head, if embittered or frivolous persons should seek to initiate the process of self-determination in the Sahara."[37]

By June the Spanish army probably had as many men on its side of the border as Dlimi had on his. They were much better equipped than the Moroccan force and there were thousands more troops in reserve in the Canary Islands, ready to be airlifted into the Sahara in the event of an emergency. However, the Spanish government was now under such a mass of contradictory pressures from Polisario, Morocco and the FLU, Algeria and Mauritania that it appeared to be losing its nerve. In May, when it was almost simultaneously confronted by the mutinies in the Tropas Nómadas, the rash of FLU attacks and Polisario's outflanking of the PUNS during the visit of the UN mission, Franco's cabinet began for the first time to consider a precipitate withdrawal, to avoid being sucked into serious military conflict. During a visit to El-Ayoun on May 26, the army minister, Lieutenant-General Francisco Coloma Gallegos, declared that, despite its wealth, Western Sahara was not worth "the spilling of a single drop of Spanish blood nor the shedding of a single tear."[38] Three days earlier the Spanish cabinet had appealed to Morocco, Mauritania and Algeria to attend a quadripartite conference with Spain, under UN auspices if necessary, to "harmonize their positions" on Western Sahara's future and warned that, if they did not do so, Spain "would be obliged to end its presence and administering role, setting a deadline by which the Spanish authorities would transfer their powers."[39] On May 24 General Gómez de Salazar was reported to have said that an evacuation plan had been drafted to "prepare for the thousand and one disasters that might occur and that might require a rapid exit from Western Sahara."[40]

However, neither the Spanish government nor the UN secretary-general, Kurt Waldheim, who shuttled between Madrid, Algiers, Rabat and Nouakchott on June 9–13, could persuade Morocco to accept Spain's invitation to a four-way conference. Hassan insisted on Algeria's exclusion.[41] This, however, the Madrid government would not accept, despite the air of impending crisis, for it was still reluctant to strike a deal with Morocco and Mauritania alone, on Hassan's terms. With characteristic paternalism, Franco still saw himself as the Saharawis' guardian, and, like the officers who administered his desert province, he regarded the very idea of capitulation to Morocco under duress as an affront. From a *realpolitik* standpoint, moreover, he still feared that Morocco, with its own large phosphate industry and its perennial fishing disputes with Spain, would rapidly curtail Spain's interests in Western Sahara's phosphate and fishing resources, irrespective of Hassan's promises, if it gained control of the territory; and he shared his foreign ministry's fears that if Spain abandoned its commitment to self-determination in the Sahara, relations with Algeria, Spain's biggest trade partner in Africa, might suffer and the efforts to woo third world support for Spain's stand on Gibraltar could be undermined too.

However, after the UN mission's visit, it had become impossible for the Spanish officials in El-Ayoun to proceed with the plans for independence without a radical revision of policy toward Polisario, since the PUNS, which was reorganized after Khalihenna Ould Rashid's desertion by his former deputy, Dueh Sidna Naucha, now evidently lacked the popular support and credibility it would need to head an effective independent government. Upon reflection, the Spanish government came to the view that Polisario did not really represent as great a danger to Spanish interests as previously assumed. A Polisario government, it predicted, would be too dependent on Spanish technical support to take over the direct running of Fosbucraa and would be likely to allow Spanish boats to continue fishing off the coast in return for Spanish aid for Western Sahara's own infant fishing industry.

Immediately after the May 23 cabinet meeting in Madrid, therefore, the Spanish information minister, León Herrera, declared that "Polisario is a reality" which the government would take into account, and, in El-Ayoun, General Gómez de Salazar and Colonel Rodríguez de Viguri were soon urging Polisario, the PUNS and the members of the Djemaa to unite.[42] Worried that the Spanish government's new overtures to Polisario might leave them out in the cold if they did not follow suit, the leaders of the PUNS and the Djemaa began to make approaches to the guerrilla movement. Their only real alternative was to follow Khalihenna Ould Rashid's example and leave for Morocco, but that would mean being ostracized by most of their kin. At the end of May, Khatri Ould Said Ould el-Joumani traveled to Tindouf to meet El-Ouali and proposed a unity pact between all Saharawi factions.[43] However, unity was not to be achieved easily. The elderly sheikhs in the Djemaa were hesitant to submit to the leadership of the young militants heading Polisario, and the *Punsistas* insisted on preserving their own party's identity within a broad patriotic front. Polisario, which was confident that it now had overwhelming popular support, was unwilling to accommodate the sensitivities of the leaders of the PUNS and the Djemaa. It insisted on the PUNS' dissolution and urged its members to join Polisario.

Relations between Polisario and the PUNS therefore remained tense for several weeks. In El-Ayoun, a demonstration by PUNS supporters on July 5 brought an angry response by Polisario activists. Two PUNS offices were attacked by mobs the next day and one was burned down. Rioting continued for three hours before order was restored by the Policía Territorial.[44] The tension increased in the capital when, on July 12 and 13, two bombs exploded, killing three Spanish policemen and the eight-year-old son of a prominent *Punsista*, Ahmed Ould Brahim Ould el-Bashir, a *procurador* in the Cortes. Polisario insignia were discovered nearby and so the PUNS immediately blamed Polisario for the attacks.[45] Relations between the two parties became even more strained than before, but in hindsight it seems most unlikely that Polisario did plant the bombs. It had never previously engaged in this kind of urban terrorism. The FLU, however, had been sporadically planting bombs in El-Ayoun since May and had every interest in foiling the Spanish authorities' attempts to bring Polisario and the PUNS together.[46]

On August 16 two hundred and fifty *Punsistas* gathered in El-Ayoun for the opening of the PUNS's second congress. The party was now in headlong decline. Just as the congress was opening, another of its officials, Khalifa Boudjemaa Mohammed, the party treasurer, turned up in Morocco, while in El-Ayoun the congress delegates had to be protected by the Policía Territorial and uniformed party guards from thousands of demonstrating Polisario supporters.[47] The congress selected Dueh Sidna Naucha as the party's new secretary-general, elected a six-member executive committee and, despite the July bombings, mandated the new leadership to renew negotiations with Polisario.[48] Accordingly, several PUNS officials traveled to Nouadhibou, Mauritania, at the end of August, to hold meetings with El-Ouali's brother, Bashir Mustapha Sayed, and other senior Polisario leaders.[49]

The incentive to reach an understanding with Polisario had been magnified by the Spanish government's success in achieving a conciliation with the guerrilla movement. Polisario attacks on Spanish outposts halted after the June 14 raid on Guelta Zemmour, and during the same month Spanish troops and administrators began withdrawing from several of the more remote bases and settlements, including Mahbes, Guelta Zemmour and Tifariti, leaving Polisario to set up "people's committees" there.[50] Early in August, the Spanish authorities freed four of their Polisario prisoners.[51] But the real breakthrough came on September 9, when, for the first time, a Spanish cabinet minister, Pedro Cortina y Mauri, held direct talks, in secret, with Polisario leaders. "The minister of foreign affairs had asked to see me," El-Ouali later recounted. "We met on Tuesday September 9 in a small village, in a foreign country. He was accompanied by several colleagues. We talked for a whole night. They wanted to preserve their interests in so far as they did not contradict the interests of the Saharawi people. So the discussions concerned the economic and cultural and also the political spheres. We succeeded in reaching an understanding."[52] El-Ouali apparently offered Spain a fifteen to twenty year "transition period" with regard to its phosphate and fishing interests.[53] The same day, at a ceremony in Algiers sponsored by the Algerian Red Crescent, Polisario released thirteen of the fourteen prisoners it had captured during the May mutinies, in view of Spain's "willingness to recognize the independence and self-determination of the Saharawi people."[54] A week later, on September 17, the Spanish authorities responded by freeing twenty-three Polisario prisoners, and on October 11 the Madrid government announced that it would also set free the seven Polisario militants who had been jailed in the

Canary Islands after the sabotage attack on the Fosbucraa conveyor belt in October 1974.[55]

The understanding between Cortina y Mauri and El-Ouali and the Spanish-Polisario prisoner exchanges sealed the fate of the PUNS. Dueh Sidna Naucha met El-Ouali near the Mauritanian border on October 10, to plead vainly again for the creation of a broad pro-independence front in which the PUNS could retain its separate identity.[56] But the ground was being cut from under his feet. Even the conservative sheikhs of the Djemaa, who had once been the PUNS's most stalwart supporters, were now drifting into the Polisario camp, with the colonial authorities' encouragement, as the Moroccan threat loomed menacingly on the horizon. Two days after Dueh Sidna Naucha's meeting with El-Ouali, Polisario successfully hosted a "unity conference" at Ain Ben Tili which was attended by several prominent sheikhs, members of the Djemaa and *procuradores* of the Cortes, including Khatri Ould Said Ould el-Joumani and Saila Ould Abeida.[57]

Though the May demonstrations had revealed overwhelming support for independence, even Polisario indicated during the summer that it might be prepared to sacrifice its goal of full independence by federating with Mauritania, if this would help block Moroccan occupation. The Saharawis' cultural ties with the *beidan* of Mauritania doubtless helped to make this a palatable second-best option, but perhaps the relative weakness of the Nouakchott regime, compared to Hassan's government, also made it seem acceptable. Polisario hoped, in any case, that, by proposing a federation, it would be able to scuttle the pact sealed by Hassan and Mokhtar Ould Daddah at the October 1974 Arab League summit. Sometime in May or June, El-Ouali visited the Mauritanian president in his Nouakchott palace and, during a two-hour conversation, proposed a Saharawi-Mauritanian federation under Ould Daddah's federal presidency.[58] But it was to no avail. Ould Daddah believed that the Moroccan juggernaut would be unstoppable and underestimated the determination of both Polisario and its new powerful ally, the Algerian government, to resist it. Furthermore, though there was nothing comparable in Mauritania to the mood of patriotic euphoria that was sweeping Morocco at this time, Ould Daddah was confident that his Saharan policy would not arouse significant domestic opposition. After another summit meeting with Hassan, in Rabat on June 11–12, Ould Daddah joined the king in announcing that they would hold "periodic consultations at the highest level, with a view to strengthening cooperation between their two countries in all fields and reaching a permanent agreement on the policy to be followed for the liberation of the Sahara under Spanish domination."[59]

Hamdi Ould Mouknass, the Mauritanian foreign minister, then accompanied Laraki on a tour of twenty African capitals to ensure that the approaching OAU summit, to be held in Kampala, Uganda, between July 27 and August 1, did not reaffirm the OAU's traditional support for self-determination and a referendum.[60] Deeply divided, the OAU summit shelved substantive consideration of the Western Saharan problem and decided merely "to await the advisory opinion of the International Court of Justice."[61]

It was now only a matter of weeks before the ICJ would publish its opinion. It seemed destined to bring the gathering friction and tension to a head, as a major international crisis. Within the territory the Saharawis were now closing ranks behind Polisario. The PUNS was disintegrating and was soon to collapse completely. The Spanish government seemed intent on proceeding with its new entente with Polisario, and on October 1 it informed the UN that it would hold the stalled referendum sometime during the first six months of 1976.[62] But the other of the principal actors in this unfolding drama, King Hassan, was as intent as ever on ensuring that the referendum was not held. Retreat, as far as the king was concerned, had become impossible. After stirring up such a groundswell of patriotic fervor among his people, it would have shattered his prestige and credibility and infuriated both the armed forces and the political parties. "I would say, and I weigh well my words," he confided on June 17, "that if we do not recover our Sahara, I will be pessimistic about the future of Morocco as a community and state."[63] Indeed, the opposition parties were already straining at the leash, urging immediate military action against Spain.[64]

On August 20 the king proclaimed confidently that Western Sahara would be Moroccan by the end of the year. "If peaceful means do not produce results," he threatened, "only armed struggle will remain for the Moroccan people." He would await the ICJ's advisory opinion, "but whatever the result Morocco will recover its rights over its despoiled provinces no later than toward the end of this year."[65] The storm clouds were gathering.

NOTES

1. Emilio Menéndez del Valle, *Sahara español: una descolonización tardía* (Editorial Cuadernos para el Diálogo, Madrid, 1975), p. 49.

2. *Sahara, 14-Nov.-1975, la traición* (IEPALA and Asociación de Amigos del Sahara, Madrid, 1980), pp. 62–63.

3. *Notre peuple face aux tout derniers crimes du fascisme impuni* (Polisario Front, December 1974), pp. 3–4; *May 20* (Arabic edition, Polisario Front), No. 16, February 1975; *20 Mai* (Polisario Front), No. 21, July 1975.

4. Report of the United Nations Visiting Mission to Spanish Sahara, 1975, in *General Assembly Official Records*, 30th Session, Supplement 23, UN Document A/10023/Rev. 1, p. 74; *New York Times*, May 17, 1975; *ABC* (Madrid), May 30, 1975; *Reuters*, dispatch from Madrid, June 16, 1975.

5. Report of the United Nations Visiting Mission to Spanish Sahara, 1975, *loc. cit.*, p. 15.

6. *Ibid*, p. 59. Representing a wide spectrum of political views, the UN mission could not be accused of bias. Indeed, the American international lawyer, Thomas M. Franck, has written that "the unanimity of the Visiting Mission is all the more remarkable because the Iranian member and the Ivory Coast chairman were both under considerable pressure from their home governments to report findings more favorable to the Moroccan cause. Yet they were so convinced by the evidence that they could bring themselves to accommodate their home governments with little more than a toning down of a few of the draft report's most critical references to Morocco's aspirations." (Thomas M. Franck, "The Stealing of the Sahara," *American Journal of International Law*, Vol. 70, No. 4, October 1976, p. 709.)

7. Report of the United Nations Visiting Mission to Spanish Sahara, 1975, *loc. cit.*, p. 66.

8. *Ibid.*, p. 67.

9. *Ibid.*, p. 59.

10. *Cambio-16* (Madrid), May 16–June 1, 1975.

11. Report of the United Nations Visiting Mission to Spanish Sahara, 1975, *loc. cit.*, p. 62.

12. *Ibid.*, p. 67.

13. *Reuters*, dispatch from Rabat, May 20, 1975.

14. Report of the United Nations Visiting Mission to Spanish Sahara, 1975, *loc. cit.*, pp. 115–118.

15. *Ibid.*, pp. 95–99.

16. *Ibid.*, p. 69.

17. *Ibid.*, pp. 104–5.
18. *Ibid.*, p. 85.
19. *Ibid.*, p. 64.
20. *Reuters*, dispatches from Rabat, November 27, 1974, and December 3, 1974.
21. MOREHOB, *Mémoire adressé à l'attention de la CIJ* (January 1975).
22. Report of the United Nations Visiting Mission to Spanish Sahara, 1975, *loc. cit.*, p. 65.
23. *Reuters*, dispatch from Rabat, September 2, 1975.
24. Report of the United Nations Visiting Mission to Spanish Sahara, 1975, *loc. cit.*, pp. 64–65.
25. *L'Opinion* (Rabat), September 15, 1975; Attilio Gaudio, *Le dossier du Sahara occidental* (Nouvelles Editions Latines, Paris, 1978), p. 390.
26. Report of the United Nations Visiting Mission to Spanish Sahara, 1975, *loc. cit.*, p. 65.
27. *Arriba* (Madrid), November 14, 1975; *20 Mai*, No. 20, June 1975.
28. *ABC*, May 7, 1975; *Reuters*, dispatches from Rabat, May 8, 1975, and May 10, 1975.
29. *Reuters*, dispatches from El-Ayoun, May 17, 1975, and June 24, 1975.
30. *La Vanguardia* (Barcelona), June 10, 1975; Report of the United Nations Visiting Mission to Spanish Sahara, 1975, *loc. cit.*, p. 74.
31. *Maghreb Arabe Presse* (Rabat), January 31, 1975.
32. *Le Monde* (Paris), February 9–10, 1975.
33. *Christian Science Monitor* (Boston), February 11, 1975.
34. *Washington Post*, April 29, 1975.
35. *Reuters*, dispatch from Rabat, April 8, 1975; *Africa Contemporary Record* (Rex Collings, London), Vol. 8, 1975–76, p. B94.
36. *New York Times*, May 17, 1975.
37. Interview with France-Inter, April 28, 1975, cited in Letter Dated 6 May 1975 from the Permanent Representative of Spain to the United Nations Addressed to the Secretary-General, UN Document A/10082, May 6, 1975.
38. Cited in Mowton L. Waring, *Spanish Sahara, Focus of Contention*, Professional Study No. 6099, Air War College, Air University, USAF, Maxwell Air Force Base, Alabama, 1976, p. 37.
39. Letter Dated 23 May 1975 from the Permanent Representative of Spain to the United Nations Addressed to the Secretary-General, UN Document A/10095, May 27, 1975.
40. *ABC*, May 24, 1975.
41. *Africa Contemporary Record*, Vol. 8, 1975–76, p. B156.
42. *ABC*, June 26, 1975.
43. *ABC*, May 30, 1975.
44. Report of the United Nations Visiting Mission to Spanish Sahara, 1975, *loc. cit.*, p. 72.
45. "The governor of the Sahara and the PUNS have gone on trying continually to reach an agreement with the party in exile [Polisario], without obtaining anything positive up to now," the PUNS protested. "On the contrary, far from any attempt at *rapprochement*, three bombs, with four deaths (among them a small child of eight years) and two very seriously wounded, appear to constitute the tragic answer." (*Informaciones*, Madrid, July 21, 1975.)
46. Menéndez del Valle, *op. cit.*, p. 18.
47. *Ibid.*, p. 18; Raoul Weexsteen, "La question du Sahara occidental," *Annuaire de l'Afrique du Nord 1976* (CNRS, Paris, 1977), p. 257.
48. Report of the United Nations Visiting Mission to Spanish Sahara, 1975, *loc. cit.*, p. 62; Soledad Balaguer and Rafael Wirth, *Frente Polisario: la última guerrilla* (Editorial Laia, Barcelona, 1976), pp. 53–54.
49. *ABC*, September 9, 1975.
50. *20 Mai*, No. 21, July 1975; John Gretton, *Western Sahara, the Fight for Self-Determination* (Anti-Slavery Society, London, 1976), p. 32.
51. *Africa Contemporary Record*, Vol. 8, 1975–76, p. B158.
52. *Le Monde*, December 2, 1975.
53. Author's interview with Madjid Abdallah, Polisario representative at the UN, in Washington, D.C., May 1979.
54. Menéndez del Valle, *op. cit.*, p. 20; *El Moudjahid* (Algiers), September 10, 1975.
55. Radio Madrid, September 17, 1975, and October 11, 1975.
56. Radio Madrid, October 11, 1975, and October 14, 1975.
57. *May 20*, No. 25, November 1975.
58. *Remarques Africaines* (Brussels), August 15, 1976; *Jeune Afrique* (Paris), April 1, 1977.
59. Joint Communiqué Issued by the Governments of Mauritania and Morocco on 12 June 1975, in Rabat, in UN Document A/10023/Rev. 1, p. 128.

60. *Chaab* (Nouakchott), July 18, 1975.

61. OAU Resolution AHG/Res. 75 (XII).

62. *Africa Contemporary Record*, Vol. 8, 1975–76, p. B158.

63. *Le Monde*, June 19, 1975.

64. The USFP's administrative commission accused the Moroccan government of "ultraconservatism" in its Western Saharan strategy on September 13, and a few days later Bouabid and Boucetta presented a joint USFP-Istiqlal memorandum to Hassan demanding measures based on "the will of the national forces to engage in the fight for liberation against the enemy." (*Le Monde*, October 18, 1975.) They urged the launching of a full-scale guerrilla war against Spain and the establishment of a "national liberation council," comprising the king, the FLU, the FAR and the main parties, to coordinate it. (*Reuters*, dispatch from Rabat, September 23, 1975.)

65. *Reuters*, dispatch from Rabat, August 20, 1975.

20

The Madrid Accords

O N OCTOBER 15 the UN mission of inquiry published its long-awaited report, disconcerting the Moroccan and Mauritanian Saharan governments with its conclusion that "the majority of the population within the Spanish Sahara was manifestly in favour of independence."[1] The next day, Rabat and Nouakchott received a new shock when the ICJ finally published its advisory opinion, rejecting their claims of historic precolonial sovereignty over Western Sahara. "The Court's conclusion is that the materials and information presented to it do not establish any tie of territorial sovereignty between the Territory of Western Sahara and the Kingdom of Morocco or the Mauritanian entity. Thus the Court has not found legal ties of such a nature as might affect the application of resolution 1514 (XV) in the decolonization of Western Sahara and, in particular, of the principle of self-determination through the free and genuine expression of the will of the peoples of the Territory."[2]

Hassan had been prepared for the worst. Within hours of the advisory opinion's publication, his government released a communiqué that twisted its conclusions beyond recognition. "The Opinion of the Court can only mean one thing," it read. "The so-called Western Sahara was a part of Moroccan territory over which the sovereignty was exercised by the Kings of Morocco and the population of this territory considered themselves and were considered to be Moroccans. . . . Today, Moroccan demands have been recognized by the legal advisory organ of the United Nations."[3] It was an interpretation worthy of the perverse Red Queen in Lewis Carroll's *Through the Looking Glass*, remarked one astonished international lawyer.[4]

Meanwhile, Moroccan radio interrupted normal broadcasting to play martial music. Morocco's cities were bedecked with flags and nationalist banners and at lunchtime workers were sent home from factories and offices. The king was about to address the nation on radio and television, and the streets were tense with excitement and expectation. When he finally spoke, he claimed that the ICJ's advisory opinion had vindicated Morocco's claim. "The whole world," he told his audience, which must have comprised practically the entire Moroccan population, "has recognized that the Sahara belonged to us for a very long time" and so the government would immediately recruit three hundred and fifty thousand civilian volunteers to march into the Spanish colony to "rejoin our kinsmen."[5] This "Green March," named after the holy color of Islam, would express the "unanimous will" of the Moroccan people and "print a new page of glory in letters of gold" in the nation's history.[6] The marchers, whom the king promised to lead in person, would be armed only with "the Holy Book of Allah."

The logistics of transporting 350,000 people to the desert from all over Morocco, with adequate supplies of food, water, fuel and tents, were daunting, but Hassan revealed that preparations had begun two months beforehand. The march, it seems, would have been staged whatever the ICJ had found. Politically, it was a masterstroke. It precipitated events before the UN General Assembly had time to consider the findings and recommendations of the ICJ or the UN mission. It brought enormous pressure to bear on Spain, and within Morocco it gave a new fillip to the *jihad*-like atmosphere that the king had been whipping up among his people since the summer of 1974. The march captured the imagination of the Moroccan people, and within three days of the king's speech 362,000 had volunteered to join it.[7] By October 21 the number had swollen to 524,000.

When news of the king's plan reached Western Sahara, it was condemned without reservation by all Saharawi leaders, irrespective of their political affiliation. Polisario, the rump of the PUNS and the *sheikhs* in the Djemaa all implored Spain to prevent the march crossing the frontier, if need be by force. Describing the march as an "indirect invasion," Mohammed Lamine Ould Ahmed, the head of Polisario's external-relations committee, appealed to the Spanish people on October 18 to "press the Madrid government to take measures to defend our territory."[8] The next day the president of the Djemaa, Khatri Ould Said Ould el-Joumani, vowed that "we will fight to the death" for independence and said that "we have been asking the Spanish government for arms to defend our frontiers."[9] For his part, Dueh Sidna Naucha, the PUNS leader, met Polisario and Spanish officials in El-Ayoun on October 20 to discuss how to respond to the threatened march. "We are ready to die to defend our country," he declared, "but we need arms to fight."[10]

In Madrid the Spanish government was appalled by Hassan's speech but was not deflected, initially, from its plans for a referendum and a devolution of powers to a Polisario-led Saharawi government. The cabinet met, with Franco in the chair, on October 17, to consider the new Moroccan challenge and decided to seek an emergency meeting of the UN Security Council.[11] The request was lodged the next day in New York by Spain's UN ambassador, Jaime de Piniés, who described the planned march as an "invasion which, besides endangering international peace and security, ignores the rights of the people of the Sahara to self-determination and is contrary to the purposes and principles of the Charter of the United Nations."[12] When the council met two days later, Piniés declared forthrightly that "Spain will meet the responsibilities incumbent upon it, and publicly denounces to this council the intolerable threats of the government of Morocco, and requests that this council act immediately."[13] In El-Ayoun, meanwhile, the governor-general, Federico Gómez de Salazar, continued to lay the groundwork for a transfer of powers to Polisario.

Following up Cortina y Mauri's rendezvous with El-Ouali and the September prisoner exchanges, the *delegado gubernativo* of the colony's northern region, Comandante Aguirre, traveled to the little settlement of Mahbes, near the Algerian frontier, on October 21, to meet Polisario's principal leaders, including El-Ouali, Ibrahim Ghali and Mahfoud Ali Beiba, and exchange their remaining prisoners. The Polisario leaders handed over Antonio Martín, the Spanish businessman seized in El-Ayoun the previous March, and a Spanish military doctor, the last of the prisoners captured in May by the mutinous Tropas Nómadas, in return for twelve of their own men, among whom were the seven militants who had been detained after the sabotage attack on the Fosbucraa conveyer belt in October 1974.[14] The next day, the governor-general himself arrived in Mahbes and reached agreement with El-Ouali that independence would be granted in six months' time, after a transitional period in which powers would be progressively transferred to Polisario. As a first step, Polisario's leaders were invited to enter the towns, and both Mahfoud Ali Beiba and Ibrahim Ghali immediately traveled to El-Ayoun.[15] There, on October 26, they held further talks with Gómez de Salazar, while several thousand Saharawis marched into the city center from the slums of Colominas, waving Polisario flags. The demonstrations continued for two days.[16] "In the end," Gómez de Salazar was later to recall of these last weeks of Spanish rule, "the Polisario Front represented the Saharawi people. The Djemaa had lost prestige and it was Polisario which shaped the Saharawi people's politics."[17] Abandoned by its Spanish mentors, the PUNS had been reduced to a shell, and when Dueh Sidna Naucha once again proposed, on October 25, to "operate jointly with the Polisario Front, but without unifying ourselves with it," his party was derided by Polisario as "a leadership without a following."[18] Polisario insisted that Dueh Sidna's grouplet dissolve itself, so that its remaining members could join the front.

As for King Hassan, he was dismayed by the chorus of opposition from Western Sahara to his march plans and so, on October 23, he broadcast an appeal to his "faithful subjects of the province of the Sahara," promising to forgive their past errors. "All those who have supported Spain or who have sided with the so-called 'liberation front' have purely and simply been led astray," he pleaded. "Return to the right path."[19] But only one Saharawi of note responded favorably. On November 1, Khatri Ould Said Ould el-Joumani flew to Morocco from the Canaries and, the next day, made the *bayaa* to King Hassan in the Agadir town hall, declaring that "I have come on behalf of all the inhabitants and tribes of the Sahara to render to Your Majesty the allegiance of our ancestors."[20] Khatri had formerly been scorned in Morocco as a puppet of the Spanish, but since he was president of the Djemaa, it was now opportune to acclaim him as the supreme representative of all the Saharawi tribes.[21] However, "an individual who makes an act of allegiance cannot represent a whole people," a Polisario leader, Mohammed Ali Ould el-Ouali, protested on November 4. "He was no more than a political corpse who has chosen to go to Morocco to recover the authority he would have lost in the event of an agreement between the Sharifian and Spanish governments."[22]

With more than half a million Moroccans volunteering to join the Green March, the Rabat authorities eventually had to choose the marchers by lottery.[23] The first contingent, 20,000 strong, set out in a fleet of buses and trucks from Ksar es-Souk, an impoverished province in eastern Morocco, on October 21, and arrived two days later in Tarfaya, where a huge tent city gradually took shape, about eighteen miles from the Western Saharan border, as the marchers poured in from all of Morocco's provinces. By October 28, 145,000 had arrived.[24] Logistically, this was a mammoth operation. The Office National de Chemins de Fer had to halt all regular rail services so that special trains could be laid on to shuttle marchers to Marrakesh, from where they had to be ferried south by road. In addition, 7,813 trucks and buses, many of them requisitioned from private companies, were mobilized, along with 230 ambulances and 470 doctors. Sacks of grain were dropped to the marchers at Tarfaya by the Moroccan air force's Hercules C-130 transport planes, which had just been delivered by the U.S., and since there was no fresh-water source at Tarfaya, 23,000 tons of water had to be brought in from the north, along with 17,000 tons of food and 2,590 tons of fuel. According to the Moroccan ministry of finance, the whole operation cost £8 million, but the indirect costs, from disruption to the economy, must have been much higher.[25]

At Tarfaya the marchers were subjected to military discipline and fed on tins of sardines and loaves of bread. But, despite the rough conditions and the frequent sandstorms that whipped through the camps, there was a holiday atmosphere. For the most part the marchers were very poor. Many were underemployed seasonal farmhands from the countryside, or jobless youths from the cities. They were getting free food and cigarettes, and many were living better than they did at home. Some, imagining that they were heading for a promised land, had arrived in Tarfaya with all their meager possessions in the expectation that they would be able to settle in Western Sahara at the end of the march.[26]

The marchers had been recruited according to provincial quotas, in much the same manner as the pre-protectorate sultans used to raise a tribal levy (*naiba*) when they embarked on a military campaign (*mahalla*). The provincial quotas reflected political as well as logistic considerations, just as the number of conscripts for the *naiba* had been determined as much by the tribes' respective degrees of loyalty as by their size. The cities, where the king's stock was much lower than in the countryside, were systematically underrepresented.[27] Students were almost entirely excluded, and though the nationalist opposition parties gave the march their full-blooded support, they were kept at arm's length. Moreover, 43,500 of the marchers, 12.5 percent of the total, were state officials, and the entire operation was run on military lines by the FAR and the Gendarmerie Royale. There was very little risk that the king's political rivals would influence the marchers. Indeed, the parties had little chance of capitalizing at all on the march. It was designed to boost the king's prestige and, unless it failed to force Spain's hand, it was bound to do so. Not only did the king enjoy the credit of conceiving and organizing the march, but by portraying it as a holy crusade, under his leadership, as *amir al-muminin*, the government reinforced his authority as a divinely sanctioned ruler. The religious dimension of the march was deliberately played up. The marchers were encouraged to regard themselves as *mujahidin*, or warriors of God, in a holy as well as national crusade to drive colonialist infidels from Islamic, Moroccan soil. "Let the Holy Book of Allah be your only weapon," declared the prime minister, Ahmed Osman, as the contingent from Ksar es-Souk set out for Tarfaya. "Go then under divine protection, helped by your unshakable faith, your true patriotism and your total devotion to the guide of your victorious march, King Hassan II."[28] On October 23, the king even likened the march to the Prophet Mohammed's return to Mecca from his exile in Medina.[29]

The regime took full advantage of this heady atmosphere to mount a frenetic campaign of allegiance-swearing to the throne. As the marchers gathered in Tarfaya, Hassan received renewals of the *bayaa* from associations, businesses and organizations of all stripes, ranging from the Union Marocaine de l'Agriculture and the Association National des Combattants to the Moroccan Jewish community and Maroc-Volvo.[30] Many of these organizations gave material support to the march itself. The canneries, for example, donated the sardines on which the marchers were fed. Fund-raising campaigns were launched, and the Fédération Royale Marocaine de Football placed a special surcharge on tickets for soccer matches. Even pop singers played their part, with Jil Jilala releasing a catchy ballad, "El-Ayoun, My Eyes," which topped the Moroccan charts soon after its release on October 24.[31]

Once the march had been announced, the king knew that he would be running serious political risks if he decided to call it off. There could be no turning back, he said on October 30. "I do not want to turn the three hundred and fifty thousand Moroccans who have responded to my call with enthusiasm into three hundred and fifty thousand frustrated Moroccans."[32] Two hundred thousand volunteers had already reached Tarfaya.

For Madrid the challenge could not have come at a worse time. General Franco, who was now eighty-two, fell ill during the cabinet meeting on October 17, and he suffered a series of heart attacks between October 21 and 24. Though it had condemned Hassan's march and appealed to the UN to get it stopped, the Spanish government's nerve began to crack as the D-Day for the marchers' frontier crossing approached. Buffeted by contradictory pressures and divided over the course to pursue, Carlos Arias Navarro's cabinet stumbled almost rudderless through the deepening crisis, in the absence of the old *caudillo*, who lay in a coma in Madrid's La Paz hospital, struggling through his long and final illness.

The army officers in the Sahara, who shared Franco's paternalistic notion of the Spanish colonial mission, were appalled at the thought of appeasing Morocco. Men like General Gómez de Salazar and Colonel Rodríguez de Viguri, who had done so much to prepare the groundwork for independence and believed that Spain could preserve its interests in the Sahara in a neocolonial framework, regarded capitulation to Hassan's pressure tactics as an affront to the honor and dignity of Spain and its army, and they made their views known to the cabinet in Madrid through the Dirección General de Promoción del Sahara. At the foreign ministry, Cortina y Mauri was equally adamant that the independence plans should proceed in defiance of Morocco. Like Piniés, his ambassador at the UN, he feared that Spain risked losing its international stature and respect, especially in the third world, and would forfeit the sympathy it had garnered over the years for its claim to Gibraltar if it reneged on its commitment to self-determination. It might also damage its important relations with Algeria, which had become a major export market, taking more than one quarter of Spanish exports to Africa. The Instituto Nacional de Industria continued to advise the government, meanwhile, that Moroccan annexation of Western Sahara would threaten Spain's control of the Bou-Craa mines, and representatives of the fishing industry in the Canaries made the same point about fishing rights off the Saharan coast. Franco might well have shared many of these misgivings about bowing to Moroccan pressure, but, since he was now in a coma, he no longer played any role in influencing policy.

Other leading politicians, among them the president of the council of ministers, Arias Navarro, the minister of presidential affairs, Antonio Carro Martínez, and the minister and secretary-general of the Francoist Movimiento Nacional, José Ruiz, who had for many years been a guardian of the Moroccan Royal Family's assets in Spain, believed, above all else, that a showdown with Morocco had to be avoided. As Franco's chances of recovery became increasingly slim, they argued that the government could not afford to run the risk of military confrontation with Morocco. It had to devote its attention to preparing the transition to the new post-Francoist order at home, avoiding the turbulence that had beset Portugal since Marcello Caetano's downfall in April 1974. Indeed, to the cabinet's alarm, unrest had been mounting, especially in the Basque country, since the garroting of two Basque nationalists and three other anti-Francoist militants on September 23, and the deterioration in Franco's health had already aroused hopes of democratization. The two principal underground opposition movements, the communist-led Junta Democrática and the socialist-led Plataforma de Convergencia Democrática, had united, calling for "true democracy and the formation of a constituent assembly," the restoration of trade-union rights and the freeing of political prisoners. [33]

If the crisis with Morocco degenerated into a war, Spanish officials knew that the Moroccan forces would be no match for their much larger and better equipped army and air force. The Spanish armed forces numbered 302,000 men, five times more than the 61,000-strong FAR, and the Spanish air force had twice as many combat aircraft. [34] There were at least 20,000 Spanish troops, including crack Foreign Legion regiments, in Western Sahara, and many more thousands in reserve in the Canary Islands. But the domestic political ramifications of a military confrontation with Morocco as Franco lay dying would be incalculable, some members of Arias Navarro's cabinet insisted. The Spanish population was in no mood for war, and, if one broke out, Spain would risk suffering diplomatic and economic reprisals from the Arab world. [35] In addition, if Spain did not accommodate Hassan, it could be assumed that he would mete out his revenge on Ceuta and Melilla, the 18,000 Spaniards living in Morocco and Spanish firms with business interests there. In any case, reports from Morocco indicated that there was such a ground swell of nationalist fervor that retreat had become almost completely impossible for Hassan. If he did not get his way in the Sahara, he might even be overthrown; and the U.S. and French governments put it forcefully to the Spanish government that radical political change across the Straits of Gilbraltar would not serve Western interests, especially in a period of political uncertainty in the Iberian peninsula.

There were thus strong arguments to bargain for the best possible compromise with Hassan, taking advantage of the concessions which he appeared to offer regarding Spanish interests in Western Sahara's fishing and phosphate resources, as well as Ceuta and Melilla. However, others, such as Piniés, were of the opinion that appeasement would only encourage Hassan, irrespective of the concessions he promised, to try his luck again later over Ceuta and Melilla. He would know that intimidation "pays dividends," he warned in a letter to Arias Navarro on October 27.[36]

However, Arias Navarro's overriding concern was to forestall military conflict, and with Morocco's target date for the Green Marchers' frontier crossing initially set for October 26, he knew that time was running out. Hassan, it was evident, could not call off the march without a humiliating and politically dangerous loss of face before his own people, and yet anything more than a symbolic penetration by the marchers into Western Sahara would be taken as an affront by the Spanish army officers there. So, on October 20, the cabinet decided to send an envoy to meet Hassan, who was then in Marrakesh, in the hope of finding a way to defuse the crisis. As an old acquaintance of the king, Solís seemed better suited to the task than the foreign minister, who had by then lost all patience with Hassan, and so the head of the Movimiento Nacional flew into Marrakesh the next day and urged the king to postpone the march, to allow more time for negotiations. The king, Solís later confided, told him that "it was impossible to do so because all the parties were involved in it."[37] But he did agree to send a negotiator to Madrid with forty-eight hours and, when Solís flew back to Madrid in the evening, he appeared optimistic that an agreement could be reached. "I believe we have left the door open for future discussions," he said at Barajas airport. Hassan was "very favorable to talking with Spain, reaching an understanding with Spain and posing all the pending problems."[38] Rumors quickly spread, in Rabat as well as Madrid, that Solís had promised a more sympathetic consideration of Morocco's territorial claim, as well as suggesting a face-saving formula for the Green March itself.[39]

On October 24 the Moroccan government announced that it had revised the Green Marchers' D-Day to October 28. The same day, Ahmed Laraki, the Moroccan foreign minister, began negotiations in Madrid, and the Spanish information minister, León Herrera, announced that a bill would be submitted to the Cortes giving the government carte blanche to "take any initiatives deemed necessary" to end Spanish administration in Western Sahara.[40] The next day, as the last rites of the Catholic Church were administered to Franco, Laraki clinched a deal with Carro Martínez on the Green March. According to Adolfo Martín Gamero, who was then Spain's ambassador to Morocco, they "reached a tacit agreement by which the Spanish armed forces demilitarized ten kilometers of the north of the Sahara, so that the Green March could enter the territory for forty-eight hours and then leave it."[41] To provide sufficient time for the Spanish to withdraw from this frontier zone and for the last of Hassan's volunteers to reach Tarfaya, the marchers' D-Day was again postponed. The frontier would finally be crossed between November 4 and 6, the Moroccan information minister, Ahmed Benhima, announced.

Laraki must have left Madrid on October 25 with more than a deal about the

Green March, however. Carro Martínez, it seems, had also promised to arrange further negotiations about the future of Western Sahara, for after reporting back to King Hassan in Marrakesh and then flying on to Nouakchott to consult President Mokhtar Ould Daddah on October 26, Laraki returned to Madrid on October 28 for a new round of talks, and this time he was accompanied not only by Colonel Ahmed Dlimi, who was supervising the logistics of the Green March, but by the Mauritanian foreign minister, Hamdi Ould Mouknass, and, significantly, Karim Lamrani, the head of the Moroccan state phosphate company, the OCP.[42] Indeed, Laraki revealed two days later, on October 30, that three joint commissions had been set up to examine the political, military and economic dimensions of Spanish withdrawal.[43]

France and Spain, which both saw Hassan as a strategic ally and regarded the success of his Saharan gamble as crucial to the maintenance of his regime's newfound stability, had advised Arias Navarro to come to terms with Morocco. The U.S. government had drafted a rearmament programme for the FAR in 1974 and increased the value of its Foreign Military Sales (FMS) agreements with Morocco to no less than $242 million in Fiscal Year 1975 (which began in October 1974) from $8.2 million in the previous fiscal year.[44] And, following a state visit to Morocco by President Valéry Giscard d'Estaing in May 1975 and visits by Moroccan military officials to the French arms exhibitions at Le Bourget and Satory the following June, the Rabat government had signed a major arms deal, known as the Marrakesh Plan, with the French Délégation Ministérielle à l'Armement.[45] Details of the diplomatic exchanges between Washington, Paris and Madrid about the Sahara at this time have never been published, but King Hassan revealed on October 27 that the U.S. had been "sandwiched" between Morocco and Spain and had encouraged its two allies to "consider a peaceful solution through dialogue."[46] Alfred Atherton, one of Henry Kissinger's assistant secretaries of state, had visited Morocco to meet the king on October 22, one day after Solís, and the deputy director of the CIA, General Vernon Walters, an experienced troubleshooter who had helped arrange Kissinger's secret mission to China in 1971 and the Paris peace talks with the Vietnamese in 1972, had been in Madrid to put American views on the Saharan crisis to Spanish leaders.[47]

By the end of October rumors abounded that Spain had agreed, at least in principle, to hand Western Sahara to Morocco and Mauritania, and they seemed to be corroborated by what had been happening within the territory. On October 28 the entente with Polisario was suddenly halted and General Gómez de Salazar clamped a dusk-to-dawn curfew on El-Ayoun, on the pretext that "extremist elements could carry out terrorist actions against the civilian population."[48] Shortly before the curfew took effect that evening, at half past six, thousands of Foreign Legionnaires, paratroopers, marines and police swarmed out of their barracks to take up positions throughout the city, and barbed wire was strung around the Saharawi neighborhoods. The same day, the governor-general ordered the immediate discharging of all Saharawi soldiers from the Tropas Nómadas, and gasoline stations were ordered not to serve Saharawi motorists and taxi drivers.[49] The Saharawis were in a state of seige. They were convinced that Spain was preparing to hand them over to Morocco, and on November 4 Saharawi workers in the phosphate industry and government departments staged a general strike in protest at the curfew, the ban on gasoline sales and the military encirclement of their suburbs.[50]

By then, the Spanish authorities had launched an emergency evacuation operation, code-named Golondrina. All Spanish civilians, except those working in essential services or the phosphate industry, were ordered to leave the country, and by November 8 about twelve thousand had already been evacuated by air or sea to the Canaries. Spanish shopkeepers transferred their businesses, complete with stock, at knockdown prices to Saharawi traders, and as the Spanish teachers left, all the schools closed down. Even the Spanish dead were evacuated. In a mass exhumation, a thousand corpses were dug up from local cemeteries and airfreighted to the Canaries. The Saharan animals in the El-Ayoun zoo, meanwhile, were shipped off to Almería.[51]

The trilateral talks in Madrid and the repressive measures taken against the Saharawis in El-Ayoun since October 28 were cause for understandable concern in Algiers, where the government had also become increasingly alarmed by the hysterical anti-Algerian campaign raging in the Moroccan press, the Istiqlal Party's revival of the old Moroccan claims to parts of the Algerian Sahara, and the Rabat authorities' decision to suspend rail links with Algeria on October 22.[52] While the Spanish-Moroccan-Mauritanian negotiations were still continuing in Madrid, Colonel Mohammed Abdelghani, the Algerian minister of the interior and a member of Boumedienne's supreme Council of the Revolution, flew to Madrid on October 29 and, in a meeting with Cortina y Mauri, requested clarification of Spanish intentions. The same day, the Algerian foreign minister, Abdelaziz Bouteflika, met the UN secretary-general, Kurt Waldheim, in New York, and on October 30, Abdelghani was received by Arias Navarro and Carro Martínez before returning to Algiers, where he reported that the "rumors" of an impending Spanish cession of Western Sahara to Morocco and Mauritania were "without foundation."[53] The same day, the Spanish-Moroccan-Mauritanian talks were adjourned.

The Spanish government had not only been jolted by Algeria's sudden diplomatic demarches. The UN had begun to take a more active interest in the Saharan crisis, as a result of Spain's initial protest to the Security Council about the Green March, and Arias Navarro wanted to see how Morocco would react. Called into session on October 20, the Security Council had shrunk from approving a terse resolution from Costa Rica demanding "as a matter of urgency, that the Government of Morocco desist immediately from the proposed march on Western Sahara," but it had agreed two days later to request Waldheim "to enter into immediate consultations with the parties concerned and interested and to report to the Security Council as soon as possible on the results of his consultations in order to enable the Council to adopt the appropriate measures to deal with the present situation concerning Western Sahara."[54] Waldheim accordingly visited Morocco, Mauritania, Algeria and Spain in turn between October 26 and 28 and then sent a personal representative, André Lewin, to Marrakesh and Algiers for further consultations with Hassan and Boumedienne. In his report back to the Security Council on October 31, Waldheim revealed that he had been informed in Madrid that "although the Government of Spain had established direct contacts with the Governments of Morocco and Mauritania because of the urgency of the situation created by the 'Green March,' it had not committed itself to seeking a solution to the decolonization of Western Sahara on a bilateral or trilateral basis.'' Moreover, ''Spain was ready to cooperate fully with the United Nations, which could be called upon to play an appropriate role that might include temporary administration of the Territory by the United Nations until such time as the wishes of the population could be ascertained.'' Waldheim reported that he was therefore pursuing his ''consultations with the parties'' about a possible UN role.[55] According to Piniés, the ''Waldheim Plan,'' as it came to be known, included the appointment of a UN high commissioner and the dispatch of thirty UN civil servants and a small peace-keeping force of seven hundred UN troops.[56]

Meanwhile, Franco's condition had worsened and, on October 30, Arias Navarro had decided, as in July 1974, to activate Article 11 of the Spanish Constitution, which provided for the temporary transfer of the head of state's powers to Prince Juan Carlos if the *generalissimo* was incapacitated. The prince's first move was to reassure the armed forces, upon whose loyalty he knew that the post-Francoist monarchy would be crucially dependent, that its prestige would not be impaired by the Saharan crisis. He was well aware of the unease of the officers in the Sahara, for General Gómez de Salazar had just forwarded to the government a petition demanding a tough response to the Green March which had been signed by officers from all branches of the armed forces at a meeting held in the ''Casino,'' a Foreign Legion mess in El-Ayoun.[57] So, only two days after taking up Franco's duties, the prince flew to El-Ayoun in his private Mystère, to address the Spanish officers there in the barracks of the Tercio Don Juan de Austria. ''I want to give you personally the assurance,'' he declared, in general's uniform, ''that everything will be done so that our army will preserve intact its prestige and its honor.''[58] The same day, in New York, the Spanish delegation at the UN requested another meeting of the Security Council ''to consider the appropriate measures to be taken in conformity with the Charter to oblige the Government of Morocco to desist from the march.''[59] When the council convened the next day, the Spanish representative, Arias Salgado, who was deputizing for Piniés, then sick in a Madrid hospital, warned that ''if the march announced by the King of Morocco is held, it will be repelled by every means at [Spain's] disposal, including the use of armed force.''[60]

However, Spanish troops had already begun pulling out of the smaller outlying posts and settlements in the territory. On October 30, military sources in El-Ayoun revealed that troops had been withdrawn from the zones of Mahbes, Jdiriya and Haousa, leaving no Spanish presence to the east of Smara.[61] At the same time, the Spanish garrison in the little fishing town of La Guera on the Cape Blanc peninsula was evacuated, and by the beginning of November, Spanish forces had pulled back to a strategic triangle of territory near the coast bordered by Daora in the north, Smara in the east and Villa Cisneros in the south. Polisario guerrillas quickly took control of most of the scattered outposts vacated by the Spanish. La Guera, for example, was occupied on November 2.[62] The PUNS briefly occupied three localities in the southeast, including Aoussert and Tichla, but the *Punsistas* were surrounded and arrested by Polisario forces at the beginning of November, and thereafter no more was heard of the party.[63] But Colonel Dlimi had also seen his chance to move forces into the territory, without risk of clashes with Spanish troops, to divert Polisario's attention from the Green Marchers. Unknown to the foreign journalists who were massing at Tarfaya, units of the FAR slipped across the border about one hundred miles to the east on October 31 and headed for Jdiriya, Haousa and Farsia, three of the outposts evacuated by the Spanish. Polisario guerrillas put up stiff but ultimately unsuccessful resistance in running battles with the columns of invading troops. The opening shots of Polisario's new, long war with Morocco had been fired.[64]

The Spanish armed forces made no attempt to stop the clashes and the government in Madrid did not even protest, in public at least, to Rabat about the Moroccan troops' violation of the Western Saharan border. Juan Carlos' bracing speech at the Foreign Legion barracks in El-Ayoun started to look rather hollow. Indeed, Spanish-Moroccan talks resumed on November 3 when Osman arrived in Madrid to meet the prince, Arias Navarro, Carro Martínez and Cortina y Mauri. "The march does not impede the negotiations and the negotiations do not impede the march," he said the next day, upon his return to Agadir, where Hassan had switched base on November 2 to keep in closer touch with Dlimi. The Spanish government, it seems, had rapidly lost faith in the UN's ability to constrain King Hassan, who had rejected the Waldheim Plan out of hand.[65] Arias Navarro had been displeased by the weakness of the resolution adopted on November 2 by the Security Council, where the U.S. and France successfully resisted pleas from Spain's closest ally on the council, Costa Rica, to order Morocco to "cease and desist." The resolution, which "avoided calling things by their proper names," as Costa Rica's representative Salazar complained, appealed lamely to "all the parties concerned and interested to avoid any unilateral or other action which might further escalate the tension in the area" and requested Waldheim to "continue and intensify his consultations with the parties concerned and interested."[66] Lewin had then shuttled on Waldheim's behalf between Morocco, Mauritania, Algeria and Spain on November 3-6, in the hope of securing agreement on the plan for a temporary UN administration. However, when he met Hassan in Agadir on November 4, in the company of Osman, who had just returned from his talks in Madrid, Lewin was told that the Waldheim Plan had been "overtaken by events" and that "the main provisions" of a trilateral agreement with Spain and Mauritania "had already been determined and stipulated a transfer of sovereignty from the administering power to Morocco and Mauritania." In Madrid, on November 6, Lewin found that, though the Spanish government still paid lip-service to the idea of a temporary UN administration, it was now of the opinion that "a trilateral agreement could also provide an appropriate formula if the United Nations was prepared to agree to it." As for the Green March, Hassan informed Lewin that "it would have a symbolic character" and the Spanish government assured him that "a march limited in area and perhaps in duration would not evoke a military response from the Spanish army, stationed in the Territory on a 'dissuasion line' some twelve kilometers from the geographical boundary."[67] As Lewin left Madrid for New York on the afternoon of November 6, the first columns of Green Marchers were already trekking across the border into a thin strip of no-man's-land.

The day before, Hassan had finally given the marchers their starting orders. "As soon as you have crossed the frontier," he ordered, as *amir al-muminin*, "you must say your prayers, facing toward Mecca, to give thanks to the Almighty." He would have liked to have led the march in person, he added, but, as "supreme commander," he had to "remain at his command post" in Agadir.[68] In the sprawling tent city at Tarfaya, the king's words were received with rapture. At once, thousands of trucks began carrying the marchers along the eighteen bumpy miles to the frontier. The operation continued all night, and as dawn broke on November 6, a vast crowd was waiting a few hundred yards from the old border post at Tah, which the Spanish had abandoned only a few days earlier when they pulled back to their dissuasion line. Ahmed Osman formally inaugurated the march at 10:40 A.M. by walking through a hastily erected arch of iron scaffolding, ornate with flags and portraits of King Hassan. With him were a score of cabinet ministers and official delegations representing three of Morocco's most conservative third-world allies, Saudi Arabia, Jordan and Gabon. "We will walk ten kilometers and see," Osman announced. Hard on his heels surged a throng of ragged Moroccan peasants and unemployed youths, a human flood half a mile wide, chanting "Allah Akhbar" (God is Great) and "The Sahara is Moroccan," and waving Moroccan flags, portraits of their king and paperback copies of the Koran. Once across the border they fell to their knees in prayer and milled around the white-domed Tah frontier post, before shuttling south for three hot dusty hours along the single-lane road in the direction of El-Ayoun. They finally halted about six miles south of the frontier, pitching their tents in a large salt-pan known to the Saharawis as Oum Deboaa, the "mother of hyenas." Forty thousand camped there the first night.[69] The marchers had no idea that this was to be as far as they would go. They had been led to believe that El-Ayoun was their ultimate destination and they fully expected to begin the second leg of their hike the next morning, braving the Spanish troops and armor massed along the dissuasion line. Tension built up during the night and a group of two thousand marchers tried to break away from Oum Deboaa toward the Spanish lines. They were violently pushed back by Moroccan gendarmes, while Spanish troops detonated three bombs at close range to warn them that they risked walking into a minefield.[70] By the night of November 7, some 145,000 marchers had reached Oum Deboaa. The same day, another 25,000 crossed the border about forty miles to the east and marched three miles south to set up a second camp to the north of Hagounia. A third incursion began a further fifty miles east, to the north of Smara.[71]

Not surprisingly, the march incurred Polisario's fury. "We hold the Moroccan government responsible for all the consequences of this adventure," declared Habib Allah, a member of the front's external relations committee, after Hassan's November 5 speech. "We will defend our rights and our territorial integrity whatever the price."[72] In Algiers, Boumedienne called the council of ministers into session on November 6 and summoned the ambassadors of the five permanent member countries of the UN Security Council to his palace. The same day, in New York, his representative to the UN, Abdellatif Rahal, charged that the "timidity" of the Security Council's resolutions had encouraged Morocco to pursue its planned march. "If the Security Council cannot or will not act in keeping with its responsibilities, my Government will be compelled to meet its responsibilities," he warned. "This is neither a threat nor a provocation. It is the clearest possible expression of the strongest possible determination."[73] During the night of November 5–6, the council had held a closed session at which the U.S. and France had once again saved King Hassan from being ordered to call off the march. Instead, the council's Soviet president had been authorized merely to address an "urgent request" to the king to "put an end forthwith to the declared march into Western Sahara."[74] Nobody expected the king to take the slightest notice and, later in the morning, after Osman had led the first block of marchers across the border, he cabled in reply to the council that "we can only inform you that the march has in fact already begun this morning."[75] For the sake of appearances, the Spanish government publicly condemned the march which it had agreed to allow into its specially created no-man's-land. As soon as the frontier had been "violated by large contingents of Moroccan nationals, including elements of the armed forces and official authorities," it requested another urgent meeting of the Security Council, to "take appropriate measures for bringing about an end to this situation and securing the withdrawal to Moroccan territory of the elements taking part in the march."[76]

When the council met in the evening, a more strongly worded resolution, deploring the Green March and calling upon Morocco "immediately to withdraw from the Territory of Western Sahara all the participants in the march," was adopted by consensus, but by then the march was already a *fait accompli* and Hassan simply ignored the council's injunction.[77] In fact, as soon as the first marchers had reached Oum Deboaa, Hassan redoubled his pressure on Madrid. In a message the same day to the Spanish government, he gave an ultimatum. If Spain refused to hold immediate formal negotiations on the territory's cession to Morocco and Mauritania, he would order the marchers to proceed toward the dissuasion line and, if Spanish troops tried to stop them, the FAR would intervene, creating a state of war. The next morning, after consulting the Moroccan ambassador in Madrid, Arias Navarro called a meeting of the cabinet for November 8. It was then, according to Cortina y Mauri, that the final decision to hand Western Sahara to Morocco and Mauritania, without a referendum, was made.[78] Carro Martínez flew to Agadir later in the day to meet King Hassan, who agreed to order the Green Marchers' withdrawal to Morocco, on the understanding that the arrangements for Western Sahara's cession would immediately be negotiated in Madrid.

"Our march has achieved what we ourselves and our friends expected of it," the king broadcast to the Moroccan people the next day. "That is why, dear people, we must return to our point of departure to handle affairs with other methods and in new ways."[79] The back-to-base instructions came as a shock to the marchers camped in Oum Deboaa, who had been expecting to walk all the way to El-Ayoun, and even more so to the 150,000 volunteers who were still waiting at Tarfaya to cross the frontier. The evacuation of the marchers from Oum Deboaa began on November 10, as Hassan returned from Agadir to Marrakesh. "There is an understanding and an accord is in sight," Benhima informed the hundreds of foreign journalists who had been covering the Green March. A Moroccan delegation would leave for Madrid "in 24 or 48 hours" and, in the meantime, "the marchers will remain at Tarfaya," so that, if the talks failed, "the 350,000 Moroccans will once again cross the frontier." It is better, he quipped, "to have a delegation of 350,000 people in the Sahara than a delegation of 40 at the United Nations."[80]

Algerian diplomacy now went into overdrive to try to dissuade both Spain and Mauritania from concluding an agreement with Morocco. On November 8, a member of the Algerian Council of the Revolution, Colonel Ahmed Daia, had held talks with Ould Daddah in Nouakchott.[81] He must have invited the Mauritanian president to Algeria, for on November 10, Ould Daddah flew to Bechar, to be lectured for five hours by Boumedienne about the grave consequences that would follow a tripartite partition agreement. "I was very surprised," Ould Daddah was to claim two years later. "How could my colleague, Boumedienne, whom I considered a very good friend, treat me like this?"[82] But Boumedienne, who had played an influential part in encouraging Hassan to recognize Mauritania in 1969 and had funneled substantial aid to Mauritania, especially to assist its withdrawal from the Franc Zone and the launching of its national currency, the ouguiya, in 1973, felt betrayed.[83] If Mauritania partitioned Western Sahara with Morocco, he warned, Algeria would give such determined support to Polisario that the Mauritanian army would be incapable of defending Mauritania's own long desert frontiers. But two days later Ould Daddah confirmed his alliance with King Hassan at a summit meeting in Morocco.[84]

On November 12, Boumedienne sent a last-minute appeal to Arias Navarro. But Osman, Laraki and Lamrani had arrived in the Spanish capital from Morocco the day before, followed shortly by Ould Mouknass from Nouakchott, and the tripartite talks resumed on November 12, with two commissions handling the details of political and economic matters respectively.[85] Meanwhile, though the last of the Green Marchers were evacuated from Oum Deboaa to Tarfaya on November 13, units of the FAR had penetrated more than a hundred miles into Saguia el-Hamra, reaching Tifariti, near the Mauritanian border, and the Spanish armed forces, which had been withdrawn to their new defense lines near the coast, were doing nothing to stop them. "We do not have any direct information about what is happening beyond these lines and, even if we did, we would not intervene," the captain-general of the Canaries, General Ramón Cuadra Medina, let it be known in El-Ayoun on November 10.[86] In Madrid, Franco was by now in the gravest condition. A respirator was pumping air through a plastic tube into his congested lungs to keep him breathing, while a kidney machine was cleaning his blood, and on November 14 he underwent his third operation in twelve days, to repair his ruptured and bleeding stomach. The same day, the tripartite talks in Madrid concluded with a Spanish agreement to cede Western Sahara to Morocco and Mauritania. In the four weeks since the publication of the ICJ's advisory opinion and Hassan's announcement of the Green March, Spanish policy had turned full circle. Franco was finally to die six days later, on November 20.

The Madrid accords were kept secret.[87] All that was made public was a brief tripartite "declaration of principles" which stated that Spain would withdraw from Western Sahara by the end of February 1976 and in the meantime "proceed forthwith to institute a temporary administration in the Territory, in which Morocco and Mauritania will participate in collaboration with the Djemaa." The Moroccan and Mauritanian governments would each appoint a deputy governor to work alongside the Spanish governor-general. Nothing was said about what would happen at the end of the transitional period. The declaration pledged that "the views of the Saharan population, expressed through the Djemaa, will be respected" and made no mention of partition.[88]

In fact, there was no intention whatever of respecting the Saharawis' views. The declaration of principles made no reference to the old plans for a referendum, to which, of course, both Morocco and Mauritania had been resolutely opposed. The Djemaa was not a properly representative body and was regarded by Saharawi nationalists, who had had nothing to do with it, as an assembly of conservative collaborators with the colonial authorities. It had not been elected by universal adult suffrage, and even in metropolitan Spain there had not been democratic elections during the Francoist era. Ironically, only a year before, on September 30, 1974, Laraki had made much of the Djemaa's unrepresentative character, describing it, in a speech to the UN General Assembly, as being "purely and simply designated by the Spanish authorities."[89] But now Hassan and Ould Daddah anticipated that its meek elders would prove as malleable as ever and ratify their plans for partition, giving them a semblance of democratic legitimacy.

The accords' real meaning was clear enough. Thousands of Moroccan troops poured across the northern border, while a smaller number of Mauritanian troops arrived from the south. They quickly took control of the main towns and settlements as the Spanish troops were evacuated, and neither Rabat nor Nouakchott had any intention of withdrawing them, whatever the Djemaa cared to say. "The Sahara has been returned to you," Hassan told the Moroccan people in a victory speech on November 17, without bothering with the niceties of self-determination.[90] And in an interview with French Television on November 27, he was adamant that there could be "no compromise regarding the final solution." It was "unthinkable that the Sahara should be independent and it shall not be, so long as there is a single living Moroccan."[91]

In return, Morocco and Mauritania made significant economic concessions to Spain. Nothing was said about this in the declaration of principles, but in 1978 the Spanish press revealed that secret agreements on minerals and fisheries had been signed on November 14, 1975. One gave "joint recognition by Morocco and Mauritania to fishing rights in the waters of the Sahara benefiting eight hundred Spanish boats, for a duration of twenty years and in the same conditions as at present, except for the payment of tax from the sixth year."[92] Another secret accord, signed by Spain and Morocco, provided that Spanish capital "would have the right in principle to 35 percent of the equity" in joint-venture companies for the exploration and exploitation of minerals in Western Sahara.[93] Accordingly, Fosbucraa, which had previously been a fully-owned subsidiary of INI, was converted into a joint concern, in which the Moroccan OCP acquired 65 percent of the shares and INI retained 35 percent.[94] The OCP reportedly agreed to compensate Spain by delivering $300 million worth of phosphate rock, priced at the bargain rate of fifteen dollars a ton, to Spain's fertilizer plants in Huelva.[95] At the same time, Hassan revealed on November 25, Morocco would freeze its claim to Ceuta and Melilla until Spain recovered Gibraltar.[96]

The Green Marchers were finally ordered home from Tarfaya on November 18, and the bill on Western Sahara's "decolonization" was approved in the Cortes the same day. "We ran an enormous risk, including that of an open war, but the

Sahara is not worth a single Spanish life," Carro Martínez told the *procuradores* during the debate.[97] Only four of them voted against the bill, while four abstained and 345 voted in favor. The Spanish officials at the UN and in El-Ayoun were shocked, however, by what they saw as a sellout to Morocco. General Gómez de Salazar, who was later, in 1978, to claim that he had never been consulted before the signing of the accords, knew that "the Saharawi people's desire for independence was unanimous" and believed that "if we had been attacked by Morocco we were in a position to destroy the Alawite army in forty-eight hours."[98]

King Hassan claimed at a press conference on November 25 that the Saharan "dossier" was closed, but he had made two serious miscalculations. He had underestimated the Saharawis' determination to resist annexation and he had not expected Algeria to give all-out support to their attempts to thwart it. "Our people, who are presently facing up to the Moroccan invasion, regard the agreement concluded in Madrid between Spain, Morocco and Mauritania as null and void and as an act of aggression and plunder," El-Ouali declared in Algiers on November 15.[99] The Algerian government's reaction to the accords was likeminded. "The Algerian Government does not recognize any right of the Governments of Spain, Morocco and Mauritania to dispose of the Territory of the Sahara and the density of its population," stated a memorandum sent to the UN secretary-general on November 19. "It therefore regards as null and void the 'declaration of principles' presented by Spain and accords no validity to the provisions contained therein."[100]

The Moroccan and Mauritanian troops in Western Sahara were already meeting determined resistance from Polisario. Tension was mounting between Morocco and Algeria, and Hassan had to turn down an invitation to attend Juan Carlos' coronation in Madrid on November 27. "I am not like Christ," Boumedienne warned Hassan. "I will not hold out my cheek for a second blow. I will respond to the utmost of my ability."[101]

NOTES

1. Report of the United Nations Visiting Mission to Spanish Sahara, 1975, in *General Assembly Official Records*, 30th Session, Supplement 23, UN Document A/10023/Rev. 1, p. 66.

2. International Court of Justice, *Western Sahara, Advisory Opinion of 16 October 1975* (ICJ, The Hague, 1975), p. 68. See the appendix for details of the ICJ's advisory opinion.

3. Press release of the Permanent Mission of Morocco to the UN, October 16, 1975, cited in UN Document S/PV.1849, October 20, 1975, p. 11.

4. Thomas M. Franck, "The Stealing of the Sahara," *American Journal of International Law*, Vol. 70, No. 4, October 1976, p. 711.

5. Hassan II, *Discours de S.M. Hassan II, La lutte pour le parachèvement de l'integrité territoriale* (Ministère d'Etat chargé de l'information, Rabat, 1975), p. 8.

6. *Ibid.*, pp. 12, 14.

7. *Washington Post*, October 20, 1975.

8. *El Moudjahid* (Algiers), October 19–20, 1975.

9. *Reuters*, dispatch from Madrid, October 19, 1975.

10. *El Moudjahid*, October 21, 1975.

11. *Le Monde* (Paris), October 21, 1975.

12. *Reuters*, dispatch from the UN, New York, October 18, 1975.

13. UN Security Council, Provisional Verbatim Record of the 1849th Meeting, UN Document S/PV.1849, October 20, 1975, p. 17.

14. *La Provincia* (Las Palmas), October 22, 1975.

15. Author's interview with Comandante Aguirre, Las Palmas, October 1978.

16. *Diario de Las Palmas*, October 27, 1975; *La Provincia*, October 29, 1975.

17. Testimony in the Comisión de Exteriores del Congreso, March 13, 1978 (*El País*, Madrid, March 14, 1978).

18. *La Provincia*, October 26, 1975.

19. Hassan II, *op. cit.*, p. 23.

20. Cited in UN Document S/PV.1854, November 6, 1975, p. 26.

21. "L'autodétermination? La voilà!" boasted Ahmed Alaoui in *Maroc-Soir* (November 4, 1975).

22. *El Moudjahid*, November 5, 1975.

23. Jerome B. Weiner, "The Green March in Historical Perspective," *The Middle East Journal*, Vol. 33, No. 1, Winter 1979, p. 31.

24. *Reuters*, dispatch from Marrakesh, October 28, 1975.

25. Hassan II, *Le défi* (Albin Michel, Paris, 1976), p. 177; *The Observer* (London), November 2, 1975; *Sunday Times* (London), November 2, 1975.

26. *Pueblo* (Madrid), November 7, 1975.

27. For a statistical analysis of the composition of the march, see Weiner, *loc. cit.*, pp. 27–28.

28. *New York Times*, October 22, 1975.

29. Hassan II, *Discours de S.M. Hassan II, La lutte pour le parachèvement de l'integrité territoriale*, p. 20.

30. Weiner, *loc. cit.*, p. 29.

31. *Ibid.*, p. 32.

32. *Le Monde*, October 31, 1975.

33. *Le Monde*, November 1, 1975.

34. *Ya* (Madrid), September 11, 1975.

35. "It was a question of avoiding a war," Colonel Eduardo Blanco, the Director General de Promoción del Sahara, later remarked, in testimony to the Cortes on March 13, 1978. "It would have been Europe's last colonial war and confronted us with the possibility of provoking unthinkable reactions in the Arab world." (*El País*, March 14, 1978.) The secretary-general of the colonial administration in Western Sahara, Rodríguez de Viguri, claimed on March 13, 1978, during the same Cortes hearings, that Spanish businesses with interests in Morocco pressured the government to come to terms with King Hassan. He cited, in particular, the Banco Ibérico and the Ocus company. (*El País*, March 14, 1978.) See also Rodríguez de Viguri's interview with *Diario-16*, September 21, 1977.

36. The letter was published two and a half years later, on March 15, 1978, in *El País*.

37. Testimony in the Cortes, before the Comisión de Exteriores del Congreso, March 16, 1978 (*El País*, March 17, 1978).

38. *La Provincia*, October 22, 1975.

39. *AP*, dispatch from Marrakesh, October 23, 1975.

40. *Le Monde*, October 26–27, 1975.

41. Testimony in the Cortes, before the Comisión de Exteriores del Congreso, March 14, 1978 (*El País*, March 15, 1978).

42. UPI, dispatch from Madrid, October 28, 1975.

43. *Lamalif* (Rabat), No. 74, November 4, 1975.

44. *Congressional Presentation, Security Assistance Program, FY 1980* (Washington, 1979).

45. *Le Nouvel Observateur* (Paris), No. 591, March 8–14, 1976.

46. Hassan II, *op. cit.*, p. 58.

47. *Africa News* (Durham, N.C.), November 2, 1979. General Walters has been unwilling to disclose the precise nature of his mission. "It would look like the King of Morocco and the King of Spain are pawns of the U.S., and that wouldn't be in anybody's interest," he told *Africa News*.

48. *La Provincia*, October 29, 1975.

49. *La Provincia*, October 29, 1975, and October 31, 1975.

50. *ABC* (Madrid), November 4, 1975.

51. *La Provincia*, October 31, 1975; *AFP*, dispatch from El-Ayoun, November 4, 1975; *Hoja de Lunes* (Madrid), November 10, 1975; *Informaciones* (Madrid), November 13, 1975.

52. *Le Monde*, October 24, 1975. On October 18, the Istiqlal Party had declared that it would pursue "the combat for the liberation of the usurped Moroccan territories, in the north, as in the east and to the south, of the country." (*El Moudjahid*, October 29, 1975.)

53. *El Moudjahid*, October 30, 1975, October 31, 1975, and November 1, 1975.

54. UN Security Council Resolution 377, October 22, 1975, in UN Document S/11863, October 31, 1975.

55. Report of the Secretary-General in Pursuance of Security Council Resolution 377 (1975), UN Document S/11863, October 31, 1975.

56. Testimony in the Cortes, before the Comisión de Exteriores del Congreso, March 14, 1978 (*El País*, March 25, 1978).

57. *El País, November 7, 1976.*

58. *New York Times*, November 3, 1975.

59. Letter dated 1 November 1975 from the Representative of Spain to the President of the Security Council, UN Document S/11864, November 1, 1975.

60. UN Security Council, Provisional Verbatim Record of the 1852nd Meeting, UN Document S/PV.1852, November 2, 1975.

61. *La Provincia*, October 31, 1975.

62. *El Moudjahid*, November 8, 1975, and November 10, 1975.

63. *Hoja de Lunes*, November 10, 1975; Jamil Moulahid, "Les sahraouis et le phosphate," *Esprit*, No. 4, April 1976, p. 800.

64. *El Moudjahid*, November 4, 1975; *May 20* (Arabic edition, Polisario Front), No. 25, November 1975.

65. *El Eco de Canarias*, October 23, 1975.

66. UN Security Council Resolution 379 (1975), November 2, 1975, in UN Document S/11874, November 8, 1975.

67. Report of the Secretary-General in Pursuance of Security Council Resolution 379 (1975), November 8, 1975, UN Document S/11874, November 8, 1975.

68. Hassan II, *op. cit.*, pp. 31–32.

69. *UPI*, November 6, 1975; *AFP*, November 6, 1975; *AP*, November 6, 1975; *Time* (New York), November 17, 1975.

70. *Pueblo*, November 7, 1975.

71. *Washington Post*, November 8, 1975; *Reuters*, November 8, 1975.

72. *El Moudjahid*, November 6, 1975.

73. UN Security Council, Provisional Verbatim Record of the 1854th Meeting, UN Document S/PV.1854, November 6, 1975.

74. Official communiqué concerning the 1853rd meeting of the Security Council, UN Document S/11869, November 6, 1975. See also Franck, *loc. cit.*, p. 714.

75. Note by the President of the Security Council, UN Document S/11868, November 6, 1975.

76. Letter dated 6 November 1975 from the Representative of Spain to the President of the Security Council, UN Document S/11867, November 6, 1975.

77. UN Security Council Resolution 380 (1975), November 6, 1975, in *Yearbook of the United Nations*, 1975, p. 187.

78. Testimony in the Cortes, before the Comisión de Exteriores del Congreso, March 15, 1978 (*El País*, March 16, 1978); letter dated 6 November 1975 from the Representative of Spain to the President of the Security Council, UN Document S/11871, November 6, 1975; *New York Times*, November 8, 1975; *Washington Post*, November 8, 1975; Testimony of Adolfo Martín Gamero (then Spain's ambassador to Morocco) in the Cortes, before the Comisión de Exteriores del Congreso, March 14, 1978 (*El País*, March 15, 1978).

79. Hassan II, *op. cit.*, p. 35.

80. *New York Times*, November 11, 1975; *Arriba* (Madrid), November 11, 1975.

81. *El Moudjahid*, November 9, 1975.

82. *Le Nouvel Observateur*, November 7, 1977.

83. *Europe-Outremer* (Paris), No. 519, April 1973.

84. *Jeune Afrique* (Paris), November 13, 1975; *New York Times*, November 13, 1975.

85. *Informaciones*, November 13, 1975.

86. *El Moudjahid*, November 11, 1975; *Washington Post*, November 11, 1975.

87. José María de Areilza, the Count of Motrico, who succeeded Cortina y Mauri as foreign minister in December 1975, said later, in testimony to the Cortes on March 14, 1978, that he had urged Arias Navarro to publish the accords but he "flatly and systematically refused" to do so. (*El País*, March 15, 1978.)

88. Declaration of Principles on Western Sahara by Spain, Morocco and Mauritania, Annex III to UN Document S/11880, 19 November 1975, in *Security Council Official Records*, 30th Year, Supplement for October, November and December 1975, p. 41.

89. Cited in Emilio Menéndez del Valle, *Sahara español: una descolonización tardía* (Editorial Cuadernos para el Diálogo, Madrid, 1975), p. 28.

90. *Le Monde*, November 19, 1975.

91. Hassan II, *op. cit.*, p. 63.

92. Acta de las conversaciones mantenidas, de una parte, entre delegaciones del Reino de Marruecos y la República Islámica de Mauritania, y de otra, de España, a propósito de los aspectos económicos derivados de la transferencia de la administración del Sahara, in *Interviú* (Madrid), January 26, 1978, p. 16.

93. *Interviú*, January 26, 1978.

94. *Wall Street Journal* (New York), July 16, 1976.

95. Ramón Criado, *Sahara, pasión y muerte de un sueño colonial* (Ruedo Ibérico, Paris, 1977), p. 247.

96. Hassan II, *Conférence de presse de S.M. Hassan II sur la Marche Verte et le Sahara* (Ministére d'Etat chargé de l'information, Rabat, 1975), p. 16.

97. *Le Monde*, November 21, 1975.

98. Testimony in the Cortes, before the Comisión de Exteriores del Congreso, March 13, 1978 (*El País*, March 14, 1978). As late as the day before the signing of the Madrid accords, Gómez de Salazar had stated in El-Ayoun that "our withdrawal should be put into effect after a referendum on self-determination and the creation of a Saharawi army capable of defending the territory's integrity."

99. *El Moudjahid*, November 16–17, 1975.

100. Position of the Algerian Government, Annex to Letter dated 19 November 1975 from the Representative of Algeria to the Secretary-General, UN Document S/11881, November 19, 1975.

101. Interview in *L'Humanité* (Paris), November 21, 1975.

Saharawi women in Polisario camp, 1979 CHRISTINE SPENGLER, SYGMA

Koranic school in Saharawi refugee camp CHRISTINE SPENGLER, SYGMA

A Saharawi elder (from Daora) Y. NAGATA, UNITED NATIONS

A ritual tea ceremony in the desert TAMI HULTMAN

Saharawis

Saharawi refugees in camp near Tindouf

Polisario guerrillas
TAMI HULTMAN

*Saharawi women and
children* Y. NAGATA,
UNITED NATIONS

*Saharawi child in an Algerian
refugee camp* UNITED NATIONS HIGH
COMMISSIONER FOR REFUGEES

Literacy class in a Saharawi refugee camp, near Tindouf TAMI HULTMAN

A black Polisario guerrilla. Polisario abolished the last vestiges of slavery TAMI HULTMAN

21

Partition or a Saharawi Republic?

T HE TRIPARTITE TRANSITIONAL GOVERNMENT took office within a fortnight
of the Madrid accords and at once began preparing the transfer of administrative powers from Spain to Morocco and Mauritania. By mid-January, all
Spanish troops had been evacuated to the Canary Islands, leaving the main towns
in Moroccan or Mauritanian hands. However, many of the smaller settlements
and former Spanish outposts in the more remote parts of the country were occupied for several months by Polisario before finally being seized by Moroccan
and Mauritanian forces, sometimes after heavy fighting. By the spring of 1976 the
majority of Saharawis had fled the country, settling in refugee camps in the Tindouf region of Algeria.

On November 22, 1975, eight days after the Madrid accords, King Hassan ap-
pointed the director of his Royal Cabinet, Ahmed Bensouda, to be Morocco's
deputy governor of Western Sahara. Three days later, Bensouda arrived in El-
Ayoun, after traveling overland from Tarfaya with Colonel Dlimi and a hundred
Moroccan officials in the first Moroccan military convoy to reach the Western
Saharan capital. On November 27, Mauritania's minister of labor and public
works, Abdellahi Ould Sheikh, followed, to join the tripartite administration as
Mauritania's deputy governor, and later the same day he joined Bensouda and
General Gómez de Salazar for their first working session in the governor-general's
office. With Spanish tanks patrolling the streets and the Saharawi suburbs ringed
with troops and barbed wire, the Saharawi population in El-Ayoun could do little
to show their dismay at the turn of events.[1]

Only a few hundred Moroccan troops arrived in El-Ayoun with Bensouda and
Dlimi on November 25. However, the next day, Dlimi met Gómez de Salazar to
discuss the timetable for the transfer of Spanish military bases and barracks to
Moroccan forces. On November 27, a column of Moroccan troops reached Smara,
and five thousand Moroccan troops finally entered El-Ayoun on December 11,
though Moroccan positions in the capital were machine-gunned by a Polisario

guerrilla group a day later.[2] The FAR took control of Bou-Craa during the last week of December, as its Spanish garrison was withdrawn to El-Ayoun.[3]. Moroccan soldiers replaced the Spanish troops guarding El-Ayoun airport on December 28, and the last Spanish troops were evacuated from the capital to the Canary Islands on January 8. Four days later, the Spanish military presence in the country came to a complete end when the remaining garrison in Villa Cisneros was evacuated.[4] About 150 Spanish officials stayed in the territory to complete the transfer of government departments and services to Moroccan and Mauritanian civil servants, though Gómez de Salazar, who had found his new responsibility for overseeing the transition to Moroccan-Mauritanian rule singularly disagreeable, had already left at the end of December, leaving Colonel Rodríguez de Viguri as head of the transitional administration.[5] He had equally little enthusiasm for the job and resigned on January 27, bequeathing his responsibilities to another Spanish officer, Colonel Rafael de Valdés Iglesias, who supervised the final stages of the handover, which was completed at the end of February.

Polisario was powerless to prevent the Moroccan-Mauritanian occupation of the towns. Though it had enjoyed overwhelming popular support since at least the beginning of 1975, only a few hundred men had been trained and organized into guerrilla units by October. Then, almost all the Saharawi soldiers of the Tropas Nómadas and the Policía Territorial, about a thousand well-trained men in all, joined the Polisario forces when they were discharged from their units at Gómez de Salazar's orders, at the end of October. Together with Polisario's earliest guerrilla recruits, they formed the core of its Saharawi People's Liberation Army (SPLA). They harassed the Moroccan and Mauritanian forces and often put up brave and determined resistance to defend the settlements that they initially controlled, but they were ultimately unable to hold fixed positions against the Moroccans and Mauritanians, who were infinitely better armed and had mastery of the skies. Their main priorities, however, were to organize the thousands of men who were now volunteering to join the guerrilla forces and to evacuate and defend the refugees streaming out of the towns. In this, they received invaluable assistance from the Algerian government, which, besides providing the guerrillas with bases, training and equipment, briefly sent units of its own army into Western Sahara to help transport the refugees to safety in Algerian territory.

The weaker of Polisario's new adversaries was Mauritania, which had only about three thousand troops in its army, a further two thousand in paramilitary units and a few ancient Britten-Norman Defenders in its air force.[6] So, even before Ould Daddah had sent any of his troops into Western Sahara, Polisario began raiding across the Mauritanian border, in the hope, perhaps, of dissuading the Mauritanian government from acting upon its signature to the Madrid accords. The Mauritanian post at Ain Ben Tili, on the Western Saharan frontier, was attacked on December 7, and raids followed two days later at Bir Moghrein and Inal, two settlements in Mauritania's remote northeast.[7] However, Mauritanian troops finally crossed the Western Saharan frontier during the third week of December. They occupied La Guera, near Nouadhibou, on December 19, after a fierce battle with about a hundred Polisario guerrillas who had barricaded themselves in the town's police barracks and two factories. The next day, about 140 miles to the east, another column of Mauritanian troops succeeded in evicting Polisario from Tichla. However, it was not until January 11 that Mauritanian troops succeeded in dislodging a force of two hundred Polisario guerrillas from Argoub, the small town facing Villa Cisneros, then still under Spanish occupation, across the Río de Oro bay.[8] In fact, the guerrillas' resistance to the invading Mauritanian forces and their diversionary attacks across the border into northern Mauritania slowed down the Mauritanian advance to such an extent that Ould Daddah's troops almost failed to reach Villa Cisneros, the main town promised him by Hassan, before the January 12 deadline set by the Spanish for the evacuation of their last two thousand troops from the city. Fearful that Polisario might seize control of Villa Cisneros, the country's third largest city, and declare independence there, Colonel Dlimi rushed Moroccan troops south from El-Ayoun. They arrived on January 9 and immediately began hoisting Moroccan flags in the city's streets, to Ould Daddah's consternation. Mauritanian troops finally broke through to the city from Argoub on January 12, just as the last Spanish troops were departing, and King Hassan reassured Ould Daddah that it would become part of the Mauritanian zone.[9] Polisario was then dislodged from Aoussert, a small administrative center protected by craggy black mountains 125 miles southeast of Villa Cisneros, but a guerrilla force almost immediately recaptured it and was not driven out again until after a long battle between January 29 and February 8.[10]

Mauritania's hold over the territory's southern towns and settlements was to remain extremely precarious. Moroccan troops had to remain in Villa Cisneros and Polisario guerrillas had a free run in the desert hinterland. Most alarming of all for Ould Daddah, however, was Polisario's ability to go on attacking targets within Mauritania itself. The Mauritanian post at Ain Ben Tili had come under renewed attack in mid-January, forcing Ould Daddah to call in Moroccan air support for his troops. For the first time in the war, the Moroccan air force lost one of its aircraft, a U.S.-built Northrop F-5 jet fighter-bomber, near Ain Ben Tili on January 21, and three days later the post fell to the guerrillas. It was not recaptured until February 14.[11] More ominous still for Ould Daddah, Polisario had begun to strike at the hub of Mauritania's iron-based economy. The power station that feeds the Zouerate iron mines had been subjected to a mortar bombardment on December 29, and on April 19 a guerrilla group raided the iron-mining company's railway from Zouerate to the port at Nouadhibou.[12] Over the following two years, the railway was to become one of Polisario's favored targets.

Farther north the guerrillas staged repeated hit-and-run attacks against Moroccan convoys and positions, despite devoting most of their resources to the huge refugee evacuation operation. During an ambush of a Moroccan convoy traveling between Hagounia and El-Ayoun on December 23, they captured two French citizens, and on April 24 they succeeded in lobbing several mortar rounds into the center of El-Ayoun.[13] By the end of January, besides, they had put the Bou-Craa mining industry out of action. Fosbucraa's sixty-two-mile-long conveyor belt and the power pylons running alongside it between the company's coastal power station and the mines, where all equipment is electrically powered, were as vulnerable to guerrilla attack as the Zouerate-Nouadhibou railway. Polisario staged its first attack on the conveyor belt since the Madrid accords on December 11, and another raid, on one of its control stations, was reported in the Spanish press on January 25.[14] The conveyor belt was not to operate again for more than six years, and though small quantities of previously stockpiled ore were trucked to the coast and exported in 1976–79, mining remained at a complete standstill from 1976 to 1982, and in 1976 Fosbucraa declared a loss of 1,772 million pesetas.[15]

However, Polisario's principal preoccupation during this early stage of the war was to assure the safety of the thousands of its supporters fleeing the cities. On January 7, 1976, the International Committee of the Red Cross and the League of Red Cross Societies announced in Geneva that forty thousand Saharawis had fled their homes. Half had reached Algeria, where they were squatting, destitute, on the Hammada, where the winter nights were fearfully cold. The rest, who were in an even worse plight, had taken refuge in remote parts of Western Sahara that had not yet been reached by the Moroccan and Mauritanian forces.[16] By the end of February, Spanish journalists in El-Ayoun were reporting that only five to six thousand Saharawis remained in the capital, barely more than a fifth of the twenty-nine thousand who had been registered there during the 1974 census. The Saharawi barrios of Colominas, Zemla and Jatarrambla were starting to look like ghost towns.[17]

One of the staging points on the exodus route to Algeria was Amgala, a waterpoint in Saguia el-Hamra about 180 miles from the Algerian frontier. Several hundred Algerian troops were there, helping Polisario to bring food and medicines to the refugees and ferry them out to Algeria, when, on January 29, a Moroccan force attacked and seized the locality, killing dozens of Algerian soldiers and capturing another ninety-nine.[18] The incident could easily have sparked off an all-out war between Morocco and Algeria, but President Boumedienne decided to withdraw all Algerian troops from Western Sahara at once. Thereafter, Algeria played no direct part in the war and limited its military support for Polisario to the provision of arms, bases and training. However, on February 14, less than three weeks after the Moroccan capture of Amgala, Polisario guerrillas massacred a large number of the three hundred Moroccan soldiers billeted there, and Hassan immediately laid the blame on Algeria. On February 15 he wrote to Boumedienne, accusing the Algerian army of "causing dozens of victims among my sons and the combatants of my country."[19] The charges were immediately denied in Algiers. "There is no unit of the National People's Army on Western Saharan territory," Boumedienne's government declared on February 16. "International observers can verify this on the spot. On January 29, when battalions of the Moroccan army staged a treacherous attack on the units that had the task of taking provisions of food and medicines to the Saharan refugees in Amgala, Algeria resolved not to yield to provocation and to avoid a comprehensive confrontation between the two sister peoples."[20]

Despite their victory at Amgala and their frequent hit-and-run raids elsewhere in the territory, the guerrillas could not halt the FAR's relentless advance toward the last of the formerly Spanish outposts in the eastern Saguia el-Hamra and the Zemmour massif. Moving in a northeasterly arc from Amgala, after the first battle there, toward the Algerian frontier, Moroccan troops successively seized Tifariti on February 5, Bir Lehlou on February 8 and Mahbes on February 12.[21] A few days later, Moroccan aircraft discovered two large concentrations of refugees, each numbering at least ten thousand, at Guelta Zemmour, the largest *guelta* in the territory, surrounded by mountains, about twenty-two miles west of the Mauritanian border, and at Oum Dreiga, farther south. Scores of refugees were killed in bombing raids, which included the use of napalm, over the following two months, and a senior Polisario leader, Bouela Ahmed Zine, who had been supervising the refugee evacuation from Guelta Zemmour, died in its vicinity on April 24, five days after the former Spanish base there had been captured by Moroccan troops.[22] However, by then most of the refugees had been evacuated from Oum Dreiga and the Zemmour massif in convoys of trucks to Algeria.[23] Between February and April, therefore, the number of refugees in the Tindouf region grew rapidly, and when the Algerian government presented a memorandum on relief needs to the executive committee of the UNHCR the following October, it reported that fifty thousand Saharawi refugees had settled in its territory. They were living in eleven scattered camps.[24]

Many of the refugees were undernourished and in very poor health upon their arrival in Tindouf. Some had spent several months in the open, without proper tents and with little food, and had witnessed the Moroccan bombing raids. Conditions in the camps on the Hammada, a barren plain that is often swept by gale-force winds, were very harsh, and the refugees were extremely susceptible to disease. The children suffered most. In 1976, the UNHCR estimated, a quarter of the babies were dying before reaching the age of three months, and when a measles epidemic swept through the camps in the spring of 1976, almost a thousand children died.[25] Algerian first-aid teams were rushed to Tindouf and eventually immunized all the refugees against cholera and the children against diphtheria, tetanus and polio.

The sudden influx of so many refugees posed enormous logistical problems to the Algerian government and relief agencies, if only because the camps were sited in the middle of the desert, more than twelve hundred miles from Algiers, and roads were poor. Very few of the refugees had been able to bring any livestock with them and in any case conditions in the Tindouf region were not propitious for either animal husbandry or agriculture on a scale that could provide more than a small fraction of the refugees' food needs. Almost all supplies, therefore, had to be brought in by truck from a huge distance. Even water had to be supplied to many of the camps by cistern-trucks since there were often no nearby fresh-water wells. Firewood had to be fetched from about two hundred miles away, and canvas tents had to be distributed to most of the refugees families since very few had been able to bring the traditional *khaimat* with them.

In Geneva, the League of Red Cross Societies launched an emergency appeal for the Saharawi refugees in December 1975 which raised 10.9 million Swiss francs. For its part, the UNHCR had contributed relief totalling $700,000 by October 1976.[26] However, when it became clear that the Saharawi refugee problem would not be resolved quickly, the Red Cross, which is normally able to tackle only short-term disasters, was not prepared to maintain its assistance. It closed its appeal in July 1976, and so, at Algerian request, the UNHCR launched a long-term relief program the following October, appealing to the world's governments to contribute $5.7 million and ten thousand tons of food, sufficient to cover the needs of fifty thousand refugees for one year.[27] The response was disappointing, however, and only $1.2 million was raised during the whole of 1977.[28] By December 1978, total contributions had still reached only $3.1 million, plus 2,140 tons of food.[29] The main responsibility for feeding, clothing and sheltering the refugees therefore fell on the Algerian government and the Algerian Red Crescent which channeled their aid through Polisario's own Saharawi Red Crescent, which had been founded on the eve of the Madrid accords, in October 1975. Despite the paucity of international aid and the continuing, though slower, growth in refugee numbers after the spring of 1976, conditions in the Tindouf camps had improved markedly by 1977–78. Administered by Polisario, rather than the Algerian authorities, the camps were acknowledged by foreign charities and relief organizations to be superbly organized. Divided eventually into about twenty-two camps, each known as a *daira*, or district, the refugees elected their own "daira popular councils," which coordinated the work of specialized committees for food distribution, education, health care, crafts and justice. Clinics were established in each *daira*, a "national hospital" was built for more serious cases, and students were sent abroad for medical training. Several schools were built, to provide primary education for several thousand children, an ambitious adult literacy campaign was launched, particularly for the women, very few of whom had ever attended school, and about forty-five hundred Saharawi pupils had been admitted to Algerian secondary schools by 1977.[30]

Just as the refugee exodus from the towns was beginning, after the establishment of the tripartite transitional administration, the two most prominent Saharawi defectors to the Moroccan camp, Khatri Ould Said Ould el-Joumani and Khalihenna Ould Rashid, returned to El-Ayoun, to try to convince their former colleagues in the Djemaa and the PUNS to throw in their lot with Morocco. The Madrid accords had committed Spain, Morocco and Mauritania to respecting "the views of the Saharan population, expressed through the Djemaa," and so the assembly's sheikhs were assiduously lobbied and wooed so that they would vote to approve the plans for partition. To the Moroccan and Mauritanian governments' alarm, however, only 32 of the Djemaa's 102 members showed up when a special session of the assembly was convened on November 29, 1975, to introduce the new Moroccan and Mauritanian deputy governors.[31] As the "unity conference" held at Ain Ben Tili on October 12 had revealed, most of the previously Spanish-aligned sheikhs had sunk their old differences with Polisario as a result of the PUNS' disintegration, Spain's brief summer entente with Polisario and the pressure from their kin to unite with the guerrilla movement to meet the threat from Morocco. So, on November 28, the day before the inquorate Djemaa meeting in El-Ayoun, 67 of the Assembly's members and over 60 tribal sheikhs, among them three members of the Cortes, Baba Ould Hasseina, Souilem Ould Abdellahi and Ahmed Ould Brahim Ould el-Bashir, met under Polisario's auspices 140 miles way, at Guelta Zemmour, and signed a proclamation that confounded the Moroccan-Mauritanian plans to have the Djemaa approve partition. "The only way of consulting the Saharan people is by allowing it to decide its own future and to obtain its independence," it declared. "Consequently, the General Assembly, not being democratically elected by the Saharan people, cannot decide upon the self-determination of the Saharan people." So, to avoid its utilization by the "enemies" of the Saharawi people, "the General Assembly decides, by unanimous vote of its members present, upon its final dissolution." It went on to declare "unconditional support for the Frente Polisario, the sole and legitimate representative of the Saharan people," pledged to "continue the struggle for the defense of our homeland until complete independence is achieved and our territorial integrity is guaranteed" and set up a Provisional Saharawi National Council, which, with forty-one members, seemed to be modeled on the old "council of 40," the *ait arbain*.[32] Its membership and first president, M'hammed Ould Ziou, a veteran of the 1957–58 insurgency and a founder-member of Polisario, were selected at a subsequent meeting of Polisario leaders and sheikhs at Mahbes, then still under Polisario control, on December 3. Three days later the Djemaa's dissolution and replacement by the new pro-Polisario council were announced by Baba Ould Hasseina at a press conference at the Hotel Saint Georges in Algiers.[33]

However, the alliance between the Polisario guerrilla leaders and the traditionalist elders of the former Djemaa was uneasy. Many of the sheikhs resented being eclipsed by the young, university-educated guerrilla leaders, most of whom, including El-Ouali, were still only in their twenties, and were suspicious of their egalitarian, reforming zeal. Some had business interests in the Moroccan or Mauritanian occupied towns and began to doubt the guerrillas' capacity to withstand the Moroccan *anschluss*. So some of the signatories of the Proclamation of Guelta Zemmour drifted away from the Polisario camps and returned to the towns, to make their peace with Morocco or Mauritania. For example, Ahmed Ould Brahim Ould el-Bashir, a member of the Djemaa since 1967 and of the Cortes since 1970, a sheikh of the Izarguien and prominent trader, who had been at the Guelta Zemmour and Mahbes assemblies and then met President Boumedienne on December 16, returned to El-Ayoun and pledged allegiance to King Hassan on January 14.[34] An attractive option for some, especially those from the south, was to align with Mauritania. Two days after the Madrid accords, the PPM set up a Front de Libération et du Rattachement du Sahara à la Mauritanie (FLRSM) to organize anti-Polisario Saharawis in the south and so facilitate its integration into Mauritania. The most prominent of its recruits were three longtime allies of the Spanish colonial administration, Mohammed Lamine Ould Horomtalla, a former leader of the PUNS, and two members of the Cortes, Saila Ould Abeida, who had been president of the Djemaa from 1967 to 1971, and Souilem Ould Abdellahi, the mayor of Dakhla, who ended his brief flirtation with Polisario shortly after signing the Proclamation of Guelta Zemmour.[35]

However, though these defections finally enabled the Moroccan and Mauritanian officials in Western Sahara to arrange a rump meeting of the Djemaa at the end of February, the assembly had lost such credibility by then and conditions in the towns had become so inauspicious for a free vote, that its approval of the Moroccan-Mauritanian partition plans was not accepted as a valid act of self-determination by the UN, or even by Spain. In New York, the UN General Assembly had adopted two confusedly divergent resolutions on December 10, though both upheld the Saharawis' right to self-determination. The first, Resolution 3458A, repeated the traditional UN views on Western Sahara's decolonization and requested "the government of Spain, as the administering power, in accordance with the observations and conclusions of the Visiting Mission and in accordance with the advisory opinion of the International Court of Justice, to take immediately all necessary measures, in consultation with all the parties concerned and interested, so that all Saharans originating in the territory may exercise fully and freely, under United Nations supervision, their inalienable right to self-determination.''[36] Eighty-eight states, including Algeria and most third-world countries, voted for the resolution, and none voted against it, but forty-one, including Spain, abstained and both the Moroccan and Mauritanian delegations to the UN absented themselves from the vote. A rival text, Resolution 3458B, ''took note'' of the Madrid accords, to which Resolution 3458A made no reference, but only narrowly passed through the General Assembly by fifty-six votes, including Spain, Morocco and Mauritania, to forty-two, with thirty-four abstentions, even though its sponsors had included a clause, to secure support, requesting ''the interim administration to take all necessary steps to ensure that all the Saharan populations originating in the territory will be able to exercise their inalienable right to self-determination through free consultations organized with the assistance of a representative of the United Nations appointed by the Secretary-General.''[37]

Since both resolutions reaffirmed the Western Saharans' right to self-determination and required the UN to supervise (3458A) or send a representative to help organize (3458B) its exercise, Waldheim requested Sweden's UN ambassador, Olof Rydbeck, to make an on-the-spot appraisal of conditions in the territory and recommend how these mandates should be implemented. Rydbeck toured Western Sahara between February 7 and 12, visiting El-Ayoun, Smara and Villa Cisneros, but he was so struck by the scale of the Moroccan military presence, the repressive political atmosphere, the exodus of refugees and the state of war between the Polisario guerrillas and the Moroccan and Mauritanian forces in the territory that he reported back to Waldheim that a genuine consultation of Saharawi opinion had become impossible.[38]

The Count of Motrico, José María de Areilza, who had replaced Cortina y Mauri at the Spanish foreign ministry in December, was told of Rydbeck's findings when he met Waldheim a few days later, on February 23, in Geneva. Like Waldheim, Areilza believed that it had now become impossible to accept a vote at a rump meeting of the Djemaa as a genuine and representative expression of Saharawi views. The rapid escalation of the fighting in Western Sahara and the guerrillas' close alliance with Algeria, with which the Spanish government was anxious to conserve its important economic relations, had made Arias Navarro and Areilza wary of endorsing an imposed Mauritanian-Moroccan partition, and so, while completing the arrangements for the transfer of administrative powers to Rabat and Nouakchott, they played on the ambiguities of the Madrid accords to deny that Spain was transferring sovereignty, which, they claimed, was vested solely in the Saharawi people. It was a convenient, if hypocritical, posture for a government that wanted to extract Spain from the Saharan quagmire as quickly and pacifically as possible while keeping open its long-term options and avoiding a serious rupture of relations with any of the states of the Maghreb.

The rump session of the Djemaa was held only in the nick of time before the February 28 deadline for Spain's final withdrawal. It was not until February 24 and 25, respectively, that the Moroccan and Mauritanian governments were able to invite Waldheim to send a UN representative to attend the meeting, which was scheduled for February 26. Meanwhile, the Spanish government wrote to Waldheim on February 25 to inform him that Spain would "definitively terminate its presence in the territory tomorrow," two days ahead of its deadline, and that Valdés Iglesias would "inform the Djemaa of this decision" when it met the same day, but it was careful to add that the Djemaa meeting "does not constitute the popular consultation provided for in the Madrid agreements of 14 November 1975 and in General Assembly Resolution 3458B (XXX) unless the necessary conditions are met, including, in particular, the presence of a representative of the United Nations appointed by you in accordance with paragraph 4 of the above-mentioned resolution."[39] It was, of course, too late by then for the UN to dispatch a representative to El-Ayoun in time for the next day's meeting. Furthermore, Waldheim informed the Moroccan government on February 26 that the "essential conditions" for the exercise of self-determination had "not been fulfilled" and so, "even if time had permitted," the designation of a UN representative to attend the Djemaa meeting would not "constitute fulfillment" of the mandates in Resolutions 3458A and 3458B.[40] So no UN representative attended the meeting. Valdées Iglesias did take part, to announce the formal ending of Spain's ninety-one-year colonial presence in the Sahara, but the same day, in New York, Spain's ambassador to the UN, Jaime de Piniés, submitted to Waldheim a memorandum from the Spanish government stating that "the persistence of circumstances beyond its control has made it impossible thus far to organize the popular consultation provided for in the agreements of 14 November 1975 and in Resolution 3458B (XXX)" and that, though Spain "as of today definitively terminates its presence in the territory of the Sahara," it deemed it necessary to place on record that "the decolonization of Western Sahara will reach its climax when the views of the Saharan population have been validly expressed."[41]

Only 57 of the Djemaa's 102 members attended the February 26 meeting, but they voted unanimously to give "full approval to the decolonization of this territory and its reintegration with Morocco and Mauritania."[42] However, they did not vote on any specific formula for partition. That was formalized two months later, on April 14, when Morocco and Mauritania signed a convention defining their new frontiers. "The frontier between the two countries," it stated, "shall be drawn by a straight line, leading from the point of intersection of the Atlantic coast with the 24th parallel north to the point of intersection of the 23rd parallel north with the 13th meridian west," on Mauritania's former border with Western Sahara. It then followed the old border northward, as far as the Algerian frontier.[43] Imposed from without, against the will of the Saharawi population, it was as arbitrary as the borders set by the Franco-Spanish conventions of 1900, 1904, and 1912. Morocco got the lion's share of the carve-up, receiving the two largest towns, El-Ayoun and Smara, and, most important of all, the phosphate mines at Bou-Craa, though they had already ground to a halt. With an additional 68,340 square miles, Morocco's land area expanded by more than a third and its coastline was extended southward by 375 miles. By contrast, Mauritania received a virtually resourceless slab of desert in the far south, covering about 34,750 square miles, though this did include Villa Cisneros, which was henceforth known by its old Arabic name of Dakhla, and its coastline of just over 285 miles was rich in fishing resources. Under a second convention signed by Morocco and Mauritania on April 14, regarding the exploitation of Western Sahara's economic resources, Morocco promised Mauritania a share in Fosbucraa's equity, in which Morocco's OCP had already acquired a 65 percent stake, but this pledge was never put into effect.[44]

Meanwhile, on February 27, one day after the rump Djemaa meeting and the formal termination of Spanish administration, the Provisional Saharawi National Council proclaimed the founding of an independent Saharawi state, to avoid a juridical *fait accompli* being created by the Spanish withdrawal and the Moroccan-Mauritanian occupation of the towns. At a nighttime ceremony near Bir Lehlou, in the eastern Saguia el-Hamra, attended by thousands of Saharawi guerrillas and refugees and a party of thirty foreign journalists, the council's president, M'hammed Ould Zion, read out a proclamation announcing "the birth of a free, independent, sovereign state, ruled by an Arab, national, democratic system of unionist, progressive orientation and of Muslim religion, named the Saharan Arab Democratic Republic."[45] The new republic's green, red, white and black flag, with Islamic crescent and star, was then strung up on a makeshift pole, as a detachment of guerrillas presented arms.

The same day, El-Ouali made a final plea to Mauritania. In a letter to Ould Daddah he warned that Morocco's occupation of Western Sahara would revive its appetite for Mauritania too, and recalling his old proposal of a Western Saharan-Mauritanian federation, he argued that "logic and truth mean that the brotherly Mauritanian people must be at the side of the Saharawi people, given the objective links between them, whether they be historical or racial links or also the inevitable unity of interests and destiny." A week later, on March 6, he wrote also to King Hassan, demanding the "recognition of our independent state." He even offered the king a share in Western Sahara's phosphate wealth. "Do not have any fear about our phosphates; we are ready to cooperate, even if we give more than we get from it."[46] But events had by now gone much too far for these appeals to have any impact.

The SADR's first government was appointed by the Provisional Saharawi National Council on March 4. Mohammed Lamine Ould Ahmed, one of El-Ouali's closest collaborators since their days together at Mohammed V University, was named prime minister. Ibrahim Ghali, who had been commanding Polisario's guerrilla forces since the earliest clashes with the Spanish army, became defense minister; and Ibrahim Hakim, a Reguibi who had been raised in Mauritania and worked in Mauritania's diplomatic service, was appointed foreign minister.[47] On February 28, Madagascar became the first state to recognize the SADR. Burundi followed on March 1 and Algeria on March 6. Morocco and Mauritania immediately broke off diplomatic relations with Algeria in reprisal. By the end of April, ten countries, nine of them African, had recognized the new republic.

With the capture of Guelta Zemmour on April 19, the Moroccan and Mauritanian armies had occupied virtually all the settlements and outposts once garrisoned by the Spanish. On April 26, Dlimi was rewarded by Hassan with a promotion to the rank of colonel-major and relieved of his Saharan command.[48] But, though Dlimi had superficially completed his mission, the real challenge still lay ahead. As his successor in the Sahara, Colonel Abdenbi Britel, was to discover, the war with Polisario was still only in its first stages. The guerrillas became masters of the desert and, though they could not seize and hold any of the towns, they proved superb desert fighters, combining the tradition of the *ghazzi* with modern weaponry and equipment to ambush convoys and make lightning raids on Moroccan defense positions. However, it was Mauritania which, over the next two years, was to bear the brunt of Polisario's attacks. The guerrillas knew from the start that the Ould Daddah regime was the weak link in the enemy chain, and as soon as their emergency refugee evacuation operation had been completed, by the end of April 1976, they went on the offensive by carrying the war deep into Mauritanian territory, in the manner of their grandfathers, who had raided hundreds of miles, as far as Trarza and the Hodh, to fall upon the French and their allies before the pacification of 1934. This time, the Western Saharawis would have the requisite leadership and weaponry to win.

NOTES

1. *Informaciones* (Madrid), November 25, 1975, and November 26, 1975; *Reuters*, dispatch from El-Ayoun, November 27, 1975.
2. *Washington Post*, December 12, 1975; *AFP*, dispatch from El-Ayoun, December 12, 1975.
3. *Africa Contemporary Record*, Vol. 8, 1975–76, p. B162.
4. *Jeune Afrique* (Paris), January 30, 1976.
5. *The Times* (London), January 1, 1976.
6. *Europe-Outremer* (Paris), No. 549, October 1975, p. 26.
7. Moktar Ould Daddah, *1957–1976: La réunification de la Patrie, un objectif sacré pour le peuple mauritanien* (Ministère d'Etat à l'orientation nationale, Nouakchott, 1976), p. 11.
8. *Le Monde* (Paris), January 30, 1976; *Jeune Afrique*, January 30, 1976, and April 16, 1976; *Washington Post*, January 12, 1976.
9. *Jeune Afrique*, January 30, 1976.
10. *Jeune Afrique*, April 16, 1976.
11. *Washington Post*, January 26, 1976; *Le Monde*, January 30, 1976; *AFP*, dispatch from Nouakchott, February 14, 1976.
12. *Le Monde*, April 29, 1976, and May 3, 1977.
13. Polisario Front, Military Communique 93/76, January 2, 1976; *ABC* (Madrid), April 27, 1976. The two captured Frenchmen were released in October 1976.
14. *Africa Contemporary Record*, Vol. 8, 1975–76, p. B164.
15. *El País* (Madrid), March 16, 1978.
16. *Reuters*, dispatch from Geneva, January 7, 1976.
17. *Cambio-16* (Madrid), February 23, 1976. Since 1975, thousands of Moroccan workers, civil servants and traders, as well as troops, have arrived in El-Ayoun. A random population survey conducted by the author in the El-Ayoun market in October 1978 revealed that about half of those interviewed had arrived from Morocco since 1975.
18. *Reuters*, dispatch from Algiers, January 30, 1976; *Maghreb Arabe Presse* (Rabat), January 30, 1976.
19. *Reuters*, dispatch from Rabat, February 15, 1976.
20. Radio Algiers, February 16, 1976.
21. Radio Rabat, February 9, 1976, and February 12, 1976.
22. Author's interview with Polisario prisoners in El-Ayoun, October 1978; *Algérie Presse Service* (Algiers), March 19, 1976; *Reuters*, dispatch from Algiers, May 21, 1976; *Le Monde* April 23, 1976; Tami Hultman, "The Struggle for Western Sahara," *Issue*, Vol. VII, No. 1, Spring 1977, p. 28; Croissant Rouge Sahraoui, Mémorandum adressé à la Conférence Internationale de la Croix Rouge réunie à Bucarest, Roumanie, 1977, p. 3. Bouela Ould Ahmed Zine had been secretary-general of health, education and social affairs in the first SADR government, appointed on March 4.
23. *Algérie Presse Service*, April 27, 1976.
24. UNHCR Document A/AC.96/534, August 9, 1978.

25. *Aide-memoire, UNHCR Programme of Humanitarian Assistance in the Tindouf Region,* Document HCR/155/42/76, GE.76-10559; *Le Monde,* August 7, 1976.

26. Under agreements signed with the Algerian government on January 22 and May 17, 1976. See *Informations* (Croissant Rouge Algérien), No. 19, 1977, p. 11.

27. *Aide-memoire, UNHCR Programme of Humanitarian Assistance in the Tindouf Region.*

28. UNHCR Document A/AC.96/553, August 9, 1978.

29. Information supplied to the author by the UNHCR.

30. *Informations* (CRA), No. 19, December 1977, p. 13.

31. *Hoja de Lunes* (Madrid), December 1, 1975.

32. *Text of the Historic Document of El Guelta (Western Sahara) Signed on 28 November 1975 by 67 Members of the General Assembly, 3 Saharan Members of the Cortes (Spanish Parliament), the Representatives of the Other Members of the Yema'a and More than 60 Sheikhs and Notables of the Saharan Tribes,* in UN Document S/11902, December 10, 1975.

33. Leila Badia Itani, *Al-Polisario: qaid wa thawra* (Dar al-Masirah, Beirut, 1978), p. 61.

34. Author's interview with Ahmed Ould Brahim Ould el-Bashir, El-Ayoun, June 1978; *Reuters,* dispatch from Rabat, January 14, 1976. For a biography of Ahmed Ould Brahim Ould el-Bashir, see Tony Hodges, *Historical Dictionary of Western Sahara* (Scarecrow Press, Metuchen, N.J., 1982), p. 25.

35. *Remarques Africaines* (Brussels), August 15, 1976; Author's interview with Souilem Ould Abdellahi, Tindouf, November 1979. Souilem Ould Abdellahi rejoined Polisario in February 1979, after the military coup in Nouackchott in July 1978. He then claimed that he had been captured by Mauritanian forces between Tichla and Aoussert in December 1975 and forced to live in eastern Mauritania, and that he had not been present in Dakhla when he was elected there, as a PPM candidate, to the Mauritanian National Assembly, on August 8, 1976.

36. UN General Assembly Resolution 3458A (XXX), in *Yearbook of the United Nations,* Vol. 28, 1975, pp. 188–89.

37. UN General Assembly Resolution 3458B (XXX), in *Yearbook of the United Nations,* Vol. 28, 1975, pp. 189–90.

38. At the end of his visit, Rydbeck even had to escort out of the country a young Saharawi who had succeeded in breaking through Moroccan police lines in El-Ayoun to give him a memorandum from Polisario. Rydbeck's report was so sensitive that it was never published.

39. Cited in Report of the Special Committee, *General Assembly Official Records,* 31st Session, Supplement No. 23, UN Document A/31/23/Rev. 1, Vol. II, p. 215.

40. *Ibid.,* p. 216.

41. Letter dated 26 February 1976 from the Representative of Spain to the Secretary-General, UN Document S/11997, February 26, 1976.

42. *Les provinces marocaines du Sud* (Ministère de l'Information, Rabat), p. 40.

43. Convention relative au tracé de la frontière d'Etat établie entre la République Islamique de Mauritanie et le Royaume du Maroc, April 14, 1976 (*Le Matin du Sahara,* Casablanca, July 15, 1978).

44. Accord de coopération économique entre la République Islamique de Mauritanie et le Royaume du Maroc pour la mise en valeur des territoires sahariens récuperés, April 14, 1976 (*Le Matin du Sahara,* July 15, 1978).

45. *La République arabe sahraouie démocratique* (Polisario Front, 1980), p. 93.

46. The texts of both letters were published in *Jeune Afrique* on April 9, 1976.

47. *Europe-Outremer,* No. 574, November 1977. For a biography of Ibrahim Hakim, see Hodges, *op. cit.,* pp. 179–80.

48. *Reuters,* dispatch from Rabat, April 26, 1976.

22

Mauritania, the Weak Link

MOKHTAR OULD DADDAH had aligned with Morocco in 1974–75 because he had predicted, correctly that Spain would eventually succumb to King King Hassan's bludgeoning and he had calculated that it would be better to join the winning side, get a small part of the spoils and cement his hard-won friendship with Morocco than to watch powerless from the sidelines as Morocco seized the whole of Western Sahara, extending its borders to within striking distance of the Zouerate mining industry on which Mauritania depended for some 80 percent of its exports. But, like Hassan, he had made two fatal misjudgments. He had underestimated Polisario's determination to resist the partition, and despite the personal warning he had received at Bechar, he still thought that he could count on his old friendship with Houari Boumedienne. By joining Morocco in the occupation and division of Western Sahara, he plunged Mauritania into a war that proved unpopular among his people, militarily unwinnable, diplomatically indefensible to most of the country's third world allies and calamitous for its fragile, drought-hit economy.

The Moroccan-Mauritanian partition treaty was ratified by the Mauritanian parliament on April 19, 1976, five days after its signing in Fez. But Ould Daddah casually disregarded a clause in the Mauritanian constitution which required that a change in the country's borders be approved by referendum. Mauritania had received the crumbs of the carve-up—a 34,750 square mile slab of desert in the extreme south with no major known resources except the fish off its coast and only two small towns, Dakhla and La Guera. Administering this annexed zone was to cost far more (162 million ouguiyas in 1977, for example) than the tax revenue it generated (9 million ouguiyas in 1977), while the cost of fighting Polisario to hang on to this wilderness brought Mauritania's economy to the brink of bankruptcy.[1]

To administer his zone of Western Sahara, Ould Daddah appointed a civil governor, Hamoud Ould Abdel-Wedoud, on January 15, 1976, three months before the formal partition. He headed a new *wilaya*, or region, named Tiris el-Gharbia, or Western Tiris, which had its capital at Dakhla and was subdivided into four departments, centered on Dakhla, Aoussert, Tichla and Argoub. In the extreme southeast, however, La Guera and the nearby settlement of Bir Gandous were attached, as a new department, to the existing Region 8 (Nouadhibou). For military purposes, meanwhile, three regional commands were established in Tiris el-Gharbia and northern Mauritania. "Group One" (G1), with headquarters at Aoussert under the command of Colonel Viah Ould Mayouf, who had dislodged the Polisario forces there in February, coordinated military operations in the south of Tiris el-Gharbia and the Nouadhibou region; G2, under Lieutenant-Colonel Ahmed Ould Bouceif, was based at Zouerate and responsible for the whole of northeastern Mauritania, as far as Bir Moghrein and Ain Ben Tili; and G3, commanded by Lieutenant-Colonel Ahmed Salem Ould Sidi, was based at Dakhla.[2]

To give an appearance of democratic legitimacy to the Mauritanian presence in Western Sahara, elections were held in the Mauritanian zone on August 8, 1976, but few independent observers doubted that they were a charade. Supposedly, 96.1 percent of the electorate, which was said to number ten thousand, went to the polls and the seven PPM candidates received 96.4 percent of the votes. The Nouakchott authorities did not hesitate to describe the poll as a "referendum in favor of unification" in which the people had dissociated themselves from the "lying propaganda and the campaign of mystification stirred up by the Algerian leaders and their mercenaries."[3] In fact, the poll was no more democratic than elections held in Mauritania itself under the PPM regime. Since Mauritania was a one-party state, only PPM candidates were allowed to stand. The official returns were almost certainly forged, as they invariably were in Mauritania in Ould Daddah's day, when improbable landslide majorities for the PPM were *de rigueur*. Most of the local inhabitants were not even physically present in their constituencies. They had already voted with their feet by fleeing to the Polisario camps in Tindouf.

Though Polisario had put up stiff resistance to the Mauritanian advance into Western Sahara and had begun diversionary or retaliatory raids into Mauritania itself since December 1975, most of its forces were initially employed in organizing and defending the refugee exodus to Algeria. However, by the end of April the refugee evacuation operation had more or less been completed, and there had also been sufficient time by then to train, organize and arm a large number of the SPLA's thousands of new recruits. Though the Moroccan and Mauritanian forces had already seized all the main towns, settlements and former Spanish bases, the Saharawi guerrillas were ready to move on to the offensive. They would confound their enemies by taking the war far beyond Western Sahara itself, deep into Mauritania and the desert regions of southern Morocco, and they believed that they had every right to do so. "It is Morocco and Mauritania who, in the first place, violated the borders of Western Sahara," Polisario would insist. "Their troops attacked our people on our territory and did not respect our right to self-determination. We have the right to strike back in self-defense. That is why we say that southern Morocco and the north of Mauritania are war zones."[4]

It was Mauritania, by far the weaker of their two enemies, which the guerrillas singled out for the brunt of their offensive. It made strategic sense to do so. Not only was Mauritania's economy in no state to sustain a war. Political conditions in Mauritania were equally inappropriate. Ould Daddah had simply been unable to generate the kind of enthusiasm for his Saharan policy which King Hassan had aroused in Morocco. Moreover, from a purely military standpoint, it would be impossible for the Mauritanian army, with only three thousand men plus some two thousand in paramilitary units and a handful of ancient Defender aircraft, to patrol the country's long desert frontiers effectively and police a territory of about four hundred thousand square miles, an area twice the size of France. The guerrillas's first objective, then, was to knock Mauritania out of the war. They would destroy the Moroccan-Mauritanian alliance.

Their military success would hinge not only on the weakness of their Mauritanian adversaries, however. The logistical support they received from Algeria, both rear bases and generous deliveries of military equipment, including Sam missiles, was vital, though they also established numerous small bases in Western Sahara and northern Mauritania and were able to supplement their military arsenal with weapons and vehicles captured in battle. Their selfless dedication to the Saharawi cause played an important part too, allowing operations of quite astonishing heroism. But perhaps the most intriguing ingredient was their combination of traditional military skills with modern equipment and techniques. Their favored tactic was to be the long-distance raid, the *ghazzi*, for which, as in Mohammed el-Mamoun's time, they would traverse hundreds of miles of desert. Though many of the Polisario soldiers were young men from the cities, the military heritage of the past had not been lost. The Army of Liberation's war had ended only eighteen years earlier, in 1958, and the last great raids of the earlier anticolonial resistance movement only twenty-four years before that, in 1934. Moreover, the stories of the great *ghazzian* of old had been passed down by the older generation, leaving the young with an extensive knowledge of military tactics, geographical zones and itineraries that complemented the modern military skills taught, at first, by Algerian army instructors and Saharawi veterans of the Tropas Nómadas. In its new, fully motorized form, the *ghazzi* was to be devastatingly effective. From bases in the Tindouf region or scattered hideouts in Western Sahara itself, SPLA units (*kataeb*) would drive their Land Rovers at great speed into Mauritania, fall suddenly upon unsuspecting targets, often under cover of darkness, and then return to base as fast as they had come, dispersing into small groups if pursued by aircraft.

As early as December 1975, Polisario guerrillas had raided close to Zouerate, mortaring the power station that supplies the nearby iron mines. There was a second raid in the Zouerate area on May 12, 1976, and during the same month guerrilla groups reached as far south as Ouadane and Chinguetti in Adrar. Something much more audacious, however, was afoot. After chairing a meeting of Polisario's executive committee on June 2, El-Ouali Mustapha Sayed himself set out on an epic expedition, with several hundred guerrillas in a fleet of Land Rovers and Berliet trucks, en route for the Mauritanian capital, some nine hundred miles away across the desert.

There were few Mauritanian troops in Nouakchott at this time. Most of the overstretched army was stationed, as might have been expected, far to the north. However, on June 5, a Mauritanian Defender pilot spotted a concentration of

Polisario vehicles near Tourine, to the east of Zouerate. Alerted at his Zouerate headquarters, Lieutenant-Colonel Ahmed Ould Bouceif, the commander of G2, sent his deputy, Commandant Mohammed Khouna Ould Heydalla, to attack them. To his stupefaction, Ould Heydalla learned from prisoners captured in the ensuing fighting that the units at Tourine were merely a backup group for a much larger force that was already heading for Nouakchott. Meanwhile, other Polisario *kataeb* were being sent toward Zouerate, Atar, Ouadane, Chinguetti and even Tichit in southeastern Mauritania to divert attention from the Nouakchott bound force. The prisoners' revelations were at first discounted in the capital, where Ould Daddah saw no reason to postpone a state visit to the Cape Verde Islands. On June 6, however, the Mauritanian general staff began to take the threat more seriously when a French civilian pilot reported seeing a powerful military column fifty miles west of Atar as he flew toward Nouakchott.

The next day, Ould Bouceif set out from Zouerate with four hundred men to race toward the capital, while farther west a second column of troops, from G1, headed south from Aoussert under Colonel Viah Ould Mayouf's command. To the south, a third force advanced from the capital, where the local garrison had been supplemented by recruits that had barely completed their training. By the evening of June 7, El-Ouali's *kataeb* had reached Oum Tounsi, fifty miles from Nouakchott. Early the next morning, El-Ouali dispatched a small group of Land Rovers to shell the northern outskirts of the capital. The bombardment lasted only half an hour, but later, after sunset, at 10 P.M., they returned, firing with great accuracy into the grounds of the presidential palace and neighboring embassies for about fifteen minutes, before disappearing once again into the night.

On the morning of June 9, as the main column, which had remained in Oum Tounsi, set out on the long return journey to the north, the three Mauritanian columns from Zouerate, Aoussert and the capital began to close in. At a place near Benichab, where the guerrillas had planned to blow up the water tanks that serve the copper-mining city of Akjoujt, a part of the Polisario force, which included El-Ouali, was cornered by an armored squadron under the command of one of Ould Bouceif's deputies, Lieutenant Ney Ould Bah. After a half-hour shootout, Ould Bah's men found the corpse of the Polisario secretary-general, who had been shot through the head. The main part of the Polisario force continued their retreat toward Tourine, oblivious of Ould Heydalla's attack on the relief force there on June 5. Viah Ould Mayouf's forces were waiting for them and opened fire on the first Polisario Land Rovers arriving for the appointed rendezvous. The rest of the Polisario column made their escape to the northeast, finally reaching a Polisario relief force at El-Mreiti, 250 miles from the Algerian border.[5]

Despite the guerrillas' heavy losses and El-Ouali's death, the Nouakchott *ghazzi* was a traumatic experience for Ould Daddah, who had returned home from the Cape Verdes the day before Polisario's mortar rounds landed in his palace gardens. He now knew that Boumedienne had been in deadly earnest at Bechar on the eve of the Madrid accords. The Mauritanian forces were evidently stretched to the limit, and on June 24 he entrusted the responsibility for beefing them up to a new chief-of-staff, Ahmed Ould Bouceif, the former commander of G2 at Zouerate. The president may have hoped that the death of such a charismatic leader as El-Ouali would demoralize his adversaries. However, the succession proceeded smoothly and there was no letup in the pace of attacks. Mahfoud Ali Beiba, the deputy secretary-general, became acting head of the movement until Polisario's third congress, which had already been in preparation, met on August 26–30 and elected Mohammed Abdelaziz, a young Reguibi, who had been one of El-Ouali's earliest collaborators, as the new secretary-general and Bashir Mustapha Sayed, El-Ouali's younger brother, as his deputy. Meanwhile, both Tidjikja and Tichit, towns in Tagant that are almost as far south as Nouakchott, were raided in August and an even more distant city, Nema, seventy miles from Mauritania's southern border with Mali, was attacked in September.[6]

However, it was the railway line from the Zouerate iron mines to the port of Nouadhibou which the guerrillas were to make their principal target. If they could bring the trains to a complete standstill, they calculated, they would deprive Mauritania of about 80 percent of its export revenue and so bleed the country economically into submission. Skirting around the Western Sahara frontier, the railway, 419 miles long, was as easy to attack as it was strategic. It was impossible to guard properly, and on three occasions in 1976 guerrillas ripped up stretches of the track. On February 20, 1977, Polisario attacked a train for the first time, destroying three locomotives with rocket fire about sixty miles south of Zouerate.[7] The trains proved extremely vulnerable, for, with almost two hundred cars, pulled by four locomotives, they were normally more than a mile long and took seventeen hours to reach the coast from the mines.

In their bid to bring the mining at Zouerate to a halt, the guerrillas also tried to scare away the 280 or so skilled Frenchmen working in the iron industry for the Comptoir Minier du Nord (COMINOR), the iron-mining subsidiary of the Mauritanian parastatal Société Nationale Industrielle et Minière (SNIM), which had been extraordinarily slow in Africanizing technical and managerial posts at the mines. Just before dawn on May Day 1977, four hundred Polisario guerrillas stormed into Zouerate itself, after successfully negotiating a thirty-five-mile-long defensive trench that had been dug, eleven feet deep, around the city after the mortaring of the local power station in December 1975. The fifteen-hundred-strong Mauritanian garrison, whose commander, Ould Heydalla, was away in Nouakchott, put up no resistance. As the guerrillas roamed through the city unchallenged for two hours, they set about damaging railway installations, administrative buildings and the power station and blew up two planes at the airport, where they also burst into the airport bar, *Le Ranch*, discovering a group of Frenchmen who had spent the night there drinking. Two of them were gunned down and six others were arrested and driven off into the desert.[8]

The next day, three French air-force Noratlas transport planes touched down in Zouerate to evacuate the French women and children in the city, 449 of them in all, and within a few days all but about 80 of COMINOR's 280 French employees there had departed too.[9] The mines ground to a halt. However, there were two months of ore supplies stockpiled at Nouadhibou, so exports were not interrupted, and with a new incentive to promote Mauritanians to skilled jobs previously held by Europeans, SNIM was able to reorganize its work force and resume mining within a month.

Two months after their success at Zouerate, the guerrillas staged another epic *ghazzi* against Nouakchott, this time without the setbacks that befell the first attack in June 1976. The force of about forty-five Land Rovers which traveled night and day for almost a week from bases near Amgala, via Bir Enzaren and Aoussert, to the very edge of the Mauritanian capital, encountered no serious resistance and on the evening of July 3 succeeded once again in lobbing a few mortar rounds into the grounds of the presidential palace. On their return home, the guerrillas even took the tarmac highway to the north, under cover of night, before vanishing into the desert twenty miles from Akjoujt. They returned to their Amgala bases with almost no casualties.[10] Less than a fortnight later, moreover, a guerrilla force attacked Zouerate once again.

In a desperate attempt to cope with the ever more confident guerrillas, the Nouakchott authorities had been hastily recruiting thousands of fresh troops. To train new officers and NCOs, a military academy was set up, with French military officers on the staff, at Atar in November 1976, and by the end of 1977 the Mauritanian armed forces' total troop strength was estimated to have grown to seventeen thousand.[11]

However, by the summer of 1977, Ould Daddah was painfully aware that his own forces could not hold the line against the Polisario *kataeb*. Often, as at Zouerate in May, the hurriedly trained and poorly motivated Mauritanian troops had insufficient resolve even to put up a fight. So, two weeks after the Zouerate debacle, on May 13, Ould Daddah signed a mutual defense pact with King Hassan which established a Moroccan-Mauritanian high command and authorized the stationing of Moroccan troops in Mauritanian territory. The joint command met for its first strategy session on June 19–20 in Nouakchott, and a month later six hundred Moroccan troops flew into Zouerate to reinforce the discredited Mauritanian garrison there.[12] Thousands more were to be airlifted to Mauritania over the following few months, and by the end of 1977 Ould Daddah had been forced to call on the assistance of the French air force too. It was an ironical twist of fate for a man who had spent the greater part of his political career trying to keep Morocco at arm's length from his country and had then tried in the early seventies to lessen his government's dependence on France, notably by renouncing the post-independence Franco-Mauritanian military accords in 1973.

NOTES

1. *Le Monde* (Paris), February 16, 1978.
2. *Africa Contemporary Record*, Vol. 9, 1976–77, p. B644.
3. *Ibid.*, p. B644.
4. *Le Monde*, May 6, 1977.
5. Author's interview with a participant in the expedition, Abderrahman Ould Saidi Ould Belgoueine, June 1978; *Jeune Afrique* (Paris), June 25, 1976, and July 8, 1977; *Le Monde*, June 22, 1976; *La République* (Oran), July 3, 1976.
6. *Africa Contemporary Record*, Vol. 9, 1976–77, p. B645.
7. *Le Monde*, February 26, 1977.
8. *Le Monde*, May 3, 1977, and May 10, 1977; *France-Soir* (Paris), May 5, 1977.
9. *Le Monde*, May 4, 1977; *SNIM Actualité* (Nouakchott), No. 12, 2nd Quarter, 1977, p. 6.
10. Interviews with two participants in the Polisario force, following their capture by the Moroccan armed forces early in 1978 (El-Ayoun, October 14, 1978).
11. *Le Monde*, December 31, 1977.
12. *Le Monde*, June 21, 1977 and July 27, 1977.

23

Operation Lamantin

Like the U.S. government, President Valéry Giscard d'Estaing had welcomed the Madrid Accords. "It seemed sensible to us," he had said in January 1976, "to let Morocco and Mauritania come to an arrangement with Spain. It is true that we regard the multiplication of micro-states as regrettable."[1] Ironically, such regret did not preclude Djibouti's independence a year later, with a population of only 220,000, and it is hard to escape the conclusion that the reference to micro-states was merely an excuse to justify Western Sahara's partition. In truth, Giscard d'Estaing saw King Hassan as a vital Western ally and knew that the stability of his regime hinged on the successful accomplishment of his Saharan ambitions. Franco-Moroccan relations were especially buoyant at the time, moreover. Fifty-five thousand French citizens still lived in Morocco, more than in any other country besides France itself, and in August 1974 the Moroccan government had agreed to pay about £10 million compensation for the Moroccamization of French settlers' lands.[2] Morocco was France's second largest export market in the Arab world, after Algeria, and fourteenth in the world as a whole, and French exports to Morocco were growing spectacularly fast, rising by 108 percent between 1973 and 1975, to 3.4 billion francs. By 1977 they had reached 4.7 billion francs.[3]

Giscard d'Estaing had been the first French president to visit post-independence Morocco, in May 1975, and he had left little doubt then that he favored direct talks between Spain and Morocco on Western Sahara's future.[4] Shortly afterward, during the summer of 1975, the Direction des Affaires Internationales of the French government's Délégation Ministérielle à l'Armament (DMA) had signed an arms procurement agreement with Morocco, which, along with the greatly increased U.S. arms sales to Morocco at this time, on the eve of the Madrid accords, permitted a major expansion and modernization of the FAR's weapons systems. Following the agreement with the DMA, which came to be known as the Marrakesh Plan, the Moroccan government signed a series of contracts with French arms manufacturers. Forty Puma helicopters, for example, were immediately ordered from the state munitions company SNIAS. In January 1976 an order was placed with Dassault for twenty-five Mirage F-1 combat aircraft, at $13 million apiece, and a year later twenty-five more of the planes were ordered. Delivery of the Mirages did not start until 1979, but in the meantime Moroccan pilots were trained to fly them at the French air-force base at Tours. In 1978, meanwhile, Morocco submitted another aircraft order to Dassault, this time for twenty-four Alpha-Jets, at a cost of $6 million each.[5] A large number of French military advisors, two hundred in 1977, were posted in Morocco, mainly to provide training and to supervise the delivery and absorption of French weapons systems.[6]

As Polisario's guerrilla attacks increased in frequency and boldness in Mauritania in 1976–77, the Nouakchott regime's military predicament began to cause particular concern in Paris. Mokhtar Ould Daddah's prospects of withstanding the Polisario offensive without external assistance seemed to be diminishing, and Mauritania looked as if it might not only have to succumb to the guerrillas and abandon its commitments under the Madrid accords but, at worst, slip into the kind of disorder and instability that had wracked Chad at the other end of the belt of impoverished and ethno-culturally divided ex-French Sahelian states. That in turn might have dangerous repercussions for such nearby-French-aligned states as Senegal and Mali.

The Ould Daddah government, however, had renounced Mauritania's military accords with France in 1973, as part of a program of nationalist measures, which included withdrawal from the Franc Zone and the launching of a national currency, the ouguiya, in 1973, and the nationalization of the iron mines in 1974, designed to lessen dependence on France and take the wind out of the sails of the clandestine but vocal left-wing opposition, the Mouvement National Démocratique (MND).[7] But after the trauma of the Polisario raid on Nouackhott in June 1976, Ould Daddah once again turned to France for military assistance. So, the following September, a new Franco-Mauritanian military agreement, providing for the sending of French military instructors—fifteen at first—to the Atar military academy, was signed, and in January 1977 it was widened in scope to enable French military personnel of all categories to be sent to Mauritania. Meanwhile, French arms deliveries were resumed in 1976.[8]

But then, on May 1, 1977, came the Polisario raid on Zouerate, which, besides resulting in the death of two French citizens and the capture of six others, highlighted the grave threat looming over the iron-mining industry, the lifeblood of the Mauritanian economy and of Ould Daddah's war efforts. The French foreign minister, Louis de Guiringaud, immediately pointed an accusing finger at Algeria, for harboring the guerrillas, and insisted that the Algerian government intercede with them to secure the French prisoners' release.[9] However, the Algerian authorities were prepared to do no more than facilitate contacts between France and Polisario, and at first the guerrillas would not even confirm that they were holding any French captives until the Mauritanian government published a list of its Saharawi prisoners. Then, on October 25, during an attack on the Zouerate-Nouadhibou railway, about thirty-seven miles south of Zouerate, a guerrilla group seized two more Frenchmen, technicians working in COMINOR's railway workshops under contract from Sofrerail, a subsidiary of French Railways. "If such criminal actions were to continue," the French foreign ministry, the Quai d'Orsay, protested the next day, "they would endanger the activity of all the French nationals who are now in Mauritania."[10] Because of the insecurity, COMINOR immediately suspended all rail services. The railway remained at a standstill for several weeks, and stocks of ore at Nouadhibou port ran dangerously low as SNIM tried to sustain exports.

Polisario justified its seizure of French *coopérants* on the grounds that they "participate actively in the Moroccan-Mauritanian war effort."[11] The SNIM and its subsidiaries, for which many of the French expatriates worked, were accused of aiding the Mauritanian armed forces by repairing military vehicles in their workshops, supplying the machinery used to dig the defensive trench around Zouerate, carrying troops and military equipment on the Zouerate-Nouadhibou railway and even allowing their aircraft to be used for military reconnaissance. Most of the prisoners later denied that they had personally engaged in military-related work, but the two railway employees captured on October 25 did acknowledge that they had repaired military equipment and mounted machine guns on army Land Rovers in their workshops.[12]

The seizure of the Frenchmen was really a form of economic warfare. The aim was to cripple COMINOR by forcing Giscard d'Estaing to evacuate all French expatriates from northern Mauritania. To Polisario's dismay, however, France not only refused to order a general evacuation but exploited the October 25 incidents as a pretext to begin direct French military intervention against the guerrillas, to shore up Ould Daddah's faltering defenses.

Since his election in 1974, Giscard d'Estaing had embarked on an increasingly activist, indeed aggressive, African policy, to defend French and wider Western interests in Africa, with which France conducts about 20 percent of its trade and from which it imports about 42 percent of its strategic raw materials.[13] One prong of this multifaceted policy was to reassure traditional African allies, many of them insecure dictators, of the steadfastness of the French guarantee in the event of "subversion" or revolts—at a time, following the Vietnam and Angolan wars, when domestic constraints in the U.S. held Washington back from military intervention abroad.

At their accession to independence, during the Gaullist era, the governments of all the formerly French-ruled black African countries, except for Guinea, had signed military agreements with the French government under which France had built up their national armies and in several cases continued to station its own troops on their territory. In addition, French troops had sometimes rushed to the aid of endangered African rulers. They had helped President Léopold Sédar Senghor of Senegal, for example, foil a coup in 1962; they had reinstated President Léon M'Ba of Gabon within forty-eight hours of his being deposed by the Gabonese army in 1964; and four thousand French troops had helped President François Tombalbaye of Chad stave off the rebels of the Front de Libération Nationale du Tchad (Frolinat) between 1968 and 1971. However, the huge cost of the Force de Frappe, developed after France's first atomic explosion in 1960, had gradually eroded the strength of France's conventional forces, and the neocolonial stigma attached to the French garrisons in Africa prompted several African governments to negotiate their withdrawal and revise their military accords with France. Nonetheless, France retained military cooperation accords with about fifteen African countries in the late seventies, and in 1978 about twelve thousand of the twenty thousand French troops overseas were stationed in Africa and the Indian Ocean, most of them in Djibouti, Réunion, Chad, Senegal, Ivory Coast, Gabon and Mayotte.[14]

Giscard d'Estaing's revival of the Gaullist practice of rushing to the aid of threatened African regimes began with the emergency in Zaire's mineral-rich Shaba province in March 1977, when fifteen hundred guerrillas of the Front National de Libération du Congo (FNLC) infiltrated from Angola, were welcomed by the local Lunda who had suffered despotism, corruption and deprivation under President Mobutu Sese Seko, and advanced to within a few miles of the mining city of Kolwezi, without meeting any serious resistance from government forces. Mobutu sent an SOS to France, with which he had signed military accords in April 1974, and after consultations with the U.S. secretary of state, Cyrus Vance, Giscard d'Estaing launched a rescue operation, code-named Verveine. French air-force planes flew a contingent of fifteen hundred Moroccan troops to Shaba, encouraging the FNLC guerrillas to slip back into Angola, with about two hundred thousand Shaban refugees.

At the fourth Franco-African summit the following May, two of Giscard d'Estaing's closest allies, Senghor and the president of the Ivory Coast, Félix Houphouet-Boigny, proposed the establishment of a French-backed African security force, a kind of Franco-African NATO on permanent standby to respond to crises as they arose. Discussed further during a state visit by Giscard d'Estaing to the Ivory Coast in January 1978, when the French president spoke of the need for an "Afro-European solidarity pact," and again during the fifth Franco-African summit in May 1978, this idea was stillborn. It was too overtly neocolonial, and it might have encouraged African allies of Cuba and the U.S.S.R. to form their own rival pact. A case-by-case approach to African emergencies was considered preferable.

One such crisis erupted a few months after Verveine. Frolinat forces launched a major offensive in the summer of 1977 and took control of the whole of the Borku-Ennedi-Tibesti (BET) region of northern Chad over the following six months, posing a serious challenge to the regime of General Félix Malloum in Ndjamena. France already had three hundred troops in Chad, on assignment to the Forces Armées Tchadiennes under the March 1976 Franco-Chadian military accords, and French pilots were flying Chad's Skyraider aircraft. However, after the fall of the BET capital, Faya-Largeau, almost a thousand more French troops were airlifted to Chad in March-April 1978, while ten Jaguars of the French air force flew into Ndjamena to begin air strikes against Frolinat. Another one hundred and fifty to two hundred French troops arrived in May, bringing France's troop strength in Chad to about fifteen hundred, and at the end of the month French forces inflicted a severe defeat on Frolinat at Ati, in central Chad, temporarily halting their southward advance.

Meanwhile, during May, the French government had once again come to Mobutu's rescue in Shaba, where government troops had surrendered before a second FNLC offensive, allowing the rebels to enter Kolwezi itself on May 13. Six days later, six hundred French paratroopers had been dropped into the city and they had been joined the next day by paratroopers from Belgium. After quelling the Lunda rebels, the French and Belgian troops were replaced in June by a two-thousand-strong "inter-African force" of Moroccan, Senegalese, Togolese and Gabonese troops, who provided a long-term garrison for Shaba's copper and cobalt mining centers.

Giscard d'Estaing responded to the challenge from Polisario in Mauritania in 1977 with equal resolve. On October 27, two days after the Sofrerail workers' capture, he summoned an emergency strategy meeting at the Elysée Palace, attended by Louis de Guiringaud, Yvon Bourges, the defense minister, Robert Galley, the minister for cooperation, and General Guy Méry, the chief-of-staff of the armed forces, who was also head of a permanent crisis command known as the Centre Opérationnel des Armées (COA). It was to the COA, based in a bunker under the defense ministry in Paris, that strategic planning for French military intervention in Mauritania was entrusted. General Méry could not envision an Entebbe-style commando operation to free the eight Frenchmen. Finding them in the desert would have been like searching for a needle in a haystack, and, if they were being held in Algerian territory, would have risked a direct clash with Algeria. Besides, the fate of the prisoners was a secondary consideration. The French government's real objective was to exploit their fate, and the concern expressed in the French media, to buttress Ould Daddah's defenses. Operation Lamantin (Sea Cow), as General Méry's plan was baptized, was to involve French air strikes against the guerrillas threatening COMINOR's economically vital operations in northern Mauritania.

The most convenient logistical base at hand for such an operation was the Ouakkam airfield on the Cap Vert peninsula at Dakar, only fifteen minutes' flying time from Nouakchott for a supersonic jet. About eleven hundred French troops were already there, under the 1974 Franco-Senegalese military accords, which allowed France to station up to thirteen hundred troops on Senegalese territory.[15] The base had been used for logistical support during earlier French military operations in Africa, including the rescue of Léon M'Ba in 1964 and Operation Verveine, and President Senghor was just as willing to assist this time. A long-standing ally of King Hassan, he had supported the Moroccan-Mauritanian annexation of Western Sahara from the beginning and he had an ingrained, almost paranoid distaste for Polisario, which, like the MPLA in Angola, he regarded as one of the spearheads of leftist "subversion" across the African continent.[16] He feared that Polisario might bring down Ould Daddah's regime, paving the way for a Chad-like disintegration of the Mauritanian state or the creation of a radical, Algerian-backed government on his northern borders.[17] In anticipation, perhaps, of such a turn of events, or to answer domestic critics of his assistance for French military intervention against the Saharawis, he began to claim, without a shred of real evidence, that Polisario was a racist Arab movement which murdered its black Mauritanian prisoners and would suppress Mauritania's black African minority if it succeeded in destroying the Ould Daddah regime. He warned that, if that happened, Senegal would champion the Mauritanian blacks' right to self-determination.[18]

During the night of November 1–2, a special force of 185 elite troops flew out to Dakar under the command of General Michel Forget, bringing the French troop strength in Senegal more or less up to its full complement of thirteen hundred. Soon afterward, Forget proceeded with sixty military specialists to Mauritania, where there were already another sixty French officers at the Atar military academy by this time. Forget's second-in-command, Colonel Huret, remained at the Ouakkam air base to coordinate backup logistics. Forget's principal task was to set up a sophisticated communications network, linked to Ouakkam, in preparation for the French air force's planned sorties against the guerrillas. Meanwhile, French navy Breguet-Atlantic aircraft, which are normally used for antisubmarine reconnaissance, began flying over Mauritania from Ouakkam, assisted by Mirages-4, long-range strategic reconnaissance aircraft, from Bordeaux, to detect guerrilla positions and photograph unmapped desert regions.[19]

While the military preparations proceeded, an official of the Quai d'Orsay, Claude Chayet, arrived in Algiers on November 1 and began talks with two Polisario leaders, Mohammed Ali Ould el-Ouali, a member of the front's executive committee, and Mohammed Salem Ould Salek, the SADR's minister of information, about the fate of the eight French prisoners. On November 8, however, he suddenly flew back to Paris, where the foreign ministry complained three days later that Chayet had been given "preconditions for the opening of all discussions about our compatriots," among them "notably the withdrawal of French citizens from the whole of Mauritanian territory as well as the south of Morocco."[20] Chayet flew back to Algiers on November 11, with instructions to tell Polisario that France would only accept the prisoners' unconditional release, but when the talks resumed on November 16, Mohammed Ali Ould el-Ouali and Mohammed Salem Ould Salek held out for a prisoner exchange. Chayet broke off the talks *sine die* on November 19, and the next day Louis de Guiringaud warned that France would not, as "Monsieur Chayet's interlocutors wanted," tackle "this problem in the framework of a prisoner exchange."[21] At the very least, Polisario hoped, however, that France would persuade the Mauritanian government to publish a list of its POWs and allow the Red Cross to inspect the conditions in which they were being held, but neither the French nor the Mauritanian governments were prepared to make even this minimal humanitarian concession to the guerrillas.[22] From November 19, there were no further direct talks between the French government and Polisario officials, who found that their French prisoners had become a dangerous liability. In desperation, they turned to the UN and the French Union of the Left (the alliance of French communists, socialists and left radicals) to escape their blunder.

Polisario had misjudged both Giscard d'Estaing's resolve and the public mood in France. The Union of the Left, which had opposed Operation Verveine and Giscard d'Estaing's close association with unsavory African dictators such as Emperor Bokassa, spoke out against the French military buildup in Senegal and Mauritania and argued that "the Western Saharan conflict cannot be resolved without applying the principles of self-determination and of the right of peoples to decide their own future."[23] However, neither the French communist nor socialist parties made any attempt to organize mass protests against Giscard d'Estaing's military preparations and both parties repeatedly called on Polisario to free the prisoners. Furthermore, the French public, which had been impressed by West German commandos' dramatic seizure of a Lufthansa airliner from Baader-Meinhof terrorists at Mogadiscio a few days earlier, on October 18, was generally favorable to the idea of a tough response to the seizure of the prisoners, who were painted as "hostages" by government and media alike.

The French far right, meanwhile, cashed in on the bellicose mood by staging a wave of terrorist attacks against Algerian immigrants. On November 4, the Air Algérie offices in Paris were bombed. On November 14 an extreme rightist organization, the Charles Martel Group, claimed that it had seized two Algerian immigrants in a Paris suburb and would execute them if the Frenchmen held by Polisario died. A bomb exploded at an Algerian tourism bureau in Paris on November 29. The worst incident, however, came on December 2, when a guardian at the Paris offices of the Amicale des Algériens, an Algerian immigrants' organization, was assassinated by Delta, a terrorist group named after the *pied noir* murder squads active in Algiers in 1961–62.[24]

King Hassan too found the circumstances propitious for making threats. In a speech on November 6, marking the second anniversary of the Green March, he warned Algeria that "every time Moroccan frontiers are violated by the pseudo-Polisario in the future, the Moroccan army will use its right of pursuit, whatever the consequences."[25]

"Any violation of the Algerian frontier will have very grave consequences for peace and security in the region," the Algerian council of ministers warned, by way of reply, on November 7, and on the same day tens of thousands demonstrated their support for Polisario in the streets of Algiers. *Chaab*, the government-run newspaper, warned the next day that Algeria "would regard any violation of its borders as a declaration of war which would unleash appropriate counteraction"; and, though Hassan repeated his threat at a press conference on November 11, he was enough of a realist to appreciate the consequences of sparking off an all-out war with Algeria, which had a much larger air force than Morocco, and so wisely refrained from ordering his forces into Algeria.

However, another six hundred Moroccan troops arrived in Mauritania in November, doubling the number of Moroccan troops there to twelve hundred, apart from those in Tiris el-Gharbia.[26] A division of labor between the French, Moroccan and Mauritanian forces seemed to be in the making. While the French prepared to use their air power against the guerrillas, Moroccan troops took over the defense of key points in northern Mauritania, gradually freeing up the overstretched Mauritanian forces for the defense of the capital and mobile counterinsurgency operations.[27] By January 1978 there were twenty-four hundred Moroccan troops in the Zouerate-Nouadhibou zone and six hundred farther south in the copper-mining city of Akjoujt, as well as twenty-eight hundred in the extreme northeast and Tiris el-Gharbia. Three Moroccan F-5s were stationed at Nouadhibou, and Moroccan construction companies were extending the runways at Nouakchott and Atar to handle F-5 and Mirage jets.[28]

On November 21, 1977, Ould Daddah announced the reopening of the Zouerate-Nouadhibou railway, almost a month after its closure, but the next day, when COMINOR sent its first train down the line from Nouadhibou, it was ambushed. The guerrillas captured the engine driver and ten Mauritanian soldiers.[29] Three days later, on November 25, four Jaguars from the French tactical air command base at Toul flew over Mauritania and landed briefly at Nouakchott, en route to Libreville, so it was said, "to participate in combined Franco-Gabonese exercises."[30] Dakar was their real destination.

The Jaguar was a much more advanced warplane than the Northrop F-5s then being flown by the Moroccan air force. In service in the French air force since 1971, it is a supersonic combat aircraft that can carry up to ten thousand pounds of bombs and rockets and has two 30-mm. guns. It is equipped with electronic countermeasures (ECM) for protection against ground-to-air missiles and can be refueled in flight to permit long-range missions. By the first week of December 1977 there were six Jaguars at Ouakkam, plus two KC-135F refueling planes, two Breguet-Atlantic reconnaissance aircraft and four Noratlas transport planes.[31]

By the beginning of December the Jaguars were ready for action, but the French government remained completely mute about what was being planned. According to Polisario, the Jaguars first entered the war on December 2, when the guerrillas attacked Boulanour, a station on the COMINOR railway about fifty miles from Nouadhibou. Resolving the prisoner controversy had now become an urgent matter, and in a letter delivered to the Elysée on December 5 by the secretary-general of the Franco-Arab Solidarity Association, Polisario assured Giscard d'Estaing that the prisoners were about to be released.[32] However, Operation Lamantin proceeded as planned. When another iron-ore train was ambushed on December 12, about forty miles south of Zouerate, the Dakar-based Jaguars strafed and bombed the retreating Polisario forces for two consecutive days, killing scores of the guerrillas and most of the sixty Mauritanian prisoners they had seized during the ambush. According to survivors of the attacks, the Jaguars used napalm and phosphorous bombs.[33] The French government refused to confirm or deny that its aircraft had gone into action, though the Quai d'Orsay menacingly declared on December 19 that "our air units are ready to ensure the security of our expatriates in Mauritania when they are in danger and at the request of the Mauritanian government."[34]

On December 14, following talks in New York between Ibrahim Hakim, the SADR's foreign minister, and Kurt Waldheim, it was announced that the eight prisoners would be released on December 23 and that the UN secretary-general would travel in person to Algiers to receive them. However, Lamantin went on. After another raid along the Zouerate-Nouadhibou railway on December 18, against Tmeimichatt, during which the guerrillas took eighty-two Mauritanian prisoners, the Jaguars flew into action again. Seventy-four of the prisoners were killed when the planes bombed the trucks in which they were being transported. The Mauritanian government claimed that only Moroccan and Mauritanian planes had staged the air strikes, and in Paris Louis de Guiringaud would only say, in the National Assembly on December 21, that the French government had been obliged "to make certain arrangements, at the Maurita-nian authorities' request, to safeguard French nationals."[35]

"The direct and massive military intervention by French forces" had stripped away "the mask of France's supposed neutrality," Polisario declared when it handed over its French prisoners to Waldheim two days later. The French air strikes had continued, it protested, after "the decision to free the French prisoners had already been brought to the attention of the secretary-general of the

UN and the French government.''[36] The French government's official cloak of secrecy about Lamantin was only removed on the afternoon of December 23, after the prisoners' arrival, with Waldheim, in Paris. Even then, the foreign minister could only announce laconically that ''the Mauritanian government requested French forces' aid and, on two occasions, units of the French airforce came to their assistance.''[37]

Lamantin was just one facet of Giscard d'Estaing's interventionist African policy at this time. ''We cannot allow our African friends, especially the weakest among them, to be subjected to threats of destabilization,'' he remarked a few days after the Mauritanian bombing raids, on January 2. ''Our friends can count on France's solidarity.''[38] By sending the Jaguars into combat in northern Mauritania, he was serving notice on both Polisario and its Algerian allies that France would not allow Ould Daddah to be defeated. However, Lamantin ultimately backfired. Neither Polisario nor the Algerian government were prepared to succumb to French military might. It was not in the FLN's tradition to do so. Parallels were drawn in Algeria about the long and bitter war of independence from France which had ended less than fifteen years earlier. On December 25, the Algerian government condemned the Jaguar raids and reaffirmed its recognition of ''the Saharawi people's right to struggle, by all available means, against the armies of aggression which have invaded its national territory.''[39] Franco-Algerian relations turned particularly sour and, over the following few months, Boumedienne took economic reprisals against French industry. As for the guerrillas, they continued to raid the Zouerate-Nouadhibou railway and simply adjusted their tactics, switching to small-scale sabotage attacks, to diminish their exposure to attacks from the air. Within a few months Ould Daddah was to be deposed by his war-weary army.

NOTES

1. *Le Monde* (Paris), February 1–2, 1976.
2. *Reuters*, dispatches from Rabat, April 7, 1975, and May 2, 1975.
3. By 1979, French exports to Morocco had risen to 5.1 billion francs. (*An-Nahar Arab Report and Memo*, January 23, 1978, and Economist Intelligence Unit, London.)
4. *Le Figaro* (Paris), May 7, 1975; *ABC* (Madrid), May 8, 1975.
5. *Le Nouvel Observateur* (Paris), March 8–14, 1976; *Afrique-Défense* (Paris), October 1978; *An-Nahar Arab Report and Memo*, March 27, 1978; *Le Monde*, June 5, 1976.
6. *Le Monde*, December 31, 1977.
7. See ''La Mauritanie à un moment décisif de son histoire,'' *Europe-Outremer* (Paris), No. 519, April 1973, p. 19.
8. Robert Taton, ''Le Sahara occidental vu du côté mauritanien,'' *Europe-Outremer*, No. 574, November 1977, p. 13–14.
9. *Le Monde*, May 6, 1977.
10. *Le Monde*, October 28, 1977.
11. *20 Mai* (Polisario Front), No. 48, October-November 1977.
12. *Le Monde*, December 22, 1977, and December 29, 1977.
13. Including all its uranium and cobalt, 95 percent of its nickel, 79 percent of its phosphate rock and 45 percent of its manganese (1977 figures). See *Africa Confidential* (London), March 28, 1979.
14. There were about 4,500 French troops in Djibouti, 2,300 in Réunion, 1,500 in Chad and 400 to 500 in both Gabon and Ivory Coast. France had military cooperation agreements with Senegal, Cameroon, Congo, Djibouti, Central African Empire, Zaire, Benin, Rwanda, Chad, Togo, Mauritania, Niger, Gabon, Upper Volta and Ivory Coast. For a detailed analysis of French military

relations with African countries, see "La coopération militaire franco-africaine," *Europe-Outremer*, Nos. 567–68, April-May 1977.

15. Taton, *loc. cit.*, p. 14.

16. As early as October 6, 1975, the Senegalese foreign minister, Assane Seck, had declared, in a speech to the UN General Assembly, that a referendum in Western Sahara was "superfluous." (*Le Monde*, October 9, 1975.)

17. *Le Monde*, December 9, 1977.

18. Quoting a "reliable witness," Senghor alleged in an interview with *Jeune Afrique* (December 23, 1977) that, when Polisario captured one group of Mauritanians, "the Moors were spared and the blacks had their throats slit." He went on: "If the status of Mauritania, its people, its regime, were modified as a result of neo-imperialism, Senegal would demand at the United Nations that the 500,000 Mauritanians who are ethnically and culturally Senegalese be allowed to exercise their right to self-determination." The main Senegalese opposition parties, the Rassemblement National Démocratique (RND) and the Parti Démocratique Sénégalais (PDS), strongly opposed Senghor's Western Saharan policy. The RND, for example, demanded (November 7, 1977) "the immediate revoking" of the Franco-Senegalese military accords, which "make Senegal a bastion of French colonialism," and declared that "the RND and the Senegalese people will not accept national territory being used as a base for aggression against the friendly Saharawi and Algerian peoples."

19. Taton, *loc. cit.*, p. 14; *Le Nouvel Observateur*, November 14, 1977; *Le Monde*, November 18, 1977; *Guardian Weekly* (London), March 5, 1978; *Flight International*, January 7, 1978.

20. *Le Monde*, November 12, 1977.

21. *Le Monde*, November 22, 1977.

22. *Le Monde*, November 25, 1977.

23. *Le Monde*, November 8, 1977.

24. *Le Monde*, December 4–5, 1977, and December 6, 1977.

25. *Le Monde*, November 8, 1977.

26. *Le Monde*, November 22, 1977.

27. *El Moudjahid* (Algiers), December 14, 1977.

28. *Le Monde*, January 5, 1978; *West Africa* (London), January 16, 1978.

29. *Le Matin* (Paris), November 24, 1977.

30. *Le Monde*, November 27–28, 1977.

31. *El Moudjahid*, December 8, 1977.

32. *Le Monde*, December 24, 1977.

33. *La Croix*, December 22, 1977; SADR Defense Ministry communiqué, December 17, 1977.

34. *Le Monde*, December 20, 1977.

35. *L'Humanité* (Paris), December 22, 1977; *AFP*, dispatch from Nouakchott, December 19, 1977.

36. Polisario declaration, December 23, 1977.

37. *Le Monde*, December 25, 1977.

38. *Le Monde*, January 4, 1978.

39. *Algeria News Report* (Washington, D.C.), January 15, 1978.

24

The Nouakchott Coup

T HE JAGUARS inflicted serious setbacks on the guerrillas in December 1977.
However, they could not stop Polisario's Mauritanian offensive. The guerrillas had to adopt less audacious tactics than in the past and operated in smaller
groups to avoid detection from the air, but though they could no longer stage
large attacks of the kind they had made against Nouakchott and Zouerate in
1976–77, they could still interrupt traffic on the Zouerate-Nouadhibou railway.
Mauritania's economy slid into an almost unmanageable crisis during the early
months of 1978, and among soldiers and civilians alike, there was a yearning for
peace. The country could no longer sustain the burden of war.

The attacks on the COMINOR railway remained as frequent as ever. A train
was derailed on December 27, 1977, at Inal, midway between Zouerate and
Nouadhibou. On January 7, a train was attacked at Choum, 110 miles south of
Zouerate. Touajil, a station fifty miles to the north, came under fire on January
26. A month later, four locomotives were derailed when a train detonated plastic
explosive. Several hundred yards of track were destroyed and the railway was
closed for four days. When it reopened, on February 25, another train was
derailed sixty miles south of Zouerate.[1] And so it continued, month after month,
until the very eve of the military coup that deposed Mokhtar Ould Daddah in
Nouakchott the following July. Indeed, there were three attacks on the railway
within three weeks of the coup.[2]

As the Polisario raids continued, so did the buildup of Moroccan troops. There
were eight thousand of them in Mauritania and Tiris el-Gharbia by the end of
February 1978, and the following June, King Hassan said that there were nine
thousand.[3] The French Jaguars were in action again on May 3–5. "When the city
of Zouerate was threatened again by a Polisario column recently, we provided air
support to the Mauritanian forces at the Mauritanian authorities' request," the
French foreign minister, Louis de Guiringaud, announced on May 7. "The incident to which I am alluding occurred within Mauritania's international borders

257

and not in the contested territory of Western Sahara.''[4] Polisario, however, claimed that the air strikes were near Oum Dreiga, inside Western Sahara.[5]

By March, nine of COMINOR's twenty-six locomotives, each of them worth $1 million, had been seriously damaged and required months of repair work. Some of the train crews had resigned.[6] During 1977 the war had forced COMINOR to delay or cancel 150 trains, with a total load of 1.6 million tons of ore worth $22 million, the equivalent of 18 percent of the country's total iron-ore exports that year. The stocks of ore at Nouadhibou port fell by almost a million tons as SNIM tried to sustain exports.[7] Still, exports fell to 8.4 million tons in 1977, compared to a peak of 11.7 million tons in 1974, and in 1978 they declined still further to 6.5 million tons, 55 percent of the quantity exported in 1974. (See Table 24.1.) In value, iron exports fell from $153.7 million in 1976 to only $93.4 million in 1978.

This was a calamity for a country that was one of the poorest in the world, with a per capita GNP of only $270 in 1977, and depended on iron ore for around 80 percent of its export earnings and 25 percent of government revenue. Whereas Mauritania's external trade had been more or less balanced until 1974, it lurched heavily into deficit thereafter and exports covered only half the cost of imports by 1977–78. (See Table 24.2.) As for SNIM, it was losing 1 billion ouguiyas a year by 1977 and so stopped paying tax revenue to the government.

The war was not entirely to blame. Like most non-oil-producing third world countries, Mauritania was suffering a dramatic deterioration in its terms of trade.

TABLE 24.1
THE FALL IN IRON EXPORTS

	1974	1975	1976	1977	1978
Output (mn tons)	11.9	8.6	9.4	7.5	7.1
Exports (mn tons)	11.7	8.7	9.7	8.4	6.5
Exports ($ mn)	123.5	137.6	153.7	127.0	93.4

Source: World Bank

TABLE 24.2
FOREIGN TRADE: THE SLIDE INTO DEFICIT
(billion ouguiyas)

	1973	1974	1975	1976	1977	1978
Exports	6.4	9.2	8.0	9.1	8.2	7.5
of which, iron	4.6	5.9	6.2	6.9	5.7	4.6
Imports	6.9	11.1	13.3	18.1	17.7	16.3
Trade deficit	0.5	1.9	5.3	9.0	9.5	8.8

Source: World Bank

Its oil-import bill had soared since the start of the oil-price spiral in 1973, whereas demand for its iron ore, and world iron prices, had fallen since 1976, as a result of the world steel recession. In addition, the collapse of world copper prices since 1974 had left the Akjoujt copper industry unprofitable, and in May 1978 SNIM had to close down the Akjoujt mines.[8]

Furthermore, Mauritania's food-growing regions, in the extreme south, in the valleys of the River Senegal and its tributaries, had suffered repeated droughts, forcing the country to import most of its food. Only 9 percent of public investment had been channeled into rural development in 1970–73 and merely 6 percent in 1974–77. Cultivation techniques were extremely primitive and yields were so low that even in non-drought years the country could only grow about 60 percent of its food requirements. However, the war years were also years of drought. Output of millet and sorghum, the main crops, fell from 36,000 tons in 1975–76 to 21,000 tons in 1976–77, leaving a deficit of 100,000 tons to be covered by imports. In 1977–78 the harvest fell further, to only 14,000 tons (Table 24.3).

Admist all these economic difficulties, the Ould Daddah government had to divert ever more resources into the war against Polisario.

The military budget was increased by half in 1976, to 1.8 billion ouguiyas, from 1.2 billion ouguiyas in 1975. It was raised by a further 26 percent in 1977, by which time it was devouring about 30 percent of total government expenditure.[9] The only compensation was that Saudi Arabia footed the bill for some of the government's arms purchases from abroad.

To help pay for the war, the government introduced a new direct tax, known as the "solidarity levy," in 1976. Businesses had to pay a 2 percent tax on their turnover and salaried workers had one to three days' pay deducted every month.[10] Overall, however, the government's revenue fell, because the mining industry slid into the red and stopped paying taxes. By contrast, government expenditure soared, partly because of the sharp rise in military outlays and interest payments on the mounting public debt. The overall treasury deficit rose remorselessly, from 0.4 billion ouguiyas in 1975 to 2.9 billion ouguiyas ($64 million) in 1976 and 4.1 billion ouguiyas ($91 million) in 1977. At first, budgetary support from conservative Arab states (6.6 billion ouguiyas in 1976) bridged the gap, but in 1977 Arab budgetary aid fell sharply, to 3.6 billion ouguiyas, and the government's financial difficulties became critical.

Meanwhile, as iron exports declined and imports of oil, food and armaments climbed higher and higher, the balance of payments current account deficit grew

TABLE 24.3
THE IMPACT OF DROUGHT

	1973–74	1974–75	1975–76	1976–77	1977–78
Output of millet and sorghum (tons)	50,000	45,000	36,000	21,000	14,000

Source: Banque Centrale de Mauritanie

dangerously large, quadrupling from $45 million in 1976 to $208 million, the equivalent of 45 percent of the country's GDP, in 1977. Again, the deficit was cushioned by the inflow of Arab funds in 1976, but in 1977, when this aid fell sharply, the overall balance of payments deficit reached $45 million. The government was in such trouble by then that it could no longer honor some of its external debt obligations.[11]

The regime's foreign exchange pressures had been made doubly serious by the fact that it had borrowed on a very large scale, on hard terms, to finance investment in a series of ambitious but ill-conceived industrial projects, including an $87-million oil refinery and a $25-million sugar refinery, neither of which could be profitably operated when they were completed in 1977 and so never entered production. In consequence, the goverment had accumulated a heavy burden of foreign debt which the war, the world steel crisis, the droughts and the rise in oil prices made increasingly difficult to finance. By the end of 1977, the country's outstanding, disbursed external public debt had climbed to $457 million, the equivalent of 112 percent of the country's GNP, the highest ratio recorded anywhere in the world. Including undisbursed borrowings, the external public debt had reached $677 million, and 22 percent of export earnings were being drafted into debt-service payments.[12]

The economic crisis came to a head in 1978. Under the 1978 budget the government resolved to cut its current expenditure by 16 percent in the hope of reducing the overall treasury deficit to 2.8 billion ouguiyas. However, as the World Bank reported later in the year, "with the continued deterioration in the economic situation, this objective soon became impossible to achieve. Indeed, a sharp reduction in revenue was unavoidable, as practically the only taxes that could be collected were import duties. In mid-1978, the situation became almost unmanageable."[13] By the end of April the total outstanding public external debt, including undisbursed borrowings, had reached $711 million. Foreign-exchange reserves dropped to an all-time low and external-debt arrears rose to 0.3 billion ouguiyas. As a crisis measure, the government blocked all expenditures with the exception of salary and debt-service payments. Even then, in July, on the eve of the coup, the Ould Daddah regime had to raise $35-million emergency aid from France, Libya and Morocco to pay civil servants' salaries.[14]

In June, a World Bank mission arrived in Nouakchott, at the government's request, to help draft an economic rehabilitation plan. However, it was quite obvious that no recovery was possible without an end to the war. The struggle with Polisario was not only placing unbearable strains on government finances and compounding the iron industry's troubles, but it was casting an ominous shadow over a massive iron-mining investment plan, upon which, with little exaggeration, the country's economic future would hinge. The existing iron mines, at Kedia d'Idjil, near Zouerate, had only enough ore left to maintain mining until the late 1980s. However, there were additional deposits of about 500 million tons of ore at El-Rhein and Oum Arwagen, about twelve miles from Zouerate. According to a World Bank appraisal study in 1977, investments totalling $938 million would be required to exploit the iron-bearing outcroppings, or *guelbs*, there and to build the necessary beneficiary plant to convert the low-grade ore (38 percent iron) into an acceptable sinter feed (65 percent iron). "The stakes on the *guelbs* are very important," remarked SNIM's director-general, Ismael Ould Amar, in June 1978. "Not to proceed with the *guelbs* would mean the country losing 80 percent of its resources and foreign exchange."[15] At a meeting at the World Bank's Paris headquarters in January 1978, several Arab and Western governments and financial institutions offered loans totalling $376 million to help finance the Guelbs Project's $501 million first phase.[16] But these huge sums could not be invested in the Zouerate region unless security was restored to northern Mauritania. In short, the war had to be brought to an end.

Meanwhile, social problems were piling up on an unprecedented scale in Mauritania's cities, which had been swollen by a huge influx of refugees, both nomads and peasants, from the drought-stricken countryside. Mauritania was in the throes of a real demographic revolution. Between 1965 and 1977, one in two of the country's nomads had become sedentary. By January 1977, 64 percent of Mauritanians were sedentary, compared to only 35 percent in 1965. Moreover, 22 percent of the country's population of 1.42 million had settled in the urban areas by January 1977. The urban population had been rising at an average annual rate of 10 percent since 1962 and had reached 310,764.

The population of Nouakchott, which had been founded near a little village of five hundred inhabitants in 1958 to serve as Mauritania's capital after independence, had grown at an annual average rate of no less than 19.4 percent since 1964, soaring from 12,300 to 134,986; and projections based on the 1976–77 census suggested that the capital's population would reach 235,000 by 1982.[17] Most of the capital's population (81,279 out of 134,986) were living in shacks and tents in Arrondissements 1 and 5, two sprawling and squalid squatter settlements on the city's outskirts, and depended on the solidarity of relatives for survival. For, in the country as a whole, there were no more than 48,700 jobs in the modern sector of the economy, 39,700 of them in the urban areas.[18]

Ironically, Mokhtar Ould Daddah had appeared to be politically secure on the eve of the Western Saharan war. His nationalist reforms in 1972–75—the renegotiation of the post-independence economic agreements with France and the revoking of the Franco-Mauritanian military accords in 1972–73, the decision to withdraw from the Franc Zone in November 1972, the launching of the ouguiya in June 1973 and the nationalization, albeit with compensation, of the iron mines in November 1974 and the copper mines in April 1975—had disarmed his left-wing critics in the MND and its Maoist "vanguard," the Parti des Kadihines de Mauritanie (PKM—Mauritanian Workers Party), which had accordingly announced their dissolution and joined the ruling PPM a few days before its fourth congress, on August 15–20, 1975. As in 1961, when he had neutralized and absorbed the Nahda, Ould Daddah had shown remarkable skill in reorienting government policy to impress and coopt the left-wing opposition.[19]

"The consolidation of the domestic front at the fourth congress," the PPM would remark in April 1976, "permitted the final trial, the reunification of the fatherland, to be tackled victoriously."[20] Despite their former collaboration with Polisario, during El-Ouali's stay in Mauritania in 1973–74, the PPM's new Kadihine recruits made no attempt to oppose Ould Daddah's Western Saharan policy—a policy which, ironically, by plunging Mauritania into war, undermined all the anti-imperialist measures that had attracted them to the PPM and forced

Ould Daddah to turn back to France, as well as conservative Arab states such as Morocco and Saudi Arabia, for military or financial aid.

Far away from the main population centers in southern Mauritania, the conflict in Western Sahara seemed distant and abstract to most Mauritanians at first. The annexation of Tiris el-Gharbia never aroused the kind of passionate enthusiasm that swelled up in Morocco at the time of the Green March. Moreover, as the war grew in intensity and Polisario began raiding into southern Mauritania, from the middle of 1976, and as the toll in human life and economic damage became less and less bearable, most Mauritanians, Moors and black Africans alike, began to question the worth of such sacrifice. In the north, where many came from tribes straddling the old borders, there was widespread sympathy for Polisario and some even left for Tindouf to enroll in Polisario.

A large proportion of the inhabitants of Mauritania's Regions 8 (Nouadhibou) and 11 (Zouerate and the far northeast) and a smaller number in Region 7 (Adrar) were Ahel es-Sahel, from such *qabael* as the Reguibat, the Oulad Delim, the Oulad Bou Sbaa or the Ahel Berikallah, who had settled in northern Mauritania, like their kinsmen in Western Sahara, over the previous decade.[21] It was in these regions that the UN mission of inquiry on Western Sahara had witnessed pro-Polisario as well as PPM-sponsored demonstrations during its visit to Mauritania in June 1975.[22] Some of these Polisario supporters left for Tindouf, to join the struggle for Saharawi independence, after the Madrid Accords, and former residents of Zouerate were among the guerrillas who attacked the city in May 1977.[23]

Some Saharawis who had lived in Mauritania assumed leadership positions in Polisario. For example, Ibrahim Hakim, a Reguibi who had followed a career in Mauritania's diplomatic service since 1966, serving as *chargé d'affaires* at the Mauritanian embassy in Algiers in the early seventies, joined Polisario in 1975 and, on account of his previous diplomatic experience, was appointed foreign minister of the SADR in March 1976.[24]

Another prominent recruit from Mauritania was Ahmed-Baba Miske, a member of the Ahel Berikallah, *zwaya* who traditionally lived in Adrar Soutouf as well as northern Mauritania. One of the leaders of the Nahda, he had joined the PPM after the Nahda's dissolution in 1961, becoming the party's secretary until 1964, when he was posted to New York as Mauritania's permanent representative at the UN. In 1966, however, he had fallen out again with Ould Daddah and gone into exile, to spend most of the following nine years as a writer and journalist in Paris, before joining Polisario in 1975. He was a member of the front's political bureau from 1976 to 1978.[25] "I have strong ties on both sides of the frontier," he wrote in 1978, explaining his motives for joining Polisario. "While participating in the struggle of the Saharawi people, I was among my own kin, but I never felt that I was betraying my ties to Mauritania. This war was waged against the interests of the two brother peoples and, by opposing it, I was acting in common with the great majority of Mauritanians. Others opposed it from within."[26]

To many of the Moors, the war with Polisario soon seemed a fratricidal one. The *zwaya*, besides, feared that the war would revive the traditions and influence of the *ahel mdafa*, the "warrior" *gabael* of the past, while some of the latter, such as the Oulad Ghailan of Adrar, saw the crisis as an opportunity to seek revenge on the marabout elite that had dominated the state under Ould Daddah, himself a member of the Oulad Birri, the principal *zwaya* of Trarza.[27] To keep the latter in check, the PPM regime recruited principally, as it hurriedly built up the army in 1976–78, from the black African minorities, the Toucouleurs (Pulaar), the Peuls, the Sarakolle (Soninke) and the Wolofs, who together constitute about one-third of the Mauritanian population.[28] But the blacks who enlisted did so for economic, not patriotic motives, to escape the drought and poverty rather than to fight Polisario. They regarded the war as an inter-Arab conflict that was completely foreign to their own problems and interests yet resulted in the death or imprisonment of hundreds of black soldiers.[29]

As the economic crisis drifted almost beyond control in 1977–78, the technocratic elite in the civil service, as well as private businessmen, recognized that there would be no chance of economic recovery without an end to the war, and as the Ould Daddah regime began to flounder, almost helpless in the face of its multiple difficulties, business interests saw their chance to rid themselves of a government that had not only dragged the country into its ruinous war, but had also given private capital little scope in an economy dominated by parastatals. At the same time, Ould Daddah began to lose support on the left too, as the government cut back expenditure on development projects to pay for the bloated army and curb the soaring treasury deficit, cemented its ties with France and the conservative Arab monarchies, and, to secure Western and Arab support for the Guelbs Project, decided, at the PPM's third extraordinary congress, in January 1978, to allow foreign interests to acquire up to 49 percent of the equity of state companies, including SNIM.[30] The progressive "gains" of 1972–75 were being rolled back, and Saudi influence was encouraging the government to adopt an increasingly conservative profile, highlighted by the introduction of a strict form of *sharia* law in May 1978. Disenchantment was rife among young, educated Mauritanians, including the ex-Kadihines and members of the PPM Youth.[31]

The army officers, meanwhile, were dismayed by their units' losses in the war and, after the signing of the Moroccan-Mauritanian defense pact in May 1977, felt humiliated by the buildup of Moroccan troops and their reduced influence over the conduct of the war on their own territory. They gradually lost the will to fight, and there were even a few cases of desertion, mainly by northerners, to the guerrillas.[32] In fact, the rapid growth of the Moroccan military presence in Mauritania in 1977–78, less than a decade since the days when the country's independence was being contested by Morocco, rubbed against the grain of many Mauritanians. Polisario went a step further, accusing Ould Daddah of paving the way for a complete Moroccan takeover.[33]

So, by 1978, Mokhtar Ould Daddah was dangerously isolated. Despite French and Moroccan military aid, he could not halt the guerrilla offensive. The COMINOR railway remained under constant threat. Iron exports were falling sharply, drought was ravaging the farming regions of the south, scarce resources were being squandered on the war, and the government was on the verge of bankruptcy. Moors and blacks, technocrats and businessmen, students and ex-Kadihines—all wanted a change of government and peace. In the past, Ould Daddah had displayed great acumen in outmaneuvering or buying off political critics. This time, however, the main parameters of the crisis, in particular the

war, were beyond his powers of control. He had become a prisoner of his alliance
with Morocco, an alliance that had reduced Mauritania to a battleground in a
wider war over whose principal contestants he could exercise no influence.

During the night of July 9–10, 1978, the armed forces seized power in Nouakchott and set up a Comité Militaire de Redressement National (CMRN—Military
Committee for National Recovery), under the presidency of their chief-of-staff,
Lieutenant-Colonel Mustapha Ould Mohammed Salek, to "save the country
from ruin and dismemberment, preserve national unity and defend the existence
of the state."[34] The CMRN assumed full powers "until the establishment of
democratic institutions," dissolved the PPM and the National Assembly, and
placed Ould Daddah under arrest.[35] "Our country has reached catastrophe," the
new president explained. "I will not even say the edge of catastrophe; it has
reached catastrophe. Its coffers are empty; its whole trampled economy is almost
totally destroyed."[36]

The coup was welcomed by virtually the entire population, and several
thousands marched through Nouakchott on July 13 to congratulate the army,
though, apart from the desire for peace, the motives for rejoicing at Ould Daddah's downfall were by no means uniform. There were hopes of democratization
after thirteen years of de jure single-partyism, during which the PPM had been
enshrined in the constitution as "state party."[37] The trade unions, which had
been forcibly subordinated to the PPM in 1973, anticipated a wider measure of
autonomy, and the Nouakchott branches of the Union des Travailleurs Maurita-
niens (UTM) greeted the coup with a mass rally asserting "the sacred right of the
workers to organize themselves freely," in addition to demanding "a halt to the
fratricidal war through rapid talks for a just negotiated peace safeguarding the independence and dignity of all the peoples of the sub-region."[38] The black
minorities, which had resented the Ould Daddah regime's policy of Arabization,
hoped that the military committee would take a more even-handed approach to
communal-linguistic problems, though, as soon became apparent, there were
Moor officers in the new government who wanted to accelerate Arabization. Two
black cultural organizations, the Association pour la Renaissance du Pulaar and
the Association pour la Promotion de la Langue et de la Culture Soninke issued a
declaration after the coup urging "a just solution to the problem of teaching the
Pulaar, Soninke and Wolof national languages," as well as applauding the
CMRN's "declared intention to work rapidly for the establishment of peace."

Business circles too praised the armed forces for taking power, both because
economic recovery required ending Ould Daddah's war and because they hoped
the military committee would liberalize the economy. "The perspectives for our
country's economic development will be glowing once peace has been restored,"
said Ismael Ould Amar of SNIM after the coup.[39] The Confédération des
Employeurs et des Artisans de Mauritanie (CEAM) organized a motorcade
through Nouakchott on July 16 to demonstrate its "total adherence" to the
military committee and two days later expressed its gratitude to the army for
"destroying the system that ruined our businesses."[40]

The military committee shared the CEAM's concerns. The CEAM's president,
Sheikhna Ould Laghdaf, was appointed foreign minister, and on July 14

Mustapha Ould Mohammed Salek announced that the CMRN would "encourage private initiative in the framework of a liberal economy."

The one aspiration shared by everyone was peace. Without it, economic recovery was impossible, and the military government made it plain at once that it planned to find a way out of the conflict. At his first press conference, on July 12, the new president promised that "we are definitely going to set out a timetable, with Morocco, . . . to lead us to peace, because, if the people want peace, the military committee will make sure they have peace."[41] If they failed to end the war, the country's new leaders must have known that, not only would they have no chance of arresting the slide toward economic collapse, but their government would end up as isolated and discredited as Ould Daddah's.

Two days after the coup, the Polisario Front announced a "temporary halt in military operations in Mauritanian territory" as a "gesture of good will" toward the new regime.[42] The Moroccan government, for its part, was understandably alarmed by the turn of events in Nouakchott and so King Hassan immediately dispatched two of his closest advisers, Ahmed Reda Guedira and Colonel-Major Ahmed Dlimi, to the Mauritanian capital to clarify the CMRN's intentions.[43]

The military committee's room for maneuver was extremely narrow, however. There was an obvious temptation to negotiate a bilateral agreement with Polisario, but Hassan could be expected to react violently to such a betrayal of the Madrid Accords and he had nine thousand troops in Mauritania and Tiris el-Gharbia, including some only 150 miles from the capital, at Akjoujt. Likewise, however, Polisario might lift its cease-fire if the new government failed to begin serious negotiations. So, with great prudence, the CMRN tried to encourage all the parties to the conflict to move toward a global peace agreement, involving compromises on all sides, including, perhaps, the creation of a Saharawi mini-state in Tiris el-Gharbia. It was to prove an impossible goal.

NOTES

1. *Le Monde* (Paris), January 5, 1978, January 17, 1978, February 23, 1978, and February 28, 1978.
2. Interview with Jean-Eudes Barbier, AFP correspondent, Nouakchott, August 22, 1978.
3. *Le Monde*, February 15, 1978, and February 26, 1978; *L'Express* (Paris), June 26-July 2, 1978.
4. *Le Monde*, May 9, 1978.
5. Polisario Front, *Memorandum to the Bureau of Coordination of the Movement of Non-Aligned Countries, Havana, May 15-20, 1978.*
6. *Africa Research Bulletin* (Exeter), Economic Series, Vol. 15, No. 3, April 30, 1978.
7. Information supplied by SNIM, Nouakchott, August 1978.
8. *Le Matin du Sahara* (Casablanca), August 12, 1978.
9. *Le Monde*, April 10, 1976; *New York Times*, January 3, 1977; *Europe-Outremer* (Paris), No. 574, November 1977.
10. *Le Monde*, April 10, 1976.
11. World Bank report No. 2479a-MAU, June 4, 1979, p. 16.
12. *Ibid.*, pp. 8, 15-17.
13. *Ibid.*, p. 18.
14. *Ibid.*, p. 18; Interview with Jean-Eudes Barbier, Nouakchott, August 22, 1978.
15. *SNIM Informations* (Nouakchott), No. 122, June 10, 1978.
16. World Bank, *op. cit.*
17. *Seconds résultats provisoires du recensement général de la population (population au 1er janvier 1977)* (Bureau de Recensement de la Population, Ministère du Plan et des Mines, Nouakchott).

18. *Libération* (Casablanca), July 28-August 3, 1978.

19. See Jean-Louis Balans, "Le système politique mauritanien," in *Introduction à la Mauritanie* (CNRS, Paris, 1979), pp. 279–319; Francis de Chassey, *Mauritanie 1900-1975, de l'ordre colonial à l'ordre néo-colonial entre Maghreb et Afrique Noire* (Editions Anthropos, Paris, 1978), pp. 383–440.

20. *Tiris el Gharbia, Hier-Aujourd'hui-Demain*, Synthèse des travaux du colloque organisé par l'INEEP du 8 au 11 avril 1976 (PPM, Nouakchott, 1976), p. 8.

21. Regions 7, 8 and 11 had populations of 55,482, 24,460 and 22,467 respectively, according to the 1976–77 census. See *Seconds résultats provisoires du recensement général de la population (population au 1er janvier 1977)*, p. 19.

22. Report of the United Nations Visiting Mission to Spanish Sahara, 1975, in *General Assembly Official Records*, 30th Session, Supplement No. 23, UN Document A/10023/Rev.1, pp. 104–5.

23. "Among them we recognized quite a few people who worked or had worked with us in Mauritania," noted Yves Haristoy, one of the Frenchmen captured in the raid, after his release. (*Le Monde*, December 27, 1977.)

24. For Ibrahim Hakim's biography, see Tony Hodges, *Historical Dictionary of Western Sahara* (Scarecrow Press, Metuchen, N.J., 1982), pp. 179–180.

25. *Ibid.*, pp. 21–23, for a biography of Ahmed-Baba Miske.

26. Letter to *Jeune Afrique* (Paris), November 8, 1978. Ahmed-Baba Miske also explained his motives for supporting Polisario in a feature article in *Le Monde*, November 16, 1977.

27. Balans, *loc. cit.*, p. 317; *Sahara Libre* (Polisario, Algiers), No. 40, July 24, 1977.

28. According to estimates based on the 1976–77 census, the black Africans numbered 467,000, compared to 933,000 for the Moors. See Francisco Vergara, "L'économie de la Mauritanie et son développement," in *Introduction à la Mauritanie* (CNRS, Paris, 1979), p. 178.

29. Balans, *loc. cit.*, pp. 316–17. Of the 17,000 men in the armed forces by the end of 1977, about 10,000 were black Africans.

30. *Le Monde*, January 27, 1978. The plan to sell off 49 percent of the equity of SNIM was enacted the following April. Within a few months, $120 million of SNIM shares had been sold to the Arab Mining Company ($28 million), the Kuwait Foreign Trading, Contracting and Investment Company ($40 million), the Islamic Development Bank ($10 million) and the governments of Iraq ($22 million) and Morocco ($20 million). (World Bank news release 80/1, July 16, 1979.)

31. An antiwar resolution was presented by dissidents at the PPM Youth Congress in August 1977 but was barred from debate.

32. In January 1978, for example, Polisario presented to the press two former cadets of the Atar military academy, Sheikh Ould Mohammed and Mohammed Ould Ahmed, who had joined the front the previous December. (*Le Monde*, January 11, 1978.)

33. "The monarchist forces effectively occupy all the important centers and above all the strategic or sensitive areas of the territory, under the cover of the slogan of 'common defense,' a slogan that is nothing other than a veil that serves to mask the process of occupation of Mauritania by Morocco. . . . When will the king proclaim Mauritania's annexation to his kingdom?" (*Sahara Libre*, October 29, 1977.)

34. *Le Matin* (Paris), July 11, 1978. Mustapha Ould Mohammed Salek, an officer in the Mauritanian army since 1961, had participated in the defense of Nouakchott in June 1976 and become commander of the 3rd military region (Adrar) in July 1977, before being appointed chief-of-staff by Ould Daddah in February 1978.

35. Ould Daddah was detained until August 1979 and allowed to go into exile the following October. In November 1980 he was condemned *in absentia* to life imprisonment for "high treason, violating the Constitution and attacking the economic interests of the nation."

36. *Chaab* (Nouakchott), August 19–20, 1978.

37. There had been a *de facto* one-party system since the "round-table" conference of 1961, when the Nahda and other opposition groups agreed to join the ruling party. The formal establishment of a one-party system was approved by a conference of the PPM at Kaedi in January 1964 and enacted, by constitutional amendment, in 1965. See Chassey, *op. cit.*, pp. 273–77; Balans, *loc. cit.*, pp. 294–95.

38. Déclaration de Soutien des Travailleurs du District de Nouakchott au Comité Militaire de Redressement National.

39. *SNIM Informations*, No. 128, July 22, 1978.

40. *Chaab*, July 17, 1978.

41. *Le Monde*, December 14, 1978.

42. *Le Monde*, July 14, 1978.

43. *Le Monde*, July 11, 1978.

25

The Agreement
of Algiers

THE MAURITANIAN ARMY'S road to peace was not to be an easy one. Fearful of how King Hassan might react to a bilateral agreement with Polisario, the new military committee attempted to bring Morocco into a global peace settlement. The officers in Nouakchott hoped, rather naïvely, that their very decision to depose Mokhtar Ould Daddah would unleash a "peace dynamic" that would bring all the parties to the conflict to the negotiating table in a spirit of compromise. The French government, which had pragmatically redefined its Western Saharan policy after Operation Lamantin, was keen to assist the CMRN by bringing its influence to bear on Rabat and Algiers. The Mauritanian and French governments began toying with the idea of a Saharawi mini-state in Tiris el-Gharbia, in the hope that such a compromise would satisfy both Polisario's aspirations to statehood and Morocco's Saharan claims. However, despite Polisario's proclamation of a cease-fire in Mauritanian territory two days after the Nouakchott coup, the goal of a global peace agreement proved utopian. Neither Algeria nor Polisario were prepared to accept anything less than Western Sahara's full independence, within its pre-1975 borders, while King Hassan feared that the establishment of a mini-state in Tiris el-Gharbia would merely encourage Polisario to fight on for a second victory in the Moroccan sector. As the search for a global agreement ran aground, the military committee faced equally daunting economic and political challenges at home. Moreover, Polisario gradually lost patience with the military committee and started threatening to lift its cease-fire if Mauritania did not abandon Tiris el-Gharbia unconditionally, with or without Rabat's approval. Finally, one year after the coup, the Saharawi nationalists lifted the truce, finally forcing the Nouakchott government to throw in the towel, to Hassan's inevitable protests.

The CMRN's desire to include Morocco in a global peace agreement was made plain by Lieutenant-Colonel Mustapha Ould Mohammed Salek immediately after the July 1978 coup. In a radio broadcast on July 14, he announced that the

267

military committee was "determined to find a solution to the question of the war in conformity with the Mauritanian people's higher interests and in agreement with the brotherly Kingdom of Morocco."[1] Indeed, before initiating contacts with the guerrillas, he wanted to reach an understanding with Morocco on the broad outlines of a negotiating strategy. "We ardently want to achieve peace," he explained on July 13. "But no dialogue between us and the Polisario Front has been started for the moment. It won't be until we have first reached agreement with our Moroccan friends and allies about what has to be done, jointly, to reach this objective."[2] The CMRN's caution was easy to understand. There were nine thousand Moroccan troops in Mauritania and Tiris el-Gharbia, and Hassan could be expected to react violently to any attempt by Mauritania to renounce the Madrid accords unilaterally.

In the hope that France would exploit its historic links with Morocco and Algeria to encourage an overall settlement, the CMRN sent one of its members, Lieutenant-Colonel Ahmed Salem Ould Sidi, to Paris, to meet Giscard d'Estaing on July 27.[3] The French government was willing to assist. Given the large number of French officers working with the Mauritanian armed forces since 1977, it had known, long before the coup, of the Mauritanian officers' desire to end the war. It may even have known beforehand of the coup plot and refrained from tipping off Mokhtar Ould Daddah. In any event, it knew that, though the French air strikes had obliged the guerrillas to adjust their tactics, they had not halted their Mauritanian offensive or diminished Algeria's resolve to support them. The war had brought Mauritania to the brink of economic ruin and, to the alarm of the French steel company Usinor, was putting the future of the Guelbs Project in question. Additionally, French military intervention in Mauritania had damaged France's relations with Algeria, at considerable cost to French business interests.

There had always, since Algeria's independence, been elements of tension in Franco-Algerian relations. To the memories of the bloody liberation struggle had been added clashes of economic interest—notably France's protectionist measures against imports of Algerian wine in 1969–70, the nationalization of French oil interests in Algeria in 1971 and the ensuing retaliation by the French oil companies, which stopped importing Algerian oil. In April 1975, just before his trip to Morocco, Giscard d'Estaing had signaled his desire to open a new chapter in Franco-Algerian relations by becoming the first French president to have visited independent Algeria. But, to President Houari Boumedienne's dismay, Giscard had then given backhanded support to King Hassan when Morocco marched into Western Sahara later in the year. Giscard had become Morocco's main arms supplier during the war with Polisario and ended up sending the French air force into action in Mauritania. On a wider canvas, Boumedienne had been angered by Giscard's covert support for the anti-MPLA factions in Angola in 1975–76, France's continuing arms sales to South Africa and the intervention of French forces in Zaire and Chad in 1977–78.

The difficulties facing Algerian immigrants in France added to the tension. There had been a gradual tightening of restrictions on immigration into France since 1972, and, though a special bilateral Franco-Algerian agreement in 1968 had given the 850,000 Algerians in France ten-year automatically renewable residence permits, the French government indicated in 1977–78 that their status would have to be renegotiated.[4] In addition, there had been frequent racist assaults on Algerian immigrants in France, some of them fatal, like the shooting of the guardian of the Amicale des Algériens in Paris in December 1977.

Another cause of friction was the hefty imbalance in Franco-Algerian trade. France had switched its oil purchases from Algeria to Saudi Arabia in the early seventies but had remained Algeria's principal supplier, despite growing competition from West Germany. Algeria bought 24 percent of its imports from France in 1977 and was still France's largest export market in the third world. Algeria's trade deficit with France rose from 3 billion francs in 1976 to 4.9 billion francs in 1977, when France sold more than twice as much to Algeria (8.8 billion francs) as it bought from Algeria (3.9 billion francs).[5]

Operation Lamantin was the first straw for Boumedienne. At the end of 1977 he sent a memorandum to the directors of the state-owned companies that dominate the Algerian economy, advising them not to award contracts, wherever possible, to French firms.[6] In consequence, French exports to Algeria fell from 8.8 billion francs in 1977 to 6.9 billion francs in 1978 and the trade deficit declined to 3.7 billion francs.[7]

The first sign of French alarm at the souring of relations with Algeria came on February 9, 1978, when, on French TV, Giscard d'Estaing proposed putting Franco-Algerian relations on a new footing.[8] Boumedienne replied on May 1 that talks on bilateral relations could start "as soon as the political and security problems posed by the French military presence in the region have been resolved."[9]

Having lost more than he had gained from direct military intervention in the Western Saharan war, Giscard d'Estaing took advantage of the Nouakchott coup to adopt a more prudent and evenhanded approach to the conflict, in the hope of repairing French relations with Algeria, helping to ease Mauritania out of the war and facilitating contacts between Rabat and Algiers. Almost immediately after the coup, in fact, Giscard d'Estaing began testing reactions to the idea of French mediation. A stream of visitors passed through the Elysée Palace—Abdelaziz Bouteflika, the Algerian foreign minister, who happened to be in Paris at the time of the coup; Abdal-Salam Jalloud, one of Colonel Qadhafi's closest associates; Ahmed Reda Guedira, a Moroccan royal councillor; the CMRN's envoy, Ahmed Salem Ould Sidi; and Félix Houphouet-Boigny, the president of the Ivory Coast, who announced after lunching with the French president on August 2 that he would try his hand at mediation too.[10] Finally, on August 11, Giscard d'Estaing wrote to inform President Gaafar Numeiry of Sudan, who was then chairman of the OAU, that "if France's relations with the interested states can facilitate a better reciprocal understanding of viewpoints, it is prepared to lend its assistance and keep the relevant African bodies informed."[11]

By February 1979, Giscard d'Estaing was describing the Western Saharan conflict as a "problem of decolonization," while his secretary of state for foreign affairs, Olivier Stirn, alluded to "the Saharawis' right to self-determination" and confirmed France's willingness "to contribute to a solution."[12] However, it was the formula of a Saharawi mini-state in Tiris el-Gharbia that exercised minds in both Paris and Nouakchott. The hope was that such a compromise would win the approval of both the Saharawis, by satisfying their aspirations for independence, and King Hassan, by allowing Morocco to keep its share of the partitioned territory. In fact, the mini-state idea satisfied neither side. From Hassan's standpoint, the creation of a Saharawi state in Tiris el-Gharbia risked legitimizing the very concept of Saharawi nationhood and providing Polisario with a territory from which to pursue its struggle against Morocco. So, in a blunt warning to the CMRN on August 20, 1978, the king ruled out the idea of a Saharawi state of any kind. There were two conditions, he insisted, for Moroccan acceptance of a peace settlement. "First of all, this solution must not involve any threat to our territorial integrity." Secondly, "Morocco has a common border with Mauritania and cannot accept this state of affairs being modified." Two days later, Ahmed Reda Guedira flew into Nouakchott to brief Mustapha Ould Mohammed Salek on Hassan's motives. The Moroccan government, he declared at Nouakchott airport, insisted on "respecting the territorial integrity of Mauritania and Morocco and rejecting the creation of a micro-state on the frontiers between the two countries."[13] To all intents and purposes, Morocco was telling the CMRN that it could not make any territorial concessions to Polisario at all. The 1976 partition had to remain sacrosanct. It was little wonder that, on his first post-coup visit to Morocco to meet Hassan, on September 18, Mustapha Ould Mohammed Salek would describe the search for peace as "long and difficult."[14]

The CMRN had made as little headway with Polisario as with Morocco. Contacts with the guerrilla movement had been made on July 23 and August 10 during visits to Tripoli by CMRN envoys.[15] Then, more extensive talks had been held with a Polisario delegation, headed by Bashir Mustapha Sayed and Mahfoud Ali Beiba, in Paris on September 9–16.[16] "Polisario is a reality which we recognize, perhaps not as exclusive representative, but we know it exists and has a role to play in the peace process," acknowledged the Mauritanian foreign minister, Sheikhna Ould Laghdaf, at the time.[17] However, the mini-state proposal did not appeal to Polisario. Settling for Tiris el-Gharbia meant giving up the most important part of the territory, including the phosphate mines and the two main towns, and making do with a tiny enclave of desert with no significant economic resources. Polisario insisted, instead, on Mauritania's unconditional withdrawal from Western Sahara, but the CMRN was too mindful of the danger from Morocco to risk agreeing to that.

Polisario was understandably disillusioned by the military committee's caution. "If they really want peace," protested the SADR's information minister, Mohammed Salem Ould Salek, on the eve of the front's fourth congress, on September 25–28, "they must prove it by acts and go beyond the stage of vague declarations that maintain confusion and equivocation."[18] Nevertheless, the congress agreed to continue the cease-fire, while spelling out in a manifesto Polisario's conditions for a permanent peace agreement with Mauritania: "1. Official recognition of the sovereignty of the SADR over the whole of the territory of Western Sahara. 2. The restitution of the part which it occupies to the authorities of the SADR. 3. The withdrawal of Mauritanian forces to their internationally recognized frontiers (frontier of 1960)."[19]

Three weeks later, in mid-October, there were further talks in Bamako, Mali, and in Tripoli, where, for the first time, Mustapha Ould Mohammed Salek came face to face with Mohammed Abdelaziz. Upon his return to Nouakchott, the president of the CMRN stated that "no peace is possible in Western Sahara without contact with all the concerned parties, including the Polisario Front." But, once again, Polisario was disappointed by the CMRN's unwillingness to sign away Mauritania's territorial claims without conditions. The CMRN "wants to get out of the war without making peace," Ibrahim Hakim, the SADR's foreign minister, commented acidly.[20] "We are still waiting for a concrete gesture from Nouakchott," complained another Polisario leader, Mohammed Salem Ould Salek, a month later, in November. "We cannot be satisfied with vague declarations of intent as an answer to our cease-fire decision on July 12. This cannot be extended indefinitely if nothing happens."[21] Contrary, perhaps, to the CMRN's hopes, the Algerian government showed no inclination to temper the Saharawi nationalists' negotiating stance.

So the CMRN's bid for an overall peace settlement rapidly floundered, caught between the irreconcilable interests of Polisario and King Hassan. By the end of 1978, Mustapha Ould Mohammed Salek was at his wit's ends. There seemed to be no middle ground between Morocco and Polisario. The Mauritanian president was particularly angered by Hassan's intransigent and insensitive approach to his country's difficulties; and his impatience with the king was evident when he referred, in a New Year's speech, to "the right of self-determination of all peoples" and promised the Mauritanian people that the CMRN would "take all necessary measures to quit the war definitively . . . if the road leading to a global agreement remains impracticable."[22] To give his government greater freedom of action, he now wanted the Moroccan troops evacuated from Mauritanian territory as soon as possible. At the first post-coup meeting of the Moroccan-Mauritanian high command, held in Nouakchott on August 5–9, the Moroccans had agreed to pull out their six hundred troops from Akjoujt, but their withdrawal from this strategic city, only 150 miles down a good tarmac road from Nouakchott, had not been completed until December. The twelve-hundred-strong Moroccan garrison in Nouadhibou was the next to go, in January, leaving about seven thousand Moroccan troops in northeastern Mauritania and Tiris el-Gharbia.[23] "From now until the end of the first quarter of 1979, all the Moroccan troops will have departed," Mustapha Ould Mohammed Salek promised in January.[24] Mauritania would pursue its contacts with Polisario, "to give its brothers in blood, religion and language the choice of deciding for themselves and considering their future freely."[25]

Nonetheless, the CMRN continued to drift, apparently rudderless, under multiple, contradictory pressures from Rabat, Polisario, Algiers, Paris, Tripoli and even Dakar. Hassan, who wrote personally to the Mauritanian president on January 6 and 22, tried to restrain the CMRN from pursuing its contacts with Polisario, while testing whether, after Boumedienne's death on December 27, the Algerian regime could be persuaded to sell the guerrillas short. The king visited Paris to hold a series of four meetings with Giscard d'Estaing on February 14–19 and gained the French president's assurance that he would pass on to the Algerian government his desire for a summit meeting with the new Algerian president,

Chadli Bendjedid.[26] However, the new Algerian leader proved as unwilling as Boumedienne to negotiate with Morocco in lieu of the Saharawi nationalists and so Hassan's demarches came to nought.

The king kept six thousand troops in Mauritania and Tiris el-Gharbia after Mustapha Ould Mohammed Salek's March 31 deadline—two thousand in Zouerate, eight hundred in the Atar region, eight hundred at Bir Moghrein and twenty-five hundred in Tiris el-Gharbia, at Dakhla and Argoub.[27] As all the available policy options carried considerable risks, the CMRN was confused and divided over what to do, though it continued to dabble with the mini-state proposal, tying it to the idea of a referendum in Tiris el-Gharbia, despite the unacceptability of a mini-state solution to both Morocco and Polisario.

Meanwhile, the CMRN faced scarcely less daunting difficulties at home. "With regard to the economic situation," the president lamented in a newspaper interview in January 1979, "one cannot overstress how catastrophic it is."[28] By the end of 1978, the disbursed public external debt had climbed to $574 million, an amount equivalent to 138 percent of the country's GNP.[29] With iron-export earnings still depressed due to the fall in steel output in Europe, and both the military and debt burdens and SNIM's losses weighing on the treasury, external trade and government finances remained heavily in deficit. The country hovered on the brink of a financial collapse that was only averted by the CMRN's success, with the help of the World Bank, whose economic recovery plan it approved in September, in raising an additional $171.5 million of foreign aid between July 1978 and January 1979 and rescheduling some of the country's external debts.[30]

In the long term, however, the country's economic future hinged on the Guelbs Project. The continuation of iron-ore exploitation, the World Bank advised, "is (and will remain in the foreseeable future) the main support of the Mauritanian economy. Indeed, the Guelbs Project is the cornerstone of the government's rehabilitation plan. Without it, all the efforts to redress the economy (including debt rescheduling) currently underway would be in vain."[31] Fifteen foreign governments, companies, banks and aid agencies promised in 1978–79 to cofinance the project's $500-million first stage, to open up the 360-million-ton deposits at El-Rhein.[32] However, such huge investment was contingent on a guarantee of long-term security in northern Mauritania, and that in turn required Mauritania's definitive withdrawal from the Western Saharan conflict.

Moreover, by sweeping away Ould Daddah's monolithic political system, the CMRN had lifted the lid off a pandora's box of submerged social tensions. In particular, the rivalry between Moors and black Africans returned once again to the forefront of Mauritanian politics.[33] The blacks were alarmed by the strong Arabist element in the CMRN, personified by the first post-coup interior minister, Jiddou Ould Salek, who proclaimed "the country's attachment in its entirety to Arab-Islamic culture" in November 1978.[34] Then, when tracts decrying the military committee's continuation of "Mokhtar Ould Daddah's chauvinist and tribalist policy" were circulated in Nouakchott and black teachers threatened to strike in protest at Arabization measures in the schools, several black activists were arrested in February 1979.[35]

President Senghor of Senegal cashed in on this ethnic tension in order to pressure the CMRN not to succumb to Polisario or align with Libya and Algeria. Recalling Senghor's December 1977 threats to support the Mauritanian blacks' right to secession, the progovernment Dakar newspaper *Le Soleil* ran a series of articles on March 8–10 accusing the CMRN of racial discrimination, and two weeks later, on March 26, a black Mauritanian exile in Dakar was allowed by the Senegalese authorities to announce the founding of a black secessionist movement known as the Walfougi Front.[36]

The CMRN itself began to divide into factional clans as it tried to find a way out of its maze of domestic and regional difficulties. On March 20, Mustapha Ould Mohammed Salek managed to have himself invested by the military committee with "full powers" to "face up to the exceptional situation" and, in a broadcast speech to the Mauritanian people, promised to "take all the measures that are indispensable in order to get out of the war definitively, in the event that a global solution between all the concerned parties proves impossible."[37] Within a fortnight, however, he had been stripped of his dictatorial powers. The military committee had not been unanimous in granting them to him in the first place, and when a scandal broke out over the ethnic imbalance in nominations to a national consultative commission, which was to advise the president, and its small minority of black members refused to take their seats, the knives were out.[38] In a palace coup, on April 6, the CMRN was displaced by a new Comité Militaire de Salut National (CMSN), which declared that the armed forces would henceforth exercise "real" power. "The association with civilians had developed a system of government unsuited to face up to present difficulties," explained the new committee's strongman, Lieutenant-Colonel Ahmed Ould Bouceif, a veteran of the war against Polisario who was now appointed premier, while Mustapha Ould Mohammed Salek remained president in a purely titular capacity.[39]

Interethnic relations remained as fraught as ever, though, and during May blacks staged new protest strikes and demonstrations against Arabization measures in education.[40] Then, on May 27, barely seven weeks after his palace putsch, Ahmed Ould Bouceif died in an air crash near Dakar, throwing the military regime into yet more turmoil. On May 31, another officer, Lieutenant-Colonel Mohammed Khouna Ould Heydalla, who had taken much of the blame for the debacle at Zouerate in May 1977 but had been appointed chief-of-staff of the armed forces after the 1978 coup, was chosen by the CMSN to succeed to the premiership, and four days later Mustapha Ould Mohammed Salek abandoned the presidency, to be succeeded by yet another lieutenant-colonel, Mohammed Mahmoud Ould Ahmed Louly, who likewise held purely titular office.

Upon taking power, on April 6, Ahmed Ould Bouceif had said that the Moroccan troops in Mauritania would stay put.[41] He believed, it would seem, that Mustapha Ould Mohammed Salek had been tilting too far toward Polisario, threatening the country's delicate relations with Rabat. The CMSN made yet another bid for a multilateral peace settlement. So Ahmed Ould Bouceif flew to Rabat to meet Hassan on May 2 and then proceeded to Paris the next day to solicit Giscard d'Estaing's assistance once again. However, the CMSN was far from optimistic about the prospects of success, and it was probably as divided and confused as ever about what to do. Indeed, Ahmed Ould Bouceif's own anxieties were paraphrased in a report by Presidents Moussa Traore of Mali and Olusegun Obasanjo of Nigeria, who met the Mauritanian premier in Nouakchott on May 1 during a fact-finding mission to northwest Africa. "Mauritania and Polisario cannot restore peace by themselves alone without the guarantees of the two powerful protagonists, Algeria and Morocco," he reportedly argued. "Mauritania cannot subscribe to a so-called peace solution that in fact drags the country into a new war. That is what would come from any solution that saw the Polisario Front continuing to wage war on Morocco because, gradually, Mauritania would find itself drawn again into the conflict, something it does not want at any price." This was why Mauritania was "in favor of a global solution to the problem." Ahmed Ould Bouceif seems to have feared that, if the CMSN signed a bilateral agreement with Polisario, it would be powerless to stop the guerrillas using Mauritanian territory to attack Moroccan positions in Western Sahara and that then Morocco might retaliate by striking across the Mauritanian border, even if it had repatriated its remaining troops from Mauritania. But Ahmed Ould Bouceif's impatience with Morocco was also evident from the report submitted by Traore and Obasanjo. "For want of a global solution," he reportedly told the OAU envoys at another stage in their conversations, "Mauritania is ready to adopt a partial solution, namely self-determination in the part of the Sahara which it administers," though only "on condition that self-determination in this framework leads to real peace."[42]

In fact, Ahmed Ould Bouceif's foreign minister, Ahmedou Ould Abdallah, had discussed the possibility of just such a partial agreement during conversations in Tripoli with the Libyan secretary of foreign affairs, Ali Abdesalem al-Treiki, on April 21–23. A furious row broke out afterward over what Ahmedou Ould Abdallah said, or agreed, in Tripoli. According to a supposedly joint communiqué issued by the Libyans after the talks, he had promised that Mauritania would "hand over to the Polisario Front the part of Western Sahara that it has annexed" and so would open negotiations with Polisario on May 26 "to sign a peace treaty guaranteeing the establishment of a permanent peace between them and the restitution by Mauritania to the Polisario Front of the part of Saharawi territory under its control."[43] At first, the CMSN denied that it had made any agreements at all in Tripoli. Then Ahmedou Ould Abdallah accused the Libyans of altering certain passages in the joint communiqué's original text.[44] In any case, no Mauritanian officials turned up in Tripoli for the May 26 rendezvous with Polisario. While retaining little faith that a global peace settlement was attainable, the CMSN was evidently still fearful, in its majority, of the consequences of adopting the only alternative option, a bilateral agreement with Polisario.

The Saharawi nationalists, however, were no longer prepared to put up with such hesitancy and indecision. On its first anniversary, on July 12, the guerrillas' cease-fire was suddenly lifted. A Polisario force attacked and overran Tichla, a small settlement in Tiris el-Gharbia, capturing scores of prisoners, including the local Mauritanian prefect.[45] The Mauritanian armed forces were now in a much worse state of preparedness than they had been before Ould Daddah's downfall. The troops, who had expected the military government to bring peace, were in no mood to resume the struggle against the guerrillas, and the officers had been preoccupied with politics in Nouakchott for the previous year.

The Tichla attack shook the CMSN out of its complacency. It could no longer prevaricate in the hope of eventually reaching the mirage of a global peace agreement. So, to Morocco's consternation, the Mauritanian delegation at an OAU summit conference, held a few days later, on July 17-20, in Monrovia, Liberia, voted in favor of a resolution advocating a referendum, on the options of independence or maintenance of the status quo, in the whole of Western Sahara. Meanwhile, the Mauritanian delegation established contact with Polisario representatives in the Liberian capital. "Morocco cannot accept the cession or alienation of the Saharan provinces," warned Ahmed Alaoui in *Maroc-Soir* on July 25, "and if Mauritania withdraws, Morocco can exercise its right of preemption in the name of history, in the name of its inalienable territorial integrity and also, above all, for a more simple reason, to assure its security."[46] In short, Morocco would seize Tiris el-Gharbia if Mauritania dared to give it up.

That was precisely what the CMSN was now preparing to do. On July 30, the new Mauritanian premier, Mohammed Khouna Ould Heydalla, declared that Mauritania had no claims to Western Saharan territory and wished to resume negotiations with Polisario "as rapidly as possible."[47] Talks opened in Algiers on August 3 and ended just two days later with the signing of a peace agreement by Bashir Mustapha Sayed and the CMSN's second vice-president, Lieutenant-Colonel Ahmed Salem Ould Sidi. "The Islamic Republic of Mauritania," it stated, "solemnly declares that it does not have and will not have territorial or any other claims over Western Sahara" and "decides to withdraw from the unjust war in Western Sahara." In a secret addendum, the CMSN undertook "to put an end to its presence in Western Sahara and to hand over directly to the Polisario Front the part of the Western Sahara that it controls within seven months from the date of signing of the present agreement."[48] Mauritania and Algeria reestablished diplomatic relations a few days later, on August 14.

The secret addendum to the Algiers Agreement could not be implemented. On August 8, Hassan ordered the withdrawal of most of the Moroccan troops still in Mauritania, but the twenty-five hundred or so troops in Tiris el-Gharbia and about a thousand at Bir Moghrein in northeastern Mauritania stayed where they were. The next day, the Moroccan foreign minister, M'hammed Boucetta, dismissed the Algiers Agreement as "null and void" and brazenly claimed that "Tiris el-Gharbia is ours juridically and historically, as the International Court of Justice testified."[49] On August 10, Mohammed Khouna Ould Heydalla flew to Rabat to try to explain the motives for the CMSN's actions to King Hassan in person. But he received a chilling welcome. He was accused of little less than treachery and heard veiled threats of hot pursuit raids into Mauritania if Polisario was allowed to use its territory. The ministry of the interior even arranged a press conference in the Moroccan capital the same day for a dissident Mauritanian air-force officer, Mohammed Ould Bah Ould Abdelkader, who opposed the Algiers Agreement. Furious, the Mauritanian prime minister flew back to Nouakchott within hours of his arrival.[50]

Meanwhile, in Dakhla, five Moroccan Hercules C-130 transport planes had arrived within twenty-four hours of the signing of the Algiers Agreement with troop reinforcements for the Moroccan garrison in the city. Alarmed by the buildup of Moroccan forces, much of the local population gathered outside the Mauritanian prefecture and at the airport, clamoring to be evacuated, but to no avail. On August 7, Colonel-Major Dlimi and the Moroccan interior minister, Driss Basri, flew into Dakhla. Moroccan troops then took control of the city's administrative buildings and Basri raised the Moroccan flag. Hercules aircraft continued to shuttle back and forth to Dakhla, flying in more and more troops and equipment, and on August 14, Tiris el-Gharbia was officially proclaimed a Moroccan province, under the name of Oued ed-Dahab, the Arabic for Río de Oro. The same day, a delegation of Dakhla residents, who had been selected by Basri and flown to Rabat, were escorted into the royal palace to make the obligatory *bayaa* to the king. "The inhabitants of Oued ed-Dahab, men and women, have met and decided unanimously," proclaimed the city's aged *qadi*, "to renew to King Hassan, the Commander of the Faithful, the allegiance that their ancestors always gave to the sultans. We promise him to remain faithful, to be his soldiers and to fight his enemies."[51]

A day later, most of the CMSN's remaining troops and administrative officials in Tiris el-Gharbia were evacuated to Mauritania.[52] However, the CMSN refused, after what had happened at Dakhla, to withdraw from La Guera, the little fishing town on the Cape Blanc peninsula. It was too close to Nouadhibou to risk allowing the Moroccans to take over, and so it remained under Mauritanian administration for several more years. On August 23 the CMSN renounced the May 1977 Moroccan-Mauritanian defense pact, and a month later, on September 25, three Moroccan diplomats were expelled from Mauritania for engaging in "subversive activities."[53] The Moroccan government, for its part, refused to withdraw its thousand-strong garrison from Bir Moghrein, and it was not until the CMSN had protested to the UN Security Council on November 27 about this "flagrant violation of Mauritanian national sovereignty", that the troops there were finally repatriated on December 26.[54]

Relations between Morocco and Mauritania were to remain strained for many years. The Moroccan government was frequently to accuse Mauritania of harboring Polisario guerrillas and, despite the CMSN's denials, to threaten "hot pursuit" into Mauritanian territory. However, though the shadow of the Western Saharan war still hung over Mauritania, it was no longer to be involved directly in the fighting. Having finally broken the Rabat-Nouakchott axis, the Polisario guerrillas could now put their full resources into the war against their principal enemy, Morocco.

NOTES

1. *L'Opinion* (Rabat), July 15, 1978.
2. *Le Monde* (Paris), July 15, 1978.
3. *L'Opinion*, July 29, 1978.
4. The 350,000 Algerians whose permits were to expire at the end of 1978 were given one-year extensions under a temporary agreement reached in December 1978.
5. Statistics from the Economist Intelligence Unit, London.
6. *An-Nahar Arab Report and Memo*, January 16, 1978.

7. Statistics from the Economist Intelligence Unit.

8. *Le Monde*, February 11, 1978.

9. *Le Matin* (Paris), May 2, 1978.

10. *Le Monde*, August 4, 1978.

11. *Le Monde*, August 28, 1978.

12. *Le Monde*, February 11, 1979, and March 6, 1979. The readjustment of French policy on Western Sahara and Mauritania at this time was paralleled by a shift in policy toward Frolinat in Chad. Recognizing that Frolinat, or at least some of its factions, had to be associated with the regime in Ndjamena, in view of the southern-based government's total lack of popular support in the mineral-rich north, and that Libyan influence over the important People's Armed Forces faction, led by Goukouni Oueddei, was diminishing, the French government, which had more than a thousand troops in Chad at the time, allowed his forces to enter Ndjamena in March 1979, paving the way for the formation of a short-lived coalition government, headed by Goukouni Oueddei, the following August.

13. *Le Matin du Sahara* (Casablanca), August 24, 1978.

14. *Le Soleil* (Dakar), September 19, 1978.

15. Interview with Jean-Eudes Barbier, AFP correspondent, Nouakchott, August 22, 1978.

16. *Afrique-Asie* (Paris), October 2, 1978, and October 30, 1978.

17. *Jeune Afrique* (Paris), September 20, 1978.

18. *Le Monde*, September 26, 1978.

19. *20 Mai* (Polisario Front), No. 51, November 1978, p. 16.

20. *Afrique-Asie*, October 30, 1978; *Le Monde*, October 20, 1978.

21. *Le Monde*, November 14, 1978.

22. *Le Monde*, January 3, 1969; *The Guardian* (London), January 2, 1979.

23. AFP, dispatch from Nouakchott, January 12, 1979.

24. *Jeune Afrique*, January 17, 1979.

25. AFP, dispatch from Nouakchott, January 25, 1979.

26. AFP, dispatch from Paris, February 16, 1979; *Le Monde*, February 22, 1979; *Jeune Afrique*, February 28, 1979.

27. *West Africa* (London), April 16, 1979.

28. *Le Monde*, January 16, 1979.

29. World Bank, *World Development Report, 1980* (Washington, D.C.), p. 138.

30. This made an overall balance of payments surplus of $19.2 million possible for 1978 as a whole. (World Bank report No. 2479a-MAU, June 4, 1979.)

31. *Ibid.*, p. vi.

32. Loans were provided by the World Bank ($60 million), Saudi Fund for Development ($65 million), the French government's Caisse Centrale de Coopération Economique and French suppliers' credits ($50 million), the Kuwait Fund for Arab Economic Development ($45 million), the Arab Fund for Economic and Social Development ($35 million), the European Investment Bank ($30 million), Abu Dhabi ($20 million), the Japanese government's Overseas Economic Cooperation Fund ($16 million), the African Development Bank ($12 million) and the OPEC Special Fund ($5 million). In addition, equity in SNIM was purchased by the Kuwait Foreign Trading, Contracting and Investment Company ($40 million), the Arab Mining Company ($28 million), the Islamic Development Bank ($10 million) and the governments of Morocco ($20 million) and Iraq ($22 million). (World Bank news release 80/1, July 16, 1979.)

33. The blacks, who had been regarded as inferior by the Moors and suffered their slave raids in precolonial times, had benefited more than the nomads from the first French schools in Mauritania and so had become predominant in the lower ranks of the colonial civil service. However, black fears of subordination to the Moor majority had spawned a series of black parties—the Union des Originaires de la Vallée du Fleuve, the Bloc Démocratique du Gorgol and the Union Nationale Maurita-nienne—in the late fifties, on the eve of independence; and though, by preaching his novel doctrine of Mauritanian national unity, Ould Daddah had successfully controlled these centrifugal forces and headed off the latent danger of black attempts at secession and unification with neighboring Mali or Senegal, the Moors became the dominant community in post-independence Mauritania. They were not only supreme in the PPM, but controlled commerce and began displacing the blacks in the upper echelons of the civil service. Tension centered in the sixties on the language question, a key determi-nant of the two communities' relative opportunities to attain educational qualifications and jobs. The PPM favored Arabization of the previously French education system, to the detriment of the blacks, and when Arabic was made obligatory in secondary schools, strikes by black students and teachers

spiraled into bloody communal riots in February 1965 in which, according to government figures, six people were killed. Despite the riots, the PPM continued, albeit with caution, with its gradual Arabization program, while some black organizations began, instead of defending the role of French, to demand the official transcription of the previously unwritten African languages and their use in the education system and as national languages, on a par with Arabic. In broad terms, the rivalries between Mauritania's black Africans and Moors have parallels in most of the countries along the southern fringes of the Sahara, though they are not reinforced, as in some states, by a religious divide (between Muslims and non-Muslims) and have not generated the kind of violence that has marked Sudan or Chad.

34. *Le Monde*, February 9, 1979.

35. *Le Monde*, February 4–5, 1979, and February 9, 1979.

36. *Le Monde*, March 30, 1979.

37. *Le Monde*, March 22, 1979.

38. *Libération* (Casablanca), June 1, 1979.

39. *Africa Research Bulletin* (Exeter), Political Series, Vol. 16, No. 4, May 15, 1979. After playing a crucial role, as commander of the Mauritanian forces in Zouerate in the early stages of the war against Polisario, Ahmed Ould Bouceif had been appointed chief-of-staff of the armed forces in June 1976 after the Polisario attack on Nouakchott. He had then resumed command at Zouerate in July 1977 after the guerrilla attack on the city two months earlier.

40. *Africa Research Bulletin*, Political Series, Vol. 16, No. 5, June 15, 1979.

41. *Demain l'Afrique* (Paris), May 7, 1979.

42. *Jeune Afrique*, August 8, 1979.

43. *Demain l'Afrique*, June 18, 1979.

44. *Africa Confidential* (London), July 4, 1979.

45. *Le Monde*, July 17, 1979, and July 21, 1979.

46. *Le Monde*, July 27, 1979.

47. *Le Matin*, August 2, 1979.

48. *Sahara Libre* (Polisario Front), No. 88, August 22, 1979.

49. *Le Matin*, August 10, 1979.

50. *Le Matin*, August 11, 1979; *Le Monde*, August 12, 1979. A member of the CMSN, Mohammed Ould Bah Ould Abdelkader had been minister responsible for the CMSN in Ahmed Ould Bouceif's cabinet. However, he had lost influence after Ahmed Ould Bouceif's death. After being demoted to the post of education minister, he fled to Morocco on June 17, to announce that he headed a "free officers' movement."

51. *Le Monde*, August 16, 1979; *El Moudjahid*, September 19, 1979.

52. *Le Monde*, August 17, 1979.

53. *Le Monde*, August 25, 1979, and September 27, 1979.

54. *Le Monde*, November 27, 1979.

26

The *"Moroccan Sahara"*

THE RABAT AUTHORITIES went to great pains, after Spain's withdrawal in February 1976, to create an impression of normality in the "Moroccan Sahara." In theory the annexed territory was to be administered in the same way as the rest of Morocco. Three new provinces were created, with capitals at El-Ayoun, Smara and Boujdour, the latter a tiny settlement of less than a thousand inhabitants living in *khaimat* around the old Spanish lighthouse.[1] They were in turn subdivided, as in Morocco, into *cercles*, and, at the local level, into communes; and as if to underscore the artificiality of the former frontiers, the little settlement at Tarfaya was attached, as a *cercle*, to the new province of El-Ayoun. Governors were appointed by King Hassan to administer the three new provinces on April 12, 1976, two days before the formal partition treaty with Mauritania.[2]

Likewise, local, provincial and parliamentary elections were held in the Moroccan-controlled regions of the territory, as in Morocco itself, during 1976–77, and the Rabat authorities pointed to the election of pro-government candidates as evidence of popular support for integration into Morocco. First, on November 12, 1976, a total of 162 councillors were elected to sixteen communal councils in the three Western Saharan provinces. Then, on January 25, these councillors chose (from their own ranks) the eleven members of the three provincial assemblies. In El-Ayoun, Ahmed Ould Brahim Ould el-Bashir, a prominent trader and sheikh of the Izarguien who had sat in both the Djemaa and the Cortes, was selected as president of the provincial assembly, while Khatri Ould Said Ould el-Joumani, the former president of the Djemaa, was chosen to preside over the assembly in Boujdour. The electoral process culminated the following June with two-stage elections to the Chamber of Representatives in Rabat, under the Moroccan constitution's semicorporatist electoral system, which provided for the direct election of two-thirds of the chamber's 264 deputies and the selection of the rest by chambers of agriculture, commerce and industry, representatives of workers and the indirectly elected provincial assemblies. However, only four

279

of the eight deputies from Western Sahara were elected directly, in the first stage of the elections on June 3—Khalihenna Ould Rashid, the former PUNS leader, and Rashid Mohammed Douihi, the former secretary-general of the FLU, in El-Ayoun, Abderrahman Ould Leibak, a former member of the FLU's executive committee, in Boujdour, and Mohammed Ali Ould el-Bashir, a former labor inspector in the Spanish administration, in Smara. With the exception of Khalihenna Ould Rashid, who ran as an independent, all were Istiqlalians. In the second stage of the elections, on June 21, Ahmed Ould Brahim Ould el-Bashir, Khatri Ould Said Ould el-Joumani and Ma el-Ainin Mohammed Taki, strangely a member of the predominantly Berber Mouvement Populaire, were selected to represent El-Ayoun, Boujdour and Smara by their respective provincial assemblies and a fourth deputy, Beyadillah Mohammed Sheikh, a former associate of El-Ouali Mustaphi Sayed at Mohammed V University, was selected to represent the work force at the Bou-Craa phosphate mines, though practically all the Saharawi miners had left for Tindouf a year and a half earlier.[3]

As valued supporters of the Moroccan annexation, some of these Saharawi politicians were rewarded with important posts. Khatri Ould Said Ould el-Joumani and Ma el-Ainin Mohammed Taki, for example, were both chosen as vice-presidents of the newly-elected Chamber of Representatives when it assembled in Rabat in October 1977, and Khalihenna Ould Rashid became the first Western Saharan to enter the Moroccan government, as secretary of state in the premier's office in April 1977 and then secretary of state for Saharan affairs in January 1979, when for the first time King Hassan also appointed two Saharans as provincial governors, in Smara and Boujdour.[4]

However, little credence could be given to the Moroccan government's claims of normality, electoral or otherwise, in Western Sahara. The territory was at war. The majority of the local population had fled to Algeria by April 1976, and among the mere 18,630 voters registered for the 1977 elections in the three Saharan provinces were a considerable number of Moroccans who had arrived since the Madrid accords as civil administrators, workers or traders.[5] The elections were held under conditions of military occupation that made a free and democratic vote virtually impossible. Furthermore, no opponents of Moroccan rule could stand for election. Indeed, even the Moroccan left-wing opposition parties, the USFP and the PPS, were barred by the ministry of the interior from presenting candidates in the Western Saharan constituencies, even though they championed the "Moroccanity" of the annexed territory. Only members of the Istiqlal Party and the Mouvement Populaire, and pro-government "independents," were allowed to stand.[6]

To the Rabat government's embarrassment, two of the four "directly elected" Western Saharan parliamentarians defected to Polisario in 1979. The deputy from Boujdour, Abderrahman Ould Leibak, fled to Algiers, via Spain, in February. Mohammed Ali Ould el-Bashir, the deputy for Smara, arrived in Tindouf the following October with several hundred of his constituents evacuated from the city by a guerrilla force that successfully breached its defenses during one of the fiercest battles of the war.[7] To replace the defectors, by-elections were held at Boujdour and Smara on May 29, 1981.

Meanwhile, communual elections had been held for the first time in ex-Mauritanian Oued ed-Dahab—or, more precisely, in Dakhla and Argoub, the only two Moroccan-held settlements there—on May 8, and three parliamentary deputies were elected (two directly and one indirectly) from the province on May 29, raising the number of seats in the Chamber of Representatives to 267. The elections were held under as undemocratic conditions as those in El-Ayoun, Smara and Boujdour, and the USFP boycotted the poll. Pro-government candidates supposedly won landslide majorities, just as the PPM candidates had in the previous elections in Oued ed-Dahab (or Tiris el-Gharbia, as it was then known) in 1976.[8]

The Saharawis in the Moroccan-controlled areas had lost all freedom of movement beyond the towns by the spring of 1976. After their arrival in the towns, Moroccan troops quickly established security perimeters around them, to halt the refugee exodus as well as to forestall guerrilla attacks. Henceforth, Saharawis could travel between the Moroccan-controlled areas only in military convoys, or leave by plane for Morocco or the Canary Islands, though only a few trusted traders, whose prosperity depended as much on cooperation with the Moroccan authorities as on contact with their traditional duty-free suppliers in the Canaries, were granted Moroccan passports and permitted to make the half-hour journey by air to Las Palmas.

Nomadism, which had gradually died away during the last decade of Spanish rule, now became entirely extinct. Most of the remaining nomads had made their way to the Polisario camps in Tindouf by the spring of 1976, and any others found by the Moroccan forces were forcibly relocated in the towns and encouraged to build fixed homes there. They could no longer graze their animals beyond the Moroccan security perimeters.

Support for Polisario remained strong among the minority of Saharawis who still lived in El-Ayoun, Smara and other Moroccan-ruled areas, and the front was able to maintain an effective clandestine network there, in contact with the external leadership thanks to the assistance of sympathetic traders with the means to travel to Las Palmas.[9] However, overt expression of hostility to the Moroccan presence was almost suicidal under such extreme conditions of military occupation, where the Moroccan troops almost outnumbered the towns' civilian population. There were periodic waves of arrests, in which known or suspected Polisario sympathizers were rounded up, detained and often tortured, though the number of detainees was difficult to gauge as they were never brought to trial and there were seldom independent journalists in the territory to record or report arrests. By way of illustration, however, I might cite the case of about fifty civilians arrested in El-Ayoun on May 20, 1978, the fifth anniversary of Polisario's first guerrilla attack against the Spanish army. During a visit to El-Ayoun in October 1978, I learned from Saharawi, Moroccan and Spanish sources that at least thirty-five of them were still being held in El-Ayoun's central prison, known locally as the *calabozo*, and that seven of them had been hospitalized following electric-shock torture.[10]

It was only among the traders and a few veterans of the Djemaa, many of whom were themselves in business, that the Moroccan authorities could summon some support. They were assiduously cultivated, as they had been previously by the Spanish. Passports, import permits and bank loans—and, in the opinion of many Saharawis, outright bribes too—were bartered for political loyalty, or silent acquiescence in the status quo. Most significant of all, the Moroccan authorities permitted the traders to continue their lucrative traffic in duty-free merchandise from the Canaries and "re-export" it, exempt from Moroccan import duties, to Morocco itself. The Moroccan army officers and civil servants in the Sahara benefited as much as the traders themselves, as a flood of luxury imports, from stereo systems to cars, arrived at El-Ayoun Playa from Las Palmas, to be sold at prices often only half those in Morocco. The number of Mercedes-Benz cars with El-Ayoun registration plates in the streets of Rabat and Casablanca had become a matter of public scandal by 1978, prompting questions in the Moroccan parliament.[11] Even commodities like cement and tea were imported into Morocco via El-Ayoun. Indeed, the scale of this traffic was such that, in 1977, 57 million dirhams (about $12.8 million) worth of tea, over half of Morocco's total tea imports (103 million dirhams), were imported through El-Ayoun by private Saharawi traders, despite a theoretical monopoly on tea imports held by the Moroccan government's Office National du The et du Sucre.[12] All told, imports through El-Ayoun soared from an average of $51.8 million in 1974–75 to $130 million in 1977.[13] Nonetheless, the traders' loyalty to the Moroccan cause was born of practical necessity rather than conviction. Like all Western Saharans still living in the towns, they had numerous close relatives fighting on the other side, with Polisario, and their own material interests suffered from about the middle of 1978 when, as a result of Morocco's worsening foreign-exchange difficulties, the Rabat government began to restrict their special "free zone" trading rights.[14]

Polisario's support extended far to the north of Western Sahara's pre-1975 borders, into the regions of southern Morocco with large Saharawi communities. As a result of droughts, Operation Ouragan and Spain's withdrawal from Spanish Southern Morocco in 1958, as many Saharawis had ended up settling, as sedentary town-dwellers, in southern Morocco as within Western Sahara itself, and as we have seen, it was from these communities, impoverished and on the margins of Moroccan society but with powerful family bonds across the Western Saharan border, that several of Polisario's foremost leaders had hailed. In towns like Tan-Tan, Goulimine and Tarfaya sympathy for Polisario was extensive from the very start of the conflict, in 1975, and some Saharawis left these areas at this time to join the front's camps in Tindouf. For example, more than eight hundred Saharawis, all Reguibat, fled to Algeria from the little town of Zaag, in the southeast corner of Morocco, twenty-three miles north of the Western Saharan border, at the end of 1975.[15]

Most of the Saharawi population of southern Morocco was politically suspect, as far as the Rabat government was concerned, and so there were numerous arrests of presumed Polisario sympathizers there as well as within Western Sahara. In Zaag, for example, seventy Reguibat were said to have been detained at the end of 1975.[16] In Tan-Tan, several relatives of the SADR's prime minister, Mohammed Lamine Ould Ahmed, including his mother, were arrested in January–February 1976.[17] Overall, Amnesty International reported in 1981 that it could "confirm the 'disappearance' of approximately 100 individuals from towns in southern Morocco since 1975, in the context of the dispute over the Western Sahara" and that "this figure probably substantially underestimates the true number of individuals taken into custody in this region by the Moroccan security forces whose arrests have not been officially admitted by the authorities."[18] Such detainees were held without trial, often for several years, in civilian or military jails in southern Morocco or Western Sahara, some of them secret detention centers, such as those known to have existed at Agdz and Ouarzazate in southeastern Morocco.[19]

Though the great majority of Saharawis from both Western Sahara and southern Morocco supported Polisario, the Forces Armées Royales had some Saharawi troops in their ranks, notably in the elite 8th Infantry Regiment and such special units as the *stations*, which were composed entirely of Saharawis, and the "auxiliaries" of the Gendarmerie Royale, former Polisario prisoners enrolled under duress in return for a limited freedom. Excepting the latter, most had been recruited in southern Morocco, where poverty and warrior traditions had encouraged Saharawis to enlist in the FAR in large numbers since the late fifties. Some undoubtedly sympathized with their Polisario adversaries, and there were occasional defections. However, many of the Saharawi troops came from one southern Moroccan tribe, the Ait Oussa, a branch of the Tekna whom the Moroccan authorities successfully roused against the guerrillas by playing on their past enmity for the Reguibat.[20]

By April 1976, the FAR had established garrisons in most of the small outlying settlements of the Moroccan zone of Western Sahara, as well as securing a firm hold over the towns. However, they could not hope to patrol the whole of the desert hinterland effectively. There, Polisario *kataeb* were able to establish an intricate network of small, scattered bases, some of them underground, to supplement their rear bases in Algeria. In particular, hideouts were established in the valleys of the Saguia el-Hamra and its tributaries, with their generally good tree cover, and such rugged zones as the Zemmour massif, near the border with Mauritania. Access to the Saguia el-Hamra from Algeria required only a few hours' drive across the Hammada, a gravel plain as flat as a pancake across which the guerrillas would drive their Land Rovers in small groups at breathtaking speed to avoid detection. The vehicles were stripped of all glass, to prevent reflection that could attract the attention of enemy aircraft; and at the sound of a plane the guerrillas would split up, taking cover with their Land Rovers under the acacia trees that flourish in this part of the Sahara.

Though the main thrust of Polisario's guerrilla campaign was directed against Mauritania in 1976–78, the Moroccans were not left in peace. Moroccan convoys were frequently attacked en route to isolated garrisons in the inteior, or even along the main supply route to El-Ayoun from the north. A favored target was the bridge over the Oued Chebeika, between Tan-Tan and Tarfaya, and by mid-1978 convoys were sometimes reaching El-Ayoun as long as a fortnight late, depriving the Saharan capital of fresh meat and vegetables.[21] Sometimes, El-Ayoun itself came under direct attack, though the guerrillas could do little more than pound a few mortar rounds into the city from beyond the Moroccan defense lines.[22] They

were able, however, to keep the Bou Craa mines closed. Frequent attacks were
staged to cut the mines' power lines from the coast, and so the huge draglines,
which removed the topsoil at Bou-Craa, were paralyzed from the beginning of
1976 and no phosphate was mined for at least six years. There were about 1.1
million tons of ore in stockpiles at Bou-Craa in 1976 and some of this was
transported to the coast in convoys of trucks, under military escort. The Fosbucraa
conveyor belt, which was a much more efficient means of transportation, was in-
operable. By mid-1978, five sections of the belt, totaling about three miles, had
been burned out and two of its ten control stations seriously damaged by the guerrillas.[23] So only very small amounts of previously stockpiled phosphate were
trucked to the coast, beneficiated in the treatment plant at El-Ayoun Playa and
exported. In 1979, for example, exports totaled only 139,000 tons, one-twentieth
of the 2.6 million tons shipped out in 1975, and in 1980 operations at Bou-Craa
closed down completely (Table 26.1).[24]

TABLE 26.1
THE COLLAPSE OF THE PHOSPHATE INDUSTRY
The Fall in Phosphate Exports, 1975–79
(tons)

1975	2,638,000
1976	277,000
1977	25,000
1978	441,000
1979	139,000

SOURCES: Interview with Larbi el-Omari, Director Fosbucraa, El-Ayoun, June 20,
1978; *Mining Annual Review*, 1980.

Despite the great superiority of their military equipment, the FAR were not
well suited to fighting a desert counterinsurgency war. The troops, peasants from
the Atlas and Rif mountains or urban conscripts for the most part, were not accustomed to the harsh Saharan climate, with its blistering heat during the day and
icy winter nights, and resented having to spend months or even years dug into
trenches in this sandswept barren landscape, far from their homes. Neither the
troops nor their officers, who came mainly from urban bourgeois or middle-class
families, knew the terrain in the manner of their elusive enemy. They were at a
decided disadvantage in that respect. Furthermore, they lacked their opponents'
guts and verve. Instead, they resorted to fighting a passive, defensive war, to
holding fixed positions, while the guerrillas displayed enormous mobility, flexibility and panache. Most of the Moroccan troops spent almost all their time in the
Sahara on trench duty, along the defense perimeters of the towns or remote outposts, waiting in boredom or fear for a *ghazzi* to make its sudden appearance on
the horizon. It was a gruesome existence that sapped morale. Even units with such
dynamic or aggressive-sounding titles as the Commandos de la Marche Verte

(CMV) or the Détachements d'Intervention Rapide (DIR) rarely ventured out into the desert wilds to seek out or pursue the guerrilla *kataeb* in classic counter-insurgency style. Additionally, the Moroccan war effort was hampered by King Hassan's heavy-handed supervision of the officer corps, in whom he could bring himself to place little confidence after the harrowing experience of the two failed coup attempts in 1971–72. Few officers received promotions, and until 1980, when Ahmed Dlimi was thus rewarded, none held the rank of general.

Morocco's military difficulties in the Sahara took a sharp turn for the worse after the July 1978 coup in Mauritania. The cease-fire and eventual peace agreement between Polisario and the military regime in Nouakchott allowed the guerrillas to give undivided attention to the struggle against Morocco. On the night of September 30, 1978, one of the control stations of the Fosbucraa conveyor belt came under attack, and a fortnight later, on October 17, mortar shells landed in the center of El-Ayoun.[25] Worse still, for the FAR and King Hassan, the guerrillas began striking repeatedly at targets in southern Morocco, just as they had earlier carried the war into Mauritania. One of the first such attacks was at Sidi Amara, in the valley of the Oued Draa, on August 27, 1978, when a supply convoy of the Forces Auxiliaires fell into an ambush. Another convoy was ambushed on two successive occasions, on September 29–30, as it tried to make its way to Guelb Ben Rzouk, a border post in the Draa Valley near the Algerian frontier.[26] "We will continue our operations in Moroccan territory as long as the king persists in denying our people's rights," the SADR's defense minister, Ibrahim Ghali, warned on October 9. "The clashes could spread as far as Agadir, Rabat and even Tangiers."[27] In fact, they did not. Polisario made no attempt to strike that far north. Rather, their favored zone of operations remained the desert or semidesert regions of Morocco's extreme south, notably the Ouarkziz and Bani mountains, the Draa Valley and the foothills of the Anti-Atlas. With their successive chains of mountains and valleys, running west to east, these regions are good guerrilla country.[28] Moreover, much of the local population was Saharawi in origin and sympathetic to Polisario, though the longer-range attacks, into the Bani Mountains or the foothills of the Anti-Atlas, took the guerrillas into predominantly Berber territory.

Following President Boumedienne's death in December 1978, this campaign against the Moroccan forces in both Western Sahara and southern Morocco was baptized the "Houari Boumedienne Offensive." The year 1979 witnessed some of the largest and bloodiest battles of the war, in which Polisario fielded as many as three thousand or even five thousand men at a time, with equipment of unprecedented power and sophistication, including "Stalin Organs," the fearsome multiple rocket launchers with a twenty-kilometer range. For the first time in the course of the war, towns and major Moroccan bases were assaulted and their defenses successfully breached. On January 28, 1979, for example, a large guerrilla force fought its way into the center of Tan-Tan, a provincial capital with an air base and a garrison of several thousand troops on the main highway from Agadir to El-Ayoun. The guerrillas remained in the city for four hours, freed Saharawi prisoners and destroyed military installations, the Gendarmerie barracks, oil depots, the power station and a local bank.[29]

The Moroccan public, which had been lulled into a mood of complacency by the optimism of government pronouncements on the war, suddenly saw that all was not well in the desert. The USFP and the PPS began accusing the government of failing to prosecute the war with sufficient drive and urged cross-border raids into Algeria. Even the progovernment parties requested an emergency session of parliament. Meanwhile, on the domestic front, the deteriorating economic climate had spawned a resurgence of labor militancy since the beginning of the year. The "social peace" that had accompanied the early stages of the Saharan saga was beginning to crumble.

With his habitual skill as a political tactician, King Hassan attempted to associate the opposition parties more closely with his conduct of the war and impose wartime sacrifice and discipline on the restive unions. The king summoned an emergency session of parliament on March 8 and admitted, in an address to its members, that Morocco faced "an increasingly difficult situation in the south of its territory which could not continue without putting our country at serious risk." To coopt the opposition parties, he announced the formation of "a council grouping the representatives of all organized political tendencies and which will have the task of assisting us in determining and conducting policy with respect to the safeguarding of our national territory and the security of the state."[30] The membership of the Conseil National de Securité (CNS), announced on March 27, included representatives of the USFP and the PPS, as well as the progovernment Rassemblement National des Indépendants (RNI), Istiqlal Party and Mouvement Populaire.[31]

Within the FAR, an immediate repercussion of the Tan-Tan fiasco was a change in command of the forces in the war zone. Colonel Abdelaziz Bennani, who had been appointed chief-of-staff of the Saharan forces in 1977, was replaced in March 1979 by Colonel Mohammed Abrouq, the fifth officer to take on the assignment in less than four years. His task, Hassan declared, was "to pacify the Western Sahara and combat whoever breaks the unity of the ranks and rebels against the orders of the Commander of the Faithful."[32]

But the FAR continued to suffer major reverses. During the night of May 30–June 1, a Moroccan convoy traveling between Tan-Tan and Tarfaya was ambushed. The Moroccan government admitted losing twenty-three dead. The road south to El-Ayoun became so insecure that by the middle of the year the FAR had to abandon its overland convoys from Tan-Tan. Thereafter, the Western Saharan capital had to depend on supplies arriving by sea. On June 14, meanwhile, a guerrilla force broke through the Moroccan defenses at Assa, the Ait Oussa's oasis town in the valley of the Draa, and on June 13 and 27 there were two more attacks on Tan-Tan.[33] Farther south, in Western Sahara, an estimated three thousand guerrillas fell upon the Moroccan base at Bir Enzaren on August 11, capturing 175 of its defendants, who were shown off to journalists visiting Tindouf on August 30, and killing, according to Moroccan government figures, a further eighty-two.[34]

The most devastating attack of all, however, came on the final day of Ramadan, which fell that year on August 24. The target was Lebouirate, a settlement in southern Morocco where the FAR's 3rd Armored Squadron was based. "We suddenly saw dozens of headlamps light up in the distance," recalled one of the squadron's T-54 tank commanders after the battle. "The Polisario Land Rovers reached us at top speed, firing all their automatic weapons and launching rockets. The noise was infernal. It was terrifying."[35] The commander of the 3rd Armored Squadron, Mohammed Azelmat, failed, in the words of the Moroccan ministry of information, to "oppose the appropriate resistance to the enemy" and abandoned "even its defensive positions as well as a large part of its equipment, thereby allowing the enemy to invest the attacked locality and stay there the whole day." The ministry claimed, however, that "intervention forces immediately dispatched to the scene succeeded in dislodging the enemy forces and liberating the invested locality after fierce fighting."[36] A relief column did set out from Zaag. But it fell into an ambush and in fact never reached Lebouirate, which remained in Polisario hands for more than a year. The settlement's civilian population, which was predominatly Reguibat, was evacuated to Tindouf, along with 111 Moroccan prisoners. A large number of the thousand Moroccan soldiers at Lebouirate must have died, and a veritable arsenal of weaponry, including thirty-seven T-54 tanks (supplied to Morocco by Soviet-bloc countries long before the Saharan war) was abandoned on the battlefield, according to foreign journalists who visited Lebouirate under Polisario auspices the following September.[37] For the FAR, the fall of Lebouirate was an unmitigated disaster, and thirty-six of the surviving members of its disgraced garrison were court-martialed in El-Ayoun in February 1980, though they were later pardoned by the king.[38]

Further shocks hit the FAR over the following weeks. On October 6, a large guerrilla force, which the Moroccan government claimed to be five-thousand strong, tried to storm through the defense perimeter around Smara. Some of Morocco's newly delivered Mirage F-1 aircraft flew into battle for the first time. However, the guerrillas succeeded in breaking through the southeastern flank of the Moroccan defense lines and reaching the city, where they rounded up seven hundred Saharawi civilians, including Mohammed Ali Ould el-Bashir, for evacuation to the Tindouf camps. The Moroccan authorities admitted losing 121 dead, among them the local army commander, Colonel Driss Harti.[39] Only a week later, on October 14, disaster struck again, when twelve hundred guerrillas overran the Moroccan base at Mahbes, in the extreme northeast of Saguia el-Hamra, near the Algerian frontier, slaughtering—according to official Moroccan figures—more than a fifth of the garrison's 780 men.[40]

Another disturbing development for the Moroccan government was a Polisario decision to extend attacks beyond the Saharawi regions of Morocco's extreme south to the Bani Mountains and the southeasterly slopes of the Anti-Atlas. On January 25, 1980, Akka, a Berber town in the Anti-Atlas, only 110 miles southeast of Agadir, was raided. It was attacked again, and occupied by a guerrilla force for about three hours, on September 3, 1980, when another Polisario group raided simultaneously against Tata, a neighboring Anti-Atlas town thirty miles to the northeast. The most northerly attack of all followed on October 9, when Polisario's target was M'hamid, the small oasis town near the bend of the Draa where Mohammed V had first spelled out his claim to Western Sahara in February 1958.[41]

Another front in this escalating war was out to sea. From April 1977, specially trained guerrilla units, using pneumatic launches, began attacking foreign fishing boats guilty of fishing illegally in the SADR's territorial waters. There was a spate of such attacks in 1977–80, mainly against Spanish boats from the Canaries, but Moroccan, Portuguese and even South Korean boats fell victim too. The guerrillas would normally board the boats, arrest their crews and, after bringing them back to shore, speed them to captivity in the desert. Polisario's virtually unchallenged freedom of action over most of the Western Saharan desert and much of the coastline was evident in the FAR's failure to foil any of these attacks or free any of the more than one hundred seized fishermen, all of whom were eventually released in Algeria, sometimes after weeks or months of negotiations.

As the challenge from Polisario grew increasingly serious, the FAR began to abandon many of the smaller, more remote outposts they had occupied in 1975–76. A process of gradual retrenchment began, while the defenses of the more important towns and settlements were reinforced. Gradually, all the outposts between Smara and the Algerian frontier were abandoned or overrun. Farsia was evacuated in April 1977, Haousa the following October, Bir Lehlou in March 1978, Amgala in May 1979. Mahbes, the last post east of Smara, was overrun five months later.

To bolster the defenses of the main towns, three large and well-equipped special forces were dispatched south to the desert in 1979–80. The first, which was assembled at Benguerir, near Marrakesh, in September 1979, a month after the annexation of Oued ed-Dahab, was designed to reinforce the three thousand Moroccan troops who had been stationed in Dakhla and Argoub during their period of Mauritanian administration or flown there immediately after the Agreement of Algiers. With six thousand men and fifteen hundred vehicles, including U.S.-supplied M-113 armored personnel carriers, the force, code-named Ohoud, after a battle in the third year of the Hejira (A.D. 625) between the Prophet Mohammed and the pagan Meccans, rolled south from Tan-Tan in November, under the personal command of Colonel-Major Ahmed Dlimi. Preceded by scouting parties of Ait Oussa from the 8th Infantry Regiment, the vast armada of vehicles, thirty-five miles long, was the first Moroccan force to risk taking the road from Tan-Tan to Tarfaya, across the Oued Chebeika, for many months. The guerrillas, judging it inopportune to take on such a powerful column, simply melted away from its path, and Dlimi, whose sole objective was to reach Dakhla, refrained from seeking them out.[42]

Its safe arrival in Dakhla, after a three-week journey across the desert, was hailed as a great victory in Rabat, after the string of humiliating setbacks over the previous year. Ohoud was followed almost immediately by the creation of another special force, named after one of the most celebrated battles in the annals of Muslim history, the Almoravid victory over the Castillians at Zellagha, near Badajoz, in 1806. Commanded by Colonel-Major Abrouq, the Zellagha Force was brought together, like Ohoud before it, at Benguerir, in January 1980, and readied for an operation in southern Morocco known as Iman (The Faith). Buttressed by the Ait Oussa of the 8th Infantry Regiment, the seven-thousand-strong force was ordered to break through to Zaag, which had been encircled for months by Polisario, and reestablish control over the Ouarkziz Mountains. Operation

Iman was a catastrophe, however, The guerrillas did not simply slip away. This time, they attacked in force. Abrouq's men were harassed constantly as they tried to push eastward from Ammeti between March 1 and 6 and then suffered heavy losses as they tried to reach Zaag through a pass in the Ouarkziz, at Ngueb, on March 9. The operation was abandoned and the force withdrew northward, to Assa, on March 11. Proud of their victory, the guerrillas escorted foreign journalists to the Ouarkziz Mountains to show off their 137 new Moroccan prisoners, as well as the charred remains of the armored cars and dozens of rotting corpses that littered the fields of battle.[43]

The FAR did finally succeed in breaking the seige of Zaag two months later, at the beginning of May, after securing control of the Ngueb Pass and a twenty-mile corridor to Zaag. Convoys of trucks ferried in supplies for the garrison there and then evacuated the town's entire civilian population, Reguibat whose sympathies for the enemy were well known, to Assa and Goulimine, north of the Draa.[44]

After securing the Ngueb Pass and reinforcing the defenses around Zaag, the FAR's next strategic objective was to block the guerrillas' other main route of access into southern Morocco, the pass through the Zini Mountains, to the southwest of the Ouarkziz range, through which Polisario had penetrated to attack Tan-Tan in January 1979 and to stage its numerous ambushes against convoys on the north-south road between Tan-Tan and El-Ayoun, via Tarfaya. For this purpose, the FAR established a third special force, named Larak, under the command of Colonel Ben Othman, which took up positions at Abatteh, to the south of Tan-Tan, and then, in August 1980, pushed forward to Ras el-Khanfra, a foothill overlooking the southern entrance to the pass (just to the north of the pre-1975 border), and Khreibichatt, on the open plain leading southward from the Zini toward Smara. Polisario put up stiff resistance and on September 16 inflicted heavy losses on part of the Larak Force near Ras el-Khanfra.[45]

However, Polisario could not dislodge the Moroccan troops from the approaches to the Zini Mountains. Indeed, Ben Othman's force was now to embark on a much more ambitious project—the establishment of a continuous defense line from Ras el-Khanfra to Smara, about sixty miles to the south, and from there, via Bou-Craa, in a southwesterly arc to the Atlantic, in order to seal off the whole northwestern corner of Western Sahara, the territory's "useful" part, with the phosphates and (apart from Dakhla) the main towns. "King Hassan's political intention is evident," the SADR's information minister, Mohammed Salem Ould Salek, remarked on November 28. "Trapped, by military and diplomatic pressure, into inevitable negotiations with Polisario, he is trying in this way to isolate what the Moroccan authorities call the Western Sahara's useful triangle (El-Ayoun, Smara, Bou-Craa) in order to put himself in a position of strength at the negotiating table."[46]

On March 2, Ahmed Dlimi, now with general's rank, announced the completion of the first stretch of this great Saharan "wall," from the Zini Mountains to the old Smara defense perimeter. It consisted of sandbanks, two to three yards high, flanked by minefields and barbed wire. At regular intervals were observation posts, artillery placements, underground quarters for the troops, and electronic sensors and radar installations to detect approaching enemy vehicles. Reserve forces were massed behind the wall, ready to respond in the event of an attack.[47] By May 11, the wall had been extended to Bou-Craa, where it linked up with a preexisting defense line alongside the Fosbucraa conveyor belt to El-Ayoun Playa, on the coast. A year later, in May 1982, the Moroccan government announced the completion of a more southerly extension of the wall, from Bou-Craa to the Atlantic, enclosing Boujdour.[48]

The guerrillas, meanwhile, concentrated their fire on one of the very few remaining Moroccan bases beyond the wall's protection, at Guelta Zemmour, near the Mauritanian border. Subjected to frequent shellings, it was attacked in force and partially overrun by Polisario units on March 24–25, 1981.[49] Seven months later, on October 13, its twenty-six-hundred strong garrison, men of the 4th Infantry Regiment, were routed in another, bloodier onslaught by Polisario forces. The guerrillas stormed through the Moroccan positions, killing many of their defendants (probably far more than the hundred whose deaths were acknowledged in Rabat) and capturing 230 prisoners. While the battle was still raging, moreover, they shot down three Moroccan aircraft—two Mirages and a C-130 Hercules transport plane. After gathering up as much abandoned Moroccan weaponry as possible, they withdrew into the surrounding mountains on October 16, allowing Moroccan reinforcements from Bou-Craa to reach the base. Nevertheless, fighting continued and by October 23 two more Moroccan aircraft—a Northrop F-5E jet and a Puma helicopter—had been downed.[50] In view of the base's vulnerability, the FAR decided to withdraw completely from Guelta Zemmour on November 7, and two days later the fifteen hundred Moroccan troops at another large base, 160 miles to the southwest at Bir Enzaren, which defended the approaches to Dakhla, were evacuated too.[51]

Besides Boujdour (soon to be enclosed within the wall) and a tiny enclave around the twin towns of Dakhla and Argoub, on the Río de Oro Bay, the bases at Guelta Zemmour and Bir Enzaren had been the only two remaining Moroccan-held localities in the vast expanses of desert beyond the "useful triangle." About 250 miles long after its extension to Boujdour, the wall enclosed about seventeen thousand square miles, roughly one-sixth of Western Sahara's total land area. The enclave around Dakhla and Argoub covered a few hundred square miles at most. The rest of the territory had been totally abandoned. Polisario's guerrilla forces roamed without challenge there, and a correspondent of the French newspaper Le Monde, who traveled over twelve hundred miles with a Polisario unit between the Hammada and Bir Enzaren in December 1981, could report that "the most complete calm reigned in the regions we crossed, where we were unable to detect any trace whatever of a Moroccan presence."[52] The guerrillas had no hesitation in driving down tarmac roads, and at night would see no risk in lighting fires or driving with their headlamps full-beam. In some regions, near Haousa for example, they were once again grazing flocks of camels and even cultivating fields of barley. By 1983, no Moroccan forces had attempted to penetrate the eastern Saguia el-Hamra for four years.

The abandonment of five-sixths of the territory might not, from one perspective, have seemed a great loss to the Moroccan regime. The "useful" sixth, with the phosphates and the main towns, still remained in its hands. Indeed, with the protection afforded by the wall, Fosbucraa was sufficiently confident to announce an imminent resumption of phosphate mining in July 1982.[53] However, the wall was ultimately no solution. It had to be manned and equipped, at enormous cost to government finances, at a time of unprecedented strain on the Moroccan economy. In January 1983, King Hassan let it be known that the Moroccan troop strength in the Sahara had grown to eighty thousand men.[54]

By 1983, Polisario had an estimated twenty-five thousand men under arms.[55] The wall could not stop the guerrillas from making harassment raids, and the Moroccan government knew that they might acquire from Algeria or Libya the sophisticated, powerful weaponry they needed to pierce its defenses. The guerrilla leaders may not have expected to win a purely military victory over the Moroccan forces massed in the useful triangle. But then, guerrilla warfare had not, in a purely military sense, driven the French from Algeria, the U.S. from Indochina or the Portuguese from Angola, Mozambique and Guinea-Bissau. The economic, diplomatic or domestic political repercussions of these wars had been decisive elements too in forcing their eventual withdrawal. Polisario was engaged in a war of attrition, in which it was gradually bleeding Morocco, militarily, diplomatically and financially. In the end, the guerrillas anticipated, their adversaries' will would crack or King Hassan might even be deposed, like Ould Daddah, opening up new perspectives for peace.

NOTES

1. There were only 590 there according to the 1974 census. See *Censo-74* (Servicio de Registro de Población, Censo y Estadística, Gobierno General de Sahara, El-Ayoun, 1975), p. 44.

2. They were Said Ouassou (El-Ayoun), Slimane Haddad (Smara) and Bouchaib Zeggouri (Boujdour). *Reuters*, dispatch from Rabat, April 12, 1976.

3. *Les provinces marocaines du Sud* (Ministry of Information, Rabat), pp. 27–28.

4. *AFP*, dispatch from Marrakesh, January 3, 1979; *Arab Report* (London), February 14, 1979.

5. Figures provided by the provincial authorities, El-Ayoun, October 16, 1978. They included 917 registered in Tarfaya, on the other side of the pre-1975 border.

6. According to Ali Yata, the secretary-general of the PPS (interviewed in Casablanca, November 14, 1978), the interior ministry barred fourteen of the party's prospective candidates from contesting seats in Western Sahara and the extreme south of Morocco.

7. Interviews with Abderrahman Ould Leibak, Tindouf, February 27, 1979, and Mohammed Ali Ould el-Bashir, Tindouf, November 1979.

8. *Le Matin du Sahara*, May 14, 1981; *Le Monde*, May 13, 1981, and May 22, 1981.

9. Interviews with Saharawi and Spanish residents of El-Ayoun, October 1978.

10. See Tony Hodges, "Sahara: le mur du silence," *Le Matin* (Paris), December 16, 1978.

11. Interview with Ali Yata, Casablanca, November 14, 1978.

12. Interview with ONTS official, Rabat, November 1978, *Le Maroc en chiffres 1978* (Banque Marocaine due Commerce Extérieur, Casablanca, 1979), p. 85.

13. Interview with Said Ouassou, governor of El-Ayoun, June 29, 1978.

14. *Ibid.*

15. According to a Reguibi from Zaag, interviewed in El-Ayoun in October 1978. "In Zaag, almost everyone left," he recalled.

16. Among them was my informant, a Reguibi interviewed in El-Ayoun in October 1978, who, after his arrest in Zaag, was held without trial in Agadir and Ifni, from October 1975 until February 1978, when he was moved to El-Ayoun and freed on condition that he enrolled in the Gendarmerie Royale's special force of Saharawi "auxiliaries." He was never tried and never saw a lawyer during his two-and-a-half-year stint in jail. See Tony Hodges, "Des supplétifs rééduqués," *Le Matin*, December 19, 1978. The repression at Zaag was confirmed by Lieutenant Mahfoud Haidar, a Moroccan officer of the 5th Détachement d'Intervention Rapide (DIR), who deserted from the Moroccan garrison there to join Polisario in February 1979 (interviewed on March 1, 1979, at Tindouf).

17. According to Gilles Gauthier, a French teacher in Agadir at the time.

18. *Report of an Amnesty International Mission to the Kingdom of Morocco, 10–13 February 1981* (Amnesty International, London, 1982), p. 42. Amnesty listed ninety such individuals by name,

noting that it had "received eyewitness reports that they were taken into custody by Moroccan security forces." (*Ibid.*, pp. 32–33, 48–51.)

19. Interviews with Lieutenant Mahfoud Haidar, Tindouf, March 1, 1979, and a former member of the Moroccan Sûreté Nationale, Zagora, December 1979.

20. *Jeune Afrique* (Paris), November 21, 1979. According to the Reguibi from Zaag whom I interviewed in El-Ayoun in October 1978, "in 1975 the Ait Oussa went to the government and said that all the Reguibat are Polisario." After the ensuing arrests in Zaag, a settlement inhabited almost entirely by Reguibat, "the Ait Oussa came and took their camels, goats, sheep, donkeys and belongings." According to Mohammed Ali Ould el-Bashir, interviewed in Tindouf in November 1979, there were five thousand Ait Oussa in the FAR.

21. Visits to El-Ayoun, June-July and October 1978.

22. On the nights of April 24–25, 1977, and February 26, 1978, for example. (*Reuters*, Rabat, May 15, 1977; interview with Colonel Abdelaziz Bennani, commander of Moroccan troops in Western Sahara, El-Ayoun, June 13, 1978.)

23. Interview with Larbi el-Omari, director of Fosbucraa, El-Ayoun, June 20, 1978.

24. *Minerpress* (Instituto Nacional de Industria, Madrid), June 20, 1978.

25. *UPI*, dispatch from Rabat, October 20, 1978; Interview with Colonel Abdelaziz Bennani, El-Ayoun, October 15, 1978.

26. *Le Monde*, August 31, 1978, and October 4, 1978.

27. *Le Monde*, October 11, 1978.

28. See Rafael Argullol and Xavier Berenguer, "Entrevista con el ministro de defensa de la República Arabe Saharaui Democrática, Brahim Ghali Ould Mustafa," *Materiales*, No. 6, November-December 1977.

29. *Sahara Libre* (Polisario Front, Algiers), No. 75, February 20, 1979; *An-Nahar Arab Report and Memo*, February 5, 1979.

30. Message de S.M. le Roi Hassan II à la Chambre des Représentants réunie en session extraordinaire le 8 mars 1979 (press release, Moroccan Permanent Mission to the UN).

31. In fact, the CNS seldom met and had no decision-making powers.

32. *Algérie-Actualité* (Algiers), August 16–22, 1979.

33. *Le Monde*, June 29, 1979, and July 1–2, 1979; *Al-Bayane* (Casablanca), July 4, 1979.

34. *Le Matin*, October 10, 1979; *International Herald Tribune* (Paris), October 6, 1979.

35. *Le Monde*, September 27, 1979.

36. *El Moudjahid*, August 27, 1979.

37. *Observer Foreign News Service* (London), September 21, 1979; *El Moudjahid*, August 28, 1979.

38. *Le Monde*, March 1, 1980.

39. *Le Matin*, October 10, 1979; *Le Monde*, October 16, 1979, and October 18, 1979; Interview with Mohammed Ali Ould el-Bashir, Tindouf, November 16, 1979.

40. Radio Rabat, October 16, 1979.

41. *Jeune Afrique*, September 24, 1980; *Africa News* (Durham, N.C.), September 15, 1980.

42. *Jeune Afrique*, November 21, 1979.

43. *El País* (Madrid), March 9, 1980; *The Guardian* (London), March 17, 1980; *The Observer*, March 23, 1980; *West Africa* (London), March 24, 1980.

44. *Le Monde*, May 27, 1980.

45. *Le Monde*, September 25, 1980, October 10, 1980, and October 22, 1980.

46. *Marchés Tropicaux et Méditerranéens* (Paris), December 5, 1980.

47. *Le Monde*, March 5, 1981.

48. *Le Monde*, June 2, 1981; *Maghreb Arabe Presse* (Rabat), May 6, 1982.

49. *Marchés Tropicaux et Méditerranéens*, April 24, 1981.

50. *Le Monde*, October 15, 20, 22, 24, 28, 1981, *Marchés Tropicaux et Méditerranéens*, October 30, 1981; *Sahara Libre*, Nos. 124–25, November 10, 1981.

51. *Le Monde*, November 29–30, 1981.

52. *Le Monde*, December 17, 1981.

53. *Cinco Dias* (Madrid), August 4, 1982.

54. *Le Monde*, January 16, 1983.

55. There were at least one hundred thousand Saharawis in the Tindouf refugee camps, but almost no men of weapons-bearing age there, implying that virtually all adult men were enrolled in the guerrilla forces.

27

Morocco at War

THE SAHARAN WAR and the ever-present danger of its escalation into an all-out conflict between Morocco and Algeria obliged King Hassan to undertake a huge and expensive military buildup that the Moroccan economy was in poor shape to support. The FAR almost tripled in size between 1974 and 1982, rising from 56,000 to 141,000 men (Table 27.1), while paramilitary forces grew from 23,000 to 30,000 men, giving a total troop strength of 171,000 by 1982. Students, who had previously been exempted from military conscription, began to be drafted from 1976.

The sheer increase in the number of troops imposed a heavy burden on the Moroccan treasury. Expenditure by the ministry of defense under the govern-

TABLE 27.1
THE GROWTH OF THE FAR
(number of troops, excluding
paramilitary forces)

1974	56,000
1975	61,000
1976	73,000
1977	84,650
1978	89,000
1979	98,000
1980	116,500
1981	120,000
1982	141,000

SOURCE: International Institute for Strategic Studies, London.

ment's recurrent budget doubled between 1974 and 1977, rising from 838 million dirhams to 1,560 million dirhams, and by 1982 it had doubled again, to 3,750 million dirhams. But total military expenditure was really much higher. By 1982, 2,145 million dirhams were being allocated to the ministry of the interior, within whose purview came the paramilitary Forces Auxiliaires, the Sûreté Nationale and the Gendarmerie Royale, which together had several thousand men in Western Sahara. In all, 5,895 million dirhams, 26 percent of the total recurrent budget, were allocated to the two security ministries (defense and interior) in 1982 (Table 27.2).

TABLE 27.2
SECURITY EXPENDITURE UNDER THE MOROCCAN RECURRENT BUDGET
(in million dirhams)

	1974	1977	1981[a]	1982[a]
Defense	838	1,560	3,014	3,750
Interior	693	871	1,766	2,145
Subtotal	1,531	2,431	4,780	5,895
Total recurrent expenditure	5,815	8,886	18,178	22,554

SOURCES: World Bank, *Morocco: Economic and Social Development Report* (Washington, D.C., 1981); Economist Intelligence Unit, *Quarterly Economic Review, Morocco*, 2nd Quarter, 1982.
a Budget estimates

However, these figures did not tell the whole story. They covered only the operating costs of the two security ministries. They excluded expenditure on the purchase of military hardware, including military imports, which rose from a mere $18 million in 1974 to $45 million in 1975, $206 million in 1976 and $540 million in 1977.[1] Such military investment was made under various annex budgets and secret "special treasury accounts," as well as the government's investment budget, and so its true cost was well hidden from public view. Nonetheless, the World Bank estimated in 1981 that the Moroccan government's total military spending, under all budgets and accounts, rose from 1,561 million dirhams, or 13 percent of overall government expenditure, in 1975, to 4,304 million dirhams, or 23 percent of total expenditure, in 1977. By 1977, 9.2 percent of Gross Domestic Product was being drained into military expenditure, compared to 4.3 percent in 1975.[2]

The burden of military expenditure grew even heavier after 1977, and, according to a report from the U.S. embassy in Rabat in 1980, "knowledgeable government financial experts" were by then claiming that "Morocco's defense-related expenditure actually diverts no less than 40% of the consolidated national budget."[3] Fortunately for King Hassan, foreign grants, mainly from Saudi Arabia, helped to pay for some of Morocco's military imports. The World Bank estimated that such grants offset 60 percent of military import costs in 1977 and totalled $1 billion in 1976–78.[4] The Saudis were estimated to be funneling $1 billion of grants a year, including $400 million to pay for military purchases, by 1980–81.[5] However, such aid was insufficient and irregular, and by 1982 the government was finding great difficulty in paying for its arms.[6]

King Hassan's real problem was that the war in the Sahara coincided with and amplified a grave economic crisis. Ironically, economic prospects had seemed remarkably good on the eve of the war. The boom in the world phosphate market had raised Morocco's annual phosphate earnings by 450 percent, from $200 million to $900 million, between 1973 and 1974.[7] The 1973–77 development plan's investment target had accordingly been revised upward more than threefold. But the optimism had been short-lived. In 1975 the phosphate boom suddenly collapsed. By 1976 earnings from phosphate exports were little more than half what they had been two years earlier, and despite world inflation they had still not returned to their 1974 level by 1983 (Table 27.3). This was no small blow to an economy depending on phosphates for around a third of total export revenue.

TABLE 27.3
THE COLLAPSE OF MOROCCAN PHOSPHATE EXPORTS
(in billion dirhams)

1974	1975	1976	1977	1978	1979	1980	1981	1982
4.1	3.4	2.2	2.1	2.0	2.3	3.0	3.4	3.4

SOURCES: International Monetary Fund.

As a non-oil-producing country, meanwhile, Morocco was hit by the huge rise in oil prices. The cost of imported fuels almost doubled between 1974 and 1980, rising from 2.3 to 4 billion dirhams, and in 1981 there was a further 55 percent increase to 6.1 billion dirhams (Table 27.4). Fuel imports, by then, cost one and a half times more than the 4 billion dirhams earned from phosphate exports.

TABLE 27.4
THE SOARING COST OF MOROCCO'S FUEL IMPORTS
(in billion dirhams)

1974	1975	1976	1977	1978	1979	1980	1981	1982
2.3	2.2	2.4	3.2	3.0	2.4	4.0	6.1	7.1

SOURCES: World Bank, *Morocco: Economic and Social Development Report* (Washington, D.C., 1981); Economist Intelligence Unit, *Quarterly Economic Review: Morocco*; *Marchés Tropicaux et Méditerranéens*, June 3, 1983.

At the same time, a gradual decline in the country's ability to grow sufficient food added to the import bill. Until the sixties, cereal production had been more or less enough to satisfy domestic needs. However, since independence, agricultural output had been rising at an average annual rate of 2 percent, while the population had been growing at around 3 percent a year. The country began to have a large and increasing food deficit. Average annual wheat imports rose from 420,000 tons in 1968–72 to 1.04 million tons in 1973–77, and, overall, food imports rose by an average annual rate of 9.6 percent in volume terms and no less than 21 percent in value between 1970 and 1977.[8] From 1977 the cost of food imports grew every year in succession, reaching a record 2.8 billion dirhams in 1980. Then, after one of the harshest droughts in living memory which reduced the grain harvest to 2.05 million tons, less than half the previous year's crop and barely a third of national needs, food imports rose 63 percent in 1981 to 4.6 billion dirhams, more than one-fifth of total imports (Table 27.5).[9] There was only a modest improvement in 1982.

TABLE 27.5
MOROCCO'S RISING FOOD IMPORTS
(in billion dirhams)

1974	1975	1976	1977	1978	1979	1980	1981	1982
1.8	2.6	2.0	1.9	2.0	2.1	2.8	4.6	3.5

SOURCES: World Bank, *Morocco: Economic and Social Development Report* (Washington, D.C., 1981), Economist Intelligence Unit, *Quarterly Economic Review: Morocco; Marchhés Tropicaux et Méditerranéens,* June 3, 1983.

Additionally, some Moroccan exports suffered from the EEC's growing protectionism, while imports of manufactured goods were swollen by world inflation. All told, the trade deficit lurched heavily into deficit, reaching 13.5 billion dirhams in 1982, compared to less than a billion dirhams in 1974 (Table 27.6). Export earnings, which had covered the cost of 89 percent of the country's imports in 1974, offset only 48 percent by 1982, and by then food and fuel imports alone were absorbing 85 percent of the country's entire export revenue. The balance of payments, which had been in surplus on current account in 1972–74, slipped into deficit in 1975, to the tune of $546 million. By 1980 the current-account deficit had climbed to $1.4 billion, by 1981 to $1.8 billion.[10]

The government's only recourse was to finance the deficit by borrowing, thereby plunging the country deeper and deeper into debt. The public external debt rose remorselessly, from $1.2 billion in 1974 to almost $8 billion, GNP, in 1981. By the end of 1982, public external debt was estimated to have risen still further, to $9.3 billion. While tiding temporarily over the foreign exchange difficulties, such large-scale borrowing made matters worse in the long run. Repaying loans, and paying interest on them, devoured an ever larger proportion of the country's insufficient export earnings. By 1981 the debt-service ratio had reached 30.1 percent, more than five times higher than it had been in 1975 (Table 27.7).

TABLE 27.6
MOROCCO'S FOREIGN TRADE DEFICIT
(in billion dirhams)

	1974	1975	1976	1977	1978	1979	1980	1981	1982
Exports	7.4	6.2	5.6	5.9	6.3	7.6	9.6	12.4	12.5
Imports	8.3	10.4	11.6	14.4	12.4	14.3	16.8	22.7	26.0
Deficit	0.9	4.2	6.0	8.5	6.1	6.0	7.1	10.3	13.5

SOURCES: International Monetary Fund.

TABLE 27.7
MOROCCO'S GROWING DEBT BURDEN

	1976	1977	1978	1979	1980	1981
Public external debt ($ bn)[a]	2.3	4.1	5.1	6.2	7.1	7.9
Public external debt/GNP (%)	23.3	35.6	37.5	37.7	38.6	51.1
Debt-service ratio (%)[b]	7.2	10.8	18.7	21.8	27.5	30.1

SOURCES: World Bank, *World Debt Tables*. 1982–83.
a Disbursed only.
b Debt-service payments (repayment of principal plus interest payments as a percentage of exports of goods and services.

The strains on government finances were as severe as those on the balance of payments. The overall treasury deficit, which had been only 516 million dirhams in 1973, had risen to 7.9 billion dirhams by 1977, due to the rise in military expenditure and the ambitious investment outlays under the 1973–77 plan, and had to be financed by large-scale external borrowing (5.2 billion dirhams in 1977, compared to 1.35 billion dirhams in 1975). By 1981 the overall treasury deficit had soared to 12.8 billion dirhams and the government's external borrowing had risen to 9 billion dirhams.[11]

The economic crisis, and the 1980–81 drought in particular, widened Morocco's deep social cleavages. By forcing many of the poorer peasants to sell their remaining livestock or their tiny plots of land, the drought reinforced the already marked inequalities in land ownership and accelerated the demographic revolution that is gradually converting Morocco into a predominantly urban society. By 1981, 44 percent of the population lived in the urban areas, compared to only 14 percent a quarter of a century earlier; and the population of Casablanca alone had reached 3.2 million, three times more than in 1965.[12] There, and in Morocco's other swollen cities, the poor squat in sprawling, insalubrious *bidonvilles*. Subsisting on occasional earnings, since very few hold regular jobs, the residents of these slums had grown in number from half a million at the time of independence to at least three million, one-third of the total urban population, by 1982.

The Green March "has made a new people of us," King Hassan had boasted on November 17, 1975, three days after the triumph of the Madrid Accords.[13] However, the marked turn for the worse in economic and social conditions during the years of war, and the apparently interminable prolongation of the war itself, had gradually eroded the ecstatic sense of national purpose and unity that had done so much to improve the king's political fortunes, at the opposition parties' expense, in the "heroic" days of the Saharan adventure, in 1975.

The initial success of national "reunification" with the Saharan provinces had briefly enabled the king to capitalize on his regained popularity by liberalizing the political climate at home and holding parliamentary elections in 1977, after five years' ruling by decree, without fear of being outmaneuvered by the weakened opposition parties. Both the USFP and the pro-Moscow communists of the PPS were allowed to function with much less harassment than hitherto, and in April 1976 fifty-four USFP detainees, who had been in jail since March 1973, were set free. In November 1977, several Marxist student leaders were released too, after four years in detention, and a year later, in November 1978, the banned students' union, UNEM, was finally relegalized. Censorship of the domestic press, meanwhile, had been lifted in March 1977. The long-promised parliamentary elections were held in June 1977, following communal elections in October 1976 and provincial elections in January 1977.

Nonetheless, there were limits to this democratization. The king retained decisive executive powers and could revert, at his will, to a more authoritarian style of rule. Indeed, even during this period of relative liberalization, many of his less compromise-prone opponents continued to suffer as inclement treatment as ever. On December 18, 1975, only a month after the Madrid accords, the director of the USFP's newspaper, Al-Moharrir, Omar Benjelloun, was assassinated by right-wing extremists. Between June and August 1976, over 370 USFP members and supporters were brought before the courts in eight major trials, on charges related to the March 1973 guerrilla incidents, and, though more than two hundred were freed, one defendant was sentenced to death and several others received long jail terms.[14] Then, the following January, 178 Marxist-Leninists, mostly supporters of the Ilal-Amam and March 23 groups, were tried in Casablanca, thirty-nine of them in absentia, on charges of belonging to illegal associations intent on overthrowing the monarchy. Most had been held without trial for over two years, since November 1974, and had been badly tortured.[15] According to Amnesty International, the trial was a travesty of justice, with numerous irregularities, and though none of the defendants was convicted, or even accused, of engaging in violent activities, almost all of them received very long prison sentences—forty-four, including the thirty-nine tried in absentia, for life, twenty-one for thirty years, forty-five for ten years and nineteen for five years. Jailed in Kenitra, they staged a long hunger strike in November-December 1977 which culminated in the death of one of the three women in their number, Saida Menebhi.[16] After another wave of arrests in 1977, eighty more Marxist-Leninists were detained in Meknes.[17] In 1979 scores of trade-union activists were briefly jailed, after a wave of strikes, and though ninety-one political prisoners, mainly USFP members, were amnestied in July 1980, many others, including 108 of the Marxist-Leninists sentenced in 1977, remained in jail.[18]

The June 1977 elections, besides, were far from being democratic. The urban areas, where the opposition parties had their traditional strength, were heavily underrepresented, in the distribution of seats, and the opposition parties were effectively barred from campaigning in many rural areas by the ministry of the interior's network of local *caids*. In addition, the semicorporatist, or indirect, system used for the election of one-third of the parliamentary seats artificially reinforced the royalists. With 15 percent of the votes, according to the highly suspect official returns, the USFP ended up with only 15 of the 264 seats, whereas the royalist "independents" secured a comfortable parliamentary majority, with 141 seats, despite receiving only 45 percent of the vote, and their government-backed allies, the Mouvement Populaire, won a further 44 seats with a mere 12 percent of the vote. With the support of 22 percent of the electorate, the Istiqlal Party, which King Hassan brought back into his government the following October for the first time since 1963, won an additional 51 seats, and so the three principal progovernment parties held 236 seats, ten times more than the USFP, the PPS and the trade-union deputies from the UMT combined. The USFP claimed that it was the victim of "forgery which took various coordinated forms involving all constituencies."[19]

By giving the Istiqlal Party eight ministerial posts in his October 1977 cabinet reshuffle, Hassan broadened his political base. Notably, Laraki was replaced in the foreign ministry by the party's secretary-general, M'hammed Boucetta, a fervent nationalist who was well-suited to the task of defending Morocco's Saharan policy to foreign governments and skeptical international forums like the UN but, like Laraki, played second fiddle to the king himself in the elaboration of policy.

Opening the Chamber of Representatives on October 14, the king proclaimed to its members that "your very presence in this hall is a challenge to dictatorship, to the one-party system, to the impoverishment of the intellect."[20] But the Chamber's powers were actually rather limited. The council of ministers remained responsible to the king rather than to the deputies, who had few real legislative powers. With such an artificially large royalist majority and a relatively minor constitutional role, the Chamber attracted little interest, even from its own members, who were frequently absent, and adopted very few laws. In any case, everybody knew that in the event of an "emergency" the king could dissolve parliament, as he had in the past, and rule by decree.

As Morocco's Saharan predicament worsened, particularly after the 1978 coup in Mauritania and Polisario's Houari Boumedienne Offensive, the ultranationalist opposition parties—notably the USFP and the PPS—began to criticize the government for failing to prosecute the war with sufficient drive and energy. The political bureau of the USFP, for example, spelled out a policy of extreme bellicosity in its report to the party's third congress, held in Casablanca on December 8–10, 1978. "Today, three years after the recovery of our Sahara, we find ourselves compelled, once again, to issue an appeal to the government, from the tribune of this congress, to abandon the hesitant and wait-and-see policy that allows events to unfold by themselves and awaits chance and solutions with unforeseeable consequences." It declared that, with the government's approval, it was prepared "to create an army of liberation and assume its responsibilities," but lamented, not surprisingly, that the idea of a USFP-run militia had fallen on deaf ears in government circles.[21] From time to time the party also advocated cross-border strikes into Algeria, a policy that the king dared not embrace, except, on occasion, at a level of pure rhetoric.

As anxious as ever to prove its nationalist legitimacy, the "communist" PPS echoed these extreme policies and had to swallow the indignity of justifying the country's dependence on supplies of French and U.S. arms to pursue the struggle against Polisario.[22] Even UNEM, under its reconstituted USFP leadership, could vote, at its sixteenth congress, in August-September 1979, in favor of "the opening of military camps for the training of the masses, including the students, so that they can get ready to go to the front of the armed struggle against the mercenaries and their masters."[23] For both the USFP and the PPS, an element of face-saving was involved in all this drumbeating, for both parties had hailed the annexation of Western Sahara with as much enthusiasm as the king and, like him, were wary of admitting that their Saharan policy had been flawed. The fear of being branded traitors by the Palace and thrust back into the repression of prewar days doubtless also militated against the adoption of an antiwar platform.[24] But there may have been a more Machiavellian consideration too, an expectation that, as the war crisis deepened, Hassan's will would falter, allowing the Left to emerge as the standard-bearer of patriotism and perhaps even as a candidate for power—though the army officers, who had little love for socialists, would have been the best-placed, given their organization and military strength, to profit from a real crisis of the monarchical regime.

The ultranationalism of the mainstream left-wing parties was at odds with the public mood of disenchantment with the Saharan war which set in from about 1979, as the conflict dragged on without issue and economic conditions progressively deteriorated. However, the USFP and the PPS nourished the illusion, among their militants and supporters, that escalation was a sure route to victory and peace. There were no other left-wing parties with the desire or the influence to organize the growing war weariness into overt opposition to continuation of the struggle against the guerrillas.[25] However, the "national union" forged by the Palace with the principal opposition parties at the onset of the Saharan affair, in 1974–75, gradually disintegrated, as the worsening economic and social conditions at home returned to the forefront of public concern. The social truce, which had held more or less effectively since the Green March, first showed signs of strain in April 1978, when one hundred thousand teachers and ten thousand workers at the Khouribga phosphate mines staged strikes for higher pay.[26] Despite its jingoism, the USFP had no qualms about encouraging such wartime labor militancy, since it was anxious at this time to rally workers from the main traditional labor federation, the independent UMT, to new party-led unions that claimed they would defend workers' interests with greater militancy. Eight of these unions came together to found a new trade-union federation, the Confédération Démocratique des Travailleurs (CDT), in November 1978, and the country was swept by a wave of strikes early in 1979, by railwaymen, bank employees, phosphate workers, coal miners, dockers, textile workers, oil-refinery workers, hospital staffs and teachers.[27]

This revival of labor militancy posed a serious challenge to King Hassan's government, just as Polisario's Houari Boumedienne Offensive was getting underway in the Sahara. The guerrillas' raid into Tan-Tan, in January 1979, came in the middle of the strike wave. So, besides coopting the opposition parties into his new Conseil National de Sécurité, Hassan attempted to refurbish his regime's image by easing his brother-in-law, Ahmed Osman, out of the premiership in March and appointing in his stead a lawyer with past links to the UNFP, Maati Bouabid. Such a change was too cosmetic to make much of an impression on the USFP-led unions. On April 10–11 the country's teachers and health workers went back on strike. The government reverted to the stick and arrested 688 strikers under a long forgotten trade-union law, dating from 1958. Of these, 230 were sentenced to prison terms ranging from one month to two years; almost nine hundred workers were fired from their jobs; and, on April 24, a sixteen-year-old militant of the USFP's Jeunesse Ittihadia (United Youth) was tortured to death in police custody in Agadir.[28]

King Hassan's stock was lowered, meanwhile, by the triumph of the Islamic Revolution in Iran and the arrival of the exiled Shah, Mohammed Reza Pahlavi, in Morocco, as Hassan's guest, in January 1979. Parallels between the Pahlavi and Alawite dynasties were quickly drawn, especially by students, and slogans painted on faculty buildings in Rabat protested that "one Shah in Morocco is enough."[29] Fueled by the continuing detention of some student leaders, despite the lifting of the ban on UNEM, and by problems regarding their grants and government attempts to restrict access to higher education, protests by students and *lycéens* became widespread in February-March 1979. Police stormed onto striking campuses and several students were reported killed.[30]

New focuses of discontent sustained the political tension. In a referendum in May 1980, the king won an improbable 96.7 percent vote of approval for a constitutional amendment to prolong the life of parliament from four to six years. The USFP was understandably infuriated by a measure which amounted to a two-year postponement of parliamentary elections and threatened to walk out of the Chamber of Representatives at the end of its original four-year term in September 1981.[31] Student protests multiplied, meanwhile, and came to a head in a wave of campus strikes in January-February 1981. The following April 10, the USFP announced that it would boycott municipal elections to be held in ten provinces in May, due to "the absence of any guarantee limiting the intervention of the administrative apparatus and assuring its neutrality."[32] The government retaliated by prosecuting the USFP's daily newspaper, *Al-Moharrir*, for defamation because it had published an article in ironical style about the $35-million wedding celebrations for the eldest son of the ruler of the United Arab Emirates.[33] Then, on June 1, Hassan warned that he might close down the USFP's offices, an action tantamount to banning the party, if its deputies dared to carry out their threat to withdraw from parliament.[34]

Morocco's shortage of foreign exchange had become so grave by 1980 that, in October, the IMF agreed to provide a stand-by credit of 810 million Special Drawing Rights (around $1 billion), its second-largest rescue operation to date for an ailing third-world economy.[35] The price, however, was the government's acceptance of a package of economic measures to reduce the deficits on its budget and the balance of payments. In particular, the IMF wanted curbs on the government's food-subsidy fund, the Caisse de Compensation, which had been swollen by the huge increase in the cost of imported food.[36] The government had already raised the prices of subsidized foods by 10 to 35 percent in September 1980.[37] But on May 29, 1981, large new increases were announced. The price of sugar was raised by 38.6 percent, cooking oil by 27.5 percent, milk by 14.3 percent, butter by 76.2 percent and flour by 40 percent.[38] This was a body-blow to the poor, and especially to the inhabitants of the urban shantytowns who had found it hard to make ends meet even before these price rises. The USFP responded by charging on June 2 that the country was "in a more serious state of crisis than at any point in the past, because of the antipopular options of the authorities and the class struggle unleashed against the workers."[39] Spontaneously, strikes and demonstrations broke out in different parts of the country. Taking fright at the scale of opposition, Maati Bouabid halved the price increases on June 6, but, instead of appeasing the opposition, this raised hopes that the government could be forced to annul the increases completely. The UMT and the CDT called rival general strikes, on June 18 and 20 respectively, and both were widely observed by workers throughout the country. In Casablanca the CDT's strike rapidly spiraled into a kind of urban uprising. Mobs from the shantytowns tore through the streets, setting fire to banks, shops, cars and petrol stations.[40] The violence was akin to the January 1977 riots in Cairo, which had likewise been triggered by reductions in government food subsidies, or to the street battles that had gripped Casablanca fifteen years earlier, in March 1965.

As in 1965, it was the army which restored order, with great bloodshed. "Toward midday the army relieved the police and immediately began firing blanks at us," recalled an eyewitness of the disturbances in the district of El-Foukara. "Some of the demonstrators were overexcited. They advanced on the soldiers, stones in hand, shouting 'kill us! kill us!' You would have thought they wanted to commit suicide. Then the army opened fire, with rifles and machine guns. It was incredibly violent. One of my pals, a fourteen-year-old, stopped a bullet in the middle of his head and his brain literally blew out before my eyes. The clashes lasted until nine o'clock. All night, tanks patrolled the neighborhood and police vehicles equipped with loudspeakers went up and down the streets ordering people to hand over to the authorities wounded relatives and friends, as well as the bodies of those who had been killed during the demonstration."[41]

Few believed the ministry of the interior's claim, two days later, that only sixty-six people had died. The USFP put the figure at 637. Troops controlled access to the city's hospitals and occupied the morgue, to avoid public burials that might spark off new disturbances, as did the great funeral processions in Tehran during 1978. All the opposition newspapers were banned, and though the PPS newspaper, *Al-Bayane*, was allowed to resume publication from July 17 (since the pro-Moscow communists constituted a relatively minor threat to the Palace), the USFP's papers, *Al-Moharrir* and *Libération*, remained banned two years later. Two thousand people were arrested, Hassan announced two weeks after the riots, on July 2. Of these, at least 1,070 were kept in detention, and by the end of July 516 of them had been brought before courts and sentenced.[42] Most were slum dwellers, seized during the riots, and they received long jail terms, up to ten years.[43] About two hundred, however, were leaders of the USFP and the CDT. Eight were members of the USFP's national administrative commission.[44] By the beginning of September, 190 USFP and CDT members had been sentenced to jail terms of between one month and one and a half years in trials before twenty-three courts across the country.[45] Others, however, were still awaiting trial, and two years later the five most prominent detainees—Mustapha Karchaoui, the editor-in-chief of *Al-Moharrir*, Noubir al-Amaoui, the secretary-general of the CDT, and three members of the CDT's executive bureau—had still not been tried.[46]

Hassan's liberalization had come to an abrupt end, for the national alliance behind the Palace's Saharan cause, which had briefly enabled the king to relax his style of rule, had been overwhelmed by the country's exacerbated economic and social difficulties. If Hassan's prestige had soared on the eve of the Saharan war, at the time of the Green March, it had sunk as low as ever by the early 1980s. There seemed to be no end in sight to the war in the desert, while the economic crisis was making life much harsher for most Moroccans. The king was held in the lowest esteem in the cities, where almost half of Moroccans were by now living, and among the rapidly growing army of youth, for whom the future held little hope.[47] It was only in the countryside and among the older generations that the king retained any real prestige from his religious role as *amir al-muminin*. Much of the educated middle class, moreover, was alienated by the corruption of Hassan's anachronistic system of patronage and his refusal to allow a real dispersal of decision-making powers.

The USFP was the main beneficiary of the radicalization from 1978 to 1981. However, the party was also challenged by groups to its left, particularly in the student movement, and as the Casablanca riots in June 1981 revealed, it could easily be outflanked by the spontaneous action of the urban poor and thrust into unintended confrontation with the Palace.

The post-Casablanca repression paralyzed the USFP and the CDT organizationally. Many of their top leaders were jailed. Their offices were closed down by the police and the USFP's newspapers banned. The party lost ground to far left groups. At UNEM's 17th congress, in August-September 1981, it ceded the union's leadership to the PPS, the March 23 group and a faction known as the Groupe des Martyres.[48] Islamic fundamentalist organizations, whose appeal had been much weaker than in some other Arab countries because the relative political pluralism in Morocco had provided more secular channels for the expression of discontent, also took advantage of the vacuum created by the USFP's paralysis. They focused their propaganda on the immorality of the Hassan regime, and the hollowness of its religious claim to rule, by attacking the prevalence of corruption, the social chasm between rich and poor and the decadence of traditional values and moral standards. In July 1982, the king deemed it wise to warn the clergy "not to transform the mosques into rostrums."[49]

None of the political parties, however, had both the will and the requisite organization and influence to overthrow the king. Nor did the small and splintered groups of Islamic fundamentalists. It was the officer corps of the army which potentially constituted the gravest danger to the Palace. It was the most powerful, organized force in Moroccan society, and it had twice revealed its political ambitions in 1971–72. It was now experiencing the degradation of a prolonged, frustrating and apparently unending war in the Sahara. Not surprisingly, rumors that a military coup had been nipped in the bud spread through Morocco when General Dlimi, the commander of the Moroccan forces in the Sahara, died in a mysterious road accident near Marrakesh on January 25, 1983. The fact that several senior officers had been arrested only a few days earlier fueled speculation that the general had been assassinated.[50] Dlimi's successor as commander in the Sahara was Colonel-Major Abdelaziz Bennani, who had held this post earlier in the war, in 1977–79.

The social, economic and political tensions within Morocco were an inauspicious backdrop to Hassan's efforts to keep up the struggle in the desert. Yet the king feared that he would be in graver political trouble at home if he withdrew from Western Sahara. With the Saharan euphoria of Green March days long gone, popular reaction to a retreat might not have been as dangerous as that to the price increases in the summer of 1981, despite the inevitable accusations of national betrayal it would have elicited from the ultranationalist opposition parties. Nonetheless, the king knew that, to abandon the "Moroccan Sahara," after years of grueling war, would have amounted to admitting a failure of such proportions that his very credibility as a ruler might be shattered. He had simply staked too much on his Saharan policy to be able to withdraw without losing face before his own people. Worse still, retreat from the Sahara might be the moment for the FAR, swollen in size and bitter after their ignominious and fruitless desert war, to seek their revenge on the monarch who had subjected them to such a humiliating ordeal. To King Hassan it seemed that the best bet was to keep fighting despite the costs, to hang on to the "useful triangle," in the hope that eventually the Algerian government would force the guerrillas to accept a settlement on Moroccan terms. In the absence of such a settlement, however, Hassan seemed condemned to a long war of attrition which he was poorly placed to sustain.

NOTES

1. *World Military Expenditures and Arms Transfers 1967-1976* (U.S. Arms Control and Disarmament Agency, Washington, D.C., 1978), p. 141; The World Bank, *Morocco: Economic and Social Development Report* (Washington, D.C., 1981), p. vi.

2. *Ibid.*, pp. 41–42.

3. Cited in *Arms Sales and the Conflict in the Western Sahara: an Assessment of U.S. Policy*, Hearing before the Subcommittees on International Security and Scientific Affairs and on Africa of the Committee on Foreign Affairs, House of Representatives, 97th Congress, 1st Session, March 25, 1981 (U.S. Government Printing Office, Washington, D.C., 1981), p. 43.

4. World Bank, *loc. cit.*, pp. vi, 35.

5. *Financial Times* (London), April 10, 1981.

6. For a few weeks early in 1982, the French government halted deliveries of military equipment to

Morocco because the Rabat government was in arrears on its payments. Deliveries resumed after the French government agreed in April to reschedule $328 million of Moroccan debts. In June 1983, Morocco was $10 million in arrears on interest payments for its military debt, totaling more than $200 million, to the United States (*Le Monde,* June 11, 1983).

7. World Bank, *loc. cit.,* p. iii.

8. *Ibid.,* pp. vi, 158.

9. Economist Intelligence Unit (London), *Quarterly Economic Review: Morocco,* 4th Quarter, 1981, and 3rd Quarter, 1982.

10. *International Financial Statistics* (International Monetary Fund, Washington, D.C.).

11. World Bank, *loc. cit.,* pp. ix, 44, 47; *Marchés Tropicaux et Méditerranéens,* May 21, 1982. In an attempt to correct the deficits in public finances and the balance of payments, the government slammed on the economic brakes in 1978, introducing a three-year austerity plan under which public investment was slashed, credit policies tightened and import restrictions extended. Investment shrunk and the economy lurched into recession. However, there was only a modest and temporary improvement in the balance of payments and government finances. The overall treasury deficit fell from 7.9 billion dirhams in 1977 to 6.3 billion dirhams in 1979, but the recessionary effects of the 1978 austerity measures prompted the government to embark on a more expansionist course. By 1980 the overall treasury deficit had risen to 8.5 billion dirhams, by 1981 to 12.8 billion dirhams. Likewise, the foreign trade deficit, which had been reduced from 8.5 to 6.1 billion dirhams between 1977 and 1978, increased year by year from 1979, reaching an unprecedented 13.6 billion dirhams in 1982.

12. *Le Monde,* March 6, 1981, and July 31, 1981.

13. Cited in Hassan II, *Le défi* (Albin Michel, Paris, 1976), p. 182.

14. *Amnesty International Briefing: Morocco* (Amnesty International, London, 1977), p. 4; *Africa Contemporary Record, 1976-77,* pp. B89-90.

15. One of those detained in November 1974, Abdellatif Zeroual, a leader of Ilal-Amam, had been tortured to death immediately after his arrest. A French doctor who examined the defendants in November 1976 noted: "These injuries included great pain in the whole leg and insomnia because of beating on the soles of the feet; tuberculosis, other lung complaints and rheumatism resulting from long periods in damp cold cells; deafness from being beaten round the ears; eye complaints after spending weeks or even months with eyes blindfolded, or from periods spent day and night under a spotlight, pains in the fingers and arms from electric shocks to the fingers, digestive troubles and dental decay from malnutrition, psychological troubles resulting from pain and fear. . . ." (*The Casablanca Trials January/February 1977,* Amnesty International, March 1977, p. 4.)

16. *Le Monde,* January 18, 1978. The following December, another detainee, Brahim Zaidi, a member of the USFP, died in Kenitra jail due to lack of medical treatment for an illness. See *Report of an Amnesty International Mission to the Kingdom of Morocco, 10-13 February 1981* (Amnesty International, London, 1982), p. 65.

17. *Africa Contemporary Record, 1977-78,* p. B24.

18. An Amnesty International mission that visited Morocco in February 1981 concluded that detainees were often held incommunicado, without access to lawyers, in police custody for many months or more than a year, that they were often tortured while in police custody, that more than one hundred "prisoners of conscience" were in jail for crimes related solely to their views, that large numbers of oppositionists had "disappeared," that some prisoners had died due to ill-treatment or lack of medical care and that some prisoners were not released after the expiration of their sentences. Amnesty International expressed particular concern for the plight of more than a hundred military prisoners jailed after the coup attempts in 1971 and 1972. None had yet been released, though fifteen had served their full terms by 1981. At least fifty-eight were being held incommunicado in a secret prison at Tazmamert, in the Atlas Mountains, where as many as fifteen could have died on account of the appalling conditions there. (Amnesty International, *loc. cit.,* pp. 27-28, 33.)

19. *Maghreb Arabe Presse* (Rabat), June 8, 1977.

20. *Arabia and the Gulf* (London), October 24, 1977.

21. Union Socialiste des Forces Populaires, *IIIème Congrès national tenu à Casablanca, les 8, 9 et 10 décembre 1978,* Rapport de synthèse du bureau politique, p. 65.

22. *Al-Bayane* (Casablanca), October 25, 1979; Interview with Ali Yata, PPS secretary-general, Casablanca, November 14, 1978.

23. *Libération* (Casablanca), September 14-20, 1979.

24. Interview with Mohammed Guessous, USFP deputy mayor of Rabat, December 1979.

25. On the Moroccan Left, only the small Ilal-Amam group and some members of the March 23 movement dared to give the Saharawis their open support. On January 15, 1977, during the *frontiste*

trial in Casablanca, the Ilal-Amam leader, Abraham Serfaty, spoke out from the dock against Hassan's "colonialist war against the Saharawi people" and proclaimed his support for the SADR. He was expelled from the court to his cell. (*L'Etincelle*, Paris, February 24, 1977.) Five months earlier, in August 1976, an Ilal-Amam delegation had attended Polisario's third congress, near Tindouf, and declared that "the struggle for the Moroccan people's demands and the reinforcement of the liberation struggle in the Sahara are two inseparable things, for we have a common enemy, imperialism and the Hassan-Abdallah-Dlimi gang." (*Maghreb an-Nidal*, Paris, No. 5, October-November 1976.)

26. *An-Nahar Arab Report and Memo*, April 17, 1978, and May 1, 1978.

27. *Agence France Presse*, dispatch from Rabat, February 10, 1979; *Le Monde*, April 18, 1979.

28. Confédération Démocratique des Travailleurs, *Livre Blanc* (Les Editions Maghrébines, Casablanca, 1979), p. 4. The king finally promised a year later, in July 1980, that the fired workers would get their jobs back.

29. *Washington Post*, March 24, 1979.

30. *Le Monde*, January 26, 1979, and April 18, 1979; *Afrique-Asie* (Paris), March 5, 1979; *The Guardian* (London), March 22, 1979.

31. *Maghreb Arabe Presse*, May 24, 1980.

33. *Le Monde*, April 12-13, 1981.

33. *Le Monde*, May 14, 1981.

34. *Le Monde*, June 3, 1981.

35. *IMF Survey*, October 27, 1980. Only Turkey had received a larger standby credit, of $1.65 billion, the previous June. The credit agreement with Morocco was revised to SDR 817 million ($988 million) in March 1981 and, then, due to Morocco's difficulties in complying with the IMF's stringent credit conditions, to $579 million in April 1982. See *Marchés Tropicaux et Méditerranéens*, March 13, 1981, and *An-Nahar Arab Report and Memo*, May 3, 1982.

36. It drained 1 billion dirhams of government resources in 1979, 1.4 billion dirhams in 1980 and 2.2 billion dirhams in 1981. (*Cedies Informations*, Casablanca, January 19, 1980; *Marchés Tropicaux et Méditerranéens*, May 21, 1982.)

37. *Le Monde*, October 9, 1980.

38. *Cedies Informations*, May 30, 1981.

39. *Marchés Tropicaux et Méditerranéens*, July 3, 1981.

40. See *Le Monde*, June 23, 1981, and *Marchés Tropicaux et Méditerranéens*, July 3, 1981.

41. *Le Monde*, June 27, 1981.

42. Amnesty International, *loc. cit.*, pp. 34-35.

43. *Marchés Tropicaux et Méditerranéens*, July 17, 1981.

44. *Le Monde*, June 24, 1981.

45. *Le Monde*, September 8, 1981.

46. *Le Monde*, May 7, 1982.

47. In 1981, 45.6 percent of the population of 20.1 million was under the age of fifteen.

48. Later in the year, there were widely followed strikes on the country's campuses, leading to the arrest of twenty-one student leaders in December and their sentencing to jail terms of up to three years in January 1982.

49. *Le Monde*, July 22, 1982. Earlier, in December 1979, several hundred Muslim fundamentalists had been detained briefly for questioning following the participation of several Moroccans in an attack on the Al-Haram mosque in Mecca on November 21 (the first day of the Muslim fifteenth century). In January 1982 there were street disorders in Tangier following the disappearance of a popular preacher, and Islamic fundamentalist cassettes were reported to be circulating in the slums of Casablanca in 1982. (*Le Monde*, February 25, 1982.)

50. For details of the controversy about Dlimi's death, see *Le Monde*, February 2, 1983, and *Africa Confidential*, February 16, 1983. Among those arrested on the eve of Dlimi's death was Colonel Bouarat, head of the Royal Guard Commandos. Dlimi's aide-de-camp, Commander Mahjoub Tobji, was arrested in March.

28

Morocco's
Diplomatic Isolation

T RAPPED INTO AN EXPENSIVE and seemingly endless war of attrition in the
desert, while economic and political difficulties mounted at home, King
Hassan also faced growing foreign criticism of his Saharan policy, especially after
Mauritania's withdrawal from the war in 1979. Polisario registered important diplomatic successes, notably in the UN, the OAU and the nonaligned movement, and
by 1983 fifty-four countries had granted diplomatic recognition to the SADR. All
of them were from the third world, and twenty-seven were African, but they
represented a rather broad ideological spectrum, ranging from Cuba and Vietnam
on the left to such countries as Mexico, Zambia and Venezuela (Table 28.1).

It was in black Africa that Morocco's Saharan policy was most poorly viewed.
The annexation of Western Sahara transgressed two of the OAU's holiest principles—the right of colonial peoples to self-determination and acceptance of the
frontiers inherited from the European powers.[1] Meeting in Maputo, Mozambique, on January 19-24, 1976, the OAU's Liberation Committee, which is
primarily responsible for assisting the freedom struggle in southern Africa, recommended OAU recognition of Polisario as an African liberation movement.

However, diplomatic alliances, with Morocco, Mauritania or their Western supporters, or fears of allowing an inter-African conflict to divide the OAU tended to
discourage some African governments from backing the Saharawi guerrillas.
Thus, when Morocco and Mauritania threatened to leave the OAU during a
meeting of its Council of Ministers in Addis Ababa on February 23-March 1,
1976, if the council endorsed the Liberation Committee's recommendation to
recognize Polisario, the proposal was shelved.[2]

However, the Liberation Committee again recommended recognition of
Polisario, on June 6 and at an ensuing meeting of the Council of Ministers, in Port
Louis, Mauritius, on June 24-29. Benin, one of the first states to have recognized
the SADR, submitted a strongly worded resolution supporting ''the struggle of
the Saharan people for the recovery of their national rights'' and demanding ''the

TABLE 28.1
RECOGNITION OF THE SADR
(As of 1983, with dates of recognition)

ASIA
(8 countries)

Afghanistan (1979)	North Korea (1976)
Iran (1980)	South Yemen (1978)
Kampuchea (1979)	Syria (1980)
Laos (1979)	Vietnam (1979)

AFRICA
(27 countries)

Algeria (1976)	Mali (1980)
Angola (1976)	Mauritius (1982)
Benin (1976)	Mozambique (1976)
Botswana (1980)	Rwanda (1976)
Burundi (1976)	Saõ Tomé and Príncipe (1978)
Cape Verde (1979)	Seychelles (1977)
Chad (1980)	Sierra Leone (1980)
Congo (1978)	Swaziland (1980)
Ethiopia (1979)	Tanzania (1978)
Ghana (1979)	Togo (1976)
Guinea-Bissau (1976)	Uganda (1979)
Lesotho (1979)	Zambia (1979)
Libya (1980)	Zimbabwe (1980)
Madagascar (1976)	

LATIN AMERICA AND CARIBBEAN
(13 countries)

Bolivia (1982)	Mexico (1979)
Costa Rica (1980)	Nicaragua (1979)
Cuba (1980)	Panama (1978)
Dominica (1979)	Saint Lucia (1979)
Grenada (1979)	Surinam (1982)
Guyana (1979)	Venezuela (1982)
Jamaica (1979)	

OCEANIA
(6 countries)

Kiribati (1981)	Solomon Islands (1981)
Nauru (1981)	Tuvalu (1981)
Papua-New Guinea (1981)	Vanuatu (1980)

immediate withdrawal of all foreign occupation forces and respect for the territorial integrity of the Western Sahara and the national sovereignty of the Saharan people.''[3] Morocco and Mauritania stormed out of the meeting in protest and the resolution was adopted in their absence by twenty-nine votes to two.[4]

Both Morocco and Mauritania threatened to quit the OAU entirely if it was ratified by the subsequent summit meeting of African heads of state in the Mauritian capital on July 2–5, and this ultimatum was sufficient once again to persuade the majority of African governments to beat a retreat. The heads of state refrained from endorsing the Council of Ministers' resolution and decided to postpone further debate until an extraordinary summit could be held, ''with the participation of the people of Western Sahara,'' to ''find a lasting and just solution'' to the problem.[5]

This was a recipe for postponing debate indefinitely. The extraordinary summit had still not been convened by the time the OAU's next ordinary annual summit met, on July 2–5, 1977, in Libreville, Gabon. On this occasion, a date (October 1977) and a venue (Lusaka, Zambia) for the special conference were agreed upon. However, there were doubts about Morocco's willingness to attend, and in September Zambia suddenly called the summit off, because, it claimed, only two states had agreed to help meet its costs and the war on the Zimbabwe border threatened the safety of visiting delegations.[6] President Omar Bongo, the chairman of the OAU at the time, then offered to host the summit in Libreville, on March 24–30, 1978, but, as a close ally of both King Hassan and President Valéry Giscard d'Estaing (then using his air force against the guerrillas in Mauritania), he had no wish to embarrass Morocco or Mauritania and so called off the conference on March 3, on the grounds that not enough African leaders were prepared to attend or help pay for it.[7]

Nonetheless, the Saharan war had become too serious to ignore by the time that the OAU held its next ordinary summit, in Khartoum, on July 18–22, 1978. The summit met only days after Mokhtar Ould Daddah's downfall and Polisario's declaration of a cease-fire in Mauritania. While voting once again to hold the extraordinary summit, the African leaders at Khartoum also decided to set up ''an *ad hoc* committee composed of at least five heads of state of the Organization of African Unity, including the current chairman of the organization, and entrust it with the consideration of all the data on the question of Western Sahara, among which, the exercise of the right of the people of this territory to self-determination.''[8]

The ''committee of wise men,'' as it came to be known, met in Khartoum on November 30 and December 1 and delegated two of its members, Presidents Olusegun Obasanjo of Nigeria and Moussa Traoré of Mali, to visit Morocco, Mauritania and Algeria. Their mission, undertaken on May 1–5, 1979, included a meeting with Polisario leaders in Algiers and was followed by talks in Madrid between the OAU's secretary-general, Edem Kodjo, and the Spanish premier, Adolfo Suárez on June 2. Obasanjo, Traoré and Kodjo reported back to the committee at its second session, held in Khartoum on June 23. The ''wise men'' then adopted a resolution which, to Morocco's consternation, recommended an immediate cease-fire, ''the exercise by the people of Western Sahara of their right to self-determination through a general, free referendum enabling them to choose one of the two following options: a) total independence, b) maintenance of the status quo,'' a meeting of all concerned parties to obtain their cooperation in implementing the cease-fire and referendum and, finally, the creation of a special *ad hoc* committee of five African states to supervise the organization of the referendum in cooperation with the United Nations.[9]

Feeling the diplomatic ground slipping from under his feet, King Hassan dropped plans to attend the next OAU summit, in Monrovia, Liberia, on July 17–20, where the wise men's proposals were duly endorsed by thirty-three votes to only two.[10] The Moroccans were unmoved. ''The Sahara is and will remain Moroccan,'' insisted M'hammed Boucetta, the Moroccan foreign minister, at a Monrovia press conference immediately after the fateful vote, on the night of July 19. Hassan himself was contemptuous of the OAU's decisions. On August 19 he dismissed the OAU's summits as ''tam-tam conferences'' and ''conferences for dancing the Saint-Guy.''[11]

Such outbursts did little good to Morocco's reputation in African circles. It slipped still further after Hassan's annexation of Tiris el-Gharbia in August. The king felt so much on the defensive that he turned down an invitation to put his views in person to the OAU *ad hoc* committee when it met once again, in Monrovia, on December 4–5, to discuss implementation of the planned cease-fire and referendum. Mohammed Abdelaziz was there for Polisario, Mauritania sent its foreign minister and President Chadli Bendjedid attended for Algeria, but there was no delegation from Morocco at all. The upshot of this boycott, which was widely regarded as a snub to the OAU, was a further erosion of Moroccan influence and the adoption of a resolution, which, besides regretting Morocco's absence from the committee's deliberations, congratulated Mauritania for its ''courageous'' decision to sign a peace treaty with Polisario and drop its territorial claims, called on Morocco to ''withdraw all its troops from Western Sahara,'' repeated the Monrovia summit's calls for a cease-fire and a referendum, and proposed the establishment of an OAU peace-keeping force to ensure the cease-fire's observance.[12]

Morocco's isolation was even more marked at the following year's OAU summit, held in Freetown, Sierra Leone, on July 1–4, 1980. Morocco was appalled to find a narrow majority of the OAU's member states (twenty-six out of fifty) recognizing the SADR and favoring its admission to the OAU as a full member state, under Article 28 of the OAU Charter, which required only a simple majority. Morocco challenged the SADR's eligibility, on the grounds that it did not constitute an independent, sovereign state, and once again threatened, with several of its conservative African allies, to walk out of the OAU if the Saharawi republic was admitted.[13] As so often in the past, the threat of a walkout was sufficient to constrain the pro-Polisario majority. A compromise, proposed by Nigeria and adopted by consensus, postponed consideration of the SADR's admission and once again asked the *ad hoc* committee to attempt to ''reconcile the parties to the conflict and find a peaceful, lasting solution to this conflict.''[14]

Morocco had little alternative but to promise henceforth to cooperate with the *ad hoc* committee. So Maati Bouabid and Boucetta turned up in Freetown for the committee's next session, on September 9–11. However, they showed no willingness to compromise on matters of substance. "In brief," the committee noted in a report on its meeting, "Morocco's views were that the Polisario did not exist and was a creation of Algeria; that the conflict was between Morocco and Algeria which was committing aggression against her; that there would be an automatic cease-fire once Algeria ceased her aggression and that there was no need to hold a referendum since the people of Western Sahara had already expressed their wish to be integrated with Morocco in the traditional manner." Bouabid and Boucetta failed to convince the committee, which concluded that "there was a clear need for a fair and general referendum," and that it should be conducted jointly by the OAU and the UN. The committee urged that a cease-fire should take effect by December 1980, under UN supervision and that the opposing forces should be confined to their bases.[15]

Several of Morocco's Western allies, including the Carter administration, President Giscard d'Estaing and King Juan Carlos, now began to advise Hassan that, unless he showed some willingness to compromise, especially on the referendum proposal, the SADR's admission to the OAU would be inevitable at the next OAU summit, scheduled for Nairobi in June 1981. "We believe the time for the execution of the OAU recommendations is overdue, especially since the question of the Polisario's admission into the OAU will probably arise at the summit in Nairobi," the U.S. State Department's deputy assistant secretary for Near Eastern and South Asian affairs, Morris Draper, told Congress in March 1981. "Admission of the Polisario would complicate OAU efforts overall to encourage a settlement, for it would confer at least qualified legitimacy on the Polisario as the spokesman of the people of the Western Sahara." So, Draper revealed, it was "after consultations with us" that Morocco informed the UN, in October 1980, of its willingness to cooperate with the OAU *ad hoc* committee's referendum plan.[16]

The Rabat government began to hint that Hassan would attend the Nairobi summit, to announce his acceptance of the referendum. When he finally took the rostrum in the Kenyan capital, on June 26, he promised, with deliberate ambiguity, to accept a "controlled referendum whose modalities should give justice simultaneously to the objectives of the *ad hoc* committee, that is to say the committee of wise men, and to Morocco's conviction regarding the legitimacy of its rights."[17] The king was applauded for his magnanimity, and for the second year in a row no decision was reached on the SADR's application for OAU membership.

Polisario and Algeria, however, doubted the king's sincerity. They believed he was stalling for time, to keep the SADR out of the OAU, and would not allow a genuine referendum, for fear that a majority of Saharawis would opt for independence. Statements by the king during the weeks preceding the Nairobi summit had revealed as firm a determination as ever to hang on to the annexed territory. "The recovery of our Sahara is well and truly accomplished," he had assured the Moroccan people in a broadcast speech on March 3. "This Sahara is ours. We are not prepared to give it up, and though we are in favor of any agreement that can put an end to the conflict, we cannot allow any such agreement to be made at the expense of an integral part of our national territory."[18]

Indeed, on the very eve of his departure for Nairobi, on June 24, he had pledged on TV that "we will not renounce a single grain of this Moroccan Sahara for which so many of us have sacrificed our blood and which has cost us so much money."[19] Moreover, when he returned to Morocco after the summit, he gave a press conference in Rabat on July 2 which revealed that he had the most restrictive interpretation of the plan for a referendum. "I see the referendum as an act of confirmation," he said. "Moroccan citizens of the Sahara will not go back on all the manifestations of loyalty they have shown." He seemed reluctant to allow the Tindouf refugees to vote. "As to the people of Tindouf, they can come to vote in Morocco [sic] if they want to or, if they are against us, stay there because we have no need for troublemakers." Polisario would not be allowed to campaign for independence before the poll. "Any people who are not Moroccans coming in from outside to preach secession will be put out of harm's way. Morocco will not tolerate foreign publicists campaigning for such a secession, because that would be to ask too much of us." He even refused to acknowledge that Polisario was a party to the Saharan conflict. "For me, the parties interested by the Saharan affair remain Morocco, Algeria and Mauritania, to the exclusion of Polisario, which has never existed for the African community."[20]

If the king had merely been playing for time, his very acceptance of the notion of a referendum had nonetheless shifted the terrain of debate to Morocco's disadvantage in the longer term. The idea of a referendum was no longer at stake. Now debate would focus on how it should be conducted, and a majority of African states would expect the king to honor his pledge by accepting conditions for a genuinely democratic plebiscite in which the Western Saharans could freely determine their future, as the UN had urged since 1966.

The Nairobi summit therefore adopted an eight-point resolution that laid down the broad guidelines for an internationally supervised cease-fire and a truly democratic referendum. The "parties in conflict" were urged to "observe an immediate cease-fire" and the UN was requested to join the OAU in providing a peace-keeping force, to ensure security during the referendum. An "Implementation Committee," composed of the presidents of Kenya, Guinea, Mali, Nigeria, Sierra Leone, Sudan and Tanzania, was set up and mandated to "take, with the participation of the United Nations, all necessary measures to guarantee the exercise of a general and regular referendum of self-determination by the people of the Western Sahara."[21]

King Hassan, Mohammed Abdelaziz and Presidents Chadli Bendjedid and Mohammed Khouna Ould Heydalla were interviewed in turn when the committee met in Nairobi for its first session, on August 24–26. The committee then adopted a compromise resolution which satisfied neither Morocco nor Polisario and Algeria. It did state unambiguously that "the referendum shall be one of self-determination which will enable the people of Western Sahara to express themselves freely and democratically on the future of their territory." All Saharawis registered in the Spanish authorities' last census, in 1974, would be entitled to vote, along with Saharawi refugees in neighboring countries whose identification would be facilitated by the UN High Commissioner for Refugees. Rejecting a proposal from King Hassan that the question on the ballot papers should not include the option of independence but be cast in terms of the traditional *bayaa*, the committee decided that "the people of the Western Sahara shall

be given the following choice: a) independence, or b) integration with Morocco.''
The committee resolved to organize the referendum itself, in collaboration with
the UN. Additionally, ''an impartial interim administration supported by
civilian, military and police components shall be set up'' and ''assisted by an adequate number of OAU and/or UN peace-keeping forces,'' while ''troops of the
parties to the conflict shall be effectively confined to their bases.''

None of these proposals were welcome to King Hassan. However, the committee refrained from endorsing Polisario's demands for the total withdrawal of the
Moroccan troops and administration from Western Sahara. Furthermore, it did
not dare risk alienating Hassan by recognizing Polisario explicitly as Morocco's
adversary. That would have been totally unacceptable to the king. Consequently,
the committee could merely urge ''the parties in conflict,'' without naming
them, ''to agree on a cease-fire through negotiations under the auspices of the
Implementation Committee.'' No target date was set for the cease-fire, let alone
the referendum.[22]

Over the following weeks Polisario pressed Morocco to accept direct negotiations. King Hassan continued, however, to reject that idea out of hand. Instead,
he wanted to talk to the Algerians. Chadli, though, was adamant that he would
not negotiate in place of the Saharawis, and so the OAU peace plan ran aground.
The fighting continued; indeed, it reached new heights with the Polisario
onslaught on Guelta Zemmour on October 13.

King Hassan tried, meanwhile, to convince the OAU that he had made as
many compromises as Moroccan public opinion would tolerate. His case was
strengthened by the USFP's decision, on September 5, to question the Moroccan
government's resolve to hold on to the Saharan provinces, in view of its stated acceptance of the OAU's referendum plan. Government declarations ''can only
suggest a predisposition to resignation, indeed the eventual abandonment of
Moroccan sovereignty over the provinces of Western Sahara,'' the party's political
bureau claimed. The Implementation Committee's rejection of the Polisario
demands for the withdrawal of the Moroccan army and administration from
Western Sahara before the poll was ''a purely formal concession'' to Morocco,
since the OAU-UN interim administration would have ''full powers.'' Furthermore, the OAU plan would entail ''a downright invasion of tens of thousands of
elements having full latitude to proclaim their hostility to our country during the
electoral campaign.''[23]

The USFP's statement was a godsend to Hassan. He could counsel patience at
the OAU. To insist on further Moroccan concessions, such as talks with Polisario,
would be unacceptable to Moroccan public opinion. At home the September 5
statement was the perfect excuse to crown the clampdown on the USFP which had
begun with the mass arrests and the banning of the party's press after the
Casablanca riots on June 20. The king knew that the USFP could not muster the
kind of popular support for its ultrabellicose Saharan policy that it had summoned in opposition to the summer price increases. Finally, there was nothing
but embarrassment at the USFP's September 5 statement among the party's social
democratic allies abroad, such as the newly elected French socialist president,
François Mitterrand.

So, on September 8, five of the nine members of the USFP's political bureau, including the first secretary, Abderrahim Bouabid, were arrested. Brought to trial in Rabat, they were found guilty of committing acts "tending to disturb order, tranquillity and security." Bouabid and two of his codefendants, Mohammed Lyazghi, the director of the USFP's banned newspaper, *Al-Moharrir*, and Mohammed Lahbabi, a university professor, were each jailed for one year.[24] They were released under a royal amnesty, at the end of February 1982, after serving almost six months of their sentences.

At a press conference in Paris, on January 29, Hassan reaffirmed his refusal to talk to Polisario.[25] The OAU's peace plan remained in a diplomatic *cul-de-sac*. However, the foreign ministers of the seven states comprising the OAU implementation committee tried to break the deadlock at a meeting in Nairobi on February 6–7. "The time has come for the heads of state of the implementation committee to name the parties to the conflict," they proposed. The "sole parties to the conflict" were Morocco and Polisario. Additionally, they recommended that the UN should take "complete responsibility" for the peace-keeping force in view of its "exorbitant cost," a consideration doubtless prompted by the OAU's inability to persuade its member states to pay for the three-thousand-strong force it had sent to Chad the previous December.[26]

Hassan, who was still in Paris, showed his displeasure by refusing to attend the subsequent meeting of the Implementation Committee's heads of state, on February 8–9. Boucetta, who led the Moroccan delegation in the sovereign's absence, bluntly told the committee that the foreign ministers' proposals were unacceptable. "Polisario is not recognized as a liberation movement. What is called the SADR is not recognized as a state. His Majesty the King has clearly stated that Morocco will only negotiate with its equals, with recognized states." Morocco would only negotiate a cease-fire with Algeria and Mauritania, "to seal or close, or render airtight, their frontiers, so that incursions cease on all sides."[27]

The committee was paralyzed. Fearing to lose Morocco's cooperation entirely, it decided, in the words of President Daniel arap Moi of Kenya, "not to name the warring parties, although we know who the parties are."[28] If it would not name them, it could not, of course, get them to negotiate a cease-fire, and so the committee could do no more than make the timeless observation that "a total cease-fire will take effect at a date to be fixed by the Implementation Committee after consultations with all the concerned parties."[29]

The Moroccan regime was jubilant. Ahmed Alaoui, Hassan's brother-in-law, trumpeted in his daily editorial column in *Le Matin du Sahara* on February 20: "No one is duped any longer. Algeria, that's Polisario, and Polisario is nothing other than Algeria." By contrast, Mohammed Abdelaziz could only express regret that the meeting "had not led to a peace agreement between the two warring parties, Morocco and the Polisario Front."[30]

However, Polisario and its African allies were almost immediately to take their revenge. Despite the failure of the June 1981 OAU summit to tackle the issue of the SADR's application for OAU membership, the OAU's secretary-general, Edem Kodjo, had written to the SADR government on August 31, by virtue of Article 28 of the OAU charter, to inform the Saharawis of their state's admission to the OAU, as the organization's fifty-first member, with the support of twenty-six African states. So, just a fortnight after the Moroccan success at the second Implementation Committee meeting, the SADR took its seat as a full-fledged OAU member-state when a session of the Council of Ministers opened in Addis Ababa on February 22. It was a calculated risk. Morocco would obviously try to organize a walkout, but it would probably be limited in scale and duration, Polisario's allies calculated. Eventually, they hoped, Morocco would take stock of its isolation and agree to talk to Polisario.

The Moroccan delegation did storm out of the Addis Ababa conference, and Hassan cabled President Moi, the OAU's chairman, to protest that the SADR's admission was "a juridical holdup and act of banditry."[31] However, to the dismay of the pro-SADR camp, eighteen other states joined the boycott. The conference ended inquorate on February 28 and the OAU was plunged into one of its gravest ever crises. Though the opponents of the SADR's admission were in a minority, there were enough of them to prevent any subsequent OAU conference from attaining the requisite two-thirds quorum (thirty-four states) if the SADR was present. Two OAU-sponsored conferences, on information media and labor affairs, were sabotaged by boycotts in March and April.[32]

On March 23, Boucetta requested Moi to convene an extraordinary OAU summit to get the SADR's admission revoked. However, there was no chance of persuading a two-thirds majority of member states, as the Charter required, to back the request. On April 24, the OAU bureau appealed to all African governments to surmount their differences at the next ordinary summit, to be held on August 5–8. This summit, though, was scheduled to be held in Libya. With the United States' encouragement, the controversy over the SADR's OAU membership was seized upon by the most Western-aligned African states as a pretext to scuttle the summit and so deprive Colonel Qadhafi of his long-cherished opportunity to chair the OAU for the following year. Prior to the summit, the U.S. government circulated a secret document to selected African governments, arguing both that "the admission of the SADR to the OAU would be a grave mistake" and that "Qadhafi's unprincipled behavior would make it impossible for us to work with him as OAU chairman," and urging African delegations to withdraw from the summit "should Libyan behavior prove to be such that responsible Africans would not want to be associated with it."[33]

At the end of July a boycott by twenty states deprived the pre-summit Council of Ministers' meeting of a quorum. The boycotters were in no mood to compromise. They showed no interest in a Nigerian-sponsored plan, accepted by Polisario, by which the SADR would voluntarily stay away from the summit in return for a seat at the Council of Ministers' meeting.[34] On August 3, the states that had supported the SADR's admission to the OAU in February issued a proclamation, known as the Tripoli Declaration, reaffirming their solidarity with the SADR, whose admission had constituted "an important step toward the reestablishment of peace in the Sahara," and appealing to the boycotters to "adopt a constructive attitude in conformity with the OAU's traditions" by coming to the Tripoli summit "in a spirit of African fraternity and solidarity."[35] The plea fell on deaf ears, and the summit collapsed, four short of a quorum.

At an informal meeting in Tripoli, on August 8, the nonboycotters set up a committee of five African presidents (Congo, Libya, Mali, Zambia and Tanzania) to reorganize the summit within three months, in Tripoli, and persuade the boycotters to attend.[36] To expedite their task, the SADR announced on October 29 that, while not renouncing its OAU membership, it would "abstain voluntarily and provisionally" from the reconvened summit.[37] This allowed the OAU secretariat to announce, on November 4, that the summit would finally be held in Tripoli on November 23-26, following a meeting of the Council of Ministers on November 15-21.

Hassan announced on November 6 that Morocco would only attend the summit if Western Sahara was kept off the agenda. In a speech marking the seventh anniversary of the Green March, he warned Morocco's "enemies" that "we are prepared to pursue the war for centuries if that is necessary, because the Sahara is Moroccan and can only be Moroccan."[38] Meanwhile, Egypt, Sudan and Somalia declared that they would boycott any summit held in Libya. Finally, though forty-four states, including Morocco, were represented at the Council of Ministers' opening ceremony, on November 15, a new dispute, over the representation of strife-torn Chad, provided yet another opportunity for Qadhafi's foes to deprive the Libyan leader of his OAU chairmanship. Fourteen states stormed out of the meeting in protest at the majority's refusal to admit a delegation from Ndjamena, where Hissène Habré had seized power in June, despite the presence of the OAU peace-keeping force, from Goukouni Oueddei's Transitional Government of National Unity. With the SADR, Chad, Egypt, Somalia, Sudan and Upper Volta (which had just had a coup) already absent, the walkout once again removed the quorum. The summit could not open as scheduled on November 23 and had to be abandoned two days later. With the OAU in disarray, divided as never before into rival blocs, the refinement and implementation of its Western Saharan peace plan seemed postponed to the Greek Calends.

Once again, the non-boycotters set up a committee, this time consisting of twelve presidents, to try to break the impasse.[39] The SADR, for its part, announced on December 20 that it would henceforth attend all OAU meetings. At a meeting in Nairobi on February 18, 1983, the Committee of Twelve resolved to reorganize the summit for a third time, in Addis Ababa rather than Tripoli, and to appeal to all African member-states to attend "without pre-conditions."[40] The summit was scheduled to open on June 6, 1983, but once again a Moroccan-led protest at the SADR's presence prevented a quorum. With the OAU facing yet another fiasco, the SADR reluctantly agreed on June 8 to stay away from the summit "voluntarily and temporarily", in the interests of "African unity."[41] The summit was saved; and, in recognition of the Saharawis' gesture, African leaders now appealed to Morocco, represented at the summit by Boucetta, to make a matching concession, by dropping its rejection of talks with Polisario, so that progress could finally be made toward implementation of the OAU's 1981 peace plan. On June 11, the summit adopted by consensus a resolution, drafted by Ethiopia, Senegal and Mauritania, which, for the first time, named Morocco and Polisario as the "parties to the conflict" and urged them to begin direct negotiations, "without delay," in order to declare a ceasefire and make arrangements for a referendum within six months. While Boucetta expressed "reservations" about the resolution, Mohammed Abdelaziz claimed a great diplomatic victory.[42]

In the Arab world, meanwhile, most states, besides Algeria and Libya, had given unqualified support to Morocco and Mauritania during the early stages of the war. Saudi Arabia had funded some of Morocco's arms purchases and had helped to shore up Mauritania's enfeebled economy.[43] However, Polisario's military and diplomatic successes gradually encouraged greater prudence on the part of most Arab governments, while King Hassan alienated some Arab rulers by encouraging President Sadat's détente with Israel in 1977–78.

Hassan lauded Sadat for his "courageous initiative" in flying to Jerusalem in November 1977 and said he was "with him body and soul."[44] Such statements angered many in the Arab world, and Hassan's decision a year later, in September 1978, to welcome Sadat to Morocco immediately after the Camp David accords, earned him equally little credit.

Algeria and Polisario did their utmost to discredit Hassan, by drawing parallels between his war against the Saharawis and his support for Sadat's betrayal of the Palestinians. On February 2, 1978, South Yemen became the second Arab state to give formal recognition to the SADR, after a visit to Aden by Mohammed Lamine Ould Ahmed.[45] Then Syria and Libya recognized the Saharawi republic at a summit meeting of the Arab Steadfastness Front in Tripoli on April 12–15, 1980.[46] Even Saudi Arabia showed its displeasure with Morocco's Mideast policy by suspending financial aid at the beginning of 1978. The Saudis stopped bankrolling Mauritania at the same time, bringing the Ould Daddah regime to the brink of bankruptcy. Hassan sent a special envoy to Riyadh in June to plead for a resumption of aid to his beleaguered ally.[47] It was too late; Ould Daddah was overthrown a month later.

Hassan's loss of support in the Arab world was reflected in the UN General Assembly on December 13, 1978, when only Egypt and Mauritania joined Morocco in voting against a resolution in favor of Western Saharan self-determination. Most Arab states, including Saudi Arabia, abstained.[48] Even King Hussein of Jordan was prepared to meet Mohammed Lamine Ould Ahmed, on June 6, 1979, during a visit to Algiers, and the following September the Saharawi premier was able to meet the prime minister of North Yemen and the ruler of the United Arab Emirates in Tripoli.[49]

Anxious to shore up Arab support and restore the flow of Saudi petrodollars, Hassan realigned his Mideast policy after the November 1978 Baghdad summit that coordinated the Arab response to Camp David. The king agreed to join the boycott of Egypt and so recalled his ambassador from Cairo. This cleared the decks for a *rapprochement* with Saudi Arabia, and King Khaled promised to revive Saudi financial aid when he visited Morocco early in 1979.[50]

Sadat, who felt betrayed by Hassan's defection, tried to regain his favor by offering, on September 1, 1979, to send arms to Morocco.[51] The Rabat government expressed "its gratitude, in the name of the whole Moroccan people, to the brotherly people of Egypt for its noble attitude."[52] However, aid from Egypt could only discredit Morocco in Arab eyes, and so Polisario exploited this new propaganda opportunity to the full. On September 24, the SADR's defense minister, Ibrahim Ghali, showed journalists a stack of captured arms that he claimed had been delivered to Morocco by Egypt. He appealed to Arab countries to "aid the Saharawis, since Egypt has chosen to turn its weapons against an oppressed people instead of pointing them at Israel, the enemy of the Arab nation that has now become Cairo's ally."[53]

The conservative Arab regimes, and in particular the monarchies, were worried, however, that Hassan might lose his throne if he was forced out of Western Sahara. Saudi Arabia continued to be Morocco's main source of external financial aid. In 1980, the Saudis reportedly provided no less than $1 billion, $400 million of it to pay for arms purchases; and, on April 9, 1981, the governor of the Saudi Arabian Monetary Authority, Abdelaziz Quraishi, promised that the aid would continue.[54]

Hassan was also able to boost his stature in the Arab world by chairing the Al-Qods (Jerusalem) Committee, set up at an Islamic conference in Fez in May 1979. In this capacity he could meet Pope John Paul on April 2, 1980, and host no less than three Islamic conferences on the status of Jerusalem during 1980.[55] Hassan played an especially prominent role in the Arab diplomatic response to the Israeli invasion of Lebanon in the summer of 1982. In September 1982, he hosted an Arab League summit in Fez which adopted a new blueprint for a comprehensive Middle East settlement.

Nonetheless, Arab states seldom gave overt support to Morocco's Saharan policy. As Polisario gained ground, in world forums as well as on the battlefield, most Arab rulers were wary of taking too rigid a stand against the movement or jeopardizing their relations with Algeria. By and large they abstained from voting on the Western Saharan resolutions debated at the UN, while a minority sided with the Saharawis. Thus, no Arab states, apart from Morocco, voted against the resolution, advocating talks between Morocco and Polisario, which was adopted in the UN General Assembly on November 23, 1982, while Algeria, Libya, Mauritania, Syria and South Yemen voted for it. The rest abstained or were absent from the vote.

Polisario's growing audience in the third world was reflected in both the non-aligned movement and the UN. In 1976–77, Morocco succeeded in dissuading these bodies, like the OAU, from adopting pro-Saharawi resolutions. Indeed, the OAU's oft-postponed plans for an extraordinary summit provided a convenient pretext to avoid substantive debate on the Western Saharan problem. Thus, the fifth nonaligned summit, held in Colombo, Sri Lanka, in August 1976, adopted a resolution that stated briefly: "The conference, having taken cognizance of the OAU resolution calling for an extraordinary summit meeting on the Western Sahara question and the situation resulting from it in the area, expresses its hope that this meeting will lead to a just and lasting solution."[56]

Likewise, Resolution 31/45, adopted by the UN General Assembly on December 1, 1976, took note of "the decision taken by the Assembly of Heads of State and Government of the Organization of African Unity to convene an extraordinary session with a view to finding a just solution to the problem of Western Sahara" and so decided to "postpone consideration of the question of Western Sahara" until the following year.[57] Morocco registered a similar success when the Western Saharan question next came up for debate at the UN, at the end of 1977. Though Morocco had done its utmost to forestall the convening of the OAU's extraordinary summit, it backed a resolution, adopted by the

General Assembly on November 28, which expressed "hope that a just and lasting solution to the problem of Western Sahara will be speedily achieved in accordance with the principles of the Charter of the United Nations at the extraordinary session of the Organization of African Unity" and accordingly postponed consideration of the Western Saharan problem for one more year.[58]

After the coup in Mauritania, in July 1978, however, Morocco could no longer prevent the General Assembly from taking a stand. Two rival resolutions were drafted by supporters and opponents of Morocco's Saharan policy. The Moroccan-backed resolution was modeled on those adopted in 1976 and 1977. It simply took note of the OAU's decisions, at the July 1978 summit in Khartoum, to hold the long-awaited extraordinary summit and set up its *ad hoc* committee, invited the OAU "to take prompt action to find a just and equitable settlement of the question of Western Sahara," and appealed to "all states in the region to refrain from any action that might impede the efforts of the Organization of African Unity to arrive at a just and peaceful solution of the problem."[59] The resolution was adopted by 66 votes to 30, with 40 abstentions, on December 13, 1978.

However, there was a much larger majority, of 90 votes to 10, with 39 abstentions, for a resolution, backed by Algeria and most third-world states, which reaffirmed "the inalienable right of the people of Western Sahara to self-determination and independence" and "the responsibility of the United Nations with regard to the decolonization of Western Sahara."[60]

The Agreement of Algiers and Morocco's annexation of the ex-Mauritanian sector of Western Sahara in August 1979 eroded Morocco's influence still further. The sixth nonaligned summit, held in Havana in September, applauded the Algiers Agreement, "deplored the extension of Morocco's armed occupation to the southern part of Western Sahara previously administered by Mauritania" and expressed hope that the creation of the OAU's *ad hoc* committee would "assure, with the briefest possible delay, the exercise by the people of Western Sahara of their right to self-determination and independence."[61]

The pro-Polisario camp carried the day in the UN General Assembly too. On November 11, 1979, a strongly worded resolution was adopted, by 85 votes to 6, with 41 abstentions, affirming not only "the inalienable right of the people of Western Sahara to self-determination and independence" but also "the legitimacy of their struggle to secure the enjoyment of that right." The resolution hailed the Algiers Agreement as "an important contribution to the process of achieving peace and a definitive, just and lasting settlement of the question of Western Sahara," deplored "the aggravation of the situation resulting from the continued occupation of Western Sahara by Morocco and the extension of that occupation to the territory recently evacuated by Mauritania," urged "Morocco to join in the peace process and to terminate the occupation of the territory of Western Sahara," and, recognizing Polisario (for the first time in a UN resolution) as "the representative of the people of Western Sahara," recommended that it "should participate fully in any search for a just, lasting and definitive political solution of the question of Western Sahara."[62] An almost identical resolution was adopted in the General Assembly a year later, on November 11, 1980, by 88 votes to 8, with 43 abstentions.[63]

After King Hassan's referendum pledge and the establishment of the OAU Implementation Committee at the June 1981 OAU summit in Nairobi, the General Assembly resolutions focused on calls for direct talks between Morocco and Polisario. A new development was that the United States, which had abstained on the resolutions adopted in 1979 and 1980, cast negative votes, alone among the Western powers, on both Resolution 36/46, which was adopted by 76 votes to 9, with 57 abstentions, on November 24, 1981, and Resolution 37/28, which passed by 78 votes to 15, with 50 abstentions, on November 23, 1982.[64]

The 1982 resolution, which was almost identical to that adopted in 1981, reaffirmed "the inalienable right of the people of Western Sahara to self-determination and independence," declared that "only negotiations between Morocco and the Frente Popular para la Liberación de Saguia el-Hamra y de Río de Oro could create the objective conditions for the restoration of peace in northwest Africa and would guarantee the fair conduct of a general, free and orderly referendum on self-determination in Western Sahara" and appealed "to the two parties to the dispute, Morocco and the Frente Popular para la Liberación de Saguia el-Hamra y de Río de Oro, to start negotiations with a view to achieving a cease-fire." Finally, the resolution affirmed "the determination of the United Nations to cooperate fully with the Organization of African Unity in the fair and impartial organization of the referendum."[65]

Overall, Polisario had made impressive progress on the diplomatic front by 1983. Fifty-four governments had recognized the SADR. A majority of African governments had done so, though the SADR had been thwarted, at least temporarily, in its bid to attend OAU conferences. Most important of all, both the OAU and the UN had backed Polisario's calls for direct negotiations with Morocco, with a view to achieving a ceasefire and determining the modalities of an internationally supervised referendum.

NOTES

1. The latter principle was explicitly endorsed by Polisario in its bid to win African governments' support. "To try to reestablish former empires or former states or even to restore the unity of nationalities today overlapping several frontiers would constitute a source of conflicts and innumerable wars between states which have been built up on the ruins of the colonial system and which are the modern reality," a Polisario representative, Mansour Salim, declared before the UN General Assembly's 4th Committee on November 11, 1976. "It was in order to hold back these demons and to ensure above all peace and good relations among African countries that, from its very foundation, the OAU proclaimed the principle of respect for the frontiers of colonialism and elevated it to the status of a dogma."

2. Seventeen states had supported Polisario: Algeria, Angola, Benin, Burundi, Cape Verde, Chad, Comoros, Congo, Ghana, Guinea, Guinea-Bissau, Libya, Madagascar, Nigeria, Saõ Tomé and Príncipe, Somalia and Tanzania. However, in view of the Moroccan and Mauritanian boycott threats, a compromise was drafted, based on the pretext that the Liberation Committee's proposal had been outdated by the proclamation of the SADR on February 27, while the council meeting was in session. Approved unanimously on March 1, this left it up to individual member states to decide whether to recognize the new state. For the text of this "consensus," see Manfred O. Hinz, Le droit à l'autodétermination du Sahara occidental (Progress Dritte Welt Verlag, Bonn, 1978), p. 60.

3. Africa Contemporary Record, 1976–77, p. B151.

4. Gabon and Senegal voted against. Ten states abstained and seven were absent from the vote. For a complete breakdown of the vote, see Hinz, op. cit., p. 63.

5. Résolution relative à la question du Sahara occidental adopté par le 13ème sommet de l'OUA tenu à Port Louis (Ile Maurice), in Hinz, op. cit., p. 62.

6. *Middle East Economic Digest* (London), September 23, 1977.

7. *Le Monde* (Paris), March 4, 1978; *An-Nahar Arab Report and Memo*, March 13, 1978.

8. UN document A/33/337, October 31, 1978. The committee comprised the presidents of Sudan, Tanzania, Mali, Nigeria, Ivory Coast and Guinea.

9. The full text of the committee's resolution was published in *Jeune Afrique* (Paris), No. 970, August 8, 1979, p. 52.

10. Comoros and Upper Volta voted against, seven states abstained and six, including Morocco, did not participate in the vote. (*Le Monde*, July 21, 1979.)

11. *Jeune Afrique*, July 30, 1979; *El Moudjahid* (Algiers), August 21, 1979.

12. *Le Monde*, December 17, 1979.

13. The argument against admission of the SADR was that it did not exercise control over the whole territory of Western Sahara and hence was not "sovereign" and "independent," as required by the OAU Charter. Though the towns were not under the SADR's control, the hinterland was, however, and there was a parallel in the OAU's history for the admission of a state with such partial control over its territory, namely the entry of Guinea-Bissau into the OAU, after its proclamation by the African Party for the Independence of Guinea and Cape Verde (PAIGC) in September 1973, a year before Portugal's withdrawal from Guinea-Bissau's towns and recognition of the country's independence.

14. *Le Monde*, July 6–7, 1980; Edem Kodjo, *Memorandum sur l'admission de la République arabe sahraouie démocratique à l'*OUA (OAU, 1982). p. 4.

15. Report of the Fifth Session of the Ad Hoc Committee of Heads of State on Western Sahara, Freetown, Sierra Leone, 9–11 September 1980, OAU document AHG/103(XVIII)B.

16. *Arms Sales in North Africa and the Conflict in the Western Sahara: An Assessment of U.S. Policy*, Hearing before the Subcommittees on International Security and Scientific Affairs and on Africa of the Committee on Foreign Affairs, House of Representatives, 97th Congress, 1st Session, March 25, 1981 (U.S. Government Printing Office, Washington, D.C., 1981), p. 7.

17. *Le Monde*, June 28–29, 1981.

18. *Le Monde*, March 5, 1980.

19. *Le Monde*, June 26, 1981.

20. *Le Monde*, July 4, 1981; *The Guardian* (London), July 4, 1981.

21. For the full text of the Nairobi summit's resolution, see *Marchés Tropicaux et Méditerranéens* (Paris), July 3, 1981.

22. Decision of the OAU Implementation Committee on Western Sahara, OAU document AHG/IMP.C/WS/DEC.1(1), also in UN document A/36/512, S/14692, September 16, 1981.

23. *Le Monde*, September 10, 1981, and September 16, 1981.

24. The two other defendants, Mohammed Mansour and Mohammed Forkani, received suspended jail sentences, of two and one years respectively. For details of the case, see *Report of an Amnesty International Mission to the Kingdom of Morocco, 10–13 February 1981* (Amnesty International, London, 1982), p. 39.

25. *Le Monde*, January 31–February 1, 1982.

26. *Le Matin du Sahara* (Casablanca), February 9, 1982; *The Guardian*, February 19, 1982; *El Moudjahid*, February 9, 1982.

27. *Le Matin du Sahara*, February 10, 1982.

28. *Financial Times* (London), February 11, 1982. See also Kodjo, *op cit.*, p. 11.

29. *El Moudjahid*, February 11, 1982.

30. *International Herald Tribune* (Paris), February 11, 1982.

31. *Maghreb Arabe Presse* (Rabat), February 23, 1982. In the opinion of Edem Kodjo (*op. cit.*, p. 12), the SADR's admission was "the direct result" of the failure to name the "parties to the conflict" at the preceding Implementation Committee meeting.

32. *The Guardian*, March 17, 1982, April 1, 1982, and April 6, 1982.

33. *Colin Legum's Third World Reports* (London), May 13, 1983. The Reagan administration was obsessed by the "Libyan menace" at this time. On U.S. opposition to the SADR's admission to the OAU, see also "Robert Flaten, Director, North Africa, Department of State, Interviewed by Tony Hodges," *Africa Report* (New York), July–August 1982, p. 21.

34. *West Africa* (London), August 9, 1982.

35. *Le Monde*, August 5, 1982.

36. *Le Monde*, August 10, 1982.

37. AFP, dispatch from Tindouf, October 29, 1982.

38. AFP, dispatch from Rabat, November 7, 1982.

39. The committee consisted of the heads of state of Kenya, Nigeria, Uganda, Tanzania, Congo, Zambia, Ethiopia, Libya, Angola, Mozambique, Lesotho and Mali.

40. *West Africa*, February 28, 1983.

41. *Le Monde*, June 10, 1983.

42. *AFP*, dispatch from Addis Ababa, June 11, 1983.

43. According to *Arabia and the Gulf* (February 21, 1978), Saudi Arabia paid for Morocco's Mirage F-1 jets. *Middle East International* reported in June 1978 that Saudi aid to Mauritania had reached $400 million since the start of the war.

44. In a speech to Arab justice ministers at a conference in Marrakesh on December 14, 1977. See *Discours de S.M. Hassan II, 3 mars 1977—3 mars 1978* (Ministère de l'Information, Rabat, 1978), p. 251. Hassan is widely believed to have facilitated contacts between Egypt and Israel in 1977. A succession of prominent Israelis visited Morocco that year, and there were rumors, denied by the Moroccan government, that Hassan met the Israeli foreign minister, Moshe Dayan, in Tangier on September 16. Sadat visited Morocco on July 4–5, 1977; and over the following weeks on the eve of Sadat's mission to Jerusalem, the Egyptian deputy premier, Hassan Touhami, shuttled between Cairo and Rabat. See *Africa Contemporary Record*, 1977–78, p. B99; *Jeune Afrique*, May 3, 1978; and *New York Times*, December 24, 1977.

45. *Sahara Libre* (Polisario Front, Algiers), February 15, 1978.

46. *Le Monde*, April 20–21, 1980.

47. *Jeune Afrique*, September 20, 1978.

48. *Le Monde*, December 19, 1978.

49. *Le Monde*, June 8, 1979; *El Moudjahid*, September 5, 1979.

50. *Africa Confidential* (London), June 20, 1979.

51. *Le Monde*, September 4, 1979.

52. Statement by Abderrahman Baddou, Moroccan secretary of state for foreign affairs, September 3, 1979 (*Le Monde*, September 5, 1979).

53. *Le Monde*, September 27, 1979.

54. *Financial Times*, April 10, 1981.

55. In March at Marrakesh, in August at Casablanca and in September at Fez.

56. *Africa Contemporary Record*, 1976–77, p. B151.

57. UN General Assembly Resolution 31/45, December 1, 1976.

58. UN General Assembly Resolution 32/22, November 28, 1977.

59. UN General Assembly Resolution 33/31B, December 13, 1978, UN document A/RES/33/31, December 12, 1978.

60. UN General Assembly Resolution 33/31A, December 13, 1978, UN document A/RES/33/31, December 12, 1978. The states voting against were Morocco, Mauritania, Central African Republic, Egypt, Gabon, Grenada, Indonesia, Israel, Nicaragua and Zaire.

61. 6ème conférence des pays non-alignés, Résolution sur le Sahara occidental, in *La République Arabe Sahraouie Démocratique* (Département d'Information, SADR, 1980, p. 101).

62. UN General Assembly Resolution 34/37, November 21, 1979, UN document A/RES/34/37, December 4, 1979. Only Morocco, Gabon, Saudi Arabia, Central African Republic, Equatorial Guinea and Guatemala (with designs on Belize) voted against the resolution.

63. Resolution 35/19, November 11, 1980. The eight states voting against were Morocco, Israel, Guinea, Senegal, Guatemala, Zaire, Equatorial Guinea and Gabon.

64. The states voting against Resolution 36/46 were Morocco, Central African Republic, Chile, El Salvador, Equatorial Guinea, Gabon, Senegal, the United States and Zaire. Those voting against Resolution 37/28 were Morocco, Chad, Chile, El Salvador, Gabon, Gambia, Guatemala, Guinea, Honduras, Liberia, Senegal, Solomon Islands, the United States, Upper Volta and Zaire.

65. UN General Assembly Resolution 37/28, November 23, 1982.

29

Flashpoint of the Maghreb

THE SAHARAN WAR was the principal focus of tension in northwest Africa from 1975. A war of attrition, it sapped the morale of King Hassan's army, exacerbated the strains on Morocco's economy and so undermined the stability of the Alawite kingdom. Yet the king feared the political consequences of admitting failure in the Sahara and ordering a withdrawal. In the opposing camp, the Algerian government—and Colonel Qadhafi too—had strong incentives to keep up the pressure on Hassan. From time to time Hassan would threaten to send his forces across the Algerian border, as well as into Mauritania. On June 6, 1979, after a Polisario attack on Assa, he even said that he had given his army "written instructions, bearing our signature, to employ the right of pursuit." Such pronouncements were little more than rhetorical outbursts, however. Hassan could not raid at will into Algeria, like the South Africans into Angola or the Israelis into Lebanon. Algeria was a powerful country. With oil and gas to finance development, its economy was incomparably stronger than Morocco's. By the early eighties its gross domestic product was more than two and a half times larger, despite a marginally smaller population. Algeria had a much stronger air force, equipped with MiG-23 aircraft, and a modern well-trained army of equivalent size to Morocco's. Algeria would have responded in kind to any Moroccan attack, sparking off an all-out war between the two countries. It could not have been confined to the desert south, for even if it had begun with a Moroccan strike against the Saharawi camps near Tindouf, the Algerians would almost certainly have retaliated, as they had done in 1963, by attacking Moroccan targets far to the north. With a large part of his army and most of his air force already committed to the war against Polisario, Hassan was poorly placed to fight on a second front against Algeria. The economic repercussions of such a generalized war would have been severe, and politically the price of failure, whether a defeat at Algerian hands or a costly stalemate, could have been the king's public disgrace, perhaps even his downfall. Moreover, key Western allies such as the U.S. and

France, which had no interest of any kind in an outbreak of direct hostilities between Morocco and Algeria, would have tried to restrain Hassan from attacking Algeria if he seemed close to taking such a dangerous gamble. Still, there was always a risk that the desert conflict might escalate into an all-out war between the two largest countries of northwest Africa. The fear of such an eventuality obliged them to drain resources into a regional arms race. Meanwhile, economic relations between Morocco and Algeria were almost entirely frozen from 1975.

Even the Nouakchott government, which had hoped to extricate itself once and for all from the Saharan conflict by abandoning its claim to Tiris el-Gharbia in August 1979, found that the war still cast a long and threatening shadow. Hassan regarded the Agreement of Algiers as a betrayal and seemed to bear a personal grudge against Lieutenant-Colonel Mohammed Khouna Ould Heydalla. He was suspicious of the CMSN's intentions, despite its protestations of neutrality, and on August 14, just a fortnight after the Algiers Agreement, he threatened to raid across the Mauritanian border if Polisario guerrillas were given sanctuary there. Appalled, the Mauritanian government accused Hassan of "flagrant meddling in our internal affairs" and harboring a "manifest desire to destabilize our country."[1]

Anxious not to get sucked back into the war it had just left, the CMSN had to maintain a bloated and expensive army, to the inevitable detriment of its efforts to rebuild Mauritania's battered economy.[2] To placate Morocco, it denied that there were any Polisario forces on its territory, claimed strict neutrality and so, despite its sympathy for the Saharawi cause (evident from Mauritania's votes in the UN and the OAU), withheld recognition from the SADR.

However, Moroccan accusations against the CMSN became frequent in 1980–81, when the guerrillas made a series of attacks on the exposed Moroccan base at Guelta Zemmour, twenty miles west of the Mauritanian border. After an attack there on June 21, 1980, the Moroccan premier, Maati Bouabid, alleged that Polisario could not have moved forces within range of the base without Mauritanian cooperation.[3] A month later, on July 29, the Moroccan air force bombed Boulanour, three miles inside Mauritanian territory, on the Zouerate-Nouadhibou railway.

Meanwhile, Morocco gave asylum to Mauritanian oppositionists—among them Lieutenant-Colonel Mohammed Ould Bah Ould Abdelkader, the former chief of the Mauritanian air force and member of the CMSN, who had fled to Morocco in June 1979, set up a "free officers' movement" and denounced the Agreement of Algiers.[4] In May 1980 he founded a new anti-CMSN movement, the Alliance pour une Mauritanie Démocratique (AMD), with another exiled officer, Lieutenant-Colonel Ahmed Salem Ould Sidi, a former second vice-president of the CMSN and the man who had signed the peace treaty with Polisario in 1979.[5] A year later, on March 16, 1981, they entered Mauritania from Senegal with a group of armed followers and drove overland to Nouakchott with the intention of deposing the CMSN. The putschists were captured and, on March 26, Mohammed Ould Bah Ould Abdelkader and Ahmed Salem Ould Sidi were executed, with two of their associates. The CMSN was convinced that Morocco had masterminded the plot, and in a speech to the Mauritanian nation on March 18, Ould Heydalla claimed that the rebels had been trained at a Moroccan base at

Benguerir, traveled under false Moroccan passports to Dakar and then collected weapons delivered there by Royal Air Maroc before slipping across the Senegal River into Mauritania.[6] The CMSN broke off diplomatic relations with Morocco.

Only days later, on March 24, Polisario staged another attack on Guelta Zemmour. Once again, Maati Bouabid charged that the guerrillas had made their way to the base across northern Mauritania—"via the locality of Bir Moghrein." The Mauritanian foreign minister, Mohammed Ould Zamel, was adamant that "Mauritanian territory has never served as a place of transit for the troops of the Polisario Front." But Bouabid served notice that "Morocco, which intends to exercise its natural right of legitimate defense, will not remain inactive."[7]

The Moroccan government's accusations against the CMSN sometimes reached fantastic proportions. During 1980–81, it put around the idea that Libyan arms supplies for Polisario were being flown to a secret landing strip at Chegga in the extreme northeast of Mauritania. The CMSN dismissed such stories as pure fantasy and suggested that, if this aerial "Piste Qadhafi" really had existed, the Moroccans would have bombed Chegga, or at least photographed it to buttress their claims.[8]

It seemed briefly, after King Hassan's referendum pledge at the OAU summit in June 1981, that Morocco and Mauritania might end their feud. At the invitation of King Khaled of Saudi Arabia, Hassan and Ould Heydalla met in Taef and signed an agreement to "prohibit any force hostile to one or other party from transiting through or stationing itself in their respective territories."[9] Diplomatic relations were restored.

However, the Taef agreement failed to ease the tension. The AMD was not expelled from Morocco. Flights between Morocco and Mauritania remained suspended. And when Polisario launched its final assault on Guelta Zemmour on October 13, Hassan immediately revived the accusations that the CMSN had been conniving in the Saharawi guerrillas' activities.[10] On October 19 he sent a message of protest to Ould Heydalla, alleging that the guerrillas had retreated from Guelta Zemmour into Mauritania, to the locality of Bir Aidiat; and a day later General Dlimi announced that Moroccan aircraft had bombed the guerrilla forces there.[11]

In a message to the UN on October 21, Ould Heydalla formally denied that Polisario had attacked Guelta Zemmour from Mauritanian territory or withdrawn there after the battle. However, on the same day, Boucetta leveled even graver accusations against the CMSN. Mauritanian troops, he claimed, had actually participated in the fighting at Guelta Zemmour, and both Colonel Moulay Ould Boukhreiss, the deputy chief-of-staff of the Mauritanian armed forces, and Sid'Ahmed Ould Bneijara, the Mauritanian president's ministerial adviser, had been in the region "to direct operations."[12] Though the Mauritanian army might not have been able to detect Polisario units crossing the vast and remote desert regions between Algeria and the Zemmour massif, the idea that the CMSN was actively aiding the guerrillas received little credence outside Morocco. Ould Heydalla, who wanted peace on his northern borders while the CMSN wrestled with its plethora of economic and political challenges at home, accused Morocco, on November 28, of trying to "pull us back into a war which isn't ours."[13]

As the war dragged on, the Moroccan government also held Libya responsible for its tribulations. In fact Qadhafi's Western Saharan policy has been ambiguous or inconsistent. As a radical Arab nationalist, the Libyan leader had warmed to El-Ouali Mustapha Sayed when he arrived in Tripoli in 1972 seeking aid for his planned guerrilla war against Spain. He had been the first Arab leader to offer El-Ouali material assistance in those pioneer days, before Polisario's formal founding. Moreover, as a bitter foe of the Moroccan monarch, he had every reason to wish to thwart Morocco's Saharan designs. He had established a very close alliance with Boumedienne after the Madrid accords, at a summit meeting in the Algerian oil town of Hassi Messaoud on December 28–29, 1975, and he had then begun to funnel substantial military and financial aid to the Saharawi guerrilla forces. His alliance with Algeria had been reinforced, moreover, by his profound fear of Egypt's President Sadat, with whom his relations had progressively deteriorated since 1974. At Hassi Messaoud, Qadhafi and Boumedienne pledged mutual assistance in the event of an attack against either of their countries, and so, when Egyptian forces bombed Libyan airfields and occupied a Libyan oasis during a brief border war in July 1977, it was to Boumedienne that Qadhafi turned to put pressure on the Egyptians to withdraw.[14] Additionally, the Algerian and Libyan leaders had a common interest in resisting Giscard d'Estaing's interventionist African policy in 1977–78, which inflicted setbacks on the Libyan-backed Frolinat forces in Chad as well as the Polisario guerrillas. So they jointly expressed their "total condemnation of neocolonialism's military intervention in Western Sahara, in the Shaba region and in Chad" and confirmed their mutual solidarity when Qadhafi made another of his frequent visits to Algiers in May–June 1978.[15]

Yet Qadhafi did not see completely eye-to-eye with the Algerian leadership and Polisario. His Arab unionism, his dream of abolishing the frontiers dividing the Arab world, made him wary of embracing the Saharawi nationalists' goal of creating their own independent state. On February 27, 1976, the very day of the SADR's founding, he informed King Hassan, in a personal message, that he had "tried to convince the leaders of Polisario to join you after independence." But Libya, he added, could not support Morocco's attempt to impose unity on the Saharawis by force of arms. "The populations of the Sahara, with Polisario at their head, have proclaimed before the world that they are neither Moroccans nor Algerians nor Mauritanians. . . ,. The integration of the Sahara into Morocco has now plainly become an operation of annexation by force. . . . You are fighting a people that refuses to submit and we cannot support you."[16] He refrained, however, from recognizing the SADR, though he reassured Polisario and Algeria on March 9 that "Libya's recognition of the Saharan Arab Democratic Republic is only a formal question, given that the Libyan Arab Republic was one of the first countries to support the Saharawi people's struggle."[17]

In truth, Qadhafi still hoped that Mokhtar Ould Daddah could be persuaded to desert the Moroccan camp, paving the way for a Saharawi-Mauritanian federation along the lines suggested by El-Ouali himself in 1975. To this end, Qadhafi invited Ould Daddah to Tripoli in April 1978, and, when he arrived, offered him Libyan financial aid, to lessen Mauritania's dependence on France, Morocco and the conservative gulf oil states. Qadhafi's initiative was not well received in Algiers, where the government newspaper *Al-Chaab* complained that "all aid to

Nouakchott can be considered in the current situation as an indirect recognition of the *fait accompli* in the Western Sahara.''[18] After Ould Daddah's downfall the following July, the Libyan regime continued to encourage a Mauritanian-Saharawi rapprochement, by sending the CMRN a budgetary support grant of $10 million and sponsoring a series of meetings in Tripoli between Polisario and Mauritanian envoys.

It was not until April 1980, four years after the SADR's founding, that Qadhafi finally recognized the Saharawi republic, and even thereafter he continued to hope that the SADR would eventually fuse with Mauritania. ''We agree in principle on a union between Mauritania and the Polisario Front when objective conditions permit,'' he said during a visit to Nouakchott on April 19–21, 1981.[19]

At times, however, constraining tactical considerations could send Qadhafi in quite opposite directions. Within weeks of his ''unionist'' declaration in Nouakchott, which was welcomed neither by Polisario nor by the CMSN, he engineered a quite unexpected, though short-lived *rapprochement* with Morocco, restoring the diplomatic relations that had been severed by Hassan after Libya's recognition of the SADR. This sudden *volte-face* was heralded by the arrival in Rabat of the commander of the military region of Sebha, in western Libya, Mansur Abdelhafid, in the company of officials of the Palestine Liberation Organization, on June 17, as Hassan was preparing to leave for Nairobi to make his referendum pledge to the OAU. On June 19, at the OAU's pre-summit foreign ministers' conference, the Libyan foreign minister, Abdellatif al-Obeidi, announced that Libya was ''ready to play a positive role in the search for a solution to the problem of Western Sahara'' and ''was about to begin dialogue with Morocco and the Polisario Front.''[20]

Securing the OAU chairmanship for 1982–83, which Hassan approved, along with all the other heads of state at the Nairobi summit, was undoubtedly one of Qadhafi's principal motives for striking a deal with Hassan and, later in the year, announcing a Libyan withdrawal from Chad. But there were other factors. Qadhafi was becoming increasingly alarmed by the bellicose noises from Washington, Cairo and Khartoum at this time. President Reagan had just promised military aid for any country threatened by Qadhafi's ''adventurism,'' closed down the Libyan People's Bureau in Washington and warned U.S. citizens not to travel to Libya. Sensing real danger, the Libyan leader decided to make amends with several of his former enemies, including Saudi Arabia and Iraq as well as Morocco.[21]

Polisario was taken aback by the apparent shift in Libyan policy. Mohammed Abdelaziz flew to Tripoli within a week of the Nairobi summit to seek clarification of Qadhafi's intentions, and in August, Ibrahim Ghali, the mastermind of Polisario's guerrilla strategy, followed him to the Libyan capital. They left reassured, for Qadhafi's new friendship with Hassan was skin-deep.[22] Libya continued supplying arms to the guerrillas, and after the big Polisario attack on Guelta Zemmour the following October, Hassan once again vented his rage on the Libyans. Ever-fearful of Washington, Qadhafi was, in turn, angered by Hassan's decision in February 1982 to grant transit facilities at Moroccan air bases for Reagan's Rapid Deployment Force. ''The Arab homeland is being sold to

America by auction."[23] Then came the Moroccan-inspired boycott of the OAU's Tripoli summit, in August, and (partly in retaliation, but also to mark his displeasure at the Arab regimes' inaction during the Israeli invasion of Lebanon) Qadhafi's boycott of the Arab League summit hosted by Hassan in Fez the following September. Never, perhaps, had Qadhafi felt so bitter toward Hassan, or had a more compelling incentive to arm the Saharawi guerrillas with the heavy weaponry they needed to pierce the elaborate and sophisticated defenses of Hassan's Saharan "wall."

However, though Libya's financial and military aid was of great value to Polisario, it was upon Algeria that the guerrillas had their greatest external dependence. Libya was far away from the war zones of Western Sahara and southern Morocco. Libyan arms supplies had to transit Algerian territory, with Algerian approval. It was in the Tindouf region of southwestern Algeria, moreover, that Polisario had its rear bases and training camps. Just as important, the Algerian government was sheltering and feeding the guerrillas' families, in the Tindouf refugee camps. Finally, Algeria's persistent diplomacy on the Saharawis' behalf, and its considerable prestige in the third world, had played a major role in winning recognition for the SADR and advancing Polisario's cause in the OAU and the UN.

From the very start of the war, King Hassan hoped that Algeria would tire of backing the guerrillas and stitch together a bilateral, face-saving settlement with Morocco at their expense. In return, Hassan offered such "carrots" as ratification of the 1972 Moroccan-Algerian border convention, a halt to the regional arms race and cooperation in exploiting Saharan minerals, such as the Gara Djebilet iron and the phosphates at Bou-Craa. However, to Hassan's dismay, the Algerian government persisted in its resolve to see Morocco driven out of Western Sahara. It continued arming the guerrillas, generously and consistently, and rejected any settlement that fell short of genuine self-determination.

In the early stages of the war, a succession of would-be mediators, among them Vice-President Husni Mubarak of Egypt, Prince Fahd Ibn Abdelaziz of Saudi Arabia and President Senghor of Senegal, tried, but failed, to persuade the Algerian government to settle for less.[24] In December 1977, Hassan made a direct approach to the Algerians. He sent his sister, Princess Aicha, to Lausanne, in Switzerland, to meet President Boumedienne's ministerial adviser, Ahmed Taleb Ibrahimi. Her mission was to convey the king's desire to meet Boumedienne in person. Seven secret meetings between Ibrahimi and one of Hassan's royal councillors, Ahmed Reda Guedira, followed during the first six months of 1978, and a tentative agreement was reached to hold a summit meeting in Belgium.[25]

However, Boumedienne called the plan off. It is doubtful that he would have reached an agreement with Hassan, had the meeting been held. Hassan's hopes of striking a deal with the Algerian president at Polisario's expense were shattered by the coup in Nouakchott on July 10, which dramatically shifted the relationship of forces in the Saharan conflict, militarily and diplomatically, to Polisario's advantage. Then, a few weeks later, in September, Boumedienne was infuriated by Hassan's decision to receive Sadat in Morocco, on his return home to Egypt after signing the Camp David accords with Menachem Begin. "I would have wished to renew mutual contact directly," he wrote to the king on October 5. "A direct dialogue would certainly have been preferable. But how can that be possible after the respective positions we have recently taken on the Palestinian affair and its impact on the Middle East and the Arab nation?"[26] Later the same month, moreover, Boumedienne fell seriously ill, with Waldenstroem's Disease, and flew to Moscow for treatment. Returning to Algiers in mid-November, he was admitted to hospital on November 17 and fell into a deep coma. He died six weeks later, on December 27.

Unable to meet Boumedienne, Hassan did his utmost, after the coup in Nouakchott, to avert a unilateral Mauritanian withdrawal from Tiris el-Gharbia. To this end, he even offered the Polisario leaders cabinet posts in Morocco, if they would give up their fight for independence. "Let them come and they will be ministers, they will be welcome," he declared in September.[27] Alternatively, he suggested on October 2, they should enter Mauritanian politics, "now that the regime has changed," since they were "Mauritanians who took up arms in opposition to the last head of state, Mokhtar Ould Daddah."[28] For the first time in the course of the war, Hassan sent envoys to meet Polisario leaders, to put these curious proposals directly to them. Ahmed Reda Guedira, Colonel-Major Dlimi and Ahmed Bensouda met Mahmoud Abdelfettah, a member of the front's political bureau, in Bamako, Mali, on October 20–21, but Polisario was dismissive of the king's suggestions. It would accept nothing short of self-determination and independence.

The king remained inflexible on the decisive issue of Western Sahara's future. Less than three weeks after the Bamako meeting, on November 6, he instructed his subjects, during a TV speech, to take a copy of the Koran and "swear by Almighty God to remain faithful to the spirit of the Green March."[29] Upon hearing that Boumedienne might be fatally ill, he placed all his hopes on a reversal of Algeria's Saharan policy by his successors. While the Algerian president was still in Moscow, he tactlessly speculated in a French radio interview that Algeria's leaders would be preoccupied with domestic matters during the delicate transition period after his death and so "the Saharan problem should see its logical end and solution."[30] As if to remind the Algerian leadership, while Boumedienne lay in his coma, of the trouble he could cause if Algiers remained loyal to Polisario, he arranged for a Moroccan Hercules transport plane to drop a consignment of arms to a small group of Algerian conspirators near Cape Sigli, on the Kabyle coast, on December 10. Though disgruntled by the discrimination against their language, the Berbers of Kabylia were in no frame of mind to support an armed revolt, and so local peasants immediately reported the arms drop to the Gendarmerie and all the "Cape Sigli plotters" were arrested.[31] However, the Cape Sigli affair hardened attitudes to Morocco in Algiers. When Boumedienne died just over a fortnight later, Hassan was not even invited to the funeral. The most prominent Moroccan to attend was the exiled leftist, Mohammed Basri.

The sensitive post-Boumedienne transition period was not propitious for radical shifts in foreign policy. "Continuity," or faithfulness to Boumedienne's legacy, were the Council of the Revolution's watchwords, as it made preparations for a congress of the FLN, the first since 1964, to find a successor. On January 26, the eve of its opening, a bomb, allegedly planted by a Moroccan agent, exploded in the western Algerian town of Maghnia, injuring seventeen people, and a suitcase of explosives was discovered in a bus station in nearby Oran. Two days later a Moroccan was arrested in Maghnia while carrying a bomb.[32] The congress, meanwhile, selected Colonel Chadli Bendjedid, a member of the Council of the Revolution since 1965, as the sole candidate in presidential elections slated for February 7. Meeting just a fortnight after Polisario's sensational attack on Tan-Tan, the congress vowed to remain true to Boumedienne's Saharan policy. A resolution proclaimed the FLN's "indefatigable solidarity with the people of Western Sahara, their vanguard, the Polisario Front, and their combatants," and pledged that the Algerian people would support the Saharawis "until they exercised their right to self-determination" and achieved "national sovereignty and independence."[33]

Hassan, who had hoped that his stalled summit would finally materialize after Boumedienne's death, was stunned by the hardened mood in Algiers. Still, he did not give up hope of meeting the new Algerian president. He persuaded President Gisard d'Estaing, during a trip to Paris in mid-February, to pass on his request for a summit to the Algerian leadership.[34] Nothing, however, came of such demarches. Abdelaziz Bouteflika, the Algerian foreign minister, informed his Moroccan counterpart, Boucetta, on February 15 that "statements by the highest authorities in Morocco, all of whom go to great pains to deny the existence of the problem of Western Sahara, of the Western Saharan people itself and its national rights, and of the Polisario Front—recognized by the international community as that people's sole legitimate representative, and without whose participation no just and durable peace seems possible—clearly show that the decision of President Houari Boumedienne to postpone the planned meeting was indisputably sound." There was no point arranging it until Morocco showed "a real desire to attack the causes of the crisis without making futile efforts to deal with its effects."[35]

When Habib Bourguiba, the president of Tunisia, offered, six months later, on August 22, to host a Chadli-Hassan summit meeting in Tunis, the idea was once again brushed off by Chadli. "Do not ask Algeria to play the same role with regard to the Saharawi people, driven from their homes and persecuted, as the role played by the Egyptian regime with respect to the Palestinian people," advised the government news agency, APS, on September 12. Hassan's decision to push Morocco's frontiers even farther to the south, by annexing Tiris el-Gharbia in August, had only served to confirm the Algerian government's belief that nothing would come of a summit if it was held.

From time to time there were exploratory "talks about talks." Ahmed Reda Guedira, for example, met Ahmed Taleb Ibrahimi in Geneva in January 1980, but, since he had nothing really new to offer the Algerians, he failed once again to convince them of the value of a summit.[36] That Morocco had not changed its tune was made abundantly clear by Maati Bouabid a few weeks later, on June 5. "There will not be a solution which stipulates that we give up the slightest portion of our territory," he warned. Morocco would never talk to Polisario because "the problem basically pits Morocco against Algeria, but against no one else."[37]

The Algerian government sensed a glimmer of hope when Morocco, after the September 1980 meeting of the OAU's "wise men" in Freetown, hinted at last that it would accept their proposals for a cease-fire and a referendum. Guedira and Ibrahimi met again, in secret, in Geneva in October and November. Meanwhile, to help defrost relations, Hassan rushed relief supplies to Algeria after a severe earthquake, at El-Asnam, on October 10. Guedira, however, left the impression that Hassan's acceptance of a referendum was cosmetic. The king, he said, was still firmly opposed to Western Sahara's independence and would not permit talks with Polisario, even if they were held indirectly, through Algerian intermediaries.[38] Once again, Chadli saw no point in meeting the king, and to quash rumors given currency by the Geneva meetings that Algeria might ditch the guerrillas, the FLN published a joint communiqué with Polisario on February 11, 1981, reaffirming "the Algerian Revolution's total and unconditional commitment to the national liberation struggle that the Saharawi people are waging under the leadership of their sole legitimate representatives, the Polisario Front."[39] The FLN's political bureau had no hesitation, a month later, in pinning the blame for the March 16 coup attempt in Mauritania on the Moroccan government, and the Algerian authorities became increasingly angered by the new Reagan administration's stepped-up arms supplies to Rabat.

If Hassan hoped that by pledging his support for a referendum at the OAU summit in Nairobi in June 1981 he would be giving Chadli a pretext, or cover, for a reasonably graceful exit from his Saharan commitment, so allowing some kind of back-stage deal under which Algeria would force Polisario to put up with a referendum held under conditions stacked in Morocco's favor, he must have been shaken by Chadli's unbending insistence on meeting the elementary conditions for a free and genuine referendum and by his continuing refusal to negotiate with Morocco in the guerrillas' stead. Chadli arrived at the first session of the OAU Implementation Committee in Nairobi, in August, with a ninety-one-page memorandum, describing Hassan's referendum pledge as no more than "a glimmer of hope, as yet a tenuous one," and listing the conditions that would have to be met for the committee to carry out its mandate to "guarantee the exercise of a general and regular referendum of self-determination."[40] These conditions included universal adult suffrage, the return of all refugees to Western Sahara, the holding of the referendum throughout the territory (and not just in parts of it, such as the "useful triangle," or among refugee communities outside the territory), the Moroccan authorities' exclusion from the conduct of the referendum, Polisario's right to enter the territory freely to campaign before the poll, the establishment of an international, interim administration headed by a senior UN official, the stationing of a UN peace-keeping force, and the "substantial withdrawal of Moroccan troops, together with a negotiated confinement to barracks of the remainder of the Moroccan forces."[41] In view of the traditionally nomadic ways of the *qabael* of Western Sahara and their trans-frontier sedentarization since the sixties, the Algerian government admitted that the identification of eligible voters "will not be without difficulties," but, like Spain in 1974–75, it favored using the criterion of affiliation to the territory's tribal fractions or subfractions to determine nationality and eligibility to vote. A voter registration committee, with observers from Polisario, Morocco, Algeria and Mauritania, could be set up by the interim administration and call on the territory's *sheikhs* for expert advice "inasmuch as they represent the memory of the Saharan population."[42]

When Hassan failed to give real substance to his referendum pledge, by refusing to negotiate with Polisario, the Algerian government concurred with the guerrillas' decision to tighten military pressure on Morocco by staging the assault on Guelta Zemmour in October. On January 29, 1982, Hassan acknowledged, at a Paris press conference, that a *rapprochement* with Algeria remained a "pious wish."[43] Indeed, the Algerian government was instrumental in assuring the SADR's admission to the OAU at its Council of Ministers' conference in Addis Ababa the following month.

Within Algeria, public support for the government's Saharan policy was seldom more than lukewarm. The French air force's bombing raids in Mauritania in 1977–78 aroused some passion, because they reminded Algerians of their own liberation struggle against France and the raids coincided with a wave of racist attacks on Algerian immigrants in France. There were large anti-French demonstrations in Algiers in November 1977. However, for the most part, the Saharan war seemed distant, almost irrelevant, to the average Algerian, even if he did acknowledge the Saharawis' right to independence in principle. To many, the government's support for Polisario, and the related buildup of Algeria's own military capability, seemed an extravagant diversion of resources from domestic priorities. Some, regardless of the Saharawis' plight, also regretted that the war, and their own government's support for Polisario, barred closer cooperation between the countries of the Maghreb.[44]

However, to the Algerian leadership, in which the military had retained preponderant influence since 1965, capitulation to Morocco seemed both weak-kneed and a threat to national security.[45] It risked emboldening King Hassan to revive other territorial claims, to parts of the Algerian Sahara, when domestic difficulties required deflecting by a diversionary external "cause."[46] Formal ratification of the Algerian-Moroccan border convention, which Hassan had withheld since its signing in 1972 but frequently offered to trade in return for Algerian acceptance of his sovereignty in Western Sahara, was not enough. The king would be taught an indelible lesson that attempts to annex territory by force, in the name of Greater Morocco, would not pay. Besides, Polisario's struggle for nationhood was analogous to the FLN's own independence war. Supporting the Saharawi nationalists buttressed the regime's claim to revolutionary legitimacy, while abroad it was entirely consistent with Algeria's long established role as a champion of third-world emancipation.

If Polisario had failed to sustain its guerrilla war, the Algerian government would ultimately have revised its Saharan policy. However, Polisario became arguably the most effective guerrilla movement in Africa. In military terms, it achieved far more than SWAPO in Namibia, or even Frelimo in Portuguese-ruled Mozambique. In 1979 it finally forced Mauritania to abandon its territorial claims and sue for peace. By 1982 it had driven the FAR into two small enclaves near the coast covering no more than a sixth of the territory's land area. The SADR had won recognition from more than fifty states and won important diplomatic victories in the UN and the OAU. It would have been senseless for Algeria to back away from Polisario after such success—and diplomatically embarrassing in view of Polisario's wide-ranging support in the third world. Despite increased assistance from the U.S., Hassan faced such an array of military, diplomatic and economic pressures that Algeria had every reason to help Polisario keep up its war of attrition in the hope that Hassan's will to keep fighting would finally snap.

Early in 1983, Chadli tried to break the logjam in the Sahara by offering King Hassan his services as a mediator with Polisario. To this end, he finally accepted the king's oft frustrated request for a summit. The idea of a tête-à-tête probably resurfaced during Hassan's conversations with Ahmed Taleb Ibrahimi, then Algeria's foreign minister, at the Arab League summit in Fez in September 1982 or while they traveled together to Washington the following October, with representatives of five other Arab nations, to brief President Reagan on the Fez summit's Middle East peace proposals. However, the idea of a summit seems to have been agreed on both sides when King of Fahd of Saudi Arabia paid visits to Morocco and Algeria in November. There were rumors that Chadli would meet Hassan in Ryadh.[47]

However, after further consultations, between Chadli and Ahmed Bensouda, who visited Algiers to attend a session of the exiled Palestinian parliament, the Palestine National Council, on February 14–22, the two leaders finally met in a village on their common border, near Oujda, on February 26.

The summit of Akid Lotfi was a milestone in the history of Moroccan-Algerian relations. It was the first time since the start of the Saharan war that the two countries' leaders sat down to talk to each other. The five hours of conversations were held in private, and no detailed account of what transpired was published. However, subsequent events indicated the tenor of the encounter. First, there was a gradual lifting of the measures that had barred almost all travel between Morocco and Algeria since 1975. On April 7, during a visit to Algiers, the Moroccan interior minister, Driss Basri, signed an agreement permitting the 20,000 Algerians living in Morocco and the 200,000 Moroccans resident in Algeria to cross the border for the first time in seven and a half years.[48] Then, on May 27, during a reciprocal visit to Morocco by the Algerian interior minister, M'hammed Yala, agreement was reached on the general reopening of the border and the resumption of suspended air and rail links.[49] There was inevitably speculation, perhaps somewhat premature, that formal diplomatic relations would be reestablished.

Meanwhile, on March 19, Chadli signed a twenty-year "treaty of friendship and concord with Tunisia," which, by its sixth article, was "open to other states of the Maghreb which accept its provisions." This amounted to an invitation, not least to Morocco, to join a regional security pact, for the treaty's sixth article required signatories "not to tolerate activity by any group which challenges the security or integrity of the other party or attempts to change its regime by violence.[50]

In this new climate of detente, reminiscent of the early stages of the Algerian-Moroccan rapprochement at the end of the sixties, Chadli hoped that Hassan would finally swallow his pride and summon up the courage to run the domestic

political risks of coming to terms with the Saharawis. To this end, Chadli offered
the king his services as an intermediary. "The problem of Western Sahara, which
is a problem of decolonization, opposes our brothers in Western Sahara and our
brothers in Morocco," declared a communique released by the Algerian foreign
ministry the day after the summit of Akid Lotfi. "Algeria has always emphasized
its complete readiness to work to bring our Western Saharan brothers and Moroccan brothers closer together in order to find a solution conforming to the Western
Saharan people's inalienable right to self-determination and independence.
Algeria is convinced that, while reestablishing peace in our region, such a solution
will open the way to cooperation in keeping with the ideal of constructing the
Maghreb. It is in this spirit that President Chadli Bendjedid, President of the
Republic and Secretary-General of the FLN, met King Hassan II on Saturday
February 26, 1983, on the Algerian-Moroccan border."[51]

Addressing the subsequent OAU summit in Addis Ababa, on June 11, Chadli
himself explained the purpose of his meeting with Hassan at Akid Lotfi. "I was
very clear about Algeria's position on the question of Western Sahara," he said.
"I explained to the Moroccan king that I had no mandate to speak in the name of
the Saharawis and that I would not arrogate to myself the right to speak in their
name or to assume their trusteeship." However, Chadli said he would "spare no
effort" to reconcile Morocco and the Saharawis, in the same way as he had helped
to bring together "the brothers in Mauritania and Western Sahara" in 1979.[52]
His bid to do so was given added weight by the Addis Ababa summit's decision to
place the OAU on record, for the first time, in support of direct negotiations between Morocco and Polisario on implementation of the OAU's long-stalled plan
for a ceasefire and a referendum.

NOTES

1. *El Moudjahid* (Algiers), August 21, 1979.
2. Public external debt (disbursed only) had risen to a record $714 million (equivalent to 140 per-
cent of GNP), by the end of 1980, while the debt service ratio reached 33 percent in 1980. (World
Bank, *World Development Report 1982*, pp. 134, 138.) The government felt unable to demobilize
any of its 15,000 troops.
3. *Le Monde* (Paris), June 26, 1980.
4. Another such oppositionist to receive Moroccan patronage was Fadiga Moussa, the secretary-
general of a black secessionist grouplet known as the Front Fédéral du Sud Mauritanien, set up in 1979.
5. Ahmed Salem Ould Sidi had been dismissed from the CMSN on January 4, when Lieutenant-
Colonel Mohammed Khouna Ould Heydalla had consolidated his hold on power by assuming the
presidency from Mohammed Mahmoud Ould Louly. The posts of first and second vice-presidents were
abolished under a new constitutional charter, published on January 9.
6. *Le Monde*, March 20, 1981.
7. *Le Monde*, March 27, 1981.
8. *Le Monde*, March 18, 1981.
9. *El País* (Madrid), July 1, 1981.
10. *Le Monde*, October 15, 1981.
11. *Le Monde*, October 21, 1981; *The Guardian* (London), October 21, 1981.
12. *Le Monde*, October 23, 1981.
13. *El Moudjahid*, October 23, 1981, and December 2, 1981.
14. *Africa Contemporary Record, 1977-78*, pp. B73–74.
15. *Le Monde*, June 8, 1978.
16. Letter from Colonel Qadhafi to King Hassan II, February 27, 1976, published in *Jeune Afrique*
(Paris), April 9, 1976.

17. *Algérie Presse Service* (Algiers), March 9, 1976.

18. *Africa Confidential*, May 12, 1978.

19. *Africa Research Bulletin* (Exeter), Political Series, Vol. 18, No. 4, May 15, 1981.

20. *Le Monde*, June 21–22, 1981.

21. *Le Monde*, July 1, 1981.

22. *Le Monde*, August 15, 1981; *El País*, August 30, 1981.

23. Radio Tripoli, February 13, 1982.

24. Mubarak failed in an attempt to bring Hassan and Boumedienne together, with Sadat, at a summit meeting in Cairo after the clash between Moroccan and Algerian troops at Amgala in January 1976. Meanwhile, between January and March 1976, Senghor and his foreign minister, Assane Seck, tried vainly, at Hassan's behest, to persuade Algeria to dump Polisario in return for joint exploitation of Saharan mineral resources. The following November, Prince Fahd made no greater progress when he shuttled between Morocco, Mauritania and Algeria, proposing, *inter alia*, limited autonomy for the Moroccan and Mauritanian provinces in Western Sahara and implementation of the 1972 agreements on the Algerian-Moroccan border and Gara Djebilet. Similar ideas were rebuffed in Algiers in August–September 1977, when both Senghor and Fahd resumed their Saharan diplomacy.

25. *Le Monde*, January 9, 1979, and November 11–12, 1979.

26. Reply of President Houari Boumedienne to the Message of His Majesty King Hassan II of Morocco, UN Document A/33/289, October 5, 1978.

27. Interview with *Al-Watan al-Arabi*, cited in *El Día* (Tenerife), October 1, 1978.

28. *Reuters*, dispatch from Rabat, October 2, 1978.

29. *Le Matin du Sahara* (Casablanca), November 8, 1978.

30. Interview on France-Inter, October 31, 1978.

31. After three and a half years in detention six of them were finally tried and sentenced (to jail terms of between three and twelve years) in June 1982. A seventh committed suicide in a military jail. (*Le Monde*, February 19, 1978, and July 13, 1982.) The Moroccan government denied that a Moroccan aircraft had dropped arms at Cape Sigli. However, Gilbert Lecavelier has confirmed, in *Aux ordres du SAC* (Albin Michel, Paris, 1982), that the arms were parachuted from a Moroccan C-130 from the air-force base at Kenitra. According to Lecavelier, the French government had received word of the plot in advance and tipped off the Algerian authorities.

32. Letter Dated 28 January 1979 from the Minister for Foreign Affairs of Algeria Addressed to the President of the Security Council, UN Document S/13057, January 29, 1979.

33. Cited in *Sahara Info* (Paris), Nos. 32–33, March–April 1979, p. 9.

34. *AFP*, dispatch from Paris, February 16, 1979.

35. Message Dated 15 February 1979 from the Minister of Foreign Affairs of Algeria Addressed to the Minister of State for Foreign Affairs and Co-operation of Morocco, UN Document S/13091, February 16, 1979.

36. *Le Monde*, March 5, 1981.

37. *Le Monde*, June 11, 1980.

38. *Le Monde*, April 10, 1981.

39. *Le Monde*, February 14, 1981.

40. *Referendum of Self-Determination for the People of the Western Sahara*, Memorandum of Algeria Presented to the "OAU Committee of Implementation," Nairobi, August 1981, pp. 1, 5.

41. *Ibid.*, p. 41.

42. *Ibid.*, p. 67.

43. *Marchés Tropicaux et Méditerranéens* (Paris), February 5, 1982.

44. The small opposition groups in exile, such as Mohammed Boudiaf's Parti de la Révolution Socialiste (PRS) and Ait Ahmed's Front des Forces Socialistes (FFS), were particularly vocal in opposing the government's Saharan policy. So too were four former leaders of the FLN, Ferhat Abbas, Youssef Ben Khedda, Husain Lahoul and Mohammed Kheiredden, who issued a manifesto, urging a "halt to the war against our Moroccan brothers" and democratic reforms within Algeria, on March 9, 1976.

45. The armed forces played a decisive role in ensuring a smooth transition after Boumedienne's death and securing Chadli's election at the January 1979 FLN congress, at which there were 600 military delegates (out of a total of 3,298). A veteran of the independence war, Chadli had been commander of the Constantine military region in 1963–64 and of the Oran military region since 1964. He had become chief-of-staff of the ALN in December 1978 as Boumedienne approached his end.

46. Such demons had not been entirely buried. The RNI, for example, voted for the liberation of "all the Moroccan provinces still under the domination of Algerian colonialism" at its constitutive congress in October 1978. (*Jeune Afrique*, October 25, 1978.)

47. *AFP*, December 12, 1982.

48. *Le Monde*, March 10–11, 1983.
49. *Marchés Tropicaux et Mediterranéens*, June 3, 1983.
50. *Afrique-Asie* (Paris), April 11, 1983.
51. *Le Monde*, March 1, 1983.
52. *El Moudjahid*, June 12, 1983.

Mohammed Abdelaziz,
secretary-general of the
Polisario Front since 1976

Saharawi refugee children showing victory sign

Saharawi women demonstrate support for Polisario at refugee camp near Tindouf

Exploded cluster bombs, delivered by the United States to Morocco

King Hassan II and President Ronald Reagan, on horseback in Virginia, May 1982
MICHAEL EVANS, THE WHITE HOUSE

30

Polisario in Perspective

THE BITTERNESS OF THE GUERRILLA WAR with Morocco crowned the process of formation of a Saharawi national consciousness. It brought Saharawis of differing tribal and social origins together in refugee camps and guerrilla units for an especially grueling and difficult struggle. It deepened their sense of national pride and unity. Moreover, the strong sense of kindred between Saharawis living within and beyond Western Sahara's pre-1975 borders roused many thousands from southern Morocco, northern Mauritania and southwestern Algeria to make their way to the Polisario camps near Tindouf. Almost all the eighteen thousand or so Reguibat who had settled in the Tindouf and Bechar regions of Algeria in the early seventies had already joined the Polisario camps by the end of 1975.[1] Several thousand more arrived from northern Mauritania, among them former employees of the iron-mining industry in Zouerate. From southern Morocco, where El-Ouali and his earliest associates had found some of their first recruits in 1971–72, came many more—among them, for example, the inhabitants of Zaag, who fled to Tindouf in 1975, and Saharawis evacuated from Tan-Tan and Lebouirate during Polisario's raids in 1979.

Thus, the number of Saharawis in the Tindouf camps and Polisario's *kataeb* came to exceed one hundred thousand—ironically, but explicably, more than the total number of Saharawis counted within Western Sahara's borders by the Spanish census authorities in 1974.[2] In new supratribal dimensions, the old imperative of *asabiya*, or blood solidarity, had brought together the Ahel es-Sahel from all corners of their diaspora, as well as from within Western Sahara, to fight for nationhood.

Allegations by the Moroccan government that many of the Saharans in Polisario's guerrilla units or the Tindouf camps were Tuareg from the central Sahara could evidently be given little credence. A Berber people, speaking a Berber language, Tamashagh, the Tuareg live in Niger, Mali and southeastern

Algeria, about a thousand miles east of the zones of migration or settlement of the Hassaniya-speaking Ahel es-Sahel, beyond the almost impenetrable dunes of the Erg Iguidi.

The Moroccan armed forces were never once able to show off a captured Targui, as they surely would have if they had caught one, just as they could never give evidence—except after the unique events at Amgala in January 1976—to buttress their government's claims that regular Algerian troops, or even Cubans and Vietnamese, were fighting with Polisario. No national liberation movement relying significantly on soldiers without historical links to the territory in which they were fighting, and thus without deep commitment to the movement's cause, could possibly have sustained a long guerrilla struggle, against formidable odds, with the kind of success displayed by Polisario.

Rather, it was the Ahel es-Sahel's newborn but profound patriotism which bore the guerrillas through their prolonged ordeal and drove them to the heights of courage and self-sacrifice. A succession of defeats might have blunted their determination and morale. However, with a record of considerable military and diplomatic successes behind them, even the escalation of U.S. military aid for King Hassan, from 1979, and the construction of the Moroccan wall around the "useful triangle" did not blunt their confidence. Encouraged by the continuing support from Algeria and Libya, they believed they could sustain the war longer than Morocco, and so they were not prepared to dilute their objective of total independence.

After King Hassan's reluctant and ambiguous acceptance of a referendum at the OAU summit in Nairobi in June 1982, the SADR's Council for the Command of the Revolution (CCR) laid down stringent conditions for its conduct. First of all, there would have to be "direct negotiations between the two parties to the conflict—the Polisario Front and the Moroccan government—to determine the practical measures for a cease-fire and for the withdrawal of the Moroccan occupation troops and administration, so as to create appropriate conditions that will enable the people of Western Sahara to exercise its inalienable right to self-determination through a general, free and regular referendum." All Moroccan troops and the entire Moroccan civil administration would have to be withdrawn from Western Sahara, all Saharawi political prisoners set free and all refugees allowed to return home. A "provisional international administration" would have to be set up by the UN and the OAU, "with the collaboration of the SADR," and UN peace-keeping forces stationed along the Moroccan frontier.[3]

Polisario doubted that King Hassan had any intention of withdrawing from Western Sahara at this time. The front interpreted his referendum pledge as a ploy to keep the OAU at bay and bar the SADR from OAU membership. The subsequent meetings of the OAU's Implementation Committee in August 1981 and February 1982 revealed that Hassan was, indeed, resolutely opposed to negotiating with the Saharawi nationalists. At its fifth congress, held on October 12–16, 1982, Polisario vowed to "defeat all maneuvers and plots aimed at limiting our national independence over the whole of the territory of the Saharan Arab Democratic Republic." Held under the slogan "The Whole Country or Martyrdom!," the congress resolved that the only way forward, after a year of relative lull on the military front, while the diplomatic battle had been fought out in the OAU, was to prepare to drive the FAR out of the useful triangle militarily. This would be Polisario's most audacious, perhaps its decisive, campaign, requiring thousands of highly-trained troops equipped with powerful and sophisticated military hardware. Polisario's task was to ready its *kataeb* for a "modern war, with modern equipment and revolutionary discipline."[4]

The leadership body that masterminded both military and diplomatic strategy was Polisario's executive committee, a relatively small, youthful and cohesive body, whose composition remained almost unchanged during the course of the war. The nine members, all in their twenties or thirties, who were elected to the committee by the third congress, in August 1976, were reelected *en bloc* by the fourth congress, in September 1978. All but two of them were reelected again by the fifth congress, which reduced the committee's membership to seven.[5] Mohammed Abdelaziz, the guerrilla veteran who was elected secretary-general at the third congress, after El-Ouali's death, was reelected by both the fourth and the fifth congresses. Likewise, Mohammed Lamine Ould Ahmed remained prime minister of the SADR for more than six years, from its founding in 1976 until a cabinet reshuffle on October 31, 1982, following the fifth congress, when he was appointed minister of education. He remained a member of the executive committee. His successor in the premiership was Mahfoud Ali Beiba, another Polisario veteran who had served as interim secretary-general for two months in 1976, between El-Ouali's death and the third congress. By contrast to many national liberation movements, Polisario had a noticeably homogeneous, collaborative and dedicated leadership. It suffered no serious factional splits; its unity was not sapped by divisive tribal or family loyalties, or by corruption; and though there was naturally a division of labor between military and political tasks, there was sufficient rotation to ensure that almost all senior Polisario cadres had personal experience of the military struggle.[6]

Within the executive committee, overall responsibility for conducting the war lay with Ibrahim Ghali, who had commanded the SPLA since the days of the guerrilla war against Spain and served as the SADR's defense minister without interruption, from the republic's founding. To mobilize mass support among the

TABLE 30.1

EXECUTIVE COMMITTEE OF THE POLISARIO FRONT

(Elected by the 5th General People's Congress, October 12–16, 1982)

Mohammed Abdelaziz, secretary-general

Mohammed Lamine Ould Ahmed

Mahfoud Ali Beiba

Ibrahim Ghali Ould Mustapha

Bashir Mustapha Sayed

Ayoub Ould Lahbib

Mohammed Lamine Ould Bouhali

Tindouf refugees for the executive committee's policies, there was a subordinate, somewhat larger political bureau, which was elected by the front's congress and met under the chairmanship of the secretary-general. It had twenty-one
members between the third and fifth congresses, and twenty-five after the fifth.
Finally, to coordinate the front's diplomatic work, there was a foreign relations
committee—headed, after the fifth congress, by Mohammed Salem Ould Salek.[7]

TABLE 30.2
COUNCIL OF MINISTERS OF THE SADR
(October 31, 1982)

Prime minister and minister of information and culture	Mahfoud Ali Beiba
Ministers	
Defense	Ibrahim Ghali Ould Mustapha
Education	Mohammed Lamine Ould Ahmed
Interior	Abdelkader Taleb Omar
Foreign affairs	Ibrahim Hakim
Justice	M'hammed Ould Ziou
Secretaries of state	
Trade	El-Kenti Ould Jouda
Health	Nema Ould el-Joumani
Secretary-general of the prime minister's office	Mohammed Ould Sidati

After its conversion from a small vanguard group into a mass movement in
1975, Polisario regarded itself as a "front of the whole people." All Saharawis,
other than "traitors" collaborating with the enemy, were automatically considered members. The entire adult population of the Tindouf refugee camps was
therefore enrolled, for purposes of political orientation, into "cells," of eleven
members each, and from 1976 the delegates to the front's congresses—known
henceforth as the General People's Congress—were elected by mass assemblies in
the refugee camps and the SPLA.

After the founding of the SADR, the front's bodies tended to overlap, in function and composition, with those of the new republic. This was inevitable,
perhaps, in conditions of war and partial exile. Article 31 of the SADR's constitution, which was adopted by the third congress, established, for example, that the
functions of the SADR's supreme executive body, the CCR, would be performed,
transitionally, by the front's executive committee, "until the holding of the first
General People's Congress after the recovery of sovereignty."[8] Such measures did
not, in and of themselves, deny the validity of the SADR's claim to statehood—for, despite its inability to administer the principal towns of Western
Sahara, the SADR had such state attributes as the control of a large and well-

equipped army and a functioning system of civil administration in exile, in the refugee camps, scattered across a swath of territory covering at least several hundred square miles, which, for administrative purposes, had virtually been "ceded" to the Saharawis by the Algerian government. However, it was Polisario, as much as the SADR, which possessed these attributes of statehood. There was, as it were, a "party-state."

As both a legislative body and "the supreme organ of executive power of the SADR," the CCR laid down "the general policy of the state," according to Article 12 of the SADR's 1976 constitution. Polisario's secretary-general presided over the CCR (Article 13) and, under a constitutional amendment adopted by the fifth congress, following the SADR's admission to the OAU in 1982, acquired the formal title of "president of the SADR." The government, known as the council of ministers, was subordinate to the CCR. Appointed by the CCR (Article 14) and presided over by a member of the CCR (Article 17), its task was to conduct "all executive business under directives drawn up by the Council for the Command of the Revolution" (Article 18). The SADR's "parliament," the Saharawi National Council, which replaced the Provisional Saharawi National Council after the third congress, theoretically had "legislative and consultative power" (Article 21). However, since the CCR also had legislative authority, the Saharawi National Council had a purely consultative role in practice.[9] It was likened to the *ait arbain* of old, for it had around forty members—the members of the political bureau, plus representatives from the refugee camps. However, the resemblance was purely symbolic.

At the subnational level, the SADR was divided into three *wilayat*, or regions, each of which was administered by a *wali*, or governor, appointed by the CCR from among the members of the political bureau.[10] Though they only existed as administrative units for the refugee settlements in southwestern Algeria during the war, they were named after the three principal towns of Western Sahara (El-Ayoun, Smara and Dakhla) and were evidently intended to assume administrative responsibility for regions of the territory after the war. The *wali* presided over a *wilaya* people's council, composed of the officials administering the *wilaya*'s component districts, or *dairat*. Each of the latter, of which there were twenty-three in 1982, was constituted by a single refugee camp of approximately five thousand inhabitants. The *daira* was governed by an appointed official and an elected *daira* people's council, which supervised the work of five specialized camp committees, responsible for education, health, justice, artisanry and supplies.[11]

For purposes of political guidance, each *daira* was subdivided into a mass of eleven-member cells, headed by *arifat*, responsible to the respective *wilaya*'s "orientation department"—a body, headed by the *wali*, which was in turn responsible to the political bureau. It was in the *daira*, finally, that a kind of "direct democracy" was practiced, according to Polisario.[12] Mass meetings, known as people's base congresses, were held in each camp every one or two years; and it was at these assemblies that elections would be held, by show of hands, for delegates to the General People's Congress, as well as the local *daira* councillors. It was the *daira* council's presidents who represented the *dairat* in the Saharawi National Council.

Polisario's "population base" was of diverse social origins. Former town-dwellers were in the majority, but a sizable minority had been nomads until 1975. Some had been workers in the phosphate industry, in the Zouerate iron industry, in transportation, construction or public administration. Others had been traders, some of them relatively prosperous. There were veterans of the Spanish Tropas Nómadas and the Policía Territorial, ex-students, from universities in Spain, Morocco and Algeria, and elderly sheikhs who had sat in the Djemaa. It was the struggle for independence that had brought them all together, in the refugee camps or the SPLA. They must have differed widely in their broader philosophy and aspirations. As a relatively stable group of young militants, many of whom had been through university, Polisario's top leadership may have shared a common ideological outlook, but like a good many other nationalist movements, the front glossed over potentially controversial matters that might have undermined the movement's wartime unity—or aroused the suspicions, or hostility, of powerful and influential foreign governments.

The movement's ideological profile was kept deliberately blurry. "There are people," remarked a member of the political bureau in January 1976, "who ask us if we are Marxist-Leninists, pro-Chinese, or I don't know what else. The truth is that this makes us smile. We are ourselves, and that is all."[13] By and large, Polisario kept silent about the kind of policies and programs it might implement upon achieving full independence.

There were a few pointers, however. "The Saharawi people are an Arab, African and Muslim people," proclaimed the preamble to the SADR's constitution. "They choose a policy of non-alignment; they struggle for the unity of the peoples of the Arab nation and of the African continent; and they are convinced that the militant solidarity of the peoples of the world will bring about a just and equitable world order which will contribute to the building of a humanity where justice reigns and where nations are united in equality and mutual respect."[14] The General National Program adopted by the fourth congress, in 1978, proclaimed Polisario's "opposition to imperialism, colonialism and exploitation" and its commitment to both "national construction and the achievement of socialism."[15] The program listed such nationalist and egalitarian pollicies as "the suppression of all forms of exploitation," the "just distribution of national resources and the suppression of disparities between the countryside and the towns," Arabization of education and the provision of free medical care, adequate housing and free, universal, compulsory education. Suppression of "exploitation" meant, notably, the eradication of the last vestiges of slavery and of such practices as the *horma*. "All citizens are equal before the law," declared the SADR's constitution. "They have the same rights and obligations."

The front gave few details, however, of the kind of economic policies it would follow after full independence. The movement was unlikely to be immune to the mercantile spirit that has always been of great influence in Saharawi society. It may, thus, have anticipated encouraging private trade, and smuggling into neighboring territories, by retaining Western Sahara's "free zone" status and the traditional commercial links with the Canaries. Given the territory's huge phosphate wealth, Polisario knew that an independent Western Sahara would be economically viable, with a per capita income possibly higher than anywhere else in Africa. However, it was equally aware that the territory would be dependent technologically. If nationalization of the ultramodern phosphate industry was contemplated, there was recognition too that it could not be run without foreign technical assistance. A management contract might have to be awarded to a foreign firm, perhaps even Spain's INI. "The Sahara will be a primary-commodity producing country, it is necessary to develop these primary resources and it is obligatory to cooperate with the industrialized countries," the SADR's foreign minister, Ibrahim Hakim, remarked in September 1977. "If the western companies respect Saharan sovereignty, they will be welcome in the Sahara."[16]

In its social and cultural policies, Polisario appeared to gravitate ambiguously between religious or cultural traditionalism and a reformist modernism. Islam was defined, by Article 3 of the SADR's constitution, as the "state religion," and the fourth congress's General National Program proposed basing the SADR's judicial system on the *sharia*. However, while taking care not to offend traditionalist sensibilities, Polisario sought to improve women's status—partly because it understood the need to mobilize all available human resources, female as well as male, in the struggle for national liberation. Thus, the fourth congress's General National Program advocated "achieving women's political and social rights and favoring their access to all domains, so that they may assume their responsibilities in national construction, in conformity with our national reality and religion." To this end, the front had an active women's wing, the Unión Nacional de Mujeres Saharauis.

Since practically all the able-bodied men who joined Polisario became guerrillas, the Tindouf refugee camps were populated almost entirely by women, children and the elderly. Consequently, women were called upon to play a major part in the administration of the camps. Nearly all the members of the specialized *daira* committees were women. Moreover, the women refugees benefited enormously from the mass literacy campaign carried out in the refugee camp during the early years of the war. Nonetheless, the traditional sexual division of labor remained. The men were enrolled in the SPLA and went off to fight, while the women took responsibility for the *friq*, albeit one in the form of a large refugee camp. The women did receive military training, and they served in the camps' militia; however, they were not enlisted into the SPLA and so did not take part in the war itself. Their role in political decision-making remained limited too. No women were elected at any time to the front's executive committee and there was only one woman among the twenty-one members of the political bureau elected at the fourth congress.[17]

Article 5 of the SADR's constitution stated that "the family, the basis of society, is founded on morality and religion." Polisario strove, in the words of the fourth congress' General National Program, to "protect the family and work to improve its position in all fields, given that it constitutes the fundamental cell of society." Apart from purely religious motives, the front hoped thereby to reduce the social weight of the *qabila*, and the *fakhd*, which were regarded as divisive relics of the "tribalist" past. Additionally, it saw an imperative need to protect the family from the strains of war and exile. So, though it was not illegal, divorce was strongly discouraged by the *daira* justice committees, through marital counseling.[18]

This strong emphasis on family cohesion was also a logical concomitant of Polisario's population policy. Given the Saharawis' small numbers, it was not surprising that Polisario should have regarded a high birth rate as a crucial weapon in the struggle for national survival. The fourth congress voted to "encourage the policy of demographic growth" and this was reaffirmed by the fifth congress in its General Program of National Action.[19] Reproduction, at the highest possible rate, became a patriotic duty.

Marital relations underwent many revolutionary changes, however. The *daira* justice committees, which occupied themselves with a wide range of social matters, succeeded in transforming the traditional dowry, which had become untenable for refugees living only marginally above the threshold of survival, into a symbolic gift, usually a goat, given by the entire *daira* to the newlywed couple. The justice committees actively discouraged such practices as polygamy, arranged marriages and child marriages; and the old endogamous marriage rules of the past, which had generally kept marriages within the *qabila*, cast little influence on the young, who, in their nationalist enthusiasm, seemed to hold the traditional fixation with ancestral lineages in contempt.

Indeed, their nationalism was so intense that the mere mention of fraction or tribal identity was censured in the Tindouf camps. "From one excess one often passes to another," noted one Polisario leader. "Not only does one abstain henceforth from referring to tribal affiliation, but one pushes zeal to the point of refusing to name one's father."[20]

Yet, Polisario's nationalism was not of a blind, xenophobic stamp. The Saharawis' Moroccan prisoners—of whom there were well over a thousand, including several pilots, by 1982—were treated well, while receiving lectures on the injustice of their government's war.[21] Meanwhile, diplomatic expediency taught the front to endorse the OAU's famous rule of respect for the frontiers drawn by the European powers. It was in the name of that precept, as much as the democratic principle of self-determination, that Polisario appealed to African governments to back the Saharawi struggle, even though this meant forgetting emotional inclinations to lay claim to former Spanish Southern Morocco, the Saharawi-inhabited region ceded to Morocco by Spain in 1958.

Likewise, Polisario's nationalism did not, in theory at least, preclude the idea of a pan-Arab union. Polisario's leaders were influenced by the "unionism" propounded by Qadhafi and, before him, by Nasser. The SADR's constitution declared, among its "fundamental principles," that "the search for the unity of the peoples of the Arab Maghreb is a step toward Arab and African unity" and that the SADR was "committed to respecting the open unionist program."

In particular, Polisario leaders continued to refer, on occasion, to El-Ouali's old suggestion of federation with Mauritania. "The idea of unity with Mauritania is not new and, in principle, is not unacceptable to the Saharawi people," the SADR's premier, Mohammed Lamine Ould Ahmed, wrote to President Senghor of Senegal on November 6, 1977. However, "it cannot be an imposed unity," and, alluding to the 1976 partition, "still less a unity in division."[22]

However, despite Qadhafi's active encouragement, the idea of a federation between Mauritania and the SADR had no practical import, even after Mokhtar Ould Daddah's downfall and the Agreement of Algiers. Though the Saharawis had a close cultural affinity with the Moors of Mauritania, their recent history had been very different. Both Polisario and the Algerian government also feared that a Saharawi-Mauritanian federation, enacted without clear evidence of a popular mandate, would undermine Polisario's hard-won diplomatic gains in the OAU and the UN. Besides, the military regime in Nouakchott had not the slightest interest in the idea. Joining with the SADR, under whatever constitutional arrangement, would have amounted to a declaration of war against Morocco and so plunged Mauritania back into the conflict it had finally and thankfully succeeded in escaping.

In any case, there was an air of unreality about Polisario's "unionism." It seemed hardly likely, after such a long, bitter struggle, which had stoked the fires of Saharawi patriotism to a burning passion, that Polisario would willingly renounce its quest for full national sovereignty—and control of the Bou-Craa phosphates—in the name of federation or union, with Mauritania or any other Arab country.

Still, a strategic perspective for the unification of the Arab world, requiring the overthrow of reactionary Arab regimes, was spelled out in the General National Program adopted at Polisario's fourth congress. "The masses' real interest lies in liberty and unity, of which they are the sole guarantor," it declared. "That is why we regard the unity of the peoples of the Arab Maghreb and the effective building of this unity to be an important step toward the achievement of the unity of the whole Arab nation. Consequently, we are convinced that coexistence between the progressives and nationalists on the one hand and the reactionary forces on the other is impossible. Hence the necessity of consolidating the progressive front in this region of the Arab world, and working for the unification of all the revolutionary Arab foci, breaking their isolation, in order to be able to achieve our nation's aspirations to unity, a unity which cannot be accomplished without putting an end to the static situation suffered by several peoples of the Arab nation."

Specifically, Polisario advocated the construction of a "tripartite Arab front (Sahara-Algeria-Libya)" and "its reinforcement so that it becomes a pole of attraction for the rest of the peoples of the Arab Maghreb and a shining example for the Arab and African peoples."[23] This perspective was reaffirmed four years later in the General Program of National Action adopted by the fifth congress, which resolved to "strenghen the tripartite, progressive front of the Saharawi, Algerian and Libyan revolutions, as a basic step toward the concretization of the revolutionary alliance of the peoples of the Maghreb."

Needless to say, such a policy entailed uncritical support for the Algerian and Libyan governments, or at least keeping quiet about points of disagreement. That, doubtless, was unavoidable for a movement so dependent, logistically, on Libyan and, above all, Algerian assistance—and on the constancy of these two allies' concurrence of views on the Saharan war. Indeed, the whole notion of a Saharawi-Algerian-Libyan bloc was essentially of wartime inspiration and relevance.

While it was reasonable to forecast that a fully independent Western Saharan state, under Polisario rule, would retain its inherited cordial relations with Algeria and Libya, there was no likelihood that it would be beholden to either country. Not only would Polisario's own nationalism militate against that, but the very achievement of independence would remove the old wartime ties of dependence. Apart possibly from some technical or financial assistance, economic ties with Libya or Algeria would be almost nonexistent, unless a railway was built, probably many years hence, if ever at all, from the iron deposits at Gara Djebilet to the Western Saharan coast.

Furthermore, Polisario let it be known that, after a peace agreement with Morocco, it would not foment or assist revolutionary action against the Moroccan monarchy. At the fourth congress, despite the General National Program's call for struggle against the reactionary forces of the Arab world, a manifesto declared that "our fight is a liberation war, for national independence, and is not intended to overthrow foreign regimes."[24] A keynote slogan at the SADR's third anniversary celebrations in the Tindouf refugee camps, five months later, even proclaimed that "the SADR is a factor of stability in the region."

This was designed to reassure Western governments, as well as King Hassan, about Polisario's long-term objectives. Polisario wanted to convince Washington, Morocco's closest ally from about 1980, that it was the prolongation of the war, rather than Western Sahara's independence, that really threatened to destabilize the Moroccan monarchy. "It is the war that is having serious repercussions for Morocco and putting the king's throne in danger," Mohammed Abdelaziz remarked in April 1982. "The Moroccan people and soldiers want peace. They want solutions to the social and economic problems brought about by the effort devoted to this war by the King of Morocco. If the United States wants to save the King of Morocco, it must make him pull out of this war."[25]

The war was, indeed, sapping the strength of the Hassan regime. Whether or not Polisario pledged to promote regional stability after the war, its guerrilla war had in fact become the potential catalyst for revolutionary change in Morocco, one of the Western powers' closest allies in both Africa and the Arab world. However, a Moroccan withdrawal from Western Sahara was as likely to put the king's future at risk as fighting on to stay there. So, despite Polisario's pleas, Washington continued, under President Reagan, to escalate its military assistance to Morocco, in the hope of saving Hassan from humiliation.

NOTES

1. Eugénie Muret, *Le processus de sédentarisation des nomades reguiebat de la région de Tindouf*, unpublished dissertation, 1976, p. II. By way of example, the experience of Lieutenant Bashir, a Polisario commander captured in Mauritania in June 1976, may be cited. A Reguibi, born in the Ain-Ben-Tili region while his parents were still nomads, he had settled in Tindouf in 1961, attended primary school there and then moved to Bechar for his secondary education. He had later attended a military school in Tafraoui. He volunteered to join Polisario at the end of 1974 and fought against Spain before the start of the war with Morocco and Mauritania. See *Jeune Afrique* (Paris), July 8, 1979.

2. Some of those Saharawis, moreover, had remained in the Moroccan-controlled towns. A few Saharawis succeeded in escaping these towns during the war—notably during Polisario's raid on Smara in October 1979, when seven hundred reached Tindouf.

3. Memorandum Dated 25 July 1981 from the General Secretary of the Polisario Front Addressed to the Secretary-General of the United Nations, UN Document A/36/488, 10 September 1981, p. 8.

4. General Program of National Action, adopted at Polisario's fifth congress.

5. The two who left the committee, Mohammed Ali Ould el-Ouali and Batal Sidi Ahmed, were both elected to the twenty-five member political bureau, however.

6. El-Ouali's death in action, during the raid on Nouakchott, is eloquent evidence of the top leadership's direct participation in the guerrilla war.

7. He had previously served as the SADR's information minister, from March 1976 to October 1982. For a detailed biography, see Tony Hodges, *Historical Dictionary of Western Sahara* (Scarecrow Press, Metuchen, N.J., 1982), pp. 240–41.

8. For the full text of the SADR's constitution, see Hodges, *op. cit.*, pp. 307–9.

9. See *Sahara Libre* (Polisario Front, Algiers), No. 137, October 2, 1982, for an interview with the president of the Saharawi National Council, El-Kenti Ould Jouda, on the council's role.

10. The following account of the SADR's regional and local structure is primarily based on information obtained during visits to the Tindouf refugee camps in November 1979.

11. Prior to April 1978 there had been nine such specialized committees. See *La République Arabe Sahraouie Démocratique* (Département d'Information, SADR, 1980), pp. 40–42.

12. *Sahara Libre*, No. 97, January 22, 1980.

13. Cited in Soledad Balaguer and Rafael Wirth, *Frente Polisario: la última guerrilla* (Editorial Laia, Barcelona, 1976), p. 39.

14. See Hodges, *op. cit.*, p. 307.

15. For the full text of the General National Program adopted at the fourth congress, see *20 Mai* (Polisario Front, Algiers), No. 51, November 1978, pp. 18–22.

16. Interview with Ibrahim Hakim, Algiers, September 1977.

17. *Sahara Info* (Paris), Nos. 29–30, December 1978–January 1979, p. 6.

18. Marigrine Auffray-Milésy, *Compte rendu de voyage en République Arabe Sahraouie Démocratique, 25 fevrier–3 mars 1979* (Paris, 1979), p. 16.

19. Unlike the fourth congress's General National Program, this document barely touched on the front's long-term programmatic goals. It was primarily devoted to short-term political and organizational objectives.

20. Ahmed-Baba Miské, *Front Polisario: l'âme d'un peuple* (Editions Rupture, Paris, 1978), p. 247.

21. Interviews with Moroccan prisoners during visits to the Tindouf region and Polisario-controlled regions of Western Sahara in September 1977, December 1977, February–March 1979 and December 1979.

22. *Le Monde*, November 9, 1977.

23. *20 Mai*, No. 51, November 1978, pp. 19, 22.

24. The text of the mainfesto issued by the fourth congress may be found in *20 Mai*, No. 51, November 1978, pp. 10–17.

25. Interview with Mohammed Abdelaziz, Algiers, April 1982. For the full text of the interview, see *Africa Report* (New York), July–August 1982, pp. 15–18.

31

The World Powers

A CONFLICT IN A SMALL DESERT TERRITORY like Western Sahara might not have been expected to arouse the concern or interest of the major world powers. Western Sahara does, of course, have some of the world's largest phosphate deposits, rich fishing resources off its coast and, quite possibly, important reserves of iron ore and other minerals, as well as oil. However, it was the Saharan war's broader regional ramifications that drew the attention of policy makers in Washington, Paris and Moscow. The destabilization of the Alawite monarchy, a long-standing and greatly valued ally of the West, aroused the concern of U.S. and French strategists as the war dragged on. The U.S., in particular, felt compelled to assist Hassan's flagging war effort. France, however, was more prudent after its direct intervention in the war in Mauritania in 1977–78, which, besides failing to sustain the Moroccan-Mauritanian alliance, damaged French business interests in Algeria, France's largest export market in Africa and the Arab world. For Paris, as well as Madrid and Moscow, an ambiguous neutrality became the favored strategy for the preservation and extension of interests on both sides of the conflict.

Giscard put great store, during the last three years of his presidency, on repairing relations with Algeria. In January 1980, his foreign minister, Jean François-Poncet, set up six joint commissions with the Algerian government to resolve issues in dispute.[1] The following September, France signed an immigration agreement pledging automatic renewal of Algerian immigrants' residence permits.[2] Though differences remained over Algerian demands for a substantial increase in contract prices for its natural-gas sales to France, French exports to Algeria, which had fallen to 6.9 billion francs in 1978, revived to 8.2 billion francs in 1979 and a record 11 billion francs in 1980.[3]

After counting the cost of trying to beef up Mokhtar Ould Daddah's resistance to Polisario, Giscard was aware, by 1978–79, of Mauritania's inability to sustain further war. To prevent a slide into Chad-like chaos, he backed the new military regime's attempts to extricate itself from the conflict, and so, on August 29, 1979, three weeks after the Algiers Agreement, France countered Hassan's threats to cross the Mauritanian border by declaring that "Mauritania's desire for independence and sovereignty should be respected by the international community." Between December 1979 and May 1980, a garrison of 150 to 180 French troops was installed in Nouadhibou, at the Mauritanian government's request, to dissuade Morocco from occupying nearby La Guera.[4] The Giscard government abstained on all the resolutions adopted in the UN General Assembly from 1978.

The French government could not afford to alienate King Hassan, however. There were still fifty-five thousand French expatriates in Morocco, more than anywhere else in the world, and though the Moroccan economy was much smaller than Algeria's, Morocco was France's third main export market in Africa.[5] Giscard feared for the Moroccan monarchy's future, as the military, diplomatic and economic pressures on the Hassan regime mounted. So, while adopting a lower profile in the Saharan conflict, France remained Morocco's main arms supplier apart from the U.S. Delivery of Morocco's new Mirage F-1 aircraft and Alpha-Jets began during 1980, and the French premier, Raymond Barre, reassured Morocco on January 24, 1981, during a visit to Rabat, that French arms sales would not be halted.[6] Above all, however, the French government wanted to get the war ended, because it complicated France's relations with the rival states of the Maghreb while destabilizing the Hassan regime.

Hassan feared a radical shift in French policy when a socialist-communist government took power in 1981. The French Parti Socialiste (PS) had close ties with the USFP, had supported Polisario since 1976 and made no secret of its intention of establishing a privileged relationship with Algeria for commercial gain. During a trip to Algiers in October 1981, Mitterrand's foreign minister, Claude Cheysson, announced a new deal for Algerian immigrants, including an amnesty for "illegals."[7] Then Mitterrand himself flew to Algiers, for a state visit on November 30–December 1, and struck an astute deal by which France would pay much higher prices for its imports of Algerian gas in return for the awarding of major Algerian contracts to French firms. The stakes were enormous for French industry. In January 1982 the Algerian government agreed in principle to award contracts for fourteen major projects, with a combined value of 20 billion francs, to French firms, and in February a twenty-year contract was signed by Gaz de France for the purchase of 9.1 billion cubic meters of gas per year (compared to 4 billion cubic meters previously) at a much higher price than before, indexed against a basket of crude-oil prices.[8]

The French foreign ministry received a Polisario official for the first time on August 5, 1981, three months after the inauguration of the Mitterrand presidency, and on December 1, Cheysson announced that Polisario had been authorized to open an office in Paris.[9] Meanwhile, the PS had condemned the Casablanca massacre and the arrests of USFP and CDT leaders. "The freeing of the leaders of the USFP is a precondition for today's France to be able to have normal relations with Morocco,'' declared the president of the socialist group in the National Assembly on September 11, 1981.[10]

Nonetheless, the new government was careful not to jeopardize France's important interests in Morocco. Upon coming to power, it pledged to honor all of the previous government's arms contracts with Morocco.[11] Cheysson counterbalanced his visits to Algiers with trips to Rabat and presided over a meeting of the Grande Commission Franco-Marocaine on October 28–29, 1981. France continued to abstain on the Western Saharan resolutions at the UN, refrained from recognizing the SADR, despite pressure to do so from some PS deputies, and only briefly interrupted the flow of French arms to Morocco early in 1982 when the Moroccan government fell behind in its payments.[12]

The Spanish government too had compelling reasons to want to preserve cordial relations with both Morocco and Algeria. On the one hand, Algeria was Spain's main export market in Africa. On the other, Madrid feared a revival of Morocco's old claims to Ceuta and Melilla or the placing of new restrictions on Spanish fishing rights off the Saharan and Moroccan coasts.

So, under both Carlos Arias Navarro and his successor, Adolfo Suárez, who assumed the premiership in June 1976, the Spanish government tried to exploit the ambiguities of the Madrid accords to placate Algeria while retaining the friendship of Morocco. Though it had handed over Western Sahara's administration to Morocco and Mauritania, the Spanish government insisted that it had not ceded sovereignty, which, it acknowledged, was vested in the Saharawi people. Madrid therefore recognized the Saharawis' right to determine the territory's ultimate status.[13] Nonetheless, José María de Areilza, the first foreign minister of the post-Franco era, described the old Spanish-Moroccan "misunderstandings" on Western Sahara as "definitively overcome" when he visited Morocco in May 1976 to promote economic relations. "For us, this is a closed matter," he declared.[14] Furthermore, Spain delivered at least $27 million worth of military equipment to Morocco between February 1976 and January 1977.[15]

To the Madrid government's irritation, however, the Western Saharan problem simply would not go away. At home, the left-wing opposition parties, which emerged from clandestinity shortly after Franco's death, campaigned actively for the annulment of the Madrid Accords. Polisario tried to force Spain to renounce the accords by attacking Spanish fishing boats off the Saharan coast, and Algeria applied additional pressure by campaigning for the independence of the Canary Islands.

On March 12, 1977, six opposition parties, including the Partido Comunista de España (PCE) and the Partido Socialista Obrero Español (PSOE), issued a joint declaration demanding revocation of the Madrid accords and the immediate withdrawal of all Moroccan and Mauritanian troops from Western Sahara. On September 8, 1977, the leader of the PSOE, Felipe González, promised, after a meeting with Polisario's deputy secretary-general, Bashir Mustapha Sayed, to "make every effort in Spain and the international arena to secure the Polisario Front's recognition as the legitimate representative of the Saharawi people."[16]

Along with the PCE, the PSOE launched a concerted campaign in the Cortes against the Suárez government's Saharan policy after the first post-Franco general elections in June 1977. On March 13–16, 1978, at the PSOE's behest, the foreign affairs committee of the Cortes' lower house, the Congress of Deputies, held special hearings on the Madrid accords which, in the absence of Arias Navarro, who refused to attend, became a forum for critics of the Madrid accords, such as General Gómez de Salazar, Colonel Rodríguez de Viguri and Spain's ambassador to the UN, Jaime de Piniés.[17]

Suárez was under pressure from Algiers too. Since December 2, 1975, Radio Algiers had been broadcasting a daily half-hour program, "The Voice of the Free Canaries," devised by the Movimiento por la Autodeterminación y la Independencia del Archipiélago Canario (MPAIAC). A bizarre grouplet founded in 1964 by a lawyer from Tenerife, Antonio Cubillo, who had settled in Algiers in 1963, MPAIAC had a bare handful of members and was almost completely inactive in the Canaries, despite claiming to have an armed wing, the Fuerzas Armadas Guanches, named after the islands' original Guanche inhabitants.

As in the Basque country and Catalonia, however, nationalist sentiment was growing in the Canaries, which have a population of 1.25 million. Unemployment, which had always been much higher than in the peninsula, had risen since the slowing of the islands' tourism boom in the mid-seventies, and accusations were rife that the islands had been "abandoned" by Madrid. The main nationalist movement was an alliance known as the Unión del Pueblo Canario (UPC), which won one of the Canaries' thirteen parliamentary seats in the March 1979 general elections and became the second party, after Suárez's Unión del Centro Democrático (UCD), in the municipal councils of Las Palmas and Santa Cruz de Tenerife in local elections the following June.

After making frequent protests about Cubillo's broadcasts, the Spanish ambassador to Algeria, Gabriel Manueco, was recalled to Madrid in December 1977. To the Spanish government's dismay, however, the Algerian government then persuaded the OAU's Liberation Committee, at a meeting in Tripoli on February 13–18, to adopt a resolution calling for the Canaries' decolonization and urging African states to give material support to MPAIAC. The resolution was endorsed by the OAU's Council of Ministers on February 22.[18]

However, the Algerian government must have had second thoughts about this campaign, which alienated the Spanish left as much as it irritated Suárez. Felipe González protested in person when he met President Boumedienne in Algiers on January 30, 1978, and the deputies of both the PSOE and the PCE joined the UCD and the far-right parties in voting in the Cortes on February 22 for a resolution condemning the Liberation Committee's resolution as "unjustifiable interference in Spain's internal affairs."[19]

An all-party Spanish parliamentary delegation toured Africa during April and May to put Spain's case on the Canaries, and at the next OAU summit conference, in Khartoum in July, the Council of Ministers' resolution was quietly shelved.[20] Meanwhile, MPAIAC's radio broadcasts had been halted and, on April 5, Cubillo had narrowly escaped death at the hands of two knife-wielding

Spaniards outside his Algiers home. He was paralyzed from the waist down. Deprived of Algerian support, MPAIAC disintegrated.

A more serious threat to Spanish interests came directly from Polisario, which began a concerted campaign against Spanish fishing operations off the Saharan coast following the signing of a Spanish-Moroccan fishing agreement on February 17, 1977, which allowed Spanish boats to fish under license in Moroccan and Western Saharan waters in return for Spanish aid for the Moroccan fishing industry. Polisario had warned Spain in March 1976 that it would "not be responsible for what happens to the individuals and companies who share in plundering our resources."[21] So, within two months of the agreement's signing, guerrillas using pneumatic launches began seaborne raids against Spanish fishing boats. In April 1977 four fishermen were wounded when their boat was raked with machine-gun fire.[22] The following autumn, on the night of November 13–14, a guerrilla unit marked the second anniversary of the Madrid accords by boarding a Spanish fishing boat, the *Saa*, which had "violated the territorial waters of the SADR to pillage its maritime wealth." After abducting three of the crew, Polisario decided to embarrass the UCD government by releasing them to representatives of the PCE and the Canaries' fishermen's union, the Sindicato de Trabajadores del Mar (STM), at a ceremony in Algiers on November 28.[23]

The PSOE, the PCE and the STM virulently opposed the fishing agreement, which they believed spelled the demise of the Canaries' fishing industry by requiring the "Moroccanization" of 40 percent of the licensed fishing boats within five years, along with the provision of $40 million of Spanish credit to the Moroccan fishing industry. However, the agreement was finally ratified in the Cortes in February 1978, whereupon Polisario escalated its war on the Spanish fishing fleet. On April 20, a guerrilla squad boarded a Spanish boat, *Las Palomas*, forty-five miles off Dakhla, and seized eight of its crew. Mohammed Lamine Ould Ahmed announced on June 15 that they would be tried for "plundering the wealth of the SADR's territorial waters without the Saharawi authorities' permission."[24] Between June and September, seven more Spanish fishing boats came under fire from the coast, and then, on October 5, three Spanish fishermen were wounded when yet another boat, the *Genesis*, was raided.[25]

The widespread sympathy for the Saharawis in Spain, the propaganda of the PSOE and the PCE, Spanish industry's commercial stake in Algeria, the MPAIAC affair and Polisario's war on the Spanish fishing fleet encouraged Adolfo Suárez and his foreign minister, Marcelino Oreja, to adjust their Western Saharan policy. Additionally, the Nouakchott coup and the Algiers Agreement fostered a more sober assessment in Madrid of Polisario's long-term prospects, while the Moroccan annexation of Tiris el-Gharbia made nonsense of the tripartite accords of November 1975.

Under pressure in the Cortes, Oreja had already announced a halt in arms shipments to Morocco and Mauritania on December 14, 1977. Then, after two months of negotiations with Polisario on the fate of the eight *Las Palomas* fishermen, the UCD's foreign affairs secretary, Javier Rupérez, signed a communiqué in Tindouf on October 12, on behalf of the UCD, recognizing Polisario as "the sole legitimate representative of the struggling Saharan people."[26] The fishermen were released two days later. Algeria and Spain exchanged ambassadors again at the end of 1978 and Suárez arrived in Algiers for an official visit the following April 30–May 1, to meet Mohammed Abdelaziz as well as Chadli.[27]

However, the ambiguity in Spain's Saharan policy remained. The government dared not alienate King Hassan. Eighteen thousand Spaniards lived in Morocco, and there were still about 750 in Western Sahara, mainly at El-Ayoun and Bou-Craa. Morocco was also an important trading partner for Spain.[28] Most important of all, however, the Suárez government feared that Hassan might revive the old Moroccan claims to Ceuta and Melilla. As if to warn Spain not to go too far in its new dealings with Polisario, a hitherto unknown "Moroccan Patriotic Front" planted bombs in the two enclaves in February 1979. The Moroccan Chamber of Representatives unanimously accused Suárez, after his meeting with Mohammed Abdelaziz in Algiers, of violating "the Spanish government's international commitments" and reminded Spain that Morocco's unity would not be complete "without the restoration of all its usurped lands, foremost of which are Ceuta and Melilla and their dependent islands."[29]

The Moroccan government, moreover, may have been responsible for an assault on a Spanish fishing boat, the *Cruz del Mar*, off the Western Saharan coast on November 28, 1978, in which seven Spanish fishermen were shot in cold blood. Polisario, which had little interest in jeopardizing its newly improved relations with the UCD, only six weeks after Rupérez's Tindouf communiqué and the release of the *Las Palomas* fishermen, claimed that Morocco was trying to discredit the Saharawi cause.[30]

To exert further pressure on Madrid, the Moroccan government withheld ratification of the 1977 fishing agreement, despite its favorable terms, and forced Spain to negotiate successive short-term agreements lasting only a few months. Spanish fishing boats were frequently boarded by Moroccan coast guards and towed into Moroccan ports.

So Suárez's visit to Algiers was carefully balanced with a trip to Morocco by King Juan Carlos on June 14–16, 1979. The Madrid accords were not annulled, even after Mauritania's withdrawal from Western Sahara and the Moroccan annexation of Tiris el-Gharbia, and the UCD's recognition of Polisario was not endorsed by the government itself. A proposal that it should do so was voted down in the Cortes on October 12 by 136 votes to 121.[31] At the UN, Spain prudently abstained on all the General Assembly resolutions on Western Sahara.

Distraught by the ambiguity of Spanish policy, Polisario revived its campaign against Spanish fishing boats in the summer of 1980, after a pause of one and a half years. On May 22 a guerrilla group boarded the *Galgomar* near Dakhla and seized fifteen of its crew. Another twenty-three fishermen were captured when two more boats, the *Sarita* and the *Terranova*, were boarded on September 29. After prolonged negotiations, which began on October 25, Spain declared its support, on December 17 for "the Saharawi people's right to self-determination, as a basis for a political solution covering the whole of the territory of Western Sahara."[32] The fishermen were freed.

Adolfo Suárez and his successor, Leopoldo Calvo Sotelo, continued to tread with great caution, fashioning their Saharan policy to give the least offense to either side in the conflict, and such pragmatism was likely to continue even under the premiership of Polisario's old ally, Felipe González, after the PSOE's election victory in October 1982. On November 14, Polisario appealed to the incoming socialist government to "denounce the criminal tripartite accords." However, González was determined to reassure Morocco. On November 30, his foreign minister, Fernando Morán, declared that the PSOE government would "do nothing to destabilize the king of Morocco," and on March 28–30, 1983, González visited Morocco—on his first official mission abroad—to "create a relationship of confidence."

Ironically, the USSR displayed equal prudence. It might have been expected, in view of its generally close diplomatic ties with Algeria, to give full support to Polisario and recognize the SADR. The USSR did oppose the Green March. "The people of Western Sahara have the right to determine their fate," the Soviet ambassador to the UN declared in the Security Council on November 2, 1975. "The Soviet Union opposes any action which would hamper the efforts of the indigenous population of Western Sahara to exercise that right."[33] After the Madrid accords, the USSR voted, along with the other states of Eastern Europe, for every resolution in the General Assembly advocating self-determination. On the eve of the French air force's intervention against Polisario from Senegal, moreover, the Soviet ambassador in Dakar spoke out, on November 3, 1977, against "foreign intervention in Western Sahara." He added that "it is not possible to ignore the Polisario Front in the search for a solution in the Sahara."[34]

In a joint communiqué issued after a visit to Moscow by Boumedienne on January 12–14, 1978, the USSR expressed support for "a swift negotiated settlement of the Western Saharan problem through the implementation of the right of self-determination of the territory's people, in conformity with the resolutions of the United Nations." Similar declarations were made after Boumedienne's stay in Moscow for medical treatment in October 1978 and a visit by Chadli to the Soviet capital in June 1981.[35]

Apart from a plentiful supply of arms captured from Morocco, Polisario's weaponry was of Soviet-bloc origin. However, none of the Eastern European countries supplied military equipment to Polisario directly. Algeria and Libya, which rely on the Soviet bloc for about 90 percent of their arms, simply passed equipment on to Polisario. Furthermore, neither the USSR nor its Eastern European allies recognized the SADR.

The main reason for such circumspection was that the USSR wanted access to Morocco's phosphates. Though the USSR is the world's second-largest phosphate producer, it has to meet its COMECON partners' import needs and will become a net phosphate importer by the 1990s. So, on March 10, 1978, it sealed a multi-billion-dollar deal with Morocco, the country with the world's largest phosphate reserves, to ensure a long-term phosphate supply. This "contract of the century," as it was dubbed in Morocco, was the largest economic agreement ever signed by the Soviet Union with a third-world country. The USSR agreed to export oil, chemicals, timber and ore-carrier ships to Morocco in return for phosphates and phosphoric acid over a period of thirty years and to finance an estimated $2-billion investment in the development of a new phosphate mine at Meskala, where there are eight to ten billion tons of high-grade ore (more than five times as much as at Bou-Craa), to produce ten million tons a year.[36] Despite closer diplomatic links, the USSR's economic dealings with Algeria have never approached anything of this magnitude.

By contrast, broad strategic considerations impelled the Ford, Carter and Reagan administrations in Washington to align, more or less overtly, with Morocco in spite of Algeria's much greater importance to U.S. business interests. The Ford administration, which was in office at the time of the Madrid accords, recognized that Hassan's Saharan crusade in 1974–75 had given a new lease on life to the Moroccan monarchy and feared that, if the crusade failed to attain its objectives, Hassan would once again face a resurgence of domestic opposition. The value of the Hassan regime to the U.S. was self-evident. After the closure of the Strategic Air Command's Moroccan bases in 1963, the U.S. Navy retained communications facilities in Morocco which were only closed in 1978 because they were no longer needed. Morocco's geographical location, astride the entrance to the Mediterranean, was of obvious strategic importance, and the Hassan regime had always allowed U.S. warships to call at Morocco's excellent deepwater ports. Furthermore, Hassan had assisted Henry Kissinger's diplomacy in the Middle East. Since 1956, Morocco had received more than $1 billion of U.S. aid, more than any other African country except Haile Selassie's Ethiopia.

The Ford administration had good reason, moreover, to advise the Spanish leadership, at the end of the Franco era, to avoid getting embroiled in a confrontation with Morocco. The Spanish left and the nationalist movements in the Basque country and Catalonia had been inspired by the revolution in Portugal and given new hope by Franco's long final illness. Washington feared that the *caudillo*'s death might trigger the kind of political turmoil that had gripped Portugal since April 1974 and strongly advised the Arias Navarro government not to be distracted by foreign adventures from its task of steering Spain to a stable new post-Francoist order.

There was a military consideration too. The political upheaval in Portugal threatened the U.S. base rights at Lajes in the Azores, which had proved invaluable to the U.S. air force as a refueling stop for its emergency airlift to Israel during the 1973 Arab-Israel war, and so gave added importance to the four huge U.S. bases built in Spain since 1953 at a cost of $465.6 million. The lease for these bases, which ran out in September 1975, was renewed on January 24, 1976, in return for aid worth $1 billion and the delivery of seventy-two F-16 aircraft to the Spanish air force.[37]

The U.S. therefore supported the Madrid accords. On December 10, 1975, it abstained in the UN General Assembly on the Algerian-backed resolution (3458A) reaffirming the UN's traditional calls for a referendum and voted in favor of the rival resolution (3458B), backed by Morocco, because, as a State Department official later explained, "it took note of the Madrid Agreement, which we believed at the time offered the best basis for an eventual peaceful settlement."[38]

In 1974, U.S. experts had drawn up a rearmament program for the FAR, supposedly to defend Morocco in the event of a war with Algeria, though, if it had occurred, it would have almost certainly been the consequence of Morocco's designs on Western Sahara. Foreign Military Sales (FMS) agreements signed by the U.S. government with Morocco rose from a mere $8.2 million in Fiscal Year (FY) 1974 (which commenced in October 1973) to $242 million in FY 1975 (Table 31.1). FMS deliveries followed the agreements, with an inevitable time lag, rising from $2.4 million in FY 1975 to $87.5 million by FY 1978. U.S. government credit guarantees for Moroccan arms purchases rose too, from $3 million in FY 1974 to $30 million in FY 1976.

When Hassan discovered, after the Madrid accords, that the war with Polisario might be long and costly, or even escalate into a head-on confrontation with Algeria, he sent a former premier, Karim Lamrani, to Washington in January 1976. He was received by Kissinger on January 29, just as Moroccan and Algerian troops were clashing at Amgala. Two weeks later Kissinger informed Congress that the U.S. would sell Morocco a squadron of twenty-four Northrop F-5E combat aircraft for $120 million, along with $36 million worth of armored vehicles.[39] In fact, Morocco ended up buying Mirages from France instead of the F-5s, but U.S. sympathies were clear enough.

Meanwhile, the State Department took special measures to rush military equipment to Morocco and Mauritania. Approval was given for numerous transfers of U.S. arms, including F-5 aircraft, from Iran and Jordan (see Table 31.2).[4]

Officially, successive U.S. governments recognized only Morocco's administrative powers, rather than its sovereignty, in Western Sahara.[41] Technically, therefore, U.S.-supplied arms were used in Western Sahara in violation of both the U.S. Arms Export Control Act and a U.S.-Moroccan military agreement signed in 1960 which barred the use of U.S. arms for nondefensive purposes beyond Morocco's recognized frontiers.

Under congressional pressure the Carter administration, which took office in January 1977, briefly placed some restrictions on U.S. arms sales to Morocco in February 1978. A planned sale of twenty-four OV-10 "Broncos," low-flying aircraft designed by Rockwell International in the sixties for counterinsurgency operations in Vietnam, and twenty-four Bell Cobra helicopter gunships was canceled and the Moroccan government was asked to stop using its Northrop F-5 aircraft in Western Sahara.[42]

However, some military sales went ahead. Westinghouse was allowed to install a $200-million air defense system in Morocco and Western Sahara.[43] In February 1979 the State Department approved the sale of six Chinook CH-47 helicopters, the giant troop carriers used in the Vietnam war, and a month later $3 million worth of ammunition for F-5s and $2.4 million worth of spare parts for F-5s and Hercules C-130 transport planes were shipped to Morocco despite Morocco's refusal to stop using F-5s against Polisario.[44] In May 1979 the State Department approved plans made by Northrop Page Communications, a subsidary of Northrop Corporation, to sell Morocco a $200-million electronic "integrated intrusion detection system," which was eventually installed along the defense wall around the "useful triangle" in 1980–82.[45]

Limited though the restrictions on U.S. arms sales were, there were soon pressures to drop them. The fall of the Shah of Iran and Anastasio Somoza of

TABLE 31.1
U.S. ARMS SALES AND MILITARY AID TO MOROCCO
(in $ million, for fiscal years)

	1974	1975	1976	1977	1978	1979	1980	1981	1982	1983	1984
Foreign Military Sales (FMS)											
Agreements	8.2	242.0	105.4	37.2	7.7	3.6	274.4	48.0	14.0	14.0[a]	100.0[a]
Deliveries	4.0	2.4	15.8	33.7	87.5	133.5	61.7	135.5	na	na	na
Credits	3.0	14.0	30.0	30.0	43.0	45.0	25.0	33.4	30.0	75.0[b]	60.0[c]
Grants (MAP)	-	-	-	-	-	-	-	-	-	25.0[d]	30.0[c]
International Military Education Program (IMET)	0.5	0.8	0.9	0.8	1.1	1.0	0.9	1.0	1.1	1.2[d]	1.7[c]
Licensed Commercial Arms Exports	0.04	1.0	4.1	21.6	12.0	8.9	17.4	3.1[e]	5.0[e]	5.0[a]	25.0[a]

SOURCES: Congressional Presentation, Security Assistance Program, FY1983 and FY 1984.
[a]Projected.
[b]Of this, $23 million had been approved by Congress, as of July 1983, and a supplemental $52 million were being requested by the U.S. government.
[c]Proposed by the U.S. government, subject to Congressional approval.
[d]Approved by Congress.
[e]Estimates.

TABLE 31.2
TRANSFERS OF U.S. ARMS TO MOROCCO AND MAURITANIA
FROM "THIRD PARTY" COUNTRIES, 1975-76
(Transfers authorized under the U.S. Arms Exports Control Act,
November 1975-November 1976)

COUNTRY OF ORIGIN	DATE	ITEM	NUMBER	COUNTRY OF DESTINATION
Iran	Nov. 22, 1975	F-5A aircraft	10	Jordan
Jordan	Mar. 26, 1976	106mm recoilless guns	36	Morocco
Iran	May 13, 1976	F-5A aircraft	6	Jordan
Jordan	May 13, 1976	F-5A aircraft	20	Morocco
Jordan	May 21, 1976	F-5A aircraft	6	Morocco
Iran	July 9, 1976	155mm mortars	16	Jordan
Jordan	July 16, 1976	M-1 rifles	5,000	Mauritania
		30-caliber rifles	30	Mauritania
		30-caliber machine guns	150	Mauritania
Jordan	Oct. 12, 1976	155mm mortars	16	Morocco
Iran	Nov. 15, 1976	F-5B aircraft	2	Jordan

SOURCE: *Foreign Assistance and Related Agencies Appropriations for 1978*, Hearings before a sub-committee of the Committee on Appropriations, House of Representatives, 95th Congress, 1st Session, Part I (U.S. Government Printing Office, Washington, D.C., 1978).

Nicaragua in 1979 shook Washington. The Carter administration backed away from its earlier human-rights rhetoric and reinforced security assistance to valued U.S. allies in the third world. There were growing fears in Washington after the 1978 coup in Mauritania, the Algiers Agreement and the succession of guerrilla victories in 1979 that the Saharan war, along with Morocco's domestic economic strains, was undermining the stability of King Hassan's regime. An unduly alarmist report from the CIA, leaked to the press in October 1979, argued that the king was likely to "lose control of events, probably in the space of a year, and perhaps even his throne."[46]

The Carter administration had persuasive reasons to come to Hassan's aid. The king had supported Sadat's initial steps toward détente with Israel, and Morocco's later decision, after Camp David, to break off diplomatic relations with Egypt was seen in Washington as a mere gesture to improve Morocco's relations with Saudi Arabia. Second, the Carter administration valued Hassan's willingness to act as a regional gendarme in Africa. On two occasions, in April 1977 and May 1978, the king had sent fifteen hundred Moroccan troops to help crush the rebellions against the pro-Western ruler of Zaire, Mobutu Sese Seko, in the mineral-rich province of Shaba. Thirdly, like its predecessor, the Carter administration appreciated the strategic importance of a Western-aligned regime remaining in power on the southern flank of the entrance to the Mediterranean.

On October 16, 1979, the Policy Review Committee of the National Security Council advised President Carter to drop the restrictions on arms sales to Morocco.[47] Accordingly, on January 24, 1980, the Pentagon announced plans to sell $232.5 million worth of aircraft to Morocco—twenty F-5E jets ($175 million), six OV-10 Broncos ($17.5 million) and twenty-four Hughes 500MD helicopter gunships ($45 million) equipped with TOW missiles.[48] The following March the Carter administration announced that it would sell 125 Maverick air-to-ground missiles, costing $7 million, for Morocco's F-5 aircraft.[49] FMS sales rose to a total of $274.4 million in 1980, while licensed commercial arms exports totaled $17.4 million.

Ronald Reagan, who succeeded Carter in January 1981, carried on and strengthened this pro-Moroccan policy. He believed that Carter's early concern with human-rights issues had strained relations with traditionally staunch allies of the U.S. and sometimes weakened their capacity to resist challenges to their rule. He was determined to step up security assistance for such allies, however dictatorial they might be, to lessen the risks that the more endangered among them, like Hassan II, might end up suffering the fate of the Shah. "It is the prevailing view of this administration that America's allies and close associates should expect understanding and reliable support," explained the deputy assistant secretary in the State Department's Bureau of Near Eastern and South Asian Affairs, Morris Draper, during a congressional hearing on Western Sahara on March 25, 1981. "It would not be in the spirit of this administration's policy if support for America's traditional and historic friends—to meet reasonable and legitimate needs—were to be withheld or made conditional other than under extraordinary circumstances."[50]

"Reasonable and legitimate needs" included fending off the Polisario guerrillas, even though Morocco's claim to sovereignty in Western Sahara was still not recognized by Washington. "Morocco," Draper stressed, "is important to broad American interests and occupies a pivotal strategic area. We intend to maintain and reinforce our historically close relationships with reliability and consistency as our watchwords."[51]

Draper favorably cited Morocco's concern over "the challenges posed by the Soviets and their surrogates and client states," Morocco's opposition to the Soviet presence in Afghanistan, its help in defeating the Shaba rebels in Zaire, "its pragmatic policies as regards the Middle East issues" and its willingness to allow U.S. warships, "including those which are nuclear powered," to call at its ports. "For all these reasons, and others, we intend to carry out a relationship that assures Morocco that it will be able to count on the United States as a steadfast and reliable ally."[52] Indeed, only two days after taking office, the Reagan administration approved a major new arms sale to Morocco—108 Chrysler-manufactured M60 tanks worth $182 million—and gave the green light for the delivery of the F-5 and OV-10 aircraft promised by Carter a year earlier.[53]

A remarkable succession of high-ranking U.S. officials began calling on King Hassan. Reagan's roving ambassador, General Vernon Walters, who had known the Saharan dossier well in 1975, during his days as deputy director of the CIA, paid the first of several visits to the king on March 21, 1981. Another frequent visitor was to be Francis "Bing" West, the assistant secretary of defense for international security affairs, who held his first tête-à-tête with Hassan on May 25.[54] The shuttling between Washington and Rabat became almost frenetic after the Moroccan debacle at Guelta Zemmour in October 1981. "The Moroccans ran to us shouting for help," according to one senior Pentagon official.⁵⁵ General Walters flew to Rabat for a meeting with Hassan on October 29.⁵⁶ On November 5, Reagan's new ambassador to Morocco, Joseph Verner Reed, a former vice-president of Chase Manhattan Bank and senior adviser to David Rockefeller, assured the king that "the United States is a true friend of Morocco" and "will do its best to be helpful in every way" when he presented his credentials at the royal palace in Ifrane. "Count on us; we are with you."⁵⁷ The same day, West, who had arrived in Morocco at the head of a twenty-three-strong delegation of officials from the Pentagon and the State Department, was touring Western Sahara in a Moroccan helicopter to assess the Moroccan forces' requirements on the spot. "The Moroccan government has asked us for assistance to counter the threat posed by the introduction of Sam-6 missiles in the fighting," he confided on November 6, upon his departure from Morocco. After a visit to Tunis, he was back in Morocco on November 11 for a long interview with the king.⁵⁸

West was critical of the passivity of the Moroccan forces in the Sahara, who were mainly dug into fixed positions along the defense perimeters of the "useful triangle" and the Dakhla-Argoub enclave. This wait-and-see posture eroded Moroccan troop morale and allowed the guerrillas to maintain the initiative.⁵⁹ West therefore proposed training elite Moroccan troops to launch mobile commando-style operations beyond the defense perimeters, to force Polisario onto the defensive. Accordingly, a team of twenty-five U.S. instructors arrived in Morocco in the spring of 1982. The previous December another team, thirty-strong, had begun a six-month training program in antimissile tactics for Moroccan pilots, in the hope of preventing another disaster of the kind that had befallen the Moroccan air force during the fighting at Guelta Zemmour, when five planes were shot down in ten days.

After West's visits to Morocco, the defense secretary, Caspar Weinberger, arrived to meet Hassan on December 3. The next caller, on December 19, was Senator Charles Percy, the Republican chairman of the Senate Foreign Relations Committee. Two prominent officials of the intelligence establishment, Vice-Admiral Bobby Inman, the deputy director of the CIA, and General James Williams, the director of the Defense Intelligence Agency, also made visits at the end of 1981. Then, in mid-January, six U.S. warships, including two nuclear-powered aircraft carriers, showed the flag at Tangier, and on January 18, 1982, the commerce secretary, Malcolm Baldrige, arrived in Morocco to announce economic assistance totalling $355 million—$55 million worth of grain and $300 million in loan guarantees.⁶⁰

The climax to all this camaraderie came on February 11–12, when the secretary of state, Alexander Haig, visited King Hassan in Marrakesh. Haig promised Hassan a substantial increase in U.S. military aid and successfully persuaded him to grant transit facilities at Moroccan air bases to the Rapid Deployment Force (RDF), the intervention force then being readied by the Reagan administration for possible use in the Middle East. A joint military commission was set up to oversee the two countries' growing military cooperation.⁶¹ Facilities were formally made available to the RDF when Haig and the Moroccan foreign minister, M'hammed Boucetta, signed a military agreement on May 27, 1983, after a visit to Washington by Hassan himself on May 18–21. Valid for six years, the agreement gave the RDF access to Casablanca's Mohammed V Airport and later, after a $20-million investment, to the air base at Sidi Slimane, complementing the facilities already negotiated for the RDF at bases in Egypt, Somalia and Oman.[62] "Morocco happens to be properly situated," commented a Pentagon official. "Morocco to Egypt is a good hop."[63]

The granting of facilities to the RDF capped the Hassan regime's strategic importance to the Reagan administration. U.S. military aid was stepped up, in accordance with Haig's promise in Marrakesh. On April 20, 1982, Draper's successor as deputy assistant secretary, Peter Constable, informed Congress that FMS credits to Morocco would be increased from $30 million in FY 1982 to $100 million, half in loan guarantees and half in direct credits, in FY 1983. "Morocco's security needs are pressing, but Morocco bears a heavy debt burden and faces serious balance-of-payments problems," he told the House of Representatives' subcommittee on Africa. "Our support is critical." Besides "servicing previously supplied U.S. weapons systems," including OV-10 and F-5 aircraft, Chapparal missiles and Vulcan guns, the aid would help Morocco "purchase new items, such as electronic countermeasures equipment for the air force, night-vision systems and ground sensors."[64] In addition, Constable announced that aid to Morocco under the International Military Education and Training (IMET) program would be increased from $1.1 million in FY 1982 to $1.6 million in FY 1983 and that the number of Moroccan military personnel to receive training in the U.S. would more than treble, from 168 to 514.

The scale of U.S. concern over Morocco's predicament in the Sahara was well illustrated by the participation of no less than eighty U.S. officials, including eight generals, an assistant secretary of state and both assistant secretaries of defense, in the first session of the U.S.-Moroccan military commission, held in Fez on April 26–27 to examine the nuts and bolts of Washington's security assistance program.[65] The same month, the U.S. government announced that it was selling 381 Maverick missiles to Morocco, for $28 million, and that it had authorized the delivery of eighteen more Bell helicopters, manufactured under license in Italy. In July it transpired that antipersonnel cluster bombs had been sold to Morocco too.[66]

While increasing arms sales to Morocco, both the Carter and the Reagan administrations recognized that Hassan could not win an outright victory in Western Sahara in purely military terms. Harold Saunders, Carter's assistant secretary of state, informed the House of Representatives' subcommittee on Africa on January 24, 1980, that "the President's policy is based on the conviction that neither Morocco nor its adversaries can win an outright military victory and impose a solution on the other side." Thus, "the comprehensive purpose of the President's decision on arms sales to Morocco is to help that country's efforts to defend itself while at the same time nurturing and encouraging a psychological climate in the region conducive to negotiations. Our efforts to strengthen Morocco militarily go hand-in-hand with our efforts to encourage both sides to come to the negotiating table."[67]

The idea was to signal to Polisario and Algeria that the U.S. would not allow

Morocco to be driven out of Western Sahara. Such signals, the Carter administration hoped, would encourage a "psychological climate" in Polisario's ranks, or at least in Algiers, conducive to hammering out a settlement on terms acceptable to King Hassan. The Polisario leaders' "public posture remains uncompromising," Saunders noted, "but we hope and expect that as the prospects on the battlefield increasingly demonstrate the impossibility of their imposing a military solution, they will draw the necessary conclusions."[68] However, the expectations were not fulfilled. When a State Department official, Edmund Hool, met Polisario leaders in Tindouf a year later, in December 1980 (the first-ever U.S. encounter with the movement), and tried to persuade them to settle for a limited form of Western Saharan autonomy, his proposals were dismissed as "impossible." Independence was "the only possible way."[69]

The Reagan administration broke off contact with Polisario. However, it too "did not believe that this conflict is winnable in a military sense."[70] Its objective was to "beef up the confidence of the king and restore the military equilibrium" in the hope of helping Morocco to sustain, rather than win, the war.[71] The intention was to convince Algeria that it was backing an unwinnable cause and would do better to sell the Polisario guerrillas short.

Under both Carter and Reagan, however, there were politicians in Washington, liberal Democrats in the main, who opposed increasing the flow of U.S. arms to Morocco. "There is no way we can provide arms to Morocco for use against the Polisario without implicitly recognizing her claims to the Western Sahara, in contradiction to UN resolutions supported by the U.S. that endorse self-determination," argued Senator Dick Clark of Iowa, the chairman of the Senate's Africa subcommittee, in a letter to President Carter on February 8, 1978, that was influential in persuading the White House, temporarily, to suspend aircraft sales to Morocco. Besides associating the U.S. with "an effort by Morocco to suppress what many African states perceive to be a war for self-determination," the sale of arms to Morocco "for pursuit of a conflict of questionable legitimacy" risked "escalating the war far beyond the local conflict it is at the moment, possibly triggering a greater Soviet response in support of Algeria."[72]

Stephen Solarz, the chairman of the corresponding subcommittee in the House of Representatives, argued likewise when the National Security Council recommended lifting the restrictions on U.S. arms supplies in October 1979. "If we change our policy, the Eastern Bloc countries could see an opportunity to gain an advantage, particularly in view of the Polisario's favorable military prospects and widespread diplomatic support, and move to become involved in a conflict from which they have thus far abstained."[73]

Solarz also feared that "a change in our arms sale policy would probably halt the improvement that has taken place in our economic relationship with Algeria, which has become a much more important economic partner of the United States than Morocco."[74] With a relatively large, expanding economy, based on oil and natural gas (of which it has the world's third largest reserves), Algeria did, indeed, offer much greater export opportunities to U.S. firms than did oil-importing, recession-hit Morocco.[75] However, there were not only commercial reasons to woo Algeria. The Algerian government wielded enormous influence in the third world, on issues ranging from Palestine and the Middle East to north-south relations and oil prices. Furthermore, Algeria was looking for closer relations with the U.S. In 1980, during the Tehran hostage crisis, it offered to mediate between the U.S. and Iran. When its efforts culminated successfully in the hostages' release on January 20, 1981, the day of Reagan's inauguration, Andrew Young, Carter's former UN ambassador, expressed hope that "the Reagan administration will appreciate Algeria's role and the value of continuing our friendship."[76]

Above all, the liberals questioned the government's main strategic premise—that increased U.S. military aid to Morocco would encourage movement toward a peace settlement. By sending arms to Hassan, they argued, the U.S. was feeding the monarch's illusion that he might eventually win the war. This was prolonging an inherently unwinnable war and so undermining still further the stability of the Hassan regime in the long run. "It is quite possible," Solarz argued, "that the King faces greater risks to his throne—from both the Right and the Left—by continuing an unwinnable and expensive war than by moving carefully to end it. In this sense, the sale of offensive American arms to Morocco for use in the Sahara may do more ultimately to undermine the monarchy than to shore it up." In Solarz's view "the real threat to the King is not from without but from within," and "by encouraging the King to maintain the illusion that a military victory is possible, we are much more likely to prolong the war than to shorten it. And with Morocco spending a million dollars a day on a war it cannot win the King will be less able to deal with the festering problems within Morocco itself."[77] Such views were shared by Young, who, after a visit to the Tindouf refugee camps, asked rhetorically in February 1980: "If Hassan is our friend, why do we aid in erecting a scaffold of weaponry upon which he can only hang himself?"[78]

Reagan's decision to escalate U.S. military aid for Morocco prompted like-minded criticism. "The more the king is encouraged to think the war can be continued indefinitely, the greater the long-term dangers to the regime," argued Howard Wolpe, Solarz's successor as chairman of the House of Representatives' subcommittee on Africa, in May 1982. Continuation of the war "at higher and higher levels" meant "directing very scarce economic resources into the conflict, thereby creating another major source of social and political strain within Morocco." A Moroccan disengagement from the Sahara would carry political risks for Hassan, but continued prosecution of the war would ultimately worsen his chances of survival.[79]

Wolpe's subcommittee decided on April 30, 1982, that "by encouraging Morocco to sustain indefinitely an unwinnable war, U.S. policy may well be contributing to the possibility of sudden radical change in Morocco itself." In addition, the subcommittee was of the opinion that increased U.S. military aid to Morocco could "hurt our large economic and other interests in Algeria, increase our diplomatic problems in Africa, where there is limited enthusiasm for the Moroccan claim of sovereignty over the Western Sahara, weaken the forces trying to heal the split in the OAU over the Saharan war (which threaten the future of OAU peacekeeping as in Chad) and increase the opportunities for Soviet and Cuban involvement on the side of the Polisario and Algeria in a widening war." To mark its disapproval of the Reagan administration's strategy, the subcommittee agreed to approve only $50 million of FMS credits for Morocco in FY 1983, half the amount requested by the State Department, and recommended a ban on the provision of training "which has as its principal purpose improving the ability of the Moroccan armed forces to carry out offensive counter-insurgency military activities in the Western Sahara." In addition, the subcommittee proposed that the government report every six months to Congress on its military-training programs in Morocco and that no U.S. military personnel should be sent to Western Sahara.[80] The recommendations were endorsed by the House of Representatives' full foreign affairs committee on the eve of Hassan's visit to Washington the following May. However, a House-Senate conference the following December restored the full military aid allocation of $100 million, with $25 million as an outright grant that the administration had not previously requested. Unexpectedly, $52 million of this aid was suddenly diverted to El Salvador, obliging the administration to request congressional approval of a supplemental allocation to restore Morocco's FY 1983 aid in full, in addition to requesting new funds ($60 million in loans and $30 million in grants) for military aid to Morocco in FY 1984. Once again, the House of Representatives' subcommittee on Africa showed its skepticism of administration policy by agreeing to approve only $2 million in supplemental funds for 1983 and $50 million of the $90 million requested for 1984.[81]

U.S. strategists worked from the assumption that King Hassan could not risk a withdrawal from Western Sahara. They were undoubtedly correct that a humiliating retreat, after years of war, might shatter his public prestige and spur revenge from his armed forces when they returned home, without honor, from their desert trauma. Washington's willingness, from the end of 1979, to accede to virtually any Moroccan arms request encouraged the king to soldier on, in the hope that his enemies' will would finally crack. Despite his ambiguous referendum pledge at the OAU summit in Nairobi in June 1981, he seemed unwilling to risk a genuine, democratic poll in Western Sahara. As of mid-1983, he was still refusing to accept talks with Polisario.

However, neither Polisario nor Algeria were inclined to cower before Washington's gestures of support for Hassan. The guerrillas had already boxed the FAR into two enclaves covering only one-sixth of Western Sahara's land area. The dispersal and flexibility of Polisario's *kataeb*, scattered in hideouts across a territory the size of France, inevitably limited the effectiveness of commando-style counterinsurgency operations. It was doubtful, moreover, that Moroccan troops had the requisite morale and courage to engage in really aggressive antiguerrilla sweeps into the desert hinterland. In addition, there were limits to the capacity of the FAR and the Moroccan air force, which had a shortage of pilots, to absorb a great deal more advanced military hardware.

The defense perimeters around the "useful triangle" and the Dakhla-Argoub enclave did present a new and difficult challenge to Polisario. However, the Moroccan government had to keep eighty thousand troops in these enclaves, at enormous cost, in constant readiness for a major guerrilla assault. The "wall" was unlikely to prove impregnable to guerrillas of Polisario's proven audacity and fighting skill, if they received equipment of the requisite power and sophistication.

U.S. policy makers should have noted, perhaps, that neither Polisario nor

Algeria had bowed to Morocco when the going was much rougher, in the early years of the war. They had not given in when France sent its own air force into combat in Mauritania in 1977–78. To the contrary, Algeria had taken retaliatory economic measures against France. That, and the debacle of the Ould Daddah regime in Mauritania, had prompted greater prudence on Giscard's part.

Polisario was simply doing too well, diplomatically and militarily, to pull back and accept a settlement that fell short of full independence. Pleased with Polisario's military success and partly responsible for its diplomatic victories, in the OAU, the UN and the nonaligned movement, Algeria too saw little reason to back down. Rather, President Chadli Bendjedid insisted that King Hassan open talks with Polisario, to pave the way for genuine self-determination, through a referendum. So long as Hassan refused to negotiate with the guerrillas, the war would continue.

However, it was King Hassan who looked the most poorly placed to survive a long war of attrition, as economic difficulties, exacerbated by the war, and popular discontent mounted in Morocco. U.S. military aid therefore served to prolong the war without much chance of altering its final outcome. Ironically, it seemed likely to worsen, rather than relieve, Hassan's predicament in the long run. It risked promoting the process of destabilization in Morocco that it was designed to halt.

NOTES

1. *Le Monde* (Paris), January 22, 1980.
2. *Jeune Afrique* (Paris), October 1, 1980.
3. OECD, *Statistics of Foreign Trade, Monthly Bulletin*, December 1982.
4. *Le Monde*, May 23, 1980.
5. French exports to Morocco were 6.6 billion francs in 1981, compared to 12.8 billion francs for exports to Algeria.
6. *Afrique-Défense* (Paris), April 1980. In March 1980 the Groupement Industriel des Armaments Terrestres (GIAT) signed a contract for the delivery of one hundred AMX-10RC light armored vehicles.
7. *Le Monde*, October 11, 1981.
8. *Le Monde*, January 21, 1982, and May 20, 1982.
9. *Le Monde*, August 8, 1981, and December 4, 1981.
10. *Le Monde*, September 12, 1981.
11. *Marchés Tropicaux et Méditerranéens* (Paris), October 9, 1981.
12. Deliveries resumed after an agreement was signed on April 4, 1981, to reschedule 2 billion francs of debts incurred for arms purchases. (*Le Monde*, April 11–12, 1982.)
13. Statement by Marcelino Oreja, Spanish foreign minister, May 5, 1977. (*Le Monde*, May 10, 1977.)
14. *Le Monde*, May 8, 1976.
15. See *Sahara* (Asociación de Amigos del Sahara, Madrid, 1977), p. 14, for a detailed listing of Spanish arms deliveries.
16. Comunicado conjunto del Frente Polisario y del Partido Socialista Obrero Español, Madrid, 8 de Septiembre de 1977.
17. *El País* (Madrid), March 14, 15, 16 and 17, 1978.
18. Radio Madrid, February 19 and 26, 1978. The immediate cause of Manueco's recall was the publication of an article in *El Moudjahid* on December 19, 1977, citing Cubillo's claim that MPAIAC was the "sole legitimate representative of the Guanche people."
19. Julio Cola Alberich, "Las Islas Canarias y los acuerdos de la OUA," *Revista de Política Internacional*, No. 4, 1978, pp. 49–50.
20. *Le Monde*, July 23–24, 1978.

21. *Algérie Presse Service*, March 18, 1976.

22. *The Times* (London), April 15, 1977.

23. *Le Monde*, November 23, 1977, and November 30, 1977.

24. *Le Monde*, June 17, 1978.

25. *El País*, September 10, 1978; *El Eco de Canarias* (Las Palmas), October 8, 1979.

26. Radio Madrid, October 14, 1978.

27. *Le Monde*, May 3, 1979.

28. Spanish exports to Morocco totaled $309 million in 1981, compared to $561 million of exports to Algeria.

29. *West Africa* (London), May 21, 1979.

30. See *El País*, November 30, 1978, and December 1, 1978.

31. *The Observer* (London), October 8, 1979.

32. *Le Monde*, December 19, 1980.

33. UN Security Council document S/PV.1852, November 2, 1975, p. 91.

34. *Le Monde*, November 5, 1977.

35. *Sahara Libre* (Polisario Front, Algiers), No. 50, February 2, 1978; *Le Monde*, October 21, 1978, and June 12, 1981.

36. The USSR was already supplying about 85 percent of Morocco's oil. The USSR is a major market for Morocco's citrus fruit, built three power stations in Morocco in 1974–76 and has prospected for several minerals in the country. On April 27, 1978, the USSR signed a five-year fisheries agreement with Morocco, to aid research into fish stocks, set up joint fishing companies and import fish from Morocco, but, unlike the Spanish-Moroccon agreement, this did not cover Western Sahara's waters.

37. *The Defense Monitor* (Washington, D.C.), Vol. V, No. 2, February 1976. See also Lewis B. Ware, *Decolonization and the Global Alliance in the Arab Maghrib: the Case of Spanish Sahara* (Directorate of Documentary Research, Air University Institute for Professional Development, Maxwell Air Force Base, Alabama, 1975).

38. Statement by Nicholas A. Veliotes, deputy assistant secretary, Bureau of Near Eastern and South Asian Affairs, Department of State, October 12, 1977, in *The Question of Self-Determination in Western Sahara*, Hearings before the Subcommittees on International Organizations and on Africa of the Committee on International Relations, House of Representatives, 95th Congress, October 12, 1977 (U.S. Government Printing Office, Washington, D.C., 1977), p. 39.

39. *New York Times*, February 22, 1976.

40. *New York Times*, May 23, 1976. See table in this chapter.

41. "The USG accepts the existing *de facto* administration of the Western Sahara, which is based upon the Madrid Agreement. We have not taken a position on the 'legality' of the Madrid (or Tripartite) Agreement of November 1975 to which we are not a party." (Responses by the Department of State to Questions Submitted by Subcommittee Chairman Fraser, in *The Question of Self-Determination in Western Sahara*, p. 71.)

42. *New York Times*, January 31, 1978, and February 28, 1978.

43. *The Middle East* (London), April 1978.

44. *Washington Post*, February 10, 1979; *Africa News* (Durham, N.C.), April 6, 1979.

45. For a detailed account of this electronic detection system, see *Washington Star*, October 15, 1978.

46. ABC TV, October 28, 1979.

47. The strategic arguments for the change in policy were listed by the assistant secretary of state for Near Eastern and South Asian Affairs, Harold Saunders, on January 24, 1980, in testimony to the House of Representatives' subcommittee on Africa. "We believe an outright military victory over Morocco by Morocco's adversaries would constitute a serious setback to major U.S. interests. First and foremost, such a development would destabilize the region in general, and the political equilibrium in Morocco in particular. Beyond that, the United States cannot turn a blind eye to the fact that Morocco has historically been a good friend and indeed, in a practical sense, an ally. Morocco identifies itself with the United States and the West on key East-West issues. Its support for U.S. positions on Iran and Afghanistan in recent weeks has been strong and public. With Southwest Asia in turmoil, we need to nurture our relations as never before with all Islamic and nonaligned states, but we particularly need to stand up for and support our avowed friends and supporters." In a parallel Senate hearing, on January 29, Saunders listed the services rendered by Morocco over the years: "It permitted U.S. bases of one kind or another on its soil until 1978, when the last installation was closed at our initiative. It has historically taken a moderate position on Arab-Israeli issues. King Hassan welcomed President Sadat's trip to Jerusalem and received him in Morocco after President Sadat had concluded the Camp David accords. While associating himself with the majority of Arab countries in opposition to the Egypt-

Israel treaty, he still maintains his personal friendship with Sadat and supports the principle of a peaceful and negotiated solution to the Arab-Israeli dispute. In Africa, Morocco has consistently supported moderate forces, twice sending troops to Zaire to maintain stability in that country's Shaba province. Morocco has publicly called for the release of our hostages in Tehran, and voted in the UN General Assembly for condemnation of the Soviet invasion of Afghanistan. Morocco occupies an important geographical position, controlling the lower half of the Straits of Gibraltar. It has permitted port visits by U.S. naval vessels and transit by U.S. military aircraft to destinations such as Saudi Arabia."

48. *Washington Post*, January 25, 1980.

49. *Afrique-Défense*, April 1980.

50. *Arms Sales in North Africa and the Conflict in the Western Sahara: an Assessment of US Policy*, Hearing before the Subcommittees on International Security and Scientific Affairs and on Africa of the Committee on Foreign Affairs, House of Representatives, 97th Congress, 1st Session, March 25, 1981 (U.S. Government Printing Office, Washington, D.C., 1981), p. 5.

51. *Ibid.*, p. 3.

52. *Ibid.*, p. 4.

53. *Washington Post*, January 28, 1981. Morocco had decided meanwhile to drop its request for Hughes helicopters in preference for twenty-four Gazelle helicopters manufactured by Aérospatiale of France.

54. *Le Monde*, June 17, 1981; *Marchés Tropicaux et Méditerranéens*, June 19, 1981.

55. Interview in Washington, D.C., May 20, 1982. The official asked not to be named.

56. *El País*, October 31, 1981.

57. *Le Monde*, November 8–9, 1981.

58. *International Herald Tribune* (Paris), November 6, 1981; *El País*, November 7, 1981; *Marchés Tropicaux et Méditerranéens*, December 11, 1981.

59. Interview at the Pentagon, May 20, 1982.

60. *Le Monde*, January 22, 1982; *An-Nahar Arab Report and Memo*, January 25, 1982.

61. *Le Monde*, February 13, 1978.

62. *New York Times*, May 28, 1982.

63. Interview at the Pentagon, May 20, 1982.

64. Testimony of Peter D. Constable, Deputy Assistant Secretary, Department of State, before the Wolpe Subcommittee on Africa of the House Foreign Affairs Committee.

65. *El Moudjahid* (Algiers), April 25, 1982; *Le Monde*, April 25–26, 1982.

66. *New York Times*, July 22, 1982; Note from John J. Brady, Chief of Staff, to Committee on Foreign Affairs, April 21, 1982.

67. *Proposed Arms Sale to Morocco*, Hearings before the Subcommittees on International Security and Scientific Affairs and on Africa of the Committee on Foreign Affairs, House of Representatives, 96th Congress, 2nd Session, January 24 and 29, 1980 (U.S. Government Printing Office, Washington, D.C., 1980), pp. 2–3.

68. *Ibid.*, p. 4.

69. Radio Algiers, December 11, 1980.

70. Interview with Robert Flaten, Director, North Africa, State Department, May 1982. The text is published in *Africa Report*, July-August 1982, pp. 19–21.

71. Interview at the Pentagon, May 20, 1982.

72. Letter from Senator Dick Clark to President Carter, February 8, 1979.

73. Stephen J. Solarz, "Arms to Morocco?" *Foreign Affairs* (New York), Vol. 58, No. 2, Winter 1979–80, p. 296.

74. *Ibid.*, p. 289.

75. U.S. exports to Algeria totaled $909 million in 1982, while exports to Morocco were $396.5 million.

76. *Washington Post*, January 26, 1981.

77. Solarz, *loc. cit.*, p. 295.

78. *International Herald Tribune*, February 20, 1980.

79. Interview with Representative Howard Wolpe, Washington, D.C., May 20, 1982. For the full text of the interview, see *Africa Report*, July-August 1982, pp. 22–23.

80. Recommendations of the Subcommittee on Africa on Foreign Legislation Fiscal Year 1983: Morocco and Western Sahara.

81. United States Military and Economic Aid to Morocco. House Foreign Affairs Recommendations for Fiscal Year 1984.

APPENDIX

The Advisory Opinion of the International Court of Justice October 16, 1975

A T THE BIDDING OF MOROCCO AND MAURITANIA, the UN General Assembly adopted a resolution on December 13, 1974, which requested "the International Court of Justice, without prejudice to the application of the principles embodied in General Assembly resolution 1514 (XV), to give an advisory opinion at an early date on the following questions: 'I. Was Western Sahara (Río de Oro and Sakiet El Hamra) at the time of colonization by Spain a territory belonging to no one (*terra nullius*)?' If the answer to the first question is in the negative, 'II. What were the legal ties between this territory and the Kingdom of Morocco and the Mauritanian entity?' "

The relevance of such historical questions to the problem of Western Sahara's decolonization in the last quarter of the twentieth century was far from evident, and though the resolution did make a point of reaffirming the Western Saharans' right to self-determination, the very decision to put these questions to the ICJ and meanwhile to request Spain to postpone its plans for a self-determination referendum until the court gave its advisory opinion suggested that the territory's precolonial legal status, rather than the will of the Saharawis, should determine its future. The Saharawis would not even have the right to appear before the ICJ since the court, which sits in The Hague, can only hear evidence from states. Nonetheless, the court responded positively to the UN's request for an advisory opinion and, after twenty-seven sessions in June-July 1975 at which Spain, Morocco, Mauritania and Algeria were represented, published its opinion on October 16, 1975.

The court defined the "time of colonization" as "the period beginning in 1884, when Spain proclaimed a protectorate over the Río de Oro," and decided unanimously that Western Sahara was not then *terra nullius* since it "was inhabited by peoples which, if nomadic, were socially and politically organized in tribes and under chiefs competent to represent them" and since even Spain itself

368

had based its proclamation of a protectorate over Río de Oro on December 26, 1884, on the agreements which it had made with such chiefs.

Turning to the second question, the court first examined the precolonial legal ties between Morocco and Western Sahara. The court recognized that Morocco had been a special kind of state, based on the allegiance of tribes to the sultans, rather than on the notion of territorial sovereignty as such, but it ruled that such allegiance had to be shown to involve acceptance of real political authority to establish that the sultans had exercised sovereignty in Western Sahara. Much of the historical evidence presented to the court, it noted, was "far-flung, spasmodic and often transitory." The Moroccan government provided evidence of two kinds to back up its thesis that Western Sahara had been subject to the sultans. There were, first, examples of what was said to be the internal display of Moroccan authority in Western Sahara and, secondly, international treaties, which were said to constitute recognition of Moroccan sovereignty there by foreign states. Among examples of the former were *dahirs*, or royal decrees, appointing *caids* to head Saharawi tribes and declarations of allegiance by Saharawi tribes to various sultans. Particular stress was placed by Morocco on the expedition to the Noun region of southern Morocco by Moulay Hassan in 1882 and 1886, when some Tekna *caids* were invested, and on the relationship between Sheikh Ma el-Ainin and the Moroccan sultanate in the 1890s and 1900s. Spain, which disputed Morocco's claim to precolonial sovereignty over Western Sahara, responded by noting that the 1882 and 1886 expeditions had gone no farther south than Tiznit and Goulimine respectively, that the appointment of *caids* was purely formal, since independently established chiefs were merely confirmed in office, that the nomadic Tekna who traditionally migrated through Western Saharan territory had not submitted to Moulay Hassan, by contrast to the settled or seminomadic Tekna of the Noun, and finally that Ma el-Ainin had really been an independent leader who made opportune alliances with the sultans. Moreover, Spain argued, there was no evidence that Western Saharan tribes had paid taxes to the *makhzen*. The court itself came to the following conclusion:

> The material before the Court appears to support the view that almost all the dahirs and other acts concerning caids relate to areas situated within present-day Morocco itself and do not in themselves provide evidence of effective display of Moroccan authority in Western Sahara. Nor can the information furnished by Morocco be said to provide convincing evidence of the imposition or levying of Moroccan taxes with respect to the territory. As to Sheikh Ma ul-'Ainin, the complexities of his career may leave doubts as to the precise nature of his relations with the Sultan, and different interpretations have been put upon them. The material before the Court, taken as a whole, does not suffice to convince it that the activities of this sheikh should be considered as having constituted a display of the Sultan's authority in Western Sahara at the time of its colonization.

> Furthermore, the information before the Court appears to confirm that the expeditions of Sultan Hassan I to the south in 1882 and 1886 both had objects specifically directed to the Souss and the Noun and, in fact, did not go beyond the Noun; so that they did not reach even as far as the Dra'a, still less Western Sahara. . . . Again, although Morocco asserts that the Regheibat tribe always recognized the suzerainty of the Tekna confederation, and through them that of the Sultan himself, this assertion has

not been supported by any convincing evidence. Moreover, both Spain and Mauritania insist that this tribe of marabout warriors was wholly independent.

Consequently, the information before the Court does not support Morocco's claim to have exercised territorial sovereignty over Western Sahara. On the other hand, it does not appear to exclude the possibility that the Sultan displayed authority over some of the tribes in Western Sahara. That this was so with regard to the Regheibat or other independent tribes living in the territory could clearly not be sustained. The position is different, however, with regard to the septs of the Tekna whose routes of migration are established as having included the territory of the Tekna caids within Morocco as well as parts of Western Sahara. . . .

. . . the Court considers that, taken as a whole, the information before it shows the display of some authority by the Sultan, through Tekna caids, over the Tekna septs nomadizing in Western Sahara.

Thus, even taking account of the specific structure of the Sherifian State, the material so far examined does not establish any tie of territorial sovereignty between Western Sahara and that State. It does not show that Morocco displayed effective and exclusive State activity in Western Sahara. It does however provide indications that a legal tie of allegiance had existed at the relevant period between the Sultan and some, but only some, of the nomadic peoples of the territory.

Moving on to the evidence provided by international treaties, the Court gave its opinion on the "shipwreck clauses" of the eighteenth- and nineteenth-century treaties between Morocco and the major maritime powers, as well as the March 13, 1895, Anglo-Moroccan agreement on the cession of Donald Mackenzie's trading station at Tarfaya, and an exchange of letters about Morocco between France and Germany in 1911. By and large, the shipwreck clauses obliged the sultan to use his authority to secure the rescue of sailors shipwrecked on the dangerous coast of the Noun and, in some of the treaties, the regions to its south, though none referred specifically to the region now known as Western Sahara. "Morocco is correct in saying," the court believed, "that these provisions would have been pointless if the other State concerned had not considered the Sultan to be in a position to exercise some authority or influence over the people holding the sailors captive. But it is quite a different thing to maintain that those provisions implied international recognition by the other State concerned of the Sultan as territorial sovereign in Western Sahara." Though the 1895 Anglo-Moroccan agreement explicitly stated that the region between the Oued Draa and Cape Bojador was part of Morocco, the court came to the conclusion that "numerous documents . . .

show that the position repeatedly taken by Great Britain was that Cape Juby was outside Moroccan territory, which in its view did not extend beyond the Dra'a. In the light of this material the provisions of the 1895 treaty invoked by Morocco appear to the Court to represent an agreement by Great Britain not to question in future any pretensions of the Sultan to the lands between the Dra'a and Cape Bojador, and not a recognition by Great Britain of previously existing Moroccan sovereignty over those lands.

The letters exchanged by France and Germany at the time of their agreement of November 4, 1911, were said by the Rabat government to recognise Saguia el-Hamra as part of Morocco since they defined the latter as compising "all that part of northern Africa which is situated between Algeria, French West Africa and the Spanish colony of Río de Oro." Spain countered that Article 6 of the earlier Franco-Spanish convention of October 3, 1904, had defined Saguia el-Hamra as being outside Moroccan territory. The court concluded that the purpose of these agreements, in their different contexts, was to "recognize or reserve for one or both parties a 'sphere of influence' as understood in the practice of that time." So the court found "difficulty in accepting the Franco-German exchange of letters of 1911 as constituting recognition of the limits of Morocco rather than of the sphere of France's political interests vis-à-vis Germany."

Summing up the evidence on Morocco's relations with the Western Sahara before colonization, the Court concluded:

> The inferences to be drawn from the information before the Court concerning internal acts of Moroccan sovereignty and from that concerning international acts are, therefore, in accord in not providing indications of the existence, at the relevant period, of any legal tie of territorial sovereignty between Western Sahara and the Moroccan State. At the same time, they were in accord in providing indications of a legal tie of allegiance between the Sultan and some, though only some, of the tribes of the territory, and in providing indications of some display of the Sultan's authority or influence with respect to those tribes.

Turning to the precolonial ties between Mauritania and Western Sahara, the court began by noting that Mauritania had accepted that it did not constitute a state at this time. The Mauritanian "entity," as it was therefore called, was a vast region between the Saguia el-Hamra and the Senegal with distinct social, linguistic and cultural traits, the Mauritanian government argued. In the court's opinion, the evidence disclosed that:

> . . . at the time of the Spanish colonization, there existed many ties of a racial, linguistic, religious, cultural and economic nature between various tribes and emirates whose peoples dwelt in the Saharan region which today is comprised within the Territory of Western Sahara and the Islamic Republic of Mauritania. It also discloses, however, the independence of the emirates and many of the tribes in relation to one another and, despite some forms of common activity, the absence among them of any common institutions or organs, even of a quite minimal character.

The court concluded that "at the time of colonization by Spain there did not exist between the territory of Western Sahara and the Mauritanian entity any tie of sovereignty, or of allegiance of tribes, or of 'simple inclusion' in the same legal entity." However, there had been legal ties of a different order between tribes living in the Mauritanian-Western Saharan region, relating to such matters as migration routes, the use of wells and the settlement of disputes, and these "knew no frontier between the territories and were vital to the very maintenance of life in the region."

The court then went on to reject Morocco's assertion that "there is a north and there is a south which juxtapose in space the legal ties of Western Sahara with Morocco and with Mauritania," leaving no "no-man's land" in between. Insofar as there were certain legal ties, though not ties of sovereignty, between some of the Western Saharan tribes and the sultans of Morocco or the tribes and emirates of the Mauritanian entity, they overlapped geographically in a complex way because of the tribes' nomadic migrations, which, to add to the difficulties, sometimes "passed also within areas of what is present-day Algeria."

The court summed up its advisory opinion as follows:

The materials and information presented to the Court show the existence, at the time of Spanish colonization, of legal ties of allegiance between the Sultan of Morocco and some of the tribes living in the territory of Western Sahara. They equally show the existence of rights, including some rights relating to the land, which constituted legal ties between the Mauritanian entity, as understood by the Court, and the territory of Western Sahara. On the other hand, the Court's conclusion is that the materials and information presented to it do not establish any tie of territorial sovereignty between the territory of Western Sahara and the Kingdom of Morocco or the Mauritanian entity. Thus the court has not found legal ties of such a nature as might affect the application of resolution 1514 (XV) in the decolonization of Western Sahara and, in particular, of the principle of self-determination through the free and genuine expression of the will of the peoples of the Territory.

One might ask what kind of legal ties would "affect" the application of the principle of self-determination? The court did not elaborate. Nonetheless, the advisory opinon did unambiguously reject the Moroccan and Mauritanian claims to precolonial territorial sovereignty over Western Sahara and uphold the Western Saharans' right to determine their own future. The court's sixteen judges voted by fourteen to two to endorse the opinion's conclusions on the legal ties between Morocco and Western Sahara and by fifteen to one to endorse those on the legal ties between Mauritania and Western Sahara. Within hours of the publication of the court's opinion, however, King Hassan II brushed aside its conclusion on the application of the principle of self-determination by announcing the plans for his Green March into the territory.

BIBLIOGRAPHY

There is an extensive literature on Western Sahara, most of it in French and Spanish. The following bibliography is highly selective. A much larger bibliography may be found in the author's *Historical Dictionary of Western Sahara* (Scarecrow Press, Metuchen, New Jersey, 1982), which lists some seven hundred books and articles, classified according to subject. An exhaustive bibliography of works published before 1960 is included in B. Blaudin de Thé, *Essai de bibliographie du Sahara français et des régions avoisinantes* (Arts et Métiers Graphiques, Paris, 1960).

Abascal, Federico, Sol Gallego and Enrique Bustamante. "Sahara: documentos secretos," *Cuadernos para el Diálogo* (Madrid), January 21, 1978.

Algerian Government. *Referendum of Self-Determination for the People of the Western Sahara. Memorandum of Algeria Presented to the 'OAU Committee of Implementation,' Nairobi, August 1981.* Algiers: 1981.

Arms Sales in North Africa and the Conflict in the Western Sahara: an Assessment of U.S. Policy. Hearing before the Subcommittees on International Security and Scientific Affairs and on Africa of the Committee on Foreign Affairs, House of Representatives, 97th Congress, 1st Session, March 25, 1981. Washington, D.C.: U.S. Government Printing Office, 1981.

Assidon, Elsa. *Sahara occidental, un enjeu pour le Nord-ouest africain.* Paris: François Maspero, 1978.

Barbier, Maurice. "L'avenir du Sahara espagnol," *Politique Etrangère* (Paris), No. 4, 1975, pp. 353–80.

Barbier, Maurice. "L'avis consultatif de la Cour de La Haye sur le Sahara occidental," *Revue Juridique et Politique, Indépendance et Coopération*, 1976, No. 1, pp. 67–103.

Barbier, Maurice. *Le conflit du Sahara occidental.* Paris: L'Harmattan, 1982.

Bataillon, C. (Ed.). *Nomades et nomadisme au Sahara.* Paris: UNESCO, 1963.

Ben Hamouda, Boualem. *La question du Sahara occidental et le droit international.* Algiers: Algerian Government, 1976.

Caro Baroja, Julio. *Estudios Saharianos.* Madrid: Instituto de Estudios Africanos, 1955.

Chaffard, Georges. *Les carnets secrets de la décolonisation.* Vol. I. Paris: Calmann-Lévy, 1965.

Chappez, Jean. "L'avis consultatif de la Cour Internationale de Justice du 16 octobre 1975 dans l'affaire du Sahara occidental," *Revue Générale de Droit International Public*, Vol. 80, No. 4, October-December 1976, pp. 1133–85.

Chassey, Francis de. "Des ethnies et de l'impérialisme dans la genèse des nations, des classes et des Etats en Afrique: le cas du Sahara occidental," *L'Homme et la Société*, Nos. 45–46, July-December 1977, pp. 113–25.

Criado, Ramón. *Sahara, pasión y muerte de un sueño colonial.* Paris: Ruedo Ibérico, 1977.

Damis, John. *Conflict in Northwest Africa: The Western Sahara Dispute*. Stanford: Hoover Institution Press, 1983.

Dessens, Paul. "Le litige du Sahara occidental," *Maghreb-Machrek* (Paris), No. 71, January-March 1976, pp. 29–46.

Dessens, Paul. "Le problème du Sahara occidental trois ans après le départ des espagnols," *Maghreb-Machrek* (Paris), No. 83, January-March 1979, pp. 73–86.

Díaz del Ribero, Francisco-Lorenzo. *El Sahara occidental: pasado y presente*. Madrid: Gisa Ediciones, 1975.

Fessard de Foucault, Bertrand. "La question du Sahara espagnol," *Revue Française d'Etudes Politiques Africaines*, 10th Year, No. 119, November 1975, pp. 74–106, and No. 120, December 1975, pp. 71–103.

Flores Morales, Angel. *El Sahara español: ensayo de geografía física, humana y económica*. Madrid: Ediciones de la Alta Comisaría de España en Marruecos, 1946.

Flory, Maurice. "L'avis de la Cour Internationale de Justice sur le Sahara occidental," *Annuaire Français de Droit International*, Vol. XXI, 1975, pp. 253–77.

Franck, Thomas M. "The Stealing of the Sahara," *American Journal of International Law*, Vol. 70, No. 4, October 1976, pp. 694–721.

García Figueras, Tomás. *Santa Cruz de Mar Pequeña, Ifni, Sahara. La acción de España en la costa occidental de Africa*. Madrid: Ediciones Fe, 1941.

Gaudio, Attilio. *"Sahara espagnol," fin d'un mythe colonial*. Rabat: Arrissala, 1975.

Gaudio, Attilio. *Le dossier du Sahara occidental*. Paris: Nouvelles Editions Latines, 1978.

Gretton, John. *Western Sahara: the Fight for Self-Determination*. London: Anti-Slavery Society, 1976.

Harrell-Bond, Barbara. *The Struggle for the Western Sahara*. American Universities Field Staff Reports, Nos. 37–39, 1981.

Hart, D. M. "The social structure of the Rgībāt Bedouins of the Western Sahara," *The Middle East Journal* (Washington, D.C.), Vol. XVI, No. 4, Autumn 1962, pp. 515–27.

Hassan II, King. *Discours de S.M. Hassan II. La lutte pour le parachèvement de l'integrité territoriale*. Rabat: Ministère d'Etat Chargé de l'Information, 1975.

Hassan II, King. *Discours de S.M. Hassan II, 3 mars 1974–3 mars 1975*. Rabat: Ministère d'Etat Chargé de l'Information, 1975.

Hassan II, King. *Conférence de presse de S.M. Hassan II sur la Marche Verte et le Sahara, 25 novembre 1975*. Rabat: Ministère d'Etat Chargé de l'Information, 1975.

Hassan II, King. *Le défi*. Paris: Albin Michel, 1976.

Hernández-Pacheco, Francisco, and José María Cordero Torres. *El Sahara español*. Madrid: Instituto de Estudios Políticos, 1962.

Hinz, Manfred (Ed.). *Le droit à l'autodétermination du Sahara occidental*. Bonn: Progress Dritte Welt Verlag, 1978.

Hodges, Tony. "Western Sahara, The Sixth Year of War," in Colin Legum (Ed.), *Africa Contemporary Record* (New York: Holmes and Meier), Vol. XIII, 1980–81, pp. A80–A93.

Hodges, Tony. *Historical Dictionary of Western Sahara*. Metuchen, N.J.: Scarecrow Press, 1982.

Hodges, Tony. "The Origins of Saharawi Nationalism," *Third World Quarterly*, Vol. 5, No. 1, January 1983, PP. 28–57.

Hultman, Tami. *Democratic Arab Republic of the Sahara*. Dobbs Ferry, N.Y.: Oceana Publishers, 1978.

Instituto Nacional de Industria. *Fosfatos de Bu-Craa, S A*. Madrid: INI, 1972.

International Court of Justice. *Western Sahara, Advisory Opinion of 16 October 1975*. The Hague: ICJ, 1975.

Itani, Leila Badia. *Al-Polisario: qaid wa thawra*. Beirut: Dar al-Masirah, 1978.

Jacquier, Bernard. "L'autodétermination du Sahara espagnol," *Revue Générale de Droit International Public*, Vol. 78, No. 3, July-September 1974, pp. 683–728.

Kodjo, Edem. *Memorandum sur l'admission de la Republique arabe sahraouie démocratique à l'OUA*. Tripoli: Organization of African Unity, 1982.

Komorowski, Zygmunt. "Formation de la conscience sociale supratribale en partant des conditions ethniques du Sahara occidental," *Africana Bulletin* (Warsaw), 1975, No. 23, pp. 95–123.

La Chapelle, F. de. "Esquisse d'une histoire du Sahara occidental," *Hespéris* (Paris), Vol. XI, 1930, pp. 35–95.

La Chapelle, F. de. *Les Teknas du Sud marocain*. Paris: Comité de l'Afrique Française, 1934.

Lazrak, Rachid. *Le contentieux territorial entre le Maroc et l'Espagane*. Casablanca: Dar el Kitab, 1974.

"Les territoires espagnols d'Afrique," *Notes et Etudes Documentaires* (La Documentation Française, Paris), No. 2951, January 3, 1963.

Maazouzi, Mohamed. *Tindouf et les frontières méridionales du Maroc*. Casablanca: Dar el Kitab, 1977.

Mackenzie, Donald. *The Khalifate of the West*. London: Simpkin, Marshall, Hamilton, Kent and Co. Ltd., 1911.

Maestre Alfonso, Juan. *El Sahara en la crisis de Marruecos y España*. Madrid: Akal, 1975.

Menéndez del Valle, Emilio. *Sahara español: una descolonización tardía*. Madrid: Editorial Cuadernos para el Diálogo, 1975.

Mercer, John. *Spanish Sahara*. London: George Allen and Unwin, 1976.

Mercer, John. "Confrontation in the Western Sahara," *The World Today* (London), Vol. XXXII, No. 6, June 1976, pp. 230–39.

Mercer, John. "The Cycle of Invasion and Unification in the Western Sahara," *African Affairs* (London), Vol. 75, No. 301, October 1976, pp. 498–510.

Mercer, John. *The Saharawis of Western Sahara*. London: Minority Rights Group, 1979.

Miège, J. L. "Les origines de la colonie espagnole du Río de Oro," in *Le Sahara: rapports et contacts humains, 7ème colloque d'histoire organisé par la Faculté des Lettres d'Aix-en-Provence*. Aix-en-Provence: Publications des Annales de la Faculté des Lettres, 1967.

Miguel, H. L. *Legislación de Sahara, años 1965 a 1973*. Madrid: Minerva, 1974.

Míguez, Alberto. "Le Sahara occidental et la politique maghrébine de l'Espagne," *Politique Etrangère* (Paris), Vol. 43, 1978, No. 2, pp. 173–80.

Miské, Ahmed-Baba. *Front Polisario, l'âme d'un peuple*. Paris: Editions Rupture, 1978.

Montagne, Robert. "La limite du Maroc et du Sahara atlantique," *Hespéris* (Paris), Vol. XI, 1930, pp. 111–18.

Monteil, Vincent. *Notes sur les Tekna*. Paris: Editions Larose, 1948.

Moroccan Government. *Le Sahara occidental devant la Cour Internationale de Justice. Mémoire présenté par le Royaume du Maroc*. Rabat: 1975.

Moulahid, Jamil. "Les sahraouis et le phosphate," *Esprit* (Paris), No. 4, April 1976, pp. 779–803.

Ould Daddah, Moktar. *1957-1976: la réunification de la patrie, un objectif sacré pour le peuple mauritanien*. Nouakchott: Ministère d'Etat à l'Orientation Nationale, 1976.

Pelissier, René. "Spain's Discreet Decolonization," *Foreign Affairs* (New York), Vol. 43, No. 3, April 1965, pp. 519–27.

Pérez Díaz, Victor. "La sedentarización en una población nómada: observaciones sobre el Sahara occidental," in *Pueblos y Clases en el campo español*. Madrid: Siglo XXI, 1974.

Polisario Front. *El pueblo saharaui en lucha: documentos del Frente Popular para la Liberación de Saguia el Hamra y Río de Oro*. Polisario Front, 1974.

Polisario Front. *Le peuple saharaoui en lutte*. Polisario Front, 1975.

Polisario Front. *Memorandum Concerning the Proclamation of the Arab Saharan Democratic Republic and the Constitution of its Government*. Polisario Front, 1976.

Polisario Front. *Troisième congrès du Front Polisario, 26 au 30 août 1976*. Polisario Front, 1976.

Proposed Arms Sales to Morocco. Hearings before the Subcommittees on International Security and Scientific Affairs and on Africa of the Committee on Foreign Affairs, House of Representatives, 96th Congress, 2nd Session, January 24 and 29, 1980. Washington, D.C.: U.S. Government Printing Office, 1980.

Reyner, Anthony S. "Morocco's International Boundaries: a Factual Background," *The Journal of Modern African Studies*, Vol. I, 1963, No. 3, pp. 313–26.

Rézette, Robert. *The Western Sahara and the Frontiers of Morocco*. Paris: Nouvelles Editions Latines, 1975.

Sahara, 14-Nov-1975, la traición. Madrid: Asociación de Amigos del Sahara and Instituto de Estudios Políticos para América Latina y Africa, 1980.

Sahara occidental: un peuple et ses droits. Colloque de Massy, 1 et 2 avril 1978. Paris: L'Harmattan, 1979.

Saharan Arab Democratic Republic. *La République arabe sahraouie démocratique*. Département d'Information, RASD, 1980.

Saharan Arab Democratic Republic. *VIIe anniversaire du déclenchement de la lutte de libération nationale. L'ALPS de la colonisation espagnole . . . à l'agression marocaine.* Département Informations, RASD, 1980.

Servicio de Registro de Población, Censo y Estadística. *Censo-74.* El-Ayoun: Gobierno General del Sahara, 1975.

Solarz, Stephen J. "Arms for Morocco?" *Foreign Affairs* (New York), Vol. 58, No. 2, Winter 1979–80, pp. 278–99.

The Question of Self-Determination in Western Sahara. Hearings before the Subcommittees on International Organizations and on Africa of the Committee on International Relations, House of Representatives, 95th Congress, October 12, 1977. Washington, D.C.: U.S. Government Printing Office, 1977.

Thompson, Virginia, and Richard Adloff. *The Western Saharans.* Totowa, N.J.: Barnes and Noble, 1980. London: Croom Helm, 1980.

Trout, Frank E. *Morocco's Saharan Frontiers.* Geneva: Droz, 1969.

Union Socialiste des Forces Populaires. *For a Just and Durable Peace in Maghreb.* Casablanca: Les Editions Maghrébines, undated.

United Nations. "Report of the United Nations Visiting Mission to Spanish Sahara, 1975," in *General Assembly Official Records,* 30th Session, Supplement 23, Vol. III, UN Document A/10023/Rev.1, pp. 12–128.

United Nations. "The Question of Western Sahara at the United Nations," *Decolonization* (UN, New York), No. 17, October 1980.

U.S. Policy Toward the Conflict in the Western Sahara. Report of a Staff Study Mission to Morocco, Algeria, the Western Sahara, and France, August 25– September 6, 1982, to the Committee on Foreign Affairs, U.S. House of Representatives. Washington, D.C.: U.S. Government Printing Office, 1983.

Vallée, Charles. "L'affaire du Sahara occidental devant la Cour de La Haye," *Maghreb-Machrek* (Paris), No. 71, January-March 1976, pp. 47–55.

Vilar Ramírez, Juan Bautista. *El Sahara y el hamitismo norteafricano. Estudios antropo-históricos sahárico-magrebíes.* Madrid: Instituto de Estudios Africanos, 1969.

Villar, Francisco. *El proceso de autodeterminación del Sahara.* Valencia: Fernando Torres, 1982.

Weiner, Jerome B. "The Green March in Historical Perspective," *The Middle East Journal* (Washington, D.C.), Vol. 33, No. 1, Winter 1979, pp. 20–33.

Wenger, Martha. "Reagan Stakes Morocco in Sahara Struggle," *MERIP Reports* (Washington, D.C.), No. 105, May 1982, pp. 22–26.

Western Sahara and the Struggle of the Sahraoui People for Self-Determination. Rome: International League for the Rights and Liberation of Peoples, 1978.

Yata, Ali. *La Sahara occidental marocain.* Casablanca: 1973.

INDEX